Learning Throughout Life

An Intergenerational Perspective

A Volume in
Lifespan Learning

Series Editors:
Paris S. Strom, *Auburn University*
Robert D. Strom, *Arizona State University*

Lifespan Learning

Paris S. Strom and Robert D. Strom, Series Editors

Learning Throughout Life

An Intergenerational Perspective

by

Robert D. Strom
Arizona State University

and

Paris S. Strom
Auburn University

Information Age Publishing, Inc.
Charlotte, North Carolina • www.infoagepub.com

Library of Congress Cataloging-in-Publication Data

Strom, Robert and Strom, Paris.
Learning throughout life : an intergenerational perspective / by Strom, Robert D., and
Paris S. Strom, Auburn University, and Robert D. Strom, Arizona State University.
p. cm. -- (Lifespan learning)
Includes bibliographical references.
ISBN 978-1-62396-046-9 (paperback)—ISBN 978-1-62396-047-6 (hardcover)
—ISBN 978-1-62396-048-3 (ebook) 1. Learning. 2. Learning, Psychology
of. 3. Intergenerational relations. I. Strom, Robert D. II. Title.
LB1060.S858 2012
370.15--dc23

                                                                    2012033289

Printed in the United States of America

CONTENTS

PART III: ADOLESCENCE (AGES 10-20)

PREFACE

A longevity society should provide opportunities to learn for people of all ages. How can this comprehensive goal be implemented? What knowledge should people acquire at different stages of life to enable growth and well being? What lessons do cohorts want groups older and younger than themselves to learn? How can the mission for education be enlarged to reflect a dual emphasis on learning in teams and independent learning? The answers to these questions are needed to optimize human development.

Before children and adolescents were able to visit the Internet, the scope of their learning was determined by adults. Grownups also believed they were capable of recognizing their own learning needs. The orientation offered here explores greater benefits that can be gained by all generations from *reciprocal learning*—this means mutual growth based on consideration of the feelings, ideas, and observations of other age groups. Reciprocal learning is the key to mutual understanding and should take place at home, in school, at work, and the community.

The dangers of age segregation and importance of age integration are examined. Each generation should recognize the others as a potential source of learning. Intergenerational harmony is possible through public awareness of experiences that define the goals, satisfactions, and concerns of other subpopulations. All of us should become familiar with how other individuals interpret events, recognize values that motivate their behavior, and appreciate their vision of the future.

The interdependence America needs to remain globally competitive requires that schools enlarge their mission in order to prepare students

Learning Throughout Life: An Intergenerational Perspective, pp. xv–xvi
Copyright © 2012 by Information Age Publishing
All rights of reproduction in any form reserved.

for individual productivity and to work effectively in teams. Cooperative learning and creative thinking are linked in the text to build social connections, encourage healthy norms of behavior, and motivate a sense of optimism that most problems can be solved by collective action. Employers want schools to equip students with teamwork skills so they can collaborate in the workplace. When students realize the importance of teamwork, they include collaboration in their definition of success.

This book describes: (a) personality assets and mental abilities to focus learning at each stage of development; (b) obstacles to anticipate and overcome; (c) a rationale to make reciprocal learning common; (d) research findings which identify intergenerational learning needs; and (e) benefits of providing lifelong education. Six age stages are explored: infancy and early childhood (birth–age 6), middle and later childhood (ages 6-10), adolescence (ages 10-20), early adulthood (ages 20-40), middle adulthood (ages 40-60) and older adulthood (age 60+). Some of the cumulative personal attributes emphasized in this book include self-control, patience, integrity, resilience, reflection, acceptance of criticism, and generativity. Research has found that these qualities contribute to healthy development over a lifetime. The intended audiences for this book are professionals working with individuals and families.

Robert D. Strom
Paris S. Strom

ACKNOWLEDGMENTS

We are a father and son team who express gratitude to many students of all ages, teachers, parents, and grandparents that have shared personal stories about educational challenges, aspirations, satisfactions, and disappointments. Theoretical perspectives on learning, thinking, and schools have been shaped by our academic mentors that include Gordon Allport of Harvard University, Paul Torrance at the University of Georgia, Sydney Pressey of The Ohio State University, and Bernard Young and Elsie Moore from Arizona State University.

Relatives, friends, and colleagues have provided valuable guidance. Mary urged us to recognize the best in people and situations, apply patience in managing difficulties, and build resilience to overcome setbacks. Fred and Lee always took time to listen and suggest ways to improvise tasks. Ken's invitation to visit a camp for inner city children and meet a counselor working there turned out to be the greatest gift for our family. Steven and Jean have shown how a balanced definition of success can be attained by fulfilling their complimentary roles in business and family affairs. Caroline and Haley are part of the Millennial Generation; they continually enlarge our frame of reference by explaining their ideas about merging cultural evolution and cultural preservation. Shirley shares our ambition to help families, schools, and the community support reciprocal learning and respectful relationships throughout the lifespan.

Robert D. Strom
Paris S. Strom

Learning Throughout Life: An Intergenerational Perspective, pp. xvii–xvii
Copyright © 2012 by Information Age Publishing
All rights of reproduction in any form reserved.

PART I

INFANCY AND EARLY CHILDHOOD (BIRTH-AGE 6)

CHAPTER 1

LANGUAGE AND SOCIALIZATION

The goals of this chapter are to describe ways for parents to help their children solve problems, persist with difficult tasks, gain language to communicate ideas and feelings, and acquire skills to learn how others see situations. Emotional attachment, empathy, and trust are identified as basic elements of mental health and socialization. Introducing children to the Internet is a new obligation of parents that requires support. Recommendations include suitable expectations to enrich the learning experience of children and their parents as they go online together.

CONVERSATION AND ATTENTION

The importance of parent-child conversations have been demonstrated by experiments conducted over the past 50 years. Robert Hess at the University of Chicago wanted to explore the relationship between teaching methods of mothers and educational achievement of their children. More specifically, he sought to answer this question: If children from low-income households typically arrive at school unprepared to do the work that teachers expect of them, and, if middle class children typically are prepared to do these same tasks, what readiness experiences are provided in middle-class homes that are less available in the poverty households? (Hess & Shipman, 1973). To study this problem, Hess recruited 160 mothers and their 4-year old children; 40 mothers were upper-middle class, 40 mothers had skilled occupation backgrounds, another 40 repre-

Learning Throughout Life: An Intergenerational Perspective, pp. 3–25
Copyright © 2012 by Information Age Publishing
All rights of reproduction in any form reserved.

sented unskilled work roles, and 40 were public support recipients. Most of the Black and White adults lived in two-parent households. The exceptions were single mothers on welfare.

Maternal Teaching Methods

One way Hess compared mothers was to observe teaching methods they relied on to help their child complete a jigsaw puzzle that pictured fish of various sizes and colors. Each mother was asked to teach her child to put the puzzle together. One mother placed the puzzle in front of her child before she explained,

> This is a jigsaw puzzle. You have never seen one before. We are going to take all the pieces out of the picture and then put them back together. First, look carefully at the picture so that later on you will remember how it looks. Notice the shapes and colors of pieces so you know where they belong.

This mother defined the task and told her child how to proceed. Then she spilled the pieces out on the table, allowed the child to move materials about and guided him to success.

Another mother was equally supportive of her child according to notes recorded by an interviewer who had repeatedly visited her home. However, she began by dumping the puzzle on the table in front of her child without saying anything. Then she indicated, "Now, you go ahead and put it together." She watched while her child picked up pieces and tried to place them where they fit. The mother's continual directive was "Turn it around, turn it around." Thirty five times she repeated this statement until finally, in frustration, the child replied "You do it."

This mother wanted to help but was unable to communicate concepts needed to solve a simple problem. From his observations it soon became clear to Hess that the ability to convey concepts, share information, and program an uncomplicated task was demonstrated least often in the low-income families. This was not, however, the only important result. Imagine a child who, in repeated interactions with his mother encounters situations s/he makes an effort to solve but, owing to a lack of maternal assistance, finds it impossible. The reaction of defeat, "you do it," is likely to recur and be magnified many times. This orientation can cause a child to conclude that most problems lack solutions. Compare this response to the example given of the first parent-child conversation. That child knew no more about the puzzle in the beginning but, through experience that was structured by his mother, came to recognize there was a solution. It seems that the way children approach new learning tasks depends on the kind of interaction they have with their parent(s).

Perceptions of the Classroom

The mothers that Hess observed also differed in the way they perceived school. Their responses were compared reacting to the following situation:

> Imagine that your child is old enough to go to school for the first time. How would you prepare for this situation? What things would you tell the child? One mother who was person-oriented said, "First, I would remind her that the reason she is going to school is to learn, the teacher will be taking my place, and she will expect you to follow directions. Also, she should realize that most of her time will be in the classroom with other children, and she should ask the teacher for help if she has a question or a problem."

In terms of promoting educability, what did responses of this mother offer her child? First, she was informative, presenting the school situation as comparable to one already familiar to the child. Second, she provided reassurance and support that would help the child to deal with anxiety. Third, she described the classroom arrangement as involving a personal relationship between the child and the teacher. Fourth, she portrayed the school as a place where the child would be expected to learn.

Another mother who was status-oriented, not person-oriented, offered a different response to the same question. She reported, "Well, John, it's time for you to go to school. You must know how to behave in class. The first day you have to be a good boy and do exactly what the teacher tells you. Mind the teacher and be sure you don't get into fights with other kids."

In contrast with the previous mother, what orientation did this one give? She began by defining the student role as passive and compliant. Second, the central issues she presented emphasized authority and the institution, rather than learning. Third, relationships she portrayed were defined in terms of status and role expectations, rather than in personal terms. Fourth, her message was vague about handling the problems of school, except through obedience.

Compensatory Programming

Difficulty arises when a mother is unable to tell a child the path that should be taken to succeed. If young children experience achievement in problem solving at home because there is positive motivation, a reward for learning, then intrinsic curiosity can take them through most early stages. Hess and Shipman (1973) concluded that inner-city mothers were capable of being taught skills to provide child instruction. He presented an appeal to provide suitable parent education so they could fulfill their teaching role. However, federal officials decided instead to introduce a national education program for children intended to compensate for learning that was missing in disadvantaged homes. External evaluations have consistently concluded that the benefits of this program, called Head Start, lack durability and tend to be lost soon after children end program involvement (Williams, 2011).

LEARNING TO COMMUNICATE

Betty Hart and Todd Risley (2002) at the University of Kansas offered evidence of how parents can impact the way their children think. They wanted to examine literature about daily lives of children living in well-functioning families. Many studies were located that detailed conditions in minority or atypical families but descriptions of stable home environments were scarce. Hart and Risley decided they would study origins of differences in verbal ability among these children who represent the majority of Americans.

The 42 families recruited included Whites (60%) and Blacks (40%). All families functioned well, had a father or other male regularly involved with domestic affairs, and represented a wide range of incomes. Parents from 13 families had attended college and held professional or managerial roles; 23 families held blue-collar positions; and 6 families were on welfare. Every family had one or more children, including a 7-to 12- months of age infant who became the focus of the study. Monthly visits were made to each home, observing for one hour as the parent (usually mother) carried out a daily routine. Everything the parent said was tape-recorded while the observer took notes but never interacted. These monthly visits continued until the children were 3 years of age. Project data included 1,300 hours of data recorded by the observers who repeatedly visited the same homes.

Amount of Parent Talk

The greatest difference among the families was amount of parent talk with children (Hart & Risley, 2002). Regardless of their background, all the parents devoted about the same amount of talk to making sure their child did not participate in unsafe activities, was properly fed and dressed, and corrected for unacceptable behavior. However, interaction in the welfare families concerned little else. In contrast, extra talk in professional families and most talkative blue-collar families centered on getting to know each other where feedback was natural as they did activities together. This talk included more varied vocabulary, complex ideas, subtle guidance, and positive feedback important for mental development.

The more formal education a mother had attained, the more often she spoke with her child. On average, welfare mothers said 600 words an hour to their infants; blue-collar parents directed 1,200 words to their child; and professional parents used 2,000 words. These patterns remained stable over time and were not attributed to gender of child, number of siblings, parent employment or number of people present during observations. The variations in exposure to language translated into estimates that, by the time children were 3 years old, those in welfare homes had heard 10 million words, compared to 20 million in blue-collar families and 30 million in the professional homes. The value of this word play is such that children left behind by age 3 might never catch up.

Focus of Parent Attention

Parents who spoke more to children also gave more explanations, raised more questions, and communicated more feedback (Hart & Risley, 2002). Parents with professional backgrounds were attentive to favorable conduct of their child and made positive comments on this behavior about 30 times an hour—"I like the way you are cleaning the play room; you do a good job following my directions." This record of favorable reaction was more than twice as frequent as observed for blue-collar parents and six times that of the welfare families.

A corresponding pattern obtained for disapproval. The parents with professional backgrounds observed child misconduct and they made 5 indications of disapproval per hour, compared to 30 signs of approval. This was a 6 to 1 ratio in favor of positive remarks. In contrast, children in blue-collar homes heard 12 favorable comments and 7 disapprovals an hour, a positive ratio of 2 to 1. Response patterns reversed in welfare homes where parents made 5 approval statements and 11 disapprovals each hour for a negative ratio of 1 to 2. This means that welfare children heard prohibitions twice as often as they got favorable feedback. When low-income parents talked about the actions of their children, they more often criticized than praised them. These differences present profound lessons for language learning. Children of professionals get encouragement and praise while welfare children do not. Instead, they are taught to follow commands.

Parent affection was not a factor contributing to interaction. Those who talked with children less often were observed to be just as loving as parents whose conversations were extended and elaborate. Everyone showed concern for their children but families differed in the amount and type of communication with their child.

Effects on Child Behavior

Differences in parent behavior were reflected by differences in the achievements of their children (Hart & Risley, 2002). Boys and girls whose parents talked to them a lot, offered positive feedback, and gave frequent explanations scored higher on a measure of intelligence and vocabulary size at age 3. They were examined again at age 8 in third grade. Early patterns of parent-child interaction remained a good predictor of results on intelligence tests, language measures, and school grades. Parent race or economic status did not account for differences in the mental achievement of children. The correlation (closeness of relationship between two things) of family income and child performance declined from age 3 to age 8 while the relationship between the parent-child interaction and child academic performance remained stable. Based on this result, it seems that whether families are Black or White, poor or affluent, the condition with the most influence is parent behavior, a factor each mother and father can control.

The findings of the Kansas study include good news and bad news. On the positive side, it seems that poorly educated parents who have low-incomes are capable of providing children experiences required for normal mental development. The bad news is that, if parents fail to arrange such opportunities, remedial programs at school are unlikely to remove the deficiencies. A promising solution is to acquaint parents with their potential for influence and show them things they can do to become more effective teachers. Many more parents should be helped to understand that frequent conversations with children about seemingly unimportant things provide opportunities significant for mental and emotional development. The fact is children get better doing the things they practice. Therefore, having more conversations, more language tools, and greater ability to communicate can contribute to their success. This view is supported by other studies concluding that children whose parents offer greater exposure to extensive vocabulary and conversation become better readers in school (Beaty, 2009).

EMOTIONAL ATTACHMENT AND TRUST

Parents communicate in other ways besides language to let children know that they are important. Between birth and 2 years of age infants acquire basic trust or mistrust of their environment. When the adults who provide care are reliable, can be counted on to feed a hungry stomach, change a diaper that is uncomfortable, and regularly offer affection, boys and girls learn that others are dependable and can be trusted. In contrast, if caregivers ignore needs, are inconsistent in showing attention or act in abusive ways, infants learn fear and perceive their environment as unpredictable and dangerous.

From 6 months until 19 months of age is a critical period to acquire the human response of love and attachment, to form an emotional bond that establishes the foundation needed for socialization. Attachment is defined as a tie of affection that babies form with another person, their mother or a caretaker. The concept of attachment was proposed by John Bowlby, a British psychiatrist. He gained experience in treating children who were maladjusted during the Second World War when they had to be evacuated from London to keep them safe from air raids by Germany. The nation also began early childhood centers so that mothers could contribute to the war effort through their work in factories. Bowlby's (1988, 1999) experience with consequences of maternal separation led him to conclude that the human infant has a need for a secure relationship with adult caregivers, without which normal social and emotional development will not occur.

Social and Emotional Deprivation

Nonattachment and emotional deprivation are devastating forms of abuse. The cost was first identified by Harry Harlow, a psychologist at the University of Wisconsin. In a classic experiment, he separated two groups of baby monkeys from mothers. In one group a terrycloth mother provided no food, while a wire monkey had an attached baby bottle that contained milk. In the second group, a terrycloth mother provided food but the wire monkey did not. It was found that young monkeys clung to the terry cloth mother, whether it provided food or not and chose the wire surrogate only when it was the only source of food. These findings differed from prevailing advice to parents that limiting bodily contact with infants was necessary to keep from spoiling them and the dominant view of behaviorism contending that emotions were unimportant (Harlow, 1986).

Harlow concluded that giving care, not just feeding, strengthens a bond because of the intimate contact. However, the cloth monkey was an insufficient replacement for a mother as demonstrated by social isolation of monkeys that grew up with severe emotional and behavioral problems. Even when monkeys were brought up in cages where they could see, smell, and hear others but were prevented from touch contact, infants developed an 'autistic like' syndrome including grooming, self-clasping, social withdrawing and rocking behavior (Harlow, 1958; Harlow, Harlow, & Suomi, 1971).

The institutional review boards that monitor all research projects in universities would likely identify the monkey experiments as cruel and not approve them. But, consider a more extreme experiment related to human maternal deprivation. It was assumed that everyone realized institutional care is inadequate to maintain the social capacity of a human infant. This was not the case in Romania, where President Nicolae Ceausescu, the communist dictator from 1974-1989 was a believer in technology. He was skeptical of mental health professionals and eliminated financial support for projects in psychology and social work in favor of building engineering and science resources for his country. Incentive policies were implemented to increase the birth rate and all parents were required to be employed. Social policy reflected economic gain instead of the best interests of children and families. For parents who were unable or unwilling to care for their children, orphanages and inferior day care centers were built to house them. More than 100,000 undernourished boys and girls were maltreated in these kinds of facilities. Although thousands of people were infected with HIV and Aids, Ceausescu maintained that these diseases were nonexistent in Romania, a denial that allowed the virus to spread (Klich & Muller, 2002).

After Ceausescu was executed during a coup that took place in 1989, Romanian orphanages were shown on global television, allowing the world to observe these warehouses for the unwanted. Children would rock back and forth and grasp themselves in the same manner as Harlow's monkeys. When they were older, most of the children demonstrated sad and bizarre social interaction. To express affection, a boy might kiss another person on top of the head. Smiling and ingratiating, they appeared friendly but were unable to form permanent attachments. Like characters in a science fiction novel, many found employment with the secret police where their lack of loyalty and inability to make friends were saleable traits (Deletant, 1995).

Stress, Touch, and Attention

Health studies of the orphans were based on prior research showing that, during stress, the body secretes adrenaline and cortisol hormones to regulate blood sugar levels. In contrast, with the fast, pumping energy that is immediately provided by adrenaline, coritsol acts to suppress the reaction to stress by shutting down the energy-expensive systems used for growth, digestion, reproduction, and immunity against disease. Mary

Carlson (2000), a neurobiologist from Harvard gained insight about maternal deprivation while she was a graduate student of Harry Harlow at the University of Wisconsin. In the Romanian care system, Carlson's purpose was to examine 60 youngsters, 2 to 3 years of age. Daily cycles of cortisol secretion were chemically measured by using saliva analyses. The results showed the stress response of children was poorly regulated. Hormone levels in the morning were much lower than normal. Cortisol peaked at noon compared to the norm at morning wake up. Cortisol secretion in the afternoon stayed high when it should be the lowest. Carlson concluded that the disregulation of cortisol was interferring with physical growth, mental development, and motor activity. The tasks that normal 2- to 3-year-olds can do well, like picture recognition, word repetition, socializing, standing on one foot, and walking upstairs without holding on, could not be performed by the orphans. Most children were in the third to tenth percentile for physical growth and grossly delayed in motor and mental development. The more abnormal the cortisol levels, the worse the outcomes.

Carlson (2000) found that lack of touch and attention could modify the stress reaction of children, stunt growth, and adversely affect behavior. The results were confirmed when she investigated another group of Romanian children who attended poor quality group care the Romanians called day orphanages. During the week while at daycare with understaffed and poorly trained workers, child cortisol levels were abnormal but became more normal on weekends when they went home to be with relatives. The children who got away from the day care part-time to more supportive conditions at home were compared with those who stayed full time at the day orphanage. Overall, the part-timers showed more normal cortisol indicators.

To explore how stress levels might change by introducing hugs and other nurturant contact, 30 Romanians engaged in an enrichment program (Cromie, 1998). Unlike usual day care where one caretaker is responsible for many children, each caretaker was assigned just four children. The goals were to cuddle, play with, read to, hug, comb hair, and make sure that each child was properly fed and well dressed. Participants in this 1-year enrichment showed significant improvement. However, after being returned to previous care conditions that excluded touching, assessments showed the behavioral and physical advantages of nurturant care faded.

Other studies of severely depressed people and soldiers returning from Iraq and Afghanistan with posttraumatic syndrome have discovered abnormalities in daily cortisol cycles (Mate, 2011). Brain images of patients who have suffered from lengthy depression and posttraumatic syndrome revealed a shrinkage in the hippocampus region of the brain that implicates memory and the regulation of cortisol secretion.

Given the consistent relationship found between poor group care and abnormal cortisol, what is happening to American children who experience poor day care on a regular basis? According to Carlson (2000),

> The social networks in which children grow up bear on the development of the neural networks that mediate memory, emotion, and self. As parents, as citizens, and as policy makers, we must ensure that our social policy pathways do not lead to social deprivation.... When faced with choices about children in day care and residential care, we must ensure that our decisions have positive consequences.

Importance of Emotional Learning

Further research has shown that, when children are denied emotional learning, effects on development can be profound (Proctor, 2008). Soon after the revelation of orphanage neglect, 1,500 Romanian orphans were adopted by Americans. Despite the affection and care provided by these parents, most of the adopted children grew up with permanent social and emotional deficits. The adoptive parents often described them in this way: "My daughter is oblivious to the concept of love. She is intelligent but unable to show concern for the needs of other people" (Galbraith, 1998). Harry Chugani (1998), a pediatric neurologist at Wayne State University and the Children's Hospital in Detroit, Michigan, conducted brain scans of adopted Romanians and found significant eccentricities in the brain region related to emotional development. Chugani concluded there is a limited period of time early in life when children must be given healthy emotional stimulation to ensure they will be able to recreate and share these same emotions through life. The Romanians were denied such opportunities at the cost of their potential for caring, compassion, and engagement in trusting relationships.

PARENT AND CHILD DEVELOPMENT

Early Intervention Approaches

Studies of intervention have consistently found that giving education for parent and child, rather than only one generation, yields the greatest gains. Exemplary large-scale programs can offer direction for states that seek replication models. For example, the Minnesota Early Childhood Family Education Program (2011) offers free courses for parents of children from birth to kindergarten. Classes are held in public schools throughout the state and reach 95% of families with preschoolers. The short courses focus on development and potential during a particular 6 month interval, allowing parents to find out how to support learning at their child's present age. These classes add to parent knowledge of childhood and they include demonstrations of teaching methods for successive ages.

While children are cared for by program staff, parents participate in discussion groups sharing hopes, anxieties, and concerns. Discussions are attended by mentor parents, those with children a few months older, so they can readily recall problems they had at the same age of their child's development. Graduates agree to become mentors for the families that follow them.

Healthy Start was established in 1985 by the state of Hawaii Department of Health (2011) and remains a model program for the prevention of child abuse. Family involvement begins when a case worker interviews the parents of newborns in the hospital shortly after their child is born. The initial goal is to identify parents that seem at risk of abusing their children. These are drug takers, alcoholics, teenage mothers, welfare recipients or people that were abused themselves as children or by their spouses. Parents who are detected as in the high-risk category are offered, at no cost, services of a home visitor. The home visitors must have graduated from high school and grew up in stable homes. They may serve as a family advisor for up to 5 years. No parent is obligated to enroll in the program but very few refuse the resource. The role of the home visitor is to be an all-purpose advocate for the family. They show the parents how to feed and nurture their infants, ensure that children get regular medical checkups and shots. In some cases, they assist parents in finding work or housing. Studies in other states have found that, without intervention, 20% of high-risk parents can be expected to mistreat children. Healthy Start reduced this proportion to less than 1%. Estimates are that the amount of money spent each year on Healthy Start is only one-third of what the cost to Hawaii would otherwise be for postabuse protective custody and foster care. Healthy Start has been adopted by 25 states.

The United States Department of Health and Human Services (2010) provides annual data on incidence of reported child abuse. The most recent report shows 3.3 million referrals about abuse of 6 million children. Victims in the birth to age 1-year group have the highest rate, twice as great as for older children. The most prominent sources of abuse are parents (81%), and other relatives (6%). The most common forms of abuse are neglect (75%), and physical mistreatment (18%).

A longitudinal study provides insight about how provision of high quality education between ages 3 and 8 can yield economic and social well-being benefits that remain evident in adulthood. The longest operating large-scale early education program for families was the focus of a 25-year follow-up with 1,000 inner city students from preschool through age 28. They were compared to 500 similar students who had no preschool but attended kindergarten. The experimental subjects were low income mostly Blacks (93%) in Chicago linked to one of 20 parent child centers funded by Title I. The instructional program included half or full day education activities emphasized mathematics and language taught by well trained and well paid certified teachers. Family services were given until children completed third grade. Parent education featured child-rearing skills.

Arthur Reynolds at the University of Minnesota led a follow-up study (Reynolds, Temple, Suh-Ruu, Artega, & White, 2011). Results showed that children who had 4 to 6 years of intervention recorded a 49% on-time graduation rate from high school as compared to 31% for those with less than 4 years of intervention. Preschoolers also recorded higher rates of entry to 4-year colleges, greater employment in skilled jobs, lower rates of felony arrests, and less depression symptoms in early adulthood. Boys and children whose parents were high school dropouts gained the most benefit. The cost-benefit analysis estimated that for every $1 invested in the preschool project, $11 is projected to return to society over the lifetime of the children.

Empathy and Social Skills

The way that mothers talk to their preschoolers about understanding feelings of other people, referred to as empathy, can have a lasting effect on social skills. Social understanding develops by reflecting on how others may see things, taking into account how events could be interpreted from the view of someone else. Researchers at University of Sussex, England, examined child ability to recognize and appreciate the perspectives of other people (Ruffman, Slade, Devitt, & Crowe, 2006). A longitudinal experiment tracked 57 children from age 3 to 12. At the outset, half the mothers were given guidelines for talking with their children about feelings, beliefs, wants, and intentions of others; the remainder half of the mothers were not given any recommendations to shape their conversations.

Researchers visited the homes to observe how each mother talked to her children while looking at a series of pictures together. For example, successive pictures of a young girl showed her favorite toy was broken, she visited swings and slides at a playground, and the high tower she has built out of blocks was deliberately pushed over by a boy. The children whose mothers talked with them about the "mental state" of characters in these as well as other pictures performed better on tasks of social understanding administered every year. The relationship between conversations that dealt with 'mental states' and social understanding was strongest in early childhood and independent of mother IQ or level of social understanding. Mother influence waned between ages 8 to 12 when children were less dependent on them and spent more time with peers, teachers, and other adults (Yuill & Ruffman, 2009).

One measure of social understanding that was applied with children age 8 and older involved watching video clips from *The Office*, a popular comedy show on television. The main character, David Brent, typifies individuals who tend to incorrectly interpret social situations. Adult viewers realized that the reason David so often embarrassed coworkers was his lack of social understanding. The children also detected David's social skill deficits in explaining why he seemed oblivious to how he continually made others uncomfortable. Every parent should take advantage of television viewing to talk with children about how characters on programs might be feeling as a result of actions or events as they unfold. Labeling the way other people might feel, identifying their "mental state," is an important step toward achievement of social maturity.

There are also daily opportunities to reinforce this lesson based on how children interact with companions. For example, when a child grabs a toy from a playmate, the observing parent could use this incident to point out that "When you took the airplane away from Terry, it made him feel sad." This interpretation provides the child with insight and offers greater benefit than saying "Give it back now or you are going to be punished." Parents should convey to their children a vocabulary of feelings so boys and girls learn how to express emotions, can use words to explain how they suppose that other people are feeling, and establish empathy as a consistent personality pattern.

Child Access to Parent Time

Low-income parents demonstrate less competence with skills that support child growth and development. For this reason they are the target group invited to participate in federally sponsored programs. Sometimes affluent parents misinterpret this policy by supposing their higher income must mean that they are successful in raising children. Fortunately, a more balanced view about what it takes to raise children is becoming known. Certain attitudes and skills that parents of every income and ethnicity should learn offer the best assurance for eliminating deprivation in childhood. We no longer suppose that every low-income youngster is deprived or all children from middle-class homes are advantaged. Parent behavior is more influential than their income.

Many affluent parents have reason to feel good about themselves and the ways they help their children. Benefit can also come from being self-critical. Our comparative studies of 5,000 parents of children and adolescents in China, Japan, and Taiwan along with diverse Americans including Asians, Blacks, Hispanics, and Whites have identified one factor as more influential than others for achieving success in raising children. "Child access to parent time" seems the most important support parents can provide daughters and sons. This variable is more powerful than child access to the income of parents (Strom & Strom, 2009). A sensible plan is to spend 1 hour each weekday and 2 hours a day on the weekends doing things with your child.

Parents of all income and education levels should choose to spend adequate time with their children. Some parents assert that they spend "quality time." However, quality time is correctly defined as when children need access to parents, rather than when parents find it convenient to schedule being with their children in the same way they arrange time for customers or clients. Managing time so priorities get the attention they must have is one of the most important lessons parents can teach children (Levine, 2006).

Affluent parents give children many advantages but seldom think about what they could learn from less privileged parents. Our studies have found that many blue-collar fathers are seen as more successful by their children and themselves than are affluent fathers. When blue-collar fathers return home from work, often at an earlier hour than affluent fathers, they do not go to their study to check e-mail, text, or make phone calls. Instead, they spend time with their children. Blue-collar parents are much less inclined to talk about "quality time" or similar euphemisms that can detract from family relationships (Strom & Strom, 2009).

The evidence that family wealth does not ensure good parenting practices is documented by studies of households with annual incomes of $125,000 or more (Levine, 2006). One assumption has been that affluent parents seldom need guidance because their social status indicates they have things under control. Some affluent parents interpret this view to mean they must maintain a false image that those at the top are able to handle their problems better than people lower on the income scale. Family studies have found that children of the affluent more often experience psychosocial risks than their low-income peers. Specifically, children of the affluent are more likely to become involved with illegal drugs, endure anxiety, and suffer depression. Two factors explain much of the risk—excessive pressures from parents to achieve at school and isolation from the parents, actual and emotional (Luthar & Latendresse, 2005).

EARLY LEARNING ONLINE

Parents encounter challenges and opportunities that seem to be more complex than were experienced by previous generations. The growing up process also appears more complicated because of the revolution in communications technology, growing influence of media, and pervasive adoption of a hurried lifestyle. Introducing children to what the digital society will expect of them is a new and demanding task for mothers and fathers. This obligation is defined by providing children with opportunities to observe, practice, and develop the attitudes and skills that will become a foundation for learning on the Internet and orientation to healthy social networking (Strom & Strom, 2010).

The New Playground

Parents bring young children to public playgrounds with an expectation that the visit will present opportunities for them to socialize and pretend with peers of their age. Children also look forward to the experience and typically express reluctance to leave the playground when told that it is time to go home. In this setting the responsibilities of grownups are commonly understood. They are supposed to be observers that monitor all aspects of the scene and arrange conditions to ensure safety, prevent mistreatment, and encourage enjoyment for everyone. The appeal of public playgrounds makes them a popular destination around the world.

There is another playground, a place where having fun, talking, and learning is what a child and parent can do together. In this more complicated environment, most parents express uncertainty regarding what to expect of themselves and their children. As boys and girls have greater access to the Internet, the amount of learning that takes place at home is bound to increase and require that parents demonstrate how to behave online, provide corrective feedback, recognize success, and give continuous supervision to ensure safety. Mothers and fathers should be made aware that, from now on, support of child development should include opportunity for practice with technology tools (Rosen, 2010).

The Kaiser Family Foundation conducted the first nationwide survey to determine the extent of media presence in lives of infants, toddlers, and young children (Rideout & Hamel, 2006). Sources of information included 1,000 parents of children aged 6 months to 6 years old. Results indicated that many young children are on the computer daily, alone when they turn on the machine, and permitted to choose their own activity. The Kaiser survey team concluded that preschoolers are the most rapidly increasing age segment on the Internet. These children are not old enough to join social networks like MySpace, Facebook, YouTube, Hi5, Xanga, Live Journal, Bebo or Nexopia, Canadian equivalent of MySpace. However, a growing number of large-scale providers like Club Penguin, Webkins, and Togetherville are catering to this young population.

Most families have Internet access and parents are eager to arrange activities to support child readiness for school. However, introducing boys and girls to the Internet is an unprecedented task that causes parents to wonder about the kinds of lessons they should try to convey. Fortunately, Internet activity is bound to promote conversation between a parent and child. A combination of visual and audio stimulation motivates young children to talk about feelings, describe ideas, interpret events, express curiosity, generate guesses, identify difficulties, recognize and correct mistakes, enjoy success, and gain confidence. There are corresponding opportunities for the parents to share their impressions, arrange discovery, express curiosity, respond to questions, urge persistence, recognize achievement, correct assumptions, make known right and wrong attitudes to guide conduct on the Internet, and make their unique contribution to the development of social skills. Close family relationships in early childhood depend on continuous access to one another and mutual self-disclosure. These same conditions can prevent the Internet from later becoming an age-segregated forum. The Center for the Digital Future (2010) has shown that many children and adolescents communicate online almost exclusively with peers and have less conversation with their parents.

Parent Internet Obligations

Preschoolers are taught the alphabet and encouraged to practice recitation of numbers as readiness activities for school. However, they lack the skills needed for reading to be used as a tool for learning. Therefore, they must rely on observation for much of what they learn. Between 3 and 5 years of age children are in a development stage known as "identification" that motivates imitation of attitudes and actions of the adults who take care of them. Accordingly, parents must learn to deal with unfamiliar obstacles of teaching in a cyber setting. Consider some questions by parents about maximizing the benefit of Internet visits with their children.

1.   What should be the focus of attention during parent-child visits to the Internet? Many adults think of the Internet as a huge library that contains infinite knowledge. Certainly, easy access to information is a great leap forward from how things were in the past. But, instead of exposure to as much content as possible, a more helpful

strategy is to emphasize the mental processes that children need to support critical thinking. This departure from the customary emphasis may seem strange because it contradicts the definition of teaching as conveying information that learners should memorize. A more effective approach on the Internet is to respect the child motivation for discovery by modeling search skills that allow individuals to find out whatever they want to know. These lessons that illustrate processes are essential in the emerging environment to frame questions, persist in locating data that is difficult to find, and to think critically about the truthfulness of content presented by Web sites. The task is to repeatedly model conditions of self-directed learning like asking questions, checking on hunches, exploring possibilities, judging credibility, and applying insights to daily affair situations.

2. How can parents support the motivation that a child needs for learning online? Parents should be aware that certain of their attitudes can interfere with teaching in a new environment and must be unlearned. First, reconsider what was taught when we were children about a relationship between pleasure and learning. Many adults believe that enjoyable activities do not qualify as learning. This view is no longer sensible and must be left behind. Instead, anyone educating children now should know that, beside providing quick retrieval of data, technology tools have enormous appeal, stimulate participation, encourage dialogue, increase attention span, and facilitate a sustained willingness to remain engaged in trying to solve problems. A common reason dropouts give for quitting school is that classroom learning seldom included pleasure. Educators of all grade levels are recognizing that continued pursuit of learning is closely related to satisfaction. And, it seems clear that children must continue to learn throughout life.

3. How can parents contribute to the joy of learning for their child? Educators frequently express concern about a lack of parent involvement and wish that there were ways to motivate more of them to take responsibility for their important teaching role. However, encouraging parents to help children learn is a vague recommendation that assumes adults are equally comfortable with participation in activities like reading, Internet searching, online games, and enjoying discussions with children. The reality is that many parents, especially those with low-incomes, feel uncomfortable in the culture of learning because the years they spent in school were mostly disappointing and lead to withdrawal before getting a diploma and completing career preparation. These parents have a need to experience the pleasures of learning before

they are able to communicate a sense of enthusiasm to their children. Carefully chosen website visits can give this experience to parents and enable them to share the joy of learning with children.

4. What conditions should be established for orienting children to the Internet? The optimal condition for children to acquire and apply knowledge is being in a setting where there are opportunities to immediately practice what is taught and get feedback from parents about achievement along with corrective guidance. Situated-learning that occurs at home often contrasts with how knowledge is gained in school where teachers must work with groups and often accept memorization as evidence of comprehension. A more practical form of assessment is to demonstrate understanding in a context where the learning should be applied. Situated-learning in early childhood, when observation is the basis of forming concepts, allows parents to act as models, the most powerful form of instruction. Those who educate young children often indicate that their purpose is to support "learning how to learn." In the future, this goal should include child involvement with Internet tools and careful supervision, the one-on-one interaction that can best be arranged in the home by parents. It is unreasonable to expect staff in early childhood centers that have responsibility for many children to also provide the individual Internet experiences children need. Parents have the leadership role in orienting daughters and sons to the Internet.

5. What behaviors should parents look for while on the Internet with children? Careful observation can reveal lessons a child learns, detect where greater attention is needed, and provide feedback to adults about their teaching success. When parents have evidence that instruction they provide is supporting child development, they report increased motivation and confidence. The checklist in Table 1.1 can be used for a periodic reference to help gauge child progress on the Internet. Behaviors in the left column are seen as desirable. Parents can place a check in the right column beside behaviors that are demonstrated. Additional competencies can be placed on the list of goals that parents want children to achieve.

Internet Safety Practices

Most parents agree that the Internet is a wonderful resource but they also fear that children may be exposed to conditions that could place them in danger. Worrisome possibilities can be reduced by careful consideration of the following guidelines.

1. Always sit beside a young child while s/he is allowed to be on the computer. Nonstop supervision is needed for Internet guidance, to observe behavior, and to protect a loved one. Before age 10 most children lack the critical thinking skills needed to be on the Internet alone. Some children will disagree but they are wrong.

2. Devise a menu of a child's favorite web sites for easy access. Young children are dependent on their parents to access web sites. This practice lets a child know that returning to familiar and safe places is easier when the computer is asked to remember the Uniform Resource Locator address, otherwise known as the URL.

3. Begin to have conversations about the importance of privacy. Small children know the frustration that occurs when others intrude on their play or fail to respect their privacy. In contrast,

Table 1.1.   A Parent Observation Checklist While On The Internet With a Young Child*

While on the Internet with me, my child—	My child does—
Asks questions that reflect curiosity	
Shows willingness to keep on trying	
Talks about preferences and concerns	
Develops a sense of self-confidence	
Accepts challenges that are unfamiliar	
Listens to directions and follows them	
Wants to participate in repetition	
Makes known difficulties of tasks	
Demonstrates willingness to wait	
Makes guesses for experimentation	
Pays attention and stays on track	
Displays carefulness and caution	
Takes time to make decisions	
Manages frustration without anger	
Views failure as part of learning	
Asks me for help when it is needed	
Displays hand-eye coordination	
Predicts what will happen next	
Accepts time limits on computer	
Can recall sequence of steps	

*Adapted from *Parenting Young Children: Exploring the Internet, Television, Play, and Reading*, by R. Strom & P. Strom, 2010, p. 7. Information Age Publishing Inc., Charlotte, NC.

children tend to trust adults without caution and seldom question their authority. Tell the child a family rule is that we never share any information about ourselves with anyone else. If some desirable website encourages children to submit their name in order to personalize content, create an unrelated nickname that does not reveal any personal data.

4.   Encourage the child to tell a parent or surrogate about online concerns or worries. Respond to the willingness to rely on adult guidance by providing positive feedback such as "I'm glad you told me about that; I would not have known otherwise."

5.   Young children benefit from composing and dictating email messages adults send for them to relatives or friends and receive messages from these sources that are read aloud. However, children should be denied involvement with Instant Messaging (IM), participation in chat rooms or message boards before they are 10 years old.

6.   Consider Internet-filter tools but not as a substitute for careful supervision by adults. Protect against offensive pop-up windows by using pop-up blocker software.

SUMMARY AND IMPLICATIONS

When parents become aware of mental potential of young children, they recognize the importance of their responsibility. Parents love their children, want to show affection and support all aspects of development. However, adults vary in amount of conversation they have with children, how they define learning tasks, extent of encouragement, attention to commendable behavior, attitudes communicated about solving problems, and emphasis on social understanding of how others see situations. Community education programs for at-risk families is a way to facilitate attachment and prevent child abuse. Research has consistently found more lasting gains when parent development is linked with child development.

Preparing children for the digital environment is emerging as an essential aspect of education that requires teaching at home. Technology can encourage boys and girls to question, challenge, and disagree, thereby increasing the potential to become critical thinkers. The orientation to the Internet needed by preschoolers cannot be adequately provided in group care where the staff have a responsibility to supervise many children. Accordingly, parents should understand some basic aspects of technology so they are able to support learning for their child, especially in the preschool years when curiosity is high and easily directed to discovery tasks, search skills, and ethical attitudes needed for healthy social networking. Parents should be informed about how to introduce their children to the Internet. Innovative education programs for families of all socioeconomic groups can persuade them that their children will benefit from guidance on the Internet and that mothers and fathers are capable of providing the initial forms of instruction.

Some parents hesitate to have a child join them on the Internet because the adult lacks confidence or computer skills. A more productive outlook is to recognize that, by demonstrating the desire to explore and discover ideas, parents offer children a worthy example of motivation for learning. Toward this goal, parents need encouragement and support to adopt high expectations for themselves as they strive to help children begin their journey toward becoming self-directed learners. As child access to technology grows, learning at home is bound to increase and require that more parents assume their unique modeling function, provide corrective feedback, and monitor Internet activity for safety.

APPLICATIONS FOR TEACHING

1. Parents who talk to children often support language and speech development. The purpose is to ask questions, explain ideas and events, define tasks, tell meanings of words, and listen. The amount of dialogue is important because children get better at the things they are encouraged to practice. Having many conversations, acquiring a larger vocabulary, feeling confident about knowing how to solve problems, and learning to communicate thoughts and emotions can contribute much to a child's success at school.

2. Children need frequent reaction to the full scope of their behavior. Boys and girls require feedback about how they behave so their progress is recognized and they know the direction for improvement. These benefits occur more often when parents pay as much attention to favorable behavior as misconduct. This broad focus for observation is needed so commendable behavior can be reinforced by comments of approval, misbehavior is detected for corrective instruction, and both parties experience satisfaction that comes with awareness of growth.

3. Parents should describe how situations and events might be seen by others. By talking together about the "mental state" of characters that are seen on television, in books and stories, during website visits, and in daily interactions children have with companions, parents can support social understanding that is needed to also respond in a socially beneficial way.

4. Situations that require waiting are opportunities to demonstrate patience. While the Internet materials are loading, adults should explain that the computer is getting things ready for the opportunity to play. Responding in this way presents a helpful example of learning to wait and being able to cope with delay. Adopting such attitudes contributes more to healthy adjustment of children than blaming the computer for inconvenience of having to wait.

5. Respect the child desire for repetition when exploring the Internet. Playing a game or carrying out an activity on the Internet repeatedly is more appealing to a child than an adult. These repetitive experiences provide children with feelings of confidence that, in certain situations, they can tell in advance what is going to happen next. Being able to predict that specific things will remain the same such as having a daily schedule for meals or going to bed at a particular time satisfies a need for order and consistency that is much stronger in early childhood than during later stages of development

6. Permit a child to navigate the mouse and practice without criticism. This experience provides a sense of control rather than watching the parent act as the sole control agent because it is easier for adults and things proceed more quickly. Sharing some control with the child in certain situations is a better guidance strategy than is constant dominance. Recognize that moving a mouse properly will be difficult at first, particularly given the lesser muscle control of children at this early age. Encourage practice. Responses like "You can do it," and "You did it correctly" are more appropriate responses to confirm achievement than vague praise like "You are amazing," or "You are really smart."

7. Following directions is the way to do tasks that are understood. Adults who read aloud the directions presented online and follow them carefully are able to orient children to a way of getting things done that is more effective than trial and error. Ask the child to explain directions to confirm understanding about a proper sequence of steps.

8. Asking questions is essential to become a self-directed learner. When parents react to their own uncertainty by asking questions, children adopt this behavior as a way to think about situations as they happen. The practice avoids premature conclusions or making decisions about appropriate ways to respond before needed reflection occurs.

9. Schedule time that is not rushed to explore the Internet together. This is important because it lets the child know the priority s/he

has in a parent's life. Be sure to avoid distractions such as cell phone calls or use of multitasking. Instead, full attention should be given to being together. Studies have determined that the amount of time spent together is the single best predictor of parent success as perceived by children and parents. Initially, we recommend 15-minute visits to the Internet with young children.

10. Realize that children are more able to control their pace of learning online. The Internet allows children to return to tasks, start a process over, and retrace their steps. In this way, Internet activity allows for the practice that is needed to build confidence and gain skills that support problem solving.

CHAPTER 2

SELF-CONTROL AND PATIENCE

Young children should be taught to begin the process of developing self-control, patience, and emotional intelligence, qualities that are needed throughout life. The evidence that these lessons are being learned can be observed by how well children get along with one another and extent to which concern is shown for mutual rights. The goals of this chapter are to evaluate the success of parents in teaching self-control, recognize the importance of child autonomy, document preschool misbehavior, and explore ways to assess student adjustment at school. Another goal is to explain why patience and willingness to wait are essential for mental health. The implications of parents overscheduling their children are examined. Dynamics of dominion play is analyzed as are related methods to support child decision making about peer conflict instead of being unduly dependent on adults to resolve all disputes.

SUCCESS OF PARENTS AS TEACHERS

Parents want their children to learn respect and responsibility. The common view is that particular aspects of character and certain values should be acquired so children are well equipped to manage predictable difficulties. A national sample of 1,600 parents of 5- to 17-year-old children responded to a survey regarding the importance of teaching eleven character traits and values. The values ranked by parents as absolutely essential for them to convey included being honest and truthful (91%),

Learning Throughout Life: An Intergenerational Perspective, pp. 27–47
Copyright © 2012 by Information Age Publishing
All rights of reproduction in any form reserved.

courteous and polite (84%), self-control and self-discipline (83%) and, always do your best in school (82%) (Farkas, Johnson, Duffett, Wilson, & Vine, 2002).

One way to evaluate the success of parents, in their own estimate, is to compare the percentage identifying a goal as absolutely essential with the percentage reporting success in teaching that attribute. This kind of analysis reveals that, even for the contexts parents regard as essential, large gaps separate their intentions from what they have been able to accomplish. The greatest challenge was identified as teaching self-control and self-discipline. A gap of 49 points exists between 83% of parents who agree this lesson must be taught and 34% who feel they have succeeded.

Other values parents hope to convey also require children to develop self-control and self-discipline. This was illustrated by the goal of teaching how to save money and spend carefully. There was a 42% gap between the proportion of parents that considered this goal important and percentage affirming they have succeeded in teaching the lesson. Another gap implicates cheating, a separation between 91% of parents reporting they should teach honesty and truthfulness and 55% who credited themselves for achieving the task. Many parents realized that they must become more effective in teaching values (Farkas, Johnson, Duffett, Wilson, & Vine, 2002).

Some related observations come from teachers in our classes responding to two questions: (1) What changes would you like to see in the way students treat teachers? and, (2) What changes would you like to see in the way parents treat their child's teachers? Educators reported a growing number of students whose lack of self-control is shown by unhealthy responses to common challenges. These signs of dysfunction include periodic outbursts of anger, cursing to express frustration, threatening classmates or teachers, and withdrawing from activities. Parents demonstrate similar responses when told about child misconduct. Becoming upset and making threats happen more than the past according to teachers with lengthy experience in the classroom (Harwood, 2005; Proctor, 2008). The most disappointing reaction of parents is denial, the refusal to accept negative feedback about misconduct of their children. Such adults often take the side of their child instead of accepting responsibility to correct child behavior. This reaction can cause troublesome students to suppose the family condones their misbehavior.

What appears to happen is that, with gradual erosion of their authority at home, many parents redefine their role to acting as a buffer for children against all outside authorities including teachers at school. Parents spend less time with children than they prefer and want to ensure that time together is mutually satisfying. Therefore, instead of imposing punishment, they usually suspend discipline in favor of issuing warnings. Perhaps they suppose this strategy will endear them to their children but the actual effect is to prevent the development of social maturity.

Educators point out that only parents can fulfill their unique role in guiding social and emotional adjustment. For this reason schools across the nation try to motivate parents to remain involved with their teaching role. Student success depends upon parents and faculty each making their distinctive contribution. When student deficiencies involve comprehension of curriculum, parents may not possess the knowledge needed for tutoring. Accordingly, schools must assume this obligation. However, when deficiencies reflect social misconduct, family guidance is implicated.

Child Independence, Doubt, and Anger

Child potential for independence begins with motor skills. Two- and 3-year-olds can climb stairs, push and pull objects, and throw things. Success with these functions motivates a desire to gain some independence, wanting to do certain things without help from adults. Sometimes simple tasks such as flushing the toilet, washing hands, carrying a plate from a table to the kitchen sink, and getting dressed are managed well and result in feelings of self-control. When adults urge self-sufficiency, the consequent independence causes children to believe they can handle certain problems on their own.

Sometimes caretakers are impatient, perhaps because of their schedule. In these cases, a typical response is to rush children or do for them what they are capable of and prefer to do alone. Adults who follow this path explain "I'll do it for you because you take too long" or they criticize the children for spilling juice, dropping a plate, or wetting pants. In turn, this response leads children to doubt whether they are capable of controlling events.

Children need patient caretakers who allow them to do some things on their own, without excessive supervision. If the adults are too demanding, expect too much too soon, refuse to let children do some tasks alone, or ridicule unsuccessful efforts to be independent, children become more uncertain about their ability to perform well. Caretakers should provide structure, safety, and discipline. To ensure that children get to experience autonomy and pride instead of feeling unworthy and lacking in confidence, they must know their own limits, be aware of rules they can count on to be kept, and have assurance of a routine. Otherwise, the world seems too large, too complex, too fast, and too impersonal. Children demonstrate ambivalence in being curious and cautious, eager and fearful, autonomous and dependent. This means caretakers should accept their fears and worries instead of being punitive. Children seek order, and need a predictable time for meals and a consistent bedtime.

Anger is a child's way of expressing that certain situations are too difficult and produce frustration. Aggression is a violent form of anger as a child attacks someone or something in retaliation. These actions are usually self-defeating because they result in counterattack or rejection. The word that 2½-year-old children say most often is "No." As a result, this is the peak age for spanking from adults who reply "You better get it straight that you are not the boss in this family."

Before adopting methods to help children manage anger and aggression, caretakers should try to find out the cause for emotional upset. Observation and listening are good strategies. For example, a sullen and aggressive boy was sent to a counselor who greeted him but received no response. The counselor asked what the boy did yesterday. "I took a walk." Was anybody with you? My dog. Do you talk to your dog? Yes. What did you talk about? My dad. This line of questioning with short answers continued slowly and soon revealed that the precipitating factor in the boy's anger was being unable to meet unrealistic expectations of his dad. When father was informed, he began to look for commendable behaviors to acknowledge. The boy grew more responsive and more confident.

Getting children to talk about the pictures they draw, coloring together, talking on a toy phone, interpreting what is happening to someone else shown on a video or photograph are ways to solicit child impressions. It is easier for them to engage in these forums of communication than talking face to face with an adult much bigger than themselves. Keep in mind that the troublesome situation may not be the root cause, as in the boy and dog conversation incident. Some guidelines to help children handle anger and frustration are:

1. Exploring anger and frustration should be motivated by an intention to discover the upsetting cause rather than just to correct misconduct.

2. Do not respond in anger. Punishment is ineffective when it is hostile. Set limits to how anger can be expressed but explain the reasons for rules. People who suppose that venting negative feelings is the way for anger to run its course are unaware of research findings showing that venting increases anger.

3. Remove the misbehaving child from a situation but permit return when s/he can show self-control. Some children find this technique sufficiently effective that they can say to a preschool teacher: I think I better leave the play area for a while.

4. Do not require inauthentic apologies. This practice denies children the benefit of reflection about their behavior in favor of saying what grownups prefer to hear. Wanting to redress a hurt that we

cause is an important attribute that can only emerge from reflection on our actions rather than follow politically correct ways. Apologies by many people are mingled with negative remarks like "I said I was sorry—What else do you want from me?" Instead of someone apologizing when they do not actually feel sorry, it is better to support change in their behavior.

Preschool Expulsion and Improvement

The Child Study Center at Yale University examined 4,000 kindergartens representing all 50 state-funded programs (Gilliam, 2005). Results showed that preschool students are expelled three times as often as K-12 students. Expulsion rates are lowest in public schools and Head Start programs, highest in faith-based, for profit, and community offerings. Boys are expelled 4.5 times as often as girls. Blacks are twice as likely to be expelled as Hispanics and Whites and five times as likely as Asian Americans.

Classroom-based behavioral consultations were identified as a promising method to reduce the incidence of student expulsion. Mental health consultants were trained to provide classroom-based strategies for dealing with challenging student behaviors. When teachers reported accessing the consultant, the likelihood of expulsion declined by 50%. Having a mental health consultant visit class in response to a teacher request was of greater benefit than no access but teachers sustaining a continuing relationship with a mental health consultant recorded the lowest expulsion rates. This situation existed because a teacher and consultant shared a building location or the consultant visited class on a monthly basis. There is evidence that mental health consultation during early childhood can be valuable. However, this approach has not been carefully investigated and knowledge is lacking about how to establish a state system of preschool mental health consultation (Hirschland, 2008).

Evaluating Adjustment to the Classroom

An adaptable person is able to adjust to change. Most parents know how difficult it can be to adjust to a new job or move to a new place. Sometimes adaptability does not involve a change in family address but a new environment like the school. Adjustment to being a student begins at ever-earlier ages. In recognition of the difficulty, some families try to ease adjustment by having their child attend a couple days a week or half days in the beginning so time with peers is balanced by time with adults at home.

Parents are usually surprised when a teacher informs them that their child presents problems with self-control. How could this be when the child seems so well behaved at home? Adaptation is less difficult at home where many children get lots of attention than when they are in a group with other self-centered boys and girls who want their own way. Since adaptability involves self-discipline, a worthwhile question is: What should the success or failure of a child's beginning days at school be based on? The usual way to assess adjustment is teacher observation. As they watch each student, most teachers try to find out:

1. Does the child like school? Whether a teacher can learn much about how a child feels depends upon their relationship.

2. Does the child feel comfortable enough to express the entire range of feelings at school including disappointment, anger, and fear as well as pride and satisfaction? This index of security shows whether a child believes a teacher will accept all kinds of feelings.

3. Does the child see the teacher as accessible and willing to give help when it is needed? Listening is always important but has even greater significance during early childhood because there are few resources for a child to access other than the teacher.

4. Does the child exhibit signs of anxiety, such as nail biting, wet pants, fear or withdrawal from activities involving groups?

5. Does the child feel a sense of belonging at school? This is shown by how s/he interacts with peers, making friends or being rejected.

6. Does the child show willingness to try new activities? If children consider the risks of exploration as too high, they avoid situations that add to learning.

7. Does the child persist in trying to complete tasks or give up when faced with difficulty? Adults should tell children that failure is a part of learning. Parents differ in how they interpret child lack of success.

8. Does the child feel comfortable enough to become involved with creative play by actively pretending? This can be observed on the playground or recess.

9. Does the child sit still and listen to a story with pictures? Other situations can also be a focus to detect length of attention span.

10. Does the child follow simple directions and finish assignments correctly?

11. Does the child know letters of the alphabet, numbers up to 20, and personal information about home address, phone number, and complete name of parents.

12. Does the child respond well to teacher correction and discipline or threaten to tell parents s/he is being mistreated?

13. Does the child take care of personal toilet needs without adult assistance?

14. Does the child show knowledge from the preschool curriculum?

Most teachers recognize the limitation of their own observations. Therefore, they rely on parents to observe a child outside of school. When parents are asked to look for certain behaviors, the resulting insight can increase understanding of a child. For example, consider the larger perspective that emerges if parents join teachers in looking for success indicators for "Does your child like school?" Children find it less threatening to tell parents about things they dislike. A teacher who supposes that children enjoy school unless they complain to her directly may overestimate willingness of students to confide in her. At home, when parents listen to apprehension of a child about school experiences, they can probe to find out, "What did you tell the teacher about this problem?" The answer can reveal how comfortable a child is expressing feelings in class. Teachers and parents view adaptation to school as important so it is good to share observations and talk often, at least monthly in the child's first year. This takes time and improvisation of schedule. However, the benefit justifies a united effort by the teachers a child has at home and in school.

PATIENCE AND WILLINGNESS TO WAIT

You may recall this conversation in 'Alice in Wonderland.' Alice observes, "Why I do believe that we have been here under this tree all this time. Everything is just as it was." "Of course it is," replied the Queen. "How else would you have it?" "Well, in our country," Alice said, still panting, "if you ran very fast for a long time as we have been doing, you would get to somewhere else." "A slow sort of country," replied the Queen. "Now here, you see, it takes all the running you can do to keep in the same place. If you want to get somewhere else, you must run twice as fast" (Carroll, 1865/ 2004).

Frustration in a Hurried Environment

Many people suffer from "time sickness," reflecting the belief that time is slipping away, there is not enough of it, and things must be done faster in order to keep up. Time sickness can restrict parent success. Consider nightly arguments with the children who want enough time to look at pictures and listen to stories read at a slow pace. Sometimes the children protest, "You read too fast." In these cases, a request to read one more story is heard as parents leave the room. Adults admit that speeding up their bedtime ritual sometimes results in guilt. But, they rationalize society dictates hurry to complete the next item on a to-do list that includes responding to text and e-mail messages, paying bills, and sitting down to relax (Olfman, 2005).

Rushing can impact other opportunities for conversation. Ellen Galinsky (2000) of Bank Street College in New York City interviewed 1,000 students from Grades 3-12. She found that children felt hurried nearly half of the time they spent with parents. It seems that, in many families, sharing ideas and feelings is fast-paced or consists of multi-tasking and continual interruption. This means conversations where parents can model qualities such as patience seldom occur.

A growing proportion of children, as young as 9, compared with their cohort a generation ago, are less fit, more likely to be obese, at greater risk for digestive disorders, have type 2 diabetes, and rely on antidepressants to manage difficulties that they have the capacity to overcome. These increasingly common unhealthy indicators confirm that excessive stress has become normative (Elkind, 2006). Efforts by faculty and parents should center mostly on ways to reduce the undue pressures children are exposed to rather than recommend they learn to adapt to unreasonable situations. This much seems certain—until adults gain greater control over stress in their own lives, they are bound to be dysfunctional models, unable to teach children to manage frustration, disappointment, and anxiety.

Frustration is a frequent experience for people who believe they should never have to wait. Instead of realizing that frustration always magnifies impatience, they prefer to blame others for causing them to get upset. For example, customers in line at a checkout counter may be heard to complain that something is wrong with the management. After all, more registers should be open so no one would ever be inconvenienced by having to wait. When people drive behind a car that does not move as soon as a traffic light turns green, the need for greater patience seldom comes to mind. Instead, the other driver may be characterized as a person who should be banned from the road. When this process is used to interpret other kinds of events as well, frustration is seen as justified since it identifies the failure of others to act as they should. Children who observe some parents and teachers conclude that frustration and impatience are appropriate responses.

Many children endure frustration of being rushed. When their teachers are in a hurry, students are denied enough time to process relevant information or examine a range of strategies they should consider for solving problems. Consequently, hasty methods of information processing are adopted. Instead of withholding judgment until all aspects of a task have been explored, hurried students that cannot wait are inclined to terminate an Internet search too soon and draw premature conclusions based on partial information. These are high prices to pay for trying to speed up the pace of learning. Efforts to rush lessons or abbreviate time to practice newly introduced skills causes some students to fall behind and others to perform below their ability level. Time and learning are always linked. Children learn what they spend time doing and from whomever participates with them.

Some reasons why being able to tolerate frustration is important are that patience enables grownups to accommodate the immaturity of children, accept limitations of colleagues, make allowances for personal shortcomings, and lead us to treat others with respect. It would be a mistake to abandon pursuit of these favorable attributes as goals that everyone should strive to attain. Parents should realize that the only persons to qualify as examples of maturity are those who consistently show patience and tolerance for frustration.

Patience and Delay of Gratification

There is mounting public concern that behaviors related to self-control such as a willingness to delay gratification and ability to show patience are in decline. When people adopt the belief that their needs have to be met immediately, it causes them to abandon the goal of learning to manage frustrating events that require impulse control. Learning how to wait should begin early in life and is illustrated by a seminal study led by Mischel and Peake (1990). The researchers met a class of young children at the Stanford University Laboratory School whose parents were faculty or staff. The challenge given to 4-year-olds was defined this way:

> If you wait until I (the experimenter) go down to the school office and come back, you will be given two marshmallows to eat. If you cannot wait until I get back, come to the front of the room and you can take one marshmallow from the teacher's desk.

This task presented a lure of enjoying the immediate reward of one marshmallow or choosing to show self-restraint to get a greater reward of two marshmallows later. The experimenter left the room and came back in fifteen minutes. This probably seemed like a long time for two-thirds of the children who resorted to covering their eyes so they could not look at marshmallows, making up fantasy games to distract themselves, singing songs or staring at the trees outside. In contrast, one-third of the children could not wait until the experimenter returned so they came forward to claim their one marshmallow.

The significance of emotional differences among children was not evident until a follow-up study 14 years later when students were adolescents. Dramatic distinctions were reported between those who years earlier resisted temptation and classmates who showed no inclination to be patient, wait or demonstrate self-restraint. Those who got two marshmallows for delaying their gratification had grown up to be more socially competent, self-assertive, and capable of handling frustrations of daily life. They were less prone to getting upset when faced with unanticipated problems and did not show any signs of disorganization when pressured by peers. Teachers viewed them as more self-reliant, confident, trustworthy, could be counted on to assume initiative in uncertain situations, and remain able to delay gratification in pursuit of their goals.

In contrast, these attributes were far less often observed in the behavior of the adolescents who earlier settled for one marshmallow. This group was more often described by teachers as stubborn and indecisive, easily upset, likely to regress or withdraw when presented with stress. They were prone to jealousy, ever ready to complain they were treated unfairly and inclined to begin arguments by showing a quick temper. In effect, even by late adolescence, they still had not acquired self-control. An ability to postpone satisfaction, to persevere to attain a longer-term goal is recognized as essential for success in a wide range of situations from staying on a weight control diet to completing requirements for a high school diploma.

Besides being more able to manage demands associated with daily living, those who waited patiently at age four differed in other ways as adolescents that contribute to achievement. In the estimate of their parents, they were more able to put ideas and feelings into words, listen to logic of other people, apply reasoning, concentrate, plan goals, assess personal progress, and display a zest for learning. Further, they performed better on the Scholastic Aptitude Test (SAT), a standard measure often required for admission to college. The one-third of children who most quickly came forward to get a marshmallow at age four had an average verbal score of 524 and 528 on their quantitative (mathematics) score. In comparison, two thirds of students who waited longest earned scores of 610 and 652, a total difference of 210 points (Mischel & Ayduk, 2004; Wargo, 2009).

The marshmallow results for child delay of gratification at age 4 were twice as powerful a predictor of SAT scores during late adolescence as IQ scores at age 4. This means that the self-imposed ability to deny impulses and to wait for gratification by remaining perseverant in gaining a longer-term, self-chosen goal significantly impacted academic achievement. Conversely, lack of self-control in childhood has been found to be a reliable predictor of delinquent behavior (Siegel & Welsh, 2007).

Self-control may be the most valuable human virtue and should be given higher priority in the education of adults as well as children. Roy Baumeister, a social psychologist at Florida State University, conducted experiments that demonstrated how personal will power governs behavior. Most of the problems that plague individuals such as addiction, overeating, crime, domestic violence, prejudice, unwanted pregnancy, sexually transmitted diseases, educational failure, debt, and lack of exercise have some degree of self control as a central factor. Psychology has found that two main traits, intelligence and self-control, are responsible for a wide range of benefits. However, despite years of effort, psychology has yet to discover what can be done to produce lasting increases in intelligence. In contrast, studies have found that self-control by will power can be strengthened with practice and be a powerful difference in the lives of ordinary people. Will power affects most aspects of our lives from time management, to saving for retirement, getting exercise, a healthy diet, and resisting temptation (Baumeister, & Tierney, (2011).

Development of Emotional Intelligence

Theories of learning are unable to explain why some people seem to have a map for living well, why students that have high IQs seldom become wealthy adults, why people are attracted to certain individuals right away and consider others difficult to trust, and why some are able to withstand adversity and show resilience while others seem to fall apart when exposed to even slight pressure. Daniel Goleman (2006a) explains that "emotional intelligence" is the answer and has documented the need to pay more attention to this context of achievement. Some elements of emotional intelligence include self-control, persistence, empathy, social concern, and the capacity to motivate self. Enabling children to possess these skills enhances maturity and improves relationships.

A popular misconception is that expressing negative emotions supports mental health. On the contrary, research has determined that tantrums are more likely to increase the influence and duration of anger (Savage & Savage, 2009). This worries teachers who report an increase in student discipline cases reflecting a lack of self-control. A sensible strategy is urging self-restraint as a reaction to frustration. This response helps to become more emotionally responsible than allowing tantrums to continue without interruption. The reason is that continuous stimulation of particular groups of brain cells, such as those required to inhibit the amygdala, the brain center of fear and aggression, makes them more sensitive and readily activated in the future. Children that are not expected to control the emotional center of their brain become candidates for maladjustment in adulthood because self-restraint was not nourished at a critical stage early in their development (Damasio, 2005).

There is considerable evidence that a hurried type of lifestyle can undermine development of patience and a willingness to delay gratification. Together these conditions increase the importance of arranging situations for children to practice patience and learning to wait. In each situation, the explanation for a child should focus on what it means to wait, why we sometimes must wait, and that health is preserved by not becoming upset during waiting. Telling a child how much longer some activity may take can contribute to a concept of time. In some situations, however, it is better to explain that waiting could take longer than anticipated and remaining calm is the way to react if faced with unforeseen delays. Consider some experiences that can be arranged to encourage greater emotional intelligence.

1. *Check out.* Choose a check out line in a store where you have to wait. Explain that "We are standing in line with others buying things they need, just like us. Sometimes we have to wait to get the things we want." This shows patience instead of frustration or complaining. While waiting, the child can be asked to hold some grocery items to place on the conveyer belt or counter.

2. *Taking turns.* When someone is talking, interrupting suggests his or her views are unimportant. Many television shows feature experts who routinely interrupt their colleagues. Waiting for a turn to talk is a courtesy, reflects patience, and maximizes the opportunity to learn. Children seeking to express thoughts can be told to wait until the teacher calls on them or their mother finishes what she has to say.

3. *Meal time.* The principle of anticipation, waiting for something that we want, can be practiced when a child sets the table or helps prepare a meal. Parents should explain that dinner must be made and everyone has a responsibility. People should show patience by staying seated and wait until everyone has finished their meal.

4. *Reading.* Children learn patience when their parents read books to them that require more than one visit. Unlike storybooks, chapters do not always have conclusions but build to a climax and an ending. This experience requires waiting for the next night in order to move ahead in the story. Anticipation of serial type movies and progressive television programs are established motivators.

5. *Bathroom and Bedroom*. Children practice waiting for parents or siblings spending time in a bathroom or bedroom to get ready for the day. Boys and girls can lie in their parents' bed while talking with the adults. Parents can say, "I'll be ready in ten minutes." Point out that there is a need to wait sometimes for adults just as grownups have to wait for children.

6. *Zoo*. An example of communicating the principle of anticipation is to tell a child, "We are going to the zoo Saturday, that is 5 days from now." Letting the child know ahead of time provides experience in looking forward to an event while having to delay gratification. You can ask the child to keep track and count days until the time arrives for going to the zoo.

7. *Puzzle*. Assemble a large puzzle or one that has many pieces. This task provides a chance to demonstrate patience while working with a child to form a missing picture. Point out that thinking carefully about where the pieces go takes time, continued trial, and will lead to success. The value of reflective thinking should often be reinforced and portrayed as a strength that everyone needs.

8. *Saving money*. A child wants a bicycle that costs many weeks of allowance. Learning to save money by placing some in a bank is evidence of patience and delay of gratification. The child can be kept informed about the current balance and the remainder sum needed. When the total of the big purchase is reached, child and parent can go to the store and buy it.

9. *Baking*. Instead of buying cookies or cupcakes, an option is to work in the kitchen that requires patience. It is easy to open a bag of cookie dough. However, waiting for gingerbread cookies to bake and cool before they can be eaten requires anticipation, readiness to wait, and time checks.

10. *Sharing toys*. When parents arrange a play date they can tell their child the schedule. Then there can be reminders of how much longer before they are able to get together with friends. And, when the time comes, sharing toys and being willing to take turns means practicing patience. Children can be taught to wait their turn and realize that every person in the group should be treated in the same way.

MUTUAL RIGHTS AND COOPERATION

More children are attending group care at earlier ages than the past. One result is that they spend more time with peers, are age-segregated as never before. Day care and preschool can provide benefits but also present the challenge of teaching self-centered children to cope with conflicts. The solution involves socialization attitudes and skills that should be taught in all group settings.

Territoriality and Dominion Play

The importance of getting along is confirmed each day of our lives. By helping children gain this ability, parents hope to improve their chances for close friendships, productive associations with peers in school and at work, a happy marriage, and peaceful coexistence. The paths to attain these broad goals are not completely known, but some clues from early childhood observations offer promise.

First, consider certain features of interaction among young children. Those who supervise 2- to 6-year-olds are often disappointed by their show of selfishness and possessiveness. The usual response is to encourage more sharing and cooperation. This advice ignores a pertinent phenomenon called territoriality, the inclination of creatures to declare a certain space as their own. Territorial behavior is evident throughout the animal kingdom. Coyotes and wolves mark territory by leaving a scent that designates the boundaries of their space. Cats attack other cats that attempt to come in their yard.

A similar intention to protect territory is observed among people. Status is recognized by the amount of space someone commands. Wealthy individuals own larger properties surrounded by high fences with signs that warn about "No trespassing." Less affluent families establish their territory by erecting smaller fences. In businesses, the lower echelon employees often work in cubicles with minimal privacy and sense of control. Elsewhere executives of the company have their offices, the largest of which belongs to the manager or the president.

Play is the activity where young children express their desire to control territory. When they assert claim to a play space or insist on ownership of a toy, it is known as dominion play. This territorial type play is normal between ages 2 and 6. However, dominion play can sometimes interfere with functioning of a group. When that happens, the adult and children should have a conversation regarding "mutual rights." Many children experience territorial situations every day at their daycare, preschool, kindergarten or play dates.

Consider Carol and Dale. Both of these 4-year-olds attend a preschool. Carol, in tears, approaches the teacher to tell that Dale will not permit her to play with him. After stating she understands Carol's feelings, the teacher suggests that they go and talk with Dale. When Dale explains he is making a zoo and does not want to have helpers, the teacher turns to Carol who indicates she wants to be his partner anyway. Since Dale is not infringing on anyone's territory, the teacher defends his right to privacy by telling Carol she must play by herself or with someone else. Forcing Dale to let Carol in the zoo against his will would violate his right to privacy and foster additional friction between them. In similar circumstances, the teacher would defend Carol's right to privacy. When young children cannot look to adults to defend their privacy, they develop a sense of helplessness instead of confidence.

At times dominion play can interfere with the rights of others. In such cases limitations must be set, not to deny space to someone but restrict it so others can also satisfy their needs. Jim, age 4, visited a railroad roundhouse over the weekend. On Monday morning, as soon as he arrived at preschool, Jim decided to build a replica out of blocks. Unfortunately, he made the roundhouse so close to the block shelves that other children were unable to reach the materials they needed for play.

After observing several unsuccessful tries by Jim's classmates to have the roundhouse removed, the teacher said, "Jim, the reason everyone wants you to move your roundhouse is because they can't get to the shelves for blocks." Jim pointed out they better not touch it or the roundhouse might fall. The teacher makes another suggestion, "Jim, can you see another place in the room to move the roundhouse so other children can play too?" Jim was definite about not moving his structure. Then the teacher said, "I know that you don't want to move it but another spot must be found." Undaunted, Jim stated, "Well, it's already built so it can't be moved." A location over by the window was suggested. Again, no deal. Next, the teacher proposed, "I'll help you move it by the cloakroom or you can do it yourself." Jim replied, "No." Without further comment, the teacher dismantled the roundhouse and moved it near the window so other students could access the blocks. Jim immediately resumed play with his roundhouse as though nothing had happened.

Most children will more readily accept suggestions than Jim but even when they do not, providing face-saving alternatives is a better method of teaching than using punishment, embarrassment, sarcastic remarks or issuing commands. Boys and girls can learn how to work alongside (not in) the private space of one another. This acceptance of mutual rights is an essential basis for social competence. As a rule, when a child's right to privacy is respected, s/he is less defensive and may soon welcome play with the same classmates recently rejected.

Adults can illustrate the importance of mutual rights by reading *This is our House* to children (Rosen, 1996). The story shows how play can be a distressing aspect of school life. George will not let any kids into his cardboard house. This means no girls, no small people, no twins, no people with glasses, and no people with red hair. Then, after George comes back from the bathroom, the tables are turned and he learns what it is like to be the individual who is left out.

In time, children commonly decide that it is ok to play with one companion but no one else. By excluding all others, the pair make it known that "Two's company, three's a crowd." Adults often disapprove of this behavior and suggest that the children involved ought to like everyone. However, adults rarely meet this unreasonable expectation themselves. A more suitable response is to accept the fact that, in most situations, children should be allowed to choose their friends. Because friendships require privacy to develop, it is appropriate to honor preferences of children to be together while distant from their unwanted peers.

Parents, babysitters, and group care workers should consider these guidelines to support social development for those under age 7.

1. Respect their need for privacy, ownership, and control of space.
2. Encourage children to respect the privacy of others. Set limits for mutual rights.
3. When possible, support the decision of a child to restrict who enters personal play space. Over time s/he may welcome another person into their play situation.
4. Before rushing in to solve a conflict, take a few moments to observe what is happening. Allow time for the children to solve conflicts in an accepted way. Support the expression of a child's feelings toward others in a civil manner.
5. If intervention is needed, offer face-saving alternatives that can restore mutual rights. This is difficult in the beginning because it requires creativity but, with practice, adults can act as exemplars.
6. Recognize that socialization requires first-hand experience for children in handling some conflicts. Generally, adults approach child conflicts as if they were policemen who will reach decisions about guilt or punishment.
7. Children need opportunities to make decisions. One aspect of decision making that should be introduced is the importance of generating possible solutions. The ability to think of options is also an asset for reducing stress.

Outcomes of Social Incompetence

What happens when surrogates that care for children fail to recognize the benefit of dominion play, overlook the need for mutual rights, deny privacy, force sharing, and resolve conflicts with coercive methods? A generation of studies suggests socialization is adversely affected. In one investigation, children who entered day care before their first birthday and continued until age 5 were compared with a similar group cared for mostly in their own home. When measured for aggression, the day care children were fifteen times as aggressive as those cared for at home. The difference was not about assertiveness, standing up for one's rights, but instead the inclination was to verbally and physically attack others. Those in day care since infancy were more easily frustrated, less cooperative, more egocentric, less task-oriented and more distractible. These children had not developed self-control and were ready to physically fight to resolve disputes. Such findings are confirmed by studies showing that spending extensive time in group care is related to increased behavior problems (Belsky, 2008).

The proportion of children attending childcare has increased during the past 30 years from 25% in 1980 to over 80% currently, with many infants receiving care between birth and age 2. The National Institute of Child Health and Human Development Early Childhood Research Care Network (2006) sought to determine effects of nonmaternal care. A sample of 1,300 mothers and their babies were recruited when the infants were 1 month old. The group was racially diverse. Follow-ups were conducted at 6 months, 15 months, 24 months, and 54 months. Assessments included videotaping of parenting practices, measurement of child outcomes, family characteristics, and provision of childcare in quality and quantity. Results indicated that extensive childcare does not support socialization.

Failure to learn "mutual rights" in child group care settings is an international concern. Barbara Tizard and Martin Hughes (2003) at Harvard summarized eight studies about the impact of day care on social development in the United States, England, and Sweden. All of the studies concluded that young children that spend many hours a week in day care exhibit less socialization skill than those attending fewer hours. Later, in the elementary grades, social incompetence takes the form of invading peer space, distracting classmates, taking things that belong to others, and preventing conditions needed to support group learning.

Wong (2005) reported a national survey involving 350 preschool teachers. Knowing the alphabet and numbers were not seen as the most important things parents should emphasize to prepare children for preschool. This exclusive focus of many parents ignores the social skills that are needed to get along in a group. Most of the teachers, 80%, reported that parents need guidance to curb the pattern of overemphasis on academic skills while not giving enough attention to social development. Parents who help develop verbal communication, ability to follow directions, and participate successfully in groups help daughters and sons gain the most from preschool (Weigel, Martin, & Bennett, 2005).

Teachers in the Horizons Corporation survey were agreed that a good way to teach social skills is exposing children to situations where they interact with age mates like play dates, playgrounds, and parent-child classes. In the opinion of these teachers, societal forces have led parents to set inappropriate priorities for child development. In a competitive environment, many parents feel pressured to push their children to get an early start on academic skills. Wong's (2005) study shows that parents can have a more beneficial effect on success at school by giving opportunities for cooperative play greater attention.

Evaluating Group Care of Children

There are 11 million American children under 5 years of age in group care. The size of this population is forecast to increase but the experience must dramatically improve. One aspect of the solution is providing quality care at a reasonable cost. The National Association of Child Care Resources and Referral Agencies (2011) reports that the average price of day care is greater than college tuition in a majority of the states. Specifically, full time care of a 4-year-old ranges from $3,900 a year in Mississippi to more than $11,000 in Massachusetts. During the past decade childcare costs have risen twice as fast as medium income of families with children. Federal Child Care and Development Block grants help states make care more affordable but do not require that funds apply in only licensed settings. Most states require fingerprinting and background checks for childcare personnel. Nevertheless, some children receive assistance in unlicensed settings where safety may be compromised. For example, Illinois spends $700 million a year to pay for babysitting of children from 150,000 low-income families. A decade-long investigation by the Chicago Tribune determined that the Illinois State Department of Human Services poorly vetted babysitters. As a result, rapists, child molesters, drug dealers, and other felons have been paid by the state to provide care for young children (Wahlberg & Mahr, 2011).

A related need is for legitimate caregivers to earn a reasonable salary. They typically receive minimum wage, resulting in high rates of staff turnover. Child-care givers in 150 Florida centers were identified. Four years later only 2% of personnel had been retained (Jinks, Knopf, & Kemple, 2006). High rates of preschool teacher attrition continue to detract from child well-being (Cassidy, Lower, Kintner-Duffy, Hegde, & Shim, 2011). To complicate the situation, high staff turnover occurs when children are most in need of continuity. Two- to 4-year-olds need a predictable routine for sleeping, eating, and persons they can rely on. Stability is an essential condition as far as they are concerned. Even a family vacation poses problems when there is departure from the familiar. For example, children like Disneyland but often express a desire to sleep that night in their own bed at home instead of a hotel. This need for continuity partially explains why young children on a trip appreciate McDonald's because the menu is predictable and remains the same as the one they are familiar with at home.

Providing Self-Evaluation Practice

High achievers are able to accurately evaluate their limitations. Self-evaluation is an important skill to apply throughout life. Parents and caregivers evaluate children daily but rarely provide opportunities to practice self-assessment. Self-control can become more common if children learn healthy self-appraisal. Consider some contexts that can be arranged for practice in self-evaluation and getting feedback that confirms or challenges self-judgment. For each situation, it is helpful to provide the child questions to rely on as a basis for self-evaluation.

Swimming lessons. After a lesson, children can reflect on these questions: How well did I listen to what was said by my coach? Did I understand and follow the directions I was given? Did I encourage others in my group to swim better? How did I act when others swimmers did well? How do I feel about my progress as a swimmer? How well do I swim compared to others taking lessons with me? The agenda allow for expression of feelings, estimation of progress, and detection of problems. A child can also gain a sense of obligation by this kind of dialogue.

Play date. After a date, each child can answer these questions: How did I get along with my friends? Did I share playthings with others? Did I take turns when it was the right thing to do? How did I handle arguments? Did I have a good time? Did everyone have fun? Did I say something mean to anyone? Did I help anyone? Parents can then ask themselves: Do I agree with a child's assessment of progress and achievement? Share your observations with the child.

Getting dressed. A child should be able to recognize whether s/he is suitably dressed in the morning and know if anything is missing with the clothing. Questions can include: Does the shirt I picked go with my pants? Do the clothes I have chosen match the weather? Will my outfit be too cold, too warm, or about right? Have I chosen clean clothes to wear today? What did I do with my clothes that are dirty? How do I feel about deciding what to wear?

SUMMARY AND IMPLICATIONS

A hurried lifestyle can stretch people to their limits. The fact is some tasks should not be speeded up because a certain amount of time is required to perform them. When activities are accelerated that should not be and people forget how to slow down, there is a price to be paid. Assets such as patience and willingness to delay gratification enrich life at every age. These aspects of emotional intelligence should be monitored because they enable us to honor personal priorities, establish suitable expectations for pace of learning, and support healthy behavior.

Self-control and self-discipline are factors that influence social maturity and formation of durable, mutually satisfying relationships. Parents are the teachers most responsible for providing basic lessons about civil behavior, concern for well-being of others, willingness to wait, and adoption of a healthy work ethic. There is evidence that many families perform poorly in carrying out these responsibilities. More parents should recognize that, even though their schedule is busy, the obligation for child guidance cannot be transferred to surrogates at school.

Some observers suppose that government subsidies are the way to improve child care. However, comprehensive changes are needed. Parents and caregivers should know the psychological and physical aspects of early development. With training, caregivers can accept the social limitations of children, respect their need for the privacy of dominion play, preserve mutual rights, demonstrate how to resolve conflict in creative ways, and express anger without harming others These strategies can help children acquire socialization skills that are essential for getting along.

APPLICATIONS FOR TEACHING

1.   The basis of social competence is child respect for mutual rights. When youngsters know that they can count on adults to defend their privacy, a sense of confidence emerges instead of feelings of vulnerability and helplessness.
2.   Thinking of alternatives is often the key to conflict resolution. One important aspect of decision making that is often overlooked is becoming capable of generating optional solutions for disputes. This is a better response than hitting, taking things from others or behaving in verbally vindictive ways. Caretakers should exemplify thinking of face-saving options when they observe children unable to resolve their disputes.
3.   Peer support can motivate social and emotional development. Children need to be with companions of their same age to make

self-comparisons, assert themselves, and assume leadership. Peers encourage children to strive for independence from their parents and the group offers feelings of belonging. Finding out what friends will tolerate, learning to cooperate, sharing secrets, expressing anger, and reconciling differences are lessons that can be taught more effectively by peers than by adults.

4. Guided practice in self-evaluation supports detection of needs. Learning to judge oneself is a powerful asset because it supports the discovery of further learning needs and helps gauge progress. Self-discipline becomes more likely when children apply healthy criteria. Schools provide external evaluation about knowledge but seldom offer guidance on the acquisition of self-evaluation skills.

5. Children need time for reflective thinking to properly consider questions. Adults who honor this condition support creative and critical thinking. Allowing children time motivates them to adopt deliberation as essential for the thinking process they rely on to reach decisions regarding what to say or do. In contrast, rushing children by expecting answers without reflection contributes to a reliance on impulsive thinking.

6. Listen and respond thoughtfully to the questions and feelings expressed by children. This practice acknowledges importance of curiosity and confirms that conversations require the undivided attention of adults. On the other hand, if grownups multitask, try to do more than listen to a child such as checking messages or read a document, the distraction ensures that some of what a child says will be missed. Children who conclude that they are often ignored may seek advisors outside the family who are more willing to pay greater attention to them.

7. Persistence is necessary to be competent and reach distant goals. Rush-oriented environments encourage a pursuit of mainly short-term goals that can be met quickly and confirmed. However, long-term challenges in life typically require repeated effort after there is failure to reach some high standard. A willingness to keep trying can contribute to achievement in school and relationships.

8. Children gain self-control by being able to delay gratification. The belief that personal needs and desires have to be satisfied immediately ignores the goal of learning to cope with situations that call for impulse control. Becoming emotionally upset, showing uncontrollable rage, and threatening others are unhealthy forms of behavior. Self-control is necessary to establish relationships that are respectful and mutually satisfying.

CHAPTER 3

REFLECTION AND IMAGINATION

People who rely on reflective thinking and imagination are better equipped to generate solutions for problems and demonstrate good judgment when making decisions. These valuable assets should be acknowledged as a suitable focus for long-term education that begins in early childhood. The goals for this chapter are to discuss learning to value time alone, the development of concentration ability, and acquisition of time management skills. Adult involvement with fantasy play is discussed as a factor that reinforces the importance of imagination for children. Recommendations are provided to help adults feel comfortable while at play with a child, recognize the limitations of praise to motivate creativity, and understand how both parties can gain from pretending together.

ORIGINS OF CREATIVE THINKING

Childhood of Creative Adults

What are creative people like and what efforts can be made to cause their extraordinary abilities to become more common? This question intrigued Donald MacKinnon (1903-1987), Director of the Institute for Personality Assessment Research at the University of California. MacKinnon (1962, 1978) and his research team studied 600 mathematicians, architects, writers, engineers, and research scientists that were nominated as highly creative by experts in their fields. Assessments were able to detect characteristics that differentiated them from less creative peers.

Learning Throughout Life: An Intergenerational Perspective, pp. 49–70
Copyright © 2012 by Information Age Publishing

In addition to being highly imaginative, creative adults showed preference for solitary activities. They were able to concentrate for long periods of time and exhibit an unusual level of task persistence. How did they get to be this way? What growing up experiences did they have in common? Some clues come from the autobiographical reports. Generally, they were either the eldest child or were distantly spaced from brothers and sisters. They spent more time alone and with grownups than they did with classmates and learned from an early age to enjoy the company of their imagination (MacKinnon, 1962, 1978).

High and Low Daydreamers

The privacy most creative adults experienced in childhood is suggestive of the environment that others may need to become more creative but the benefits of solitary play were largely overlooked until Dorothy and Jerome Singer (2011) of Yale University made some discoveries. One of their experiments involved a sample of 9-year-olds who were similar in intelligence, grade level, and social background. After intensive interviews, the children were divided in two groups.

The "High Daydreamers" included boys and girls who reported imaginary companions, enjoyed playing alone, and described more daydreams. Children who preferred more literal play, expressed disinterest in solitude, and reported infrequent daydreams were categorized as "Low Daydreamers." Everyone was told that, because astronauts have to spend lengthy periods of time in a space capsule without moving much or having frequent conversations with others, the goal of the experiment was to see how long the children could sit quietly without talking to the experimenter.

The results were significant. High Daydreamers could remain quiet for long periods of solitary activity and persist without giving up—factors that are closely related to concentration ability. In addition, High Daydreamers were less restless, less eager to end the experiment, and seemed serenely able to remain occupied inwardly to make the time pass. Later, it was found that each of them had transformed their situation of forced compliance into a fantasy game that helped increase their ability to wait. In contrast, Low Daydreamers never seemed able to settle down. They would repeatedly leap up and ask, "Is the time up yet?" They continually tried to engage the experimenter in conversation. Further testing revealed that High Daydreamers also scored higher on measures of creativity, storytelling, and need for achievement.

Learning To Value Time Alone

Parents and teachers can confirm the Singers' (2011) findings. Children from low-income households are usually crowded together and seldom have much opportunity to participate in solitary play. As a result, they come to school restless, cannot sit still, and are unable to focus on a task for very long. Instead, they are inclined to act out their impulses instead of reflecting on them. Because these children lack the ability to concentrate, much time is spent interrupting and distracting others. In many schools, this behavior means that teachers have to devote considerable effort trying to establish the discipline needed to enable learning. Many educators complain that students have not developed the inner resources necessary for sustained inquiry. The forecast is not much better in higher income homes where a growing number of children complain, "There's nothing to do" whenever playmates, television, cell phones or computers are unavailable. It is a sad commentary when the young already bore themselves.

Fortunately, when solitary play is given higher priority, boredom and inattention can become less common. This transition will be difficult because adults have traditionally not recognized that children need privacy. In fact, children are often led to feel that being alone is a form of punishment called solitary confinement. Parents resent intrusion by their children whenever they are trying to concentrate. Nevertheless, the inclination of adults to underestimate seriousness of children at play is nearly universal. Moreover, the frustration effects of interrupting solitary play include a reduction of child persistence for mental tasks and a lowering of ability to concentrate. The younger the child, the more vulnerable s/he is to play disturbance. This comes as no surprise to daycare and preschool caretakers who are unable to grant the request of many children seeking periodic privacy.

Learning to get along with classmates is a socialization skill children can value and acquire when they go to school. However, learning to spend enjoyable time alone and value solitude will probably begin at home or never eventuate (Cain, 2012). Obviously, the number of children at school and the frequency of interruptions there combine to make solitary activity a low priority in classrooms. Then too, once the years of schooling begin, organized groups such as the Girl Scouts, Little League, Soccer, Boys and Girls Clubs, and after-school programs are available. These experiences are beneficial but parents should recognize their obligation to also ensure that the schedule of their child includes some daily time alone. This is a difficult task for parents who find it impossible to schedule any uninterrupted time for their own leisure activities.

PARENTS AND SOLITUDE

Parents should show that they value and know how to arrange time alone. The self-impressions of 1,545 Black, Hispanic, and White mothers and their early adolescents (ages 10 to 14 years old) were examined. The purpose was to determine what each generation perceived as the assets and shortcomings of the parents. Mothers reported that being able to set aside time for personal leisure was their most difficult task, ranking it 60th out of 60 situations. Adolescents also detected the inability of their mothers to arrange for personal leisure by ranking it as 57th out of 60 items (R. Strom, Strom, Strom, Shen, & Beckert, 2004).

This common difficulty should be seen in a broader context than maternal sacrifice. Children need mothers to show them how to deal with stress by setting aside time for relief and demonstrate ways to manage time so they have balance and personal control of their life. There is evidence that many employed mothers suffer from stress produced by multiple role responsibilities that typically include child care, responsibilities toward a husband, offering support for aging parents, satisfying an employer, and managing a household. These combined pressures can motivate mothers to over-schedule their children, thus depriving them of free time that provides a needed sense of control over life and chance to decide what things they want to do alone.

Similar results were found in studies of 517 Black and White fathers along with their early adolescent daughters and sons. These fathers reported that, like the mothers, their greatest difficulty was scheduling leisure time for themselves. This inability to demonstrate time management, to plan personal discretionary time, has an influence on most contexts of parent guidance. When parents are stressed or fatigued, the time they spend with children typically includes more nonproductive conflict and reduction of mutual satisfaction. Most fathers accept less responsibility than mothers for childcare and supervision. Consequently, it seems improbable that a father will be able to teach children how to cope with multiple demands on their time when he is unable to arrange moments for his personal relief and renewal. Many children conclude that their parents have yet to learn how to deal with pressures of feeling hurried and sensing helplessness over lack of control of their time. As a result, some decide they have to turn to sources outside the family for lessons on how to cope with stress. Some external sources offer unhealthy solutions (R. Strom et al., 2000; R. Strom, Beckert, Strom, Strom, & Griswold, 2002).

Arranging Child Schedule

Consider what happens in many homes. Mom and Dad have been at their workplace throughout the day and, after dinner, engage in some brief activity with their child. Then, to ensure their own privacy, parents may direct the child to get ready for bed even if the time may be earlier than is necessary. A more helpful approach for parents to have time alone is to tell a child,

> It is time for you to be alone, doing things you enjoy. Mom and Dad will do the same. The light in your bedroom will be left on so you can decide whether you want to quietly look at pictures, color, draw, play with dolls, action figures or toys or something else that is interesting. In 30 minutes, we will come to tuck you in and turn out the light so you can sleep.

This strategy helps a child to realize everyone needs time alone and it can be an enjoyable experience with benefits that cannot be found in other ways. By arranging time for solitude, parents avoid depriving a child of the self-encounters everyone needs to nurture imagination and self-evaluation.

Fantasy and Solitary Play

When children participate in solitary play, they fantasize more than during play with friends or parent-child play. Nevertheless, although parents recognize solitude is the best condition for fantasy practice, some of them worry about the child who prefers to play alone. This apprehension relates to the high value our society assigns to extroversion and sociability. Most people are unaware that two-thirds of highly creative individuals are introverts (Cain, 2012). Some parents express reservations about whether solitary play is healthy. One father observed, "Playing alone may be fine in some cases but my 4 year old seems to be a victim of hallucinations. He refers to talks with Roy, a fantasy companion." If this father had listened more carefully, he would recognize that during solitary play it is the child who controls imaginary friends. In fact, total control over the fictitious companion may be what bothers some parents. Perhaps they suppose the power that comes with being a boss is not good for children because it could cause them to become uncooperative in relating to adults. The fact is that cooperation implies a sharing of power. Children who feel powerless are unable to cooperate and instead can only acquiesce.

If imaginary companions appear at all, children between ages three and six create them and these products of fiction seldom remain after the age of 10. Bear in mind that these are not also lonely, timid, or maladjusted children. They are normal, found in families of all sizes and social status. Estimates from 20% to 50% of boys and girls are the proportion that experience fictitious companions. Studies have found that highly creative children are more likely than less creative peers to interact with fantasy companions. These findings are corroborated by retrospective studies of creative adults who share similar memories of playing with imaginary companions (Taylor, 1999).

Consider this scenario. A highly competitive money manager becomes aware that his desire for promotion will depend on providing better economic forecasting than another candidate for the job. He soon determines that it is wise to turn to his 7-year old daughter and her imaginary companion for guidance. Eddie Murphy is the part-time father, full-time executive, in *Imagine That* (Kirkpatrick, 2009), a movie where viewers discover that all you need is imagination, enough time to spend with each other, and a lot of love to achieve the most in life.

During solitary play children govern the behavior of everyone involved in their stories. This expression of imagination is normal in early childhood. There will be times when children report on conversation with imaginary companions that parents consider disturbing. For example, 4-year old Derek reports that he did not pick up the toys in his room as directed by parents because Ollie, his fictitious friend, told him he did not have to do it today. Some parents respond with punishment or a reminder that lying is unacceptable, and want the child to stop making up stories. This reaction is intended to reinforce the differences between right and wrong and support development of moral character. However, Derek's mother saw the situation differently as shown by her response. She said, "Tell Ollie that your mother is the person who decides how our house is taken care of and chores that are expected of everyone in the house including Derek." Mother did not refer to Derek as being a liar nor did she discourage a relationship with his imaginary friend. Instead, she called attention to the fact that Derek can make up stories but she will not approve excuses for not doing assigned chores.

Brain Executive Function

The admission of many parents that they cannot schedule personal leisure prevents them from being an example of time management for children. There is also reason for concern about how changes in the way that children spend time impacts their cognitive and emotional development. A long-standing custom has been that children improvise their own activities, regulate interactions with one another, and make up their own rules that are applied to guide group behavior. This tradition of self-governance during play has largely vanished over the past generation. The shift attributes to increased fear among parents regarding child safety that has led to more structured play featuring adult supervision (Meltzer, 2007).

The benefits of this transformation have come at a cost. The reason is that because the greater amount of time children used to spend in play directed by them allowed plenty of practice for a cognitive skill known as executive function. The thought processes that govern judgment are mediated by executive function. Developing the ability to self-regulate is the main purpose for executive function. Youngsters who acquire good self-regulation are able to show greater control of their emotions, avoid misconduct, rely upon reflective thinking instead of impulsivity, and demonstrate self-discipline.

Research has found that the capacity of children to exhibit self-regulation is in decline. To illustrate, one experiment conducted in the late 1940s called on 3-, 5-, and 7-years-olds to stand still for as long as they could. The 3-year-olds were able to stand still for only a minute while 5-year-olds could remain still for around 3 minutes. The 7-year-olds showed that they could stand still for as long a period of time as the adults requested (Bodrova & Leong, 2006). Sixty years later the National Institute for Early Education Research repeated the experiment but with a much different outcome. In the replication 5-year-olds stood still for the same length of time as 3-year olds had in the original study. Seven-year-olds were unable to stand still as long as the 5-year-olds had many years earlier in the initial observation. These are disappointing results because self-regulation is an asset everyone needs (Bodrova & Leong, 2006).

The reduction in self-regulation skills among children seems reflected by an increasing number of students diagnosed with attention deficit hyperactivity disorder (ADHD). A poor level of executive function is closely associated with high rates of school dropout, drug taking, and participation in criminal activity. In contrast, good executive function is recognized as a better predictor of academic success than intelligence test scores. Consequently, children who can manage their feelings, pay attention for lengthy periods, and concentrate are more able to learn (Meltzer, 2007).

Unstructured make-believe and imagination-driven play can be a powerful tool for developing self-discipline since children usually engage in private speech while pretending. They talk to themselves about what they intend to do and ways they will carry out their plans. Observation studies comparing how preschoolers behave across a wide range of activities have found that the amount of private speech related to self-regulation is greatest during fantasy play. Moreover, the use of self-regulating language is predictive of better executive function. But, the more structured play is when adults dominate, the less children are involved in private speech.

Participating in child sports leagues directed by grownups offers bene-fit but can also deny opportunities for children to practice policing themselves because they do not have to rely on self-regulation. Instead, adults decide when games are played, who fills each position, whether pitches are balls or strikes, and if a hit is fair or foul. There is a loss of other conflict opportunities too that implicate regulation of behavior and decisions that many children are no longer allowed to make for themselves. In the common quest to protect boys and girls, offer them guidance on how to behave on a team, and learn to process the experience of winning and losing, adults inadvertently sacrifice some activities that are needed to shape emotional and social development (Ripkin &Wolff, 2006).

PEER INFLUENCE ON BEHAVIOR

Balance in the way that time is spent can support growth and achievement. Children are unable to schedule themselves so it is up to parents to arrange for them to have some time alone. Parents should also know benefits and obstacles that can result from child interaction with others of their same age.

Benefits of Peer Interaction

The potential influence of peers on socialization is shown by lessons that students learn mainly from classmates. They offer the first substantial experience in equality. Everyone seeks companionship and enjoys attention given by others. The peer group is in the best position to satisfy these needs. When classmates act in approved ways, the group rewards them with attention, acceptance, and emotional support.

The peer group presents a separate set of standards from the expectations that are imposed by parents and caretakers. Peer norms are more attainable and often provide reasons for conduct which oppose adult directives. The greater resources of grownups make it difficult to declare much autonomy from them. Still, peers are consistent in listening to reports by friends about common dilemmas, and encourage one another to express differences in the presence of grownups.

The positive influence of peers should not be overlooked or undervalued. Peers provide experiences that support social and emotional development. For example, children need companions their own age as a basis for self-comparison, chance to express themselves without fear of punishment, and opportunities to share leadership. They encourage one another to strive for independence and convey a sense of belonging to another important group besides the family.

Children learn about friendship mostly from each other, how to get along with someone who has the same level of status. Becoming a group member requires gaining specific skills that are motivated by peers. These skills include cooperation, sharing, questing for independence, venting anger, and making up—all lessons that are more easily learned from peers than parents. They discover what friends will tolerate as well as behaviors that will not be condoned. Most children gain a sense of belonging and feel accepted in peer groups. Students find out they must learn from others how to handle disputes peacefully, even though, like adults, aggression is sometimes a prominent pattern of behavior.

Peer Pressure Protectors

Belonging to a peer group usually requires conformity. This is fine if norms that a child is expected to adopt are healthy. When this is not so, individuals from early childhood onwards must be capable of withstanding pressure from peers because caving in could compromise health, integrity, and goals. Parents should prepare their children for pressures to adopt dysfunctional behavior or suffer rejection. All children need the following peer pressure protectors.

1. One important way to minimize peer pressure is encourage individuality. Parents do this by avoiding comparisons of the ability, achievements or limitations among their children. When one child becomes a standard for behavior of a brother or sister, the likely outcome is sustained rivalry and jealousy instead of lifelong reciprocal support and pride among siblings (Conley, 2004).

2. Encourage children to value solitude, time for reflection, self-evaluation, deliberation, and looking at things anew. Access to solitude can support the individuality and creativity that children need so being with age mates for lengthy periods of time does not result in excessive peer dependence.

3. Parents should make themselves available to listen, particularly about the difficulties of building friendships. This task demands priority, takes time, and is sometimes inconvenient. Do it anyway! Problems with classmates are likely to be continuous and, depending on the way parents respond, they may continue to be asked for advice or not at all. Children need help to get along without threatening withdrawal to force concession behaviors by others. Share your mistakes, a resource that requires self-disclosure.

4.   Allow and defend child privacy. Let children confide in you without insisting that everything that is going on in their lives be told
to you. Trust is essential for close relationships and parents have
the most prominent role in shaping this characteristic.

Thinking in Early Childhood

Parents want to support child creativity, cooperation, and independence to prevent peer domination. In addition, adults should know the
predictable changes in how normal children view and interpret the world
as they advance in their age groups. This awareness helps to establish reasonable expectations for learning, avoid undue pressure, and take advantage of opportunities for growth. Two- to 6-year-olds share the thinking
processes described in Table 3.1, based on studies by Piaget (1969).

Language. Meaningful words, ones that can be understand by people
outside the family, are initially spoken at around 12 months of age. Most
words gained in the second year are used to identify favorite objects or
events such as doggie, cookie, milk, and toys. Two-word phrases like "all
gone," "big truck," and "more water" are evident. The basic information
is there even though verbs are not. During the third year the number of
words children comprehend increases to nearly a thousand. The vocabulary they understand is larger than their spoken vocabulary. At this age
they experiment with three- and four-word sentences like "I want more
milk." A typical 3-year old asks between 400 to 500 questions a day, leading parents to temporarily feel omniscient. Four-year-olds begin to grasp
the rules of grammar but falsely suppose them to be consistent. So, they
sometimes say things adults consider humorous such as "Mama telled
me," or "I drinked my milk." At age 5, most irregular verbs of grammar
are in place, and by 6 years of age all the sounds including s, r, and th, can

Table 3.1.   Thinking Abilities of 2- to 6-Year Old Children*

Thinking Abilities	*Achievements and Limitations*
Preoperational Stage—2- to 6-Year-Olds	
Language	Speech is becoming socialized
Classification	Organizes using a single factor
Perception	Judgment is based upon senses
Centration	Focuses on one aspect at a time
Egocentrism	Unaware of how others see things

*Adapted from J. Piaget, *Psychology of Intelligence.* New York, NY: Littlefield, Adams, 1969.

be spoken (even by those who still lisp). First graders are capable of conversation with any age group.

Many children are more likely to have poor speech models than in the past. This is because it was common then to spend more time with older children or adults. A far higher rate of maternal employment has changed the situation. Because language is learned mostly through imitation, children in day care and preschool naturally copy the speech of immature companions and thereby reinforce poor habits of communication.

Classification. The ability to classify is essential to organize things and solve problems. Preschoolers are able to sort objects into groups based on a single factor like color, size or function. Limitations of children should also be recognized. When 4-year-olds are asked whether there are more boys or children in their class, they say, "There are more boys than girls." This response illustrates a lack of understanding that someone can belong to two groups at the same time. It will not be difficult to understand by age 7, when children recognize that Tom classifies as a boy and as a child. During one day preschoolers can see a number of short, tall, fat, and thin Santa Clauses at different shopping malls but not have their belief about Santa shaken because they consider every Santa Claus to be one and the same.

Perception. Preschoolers rely more on their sense of sight than reasoning so they are easily misled when confronted by a problems of conservation. The term conservation means understanding that, unless something is added or is taken away from an object, the quantitative aspects of that object remain the same despite external changes in appearance. Consider the observation of substance. Before age 6 a child will observe that two balls of clay are of equal size and then, several moments later, declare that the piece they have just seen transformed into a long, thin strip has more clay than the ball-shaped clay. In a similar way, preschoolers believe that the same amount of liquid is greater when it appears in a tall, narrow glass than when it appears in a short, wide container.

Centration. Failure to understand the conservation of volume attributes to another limitation of thinking in early childhood. Centration limits attention to just one aspect of a situation at a time. Thus, the preschooler tends to focus on either height or width of the container and fails to notice that the other is also changing in a compensating way so volume remains the same. Centration is also evident during television watching when a child often misses things noticed by the adults. Grownups can enlarge the scope of what children see by asking them questions that draw their attention to details they would otherwise overlook. Wise parents realize that because children can focus on only one thing at a time, directions they are given should be simple, clear, and repeated as often as necessary.

At age 6 some boys and girls attain the concept of conservation, but by age 7 one-third of them have still not attained the concept. Even at age 10 there may be 15% who do not understand that quantity remains the same regardless of change in appearance. This means that it is probable that slow learning children fail to achieve real understanding of schoolwork and just go through the motions when assigned rote processes of habit and repetition. Instruction can go beyond a child's level so s/he still counts and writes without really grasping the lessons.

This is why tutoring is important and usually leads to higher achievement. It allows the ability of an individual rather than peer group level to set the focus of instruction. The benefits of one-to-one tutoring are confirmed by studies of home-schooled children whose parents teach them instead of relying on public schools. On average, home-schooled students score higher than the children in school.

Egocentrism. Preschool thinking is limited by egocentrism. This is not a derogatory term but instead describes excessive reliance on one's personal view with the consequent inability to be objective. Egocentric people of any age find it hard to comprehend how anyone can see things from a different perspective. So, in their minds, they are "always right." This outlook ensures there will be conflict at day-care, preschool and other group settings.

Egocentric children lack ability to distinguish between their own views and the views of someone else. A preschooler shakes his head indicating yes or no over the cell phone as though the caller, who may be many miles away, can see these gestures. First-grade teachers find that when a child is talking to them, another students comes along and starts a conversation with her, disregarding the other child who is also speaking at the same time. An employed mother complains, "When I try to get Michelle ready in the morning, she dresses very slowly and does not understand the urgency for me to get to work on time." It is this insensitivity that adults are trying to banish when they urge children to show empathy for playmates that are crying or have been left out. But, young children cannot demonstrate qualities beyond their maturity.

It has been observed that nearly half of preschooler speech is egocentric. For example, collective monologues can be witnessed in group settings when boys and girls are expected to participate in a similar activity. Each of them talks about what they are doing but none seem to listen to others; everyone is simply talking aloud to themselves in front of classmates. This same behavior can be seen in the backyard whenever young companions are engaged in parallel play.

Teachers report that many kindergartners and some students in the first grade are egocentric and need to enlarge their perspective. These individuals benefit from daily dramatic play requiring role taking, talking about alternatives, and listening to others tell how they feel about things. Such activities establish a better base for empathy than appealing for children to feel guilty about being self-centered.

Adults often see egocentrism as a selfish trait that inconveniences those who are child caregivers. This assessment is accurate but it is important to also recognize that egocentrism can make preschoolers vulnerable to family crisis. To illustrate, children who are mistreated do not recognize the cause of their harm is lack of self-control by an abusive adult. Instead, some children are likely to feel that they are at fault, to interpret a beating as something that must be deserved. This inclination to credit oneself as the cause of most events also accounts for preschoolers feeling they have brought about separation or divorce that parents tell them was "not your fault." Because there is a potential for crisis in any family, adults should encourage children to share feelings and talk about things that bother them.

TEACHING THROUGH PLAY

Parents want children to become creative adults who adapt to change and produce unique and practical ideas. But, few families know what should be done to facilitate these achievements. Play is the universal activity of children. Parents say that they would like to respect motivation of their children to play but doubt if engagement with fantasy activity offers any benefit. They also wonder whether it is reasonable to encourage reliance on imagination as a way to prepare for being able to get along in the real world. Other parents have mixed feelings about how to respond when their children invite them to become partners in fantasy play.

Parent-Child Fantasy Play

Many parents of young children are uneasy about participating in pretend play with children. Some of their questions about what to do in this context are presented along with answers based on our large-scale family studies.

(1) *How should I respond when my children ask me to participate in play?* When children invite you to play, the best response is to participate. Even though play is the favorite way boys and girls spend their time, adults are unsure about its value and reluctant to engage in pretending themselves since it causes them to feel silly. Feelings of embarrassment reflect an unfortunate view that the only justifiable time for fantasy is in early childhood. A more beneficial perspective is to think about your child and your-

self as partners. In a partnership, there is no competition because the strengths of each partner are used to advantage both parties. Your child has more access to imagination but you possess greater language, values, and maturity. When these assets are combined, both parent and child are bound to benefit.

(2) *How long can I remain interested while at play?* A casual observer will notice that going shopping has little interest for young children. Usually they ask their mother to go home well before she is ready. Mothers recognize that what boys and girls complain about as "a long time" is actually just a few minutes. This attention deficit is reversed in fantasy play. For example, we invited 300 families with young children to be part of an experiment. As each family arrived they were greeted by a host who invited the parents to play with their child for a while using a box of toys until our staff was ready to meet them. They were unaware that the length of playtime was being measured. Later they were told, "We are glad that you kept busy playing until we could see you. By the way, how long did you play?" Most parents guessed they had been playing 20 minutes even though the actual time was 6 minutes.

When someone says another person has a short attention span, it really depends on the activity. For many parents this means that initially they can expect to play for about 10 minutes or less without becoming bored or distracted. Because it is unwise to play beyond your point of interest, tell the child, "It's time for me to stop. I cannot play as long as you can." When you take this approach, you experience satisfaction, become less inhibited, and your attention span for pretending will increase.

(3) *How important is my influence during play?* There are unique benefits of parent-child play. The children gain a broader perspective than when playing with friends or playing alone. Whatever play theme children choose, parents can help to enlarge vocabulary by defining new words in context. The more words boys and girls understand because of play, the greater their comprehension will be for reading. Plan to play at times when you are energetic and insightful rather than the times when you are intolerant and fatigued. Sometimes tired parents read to their child supposing the effort supports literacy, but reading in a monotone voice provides little benefit. In contrast, if you express emotion and act as the character you are reading about, enthusiasm for spending time with books is a likely result.

Much of what boys and girls learn before they enter the elementary grades comes from asking questions, playing, exploring, and observing. These activities match most definitions of the creative process. Because children prefer to rely on imagination, all parents should place high priority on preservation of this asset. Creativity is fostered when adults join children in play. Children often base their self-esteem on the extent to which parents get involved with activities that they enjoy. Therefore, it is not surprising that parents who engage in fantasy play are the ones establishing a closer relationship (Brown & Vaughan, 2010).

(4) *Should I praise my child during the time we play together?* Children seek recognition but it is less for praise than for acceptance. In this sense, acceptance is the greatest reward that we can offer children because then they can retain their imagination into adult life. Although praise is well intended, it is often used to shape behavior in ways that can deflect normal development. Normal development would be the continuation of creative behavior. If praise were the way to sustain creative behavior, schools would not contribute to a decline in creativity because most teachers spend a great deal of time praising students. It is when we want to develop initiative, creativity, and problem solving that praise fails us most. To liberate these qualities in others, we need to rely on internal motivation to enable people to feel free of our control.

Children at play experience the intrinsic satisfaction of play so there is no need to praise one another. They may sometimes try to control playmates and playthings but praise is not a tool they rely on. However, praising adults ignore the intrinsic satisfaction of play and instead insist on acting like a judge whose function is to verbally reinforce certain behaviors. If parents find pleasure in play, they can sustain attention for this activity. On the other hand, when parents lack enjoyment during play, it usually shows up as a short attention span and reliance on praise as an extraneous reward system.

Adults who rely on praise are easily distracted from play and tend to lapse into a pattern of near constant compliments and favorable feedback. Consider 4-year old Darin playing submarines with Jill, his grownup play partner. When Darin announced they were getting close to the island of monsters, Jill replied, "OK, you keep on watching the controls." Immediately Darin shouted, "Oh, oh, we're out of gas." Without delay, Jill answered, "Good, just keep going." Darin, who was obviously the only player aware of the imaginative dilemma declared, "Good, what do you mean good?" Many children could ask Darin's question of distracted parents who use praise as a substitute for giving their full attention.

Being an observer also implicates praise. Suppose your child comes to you with a picture s/he has colored. You are busy with other activities and don't have time to talk so you say, "That's a wonderful job," "That's great," or, "I like it better than the one that you did before dinner." Soon s/he returns to show the next product and solicit your praise. Change your strategy by sitting down and watching the act of coloring. Now the child realizes that what is being done has sufficient importance to warrant your full attention so s/he no longer has a need to seek praise. When children are young, it is not only listening to them that matters. Observation can also have a great effect by reinforcing what parents consider to be important behavior.

When people of any age become dependent on praise, they have to look outside of themselves for confidence and thus remain incapable of judging their own behavior. The need for undue praise happens most when grownups impose inappropriate expectations. For example, parents who pressure 4-year-olds to read find it necessary to praise them more often. The unintended result is that the child becomes overly reliant on praise in situations requiring perseverance. When Scott was in second grade, he asked, "Dad, why was I good at football right away?" "Because we started to play catch with the football when you were six years old instead of four years old." At age 4, Scott was less coordinated and would have required frequent praise to stay involved. To support favorable self-concept without the high cost of dependence on continual praise, emphasize the main motive and strength of young children, imagination expressed through play. Watch children at play and you will discover they never praise one another. Praise discourages independence, a quality that people need when they become involved with long-term and difficult tasks. Should parents ever praise children? Certainly, but avoid praise to make comparisons such as 'You did that better than your brother,' or to indiscriminately commend trivial behavior.

(5) *How can I encourage creative abilities in my child?* Research has found that the single most important factor that distinguishes creative children from less creative peers is family support of imagination (Brown & Vaughan, 2010; Singer & Singer, 2011). Play is the method most children prefer to express imagination. Therefore, parents are encouraged to watch their children play. By watching them as they pretend, approval of this activity and the acceptance of imagination is approved. In this environment, boys and girls realize that they do not have to change what they enjoy doing in order to get attention. They must feel that creative play is worthwhile before they can conclude that the ability to pretend is important to retain. Adults must learn to value the qualities in children that we want them to retain beyond childhood.

Multitasking and Reading

Some worries that parents may have about lessons at play involve societal changes related to multitasking and reading.

(1) *Is it ok for me to multitask while I am playing with my child?* No. Parent inattention is a major obstacle to successful teaching and close relationships. This increasingly common hindrance is illustrated by a father's observation of his 3-year old daughter:

When she is vying for my attention and wants me to look at something that she has created, finds interesting, or has questions about, I (especially when preoccupied with other matters) offer confirmations such as "uh huh," "oh, yeah," or "that's neat," without turning my head to really look. It is these moments when her tone becomes more insistent, and she tells me, "Daddy, look with your eyes." It sounds so basic, but it is her method to request my undivided attention in the only way she knows how to confirm it—when I'm looking directly at her.

(2) *Should I read to my child as well as play together?* Yes. Reading is important and provides benefit if these guidelines are considered:

(a) Read to a child when you are fresh and energetic. Don't give a son or daughter the time when you are tired and lacking in enthusiasm. Arrange time together because it reflects the high priority children have in your life.

(b) Reading children's books is fun but make certain the child also gets to see you read alone for pleasure or lessons you try to convey about the joy of reading will have much less impact.

(c) Reading is more exciting and can lead to greater learning when the process includes stopping to ask questions, talking about a story, and commenting on related events.

(d) Recognize that during reading the adult is in the power position because the child is unable to read. This means you should also spend time playing together where your child can share dominance by demonstrating strengths of imagination.

Environments and Time Management

Being aware of personal limitations can motivate improvement. Every parent has assets but sometimes overlook the advantages provided by their unique situation.

(1) *What are the difficulties I experience when pretending with my child?* Several hundred parents and teachers were surveyed to identify the top ten difficulties in playing with young children. Their responses, presented in Table 3.2, are listed in rank order with 1 being the greatest problem and 10 the least. Look over the list and rank order the problems based on your own experience using the My Rank column. This reflective task can help to recognize personal shortcomings and target goals to become a better play partner with your child (R. Strom & Strom, 2010).

(2) *How do my opportunities to teach using play compare to play at school?* Examine Table 3.3 to learn how parent opportunities are different from teachers. Given these distinctions between home and school, it is obvious

**Table 3.2.   Rank Order of Parent and
Teacher Difficulties Playing With Children***

Difficulties Playing With Young Children	My Rank	Parent Rank	Teacher Rank
Difficulty staying interested in the play		1	2
Don't have enough time for play		1	9
Trying to control the play		3	1
Boredom because of the repetition		4	5
Feeling silly and embarrassed		4	14
Orientation to completion and order		6	2
Can't think of ideas to focus play		7	5
Putting up with child dominance, bossy		8	11
Needing to control the noise level		9	5
Substitute praise for involvement		10	4
Interruption from other children		–	5
Conflicting claims of toy ownership		–	10
Accepting play themes child chooses		10	–

*From *Parenting Young Children: Exploring the Internet, Television, Play, and Reading*, by R. Strom & P. Strom, 2010, p. 116. Information Age Publishing Inc., Charlotte, NC.

that the parent has greater potential for using play for teaching, the learning context children prefer most.

(3) *Am I willing to arrange time for fantasy play with my child?* Many parents are in a constant state of fatigue. They come home tired or late, and often excuse themselves from interactive play until the weekend. Nevertheless, the child's need to play with parents is continuous rather than a Saturday or Sunday phenomenon. A better plan is to amend the daily schedule so 10 minutes can be devoted to playing together. Recognize that unscheduled play may sometimes be necessary too. Occasionally every child will make demands or provide other clues that extra attention is needed— "Watch me," "Look at this," "See what I did." In such cases, a few minutes of play can prevent frustration or conflict. Successful parents have in common the attitude that family members always come first.

(4) *How worthwhile am I as a model for leisure?* Children need to observe how parents use leisure time, become aware of the activities Mother and Dad enjoy when they are not working. Some parents give this explanation: "I sacrifice my free time so you can have things and opportunities I never had as a child." This gratuitous statement implies the child should be grateful to their parent for doing without leisure.

Table 3.3. Twenty Differences in Using Play to Teach at Home and at School*

Teaching With Play at Home	*Teaching With Play at School*
1. Ideal teacher-child ratio	1. High teacher-child ratio
2. Activities can be left unfinished	2. Activities must be finished
3. Child can be spontaneous	3. Turn taking is important
4. Child speaks without permission	4. Child gets permission to speak
5. Teaching is one responsibility	5. Teaching is main responsibility
6. Creativity can have priority	6. Memory usually has priority
7. Opportunity to share dominance	7. Teacher usually dominates
8. Child participates continually	8. Child participation is variable
9. No comparison with peers	9. Some comparison with peers
10. No peer pressure to conform	10. Peer pressure to conform
11. Learning can be unscheduled	11. Most learning is preplanned
12. Emphasis on ways to learn	12. Emphasis on learning facts
13. Continued feedback on learning	13. Variable feedback on learning
14. Child privacy can be arranged	14. Less possibility for privacy
15. Play is accepted use of time	15. Play may have low priority
16. Parent is seen in all conditions	16. Teacher may be little known
17. Individual space and movement	17. Less space and movement
18. Child can choose playmates	18. Child may be assigned groups
19. Time limits are seldom needed	19. Time limits are usually needed
20. Children choose play activity	20. Children are told what to play

*From *Parenting Young Children: Exploring the Internet, Television, Play, and Reading,* by R. Strom & P. Strom, 2010, p. 117. Information Age Publishing Inc., Charlotte, NC.

On the contrary, one of the responsibilities of parents is to show how to arrange for leisure time. Parents need to recognize that the time and interactions they share with children are more valuable than the material things they can give them. Happiness is one of the most elusive goals sought throughout the world. When parents make an effort to consistently model how to maintain a life consisting of balance, a schedule that includes time for pleasure as well as for work, their children become rich if not affluent beneficiaries.

Parents whose main goal is to provide greater family income may not be around enough to demonstrate healthy pathways to find or realize satisfaction and happiness. In these situations, children often turn to either their peers or risky experimentation to discover how to experience enjoyment. When the lifestyle that parents convey includes only how to work hard while excluding examples of how to find satisfaction or interact, the model is too narrow to support development.

SUMMARY AND IMPLICATIONS

Productive use of privacy is a lesson that can be more effectively learned at home than in any other environment. Young children seldom decide on their own to withdraw from the presence of others. Parents decide how daughters and sons spend their time and can arrange a schedule that includes daily time for solitude. However, this practice contradicts the lifestyle of families where adults admit that they find setting time aside for personal leisure is their most difficult task. Another group of parents insist on privacy for themselves but do not recognize children also need privacy. Reflective thinking calls for solitude and is a factor in making decisions (Cain, 2012).

Society tolerates the results of a broad-based failure to schedule children so they have uninterrupted time for solitary activities and reflective thinking. Hyperactivity, disruptive behavior, impulsivity, inattentiveness—teachers and parents reluctantly feel obliged to accept these problems. However, can the long-term effects, the more significant consequences in adulthood be accepted? When people lack access to their imagination, reflective ability, analytic thinking, and self-examination, mental health is compromised. A brighter future is likely if more parents see solitary play as a basis for problem solving by its direct influence on the development of concentration, task persistence, self-control, and delay of closure. Then, an emphasis on understanding others can be joined by enthusiasm for getting to know oneself. Children must learn to relate well to friends and classmates. They also have to learn productive use of privacy. Achieving both goals can support mental health and ensure a person has something to offer when in the company of others. Adults who seek to guide young children should understand the thinking processes that are normative for this age group.

Play is the dominant activity of young children, the method of learning they prefer most. Some adults consider pretending an insignificant activity, tolerable for children only. The fact is imaginative play contributes to creativity and mental health at every age. We are accustomed to thinking of adults as giving leadership in most sectors of life. However, children are the models that we should look to for how to play. Recognizing the importance of reciprocal learning is the way to establish a respectful relationship.

APPLICATIONS FOR TEACHING

1. Every child needs time alone each day to support creative thinking and mental health. Adults want their privacy respected but may not recognize that children need privacy too. Scheduling time for them to be alone in a safe setting enables children to value relief and recognize other benefits that come from the solitude of time alone.

2. Encourage children to reflect on information they find while searching the net. Young children soon become accustomed to fast communication online. This expectation for immediate access to games and ideas should not carry over to the more complicated task of information processing. Reflective thinking calls for solitude and is the basis for good judgment. Remind your child that to act on information in a hasty way without reflection is often the cause of poor decisions in every sector of life.

3. Analyzing out loud what to do before taking a course of action involves reflective thinking. Alternatives should be weighed as a part of the process for identifying the most suitable response. Reflective thought can result in better decisions than when impulsivity dictates responses. Helping a child transition from reliance on impulsivity to reflective thought is an important lesson.

4. Arrange uninterrupted time daily for imaginative play with a child. Young children have much to gain when they can count on regular playtime with parents. Plan to have the play sessions when you are energetic and insightful rather than fatigued or intolerant. Recognize that some unscheduled time may also be necessary. Occasionally almost every child will make demands or give other clues that extra attention is needed. In such cases, a few minutes of play may avoid unproductive conflicts.

5. Play offers an opportunity for parent and child to learn from each other? Think of your child and yourself as play partners. There is no competition in a true partnership. The strength of each individual benefits both parties. Your child possesses greater imaginative strength while you have more mature values, extensive command of the language, and power of approving and reinforcing creativity. By merging these assets, reciprocal learning in your family could begin with play and continue in elementary school when technology becomes an added medium for sharing.

6. Maintain a lifestyle that balances work and play. An increasing number of adults accept more responsibilities than can be managed during the expected period of time. Some consequences for

individuals who behave in this way are feelings of anxiety, stress, resentment, helplessness, anger, and loss of self-confidence. Learning to say no when others make requests that would erase family leisure time or asking for a later due date when unreasonable expectations are proposed is more sensible than hurried or last minute efforts to finish tasks. Children should learn to gauge personal limits from examples given by parents.

CHAPTER 4

FEAR AND CRITICAL THINKING

Everyone has to confront fears and worries. However, these feelings are more prevalent in childhood. There are several reasons for the difference. Children have active imaginations and are sometimes unable to distinguish fiction from reality. For them the daytime includes lots of fantasy and sleep brings more nightmares than are reported by adults. Growing up includes additional fears because children are exposed to a broader range of experiences than ever before. The apprehension of parents is another influence. Television and the Internet present mothers and fathers with reminders about situations with potential to endanger their children. In combination, these factors should motivate parents to think about ways to help children manage fears and worries.

The goals of this presentation are to describe how children can be taught to assess risk and danger, balance caution and trust, and diminish undue pressures that contribute to anxiety. Knowing the progressive stages by which children come to comprehend death is important because it prevents a misinterpretation of why war play appeals to children and avoids attributing motives to boys and girls that do not match their intentions. The important role of play and children's books are discussed as resources for coping with fears. Understanding ways to reduce the anxiety of children are examined for teachers, and counselors.

Learning Throughout Life: An Intergenerational Perspective, pp. 71–92
Copyright © 2012 by Information Age Publishing

MESSAGES ABOUT DANGER

Five-year-old Jonathan examines the milk carton in front of him while he eats his breakfast cereal. He wonders if the missing boy pictured on the carton will be found and whether his parents will ever hear from him. Down the street 6-year old Mark looks at a postcard that came in the mail. The card includes a photograph of a girl about his age who is missing along with printed details. Eight-year old Denise is watching television when an Amber Alert interrupts the program. Information is given citing the license plate, color and make of car driven by someone who abducted a young girl. Nine-year old Jeffrey has returned from a trip to the grocery store with his mother and is helping carry packages to the kitchen. Every bag he places on the counter portrays an image of a child who has been reported missing. Jeffrey reflects on how he would escape if someone tried to take him away from his family.

No one knows how repeated exposure to these kinds of messages about missing persons impact a child's outlook on life. However, it is certain that such reports have dramatically altered the way in which many parents orient daughters and sons to relationships and guidance about interpreting their environment. Parents are naturally upset when television or written materials inform them that a registered child molester has been allowed by the courts to move in their neighborhood or media reports that children are being exploited by pedophiles that they meet on the Internet. Sometimes it seems that there is no end to the list of dangers children could potentially encounter (Bakan, 2011; Rycik, 2006).

In response to what seems to be an increasingly hostile environment, some parents conclude that it is necessary to warn children against contact with strangers. Others take the precaution of fingerprinting or videotaping children, keeping up-to-date photographs or implanting dental microdots with identification numbers that are filed in computer registries. Growth of these practices underscores a need for parents to consider whether they are protecting their children or just frightening them. How can parents put justified concerns in perspective so safety rather than fear dominates their behavior? Obviously, an increased awareness about potential for harm to children is bound to cause worry. Nevertheless, parents should carefully think about personal fears in relation to the evidence before they can expect to help frightened youngsters cope with situations that may be unsafe (Bourke, 2005; Schneier, 2003).

The intention should be to present a balance of concern for safety, fear, and trust. This balance is crucial because the ways parents handle personal fears determines how they prepare their children for a world in which there are many unsafe situations. One way to begin this lesson is by teaching how to assess risk, an ability that governs the extent of fear.

Assessment of Risk

Parents whose fears cause them to believe most people cannot be trusted are incapable of teaching children how to trust others. Emotional needs of children should not be mistaken. It is essential that they have an overall impression that the world is a safe and friendly place rather than view their environment as permeated by danger and unfriendly people. Nevertheless, motivated by personal anxieties and worries, some parents discourage children from speaking to anyone who they do not know. This decision brings about a reciprocal dilemma. If children should not speak to strangers, it follows that strangers should not speak to children.

Older adults are frequently disappointed by their lack of opportunity to interact with children. Marie, a grandmother, describes one experience in this way,

> I was in the drug store and decided to check my blood pressure. An elementary student was at the machine when I arrived. By looking over his shoulder, I could see the reading was 110/70 on the machine and said, "Wow, I wish my blood pressure was that low." He looked at me in an odd way, said nothing, and walked away. Whenever I try to have a conversation with children, even those living on my street, it is always the same. They do not respond. Other friends my age report a similar reaction of children.

One consequence is that many safe, well-meaning grownups that children could turn to for help become reluctant to interact with them. Adults often report this response about their experience in shopping malls where a "Don't talk to strangers" practice prevents intergenerational conversation. It seems natural to smile at a child, say hello or exchange brief comments. Yet, more and more people reason "I should not be talking to unsupervised children because I do not want to appear as a threat. They have likely been told to avoid strangers and, in effect, I am urging them to disobey parents."

The accuracy of this perception is confirmed by the results of surveys from students in kindergarten through grade three. When asked to identify their fears, strangers are mentioned more often than any other concerns (Bakan, 2011). Children admit that their parents taught them this fear. But how accurate is this scary lesson about strangers? The National Center for Missing and Exploited Children (2012) identifies each reported case as being an abduction by an unknown individual, kidnapping by a parent, or a runaway choosing to be gone. Unfortunately, specifics of individual cases are not identified by agencies that print the warning flyers, grocery bags, and milk cartons. Thinking of missing children as being a homogenous group has produced confusion and unwarranted fear. As a result, when parents lack information, many of them inaccurately suppose strangers are the main cause of missing children (Gardner, 2009; Glassner, 2010).

The Federal Bureau of Investigation has determined this conclusion is inaccurate. Every day about 22,000 children are declared to be missing, roughly 800,000 a year. The largest subgroup of 450,000 are juveniles who have run away. Of the 350,000 kidnapped, a relative without legal custody, typically father, abducts 99% of them. Only 200 children, less than 1% of the total kidnapped, are taken by strangers (Jasper, 2006). The National Center for Missing and Exploited Children recognizes there is unwarranted paranoia about strangers. For this reason the agency shuns their previous message of years past about "stranger danger." The center states that it no longer supports the "stranger danger" message. Children do not have the same understanding of who a stranger is as an adult might; this is a difficult concept to grasp. A more beneficial response is to help children build the confidence and self-esteem they need to stay as safe as possible in any potentially dangerous situation rather than teaching them to lookout for a particular type of person. The "stranger danger" message is ineffective and, based on what is known about people that harm youngsters, the danger is greater from someone the children know or the family knows than from most strangers (McBride, 2011).

There are also misperceptions surrounding alleged dangers students face at school. News reports about prevalence of drugs and violence have led parents to believe that murder could be a potential threat to their child's life. On the contrary, of 55 million students in the elementary and secondary grades, 30 are murdered at school each year. In the same period, parents or caretakers kill 3,000 children at home. Stated another way, the children murdered at school are 1% of those killed at home. The illogical response to these statistics has been to increase the funding for metal detection and security guards to prevent someone from bringing a weapon on campus or coming there to harm students (Langman, 2009).

Balance Caution and Trust

The national rate of serious crime has declined in the past 5 years. However, media coverage of crime increased by 600% in the same period (Bakan, 2011). Some people do not watch local news because the content centers on tragedy and bad events more than favorable ones. Still, there is no point in blaming the media for our lack of critical thinking. The fact that negative stories get more attention on television, the Internet, and in the newspapers is an insufficient reason to ignore objective evidence. When 99% of child kidnappings, 98% of child abuse, and 99% of child murders implicate relatives, the rational conclusion would be to pay more attention to the improvement of family life (Carrabine, 2008).

For the same reasons, it is illogical to identify all strangers, childcare workers and community volunteers in youth agencies as people that cannot be trusted. The assumption that most people would harm children is false and should be rejected. Boys and girls must be taught to trust but also to become more able to recognize suspicious behavior. Let us examine some of the ways these important purposes can be achieved.

Family Safety Guidelines

Divorced or separated parents with child custody should not identify strangers to children as being a major threat. Since 90% of all custodies in the United States are assigned to mothers, persons most likely to kidnap children are noncustodial fathers (Cherlin, 2009). This means that mothers should assess their situation before deciding what to tell daughters and sons about missing children. It may not be in the best interest of children to tell them that noncustodial parents are responsible for most kidnappings. The idea that one of their parents would do such a thing could become an undue source of worry to children.

If a mother decides that she is not in a high-risk group because there is no custody battle and an estranged spouse has not made threats, then her conversations with children can focus on possible situations and ways of responding. On the other hand, if a former spouse appears as a potential problem, certified copies of the legal document on child custody should be placed in a child's file at school. And, if a noncustodial parent threatens to take a child, the principal and teachers should be told so they do not allow the child to leave school with an unauthorized adult.

Parents from single and intact families should stop warning children about everyone that is a stranger. The fact is strangers are not a common danger. In the vast majority of cases involving crimes against children, the youngster knows the perpetrator. It could be some relative, an older friend, brother of a playmate or a man who lives nearby. Children can readily be taught to run away from a stranger, but teaching them to say "No" and leave adults they are familiar with or persons their parents trust is another matter.

Parents should formulate family safety rules to help protect children from dangers that are both known and unknown. Boys and girls should be told these family rules must be followed at all times. "Never go anywhere without telling Mom, Dad, Grandma or the babysitter." This is a good rule because it prevents situations the parents would not condone. Encouraging children to trust their intuition and gut feelings about situations is important because parents will not always be around when there is a need to assess danger. Children should understand that "Anyone who tries to get you to break a family rule is a bad person. That person deserves to get in trouble, so go tell an adult—Mom, Dad, your teacher, the principal--right away if someone is bad." This rule defines bad people in terms of their behavior instead of their appearance. Children can apply the bad person rule to people they do not know and familiar faces without emphasizing danger from either source.

People who exploit children generally rely on methods that would be ineffective with adults. They use intimidation, which is most effective with children who have been taught to never challenge the authority of adults. Elementary school children that are trusted by parents to rely on their own judgment when any situation seems to present danger are less likely to do what they are told by a coercive adult. Inner strength is needed to oppose directives that children believe could jeopardize their safety. If children in the primary grades can gain confidence about making personal decisions, learn family rules on how to ask adults for assistance and feel this is the right thing to do, they will be better equipped to assess danger, cope with scary situations, and still view the world as a safe place (Lucado, 2009).

Since the terrorist attacks on September 11, 2001, Americans have had to confront unprecedented fears and worries. Some parents prefer to avoid talking with children about the dangers faced by our nation. However, a more practical response assumes that the more children know, the more able they will be to cope and the safer they can feel. The United States Department of Homeland Security (2012) recommends families discuss the need to be observant and what can be done to reduce danger. Children should be aware that the government tries to protect our family by providing media warnings when appropriate about threat levels, amber alerts, and that steps are taken by airport security and air marshals who are assigned to airplanes. Despite these precautionary steps, there is a need to go beyond just training the firemen and police to deal with potential disasters. Everyone should be on guard. Families are advised to prepare a disaster kit in the unlikely event of an emergency that requires leaving home. This kit should contain water, juice, canned goods, medication and bandages.

Parents should make sure that their children know how to contact a particular person if family members were to become separated. Boys and girls should know a landline phone number to reach the contact person and understand where to go if they find themselves alone. And, of course even preschoolers should be able to tell police the full names of their parents, home address, and phone. Many parents overlook the fact that they are responsible for providing children with these lessons.

Many young children are unprepared for fearful situations that they may have to face. Parents should ensure that their child knows essential information. These simple lessons are not learned quickly so patience and continued emphasis is needed. Practice brings the desired result. When a child can answer correctly, ask these questions in the presence of relatives and friends. Adults will tell the child that they are pleased important lessons have been learned. Young children should know:

- His or her full name, home address and phone number
- Parent full name and name of place where s/he works
- How to dial 9-1-1 in order to get emergency assistance
- What to do if they think that someone is following them
- How to answer the phone without letting callers know they are alone
- What to do in the case of a fire

RESPONDING TO CHILD FEARS

It is unfortunate that parents teach their unfounded fears to children and yet dismiss fears that are uniquely experienced by youngsters. Indeed, many parents are ashamed of fearful children and try to banish the fright by denial. A father recalled taking his 4-year old son Steven to a zoo. Because crocodiles fascinated him, quite a bit of time was spent at the reptile exhibit. During that time, another little boy about the same age as Steven arrived with his family. The boy was afraid and preferred to stay at some distance from the floor-to-ceiling window behind which the crocodiles were in sight. Taking notice of his fear, the boy's father lifted him up, held him against the window, and announced, "See, it's like I told you; they're locked in so you do not have any reason to be afraid." Imagine how confusing it was for this boy to be told he was not afraid when he was scared. His parents, the all-knowing authorities, must know more than he does. Some children thus develop an alienation from their own feelings. They learn to mistrust their own senses and rely upon others to tell them what to feel. It would have been better for this father to tell his child "The crocodile is dangerous, and can make us feel afraid. We are protected behind this window and we will be careful. If we want to stand back a little ways, that's ok."

Sometimes children encounter an opposite but equally firm denial that their experiences are unique. Each of us has heard people say, "I know just how you feel." Actually, no one can know exactly how another person feels. However, this limitation of empathy, ability to participate in someone else's experience, becomes less disturbing when we realize that it confirms our assumptions about being individuals. For parents this means the fears of children should be respected if we share them or not. Our acceptance of others seems to play a larger role in determining interpersonal success than our understanding of other people. If we limit our respect to those whose experiences we understand, the quest for understanding itself becomes an obstacle to successful relationships.

Besides denial and empathy, ridicule is a common response to fear. But laughing at another person's fears does not decrease the fear. Instead, the effect is to lower that individual's confidence. Telling a child "It's just a dream and not real," might be well intended, but inspires shame for having fears that grownups declare unwarranted. To laugh at somebody's fears or call the person a derogatory name such as wimp, sissy, baby, or chicken, is to undermine a relationship. Children whose feelings are ridiculed soon stop sharing their experiences. The tragedy for parents is they reduce the chance to know their child better and forfeit an opportunity to help cope with fears and worries.

The first step in overcoming fears is to acknowledge them. Because children identify closely with parents, a sound method to reduce the harmful consequences of children's fears is for parents to admit their own worries. A child who is afraid of the dark, of being alone, or starting school should be assured by adults that fear is a natural reaction and telling about fears does not make someone a coward or a sissy. Courage is not the absence of fear but instead the mastery of fear. When people lose touch with the possibilities of danger, they also lose a normal sense of caution that serves to protect them.

A certain degree of fear is needed to exercise good judgment. The Greek philosopher, Plato, wrote, "Courage is knowing what to fear." And, while parents may insist there is no danger in the dark, a child observes that Mom does not go out alone late at night, and doors are double locked at bedtime. Children should not be caused to feel ashamed of expressing feelings of fear. After all, many adults have fears about becoming old, being alone, getting fat, losing a job, developing cancer, falling down, becoming a burden, and being rejected by other people. However, adults have an idea of what fear is whereas children worry long before they comprehend the notion of fear.

A child whose fears are unsuspected or unshared bears an additional burden of loneliness. No other aspect of experience is more deserving of compassion as well as attention than a person's fears. Also, no aspect is more baffling to a child or those who want to offer assistance. Certainly children should have someone they can turn to that will hear their worries without judging them. They have this experience when their parents accept them unconditionally. No child should have to repress fear or to pretend bravery to gain esteem of parents. When worries that relatives have in common and those that are unique to each person are identified, family members are more able to help one another. Make an effort to identify the worries of your children and share some of your own fears with them.

Use of Children's Books

One way for parents to reduce anxiety of children is by reading children's books where the main character has to deal with situations similar to those experienced by young listeners. Talking about how the story character may feel and how that same feeling bothers boys and girls can help them to realize that telling parents their fears is a way to manage them better. When people share their fears, they are no longer alone and there can be some reduction of anxiety. Consider some examples of how reading about a common child fear can lessen by talking with adults.

Leela and the Watermelon is a story about a young girl from India (Hirsch & Narayan, 1971). She likes watermelons but one day she ate so fast she swallowed a seed. Her older brother teased Leela suggesting that a watermelon would now grow inside of her. Leela feels anxious because she is alone with her fear and feels helpless. Then she sees a lady at the market who has a big stomach. Had the lady swallowed a seed too? When Leela asks, the woman replies "I don't know." Leela worries about herself and about the lady. Later the lady is seen again announcing birth of her baby. Again, Leela wants to know if a watermelon seed was swallowed. Other women standing by find this funny and explain that having a baby does not result from swallowing a seed. When Leela tells grandmother that her brother said a seed would grow inside her, the old woman took her to the bazaar to buy the biggest melon that was available. Leela was allowed to eat it all herself and was not expected to give her brother any.

Jill is the main character in *The Alligator Under the Bed* (Nixon, 1974). She hears an alligator making swishing noises with its tail under the bed so mother is called. The mother listens, suggests a bad dream was the cause, and urges Jill to go back to sleep. The same thing happens again but this time Jill's father answers her call. He advises her to avoid imagining things because it was impossible for an alligator to be under the bed. The third episode of asking for help resulted in Uncle Harry coming to the bedroom. Harry announced that he heard strange noises coming from this room. Jill said, "It's the alligator." Harry suggests that the alligator is under the bed because it makes a good hiding place and he must be lost. So Jill tells the alligator to go home, Uncle Harry opens the door, and leads the alligator out so he can return home.

Fear of Bullies at School

Elementary grade students sometimes experience fear about their safety because of peers that seek to bully them. Feelings of resignation that nothing can be done or expecting adults to deal with every incident should be replaced by collective student resolve to assume their unique responsibility related to the misconduct of classmates. When teachers present a structured agenda that allows students to describe impressions of peer abuse, constructive norms of response to prevent it can emerge. In a similar way, teachers should avoid assuming that students who show cruelty and lack self-control are incapable of improvement so giving up on them is justified. A more promising outlook is to realize that teacher guided discussions can promote healthy group responses to frustrating situations.

Class discussions about bullying can support the motivation students need to assume their important role to ensure safety of classmates. These conversations can also improve perspective taking by adults. Investigations have determined that, compared with students, teachers and administrators underestimate the scope of bullying, consider the school as more safe, and judge incidents to be less serious (Willard, 2007). A suitable agenda invites student opinions that are seldom allowed expression and consideration in the classroom. Teachers can reinforce accurate impressions by providing summaries of findings from research studies. The following questions are recommended for periodic discussions with elementary school students.

1. What does it mean to be a bully? (students share their definitions based on personal experience)
2. How does it feel to be the victim of a bully? (encourage awareness based on hearing feelings of others)
3. What can happen to someone who is bullied a lot? (effects of bullying on mental health)
4. Why do you suppose people bully others? (speculation and first hand accounts about bully motivation)
5. What do you think will happen to bullies when they grow up? (guesses about long-term consequences accompanied by teacher reports of research findings)
6. What problems can school bullies expect to face later in life? (difficulty forming intimate and durable relationships; rejection by co-workers and neighbors in the community)
7. How can bullies change to become someone that other people like? (identify possibilities for rehabilitation)

8. How do you suppose their parents treat bullies at home? (conjecture about the parent-child relationships compared to what is revealed by research literature on bullies)

9. What should someone do when they are picked on? (find out the best ways to respond is of great interest to students)

10. What can students expect of adults to protect them from bullies? (identify ways teachers and parents can be counted on to enforce the civil rights of everyone)

11. What factors should bullies consider when they reflect on their behavior? (provide healthy criteria all students should use for self-examination)

12. What are some myths about bullies? (speculation followed by review of research about bullies)

13. Why should students tell on a bully when they know about peer abuse (individual obligations in a civil society)

14. What are some names that you do not want to be called in the classroom or outside of school?

15. What results from the bully poll taken by our class do you want to discuss?

The expectation that class time should be used efficiently means that teachers are confronted with choices about balancing instruction and giving attention to student concerns. Some educators and parents might wonder whether discussions about relationships is appropriate when the purpose of curriculum is to prepare students for the world of work. This perspective is shortsighted. Over the past decade, substantial evidence has revealed that students who are unable to get along with classmates also show a higher rate of absenteeism, dropout, truancy, incarceration, suicide, and murder. Devoting class time to talking about issues that bother students is justified (Gardner, 2009; Glassner, 2010).

Anxiety During Childhood

Human beings are always imagining, and in the process may feel alone or helpless. When we find ourselves in all three conditions at the same time—imagining, alone, and helpless—anxiety will be experienced. Aloneness is a variable condition. Age and needs can determine what is required to feel alone. At a certain age or because of specific needs we may feel alone whenever a particular person is out of reach. At another stage of development or when influenced by different needs, we may feel alone if companions disagree with our opinions. Similarly, over time, the same person may feel helpless when faced with the tasks of tying shoes, doing algebra, or reading a foreign language. In order for anxiety to occur, the conditions of aloneness and helplessness must combine to confront an open imagination.

When an imagining person is alone but not helpless, s/he might feel disappointed, unhappy or abused but still avoid feeling anxious. Someone who feels helpless but not alone may resent being dependent or acquire a sense of inferiority but still not experience anxiety. When we feel alone and helpless but are able to cushion effects of imagination, we may be angry, suspicious or afraid. Nevertheless, we escape anxiety. It seems that, short of madness, there are only three ways to prevent anxiety—be less alone, less helpless or less imaginative. Because the future will require greater creativity, efforts to curb anxiety should exclude reduction of imagination and focus instead on aloneness and helplessness (P. Strom & Strom, 2009).

When anxiety threatens mental health, individuals of any age should be referred for therapy. By using a medium like play, free association or a review of troublesome events, the therapist tries to recreate the client's anxieties so they can be shared. A certain amount of interrupted time is scheduled for sessions. Self-disclosure in these sessions is confidential. Together, the guarantee of time and safety encourage intimacy. In addition, therapists inspire confidence because they are trained to listen, remember details, correct inconsistencies, and present reflective questions. Once the images that previously produced anxiety are shared with the therapist, a client may re-experience guilt, shame, doubt, or other natural reaction but no longer anxiety. For many people release from anxiety brings therapy to a close. A decision about further treatment for feelings of helplessness may depend upon the case load of a therapist and whether s/he subscribes to theoretical views of Carl Rogers, Carl Jung, Alfred Adler, Sigmund Freud, or some other figure of counseling renown (Compton, 2009).

It is worthwhile to consider how children could more easily access treatment for anxieties. At the same time even greater effort should center on finding ways to reduce the number of students who are so anxious they need therapy. Teachers suppose that, because anxiety is a concern of therapists, therapists are the responsible parties to support reduction. In contrast, teachers view themselves as responsible to produce creative learning. Actually, creative thought and anxiety are related in being two ends of a continuum that should not be mistaken for one another. The methods of therapists are meant to diminish a child's sense of aloneness and helplessness while teacher methods are meant to increase the polar opposites, feelings of community and mastery. The complement of these professions can be diagrammed in this way:

Imagination + Aloneness + Helplessness = Anxiety > Psychotherapy
Imagination + Community + Mastery = Creative Learning

The diagram indicates imagination plus aloneness plus helplessness leads to anxiety that can be treated by psychotherapy. Instruction in the classroom should combine imagination, community, and mastery to yield creative learning. To the degree that teachers achieve the goal of creative learning, they also contribute to a reduction of anxiety. However, the rate of success should be much improved. The fact is there are many students who feel alone and helpless. They might feel alone because they have moved, are newcomers to a school, their parents are breaking up, or they hold opinions not shared by classmates. Others feel helpless because of class competition, their powerless role in confronting bullies or do not know how to do their homework. Somehow the uniqueness of each individual should be preserved without making children feel alone. Establishing a sense of community seems essential.

Educators can begin by enabling more students to feel they belong at school and are welcome in regular classrooms. Whenever teachers prefer sameness of mental ability level among students, the unintended result is that classrooms do not represent a microcosm of the society. Under these conditions student miss a chance to learn what being part of a community is about, especially accommodation of differences. Another way to promote feelings of community is reciprocal teaching in cooperative learning groups. Children are also less likely to feel alone when they require help if their teachers do not see themselves as isolated professionals. Teachers who view colleagues as an interdependent team are more able and willing to confront complex problems together.

Similarly, educators should enable students to attain a sense of mastery without isolating them. There is concern about the increasing population inclined toward cynicism. Students schooled for individual competition only may limit their role as adults to being social critics, complaining they have solutions to problems but no one listens to them. This choice prevents them from cooperating with others to improve their community, and denies them the sense of potency that comes with being able to produce social change. Exerting influence in a world of institutions calls for a broader definition of competence than existed in the past. What is required is not just strengths as individuals but readiness for social and corporate action. When educators arrange for students to attain mastery through collaboration, to observe and appreciate interdependence, they minimize the chance that individuals will experience aloneness, helplessness, and anxiety. In this way, teachers have an opportunity to prevent anxieties that therapists would otherwise have a responsibility to treat (Marks, 2005).

UNDERSTANDING THE PRESCHOOL SOLDIER

Children are curious about stories they see on television, particularly scenes that involve warfare and death. Many parents report their children ask them these kinds of questions: Who will take care of the boys and girls whose parents are fighting in the war? Will my father have to be a soldier? What if the enemy attacks the buses or subways in our city? No adult feels adequately prepared to respond to these kinds of questions but parents do their best to explain in a nonfrightening manner. The goals of this segment are to explain why young children from all countries rely on fantasy play as a powerful tool for the reduction of their fears and worries. Parents should understand mental development stages that govern how children interpret the meaning of death and why they find conflict play appealing. Learning to accurately interpret the motives of children should motivate adults to allow children their choice of toys and themes that guide playing alone, playing with peers and fantasy play with parents.

Child Understanding of Death

Parents wonder how observing the scenes of war on television could influence their child. Some are uncertain over whether to allow playing with toy weapons or military video games. Barbara is a 35-year old mother who has two preschoolers. Even before the fears of terrorism became a global concern, Barbara and her husband agreed that violent-type toys motivate lawlessness. "We knew the decision to deny weapon play would be difficult for our sons to comprehend and it would be easy to conform to the majority opinion. But, for us that would mean lowering our standards of integrity."

After overhearing my child tell his cowboy companions that he was going to shoot and kill them, I felt compelled to say, "Donnie, you don't really mean that." Then I reconsidered and thought maybe I should sit him down and explain that when you kill someone they are dead, and they will never breathe again. Then I wondered, if I do not let Donnie play with guns, it might give him the feeling we are convinced he is so violent he requires different toys from everyone else. Finally, not knowing what to do or say, I ignored him and went on feeling guilty.

Barbara's dilemma is common. Perhaps insight can be attained by more closely examining just what young children mean when they talk about killing and dying. The meaning of death has many interpretations and misconceptions for them. Young children view death as a reversible process. Whether they play hide-and-go-seek or cowboys and Indians, all of the dead people are expected to recover quickly and live again. The conventional television cartoon reinforces this notion when a rabbit runs and then falls off a high cliff, hits the ground with a thud, and, in keeping with the child's reversible concept of death, is immediately brought back to life. The same thing happens when children watch the death of an actor on a television program that later miraculously appears as a guest on a talk show. Some time ago, when one of my sons was a preschooler, we had this conversation:

> Son: Dad, I'm going to dress up like an army man.
> Dad: You look just like a soldier. I was a soldier once.
> Son: Why?
> Dad: The country needed me. We were having a war.
> Son: Dad, did you die?
> Dad: No, I was lucky.

The realization that death is permanent takes place in stages. Between ages 3 to 5, there is a lot of curiosity and questioning about death. Unfortunately, many adults suppress this curiosity, and think it is impolite for a child to ask old Mrs. Thompson when she is going to die. In contrast, several generations ago, it was quite common for children to witness at least one deathbed event, usually the death of a grandparent. Yet, the young child believes that death is not final; it is like being less alive. Just as sleeping people can wake up and people who go on a trip can return, so too a dead person can come back to life. The coffin limits movement but dead people must continue to eat and to breathe. People buried at the cemetery must know what is happening on the earth, they are sad for themselves, and feel it whenever someone thinks of them. Dying disturbs the young child because life in the grave is seen as boring and unpleasant. Most of all, it bothers the child because death separates people from one another. And, at this age, the greatest fear of children is separation from parents.

Young children are self-centered and preoccupied by present events, so they are unable to recognize how a death in their family might impose future demands on them including permanent loss of someone's presence, their comfort, love, encouragement, and financial support. Because these understandings do not come until a later age, little children seldom express grief immediately or even cry like their adult relatives and friends. In fact, it is common for adults to mistakenly conclude that a child is coping well with the loss of a loved one. But, bear in mind that little children are unable to fully comprehend the situation and they can only tolerate short periods of sadness. Because it is easy for them to be distracted, they may seem to be finished with grief and mourning earlier than is actually the case.

Even young children recognize that words are an insufficient way to help someone in grief and that what matters the most is just being there to console them. To illustrate, 4-year old Amanda did not come in from the backyard when called by her mother. Later, when mother asked Amanda to explain why she was late, the little girl replied, "I was helping Judy." Mother wanted more information. "What were you doing?" Amanda said, "Well, her doll's head got crushed." Mother wondered aloud, "How could you help fix that?" Amanda said, "I was helping her cry."

Children between 5 to 9 years of age tend to personify death, seeing it as an angelic character that makes rounds during the night to start life for some individuals and end it for others. The big shift in child thinking from the first stage to this one is that death is recognized as possibly being final. It is no longer seen as being just a reduced form of life. This view of death emerges with increasing personal experiences, which suggest that certain separations are permanent. When a pet goldfish dies, mother buys a new one because she says the other one is gone forever. Claude Cattaert's (1963) classic child's book *Where do Goldfish Go?* demonstrates how some adults react to death of pets by suggesting they can be replaced. When Valerie's goldfish dies unexpectedly, no one seems to be bothered except Valerie; yet the family is overcome with sorrow when grandfather dies, even though his death had been discussed and anticipated for years.

It is not just families that need to become more aware and sensitive to children's feelings about death. During conversations with prospective kindergarten and first-grade teachers, they were asked: "What would you do if some morning at school the class goldfish were found dead?" The range of responses included these comments: I would deliver a eulogy; declare a day of mourning; conduct a burial; discuss the qualities of the deceased; consider the after-life of fish; invite testimonials from friends; talk about human death and its meaning; and, flush the fish and say, "Take out your books, it's time for oral reading."

Parents know they cannot guarantee a long life for pets, but hope that they can reduce the amount of exposure their children have about death on television. The outcome of this decision to protect youngsters is usually a refusal to allow them to watch television detective and police programs, censorship of aggressive cartoons, and ambivalence about viewing the local news that frequently portrays violence or death in the community.

The typical 5- to 9-year-old child believes that the cause of death is external, and they personify death as being an outside agent. Since they conceive of death as a person, children feel it is possible to avoid death if certain protective measures are taken. Thus, one child may claim that his grandfather will not die, because the family is going to take good care of him. Children of single parents admit they worry most about "What will happen to me if my mother dies?" It is reassuring for them to know that plans have been made so they will be taken care of in the event of unexpected death.

Finally, about ages 9 to 10, children realize that death is not only final but inevitable. It will happen to them too, no matter how clever they are or how well they take care of themselves. Instead of imagining death as being controlled by an external agent, they now recognize that internal, biological forces are involved. As children accept the universality and the certainty of death, some changes can be observed. They begin to show concern about the meaning of life, their purposes for being on earth, and ways to achieve them. This means that values become more important in governing their behavior.

Many children throughout the world are growing up in the midst of death and threats of destruction. They see death on television with such regularity that fear of war has become common. Children look to adults for answers about death, but our attitude can be our most important response. Certainly parents will want to explain their beliefs about what happens after death. But, bear in mind that youngsters love mystery, and they will adopt your sense of wonder and uncertainty if you are willing to express it (Wolpe, 2009).

Children's Perceptions of Toys

There are many playthings parents believe children could do without. Some dislike all military toys because they reflect violence. Others oppose stunt-oriented toys that encourage taking risks on skateboards. Crash cars that fall apart on impact and then can be quickly reconstructed are thought to sanction a disregard for safety, and martial arts dolls create reliance on an irrational method for resolving conflicts. Parents with these complaints are often ambivalent because they want to purchase toys that reflect their own values but should also recognize that children require opportunities in decision making to develop their own value system. And where is it more appropriate for children to be given options than in their realm of play?

Grownups can justify making some decisions for children such as whether they will attend school, if they will go to the doctor, and when it is time for bed. Parents will also determine how much money can be spent on entertainment and toys for children. On the other hand, to claim that boys and girls need coherent values but deny them practice in making some personal choices is unreasonable. So, parents are bothered about the priority they should assign to feelings of their children in selecting toys for them. Instead of declaring your values by choosing children's toys or by censoring the content of their fantasy, try to enact your values while you participate in pretend-type play with them. The imposition of values always has less influence than the illustration of values. If you feel that war tends to be glorified while the darker sides of battle are overlooked, give some attention to the aftermath of war and importance of the peace-maker role in your play.

Most people share the aspiration that international disarmament will rid us of the threat of nuclear war. But, while peace means the end of war, it does not mean an end to differences of opinion. Since there is a critical distinction between the fantasy wars enacted by children and bloody wars carried out by adults, it is a serious mistake to misread the motives of the preschool soldier. Grownups who suppose that young children who play soldiers have the same purposes as the men and women at war they imitate are misinterpreting motives of children and their understanding about violence and death. Parents should strive to recognize favorable possibilities in their children's choice of playthings.

Conflict toys and games can serve to meet certain needs of boys and girls. This kind of play offers relief from feelings of powerlessness and of dependence that accounts for much of a child's experience. Surely there is nothing strange about the desire to control others, especially those who daily exercise power over you. Children delight when asserting themselves in play and make Daddy run away or fall down because he has been shot. Then too, conflict playthings can provide a safe setting in which to express disapproved feelings such as anger, fear, frustration, and jealousy. In many homes these feelings are met by punishment, ridicule, or shame. Danger play also provides an opportunity to repeatedly confront fearful issues like war, death, and injury. Although these subjects are of universal concern to children, many adults avoid talking about them and, as a result, increase the anxiety of children.

Taking risks requires practice in a low-cost setting. During danger play children can afford to take chances, to see what it is like to rebel, to be the bad guy or the outcast. These are risks they dare not take in daily family life. In this connection, it is worth noting that war play is the only context in which some children can conduct conflict without guilt. Even though parents should teach how to settle disputes in constructive ways, some boys and girls learn instead to feel guilty whenever they oppose an authority figure. For many kids fighting off a mutual "enemy" can foster competition needs. War play also allows children to experience leadership, to take charge and command others as well as to become heroes like their favorite television characters. Finally, conflict toys and games are fun, a fact that should be appreciated by a society that values enjoyment.

Influence of Toys and Players

Safety should always be a parent consideration when they buy toys for children. However, instead of overemphasizing the effect of toys, it is important to understand that the adults who play with children also can have a great influence. Otherwise, the value of playthings is exaggerated while the impact of players is underestimated. Relatives cannot fulfill their guidance role merely by purchasing the right kind of toys or forbidding the wrong ones.

Some adults complain that children are inclined to believe what they see advertised on television. Is the adult condition any better if we believe everything we read on toy packaging? For example, exposure to so-called educational or creative toys will not necessarily support child reliance on imagination. Creativity does not reside in certain toys because of their design, but mostly relates to interaction between persons that play with them. Research on creative behavior and modeling shows that parents should play with their children; they should become involved instead of limiting themselves to judging the merits of playthings. The assumption that certain toys can have a dysfunctional effect on child personality is unsubstantiated but the view that adults can have a favorable influence through play has been demonstrated.

Parents should end the practice of censoring content of children's fantasy play, except in instances of bodily danger. Once the direction of children's pretending becomes a choice of adults, boys and girls are no longer decision makers. And, in fantasy play, making choices is essential for participation. Adults can share in determining the agenda if they are willing to accept the role of play partner. It is unfair to interpret the content of children's play as representing adult motives. When an actor portrays the role of a killer in a film or a stage play, the audience may consider the performance convincing and therefore successful. However, if a pretending child chooses to play the same role, reasons for deciding to become that character may get greater attention than performance of the child. Such pessimistic interpretations of child's play can lead to unfair inferences and attribution of motives that children do not possess. The motives of children who kill each other temporarily when using toy weapons are unrelated to motivation for violent activity in adult life.

Parents want children to learn nonviolent ways to settle disputes. The way to achieve this goal is by a sustained long-term emphasis on conflict resolution. It is also important that mothers and fathers accept stages of normal development through which all children must grow in understanding the finality of death. Whenever the war play of children is construed to be a kind of personality fault or prelude to violent activity in adult life, the motives of boys and girls are unfairly judged.

Pretending helps kids to confront their common fears of war, death and injury and gives them a vicarious sense of power to control such events. Adults should avoid censoring the focus children choose for pretending and instead encourage children to build an understanding of how to solve disputes by enacting their own values during parent-child play sessions.

SUMMARY AND IMPLICATIONS

Children acquire fears that parents convey to them. Mothers and fathers should make sure they also teach how to gauge risk rather than view exceptional situations as normative. It is important to support a balance between the need of children for caution and their need for trust. Instead of supposing trust is a naive orientation, recognize that trust is the basis of intimate relationships, mental health, and sense of community. By establishing family rules for responding to potential danger, guidance can be provided without contributing to excessive worry. As children get older, they become more able to describe their fears and worries. Adults should be willing to listen to the fears and anxieties of children and share some of their own. Teachers can guide discussions about student fears of bullies and acquaint them with the need to report intimidation so it becomes less common. When teachers arrange for cooperative learning groups where children get peer support, this orientation prevents feelings of aloneness and helplessness that produce anxiety.

Parents should understand the stages of normal development through which all children grow in understanding about the finality of death. When their war play is misconstrued as a personality fault or inclination to rely on violence for solving problems in adult life, the motives of boys and girls are being unfairly judged. A common but rarely acknowledged sign of prejudice toward children is to misread their motives, to suppose they possess dreadful intentions when this is not so. The developmental reality is that pretending allows them to confront universal concerns they feel about war, death, and injury.

Everyone possesses creative abilities to some extent. Most of what children learn before they go to elementary grades comes from guessing, questioning, observing, manipulating, and playing. Given the natural creativity of children, a concern of parents should be to preserve this priceless asset that enables healthy adjustment and success through life. Robert Louis Stevenson (1915), in *The Land of Counterpane*, encouraged adults to always keep in mind the child view of how play stimulates imagination and creative behavior.

When I was sick and lay a-bed,
I had two pillows at my head,
And all my toys beside me lay,
To keep me happy all the day.
And sometimes for an hour or so
I watched my leaden soldiers go,
With different uniforms and drills,
Among the bed-clothes, through the hills;
And sometimes sent my ships in fleets
All up and down among the sheets;
Or brought my trees and houses out,
And planted cities all about.
I was the giant great and still
That sits upon the pillow-hill,
And sees before him, dale and plain,
The pleasant land of counterpane.

APPLICATIONS FOR TEACHING

1. Children should be taught to assess risk in situations where the parents may not be nearby to protect them. They should be urged to rely on their own judgment when any adult directs them to do something that they feel uncomfortable about, consider wrong or possibly dangerous. Acquiring self-confidence and being ready to oppose anyone who would undermine their safety reflects the inner strength that is needed by all children.

2. Establishing family rules, talking about them, and making sure they are understood are important strategies for safety. Children should realize that anyone wanting them to break a family rule is a bad person and should be reported immediately to a parent or a teacher. This rule defines bad people based on their behavior instead of their appearance and can be applied to known as well as unfamiliar faces without attributing danger to either source.

3. Helping children cope with fears begins by encouraging them to always share experiences that bother them. Adults should be willing to hear about worrisome events and situations without suggesting they lack credibility. Children are able to recognize that everyone confronts fears that change depending on age and circumstance. Knowing that fear is normative, and talking to relatives about fears makes us feel less alone and sometimes results in being able to overcome them.

4. Respect the motives of young children whose fantasy play is governed by their imagination. They consider death a temporary con-

dition and so delight in being able to shoot and kill one another or an adult in war play scenarios. Parents who recognize the limited understanding that children possess about death are less inclined to misinterpret their motives and instead respect their fantasy orientation by approving a broad range of content for pretending.

5. Encourage children to pretend as a way to process fears and worries. Boys and girls reduce their fears by repeatedly confronting them in play settings that they can control. Parents who recognize the benefits of this strategy avoid making judgments about the focus of pretending they will allow. They also show support by willingness to participate in the fearful scenarios and themes children choose to emphasize during family play. Greater awareness about the range of outcomes that are associated with war happens when parents at play pay attention to hospitals, rehabilitation of those who have permanent disabilities, and survivor loss of loved ones who were casualties.

6. Parent and child development should be linked for greater success. Mothers and fathers must continue to learn about the behavior that is normative for the current age group of their child. By keeping up to-date, parents can establish reasonable expectations, encourage ways of learning daughters and sons enjoy, and experience more satisfaction as their child's only long-term teachers.

PART II

MIDDLE AND LATER CHILDHOOD (AGES 6-10)

CHAPTER 5

TELEVISION AND
SOCIAL NETWORKING

In Plato's *Republic* the foundation skill for teaching is identified as having
the ability to raise questions that provoke thought. Examples are provided
of the way that Socrates applied a series of ever-more probing questions
to help students engage in critical thinking, and, eventually, to attain
understanding. This strategy became known as the Socratic method. Educators across time and cultures have continued to rely on questioning as a
means to evaluate comprehension and detect lessons that may have been
taught but not learned. The goals of this segment are to demonstrate how
questions can be effectively used while watching television with children
to assess their knowledge and feelings as a basis for decisions about what
to teach them. Emphasis is on an agenda that is applicable to most television programs and allows adults to provide advice in a context that can
help children deal with anxieties, conflicts, doubts, and concerns. The
benefits of social networking are discussed along with issues related to
underage friendships online access, uniting efforts to support online
safety, dangers of communicating with predators, and preventing exploitation on the Internet.

Learning Throughout Life: An Intergenerational Perspective, pp. 95–112
Copyright © 2012 by Information Age Publishing

CHALLENGES OF TELEVISION

What is known about the future suggests that creative abilities should become more common. Creative persons are more able than others to adapt to new knowledge, accept complexity, and propose constructive ways to manage disagreements. They more readily see new ways to improve conditions, can make decisions on their own, and feel comfortable when faced with conditions of uncertainty (Cain, 2012). There are differences of opinion about how to improve schools to meet the goal of graduating a greater proportion of students that can demonstrate creative thinking. However, educators are united in believing that the best time to begin support for imagination to guide thinking is in childhood. There is also awareness that most children consider parents as their main sources of learning.

Watching television is a shared experience in which parents can be teachers. Television presents three challenges for parents. First, they are obliged to decide on the programs that daughters and sons are permitted to watch. Second, they have a responsibility to nurture critical thinking by helping children interpret media messages. Third, the willingness of parents to ask questions and listen to their children can do much to qualify them as sources of guidance. Most parents report they watch television with their family. In fact, more time is spent together as spectators of television than is devoted to any other activity (Bakan, 2011; Singer & Singer, 2011).

Family Conversation Agenda

When families watch television together everyone sees the same visual images and hears the same words. However, because of wide variance in their experience, children and parents interpret some messages differently and reach dissimilar conclusions. This variance in age group perceptions means that sharing observations can bring mutual benefit. Accordingly, one way to find out how a child interprets what is seen is by asking questions that reveal personal impressions.

Table 5.1 contains a list of ten questions with purposes intended to stimulate family conversations while watching television together. The list is used as a guide for discussions, and only relevant questions should be used when they fit the television program. These are simple questions and serve as a good beginning for dialogue with young children such as pre-kindergarteners. Questions are open-ended and do not have a single right answer. This format provides an opportunity for a child to think more deeply about a relevant event that is being shared, and eliminates the parent inclination to make judgments about the answer(s). Parents refer to the list often and keep a copy near the television for easy access.

**Table 5.1. Television Questions for
Conversations With Preschoolers Through Grade 3***

Question	Purpose
1. How would you handle this situation?	Identify alternatives
2. What do you suppose will happen next?	Anticipation of events
3. What parts of this program did you like most?	Expression of interest
4. If you were a friend, how could you help?	Responding to needs
5. What does (a word heard on television) mean?	Vocabulary development
6. Do you think s/he is making the right decision?	Evaluation of judgment
7. What kind of person does s/he seem to be?	Assessment of character
8. What has happened in the story so far?	Sequence recognition
9. How do you want the story to end?	Identify preferences
10. What was learned from this situation?	Evaluation of learning

*From *Parenting Young Children: Exploring the Internet, Television, Play, and Reading*, by R. Strom & P. Strom, 2010, p. 157. Information Age Publishing Inc., Charlotte, NC.

(1) *How would you handle this situation?* Being able to think of alternatives is a valuable asset throughout life. People who can see many possibilities in a single situation are more able to negotiate, get along with others, and think of optional solutions to problems. These strengths are helpful when responding to disputes and can support mental health. By sharing interpretations, parents and children reveal the scope and limits of individual perception. Such knowledge helps to assess child comprehension and detect aspects of a lesson that require further consideration.

(2) *What do you suppose will happen next?* By asking questions that call on children to guess or hypothesize, adults motivate them to explore beyond what can be seen directly, to imagine what is unseen, and to express a futuristic perspective. Such an approach encourages children to talk more because the questions are open-ended, and there is no single correct answer. This strategy also allows children to express differences of opinion from adults. When parents recognize that a daughter or son is able to think of ideas the adults would not have conceived, respect for child thinking increases and the relationship can be enhanced. Mothers and fathers who ask guessing-type questions become more comfortable with uncertainty and willing to discuss issues for which they do not know the full range of responses.

(3) *What parts of this program did you like the most?* One of the conditions for building a close relationship is trying to remain aware of things that please or disappoint the other person and, in turn, to make personal choices and preferences understood. A mutual expression of likes and dislikes provides

the base of information that people need to make decisions about compromise and sacrifice. Sharing what we like best is an easy topic for conversation.

(4) *If you were a friend, how could you help?* Everyone should care about others and aspire to be helpful. A combination of loyalty, willingness to offer support, and the ability to recognize when a friend needs help can be effectively taught by example. Relatives benefit from telling each other about friendship difficulties and methods they rely on to sustain and repair relationships. Children begin to seek advice from parents about how to preserve and build friendships while also maintaining independence. This topic arises early and becomes more pronounced by age 9 or 10 when peer pressures become a strong force to influence the behavior of everyone associated with a group.

Some parents recommend, "When other kids don't treat you right, forget about them and find new friends who will be nice to you." Although this advice may be well-intentioned, it suggests withdrawal is the best way to cope with the insensitivity of classmates and even friends who, at this age, are likely to behave that way quite often. Children want to get along with peers including those who treat them poorly. They want to improve difficult relationships and strive to make them more satisfying. When parents do not embrace this same goal for themselves, they make suggestions that inadvertently disqualify them as child-chosen sources of advice.

(5) *What does (a word heard on television) mean?* Building an extensive vocabulary should be a goal throughout life and is helpful for conversations with other generations. Some of the words children hear on television may not be fully understood by them and ought to be the focus for questions like these: "What do you suppose 'danger' means? 'safety' means? 'bystander' means? 'volunteer means?'" We suggest that parents tell children to repeat aloud right away any words they hear but do not understand during a program segment. The parents can then help define these words. Most parents are amazed at the number of words for which they are able to provide definitions that would otherwise remain unknown by the children. There are also words children may understand that grownups do not and these should be detected in watching the shows children prefer. The best way to learn new words is in context. Therefore, dialogue while watching television can augment the vocabulary that children acquire in the classroom. This strategy calls for the more informed observer to define words to provide meaning for other members of the family who are watching.

(6) *Do you think s/he is making the right decision?* In this case, the goal is to evaluate judgment in actions taken by some character on television. Parents want their children to acquire good judgment and keep them from making serious mistakes. Sometimes harmful consequences happen

before important lessons have been learned. By reacting to the televised versions of real-life dilemmas, families are able to simulate predictable problems and explore the worthiness of individual judgment without having to experience disappointment, embarrassment, or other undesirable consequences. Children also need to realize that other people want to persuade them to buy things that they may not need. Families should consider together decisions about television and Internet commercials that target the young.

(7) *What kind of person does s/he seem to be?* Assessment of character is an imprecise yet very important skill. Mothers and fathers want children to evaluate situations and be able to determine whether being with certain people is in their best interest. One way to find out how to assess character is to compare how the parent and child see specific characters at the beginning and end of a program. Mom and Dad may not always know best but children generally conclude that parents have something of value to teach when it comes to sizing up situations.

(8) *What has happened in the story so far?* The recognition of sequence is a need that begins during preschool at ages 3, 4, and 5. One goal for learning how to read is comprehension, and understanding what is read. This skill is more complex than just memorizing the alphabet or recognizing words. Knowing the progression of events that are read is also important. In the books from which children learn to read, the words are simple and the story line may seem uneventful. On the other hand, most programs on television have a beginning, middle, and end. Indeed, most programs are well suited for teaching sequence and can be used for improving comprehension skills. At the end of a television program or during the reading of a book, ask the child to describe main events that have happened in the story so far. You will learn what was understood, details a child considered important and elements that were overlooked. These insights allow you to provide missing aspects of comprehension.

Encouraging children to summarize their experiences is more important than is realized by many parents. Students that get lots of practice in summarizing are often able to readily describe ideas and events in their own words, making them less inclined to plagiarize homework, projects or tests.

(9) *How do you want the story to end?* Expressing preferences is one way to reveal values. Public polls report opinions and priorities of adults. However, the likes and dislikes of children are seldom assessed. This is unfortunate because the future we hope the young will enjoy depends in part on helping them develop a sense of what is possible, acquire an attitude of optimism, and willingness to express their values. Parents have the chance to reinforce these behaviors in conversation while watching television.

(10) *What was learned from this situation?* Talking to children about the right and wrong decisions that characters in programs make can be helpful. There is concern that moral development of children is not keeping pace with progress of mental abilities. Television presents a chance to watch how other people manage difficulties and try to solve problems. Parents and children can identify with issues portrayed by describing their own related events and struggles. The most effective way to acquire moral learning is to be an observer. When misconduct of someone else is a focus of attention rather than our own behavior, we are less defensive and become more able to consider making personal changes that seem warranted.

Table 5.2 offers an opportunity to practice additional questions when talking to children in preschool through Grade 3. To pursue this task readers should determine a personal justification for talking about these particular issues. The purpose of questions is stated but the motivation for asking them depends on personal rationale about relevance and possible benefits.

Build Skills for School Success

Parents have great potential to help their child begin developing some important skills while observing television together. All the skills listed in Table 5.3 can contribute to success at school. Some of them such as

Table 5.2.   Television Questions for Conversations With Preschoolers Through Grade 3*

Question	Purpose
1. What did you like most about each character?	Perception of potential
2. Why did this person do what s/he did?	Recognizing motivation
3. How will that person's behavior affect others?	Influence on others
4. How do you think s/he should be punished?	Scaling consequences
5. Has anything like this ever happened to you?	Recognizing similarities
6. What choices does s/he have in this situation?	Generating options
7. In what ways are you like any of these people?	Personal identification
8. Why do you think s/he made that decision?	Evaluating purpose
9. How do the people in this show differ from us?	Noting differences
10. Who were the important people in the story?	Significance of character

*From *Parenting Young Children: Exploring the Internet, Television, Play, and Reading*, by R. Strom & P. Strom, 2010, p. 160. Information Age Publishing Inc., Charlotte, NC.

describing events in sequence, identifying main points, and building a vocabulary influence reading comprehension (e.g., skills #1, 2, 3). Restating opinions of others, listening to people who express opposing points of views, and recognizing strengths of classmates are assets for participation in cooperative learning teams (#4, 6, 14). Self-directed learners share a motivation for discovery they reveal by presenting questions, identifying similarities in situations, and by reviewing their lessons (#5, 8, 15). Creative thinkers are able to anticipate what will happen next, think of a wide range of solutions, acknowledge lack of understanding and need for help, and tell how new information changed their outlook (#10, 13, 17, 19).

Critical thinking has high priority for education because students must be prepared to distinguish fact from opinion, determine quality of judgment, and evaluate reasons that govern decision-making (#7, 12, 16). Emotional maturity depends on having a moral compass to guide ethical behavior as reflected by choosing to do what is right, fairly evaluating character and personality, recognizing how a particular decision might affect others, and evaluating need for moral learning (# 9, 11, 18, 20). It seems that much of what parents want children to learn in school also implicates instruction provided at home while watching television.

Benefits of Reciprocal Learning

Asking questions while watching a program can be disturbing to some adults in the beginning. They consider this behavior distracting and liken

Table 5.3. Skills Parents Can Help Children Develop While Watching Television*

1. Describe events in proper sequence	11. Fairly evaluate character and personality
2. Identify the main points presented	12. Determine the quality of judgment
3. Continue to build larger vocabulary	13. Identify a range of possible solutions
4. Restate the opinions of other people	14. Recognize strengths in other people
5. Show curiosity by asking questions	15. Comprehend similarities in situations
6. Listen to people with opposing views	16. Evaluate the reasons behind decisions
7. Distinguish the factual from opinion	17. Tell how information influenced outlook
8. Review lessons offered by a program	18. Recognize how a decision affects others
9. Recognize right and wrong behavior	19. Acknowledge personal need for help
10. Anticipate what will happen next	20. Evaluate the need for moral learning

*From *Parenting Young Children: Exploring the Internet, Television, Play, and Reading*, by R. Strom & P. Strom, 2010, p. 161. Information Age Publishing Inc., Charlotte, NC.

it to the conduct that makes watching movies at a theater disappointing. In their opinion, observers should watch quietly so they avoid disturbing concentration of others. By this reasoning, the best time to discuss a program is when it is over and the television is turned off. However, the assumption that parents and children are unable to follow a story line and talk at the same time is false. This is not a demanding example of multitasking. All of us show this ability when we watch a television picture while also reading the messages that appear at the bottom of a screen. Children and parents easily keep up with content of a program and speak about events as they unfold. Besides, it is more important to talk to each other than catch every detail of a program.

When parents make this shift, they experience the satisfaction that comes from hearing children express themselves more. Adults also quickly sense that the benefits of conversation are greater than entertainment of the program. Nevertheless, many families continue to sit side-by-side watching television without sharing their reactions to what is seen. Seeking the opinions of children can influence the amount of attention they pay to comments of the adults.

Questions and Child Reflection

Demonstrating willingness to wait for a child to respond to a question honors reflection. Some adults misinterpret the silence that may follow after a child is asked a question; some suppose that the silence confirms there is a lack of understanding. Teachers sometimes behave the same way because of their concern that waiting requires too much time or other students are unwilling to wait for their classmates to react. When adults judge the thinking of children in this way, they are inclined to modify a question or resort to offering clues about the expected answer. This practice of rushing children has the unintended effect of reinforcing premature response, and ignores individual pace of decision-making. Cognitive tempo refers to speed at which individuals process information, reach judgments, and solve problems.

Psychologist Jerome Kagan (2007) from Harvard University devised the Matching Familiar Figures Test (MFFT) that illustrates cognitive tempo. For this test, children are asked to choose from six pictures that appear to be similar to the one that is identical to a model. Youngsters with impulsive cognitive tempo act on first impressions without pausing to evaluate quality of their replies. Thus, they react quickly but make many errors. By comparison, children with reflective tempo take more time in examining each picture. Because they think before acting, reflective children are more accurate and make fewer mistakes. Cognitive tempo is often evident by 2 years of age, stabilized by age 4, and relates to parent-child patterns of interaction.

An observation study was conducted with 30 couples and their young children. Each family was given a Fisher-Price toy airplane along with colorful wooden passengers and suitcases. Time samplings of family play conversations were observed and recorded. Although society values reflective thinking, results showed that these parents expected their children to give immediate reactions to their questions. The mothers waited a minimum of 5 seconds for child answers to questions 60% of the time. Fathers, who showed a greater need for closure, waited 5 seconds in 40% of cases. In contrast, children respected reflection most, waiting 5 seconds or more in 86% of cases when asking a question of parents (R. Strom & Strom, 2010). The results of the study indicated recommendation for a 5-second rule for asking questions instead of encouraging hasty answers. When children have time to reflect, they are more likely to value and rely on critical thinking (Kagan, 2007).

Children want to please parents and can tell when adults are impatient and unwilling to wait for answers. Parents who demonstrate patience support child thinking. Waiting long enough for answers seems an important skill for provoking thought and encouraging reflection. On the other hand, parents who insist that a child answer questions without delay motivate impulsive behavior. School success requires the ability to reflect, and need for this ability increases as a student advances through the grades.

SOCIAL NETWORKING

Most of the literature on peer relationships reflects a bygone era when face-to-face interactions were a single focus of concern. Students saw each other mostly at the mall or the movies, drove around with friends, or hung out at someone's home. In contrast, friendships today are more reliant on cell phones, texting, instant messaging, e-mail, and social networking sites. Consequently, over the next decade, some of the following questions about peers are likely to become a focus of studies. How will the emerging online communication forums change the way students build and preserve friendships? What are the essential skills needed to nurture virtual friendships with age mates in other cultures? What guidance can parents provide to support online friendships and involvement with cyber dating? How can Internet friendships be linked with the goals schools have for socialization, communication, and cultural diversity?

Multiple Selves and the Internet

The ability to create multiple identities on the Internet presents a new consideration for social development. While online identities of most people will be the same as their real life identities, some of them will present themselves in other ways. An interesting focus to explore Internet social interaction involves the concept of multiple selves, originally proposed by Carl Rogers (1961). As a leader in counseling psychology, he maintained that each individual has three selves—the ideal self, real self, and perceived self. The ideal self is the person that people would like to be, the real self is the one seen by others, and the perceived self is the self impression.

Jamie's aspiration, his ideal self, is to be popular with others at school. In contrast, the way peers see Jamie, his real self, is being reluctant to join them in their common challenge against aspects of adult authority. According to Jamie, his perceived self is someone whose shyness is misinterpreted as a lack of courage or assertion. Rogers (1961) indicated that the goal for counseling therapy is to help clients pursue their ideal selves while increasing the accuracy of their perceptions of where they currently are and the extent to which their ideal self has been realized (see Figure 5.1).

Rogers (1961) would have been intrigued by how his concept of multiple selves could be applied to people using the Internet. Adolescents who join chat rooms can have multiple aliases allowing them to masquerade, try out new roles, and discover what it is like to act differently than their typical daily behavior (Liau, Khoo, & Peng, 2005; Subrahmanyam, Greenfield, & Tynes, 2004). A teenager like Jamie who is shy might wish to be assertive on the Internet before showing assertive behavior in face-to-face conversations. There are students who prefer to present themselves online as being less dominant than they are in person. Both genders claim to have learned certain courtship skills online such as finding out as much as possible about another person's interests and preferences because of conversational opportunities that may not occur in face-to-face situations. The chance to practice unfamiliar but desired roles is appealing (Kelsey & Kelsey, 2007).

Teachers should continue to remind students about their accountability for social interaction online. They need to know that anything they do on the Internet could be traced and, therefore, although a sense of anonymity might be felt, it cannot be ensured. A priority goal should be to reconcile different impressions one chooses to make on others via the Internet with interaction that is honest along with guarded privacy to avoid sharing sensitive information anyone can see. In this way, misrepresentation does not happen and the online selves are integrated with off-line conditions (Horak, 2007).

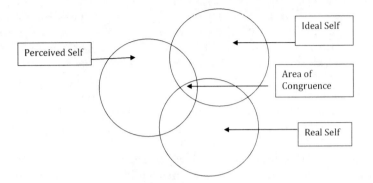

a. Small area of congruence suggests poor psychological health and the advisability of therapy to bring the selves closer together.

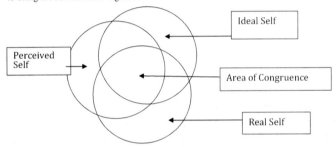

b. Large area of congruence suggests psychological health and little anxiety, and therefore efficient life functioning about where they currently are and how much of their ideal self has been realized.

Adapted from Carl Rogers (1961). *On becoming a person.* Boston, MA: Houghton Mifflin.

Figure 5.1.   Congruence of ideal, real, and perceived selves as an index of psychological health.*

Participation of Underage Friends

Facebook has 900 million subscribers, half of whom visit the social network site daily. Most of them, 75%, live outside the United States. The average user has 130 friends and some have many more. This online experience provides a much greater number of contacts than young people in the past were exposed to but most are weak associations. The time required to interact with these contacts takes away from more important relationships and can cause them to weaken. Someone with 400 friends has less time to build close and durable relationship. Communication on Facebook is easier but it is less personal than face-to-face interaction.

The appeal of social networks is enormous. Children across the nation are lying about their age so they can be on Facebook. This conclusion comes from a *Consumer Reports* (2011) titled "That Facebook Friend Might Be 10 Years Old, and Other Troubling News" survey that found over 7 million active users of this popular social network site were under the minimum required age of 13. Further, more than 5 million of the users were 10 years old or younger. Not only are kids lying about their age but they do so with the support of their parents who seem to be unconcerned by their child's involvement. Parents of the youngest group may suppose that boys and girls of this age are less likely to engage in risk taking. Only 18% of parents of preteen users made their child a Facebook friend. In comparison, 62% of parents with 13- to 14-year-olds made their child a Facebook friend because they assume this is the age span when it is time to become concerned about taking risks.

Poor monitoring practices run counter to getting parents to become more constructively involved in online activities of children, a purpose of the Children's Online Privacy Protection Act of 1998 (2012). That legislation led to the age restriction that prohibits social network sites from knowingly disclosing identifiable information of children that makes them vulnerable to exploitation. Difficulties of finding out who is lying about being underage is complicated. Still, Facebook reports that it removes 20,000 people each day, albeit a tiny fraction of 900 million subscribers worldwide (Zuckerberg, 2011).

Surveys indicate that a growing number of parents believe their children should be allowed to begin social networking before adolescence. In response, the Facebook founder, Mark Zuckerberg (2011) has expressed a willingness to support changes in federal regulations that would permit children under the age of 13 to join. He recognizes the Children's Online Policy Protection Act regulates what information websites can gather about children under age 13 and states a determination to support sensible alteration in current policy. In his view, "My philosophy is that for education you need to start at a really, really young age."

Excessive Texting and Social Networking

Texting while driving is recognized as a dangerous form of multitasking for teenagers. Additional hazards may also be related to excessive involvement with texting. Researchers at Case Western Reserve School of Medicine in Cleveland, Ohio, surveyed 4,200 high school students to determine the association between use of communications technology and health behaviors (Frank, 2010). Results indicated that excessive users of texting and social networking are much more likely to engage in unhealthy behaviors. Being a hypertexter, defined as texting 120 or more messages in a school day, was reported by 20% of the teens, many of whom were female, minority, lower income, and did not have a father in the home.

Survey outcomes showed that teenage hypertexters are:

- 40% more likely to have tried cigarettes than those who spend less time texting;
- 43% more likely to be binge drinkers;
- 41% more likely to engage in substance abuse;
- 55% more likely to have been in a physical fight;
- 3.5 times more likely to have had sex; and
- 90% more likely to report having had four or more sexual partners.

These surprising findings suggest that when texting and other methods of staying connected are not monitored, there could be adverse effects for health. According to the lead investigator, Scott Frank (2010), "The results should be a wake-up call for parents to not only help their children stay safe by not texting while driving, but by discouraging excessive use of a cell phone or social web sites in general."

Adolescents who engage in hypernetworking, defined as spending 3 hours or more a day on social networking sites, is also risky. Of the teenagers surveyed, about 12% reported spending more than 3 hours a day on social networking. This subpopulation were found to be:

- 62% more likely to have tried cigarettes;
- 70% more likely to have tried alcohol;
- 69% more likely to have used illicit drugs;
- 94% more likely to have been in a physical fight;
- 69% more likely to have had sex; and
- 60% more likely to report having had four or more sexual partners.

The study did not conclude that avid texting and networking causes unhealthy behavior but that the behaviors are associated (Frank, 2010).

Prevention of Child Exploitation

A predictable hazard arises when students divulge personal information or photos by e-mail or blogs. Most of what has been written about experimentation with multiple identities on the Internet has dealt with dangers that can happen when people exploit others. For example, pedophiles visit chat rooms and social blog sites to find and lure children to meet them. Another group of users describes or sells sexual experiences or shares pornographic images that can be downloaded. The National Center for Missing and Exploited Children (2012) released the results of its latest survey regarding the number of registered sex offenders located in the United States. The most recent survey found there are 747,408 registered sex offenders in the country, which represents an increase of 7,555 offenders since the previous survey in June 2011.

The Federal Bureau of Investigation maintains a task force to monitor the Internet for criminal behavior and protects the vulnerable, particularly minors. The FBI reports that computer sex offenders are mostly White, professional, upper middle-class males. The predators' multiple identities appear to resemble the personality polarities first described in *The Strange Case of Dr. Jekyll and Mr. Hyde*, written by Robert Louis Stevenson (1886). In this classic tale, Dr. Jekyll is the main character that people believe they know well and affirm to be a model citizen. However, he is periodically transformed into the monster Mr. Hyde, whose evil deeds are seldom observed. In a similar way, when online predators are publicly identified, neighbors often express surprise stating they never observed that side of the person's dual nature. If the Internet were not available to these people to comfortably express themselves online, they would probably be more reclusive. Many predators have been arrested as a result of Internet electronic surveillance conducted by the FBI. The United States Department of Justice (2012) offers *The Parent's Guide to Internet Safety* online with information for parents regarding child predators.

To protect students, some school districts prohibit them from using their school e-mail address to register for blogs that focus on meeting others or provide cyber dating. Participants on MySpace and Facebook are supposed to be at least 13 years old but younger students often misrepresent themselves. Some schools offer seminars for parents regarding ways for them to protect youngsters online. They emphasize that it is not a matter of whether to trust daughters and sons but to show concern for safety.

Prevention of exposure to sex offenders should become a priority for schools as well as parents. A national resource that all educators should be familiar with is the website Family Watchdog—http://www.familywatchdog.us/ . This website provides a map of the city and state that is typed in. The map legend shows school locations and addresses where identified convicted sex offenders live and work. In each case, there is a description of the conviction, picture of offender for ease of recognition, and indication of how close the person lives to the school or home address given in the inquiry. Bear in mind that it is a misdemeanor to harass anyone listed on the offense registry. The purpose of this national service is to make faculty and students aware of sex offenders in their community so children can be warned to avoid talking or interacting with them.

Internet Interaction Opportunities

In *The Case Against Adolescence*, Robert Epstein (2007) argues against blaming brain development as the main cause for foolish risks taken by many adolescents. He suggests that instead of tracing poor judgment to the delayed rate of growth in the frontal cortex, more attention should be placed on the 24/7 immersion in a peer culture facilitated by cell phones and the Internet. Many teens are in contact with friends 70 hours a week yet lack meaningful contact with the important adults in their lives. Some of them spend brief periods with their parents but often this is time watching television, eating, or checking in by phone. Epstein argues that adolescents have been infantilized by our culture, causing their isolation from adults and motivating them to communicate almost exclusively with peers.

Finding ways to improve the social networking of children and adolescents should be a high priority. Consider some possibilities:

- Partnerships between schools and businesses to help explore careers
- Students postrecreational reading reactions for classmate consideration
- Indigenous mentors answer student questions on aspects of their culture
- Question and answer site on using the Internet to improve schoolwork
- Enabling students learning a language to practice interacting with others
- Have parents help their children create profiles to go on social network
- Peer counseling as a source of guidance regarding concerns at school
- A site where students cooperate to inform adults on concerns of kids
- Pen pals across national boundaries through matching mutual interests.

- A support group for children facing similar challenges led by counselors.
- School chat rooms by grade level for students monitored by counselors.
- A site with volunteer options for children often excluded because of age.
- A place for children to display drawings or pictures and obtain feedback
- A site to upload/ download music from peers within the same age group.
- Establish an online book club where children share literature they read.

There is a need to replace what is frequently becoming a strictly peer-driven communication environment for social networking. More contact with trustworthy adults online and in person along with a gradual increase in youth responsibility is essential. Teachers can motivate intergenerational interaction by devising creative online homework for students that requires involvement with parents and grandparents.

SUMMARY AND IMPLICATIONS

Children realize that their parents have important lessons to teach them. However, they also possess experiences that significantly differ from adults so learning from each other should be encouraged. Even though reciprocal learning is essential during times of rapid change, some adults reject the concept. They feel that the traditional way society has assigned status and guided interaction between generations should be retained. In the past, values were handed down from older to younger people. The notion that parents may need to acquire some values and ways of thinking from children is without precedent. Consequently, adults lack experience in perceiving young people as sources of knowledge.

There is much for parents to learn about how television can be used to support creative thinking, critical thinking, and observational skills with children. Parents should expect some new obligations of themselves to adjust to changing rules for their child's education. In particular, they should watch television with their children—this requires time. Next, they can ask questions of daughters and sons during mutual observations—this is a skill that takes practice. Just as children are expected to express their impressions of what they see, parents should also share experiences—this requires self-disclosure. Finally, children should be allowed to select some programs that the family watches together—this demonstrates acceptance of child interests. Parents who subject themselves to these kinds of expectations communicate more easily with their children and establish themselves as a lasting source of guidance.

Significant changes are transforming the socialization of children. There is increasing reliance on technology tools for communicating online with friends and strangers. Social network sites facilitate these mostly out-of-school conversations that expose children to the opinions of others, elaborate their own impressions, report on satisfactions and disappointments, disagree over how to solve problems, and identify community needs of concern (Gardner & Birley, 2008). Preventing predators from harming youth that feel invulnerable remains a challenge for schools and parents. Although there are many complaints about the lack of etiquette in use of technology, there is little dispute that cell phones and the Internet have increased the number of people listening to youth. On the other hand, periodic cell calls to check in should not be seen as a substitute for face to face conversations needed to discuss things that matter (Weber & Dixon, 2007).

APPLICATIONS FOR TEACHING

1. Helping children interpret what is seen on television is a parent obligation. The benefit families can gain from television depends on how adults define their role. Parents are more comfortable by going beyond the task of only judging what children are permitted to watch. They should also accept the task of acting as an interpreter too. A continuing dialogue about things that your family sees together helps everyone learn the opinions of one another, develop critical thinking skills, and builds a more extensive vocabulary that makes it easier to communicate.

2. Ask questions while you and your child watch programs together. Adults and children see the same pictures and hear the same words while they watch television together. However, prior experiences cause them to sometimes reach dissimilar conclusions. These individual differences in perception enable family members to benefit from sharing. Asking questions is an efficient way to find out how children interpret what they observe.

3. Processing failure involves realizing that it is a vital aspect of learning. When a television program illustrates some failure that is taking place, it can be difficult but necessary for the people involved to process this experience. Being willing to admit personal failure without defensiveness and focusing on ways that performance can

be improved are essential aspects of problem solving. Trying to protect children from ever failing or denying when they fail prevents learning and development of resilience.

4. Most children want to be seen as responsible because it is a sign that they are growing up. One way to support this goal is ensure students understand that everyone is accountable for what they do or say in cyberspace. All behavior on the Internet can be traced by law enforcement so self control is essential and avoid any misrepresentation.

5. Underage children should not lie about their age in order to join a social network where the participants are required to be at least 13 years old. The school should acquaint parents with protected sites for younger children, and also blogs that the whole family might join together.

6. Students need to be reminded often that sharing personal information online could expose them to possible danger. The need to protect privacy is underestimated by children so periodic discussions are a helpful practice at home and in the school.

7. Prevention of student exploitation by sex offenders should be a high priority for parent and school surveillance. Website resources identify the convicted sex offenders, show their pictures, and indicate how close they live to schools. If a known offender is seen near or on the campus, the police should be notified.

8. Provide examples of good manners by demonstrating courtesy to others face-to-face and online. This means confirming when e-mail is received and thanking people who respond to requests. Children should know that the rules of good behavior in face-to-face relationships are the same to apply electronically.

CHAPTER 6

THINKING AND
SELECTIVE ATTENTION

The traditional purpose of schools has been for teachers to present lessons and expect students to show that they can retain the information for tests. This process is changing because of a rapid increase in knowledge and greater access to information. Much of what is memorized may be relevant for only a short time. Then too, technology can provide more efficient data storage than human memory. Consequently, memory is no longer accepted as the singular evidence of learning. Instead, students are expected to demonstrate the abilities to locate, comprehend, organize, and apply data for solving problems as individuals and in teams. The goals of this chapter are to examine ways theories of intelligence have influenced thinking priorities in classrooms and instructional methods. The prevalence of online distractions and consequent difficulty with paying attention are examined. A dual emphasis on linear learning and nonsequential learning are portrayed as a more promising alternative than selection of one mode of thinking.

PERSPECTIVES OF INTELLIGENCE

Quantitative Assessment of Intelligence

Education authorities in Paris, France wanted to identify students that lacked sufficient mental ability to benefit from instruction in the classroom. Alfred Binet (1857-1911) was asked to devise a method to detect students that had mental deficits. The screening test Binet (1905) invented was the first measure of intelligence (Naglier & Goldstein, 2009). He observed that the good items on a test are solved more readily as children get older. Therefore, his test items were arranged based on age at which approximately 50% of students performed them correctly. This method enabled students who were more capable to differentiate themselves from classmates. Binet's method for selection of test items was soon adopted by other nations and remains today as the dominant practice in the design of standardized tests.

Lewis Terman (1887-1956) at Stanford University revised Binet's inventory so that it could be administered to American students. He called his revision the Stanford-Binet Intelligence Test to credit the French inventor (Terman, 1916). School psychologists administer the Stanford-Binet, currently in its fifth edition, to evaluate ability of individual students so that decisions can be made about placement in special programs (Roid, 2004).

The first large-scale intelligence testing involved nearly two million soldiers during World War I when Terman was in the military. He and other psychologists worked together to categorize army recruits after completion of group intelligence tests that took about one hour to administer. The examiners scored these tests on a scale from "A" through "E." Soldiers that earned "A" scores were trained as officers. Following the war Terman successfully lobbied for schools to begin use of intelligence tests as a way to improve the efficiency of student placement.

An intelligence quotient, called IQ, was the way that intelligence test scores were expressed. IQ was obtained by dividing mental age of a student, determined by the test responses, by chronological age and multiplied by 100. Current measures like Weschler Intelligence Scale for Children (WISC), allow examiners to interpret IQ by use of a score table that corresponds with student chronological age (Thorndike & Hagen, 2011). The common way to describe mental status is standard deviation, a measure of variability showing how much student scores are spread. There are eight standard deviations in a normal distribution regardless of whether the focus is height of fifth grade boys, weight of eighth grade girls, or freshman scores on an intelligence test.

Figure 6.1 shows that, in a normal population portrayed by a bell shaped curve, approximately two-thirds (68.27%) of all cases fall between one standard deviation above the average and one standard deviation below the average score. The distance between plus or minus three standard deviations includes 99.7% of all students. This means that one standard deviation is large, two is very large, and three deviations is huge (Murray & Herrnstein, 1996).

IQs depicted on the lower axis in Figure 6.1 reveals that a student two standard deviations below the mean has an IQ of 68. This level has been used as the upper limit to classify students as mildly retarded. The mildly retarded IQ range of 50-68 includes approximately 11% of students assigned to special education programs. At the other end, students scoring two standard deviations above the mean, recording an IQ of 132 or higher, are chosen for participation in gifted and talented programs (Heward & Haring, 2011).

Qualitative Differences in Thinking

Jean Piaget (1896-1980), a psychologist from Geneva, Switzerland, wanted to determine how children think and interpret the world. At the beginning of his career, in the 1920s, Piaget's job involved working on test development. His tasks consisted of administering standardized measures until he made three observations that caused him to pursue a new direction for assessment of mental abilities. First, instead of calculating num-

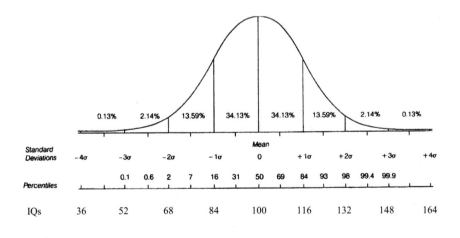

Figure 6.1.   Standard deviation and the normal curve.

ber of student correct answers, the method typically applied in analyzing responses, Piaget examined incorrect answers to detect limitations students of the same age group had in common. He concluded that the way children who are older think is qualitatively different from thinking of younger children. This decision led Piaget (1954, 1963, 1969) to abandon the concept of quantitative intelligence.

A second observation caused him to implement a new technique for the study of intelligence. He thought a strategy was needed to provide interviewers greater freedom than the methods required for standardized testing. In recalling his reading of Freudian psychology, Piaget tried a strategy that would have interviewers allow child answers to guide the flow of questioning. However, the abnormal children he was working with had verbal deficits so this strategy was not productive. Another novel feature was applied. Besides having students state their answers as best they could, Piaget invited them to manipulate objects, thereby crediting action as evidence of thinking instead of showing knowledge only by use of words. Many years later, other researchers discovered that verbal ability is greater among students from higher economic backgrounds (Eysenck & Keane, 2005).

A third way Piaget (1970) departed from other child development observers was his recognition that, because the mind appears to be an integrated unit, the best way to instruct students is by offering curriculum they can understand at their present level of thinking. His terminology is important to understand information processing. Piaget referred to the term schemas to describe how children make sense of their experiences. *Schemas* are defined as temporary cognitive structures determining the way information is processed and situations are organized. As students encounter new experiences, their schemas must enlarge or change to allow for adjustment in a complex environment.

According to Piaget (1970), people rely on two processes for adaptation. First, the process of *assimilation* calls for integration of new conceptual, perceptual or motor information into existing schemas. For example, Don is a first time visitor to the French Impressionist Exhibition at the Metropolitan Museum of Art in New York City. Previously he has seen pictures by Monet and Van Gogh in magazines. During Don's observation at the museum, his "Impressionist schema" has to expand to include the work of Manet, Toulouse-Lautrec, Cézanne, Gauguin, Seurat, Sisley, and Matisse, all artists who lived during the late nineteenth 19th century and commonly explored the visual analysis of color and light. Assimilation enlarges the size of a schema, as in Don's case, but does not result in a schema change. Instead, a second process people rely on for adaptation is called *accommodation* that requires modification or replacement of schema in order that novel conditions can be accepted.

When Don left the Impressionist gallery, he took the elevator to the next floor of the museum where the modern art exhibits are located. In this new context Don was obliged to accept a different set of criteria to appreciate work of abstract expressionists whose representations are more often symbolic than literal. This artistic group includes icons like Braque, Calder, Kandinsky, Miro, Nevelson, Pollack, and Rothko. The schema that Don had applied to enjoy the Impressionism artist presentations did not enable his appreciation of modern art so it was necessary to adopt a new schema. The imbalance between the familiar and novel creates tension until new schema categories are formed.

When students sense disequilibrium, they search for equilibration through greater assimilation or by accommodation of examining unfamiliar concepts and events in new ways. Equilibration takes place when a suitable balance is struck between the amount of assimilation and amount of accommodation. If someone is engaged in assimilation only, that person would possess a few very large schemas, tend to perceive most situations as similar, and be unable to recognize differences. Conversely, someone who uses only accommodation would have many very small schemas, tend to perceive most situations as different from one another, and demonstrate an inability to recognize similarities.

Thinking Abilities at Ages 6 to 11

Constructivism is the name applied to Piaget's theory that attempts to describe how students actively develop their own meaning for events based on their personal experience (Fosnot, 2005). Piaget became aware that thinking of children and many adolescents do not proceed in the same manner as adults. He maintained the thinking process evolves through a succession of stages roughly associated with chronological age. Elements of Piaget's stages of thinking in relation to the preschool age group were discussed in Chapter 3. Aspects of the thinking stage that characterizes most students in the elementary grades is referred to as *Concrete Operations* and summarized in Table 6.1.

Reversibility. The most important mental ability that differentiates elementary students from preschoolers is reversibility. This capacity allows the student to carry thought backward as well as forward, a requirement for arithmetic reasoning since addition and subtraction are the same operation carried out in opposite directions. Second graders can learn that 4 + an unknown number = 7 and use reversibility to determine the answer (7 minus 4 = the unknown).

As early as third grade children can play the hand bean game in which a student counts out a required number of beans. The teacher puts these

Table 6.1.   Concrete Operations Thinking Ages 6-11*

CONCRETE OPERATIONS	
6 to 11 Years Old	*Achievements and Limitations*
Reversibility	Carries thought forward and backward
Logic	Solves problems on tangible things or involving familiar situations
Decentration	Attends to several aspects of a problem at once
Classification	Uses multiple factors to organize or categorize; class inclusion
Seriation	Arranges things in order by sequence or according to some quantitative aspect

*Adapted from J. Piaget, *Psychology of Intelligence.* New York, NY: Littlefield, Adams, 1969.

beans in both of her hands. Then she closes one hand, thus hiding some of the beans, while opening the other hand to show the beans there. Regardless of the bean combinations, children know that the total will always be the same. This is not a magic trick; it is reversibility. When faced with a liquid conservation task where children must judge whether a tall slender vessel contains more liquid than a wide, short container, elementary children rely on reversibility; that is, they can pour the liquid back into the original container to find out whether the two quantities take up the same amount of space. In this way they try to solve problems by retracing conclusions.

The concepts of reversibility and conservation take on additional meaning as the children mature. During the upper elementary grades, they begin to apply reasoning to specific problems. When faced with a discrepancy between thought and perception as in conservation tasks, they make logical decisions rather than perceptual decisions. As logic is acquired, boys and girls move from egocentric thinking toward objectivity. They no longer see the world exclusively from their own view and become capable of looking at situations from the perspective of others. When this ability is exhibited with regularity, typically by age 9 or 10, children are ready to shift from doing most of their schoolwork alone to also working in small cooperative groups.

Logic. Elementary logic becomes more evident. Students are able to solve story problems in mathematics by choosing for themselves the right process of arithmetic to apply instead of just computing answers by rote or asking the teacher for directions. By fourth grade (age 9) students learn how to figure percentages and can understand that parts of an object make a whole. Fifth graders are expected to predict story endings.

Logic is needed for this activity because the ending is a rationale extension of events that have been presented.

Decentration. The ability to decenter or to focus on more than one aspect of a situation at a time can be observed in play. "Battleship" is a favorite game of children that involves locating and trying to destroy enemy ships. Players find their opponent by guessing and deduction using board grid numbers and letters in combination, such as B6 or G4. Children know numbers and letters before third grade but cannot handle them simultaneously. This is why board games list a recommended mental (not chronological) age. To play Battleship, a mental age of 8 is recommended as an appropriate minimum.

When 7-year old Kathy plays checkers, she knows the positions for each of her pieces. Because she is able to focus on more than one set of circumstances, Kathy is capable of developing a strategy for winning the game. Playing the piano or another musical instrument also calls for decentration, as the musician has to pay attention to several aspects of a situation, including reading of notes and taking timing into account.

Classification. As children move through the elementary grades, they improve in their ability to classify objects and events. When second graders are given eight pictures of animals with slight differences, most students can identify the two pictures that are alike. An increasing need for competence in this context is tested by assignments at school like recognizing vowels in a word, deciding whether each has a short or long vowel sound, and deciding which ones are silent. By the third grade students learn to group animals into classes such as mammals and reptiles. Fifth graders can subdivide by classes and tell which numbers are divisible by 5 (out of, e.g., 15, 19, 12 or 20) and which numbers are divisible by 3 (out of, e.g., 15, 19, 21 or 33).

Seriation. Elementary students can seriate. They may be expected in reading to examine separate events of a story and then put them in proper sequence or arrange pictures in correct order. Third graders have learned to place groups of five words that all begin with the same letter into alphabetical order. They are able to apply the seriation concepts of "more" and "less" and the symbols for "greater than" (>) and "less than" (<) when comparing pairs or groups of numbers. When asked to seriate the states by size, as determined by square miles, they indicate Alaska is biggest, then Texas, California, and so forth. In contrast, although preschoolers can count, arranging numbered cards in order usually defeats them; they are unable to seriate.

The reason for Piaget's eminent standing and popularity almost one hundred years after his contributions is that his methods of assessing thinking levels enables educators to determine rationally the assignments individual students can benefit from. He emphasized the wisdom of using each child's development stage to guide teaching. Children should perceive, talk about, and manipulate objects in order to develop their mental abilities. First-hand experience, however time consuming, is the key to stable learning. Therefore, a fundamental responsibility of teachers and families is to provide tasks that permit children to acquire understanding. What matters more than verbalizing rules or committing facts to memory is involvement in activities that require problem solving, critical thinking, and creativity.

Social Constructivism

Russian psychologist Lev Vygotsky (1896-1934) was a contemporary scholar of Piaget. Both men agreed that the key to durable learning is for students to build their own knowledge instead of to acquire it vicariously by listening to their teachers or by memorization. Piaget's identification of thinking stages caused him to recommend that teachers arrange opportunities for exploration allowing for personal knowledge building. Vygotsky (1978) did not propose new cognitive stages but emphasized collaboration as a condition teachers should encourage to ensure greater learning. Vygotsky saw merit in having all students perform some tasks with peers more competent than themselves (Smagorinsky, 2011).

Vygotsky (1978) joined Piaget in rejecting the use of standardized testing as an exclusive method to assess intelligence. He believed that educators should go beyond detection of mental age and link processes of development with learning abilities. To merge development and learning, he maintained two separate levels of development must be evaluated. The 'actual development level' identifies mental capacities, shown by intelligence tests, indicating what an individual can do alone without help. However, this awareness should not end assessment. Vygotsky challenged the assumption that the tasks students are able to do by themselves represent the full scope of their abilities. What if, as a result of dialogue with a teacher or tutoring by a more competent peer, students given questions or shown examples of how to solve problems become able to do so without help or can nearly finish these tasks on their own? Vygotsky's 'potential development level' defines achievements students can reach with the help from others. He maintained that this broader view represented a more suitable index of mental development than only what individuals can accomplish alone (Vygotsky, 1994).

The need to differentiate actual development and potential development can be clarified with an example (Vygotsky, 1998). Two students are administered an IQ test. Both are 10-years-old and obtain scores equivalent to being mentally 8-years-old. This means they can independently solve problems consistent with a normative degree of difficulty dealt with by students two years younger than themselves. Generally, since both students had the same IQ, it is assumed that their prospects for learning must be similar and it would frustrate them to be exposed to problems higher than their mental age of 8 years. However, in this case, a teacher demonstrates how to solve more difficult problems, invites the students to replicate her examples, arranges for repeated observation of specific steps in the process, asks them to finish the task, encourages reflection on personal logic, and offers guidance as needed. In the end, one student is able, with assistance, to solve problems considered appropriate for 9-year--olds while the other student can do tasks up to the level of 12-year-olds (Vygotsky, 1998).

Because performance of the two students varied to a high degree when given guidance, expectations for learning as individuals should differ. The "zone of proximal development" is the distance between the actual level of a student's development as assessed by independent problem solving and the level of potential development as found by problem solving with guidance from an adult or in collaboration with more capable peers (Vygotsky, 1994). The zone of proximal development concept shows learning can lead development. That is, the natural development process lags behind and this sequence results in zones of proximal development that call attention to the importance of tutoring, cooperative learning, dialogue with relatives, and interaction with out-of-school mentors.

A key process linked with the zone of proximal development is called scaffolding, techniques used to adjust guidance to match levels of performance. At the outset, a teacher might use direct instruction to introduce concepts. As the learner becomes more able, a gradual shift occurs so the teacher role shifts to monitoring progress, giving feedback, offering encouragement, and providing minimal correction. Middle school and high school teachers find the zone of proximal development and scaffolding concepts support better instruction.

For example, the formal operations content of math and science is cumulative so it presents difficulty for many students. Vygotsky's insights encourage peer teaching and cooperative learning in secondary school because of the greater ability of some students who could tutor others (Cukras, 2006). When students admit that they are completely lost, they communicate a feeling of being outside their zone. When this occurs in a cooperative group, teammates should help a student ask questions so s/he can reconnect again. Otherwise, time will be lost for the learner and the motivation to put forth an effort may decline.

Vygotsky (1994) believed the social context of schooling is essential for special education students. He felt it is inappropriate to rely on the actual level of development, as shown by test results, as the upper limit for expectations of students with disabilities. Because mentally retarded students perform poorly on measures of abstract thinking, educators are inclined to give up on arranging tasks that require abstraction in favor of tasks that reflect Piaget's concrete stage of thinking. However, when instruction is limited to concrete experiences, mentally retarded students are prevented from overcoming limitations.

In Vygotsky's (1978) view, the most influential learning for students who have disabilities is the social consequence of rejection by normal classmates that would not behave that way in a more humane society. Forty years after Vygotsky died, the high cost of social exclusion was acknowledged by the Education for All Handicapped Children Act (1975) as justification for abandoning a long-standing practice of isolating students in special education. The replacement practice, first called "mainstreaming," and more recently "inclusion," is considered the way to help the normal population to accept differences while also enabling students with disabilities to acquire social skills they need (Farrell, 2012).

Cyber Constructivism

The premise of constructivism, originated by Piaget and Vygotsky, is that students learn best when they are allowed to build their own knowledge rather than receive it as ideas told to them by their teachers. Students invent personal theories by assimilating new information into existing schema or modify their understanding by accommodation of novel data. This section reviews cyber constructivism that has gained global attention over the past decade. Vygotsky described the potential importance of peer influence on learning, but no one really knows how much students could learn from their peers in situations where adult supervision is lacking.

A cyber form of constructivism provides cooperative learning opportunities for the children in resource-scarce environments. Leadership in this context has been given by Sugata Mitra, an educational technology professor at Newcastle University in England. Before Mitra joined academia in 2006, he was director of research and development for India's largest software company in New Delhi. At social gatherings, affluent parents often told him their children could do computer tasks the adults saw as complicated and impressive (Mitra, 2003).

Mitra wondered whether the parent reports were exaggerated, reflecting their personal lack of experience with computers. If educated adults underestimate how well their children can perform with little or no formal training, perhaps disadvantaged youth can attain the same competence. Since children do not ask for or receive much instruction on computing, maybe allowing them more unsupervised use is a key to accel-erating the acquisition of basic skills. To find out, Mitra put a Pentium computer with a fast Internet connection and touch pad in a kiosk located on the wall separating his company from a wasteland that people living in an adjacent slum used as an alley. The computer was always left on so passersby would have a chance to tinker with it. All activity was monitored by a remote computer and video camera mounted in a nearby tree (Mitra 2006).

Most adults glanced at the kiosk but did not stop to investigate. In con-trast, 80 children between ages 6 to 16 and not enrolled in school, expressed curiosity. Within days, many had acquired basic computer literacy skills. Mitra had defined basic literacy as the ability to carry out window operation functions like using a mouse, point, drag, drop, copy, and browse the Inter-net. After three months the children had learned to load and save files, play games, run programs, listen to music, set up and access e-mail, chat on the Internet, troubleshoot, download and play video games. Disney and Micro-soft Paint were the favorite sites because everyone enjoyed drawing but no one had money for the supplies (Mitra, 2006).

When a second kiosk was placed in an illiterate rural village where no one had ever seen a computer, children helped one another gain basic skills. These "Hole in the Wall" projects have expanded to more than 100 sites in impoverished areas that have no schools or teachers. The cost of setting up a kiosk and maintaining it for a year was initially about $10,000. On average, 100 children used a kiosk. Mitra and Dangwal's (2010) dream was to install 100,000 kiosks. He speculated that the out-come would be 10 million more computer-literate children who would change India forever by moving themselves toward prosperity.

The theoretical paradigms merging to support minimally invasive edu-cation are unstructured collaboration and shared exploration as children use trial and error in opening the door to cyberspace. Because this approach to learning depends on discovery and sharing, working in groups is essential. Children teach one other and regulate the process. The ability to become computer literate in a short time seems to be inde-pendent of formal education, socioeconomic background, gender, ability to read or intelligence. The minimally invasive education concept has been adopted by other nations with a scarcity of teachers, schools or hard-ware. Hole-in-the-wall kiosks have been established in Egypt, Cambodia, and six countries in Africa (Mitra, 2012a).

Learners tend to divide themselves into "knows" and "know nots." However, there is a recognition a person who knows will part with knowl-edge in return for friendship and exchange. The more mature partici-pants, usually older females, commonly insist on proceeding in a civil manner. As a result, everyone enjoys the satisfaction of social experience and chance to learn more rapidly because they imitate one other, spur each other on, and pool their insights. When a group no longer produces breakthroughs, minimal intervention is welcomed from an online teacher who introduces a new skill for students to use in generating discoveries on their own. Studies have found that adults in the affected communities believe this method can spread literacy (85%), provide opportunity to learn about computers (80%), improve social cohesion (79%), develop confidence and pride (85%), and improve mental performance (79%) (Mitra & Dangwal, 2010).

Based on progress of children using kiosks, Mitra has established 12 self-organized learning environments (SOLE) in disadvantage areas of India. This concept calls for modifying conditions of classroom learning. Children work in small groups of 4 with one computer and can use Google and the Internet to search for information that can allow them to address hard but interesting questions such as: Do trees think? How does an iPad know where it is? Where did language come from? While supervision by adults is unnecessary, students benefit from friendly mentors or mediators who volunteer. Mitra placed an advertisement in a London paper asking grandmothers who were computer literature to devote one hour a week to child development. The women use Skype to help immigrant students speak and get feedback on their new language. Those who are member of the 'granny cloud' offer encouragement without giving direction and assist students at no cost to the schools (Mitra, 2012b).

These outcomes underscore the potential benefits of exposure to the Internet, the capability of students to accelerate their organization of knowledge by uniting efforts, and need for teachers to present tasks that support chances for student practice in collaborative constructivism. Creation of curriculum content is no longer as important as the provision of infrastructure and access to a world of information. Minimally invasive education is a self-structured system that assumes students can construct knowledge on their own. In this paradigm a teacher stands aside and intervenes only when assistance is needed. The custom has been to expect teachers to "make learning happen." Now teachers are expected to "let learning happen." The distinction between these two expectations is illustrated by reactions of Indian adults. Unlike children, they just gazed at the kiosk and asked, "What is this for? Why is there no one to teach us something? How will we ever use such a device?" Mitra (2012a) explains that, until now, people were taught to want teachers, and believe that they cannot learn without them. Once upon a time, in yesterday's world, that was the case.

SELECTIVE ATTENTION AND LEARNING

The communications revolution has brought access to increased information and external stimulation. This enriched type of environment requires selective attention so concentration focuses on relevant information while less pertinent data is screened out. Concerns about deterioration of selective attention implicates multitasking. Students believe that they can do homework while texting their friends, skim reading papers on an Internet site, and downloading a favorite piece of music. People of all age groups do poorly in trying to manage simultaneous tasks, overestimate how many things they can perform well at the same time, and acknowledge becoming distracted while following links and losing touch with the reference goals that are needed to guide online activity. The prevalence of such problems is prompting research about ways to help students anchor their attention and sustain concentration.

Multitasking and Comprehension

The challenges of attention is complicated by a general belief that multitasking improves productivity even though information processing experiments have reached the opposite conclusion. More serious is that multitasking appears to boost the level of stress-related hormones like cortisol and adrenaline that wear down adaptive systems through biological friction (Medina, 2009). Recognize that the adolescents growing up now have always had access to the Internet, they have become habituated to split-screen presentations, instant messaging, texting, and feel comfortable about being frequently interrupted. For them it is acceptable to shift from doing one thing to doing another by shifting attention back and forth. However, being an effective thinker in a culture of distraction requires selective attention and concentration.

Concern about the documented decline of ability to give full attention to anything implicates multitasking. As early as middle school, students send messages to friends while they also watch television or surf the web and do homework assignments. Consider David, an eighth grade student, at his desk in the bedroom. Within a few minutes, he switches from Facebook to iTunes to texting his friends. The parents say they are impressed with how David is able to balance multiple activities at the same time but they also worry that this pattern of thinking could prevent development of other important skills. His mother explains "I want David to be able to concentrate, to focus for long enough so reflective thinking is applied to solving problems." High tech jugglers like David are everywhere and most of them agree that multitasking somehow makes them more productive. But, is this an accurate view?

Researchers Ophir, Nass, and Wagner (2009) at Stanford University administered three tests to 100 students to identify the mental abilities in which multitaskers are more competent. Multitasking is receiving and using multiple streams of unrelated information simultaneously. Students were given a questionnaire about different categories of media and asked: How often when you are doing this media category, are you also using this category, and asking them to estimate amount of time. Then students were placed in two groups; those who regularly do a lot of media multi-tasking and those who do little media multitasking. In the first test both groups were shown two red rectangles sometimes surrounded by two, four or six blue rectangles. The configurations were flashed twice before the students were asked to tell whether two red rectangles in the second frame were in a different position than in the first frame. Directions stated that the blue rectangles should be ignored. Low multitaskers performed well but high multitaskers were continually distracted by blue rectangles and performed poorly.

Since the high multitaskers had shown that they were less able to ignore things, perhaps they had better memories and would be more capable of storing and organizing data. To find out, a second test presented sequences of alphabetical letters with the students asked to recall when a letter was making a repeat appearance. Again, the low multitaskers performed well while heavy multitaskers did poorly. So, if heavy multitaskers could not filter irrelevant information and were less able to organize memories, maybe they would excel at switching from one thing to another more quickly and efficiently. In the third test, students were shown images of letters and numbers at the same time and told what to focus on. When directed to pay attention to the numbers, they had to determine if the digits were odd or even. When concentrating on letters, they had to say whether these were vowels or consonants. Again, heavy multitaskers did poorly and light multitaskers performed well.

In review, the three abilities of filtering, memory management, and task switching were assessed. Filtering involves the ability to ignore irrele-vant data while focusing on relevant information. High multitaskers were captivated by distractions and irrelevant data. The more irrelevant infor-mation they see, they more they seem attracted to it. The second ability, management of working memory, relates to having neat filing cabinets where things are carefully stored so when information is needed we know immediately the cabinet to find it. Again, high multitaskers are much worse at this task. The greatest surprise involved the third mental ability of switching from one task to another. It was assumed that high multi-taskers would be superior in this context but their performance turned out to be much slower and worse. The researchers concluded that heavy multitaskers always draw on all the information in front of them. They cannot keep things separate in their minds, unable to filter out the irrelevant, and pay attention to what matters most. By doing less, they could accomplish more (Ophir, Nass, & Wagner, 2009).

Other neuroscientists have found multitasking jeopardizes the capacity for deep sustained attention while stunting ability to detect and comprehend lessons that are most relevant (Medina, 2009). Each time that attention shifts, the brain must slow down to reorient. This means that the demands of multitasking on sustained attention reduce ability to learn. Constant shifting of attention while online might create more readiness for multitasking but improving the ability to multitask actually hampers ability to think deeply and creatively. It appears the more someone multitasks, the less deliberative they become, the less able they are to reflect and to concentrate on solutions. In addition, the brain needs recovery time to consolidate memories and thoughts. If, instead, every quiet moment is taken up with another phone call or interruption related to electronic stimulation, the reprieve from external stimulation that is needed cannot happen (Jackson, 2009). Two thousand years ago the Roman philosopher Seneca expressed an insight that seems to apply to today. He said, "To be everywhere is to be nowhere." In the current environment, Clive Thompson (2008), a science writer at *The New York Times*, captured the essence of our problem—"Information is no longer a scarce resource, attention is."

Screen Skimming and Reading

Ziming Liu (2008) is a professor of Library and Information Science at San Jose State University. His studies show that skimming the Internet has become the dominant mode for reading, having replaced reading of books that many people claim takes too long and requires greater patience than they can muster. Instead of using skimming as a preliminary way to judge the relevance of material as people have always done, skimming is now the preferred method to rapidly sample data from many sources and try to make sense of it. Liu surveyed 30- to 45-year old professionals in engineering, teaching, business, industry, health sciences, and technology to find out how their reading habits had changed in the past 10 years. Over 80% reported that they now mostly engage in nonlinear reading of documents on the Internet. About 45% admitted their involvement with linear in-depth reading had declined. Only 16% said they devote more sustained attention to reading books. Liu concluded that the digital environment encourages exploration of many topics but often at a superficial level and hyperlinks further distract from reading and thinking deeply. A greater amount of time is spent reading now than in the past but screen skimming differs significantly from concentrated reading that requires sustained attention and reflection (Liu, 2008).

Adolescents will participate in multitasking and screen reading more than adults. A 2010 national survey by the Kaiser Foundation found that more than half of teenagers engage in some other media form while they also watch television. They multitask while on the computer or a cell phone (Rideout, Foehr, & Roberts, 2010). Such behavior also implicates preservation of creativity. Having the ability to concentrate, to value reflective thinking, and pay attention for long periods characterizes highly creative persons. The lesson for parents is to consistently schedule nonelectronic uninterrupted time for linear reading, family conversation, and solitary reflection. This strategy is hard to implement but promises that children will benefit from a merger of their favorite mode of learning with customary methods of linear thought that are needed by every generation.

Attention Focus and Distraction

The importance of paying attention to focus learning was described by William James (1842-1910). His *Principles of Psychology* (1890/2007) was the first textbook in psychology. James explained, "Attention is the taking possession by the mind in clear and vivid form of one out of what appears to be several simultaneously possible objects or trains of thought." He considered attention the conductor that leads orchestration of the mind. Yet, increasingly, people's lives appear to be shaped more by distraction than by attention. James saw attention as a clear and vivid possessing of the mind, an ordering, and a withdrawal from active consideration of other stimuli.

The science of interruption was introduced a century ago in studies of telegraph operators. These workers had the first high stress, time-sensitive technology positions. Psychologists found that, when someone spoke to a telegraph operator who was in the process of keying a message, errors significantly increased because operator cognition was scrambled by mentally having to switch channels. Later, it was found that workers performing any job that requires careful data monitoring, presentation is all-important. Given this knowledge, the airplane cockpit of fighter pilots was reconfigured in order that each meter and dial could be read quickly at a glance. During the 1920s experiments in Russia were conducted that revealed intriguing aspects of interruption. Bluma Zeigarnik instructed subjects to complete jigsaw puzzles and then interrupted them at various stages of their task (A. Zeigarnik, 2007). She discovered that the persons least likely to finish task were those interrupted near the beginning. Since they did not have enough time to become mentally invested in the task, they had greater difficulty recovering from a distraction. Subjects interrupted toward the end of assembling a puzzle more often stayed on track.

Mark Bauerlein (2010), professor of English at Emory University, has established a debate about attention and student achievement in the present era. In The Dumbest Generation, Bauerlein contends that, although adolescents have unprecedented access to a world of knowledge at their fingertips, they are less informed and literate than prior generations. Technology and its digital culture are not broadening the horizons of youth but instead narrowing it to a self-absorbed social universe that often blocks out virtually everything else. The immediacy and intimacy appeal of social networking sites means that student Internet use pertains almost entirely to their friends and themselves.

Many adolescents rely on the Internet less as a source for their learning than for communication with friends by texting, e-mail, ichat, and blogs. The Internet communication language with its peculiar spelling, grammar, and punctuation actually encourages illiteracy by making writing errors a socially acceptable practice.

Young adults intend to have a better balance between work and leisure than previous generations. However, excessive communication with friends can distract from school work. Researcher Buboltz (2012) at Louisiana Technical University explored how 654 college students use their cell phones. About 75% had smart phones, a rate 25% higher than the general public. On average, these students spent 5 hours every day interacting with their phone. Of the total 5 hours, over 3 hours is spent talking on the phone. Students make and receive 12 voice calls a day with an average duration of 25 minutes for each call. In addition, they send 100 text messages and receive 120 messages a day. These messages average 30 seconds to convey. This means one hour a day is spent sending and receiving approximately 220 text messages. Another 30 minutes involves watching videos with YouTube being the most popular site. Finally, men spend about 30 minutes each day playing video games while girls spend only 5-10 minutes on this activity. Local, national, and world news tend to be ignored by the students.

Bauerlein (2010) contends that most adults who are supposed to help shape the character and perspective of children have abdicated their responsibility. Some parents find it is easier to cave in, allowing their adolescents to retreat to the bedroom for hours surrounded by cell phones, computers, audio equipment, and preoccupation with peer communication. A related downside is that adults do not engage children in meaningful dialogue on serious issues needed to foster the growth of every generation. Bauerlein suggests that society must redress the imbalance of youth reliance on technology for communication in favor of devoting greater attention to learning than the current norm.

Similar concerns about communication are identified by results of annual surveys conducted by the Center for the Digital Future at the University of Southern California. Parents report that they are souring on the Internet. The worrisome trend is reflected by a one-third drop in the amount of family face-to-face communication time (from 26 to 18 hours per week) in Internet households between 2007 and 2010. A rising proportion of parents also report that Internet access at home is reducing the in-person time that their children spend with friends. Approximately the same proportion of families (60%) restricts use of the Internet as punishment as those that restrict television watching time as punishment (Center for Digital Future, 2010).

With an explosion of sophisticated cell phone technology and social network web sites like Twitter and Facebook, many people have concluded that human relationships are blossoming as never before. Sherry Turkle (2011) from the Massachusetts Institute of Technology challenges this assumption. In her book *Alone Together: Why We Expect More From Technology and Less From Each Other,* Turkle suggests people are determined to give human qualities to objects and content to treat one another as things. Based on surveys of text messages used by teenagers, she paints a sobering portrait of human disconnectedness in the face of expanding virtual connections in cellphone, intelligent machine, and Internet use. She describes the anxiety of adolescents when they do not receive an immediate reply to a text message. One girl pointed out she needed her cell phone for "emergencies"; it turns out that what she means by an "emergency" is having a feeling without being able to share it. Turkle reaffirms that humans still instinctively need each other and reports dissatisfaction and alienation among users; teenagers whose identities are shaped not by self-exploration but by how they are perceived by the online collective, mothers who feel that texting makes communicating with their children more frequent yet less substantive; Facebook users who feel shallow status updates devalue true intimacies of friendships. Turkle makes a strong case that what was meant to be a method to facilitate communication has pushed people closer to their machines and further away from each other in many ways.

Ways to Maximize Student Attention

Students are exposed to a broad range of potential distractions that can undermine concentration and reduce attention on learning. Students, teachers, parents, and administrators need to find ways to minimize interference with instruction. The suggestions presented in Table 6.2 can be posted on campus and the school website where everyone can read it and make an effort to assume their share of accountability.

Table 6.2. Ways to Maximize Student Attention

Encourage Goal Setting	This strategy respects the motivation of students and makes teachers initially aware regarding the goals that individuals want to accomplish. Such knowledge can provide feedback on progress and achievement.
Emotional Activation	The way a student feels about instruction can influence the amount of attention given to learning. Inviting teams to have a say in shaping individual and group assignments recognizes them as being capable partners.
Pause After Questions	Calling on the first students who raise their hands can cause other students to prematurely stop their information retrieval process. Retrieval should include reflection and relating instruction to situations.
Differentiate Instruction	Direct instruction is a common method in secondary and higher education but if used exclusively this tactic produces the least retention. Differentiated instruction assigns priority to collaboration enabling group and individual accountability.
Provide an Agenda Guide	Teachers should provide outline notes for each session so the planned sequence of issues is made known, interaction triggers improvisation, and a synthesis of lesson content is provided without extending the time for direct instruction.
Reflection Time	Educators are able to maximize student concentration by scheduling some time during class for solitary deliberation on topics and tasks. Thereafter, team members can benefit from sharing implications of independent and collective thought.
Avoid Disruptive Announcements	Principals can reduce distraction from instruction by limiting school-wide intercom announcements to a specific time each day. The office should contact students and faculty without having to interrupt everyone else.
Respect Attention Span	Schedule short periods of 10-20 minutes for direct instruction, alternate intervals that focus on teamwork, discussion, deliberation, group reporting, and interaction about consideration of questions, planning, interpretation, and application.
Assess Prior Knowledge	Teachers are more helpful when student skills are recognized. It is unwise to suppose that everyone brings the same knowledge base to class. Consulting portfolios is helpful when they can be accessed from other courses.
Take Renewal Breaks	Maintain a schedule with periodic breaks of 10-15 minutes. This practice allows students to step back from demands of class, stretch, walk around, go to the restroom, have a snack, and engage in private conversations.

Need for Dual Modes of Thinking

There can be benefit in reflecting about how thinking processes are changing. Marshall McLuhan (1967) at the University of Toronto in Canada became an instant celebrity with the publication of his book, *The Medium is the Massage*. He forecast the electric media that, at the time, included phones, radio, television, and movies were replacing text as the main influence on human thoughts and senses. His warning was that the content of media matters less than the medium itself in affecting how people think and act. He pointed out that it is common to assure ourselves that technology is only a tool and the way we use tools is what really matters. The comforting implication is that people are in control.

In contrast, McLuhan (1967) suggested that every new medium has altered the thinking processes of mankind. Adults do not think the same way as they did before the Internet. One difference that is felt strongly involves reading. A generation ago people found it easy to immerse themselves in a book, so libraries were quiet places. That ability has become rare. Instead, most people admit their concentration begins to drift after they read only a page or two, feelings of uneasiness take over, the inclination is to look for something else to do while also feeling we must drag our attention back to the task of reading. The deep reading that once came naturally has become a common struggle.

McLuhan (1967) seems to have been correct in suggesting that the effects of media are greater than just providing additional channels for information. They supply the essence of thought, but also have an influence on the thinking process. Nicholas Carr (2010) has documented the mental and cultural consequences of how the Internet and other electronic media such as cell phones, texting, and television programming are changing how people think while at the same time diminishing the capacity for concentration and contemplation. For example, the more people use the web, the greater the difficulty they report in staying focused when faced with complex narrative text. Even adults who, at an earlier age, read and enjoyed lengthy pieces of literature admit they can no longer do so. Coping with social network postings that are more than a few paragraphs in length can seem almost too much to absorb. Instead, a common preference is to rapidly skim and scroll.

For some people the practice of reading a whole book is considered a waste of time, a quaint way to gain information that could be found quickly by Google or another search engine. Tapscott (2009) describes a year-long series of discussions about the Internet with 300 users between 4 and 20 years of age. Their digital immersion was found to have influenced how this group absorbed information. They did not necessarily read a page from left to right or top to bottom. The most common preference involved rapid skimming to locate pertinent data. They blogged, tagged, texted, and twittered but were not interested in reading books.

High school students who jump from link to link, are easily distracted, feel that being interrupted is ok, and participate in multitasking have difficulty when faced with reading tasks required in most college courses. Based on placement test scores, 42% of all students entering community colleges, and 30% of the freshmen at universities are involuntarily assigned to take remedial reading classes without credit. According to American College Testing (2006), the principal cause of remediation for these students is their "inability to grasp complex texts." The reluctance to participate in slow reading is implicated. The most powerful predictor that a college student will drop out is their need for remedial reading. While a majority (58%) of students who are not assigned to remedial instruction earn a bachelors degree within 8 years, only 17% of remedial readers get a degree in the same time (Vandal, 2010).

We appear to have arrived, as McLuhan (1967) predicted, at an important stage in our intellectual and cultural history, a time of transition between two very different modes of thinking. What we might be trading in return for wealth of the Internet is competence with the use of linear thought processes. Calm, focused, undistracted, the linear mind is gradually being set aside by a new mindset that needs to take in and express information in short, disjointed bursts, the faster the better.

Since the printing press made reading books possible 500 years ago, the linear mind has been at the center of art, science, and society. Gradually it is being shoved aside. Computers exert a subtle influence affecting how we work and think. At some point many people discover that it is no longer possible to edit on paper because they can only do it online. They feel lost without a scroll bar, cut and paste functions, a delete key. Some of them are aware of their vanishing ability to pay attention to one thing for more than a couple of minutes.

To read a book silently requires the ability to concentrate over a lengthy period, to "lose oneself" in the pages. Developing such mental discipline takes time and is not easy. The natural state of the human brain reflects distraction. The predisposition is to shift attention from one object to another, to be aware of as much of what is going on around us as possible. Neuroscientists have found primitive brain mechanisms that respond rapidly to sensory input and shift attention involuntarily to visual features of potential importance. What draws our attention most is any alteration in surroundings. When something changes, we take notice since it could present danger or opportunity. This fast reflexive shift in focus was once needed for survival to reduce the likelihood that a predator would surprise people or overlook a food source. The usual path for most of human thought was anything but linear (Carr, 2010).

An Internet Paradigm for Schools

Adults have historically been the authorities regarding most things of value. For this reason, teacher and parent roles have emphasized guidance of youth but without a corresponding obligation to learn from adolescents. However, adults are aware that teenagers possess greater skills than themselves in using technology tools (Rosen, 2010). This authority inversion is influencing relationships of adults with adolescents who have been using digital tools since early childhood. Children learn to use computers by playing with them so they consider this kind of involvement as fun. Consequently, the assimilation or integration of new learning as part of the environment they have always known comes naturally.

In contrast, most adults consider computers as tools, not toys. As a result, the same lessons students consider easy can be difficult for adults because their learning requires accommodation, replacing long-standing thinking habits with new ways of seeing things. Many adults feel compelled to depreciate or to abandon linear thinking strengths in order to instead acquire a nonlinear mode of thinking because they fear being seen as old-fashioned and it can be difficult to retain older skills while learning new ones. In the view of the authors, both modes of thinking should be retained and communicated to youth to provide a comprehensive basis for problem solving. This situation presents ideal conditions for reciprocal learning to promote intergenerational harmony and enlarge the scope of thinking (Lancaster & Stillman, 2005; Sharez-Orozco, 2005).

When adolescents talk about the Internet, they often wish their teachers would provide them with more opportunities for interactive learning (Strom, Strom, & Wing, 2008). The six strategies described here appear compatible with the cyber preferences expressed by most adolescents, fit the instructional environment needed to support a tech-savvy society, and qualify as essential elements in the tentative formation of paradigm for Internet learning.

(1) *Expand linear learning to include nonsequential learning.* The custom has been to depend on linear-type tools as the single method of progression to acquire understanding. Linear learning, as applied to reading, means always beginning at the front page of a book, journal or magazine, and continuing until the last page is finished. Movies, programs on television and videotapes are typically linear presentations. However, Internet learning is often nonsequential and interactive, allowing students to surf and to choose links that connect to websites, blogs, or social network groups for persons with similar interests. These sites sometimes contain graphics, audio, and video elements along with the text. Students can also learn by chatting, composing electronic messages, and downloading materials (Debevec, Shih, & Kashyap, 2006). This broader view of learning can accommodate differences among students in level of knowledge, pace of development, and benefit of visual enrichment.

(2) *Establish discovery as the expectation for self-directed learning.* This kind of orientation encourages student discovery of knowledge to enhance

direct instruction provided by teachers. So long as educators were the primary source of information, it was appropriate for their training to focus mostly on ways to communicate the content of lessons. Students still expect teachers to plan instruction, design and organize tasks, make themselves available to listen and offer guidance. However, students also prefer to learn by doing, finding out some things on their own instead of always being told and getting their knowledge secondhand. The pervasive interest in discovery means that learning based on personal experience brings greater meaning and can transfer more readily to real life situations than can ideas conveyed by teachers.

(3) *Student-centered learning should include obligation to share knowledge.* This shift is needed because digital media offers unprecedented possibilities for teamwork. Instead of viewing team discussions as a forum to express personal opinion, the expectation should be that everyone would share ideas and relevant resources they have found on the Internet or library. It is unreasonable to sustain the custom of students reading only from a text or material teachers assign.

The potential benefit of the Internet depends on greater expectations for students to locate reading on their own. Further, our studies have shown that expecting students to bring reading materials they locate to class for peers to examine and refer to reading materials during discussion necessitates a reorientation to what is considered essential for cooperative learning groups (P. Strom & Strom, 2011b). This transition toward increased student responsibility does not diminish teacher influence. On the contrary, teaching becomes more complex by structuring student experiences that promote discovery, highlight competence, and encourage self-evaluation.

(4) *Support student individuality with search and synthesis activities.* The goal of learning how to find things out has joined the customary classroom emphasis on memorizing information. One aspect of this broader purpose is to provide opportunities for students to gain and practice the ability to synthesize. Teammates can be given the task of locating the same website, reading the material, and writing a paragraph summary. Everyone then critiques all the presentations to identify how the descriptions differ, note aspects that some students captured better, and detect relevant elements that no one mentioned. Writing includes the skill of being able to synthesize the views of others and to express personal interpretation.

Being able to make connections and knowing how to build on the ideas of others is an important skill. Combining the intelligence of individuals by networking often solves problems in a more efficient and less time consuming way than working alone. Instead of equating memorization with achievement, more attention should be given to honing the abilities of locating data, merging together, and synthesizing information as a basis for reaching more informed conclusions. Students who can find information, organize it, and present results in a coherent way offer credible evidence of problem solving ability.

(5) *Encourage development of durable intrinsic motivation.* Learning in response to curiosity rather than in response to direction given by someone else defines intrinsic motivation. The time available for learning in a longevity society is far greater than the past. Previous generations saw life as divided in two stages. During the growing up stage, students attended school, learned the skills needed to get a job, and then spent their adult years at work. In contrast, knowledge increases more rapidly now. The acceleration of new information motivates businesses to invest more money in continuing education for employees than is spent by all American institutions of higher education combined (Davila, Epstein, & Shelton, 2006). The duration of relevance that education programs offer is also diminishing. So, students must gain intrinsic motivation to remain eager to keep learning after graduation.

(6) *Promote critical thinking by participation in a "fact-check" system.* Teachers can tell students that, for specified lessons, one or more aspects of a presentation will be incorrect. The perpetual homework task is to rely on the Internet at home as a tool to "fact-check" the lessons. Students will relearn and reinforce in memory facts from daily lessons that are accurate through Internet exploration while also detecting elements containing errors. Student reports in class can be made the following day to identify what was revealed through the process of fact checking. Because adolescents enjoy finding flaws in the thinking of teachers, parents, and other adults, this task motivates careful monitoring and is perceived as a reasonable process to challenge authority when inaccurate information is disseminated. Students may have to check several sources to find details of a lesson that are false. A sense of accomplishment usually follows as students locate 'misleading' information. They may discover additional data that contradicts what teachers say and create discussion reflecting the premise that truth is sometimes unrecognized and errors may appear to be correct.

Rotating student assignments so two or three share the "fact checker" role daily ensures that all lessons are covered and feedback provided for the previous day. This nontraditional principle encourages self-guided learning in cyberspace and helps students gain insight about teaching. Students come to realize that teaching is not as easy as it appears, and educators must be prepared and ready to back up assertions with facts. Parents and siblings can be enlisted as helpers, thereby encouraging family interaction.

SUMMARY AND IMPLICATIONS

Intelligence testing, invented by Alfred Binet, remains the dominant resource for making decisions about student placement in special education or accelerated learning classes. Jean Piaget's qualitative view of intelligence led educators to shape curriculum so tasks correspond with stages of thinking. Lev Vygotsky reasoned that what students can achieve on their own and what they can accomplish with help from peers should be merged when estimating capacity to learn. Sugata Mitra, author of *Minimally Invasive Education,* maintains that creation of curriculum should no longer be seen as important as providing student access to information they organize on their own, without direction from adult teachers.

Paying attention to one task at a time is being replaced by multitasking, a pattern of thinking the public believes can increase productivity. In contrast, the experiments of neuroscientists have determined that multitasking undermines learning. The education deficits related to divided attention include a decline in ability of students to concentrate long enough to participate in deep thinking and problem solving. Fragmented attention is accelerated by extensive use of technology. The emerging reading preference is to skim and scroll quickly, and express impatience with in-depth lengthy materials. A new paradigm is needed for Internet learning to enable self-direction, establish obligation to share knowledge with peers, improve capacity to synthesize ideas, and promote critical thinking by verifying assertions.

APPLICATIONS FOR TEACHING

The single most important application of this chapter implicates a vital decision for the future of education. Society and its schools should provide a dual emphasis on linear learning and nonsequential learning instead of assigning priority to the pursuit of only one mode of thinking. Surfing the net to find data, exploring links to learn more, and interacting online provide benefits and have broad appeal. In addition, everyone needs another set of mental assets that include the ability to pay full attention to one task at a time, avoid distractions by screening them out to maximize learning, concentrate for a sustained period of time, and think deeply as the basis for decision-making and solving problems. Support for both modes of thinking is the best way to enhance intelligence, foster health, and improve productivity. The nurture of slow and deliberate reading of complex texts is bound to elicit opposition from persons habituated to skim reading and reaching hasty conclusions.

The youth preference is for nonsequential learning. They consider linear thinking out-of-date and try to persuade adults to give it up. This means they usually object to school assignments intended to help acquire this additional realm of competence. Being assigned a lengthy document to read or being expected to listen carefully to a lecture yields complaints of boredom by those who have short attention spans. Teachers and parents should resist the inclination to relent and, instead, mount a united effort to make certain that students are provided the comprehensive cognitive perspective they need for a more promising tomorrow.

CHAPTER 7

INTEGRITY AND
ETHICAL STANDARDS

In *Alice in Wonderland* comes to a crossroad and asks a Cheshire cat for advice: "What road should I take?" The cat replies, "That all depends on where you want to go." Alice admits, "I don't know where I want to go". The thoughtful cat replies, "Well, then, any road will do" (Carroll, 1865/2004). Children have more roads to choose from now than were available for previous generations. Selecting the values that contribute to personal growth can lead to responsibility, happiness, and maturity. When youth are expected to adopt healthy values, they are less likely to be misled by anyone who seeks to take advantage of vulnerability, confusion, and indecision. Values are accepted principles used to guide the behavior of individuals or groups. Children obtain their values from parents, other relatives, friends, classmates, teachers, clergy, musicians, sports figures, media performers, social networks, politicians, and reality program participants. When these sources offer conflicting advice, it can be difficult to decide the path to take. The goals of this chapter are to describe the prevalence of student cheating, motivation for deception in school, methods that teachers can rely on to minimize plagiarism, and collaborative efforts to educate for honesty and social maturity. The characteristics of face-to-face bullies are examined along with the emerging problems of cyberbullying. Action plans are identified for adults and peers to diminish these kinds of harassment.

CHEATING IN SCHOOL

Prevalence of Dishonesty

Honesty represents the combined qualities of being fair, just, truthful and morally upright. The Josephson Institute of Ethics in Los Angeles conducts annual surveys that monitor the ethics of 43,000 adolescents attending 100 randomly selected high schools nationwide, public and private. All students taking the survey are assured of anonymity and results have a less than 1% margin of error. About two-thirds of students admit to cheating on a test during the past year. Homework cheating is pervasive; over 80% report that they copied another student's work at least once in the past year. Lying is prevalent with 83% stating they lied to a parent about something important and 40% lied to a teacher two or more times about issues of importance. To underscore the premise that lying, cheating and stealing go together, 30% of the students admitted having stolen something from a store. Students 17 years of age and younger are five times more likely than people over age 50 to embrace the view that lying and cheating are necessary behaviors to survive (51% compared to 11%) (Josephson Institute of Ethics, 2010).

Despite this disappointing evidence that moral development is in jeopardy, the surveyed students still reported high self-esteem with 93% expressing satisfaction about their personal ethics and character. Indeed, 77% stated, "When it comes to doing what is right, I am better than most of the people I know." Even though these results mirror a trend toward deterioration of ethics among youth, it would seem that the main question for consideration is not whether things are getting worse but if they are bad enough to mobilize concern and action by families, schools, and community. Michael Josephson, the Institute Director, suggests, "These results show that our moral infrastructure is unsound and in serious need of repair" (Josephson Institute of Ethics, 2010).

Cheating is behavior to deceive or mislead others for personal advantage. In the past it was usual to suppose that cheaters had marginal abilities, causing them to resort to dishonesty as the only way to keep pace with their more accomplished classmates. However, when 3,000 students selected for recognition in *Who's Who Among American High School Students* reported their experiences, 80% acknowledged cheating on tests (Lathrop & Foss, 2005). This high proportion of achievers engaging in deception reflects a 10% rise since honor students were first presented the same question 20 years earlier. Among adolescent leaders that admitted cheating, 95% said they were never caught and therefore did not feel guilty and considered themselves to be morally responsible. Cheating among middle school, high school, and college students is widespread in Australia, England, India, Japan, Korea, Spain, and Scotland (P. Strom & Strom, 2011a).

Motivation for Cheating

Why do students of all ages and levels of achievement participate in cheating? One speculation is that academic dishonesty is a reflection of the broader erosion in ethics that support self-centeredness over concerns for fairness and equality. Another view is that fear and anxiety about high stakes testing causes dishonesty, especially among students who have difficulty acquiring minimal competency skills required for graduation. Other observers fault educators because they disregard evidence of character failure and choose not to hold the students accountable. In turn, teachers maintain that more and more parents are obsessed by the aspiration that their children should perform better than peers, regardless of what it takes to get the desired results (Anderman & Murdock, 2006).

There is a way to obtain a more accurate appraisal of how students feel about this matter. Since computers are present in all schools and electronic polling can be an option, educators should make an effort to become aware of how students perceive life in the classroom. In order to increase awareness, Strom and Strom (2009) designed 12 polls for students. These multiple-choice polls each consider student views about conditions of learning at their school. One of the polls focuses on cheating and includes items about observed prevalence, reaction to classmate cheating, punishment for test abuse and plagiarism, teacher reliance on software for detection, observation of adults who cheat, parent response to dishonesty, identifying cheating situations, circumstances that justify dishonesty, characteristics of students who cheat, and personal involvement in deception.

Every school district should establish policies and procedures about cheating so that faculty are able to respond to incidents they see or have reported to them without experiencing fear of duress from students or parents. While 80% of students responding to the *Who's Who Among American High School Students* survey admitted cheating on tests, a separate survey administered to their parents found 63% expressing confidence their child would never cheat. Perhaps these parents suppose that teaching difference between right and wrong is enough without linking awareness with responsibility to act in truthful ways (Lathrop & Foss, 2005). A noteworthy example of this assumption is a college student who scored at the 97th percentile of the SAT (Scholastic Aptitude Test) commonly used for admission to college. He later took the test for six students in the Great

Neck New York high school, charging $2,500 each for the deception. All seven individuals were arrested (Khadaroo, 2011).

A familiar outcome is that educators feel vulnerable to parent threats of lawsuits if the honesty of their child is challenged without indisputable proof. Many teachers worry that they may erroneously accuse a student and then suffer the dreadful consequences. Indeed, 70% of educators agree that concern regarding parent reaction discourages them from identifying and punishing many cheaters. An unintended result is student awareness that their misconduct rarely brings punishment and presents a low risk of detection (Whitley & Keith-Spiegel, 2002).

Technology and Monitoring

Teachers are advised to be vigilant when they monitor students taking tests. A perennial form of dishonesty involves referral to messages cheaters write on their body, clothing or belongings. A common practice has been to remind test takers not to glance at papers of others during a test. The emergence of technological devices has spawned new and more sophisticated approaches. Students with handhelds or cell phones can "beam" or call data silently from across a classroom or, with a cell phone from anywhere off campus. During a test these tools are hidden under the table or in baggy pockets. Both devices can be equipped with text messaging, instant messaging, e-mail, and a camera or video recorder that makes capture or transmission of answers a relatively simple task. Cell phones could have a hands-free function allowing a user to listen to sound files (i.e., prerecorded class notes). Applying this same method of sound files, others use music devices such as iPods.

Giving open book examinations and allowing students to bring notes increases familiarity with the content of a course, improves the review process, and reduces the incidence of cheating. While some of the considerations that have been described may seem unduly cautious, collectively these steps can do much to prevent dishonesty and support the integrity of a test environment. Students take honesty more seriously when they see that their teacher is making an effort to ensure fair conditions for assessment. Fairness is an essential value that most students agree should be upheld by everyone.

While forms of student cheating increase in complexity, a related but unexpected threat has also become more common. During the era of high stakes testing, faculty and administrator salaries and career paths are tied to test performance of students (Headden & Silva, 2011). Some teachers and principals have been fired for giving students answers to tests, prompting change in responses of students while being tested, changing answers after tests are completed and before submission to the district for processing, and allowing students more time than is specified by directions (Carey, 2011).

Many states contract with Caveon Test Security (2012), the nation's premiere company that monitors annual assessments of student achievement, cheating detection and prevention. This company has developed data forensics, a process that searches for unusual test response patterns like getting difficult questions correct while missing easy questions, an abnormally high pass rate for a classroom or school, tests where incorrect answers have been erased and replaced with correct ones. The service includes protection of instruments from fraudulent practices, erecting barriers to prevent unauthorized access to copyright materials, and applying sophisticated statistical and web patrolling tools that track cheaters, and hold them accountable by providing evidence to school administrators.

INTERNET ETHICS

The Children's Internet Protection Act (2000) requires public schools and libraries to install filters to minimize exposure to objectionable material like pornography. Another feature of cyber legislation, the body of law pertaining to computer information systems and networks, is safeguards for copyright material of authors and artists whose music or ideas are made available online. A national rush to make certain every age group can be online has overlooked the training everyone needs to support ethical behavior on the Internet. Dishonesty is not unique to students. This misconduct is widespread among adults at work and presents similar challenges to integrity, trust, and giving credit where credit is due (Gallant, 2010).

Students and Plagiarism

When students lack ethical commitment needed for searching the Internet, they may suppose that it is acceptable to present the words and views of someone else as if it was a representation of their own thinking. Plagiarism is a major problem in middle school, high school, and college that teachers are struggling to confront (Davis, Drinan, & Gallant, 2009). Cyber law proposals defining offenses and penalties are emerging as agenda that, in the future, could be determined in the courts instead of in the schools.

Parents share responsibility for helping daughters and sons realize that looking up a topic on the web is only a first step in research, similar to visiting a library. Copying from books, journals or sources on the Internet and portraying these products as one's own invention is dishonest and defined as cheating (Moore & Robillard, 2008). Because of broad Internet access, deceptive practices by students have been reported as moving downward to earlier grades. In 2012, the Philadelphia School Reform Commission has appointed a new oversight position called the testing integrity advisor; the state is currently investigating over 50 public schools, including elementary schools, over alleged malfeasance regarding student assessment testing (Graham, 2012).

Prevention of Plagiarism

Teachers want students to practice search skills on the Internet but are finding it difficult to cope with plagiarism. To encourage originality and prevent students from taking credit for the writing of other people, schools are contracting with a service that quickly detects work that is plagiarized. The plagiarism detection tool Turnitin.com identifies when more than eight copied words in succession are used in a paper, the original source, and evidence for confronting students and parents. Public schools and universities use this resource. While 31% of the high school students' papers submitted indicate cheating, 26% of college students' papers show cheating. For both high school and college students, Wikipedia and Yahoo Answers were the top two most popular sources of lifted copy (Watters, 2011).

Students are rarely asked to evaluate the practicality of classroom assignments. Another way to better understand student reaction is from conversations in which they describe their experience. Jamal, a sophomore in Montgomery, Alabama, believes it is misleading to limit the cheating focus only on inappropriate motives of students. Jamal suggests,

> Maybe a bigger problem is teachers requiring students to memorize instead of teaching them to think. You can cheat if all you are going to be tested on are facts but it is harder when asked to attack or defend a position and actually write an essay.

Jamal's outlook may not reflect consensus. Nevertheless, his view that teachers could minimize cheating by devising more challenging tasks that are less vulnerable to cheating is gaining support. Assignments that motivate learning by doing, encourage reciprocal learning in cooperative groups, support self-directedness, and foster original thinking are essential shifts in teaching that allow students to become actively involved in construction of their own knowledge. Teachers have devoted preparation time mostly to instruction they present in class and little time building assignments allowing students to learn on their own.

Individual and team projects are another context for cheating. Teachers can reduce deception by considering these recommendations.

1. The purpose of every project should be clear, identify anticipated benefits, and invite dialogue about methods, resources, and products acceptable for submission.

2. Relevance should be established for students. A connection between curriculum and real life is confirmed when students are able to get credit for interaction with informants from other generations or cultures whose experience goes beyond the perspective offered by a teacher or text.

3. Encourage students to express feelings and describe the processes they rely on to reach conclusions. These presentations are more interesting to write and more satisfying to read.

4. Go beyond the customary scope of problem solving. Students are often presented questions the teacher already knows answers for or could readily locate. Yet, generating alternative solutions and then making choices is often the key to overcoming personal challenges in life.

5. Encourage varied types of information gathering. Submissions might include a hard copy of the located web data accompanied by the same information summarized and interpreted in a student's own words, results drawn from polls or interviews, and descriptions of steps in an experiment.

6. Identify criteria to be used for evaluating the quality of performance. When students know in advance the criteria that will be applied to judge work, they can focus instead of reporting at the end, "I wasn't sure if this is what you wanted."

7. Allow students to reflect, revise, and improve a project product they submit. Having access to suggestions of classmates who read their work and being expected to revise products fosters perseverance, and motivates acceptance of criticism.

8. Consider an oral critique. This method allows students to express their views verbally, permits classmates to practice giving helpful criticism, enables teachers to call for clarification if points are unclear, and eliminates use of tech tools for deception.

Integrity and Maturity

Legalistic syllabi and tough policies alone are insufficient procedures to prevent cheating. Instruction is also needed. Students are able to understand that honesty is an important indicator of developing maturity. Indeed, maturity cannot materialize without a sense of obligation to treat other people fairly (Sternberg & Subotnik, 2006). Students benefit from discussions about a need for integrity across all sectors of life. They should also be informed about the seldom considered damaging effects of cheating, the gaps in knowledge and skills that adversely affect later success when the knowledge foundation necessary to understand processes in higher-level courses has not been acquired (Gallant, 2010).

Academic dishonesty presents another major disadvantage. The moral compass students need to guide conduct in class and outside of school can be thrown off course. This is the message portrayed in *The Emperor's Club,* a film starring Kevin Cline (Hoffman, 2002). As a teacher and assistant principal at St. Benedict's High School for Boys, he motivates students to choose a moral purpose for their lives in addition to choosing career goals. The story illustrates how great teachers can have a profound influence and cheating during youth can become a life-long habit.

Fairness and equality are core values families and schools expect to pass on to youth. However, neither value is conveyed in situations where students are placed at a disadvantage because others cheat. When dishonesty is common, high achievers are unable to distinguish themselves, gaps in student learning remain hidden, tutoring needs go undetected, and progress reports are inaccurate. Scandals in the workplace and government continually show how unethical practices by leaders can erode public trust and motivate cynicism. Early adolescence is the time when most people establish their sense of moral direction, define commendable behavior and misconduct, and determine relationships they approve of and ways of treating others they reject. For these reasons, students benefit from guidance that leads them to choose integrity to shape behavior rather than rely on cheating to get ahead (Adams & Hamm, 2006).

FACE-TO-FACE BULLYING

Most adults recall school bullies they tried to avoid and still wonder what caused them to torment their classmates. Similarly, opinion varies about the normality of bully behavior, the kinds of individuals who become involved, and the quality of relationships they have with their relatives and friends. There is also speculation about influence of bullies on classmates who observe while they victimize others. Research has led to knowledge about some of these issues.

Misconceptions About Bullies

When bullies stop bothering peers, schools can become safer places. One way to begin is abandon the misconception that bullying is normal, a stage that some people go through but will likely outgrow as they become adults. Studies support an opposite conclusion and suggest ways must be found to change behavior of bullies while they are still young. Psychologists at University of Michigan carried out a longitudinal study of 500 students, following them from age 8 until age 30 (Huesmann, 2007). Assessments showed that bullies experienced more adjustment problems than their peers. About 25% who started fights during elementary school by pushing, hitting or stealing belongings of others had a criminal record by age 30; the comparable record was less than 5% among the nonbullies. Furthermore, waiting longer to intervene seems to make matters worse.

Bullies often have unstable relationships as adults. In comparison with the general population, male bullies abuse wives more often, drive cars erratically, get fired from jobs, commit more felonies, and less often attain vocational success. Females who bully classmates in childhood are more inclined to severely punish their own children. Male and female bullies have higher than average rates of alcoholism, more often suffer personality disorders, and require greater use of mental health services (Larson, 2008).

Although bullies receive attention from their teachers and principals, institutional responses seldom include instruction to improve their behavior. Later on, the same dysfunctional patterns that make bullies troublesome to classmates are portrayed on a larger scale in employment histories when rejection is the most common response of coworkers. Parents of school-age bullies should be made aware that harassing others would eventually harm the perpetrators as well as victims (Dutton, 2007). Teachers should recognize that helping students develop their own internal guidance system is a more constructive response to violence than increasing the number of guidance counselors.

Contrary to popular opinion, bullies are often intelligent, receive good grades, and express self-confidence (Huesmann, 2007). These assets can cause some teachers to underestimate the dangers that may occur if such children grow up without a sense of empathy and continue to mistreat others. Policymakers encourage educators to take the problems of bullies as seriously as if they had another disability teachers feel more comfortable trying to remediate. If students experience difficulty reading, tutoring is provided with the expectation that intervention will result in improvement. However, educators less often express hope if a student is lacking in self-restraint or concern for feelings of others. In such cases, potential for learning is ignored in favor of options for punishment.

Confronting social skill deficits and emotional immaturity are matters teachers feel unprepared for when students begin to show signs of failure. Many schools give up on these individuals. Yet, classes are provided for students who have taken illegal drugs because it is assumed they are capable of recovery. This same optimistic attitude should apply to the curriculum for students whose emotional and social difficulties are exhibited by lack of self-restraint and empathy (Ybarra, Diener-West, & Leaf, 2007).

Low self-esteem is sometimes suggested as an explanation for motivation of bullies. Research does not support this opinion. In fact, there is a strong relationship between high self-esteem and violent behavior (Baumeister, 2005; Baumeister, Campbell, Krueger, & Vohs, 2003). People that have high self-esteem often perpetrate violence. This troublesome group includes bullies, racists, gang members, people that are associated with organized crime, rapists, and psychopaths. Intervention with these individuals that concentrates on self-control rather than self-esteem is more successful.

The favorable self-impression of bullies is usually based on lack of awareness about what peers think of them until late adolescence. While bullies are growing up, they hang out with one or two companions, often lackeys who feel constrained to help them carry out hostile wishes. Bullies mistakenly suppose that their own social situation is normal (Henkin, 2005). Owing to the social blind spot that makes them oblivious to how they are seen by peers, bullies characteristically lack empathy and ignore views of classmates they intimidate. Acquiring empathy is an essential purpose for education of bullies (Orpinas & Horne, 2006).

Female bullies need rehabilitation too (Chemelynski, 2006). Male bullies rely on physical aggression like shoving, hitting and kicking whereas females more often resort to relational aggression. To get even they spread rumors about someone so classmates will reject the victim. The way female bullies strive for domination is threatening social exclusion, "You cannot come to my party unless you ..." Threats are made to withdraw friendship in order to get one's own way, "I won't be your friend unless ..." The silent treatment is applied to produce social isolation. These expressions of coercion are effective because they jeopardize what girls value, their relationship with other girls. Social exclusion is especially powerful when girls transition to adolescence and are more susceptible to conflict (Goldstein & Brooks, 2012).

Bully Family Relationships

Abuse is a behavior often learned at home where young bullies are victims of mistreatment. Family studies have found that parents of bullies interact with children much differently than families of nonviolent children. Parents of bullies do not use even a fraction of the praise, encouragement, or humor other parent's use in communicating with sons and daughters. At home bullies often experience put-downs, sarcasm, and criticism (Dutton, 2007). The punishment of a young bully may depend more on the mood of a parent than gravity of misconduct. If a parent is angry, harsh punishment is usual. If the parent is in good spirits, the child may get away with almost anything (Centers for Disease Control, 2011c).

Dysfunctional homes sponsor an outlook that life is essentially a battleground and threats are anticipated from any direction at almost any time (Hardy & Laszloffy, 2006). Even when bullies grow too strong for parents to physically abuse them, they continue to observe mistreatment of younger siblings or a parent. The lesson is always the same—whoever has the greatest power is right. Based on erratic attacks from parents, bullies become wary and they misinterpret motives of people outside the family too. They often see hostility where there is none and this suspicion precipitates conflict with classmates (Larson, 2008). Schools must be given authority to educate dysfunctional families by giving instruction to parents of bullies as well as their children. This approach can help parents adopt constructive goals, better communication, and suitable forms of discipline. In the long-term, counseling cannot compensate for failing to offer parents skills needed to give humane guidance (Larson & Lochman, 2005).

Influence on Classmates

Students who are spared as targets of bullies can still be harmed by social lessons that are learned from them. Researchers at York University in Toronto, Canada found that bullies who do not get negative feedback about their misconduct present a dysfunctional model for classmates that suggest there are no consequences for aggression (Mishna, Scarcello, & Pepler, 2005). This observation can motivate bystanders to behave in the same way themselves. Evidence about the influence of bullies comes from studies where peers have been observers in over 80% of bully episodes at school (Lodge & Frydenberg, 2005). The willingness to remain spectators and acquiesce encourages greater intimidation (Coloroso, 2009).

In the United States, a study of 1,000 elementary students found that an experimental group provided guidance about ways to respond to bullies later reported enhanced bystander responsibility, greater perceived adult responsiveness, and less acceptance of bullying and aggression than peers in an untreated control group (Frey, Kirschstein, & Snell, 2005). Barbara Coloroso (2009) portrays the bully, bullied, and bystander as three characters in a tragic play and explains how their scripts could be rewritten, new roles created, and the plot changed to produce responsible behavior.

It is important to identify conditions that would motivate bystanders to intervene in behalf of those being mistreated. Few students challenge bullies but most who do take action have high social status. To increase peer intervention, it is necessary to make students aware of their individual responsibility to take action and demonstrate empathy for anyone being abused. In addition, students need effective intervention strategies and should be encouraged to show the courage necessary to offset a silent majority whose lack of caring can deprive victims of support while at the same time jeopardizing their own future as compassionate individuals (Beran & Shapiro, 2005).

When bully behavior is viewed as a group phenomenon, the participant role of observers is recognized and attention can be given to training them to facilitate social change by becoming willing to report incidents. Besides victims (who suffer humiliation, anxiety, and pain), bullies (who harm others and endanger their social and emotional development), the witnesses (who are in the process of forming lifelong responses to injustice) deserve consideration. Bully behavior may begin with minimal harm but records show that it can escalate to devastating treatment of others (Salmivalli, Kaukiainen, & Voeten, 2005).

When parents and students discuss worries about school safety, the fear that someone will bring a weapon is mentioned more than other concerns. This attributes to many killings by middle school and high school students and recognition that, annually, more than 4,000 students are expelled for having a gun at school. Nevertheless, nearly half of students report they would not tell teachers or principals if they knew a classmate brought a weapon. The reason they give is possible retaliation, a fear the person would "Get them back." Clearly, unwillingness to report peer abuse is a perilous norm. Following cases of violence, it has quite often been discovered that students had been aware of threats but did not take them seriously or decided not to inform faculty or parents (Fein et al., 2002).

The attainment of school and family cooperation can nurture development of healthy social norms that motivate students to treat others with fairness and respect and assume responsibility for the safety of others. Table 7.1 is included to help teachers and principals.

BULLIES IN CYBERSPACE

Many adolescents possess greater skills than their teachers or parents in using tools of communication technology they will need for continued learning in the future. This unprecedented lag in proficiency of grownups

Table 7.1. Peer Support Practices to Decrease Bullying and Increase Concern for Others

1	Use healthy criteria for self-evaluation so confidence is not based on demeaning others.
2	Urge students to periodically identify positive qualities that they observe in classmates.
3	Portray social maturity as an achievement demonstrated by acceptance of differences.
4	Help students realize that teasing shows an inability to care about other people's feelings.
5	Show courage in challenging the mistreatment of others when it is observed or suggested.
6	Build feelings of belonging and support for teammates from cooperative learning groups.
7	Provide reminders on class walls about no name-calling, eye rolling, or laughing at peers.
8	Teach students how to process teaser comments presented in many situations at all ages.
9	Discuss how being teased can have harmful effects regardless of intentions of the teaser.
10	Create a list of words students agree are not to be used when they talk about each other.
11	Encourage students to identify the person they wish to become and set personality goals.
12	Ask students about a time they teased someone, their reasons for doing so, and outcomes.
13	Invite students to share an incident when they were teased and how they felt at that time.
14	Enable students to learn conflict resolution skills instead of reliance on negative remarks.
15	Suggest that parents talk with their child who is a teaser or was teased by someone else.

has created a virtual island where the adolescents can roam without supervision, akin to the island portrayed in *Lord of the Flies* by Nobel Prize winner William Golding (1954). His story begins as a group of boys are being evacuated during wartime. The plane they are on is shot down but no one is seriously hurt. After searching the remote island on which they are stranded, the boys realize there are no adults around to tell them what to do, make decisions for them, or punish misconduct.

Adapting to their new social environment means the boys have to develop their own rules and expectations. Some discover that control and intimidation of companions is easier if they paint their faces as a disguise, taking on a mask of anonymity while creating fear in the mind of enemies. In a similar way, adolescents who visit the virtual island called the Internet often conclude that adults are not watching, cannot know if misbehavior occurs, and will be unable to intervene when corrective action is needed (Rosen, 2010). Many parents overschedule themselves and are so busy that they are unable to arrange time to explore what their children are doing on the Cyber Island.

Most students on the Cyber Island engage in healthy activities such as making and maintaining friendships, posting messages on network sites, sharing music, videos and photos, and learning by self-directed searches for information. Students also recognize technology can be used to express the dark side (Shariff, 2008). Bullies may suppose hiding behind pseudonyms and well-disguised IP addresses can conceal their identity while victims remain unable to detect the source of threat. On this modern day Cyber Island, students can behave in shameful ways, often without accountability for their actions while their victims suffer damaging consequences (P. Strom, Strom, Walker, Sindel-Arrington, & Beckert, 2011).

Unfortunately, some young victims do not communicate their suffering to adults (Bauman, 2010; Kowalski, Limber, & Agatston, 2008). In addition, experts have drawn attention to a decline in meaningful communication of many teenagers with adults (Epstein, 2007). Because adults, even when present, are uninformed regarding what life is like on the Cyber Island, teenagers increasingly turn to peers as their main source of advice (P. Strom & Strom, 2009). A national survey by the Kaiser Family Foundation found that adolescents, on average, spend 8 hours a day with media and immersed in a peer culture facilitated by cell phones and the Internet. Some youth are in touch with friends 70 hours each week but spend little time interacting with the important adults in their lives (Rideout, Foehr, & Roberts, 2010). One worrisome view is that the society is unintentionally isolating youth, causing them to communicate exclusively with peers on the Cyber Island. Creative initiatives are urgently needed so intergenerational communication can be more common and satisfying (R. Strom & Strom, 2011).

Uniqueness of Cyberbullying

Students have always been in contact with bullies in schools and neighborhoods but currently they must also be concerned about unseen enemies (Coloroso, 2009). The assumption that knowledge about face-to-face bullies is applicable to online bullies is unfounded. A national online survey of 1,600 students from ages 10 to 15 found that two-thirds of those who reported being harassed online did not report being bullied at school (Ybarra, Diener-West, & Leaf, 2007). Messages to undermine the reputation of a victim could do more harm than face-to-face altercations. Instead of a case being witnessed by a small group, a much larger audience become observers if cyberbullies communicate embarrassing photographs or text messages. Victims can identify their tormentors at school but cyberbullies can be difficult to trace. As a result, they avoid responsibility and do not fear getting caught or punished (Wolak, Mitchell, & Finkelhor, 2007).

Misconduct in cyberspace presents school principals with uncertainty about the boundaries of their jurisdiction. They are unable to respond when unknown parties send hate messages from a location outside school like a home-based computer or mobile phone. Some students are reluctant to inform adults about anxiety they experience at the hands of cyber enemies, fearing that parents may overreact by taking away their computer, Internet access, or cell phone. Many students are unwilling to risk having their parents choose such extreme forms of protection. The reason is without tech tools, they would be socially isolated and unable to stay in contact with friends (Rosen, 2010).

Until recently, victims considered their homes to be a place of safety, sanctuary from those who would mistreat them. This is no longer the case. Most students go online as soon after they return home from school. Some find themselves to be a target of threats, rumors, and lies without knowing the identity of persons creating fear and frustration or how to end the damage (Bauman, 2010). The following examples of cyberbullying from several countries reveal the scope and complexity of arranging safety in cyberspace (P. Strom, Strom, Wingate, Kraska, & Beckert, 2012).

Sixteen-year-old Denise is a high school junior in Los Angeles. She argued with her boyfriend and they broke up. The rejected boy was angry and wanted to get even. The devious method he chose was to post Denise's contact numbers, including her e-mail address, cell phone number, and street address on several sex-oriented websites and blogs. Denise was hounded for months by instant messages, prank callers, and car horns of insensitive people who drove by her house to see whether they could catch a glimpse of her. In this case, the identity of the cyberbully, Denise's former boyfriend, was detected quickly. Nevertheless, his apprehension did not eliminate the sense of helplessness and embarrassment felt by Denise.

Shinobu is a high school freshman in Osaka, Japan. When his gym period was over, Shinobu got dressed in what he believed was the privacy of the changing room. However, a classmate seeking to ridicule Shinobu for being overweight secretly used a cell phone to photograph him. In seconds, the naked boy's picture was sent wirelessly by instant messaging for many students to see. By the time Shinobu finished dressing and went to his next class, he was already a laughing stock at school.

Donna attends eighth grade at a parochial school in Montreal, Canada. Donna and her mother went to Toronto to visit her grandmother who was recuperating from cancer surgery. When Donna returned home, a cyber-bully had circulated a rumor that she had contacted SARS (severe acute respiratory syndrome) in Toronto. Donna's girlfriends were afraid and unwilling to be around her or talk on the phone. Without exception, class-mates moved away when Donna came near them.

Some cyber cases involve more than one bully and a single victim. Others could involve a group of bullies that persecute multiple parties. The latter occurs when students respond to online trash polling sites. These websites invite students to name individuals they feel qualify for unflattering char-acteristics, such as the most obese person at school, boys mostly likely to be gay, and girls who have slept with the most boys. The usual consequences for those who suffer from this shameful treatment are depression, hope-lessness, and withdrawal (McQuade, Colt, & Meyer, 2009).

Reassessment of Teasing

Detection and rehabilitation of cyberbullies is complicated by the way teasing is generally perceived. Many see teasing as just making fun of someone in a playful way. Teasers often explain their motivation, saying "I was just kidding." In contrast, students report that being teased is stress-ful. When students report physical abuse to teachers, they are encouraged to identify classmates who hurt them. However, if students report teasing, they are often given a contradictory response. The dilemma begins with a false assumption that teasers lack any motivation to harm and would stop if a person being made fun of expressed their disappointment. So, the victim may be encouraged to suck it up, view the incident as an aspect of life everyone must cope with, and consider their ordeal an opportunity to build character and develop resilience. Research regarding teasing has found that two-thirds of cases implicate name-calling, focused on a per-son's physical appearance or dress, followed by attention to deviance from group norms, and deficits in academic skills and other imperfections (Agliata, Tantleff-Dunn, & Renk, 2007).

Espelage and Swearer (2010) discovered a high correlation between popularity and bullying among sixth grade students. Those nominated by peers as doing the most teasing were also the students nominated as most popular and having the most friends at school. Given the reluctance of adults to condemn teasing in the same way physical bullying is renounced, it is not surprising that students adopt the same perspective. As a result, many trivialize such mistreatment when it is applied to harass others on the Internet. In effect, students are led to believe that to physically hurt someone is unacceptable but teasing them is relatively harmless and could even enhance the victim's ability to cope with adversity (Agliata, Tantleff-Dunn, & Renk, 2007).

There can be a high emotional cost when students call one another undesirable names. These name callers are seldom referred to as bullies even though their behavior undermines the mental health of others. When some victims of teasing respond with violence, their reasons more often relate to being teasing than being physically bullied. Reports by teenager murderers who said they could no longer bear being called nasty names frequently identify ridicule as their motivation for taking such desperate actions. The United States Secret Service conducted an investigated of school shootings. The findings revealed that most attackers had experienced long-term severe peer harassment and bullying. More than 70% of them reported being persecuted, threatened and, in certain cases, injured before choosing violence as their solution. In some cases, being bullied had a significant impact on the attacker and seemed to be a factor in deciding to attack the school. More than three-fourths of school shooters were found to have announced suicidal thoughts that were ignored by their friends or family (Vossekuil, Fein, Reddy, Borum, & Modzeleski, 2002).

In 1999, at Columbine High School in Littleton, Colorado, two students used guns and bombs for killing 12 classmates and a teacher while wounding 30 others before killing themselves. Following the massacre a suicide note from one shooter was found. In his explanation for why he and Dylan Klebold carried out their bloody rampage, Eric Harris warned against blaming rock music they listened to like Marilyn Manson or trench coats worn by their outcast group. Instead, he repeated the message communicated to the students while killing was going on. According to Eric's note,

> Your children who have ridiculed me, who have chosen not to accept me, who have treated me like I am not worth their time are dead. I may have taken their lives and mine—but it was your doing. Teachers, parents, let this massacre be on your shoulders until the day you die. (Johnson & Brooke, 1999)

When Marilyn Manson was asked what he would say to students at Columbine and the community, he replied, "I wouldn't say a single word. I would listen to what they have to say and that's what no one did" (Moore, 2002).

Failure to Confront Parents

What happens when schools fail to confront parents about their responsibility to correct their child who is mistreating classmates? Perhaps an important lesson can be learned from England where 34 local education authorities conducted a survey to find out why the number of families deciding to home school their children was increasing at such a rapid pace. The major factors identified by parents who chose this option included a range of motivations such as a rise in the number of students in classes diagnosed with special needs and requiring more teacher attention, parents wanting to spare their child the state's school focus on testing, readily available teaching materials to use at home, guidance on the Internet, and doubling of private school fees.

However, the most prominent motivation related to bully behavior. A substantial proportion of parents, 44%, cited bullying as the main reason for withdrawing their child from public school. They explained that they do not believe schools respond to problem children or hold families accountable, as should be the case. Therefore, if their child is bullied, some parents try to manage the situation themselves in a way they feel is best (Blackhurst, 2008). The extent to which American parents who transfer daughters and sons from public schools to home school, charter, private or parochial institutions based on wanting to ensure safety and psychological well being of their children is unknown.

INNOVATIONS FOR CONSIDERATION

Antibully School Legislation

New Jersey has the nation's most comprehensive school Anti-Bullying Bill of Rights law (2011). All faculty and staff must report bully incidents on the same day they become aware of a complaint. A formal investigation must begin within a school day of an episode and completed within ten days including a resolution. All schools must appoint and provide training for an antibully coordinator in the school district and a specialist at each school to lead a safety team that includes the principal, teacher, and parent to review complaints. Superintendents have to report twice a year to the state department of education. A grading system ranks every school based on efficiency in combating harassment and intimidation.

This law is viewed as a game changer. During the past using a four-letter word at school could get students into more trouble than calling someone else ugly, fat, retarded, or gay. Administrators are considered responsible for the culture of their school but the law takes away discretion of principals to ignore something that could be harmful and empowers faculty who, in the past, may have turned a blind eye to episodes knowing a principal would not act. This orientation may have flaws but promises to change what is considered normal acceptable behavior.

These extraordinary reforms were largely motivated by the bully related suicide of a freshman at Rutgers University whose roommate secretly videotaped his relationship with another man to disseminate on the Internet. Many studies have found students who depart from norms are the ones most often harassed (Mason, 2007). When 6,200 students in middle and high school were surveyed, 86% that identified themselves as gay or lesbian reported being physically abused during the past year and 44% reported physical mistreatment (Kosciw, Dias, & Greytalk, 2008). The *It Gets Better Project* was established to prevent the suicide of gay and lesbian youth by giving them hope and assurance that they can have a positive future if they are able to get through middle and high school when persecution is most frequent and usually unpunished (Savage & Miller, 2012).

Acceptance of Group Differences

In addition to antibully policies, boards of education can amend how history is presented in schools. Elementary and secondary students become more accepting of differences when they learn how groups targeted for abuse have benefitted the nation. During the 1960s schools began to acquaint students with African Americans who were previously unrecognized even though their initiatives had improved national quality of life. In the 1970s, Latinos were first portrayed to the public in a way that acknowledged the contributions by leaders in this subpopulation. The California Fair Accurate Inclusive Respectful (FAIR) Education Act (Senate Bill 48) of (2011) mandates that schools address certain gaps that still exist in current textbooks. Specifically, outstanding figures within the lesbian, gay, bisexual, and transgender community, advocates for disability rights, racial justice organizations, and other groups that have shaped history should be acknowledged in the textbooks and curriculum that chronicles the evolution of society.

Students should also be taught to recognize that fear is a valuable emotion when it motivates cautious behavior that protects us from harm. People are wise to be guided by fear of consuming illegal drugs, chatting with online predators or traveling with drunk drivers. These kinds of dangers warrant consideration because they have the potential to threaten self-preservation. On the other hand, fear of groups whose behavior departs from norms does not serve the survival purpose, compromise safety, place the general welfare at risk or undermine individual freedom to pursue a lifestyle of our choosing. The fact is fear of differences can only be sustained by dissemination of misinformation that is used as a basis to justify the abuse of selected groups (Strom, Strom, Wingate, Kraska, & Beckert, 2012).

In the past, a popular statement was "Sticks and stones can break my bones but names will never hurt me." We now know that statement is false because research has shown that being called names hurts and the extent of harm depends in part on age of the victim. Prior to adolescence, students lack access to a defense mechanism called rationalization. Consequently, they are inclined to believe negative comments that others say about them. Parents struggle to convince children that such insults are false. Consider 8-year old John who, in tears, tells his mother that Roger has been calling him a "retard," John's mother may point out that you, John, are assigned to the highest reading group in class while Roger is not in that reading group. This means that him calling you a retard is foolish. However, John is not old enough to rationalize and so remains convinced that he is whatever Rogers calls him. This sad story implicates education to treat everyone with similar respect and kindness. Being subjected to mistreatment as a child can have lifelong consequences in terms of self-esteem and confidence to achieve.

Teacher-Parent Communication

Surveys of 250,000 students have shown that, between Grade 6 and Grade 12, a decline in parent-child dialogue is common (Benson, 2010). Communication between teachers and parents also declines in middle school onwards because the students no longer have just one teacher. They have four to six teachers who provide instruction daily. In this more complex setting, faculty should share their observations about the notable behavior of students they have in common with their colleagues and inform parents too. Yet, this essential kind of interaction rarely occurs.

Communication with families is poor because schools continue to use ineffective and outdated methods to contact parents. Most parents work so they cannot be reached during the day at home. Some do not have e-mail, answering machines or voice mail. Others are unable to talk while they are at work or check e-mail promptly. When parents cannot speak privately on the phone while at their job, it is unlawful for teachers to leave messages regarding student behavior with a coworker. A related problem is that misbehaving students come home before their parents, intercept the school message left on the answering machine about their misbehavior, and erase it.

Teachers have limitations too. They are in class most of the day so repeated efforts to reach parents is impractical. Using electronic mail during class can be difficult. Phone tag is tiring and takes too much time. Teachers are also reluctant to speak with parents who react to bad news by becoming upset and confrontational. Given these obstacles, an innovative approach is to send and receive some information without dialogue or confrontation.

An erosion of communication with parents produces unfavorable results. If the school gives parents information late, they cannot offer a timely, well-reasoned response. On the other hand, lack of information leaves them unable to respond to student misconduct or commendable behavior. Poor school communication motivates some parents to withdraw from their corrective guidance role and expect teachers to take their role. Teachers may try to address misbehavior but without support eventually give up. No one benefits if teachers and parents look the other way about misconduct. Without synchronized adult efforts, the emotional and social needs of adolescents remain unmet.

Most parents agree that they would like to be informed about good behavior of their child as well as misconduct. They realize that character development depends on being able to reinforce favorable actions when they occur. In this context an experiment, supported by Motorola, involved 108 high school students, their parents and teachers. (P. Strom & Strom, 2009). All faculty serving these students were provided with training to use a personal digital assistant (PDA) for recording events in the classroom. The School Code of Recordable Events (SCORE) consisted of a numeric code that included 50 statements, written on both sides of a wallet-size card, to interpret classroom events. When teachers observed any criteria on the SCORE card, they entered the corresponding number on their hand-held wireless organizer. Later, information was electronically transferred to a personal computer. The SCORE statements identify misconduct, good behavior, and teacher responses to incidents.

In order for results of SCORE to involve families, the Parent Alert Signal System (PASS) was devised. This system informs parents about the nature of a challenge they face in guiding their child to adopt acceptable behavior or commend exemplary conduct. The teacher's numeric coded message is sent to a parent's e-mail or cell phone. Getting a message the same day as an event occurs enables the families to focus on corrective guidance or good conduct. Once sent, a parent checks the cell or e-mail to see the message and consult the SCORE card to identify the issue to discuss with a child. Next, the parent contacts the teacher's cell or email to confirm a message was received (P. Strom & Strom, 2009).

Teachers present certain lessons in school according to a planned schedule but parents usually have to teach teenagers lessons when needed in response to situations. However, they can know when certain life lessons are needed if teachers report notable events in a timely manner. The requirement of immediacy for feedback to parents about student behavior is an important condition to implicate positive/negative reinforcement and punishment.

Collective Teacher Intervention

Teachers differ in the academic subjects they provide but all faculty are expected to support social development of students. Technology can help to achieve this goal by enabling faculty collaboration. When the SCORE observations of teachers who instruct the same student are combined, a more complete picture of the behavior of that person emerges. In turn, united intervention strategies can be planned and monitored for effect. Educators who might otherwise feel helpless in dealing with disciplinary situations alone can gain confidence as part of a team that shares its observations with the principal and parents and identifies action that are expected of families.

In the 1 year SCORE/PASS project most of the parents (98%) and students (83%) felt encouraged by getting messages from teachers about commendable behavior. Teachers (92%), parents (92%), and students (82%) expressed a common belief that most adolescents will behave better if good conduct gets timely recognition. One mother stated the consensus view, "Before this project, I supposed that 'no news is good news. Now I realize that no news is just lack of information. It is a great boost to sometimes receive feedback indicating that our son is becoming mature" (P. Strom & Strom, 2009).

Reporting favorable student behavior as a way to encourage and maintain good conduct corresponds with research that nurturing healthy relationships at school is a better way to reduce discipline than zero tolerance policies and punitive penalties. This impression is confirmed by a National Longitudinal Study of Adolescent Health that found attachment to school is a protective factor against involvement with violence (Franke, 2000). The most significant predictor of student well-being was feeling connected with school. Other studies have shown that when students feel accepted by peers and vested in the institution, they engage less in risky behavior (Orpinas & Horne, 2006).

Harry Potter used magical powers to silence his bully, the abominable Dudley Dursely (Rowling, 1999). In real life, however, children, teachers, and parents do not have magic at their disposal. Education for civility and social maturity represent the most powerful foundation that can be provided to protect students so they are safe in school and at home.

SUMMARY AND IMPLICATIONS

High rates of cheating, even among honor students, reveals moral development is not keeping pace with other areas of mental development. In response, initiatives are taking place to motivate ethical behavior and define the conditions of integrity to govern student conduct. Explanations for why so many students cheat include erosion of ethics in society, high stakes testing, parental pressures to excel, and the student desire to get ahead no matter what the cost. Schools should poll students to detect the prevalence of cheating, reactions to academic misconduct, and personal definitions about cheating, individual involvement, and ways to reduce misconduct. Technology to detect cheating, devising multiple versions of tests, teacher surveillance, and alternative assessments deserve consideration. Faculties should police themselves and not provide students answers to raise their scores. Companies that monitor test security and detect fraud are a necessary form of protection.

Everyone needs training to understand ethical responsibilities on the Internet. There are websites that offer students, for free or a price, papers to submit so they do not have to write their own. Consequently, plagiarism presents teachers with situations of uncertainty over whether they are grading their students or efforts of someone else. Educators are reluctant to express doubts about the dishonesty of any student without proof because they fear retribution from parents and administration. To assist teachers, schools pay for services that can detect plagiarism. Another way to reduce cheating is for teachers to devise more challenging assignments in which students defend or they oppose particular views and provide opportunities for reciprocal learning as generational reporters or cultural reporters gathering input from older relatives or community sources. Use of legalistic syllabi that clearly state school policy and punishment for participating in deceptive practices can impact thinking and motivate accepted conduct. Instruction is necessary as well. Students are able to recognize that becoming mature cannot be achieved unless they demonstrate fairness and equality toward others. They should become acquainted with cyber laws, why these are needed, and situations that could place decision making on punishment for school offenses in the courts instead of the schools. There is a need to educate parents, providing agenda for family discussions about the importance of honesty, trust, and integrity.

The customary way to learn civil behavior has been to observe and imitate more mature people who are admired as models. This pattern of development does not guide the way students are learning to treat others in cyberspace. They are technologically savvy, communicate more with peers than with adults, and turn to one another more for advice on interaction for using tools of technology. Adults accelerate excessive reliance on peers for communication and guidance when they refuse to listen to students about conditions of learning at their school. If school improvement committees know student opinions offered on anonymous Internet polls, a more accurate portrayal of institutional assets and limitations in relation to cheating and civil behavior can become known.

APPLICATIONS FOR TEACHING

1. Extensive schooling does not ensure that students will choose honesty as a lifestyle. These aspects of development depend more on exposure to tasks that are emotionally maturing than academic study alone. Giving students opportunities to respond directly to social problems through community service generates concern for the welfare of others, keeps the caring capacity alive, and provides the satisfaction of meeting needs.

2. Character development is motivated by observation of commendable behavior. This is why the public should expect teachers, parents, politicians, athletes, film stars and music icons to behave as models of integrity, and maintain ethical standards. Teachers have a responsibility to consistently demonstrate maturity for impressionable observers.

3. Teachers, students, parents, administrators, and librarians should make a concerted effort to reform the school culture from one where cheating is ignored or tolerated to an environment where creative initiatives are taken that emphasize the values of honesty, fairness, and equality. Faculties can develop agenda for dialogue about moral issues in school and family discussion that can facilitate progress in becoming responsible adults.

4. Educators can reduce the odds that students will portray the work of others as being their own by preparing assignments that require higher order thinking related to issues studied in class. Students can be asked to oppose or support propositions and ideas, requiring them to engage in evaluation. They can be challenged to exhibit an ability to synthesize by preparing a list of questions that can be answered based on lessons in class and related list of questions that they are unable to answer. Scenarios can be presented for which students select and justify an answer and generate alternative solutions with their explanation.

5. School initiatives in character development should give students opportunities to discuss, consider, and apply suitable criteria for self-evaluation. Many students admit they cheat on academic work yet still consider themselves satisfied with their ethic. This contradiction suggests there is a need to revise the criteria students rely on to evaluate personal success. Although educators are reluctant to permit self-evaluation related to classroom performance, it is pertinent to promote such involvement to improve self-perception of progress toward social maturity.

6. Teachers and administrators who break the rules for administering tests so scores of their students improve are increasingly obliged to resign their position, lose certification, and have their identity revealed to the public. Educators cannot justify misconduct with claims of trying to help students perform well. With the increase in number of security breaches, some districts are employing independent test proctors or hiring organizations that monitor test fraud by erecting barriers to unauthorized access and applying web-patrolling tools that assess answer patterns that detect cheaters.

7. Encourage healthy criteria for self-evaluation so student confidence does not come from demeaning others. Social maturity should be a common goal. Help students to realize that teasing reflects an inability to accept differences between peers and us.

8. Discuss why people want to fit in and how being made fun of is harmful no matter the intention. Create a list of words students agree are not to be used in talking to each other. Provide gentle reminders about no name-calling, eye rolling, or laughing at peers.

9. Children should avoid sending impulse messages or staying online when angry. Wait until self-control and sense of calm is restored so the message is more sensibly written and excludes hostility.

10. Victims should never respond to cyberbullies, but keep messages as evidence, including text and source of information detailing the originating address of the e-mail. Whether they are read or not, bully messages should never be erased. The police, Internet service provider, or telephone company often can use the narratives for tracking purposes. Victims may notice words that are used by people they know. Most cyberbullies who post messages are not anonymous as they suppose. If a legitimate threat exists, law enforcement can subpoena records of all web users for a particular website. From there, users can be tracked to individual computers.

PART III

ADOLESCENCE (AGES 10-20)

CHAPTER 8

IDENTITY STATUS AND GOALS

Dumbledore is the school principal in *Harry Potter and the Chamber of Secrets*. His advice is to always remember, "It is our choices, Harry, that show what we truly are, far more than just our abilities" (Rowling, 1999, p. 333). Parents, teachers, and counselors who are familiar with the goals of individual students can give feedback and offer relevant advice.

The research literature about adolescent identity has not kept pace with societal change so development continues to be explained by theories proposed during the 1950s (Erikson, 1968; Havighurst, 1972). Common assumptions of these theories were that a high school diploma was enough education to prepare for a career, full-time jobs could easily be found at an early age, and girls would follow traditional gender expectations. In addition, the workforce would be mostly men, getting married would be the path chosen by nearly everyone, two-parent families would be the norm, and people could expect an average lifespan of 55 years.

The goals of this chapter are to describe factors that contribute to the identity of contemporary adolescents. These factors include recognition of generation as a culture, replacement of customary criteria for granting adult status, moving to horizontal relationships among age cohorts, respecting differences in thinking among students, encouraging personality development, fostering satisfaction at school, building friendships and dating, exploring career options, and recognizing when to amend goals.

Learning Throughout Life: An Intergenerational Perspective, pp. 167–189
Copyright © 2012 by Information Age Publishing
All rights of reproduction in any form reserved.

CONDITIONS INFLUENCE IDENTITY

Generation as Culture

The customary way of thinking about culture is no longer sufficient because it does not take into account the enormous impact of recent technology and consequent effect on social evolution. There was a time when adolescent identity was influenced more by family, ethnicity, language, nationality, and religion. Currently, because of the communications revolution, youth are often exposed to similar experiences regardless of their background. Global media supports greater influence by peers while diminishing the overall effect of adults. Teenagers are more reliant on one another for conversation, feedback, and advice (Kovarik, 2011).

All children adopt some aspects of culture they are oriented to by their relatives and caregivers. However, because growing up has become so different from one generation to the next, peers have greater influence on identity. The norms of peers are communicated and reinforced by global social networks and entertainment media. Consequently, adolescents from Atlanta, Moscow, London, Tokyo, and Sydney share more views with peers than with older relatives in their family. Adolescents resemble their times more than they resemble their parents (Underwood & Rosen, 2011).

When generation is recognized as an important factor in defining culture, the ideas and feelings of youth are seen as deserving attention. Accordingly, it is wise for adults to give up their role of advocates for youth in favor of encouraging adolescents to speak for themselves. In hierarchical-oriented societies, youth are discouraged from expressing different opinions from older relatives, educators or other authority figures. In these situations, teenagers who state ideas that conflict with adults are often viewed as lacking respect for their elders. This constraint to dialogue leads some youth to stay silent and, in turn, misleads adults to suppose a lack of opposition means there is agreement across generations (Dolgin, 2010).

A more promising outlook is to recognize that, if the voices of adolescents are heard, they may be less inclined to discount their legacy or abandon customs that might otherwise be revised and preserved. Discovering student impressions seems to be an essential requisite for uniting the goals of cultural preservation, cultural evolution, and cultural adjustment.

Criteria for Adult Status

There is agreement that a well-defined role can support a favorable sense of self. This is especially significant during adolescence when the common goal is identity, aspiring to have the status of an adult along with an individual sense of meaning, purpose, and direction. Nevertheless, permitting youth a significant role seems to be more difficult in a technological society than in previous generations. The traditional criteria for granting youth identity status are no longer appropriate. The reasons are that preparing for a career, leaving home, gaining full time work, and perhaps getting married are necessarily delayed until later than in the past. Accordingly, it is necessary to determine how identity status for adolescents can be reasonably achieved in the contemporary setting.

Adolescents rely on technology tools for conversations with friends. These same tools could be used to expand the social context that contributes to identity by interaction with adult mentors, relatives, community leaders, and persons from different subcultures (Hirsch & Hudnell, 2009). Projects to enlarge the contextual base for identity should reflect a recognition that the emerging social self can be too narrow when defined almost exclusively by peers in face-to-face or online interaction.

Robert Epstein (2007) believes adolescents and young adults are unfairly denied identity. He has described common fallacies of viewing youth as being inherently irresponsible, in need of protection from adult tasks, and incapable of making their own reasoned decisions. Epstein refers to an *artificial extension of childhood* by which teenagers are isolated from the people they are about to become and trapped in a meaningless world that is controlled by their peers and the media. Most adolescents realize they have strengths and are frustrated when adults overlook these important assets.

Because computer skills are important, those who possess them deserve status recognition, should be given responsibility, and expected to communicate with people of other ages to meet a need for societal harmony and development. This seems a more suitable strategy than to insist on no longer attainable conditions. Dependence on peers for interaction is evident from the high involvement with social network sites. Talking to peers is easier because relationships are based on equality, a condition that is less common in conversations with adults. Sharing dominance means allowing someone else to assume leadership. The most successful relationships are characterized by shared dominance rather than unilateral control based on age or gender. When people value and rely on strengths of one another, they can establish a partnership. Before public access to the Internet, before 2000, it was rare for adults to think of adolescents as a possible source for learning. Men and women should understand that, in some situations, hierarchy prevents mutually satisfying intergenerational relationships.

Generational Relationships

Figure 8.1 (A, B, and C) illustrates how cultural evolution has altered generational relationships and influenced the identity of adolescents. Figure 8.1A portrays the conditions of a past-oriented society. Trace the sphere depicting adult experience. Notice that a large portion is unfamiliar to children. This is because they have yet to encounter certain situations of adulthood. In contrast, tracing the sphere of child experience shows the adults know most of what happens at this age. The experiences generations have in common are identified as a shared sector. In a slow changing, static environment, parents are expected to socialize children by conveying to them an unchallenged impression about how to live. Children believe that their future will be a repetition of the past. When things are so predictable, so free of uncertainty, anxiety is rare. Freedom from anxiety has great appeal to people who suffer from uncertainty and exposure to stress.

Past-oriented cultures continue to exist in some parts of the world where adults remain the only source of learning for children and adolescents. Visitors to Bali, an island in Indonesia, can observe parents as they pass on woodcarving and painting techniques to children that anticipate making a living in the same way. The hands of time appear to have stopped for some aboriginal tribes in Australia and New Guinea where people are dedicated to perpetuating customs of ancestors (Peterson, 2005). Religious groups like the Amish in Ohio and Pennsylvania retain aspects of a lifestyle that is similar to their forefathers (Davidson, 2005).

Past-oriented societies do not recognize adolescence as a stage in life. Instead, they celebrate initiation rites that recognize the transformation from being a child to becoming an adult. Some of these rites may seem cruel to outsiders. However, the result is always elevation from childhood status to the assumption of rights and responsibilities of adulthood (Savage, 2007). Initiation is no longer a tradition in technological societies where young people are typically uncertain and anxious about their place in the society and have to think about achievement of identity for a longer period.

Reliance on identity rites and rituals obtain in cultures where: (a) children can reasonably expect to have a lifestyle in adulthood that closely resembles their parents, (b) specific gender roles define the division of labor in a family, (c) cultural homogeneity is in place, (d) there is a uniform structure to socialize youth, and (e) life is relatively short with everyone fulfilling predictable roles. None of these conditions is common in modern America (Campbell, 2004).

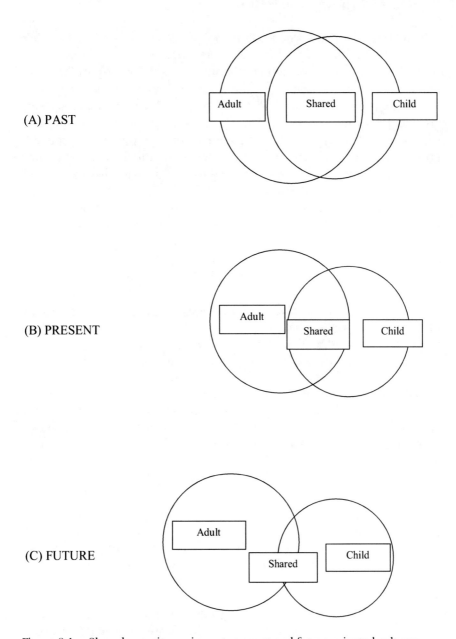

Figure 8.1. Shared experiences in past, present and future-oriented cultures.

Present and Future Orientation

Something happens when technology is introduced on a large scale and accelerates the pace of living. Social conditions change and traditional lifestyles are permanently modified. In addition, experiences that adults and children have in common diminish and produce misunderstandings. More child experiences in Figure 8.1B than in Figure 8.1A are outside the memory of adults. This is because youth are exposed to many experiences that have never happened before for people of their age group. Because adults are too old to know some things first-hand about the current youth experience, they need to learn vicariously what it is like to be growing up now (P. Strom & Strom, 2011b).

Even a casual observer of age-segregated communities recognizes that younger groups seek peers as their main listeners and advisors. Certain benefits flow from this reliance. However, the arrangement can also undermine cultural continuity because it divides the population into special interest groups. As an emphasis on the past is replaced by greater attention to the present, older adults lose their prominence and are less often seen by youth as sources of knowledge. Instead, each generation identifies with well-known persons of their age or next older group viewed as newfound models (Tapscott, 2009).

Figure 8.1C portrays the current stage of civilization with widespread reliance on the Internet, cell phones, text messages, instant messaging, e-mail, and iPads. In this era, students go to school at an earlier age and continue for a longer time. Their education features digital literacy and ease of access to knowledge that was unavailable in prior generations. Together these changes cause adolescents to acquire a different outlook. This situation urges that outdated requirements for assigning adult status like full time work and economic independence should be abandoned. Otherwise, if adolescents continue to be denied the recognition that was granted people their age in the past, the quest for identity must increasingly center on the only place recognition can be attained, in the peer culture. Learning in the social context is defined more often in terms of being influenced by others of the same age. Adolescents face similar experiences but also share immaturity and judgment that is less well developed.

The digital divide is the most profound gulf in communication between children and adults throughout history. We proposed a paradigm for guiding education and relationships to minimize the scope of the communication gulf (Strom & Strom, 2009). This imperative of teaching adolescents while learning from them is based on four assumptions:

1. Adolescents have unique experiences that qualify them as the most credible source about what going to school and growing up is like at the present time.

2. Adolescents are more competent than many adults in using the tools of technology that will be necessary for self-directed learning during the future.

3. Adolescents and adults support mutual adjustment by adopting reciprocal learning as a practice that is essential for the development of every age group.

4. The common quest of adolescents for identity as adults is attainable when their knowledge of technology is accepted as one criterion for granting status.

Thinking of Adolescents

Identity is determined in part by a student's academic standing. Setting reasonable expectations for children and adolescents requires knowing what they are capable of doing and being aware of their limitations. According to Piaget (1969), cognitive abilities emerge in a predictable sequence of stages, roughly associated with age. These stages are called preoperational (ages 2-6), concrete operations (ages 6-11), and formal operations (ages 11-adult). Preoperational refers to the thinking that precedes use of logic. The logic used by concrete operations thinkers is restricted to involvement with concrete materials and situations. Unless they have some direct experience with a specific situation or the material is intangible, concrete thinkers are usually unsuccessful in solving abstract problems. Students at the higher stage of formal operations can reach solutions without use of props, manage hypothetical situations, and manipulate abstractions. Evidence of formal operations appears between ages 11 and 15 for most students, somewhat later for others (during their 20s), and never for some (Medina, 2009). Before examining the challenge, consider some of the characteristics of formal operations thinking shown in Table 8.1.

This conclusion presents a serious challenge for secondary schools that, in the past, were less willing to provide instruction for concrete thinking students. However, dropping out is no longer a sensible option so teachers must become more effective in serving a broader range of student thinking.

Propositional thinking. Students can reason through a problem either verbally or propositionally without the presence of objects. They are not limited to concrete thinking, things they can see or feel. The emphasis is on

Table 8.1.   Thinking Abilities of Children and Adolescents*

Thinking Abilities	Achievements and Limitations
2- to 6-Year-Olds	
Language	Speech is becoming socialized
Classification	Organizes using a single factor
Perception	Judgment is based upon senses
Centration	Focuses on one aspect at a time
Egocentrism	Unaware of how others see things
6- to 11-Year-Olds	
Reversibility	Carries thought forward and backward
Logic	Solves problems in objective ways
Decentration	Attends to several events at once
Classification	Uses multiple factors in organization
Seriation	Arranges by hierarchical order
11- to 18-Year-Olds	
Propositional Thought	Able to manipulate abstract symbols
Metathinking	Critically examines someone's logic
Experimental Reasoning	Relies on testing to reach solutions
Recognizes Combinations	Imagines full range of possibilities
Understands Historical Time	Contemplates the future and past
Idealistic Egocentrism	Applies excessive self-criticism

*Adapted from J. Piaget, *Psychology of intelligence*. New York, NY: Littlefield, Adams, 1969.

learning to use symbols for other symbols, as in algebra. Student logic allows for transcending present circumstance and being able to think about future possibilities. Even propositions contrary to the fact can be treated as if they were true. Whereas formal thinkers can confront a proposition such as "Let's suppose snow is black," concrete thinkers would insist "Snow is not black, it is white." The ability to examine opposing views increases reliance on the scientific method, decreases self-centered thinking, and improves interpersonal relations (Piaget, 1970; Rescoria & Rosenthal, 2004).

Metathinking. Formal thinking teens exhibit metathinking, the process of critically examining someone else's logic instead of paying attention to only the content of their views. The benefits of metathinking are evident when someone consults with a therapist, relative or friend for assistance to monitor their thinking about specific concerns. There is a risk if teens restrict themselves to guidance from peers just because they have similar experiences. The classmates may be unable to participate in metathinking, critically examine logic of a friend or fear a loss of friendship if they seem to be critical. Teachers lack many experiences of students but their ability to monitor logic and provide feedback is applicable for most situations (Geldard & Geldard 2009).

As a rule, adolescents initially acquiring a capacity for metathinking are inclined to practice the skill by arguing about almost everything. This is seen by their effort to detect the weakness of logic that adults use at home or in school. Seventh and eighth graders want to confront any school policies they consider unfair. It is a delight to catch teachers or parents in faulty propositions that can be turned against them. Some parents are disappointed by the transformation of their children from passively accepting ideas to challenging how authorities see things (Nisbett, 2009). A more accurate interpretation is the student has reached formal operations and deserves encouragement for independent thinking.

Experimental reasoning. The ability to use experimental reasoning is a powerful asset. This enables students to go beyond personal observation as a basis for reaching conclusions. New information can be deduced from a set of data by testing it. In biology, chemistry, and physics students show the ability to form hypotheses, test variables, and determine probable consequences. Their breadth of reasoning includes factual relationships as well as understanding the logical relationships that might exist. The result is increased potential for solving personal and group problems.

Conceptualizing combinations. Formal thinkers differ in the way that they conceptualize combinations. Here it is important to recognize that the reasoning of concrete level thinkers is limited to the realm of their direct experience or what they prefer to call reality. In contrast, reasoning of formal thinkers is not limited to personal experience. In addition to reality, they can also consider potentiality, conditions that do not yet exist but might in the future (Kamphaus & Frick, 2006).

For example, students are told to assume that all animals can be classified into these groups: those that live on land (terrestrial), others that live in the water (aquatic), those with backbones (vertebrates), and those that lack backbones (invertebrates). When asked to identify all of the possible combinations of animal life on a newly discovered planet, the concrete thinkers identify four possibilities: vertebrates that live on land; vertebrates that live in the water; invertebrates that live in water; and invertebrates that live on land. However, these are not the only possible life forms according to formal thinkers. They realize there might be no animals at all or a planet may have just aquatic vertebrates and so forth.

Understanding historical time. During elementary and middle school, students rank social studies near the bottom of their list of preferred subjects (Privateer, 2006). When they get to high school and begin formal thinking, some students start to comprehend historical time. The distant past assumes meaning, possible futures are contemplated, life in other cultures can be understood, and history is regarded as an interesting subject rather than boring (Tally & Goldenberg, 2005).

Students may function at formal thinking in some subjects and not others. Tom's spatial intelligence allows him to be a formal thinker in three-dimensional drawing for advanced art class but not function at formal level in mathematics.

Idealistic egocentrism. Because formal operations thinkers can look ahead and identify possibilities, they are sometimes frustrated when comparing the world as it could be with the existing inequitable conditions. Idealistic adolescents yearn for a better world and contend it is attainable if adults would do certain things to produce the necessary change. This perspective generates conflict with adults who do not think at formal operations level and are therefore present-oriented. Such persons consider idealistic teenagers to be dreamers and recommend becoming realistic by looking at the world in realistic ways (Alexander, 2005).

Adolescents who have reached formal operations thinking often direct their newfound ability for criticism and judgment to themselves. As a rule, the standards they set for their behavior are too high. This causes them to feel unsuccessful at the same time friends and relatives believe they perform well. Excessive self-criticism comes from an egocentric assumption that personal faults are observed by everyone. The *imaginary audience* is a phenomenon that leads people to believe their limitations are the object of attention. Consider a high school cheerleader that detects a pimple on her chin before performing on the football field. Moments later, in the routines in front of fans, she supposes all of them are looking at her pimple. Adults should know adolescents are more defensive than people of older ages in processing criticism (Wormeli, 2006). The emergence of introspection in adolescence should be linked with development of self-evaluation skills. Parents and teachers can help by suggesting reasonable criteria for self-evaluation to preserve confidence and lessen peer dependence.

The proportion of formal thinkers during adolescence might increase if schools incorporate more streaming video, provide DVDs that repeat steps of problem solving in mathematics that students can check out of the library and bring home to repeat as needed, graphic organizers, visuals keyed to match verbal lessons, and Internet applications as contexts for skill practice. In addition to providing new tools to support formal thinking, educators should assume the task of devising technology assessments that fit the current schooling context.

GOAL SETTING FOR STUDENTS

Personality Goals

Parents and teachers realize that goal setting is an important component of identity and wonder how they can provide opportunities in this
context without sacrifice to academic success. Children cannot be allowed
to select subjects they study at school. However, students could be encouraged to choose personality goals before they make decisions about selection of occupational goals. This sequence of setting personality goals first
and then career goals later invites students to initially focus on the kind of
person they want to become, the way they want to act, and the kind of
influence they hope to have on others. These aspects of maturing can be
observed well before there is evidence about the kind of occupation a student might someday be qualified to perform. When adults encourage
children to establish personality goals and the values they reflect, the
importance of achievement in the social context will be better understood.

Major problems of getting along with others shown by abuse, divorce,
crime, racism, and being fired more often relate to poor emotional health
and immature behavior than to lack of proficiency in academic subjects.
Reading, writing, and mathematics are essential skills; they also seem to
be the easiest lessons for most people to learn. In addition, the education
that adolescents need should equip them to cope with unforeseen adversity by developing hardiness that contributes to resilience (Ginsburg,
2011).

Parents need to think about the future and realize the real goal is raising their children to be successful at 40 years of age. It is less about immediate smiles or good grades and more about bringing up emotionally and
socially intelligent people with an ability to recover from disappointment
and still forge ahead throughout life. Resilience is about confronting significant stressors that children encounter for academic performance,
achievement standards, media messages, peer pressure, and family tension (Ginsburg, 2011).

Some goals students might want to consider are in Table 8.2. These
collective personality goals suggest that relatives should not excuse themselves from teaching with claims that the curriculum at school has
changed so much they are unable to help or they lack formal education
needed to assist with home work. The interpersonal skills on the personality goals list can improve personal success no matter what occupation a
student may choose to pursue.

Individually chosen personality goals are a more appropriate long-
term focus for self-evaluation than for academic subjects. Personality is

**Table 8.2.   Personality Goals and Achievement for
Consideration by Adolescents**

Goals for Individual Consideration	Achievement Perceived by Parents	Achievement Perceived by Self
• Get along with classmates		
• Treat people around me fairly		
• Show a willingness to help others		
• Look at the bright side of things		
• Make time for what is important		
• Develop a healthy sense of humor		
• Make feelings known to relatives		
• Learn to become a better listener		
• Settle arguments in a peaceful way		
• Ask questions if I don't understand		
• No unkind statements about others		
• Keep trying as things get difficult		
• Ask for help when it is needed		
• Be patient in dealing with others		
• Be a person who others can rely on		
• Keep mind and body healthy		
• Reflect on behavior to improve self		
• Seek and accept criticism of others		
• Have self-control and self-discipline		
• Being a self-directed person		

the key to identity, the way we perceive ourselves and how others see us. Personality and identity are connected because both are lifelong concerns while having a job is not. Uniting family and school support for personality development conveys the message that social and emotional development require attention and will be recognized along with mental achievement.

When adults identify attributes they want to be remembered for by family and friends, they usually mention nonintellectual qualities that endear people to one another. These qualities can become more common when they are chosen as goals. The example that adults set is important. They can acknowledge their shortcomings to younger relatives, describe plans they have for improvement, and ask for feedback as a valued source of observation to help them gauge their progress. This means that, besides helping teenagers establish short-term and long-term goals, wise adults review their own goals and make them known to their family. Everyone should strive to improve their personality for as long as they live.

Some goals from Table 8.2 are elaborated here as reminders of how important they can be in preparing children for the challenges of growing up.

- *Get along with classmates.* A 14-year old granddaughter of an 82-year old African-American told her, "Grandma Flora, I want to be just like you when I grow up." Flora replied, "Why? I have so little in the way of material things and did not make much of myself." Her granddaughter said, "Grandma, you have more friends than anyone I know." What a nice compliment.

- *Treat people around me fairly.* Society is struggling to get this right; it is an important lesson to learn and a difficult one to teach.

- *Show a willingness to help others.* This is what growing up and maturity are all about, moving away from being self-centered in favor of showing concern for the welfare of others.

- *Look at the bright side of things.* Every problem is not a crisis that is unfair. Look at possibilities in other people and situations. Few things are worse for adolescents than to be around cynical adults who cause them to lose hope for the future.

- *Make time for what is important.* Setting priorities in life is a vital lesson that usually comes with growing older, discovering what really matters most. This lesson could be learned much earlier in life. Many parents do not devote enough time to being with their family and children suffer because of it.

- *Develop a healthy sense of humor.* As people mature, they discover that laughing at them is a way to support mental health.

- *Settle arguments in a peaceful way.* Many youth are not learning this lesson and parents should not expect teachers to be the only instruction source.

- *Avoid making unkind statements about others.* Teenagers report that they learn values from relatives indirectly by how they respond to characters on television, and how they react to stories about neighbors or people in the news.

- *Be patient in dealing with others.* Impatience is becoming more common and generally undermines relationships.

- *Be a person others can rely on.* This is one of the greatest accomplishments a person can achieve.

- *Become a self-directed person.* Show the capability of making independent decisions and pursuing a direction without external control.

Mary Ann Marian (1819-1880) was a 19th century English writer. She thought that people of her era underestimated women by supposing they were only capable of writing stories about romance. She wanted her work to be taken seriously as if written by a man. She wrote using the male pen name of George Eliot. Her observations about optional pathways to self-improvement were widely recognized for her classic book titled *Silas Marner* (1861/2005). Marian suggested, "It is never too late to be who you might have been." There is still time, no matter what our age, to set more mature goals and, in the pursuit of them, be someone with a more favorable influence. During a workshop on improving how success is defined, one man shared his observation, "All my life I said I wanted to be someone; now I can see I should have been more specific."

Some parents tell their children, "This is America, and you can become whatever you want to be." Perhaps they should also say, "You can be the kind of person you want to be, and we will help." Adults should encourage children to identify additional goals to place on Table 8.2. Some additional goals children have chosen are: defending rights of others, showing greater empathy, assuming more responsibility, become willing to compromise, and strive to demonstrate integrity. Monitoring the child's achievement of personality gains is a task that requires respectful parent observation and feedback.

Some current indicators of adolescent success are trophies, certificates, high grades, and competitive test scores. These are signs of growth but reflect a narrow definition of achievement. In addition, social skills are needed, such as adaptability, flexibility, and collaboration.

Satisfaction at School

Some goals students are expected to attain are chosen for them by educators. School presents students with two cultures, an instrumental culture and an expressive culture. The instrumental culture is made up of the academic requirements everyone must meet to graduate. Instrumental goals are related to mathematics, science, and English. These subjects are mandatory because they contribute to the skills, knowledge, and values stated as purposes for schooling. Students participate in the instrumental culture to attain desired satisfactions in the future like getting a diploma, being admitted to a college, and finding a job (Jennings & Likis, 2005).

The expressive culture at school includes activities students participate in for the pleasure of involvement (Mahoney, Larson, & Eccles, 2005).

Art, drama, music, and athletics are aspects of the expressive curriculum. Although being engaged in the expressive culture increases knowledge and skills, this outcome is not considered as important as in the instrumental culture where everyone must pass state examinations in mathematics, reading, and science. Many students enjoy singing in a choir, working with clay in art, helping with a theatrical performance or playing volleyball. The criterion for success in the expressive culture depends more on how much a person enjoys participation than how well s/he performs.

Sometimes the instrumental culture has an expressive impact such as when a student enjoys science experiments, reading novels or doing algebra. Similarly, there can be an instrumental outcome in expressive activities when students gain considerable skill and knowledge regarding art, music, and drama. However, students distinguish between expressive and instrumental cultures. Because most students find satisfaction in the expressive culture, competition is deliberately minimized in this context making it the most viable venue in which to teach values like appreciation for learning, commitment to individual growth, and valuing participation. Parents are easily involved in the expressive culture.

The motivation to stay in most situations usually depends on satisfaction. People will endure disappointment if satisfaction remains a part of their overall experience. This means that some experiences in school must be satisfying so students are motivated to stay and graduate rather than withdraw and drop out. Various combinations of satisfaction with instrumental and expressive cultures can sustain involvement or motivate withdrawal. Table 8.3 shows that a high level of satisfaction in both cultures defines academic achievers who also feel good about extracurricular activities. A high instrumental and low expressive combination portrays someone who gains satisfaction from results of academic tests but does not care about extracurricular activities. A low instrumental and high expressive combination identifies those who have mediocre test scores but feel satisfaction from the extracurricular activities. Such a person has difficulty in mathematics or English but shines on the basketball court or football field. In this situation, the single incentive to stay in school is the pleasure and favorable self-impression from being involved with athletics, band, or drama (Rathvon, 2008).

Some students do not find satisfaction in the expressive or instrumental culture. They dislike required courses and refuse expressive opportunities. They consider school to be a place of disappointment so they want to quit as soon as permissible. Feelings of alienation motivate them to withdraw and hope they can find satisfaction in some other environment. Schools must discover better ways to appeal to these students so that they can find

Table 8.3.   Level of Student Satisfaction With the Instrumental and Expressive Cultures at School

Culture and Satisfaction	Example of Student Reported Experience
High Expressive High Instrumental	Renaldo enjoys the math courses he has taken and wants to become an engineer. He also likes playing trumpet in the school marching band.
Low Expressive High Instrumental	Melinda likes the curriculum and has a part time job. Her busy schedule means that there is no time left to participate in extracurricular activities.
High Expressive Low Instrumental	Jason is 6 feet, 8 inches tall, lives for basketball, and is the top scorer for the conference. He struggles with required subjects but is grateful to get tutoring.
Low Expressive Low Instrumental	Avery does not like school and feels that his classmates look down on him. His friends left before graduating, and he thinks this would be the best choice for him too.

satisfaction within the institution and prepare for the future (Goldstein & Brooks, 2012).

Unlike dropout prevention programs or remedial education to overcome academic deficits, extracurricular activities can support adjustment to school demands by promoting individual interests and satisfaction. Creative use of the expressive culture can make school a place of greater satisfaction for more students and improve their results in the instrumental culture. This was shown at a junior high school in Harlem, New York. Black and Puerto Rican students were involved. The top half of the 1,400 students were chosen for a Higher Horizons Project (Morrisey & Werner-Wilson, 2005). These students typically scored 2 years below grade level for reading and mathematics. The principal told them,

> We realize most of you don't like mathematics or reading but it does not change the fact that these skills are important for your future. However, instead of increasing the time that you spend on these subjects by cutting back on other curriculum like art, music, and physical education, we plan to take the opposite approach.

So, motivating influences from the expressive culture were introduced to increase satisfaction and motivation to learn. Students were taken to sporting events, concerts, and movies. They visited parks and museums, went on sightseeing trips while also continuing exposure to instrumental subjects.

Follow-up studies found that project members who went on to senior high school graduated in substantially greater numbers than those in the same junior high during pre-project years. Then too, 168 graduates advanced to attend higher education, compared with 47 in three classes preceding the experiment. It seems that expressive activities offered enough satisfaction to motivate students to stay in school instead of leaving. Effects included higher instrumental performance (Morrisey & Werner-Wilson, 2005). This is why middle and high schools devote considerable attention at the beginning of the year to encouraging involvement with extracurricular activities and after school programs. A lack of involvement with the expressive culture renders some students less able to deal with daily pressures and more vulnerable to stress (Christie, Jolivette, & Nelson, 2005).

Friendships and Dating

Adolescents see friendships and dating as important factors that support or diminish identity. Friendships are based on mutual trust and affection. An ability to make friends is needed for socialization. Dating, to go out with someone as a social partner, provides practice in development of friendships and explores romantic connections. By age 16, many adolescents interact more with a romantic partner than with parents or friends. Cyber dating, online exploration of romantic relations, is increasing (Fohee & Langwick, 2010).

Some students do not learn to build friendships because parents ignore the sequence of attitudes and knowledge needed to achieve this purpose. The orientation about dating provided by the family should include an emphasis on equality, mutual respect, and consideration of the dating partner goals. Instead, quite often parent fears about sexual experimentation and pregnancy motivate them to skip lessons on friendship building in favor of talking about premature sexual involvement and condoms. Concerns of parents are reinforced by health reports that each year approximately three million teenagers are diagnosed with a sexually transmitted disease (STD) and one million adolescent girls get pregnant. Parents are also frustrated by intimacy scenes on television, situations in which couples become sexually involved quickly after they meet for the first time. The fear is that teenagers will conclude that speeded up involvement is an acceptable practice and an expectation for dating (Pierce, 2011).

Sexual harassment is unwanted sex-related advances toward someone. Improper touching or suggestive comments are examples of harassment. Most schools have sexual harassment policies but few provide curriculum to address the issue. In addition, communities should increase their after school, no-cost places where students can hang out, talk, play games, dance or engage in adult led discussions regarding healthy relationships and day-to-day worries. Most of the after-school programs are too competitive and gender-segregated. Teens benefit from opportunities to practice being with and feeling comfortable talking to the other gender. There is a need for more diverse programs after school on campus or at community centers.

Dating abuse is when someone resorts to a pattern of violent behavior by means of verbal, physical, or sexual intimidation to gain power and control of a partner. Some boys suppose it is cool to call girlfriends bad names or mistreat them in the presence of guys they want to impress. Such put-downs make further mistreatment of girls easier to justify (Strauss, 2011). It seems many boys get conflicting and harmful messages about what constitutes "being a man" and need better advice on how to treat girls (Kindlon, 2006; Sax, 2005).

Some education about dating should take place at school where there can be guided discussions with classmates. There is a need to understand that roles like driving a car, going to school, playing on a team, and dating all involve rights and responsibilities. The state of Washington provides a guide on student dating rights and responsibilities which could be posted on campus and the school website (Washington State Office of the Attorney General, 2012).

Most teenagers have questions about dating and want to avoid abuse. For example, "I thought my boyfriend must really love me when he started to call me a lot on my cell phone. Now he wants to know where I am all the time. Is this normal behavior?" No, he is possessive. Someone is possessive when they treat another person like one of his or her belongings. A possessive person does not want a partner to share time or attention with anyone else. The control attitude is evident when one person insists on making all decisions while the dominated person's view is ignored. Often a controlling person tells the partner how to dress, who to talk to, where to go and what they cannot do. Frequent calling or texting on the cell is a way to maintain control, keeping tabs on her activities and whereabouts. Some boys monitor the chat room and e-mail activities of their girlfriend. If a girl finds herself in this predicament, she should seek advice from a teacher, parent, or other trusted adult (Fohee & Langwick, 2010).

Career Exploration

Many adolescents express anxiety about their future occupational identity (Fitzpatrick & Costantini, 2011). A valuable innovation for all secondary schools would be to create a new position called Director of Career Education. This person would be responsible to arrange biweekly evening presentations. Professional and technical and trade workers could be invited to share insights about specific jobs, make known the length and type of training required, expected rate of pay, and report satisfactions as well as disadvantages of the position. During these meetings, students can express personal goals and get feedback on whether their expectations match reality of experiences of employees in that field (Johnson, Duffett, & Ott, 2005). The questions in Table 8.4 serve as a guide for presenters, students, and parents.

Three hundred middle-school students completed an online poll on career exploration (Whitten, 2011). They identified parents and other relatives (78%) as preferred sources for their conversations regarding work. When asked about the steps they had already taken on their own to explore possibilities, the most common response was web searching focusing on job requirements (55%). Given this response, it seems sensible for counselors in

Table 8.4. Career Exploration Agenda for Adolescents

Questions for Discussion	*Considerations*
1. How long will it take me to prepare for this occupation?	Time and money are important factors.
2. Am I informed about requirements to reach this career goal?	Know the necessary steps.
3. Would I enjoy the tasks involved with this career?	Awareness of satisfying and disappointing aspects is crucial.
4. What are my reasons for wanting this job?	Personal motivation should be clear.
5. Do my goals include intellectual, social, and emotional growth?	Balance is a key to personal success.
6. Is this goal being pursued for myself or for other people?	Believe in your own sense of direction.
7. What do trusted adults see as benefits and drawbacks of my career goals?	Weigh the judgments of others.
8. Does this career provide opportunities for advancement?	Explore promotion possibilities.
9. Will this job offer the income needed for my desired lifestyle?	Calculate the match.
10. What resources will I need to achieve this goal?	Search for information online and in the community.
11. Is this a realistic and attainable career goal?	Seek feedback about your capabilities.
12. What are the differences between my original career goal and the amended goal?	Be specific and understand your reasons for change.
13. Am I aware of the stresses and demands related to this career?	Think about necessary adjustments.
14. How can achieving this goal affect my happiness?	Discuss it with people in the field.

a school district to collaborate in formulating a list of websites for students to visit, augmented by explanations about unique benefits of particular sites. For students who are not self-starters, access to these kinds of resources could be the key to motivating their search process and dialogue with parents.

Almost all of the students, 96%, reported that they often think about their career. Doubt, anxiety, and worry, were commonly expressed about occupations. Many students believe that society is changing so fast they wonder whether the jobs they prepare for will be available when they graduate. Some students, 39%, stated they know the job they want. The 61% who have yet to choose should be informed that indecision is normal during high school and reflects the need for further exploration. Living with ambiguity and uncertainty is difficult and often produces unpleasant stress. Students should know that their desire to be certain should not preclude finding the best career that might take longer than expected (Whitten, 2011).

While 53% of students reported a college degree is needed for the job they want, only 5% saw vocational or trade school as suitable training for them. These reactions suggest that visits to explore educational opportunities should include trade schools and vocational training sites along with tours of colleges.

In the Whitten (2011) study, 47% of the students observed that the jobs they prefer will require extensive education. During the career nights in middle school, higher education recruitment officers should be invited to discuss tuition and conditions associated with student loans. This is a concern for youngsters who do not want to burden parents about paying for an education when they do not have a definite job goal. In fact, half of students in the upper half of their high school graduating class across the nation choose to not attend college because of debt concerns (Fitzpatrick & Costantini, 2011).

Goal Amendment

The need to amend goals is overlooked as an aspect of decision-making and planning. Steven, age 14, informed his parents the occupation he wanted to pursue was to be a commercial airline pilot. The family had conversations identifying the appealing features of this occupation including satisfactions of flight, promising economic future, chances to visit new places, and responsibility for ensuring that passengers reach their destinations safely. Then Steve found a newspaper advertisement about flying lessons. The price was $500 for 20 lessons that included solo flights and landing experience needed to get the basic licensure to operate a small aircraft. The parents agreed that taking lessons would enable Steve to understand what is expected of aviators and figure out if this line of work would be satisfying for him.

Because Steve was not old enough to have a license for driving the car, his dad brought him to the airport for each lesson. After finishing the second lesson, Steve returned to the lounge where his father was reading. Steve looked pale but he said nothing. The same sickly appearance was evident after the third and fourth lessons. Then, on Thursday, the day before lesson five, Steve said, "My lessons are not turning out as I supposed. Flying a plane is easier than I thought but each time we go up, I get sick to my stomach. At first I thought it was caused by something I ate before the lesson but it happens every time."

Further conversation revealed that Steve wanted to end his lessons. But, he said, "I know you spent a lot of money to give me this chance so I will keep going if you want me too." The father said,

> No, the tentative goal you had to become a pilot is no longer appealing. The money was well spent because the result showed that flying is not the right occupation for you. Finding that out is good because otherwise you might have continued to suppose the life of a pilot had greater promise than is the case. Many adults dislike the career choice they made and wish it were possible to change. Fortunately, you can amend the goal to be a pilot and consider other careers.

In every aspect of life goals should be altered when they cannot be attained or become less appealing as awareness of other possibilities emerge.

The processes to enable amendment of goals should be understood. This issue is becoming more important with increasing exposure to overchoice. Wise amendment of goals is necessary for adjustment to previously unrecognized requirements, underestimated difficulties, and opportunities that may have been overlooked in other sectors of the workplace. The following questions can help adolescents reflect on whether to amend goals.

1. Have I written my goals so they are specific and could be conveyed to a confidante? It is difficult for relatives or friends to provide feedback about ambiguous goals.

2. Have I set goals in all significant areas of life including mental, social, emotional, physical, spiritual, career and family? When goals are too narrow, growth is limited in a corresponding way.

3. How long will it take to achieve each goal I have on my list? Unless a reasonable time limit is assigned, it is hard to know when to amend particular aspirations.

4. What are my reasons for pursuing these goals? Writing down pros and cons for each goal encourages reflective thinking. Sometimes

goals cannot be attained and failure should be acknowledged. Then, it becomes necessary to amend goals and commit to achieving the revised purpose.

SUMMARY AND IMPLICATIONS

Society can influence important aspects of identity during adolescence.

1.   New criteria that reflect student ability should be used to assign adult status.
2.   Youth should be urged to choose personality goals in defining achievement.
3.   A sense of satisfaction at school can motivate learning and promote health.
4.   Expectations for students should respect individual levels of mental ability.
5.   Knowing how to build friendships and dating confirm personal importance.
6.   Career exploration motivates realistic goals leading to future work identity.

APPLICATIONS FOR TEACHING

1.   The identity status of adolescents has changed because of the need for extended education. Still, for the first time, students know more than some teachers about digital tools on which future learning depends. Teachers can support the identity of adolescents by recognizing their technology skills and assigning tasks allowing them to further develop these assets.
2.   Society seeks change when it promotes growth, health, and productivity. There is also a desire to retain important aspects of heritage. The goals of cultural preservation and cultural evolution are compatible but necessitate reciprocal learning among the generations. Benjamin Franklin's advice remains timely, "When you're finished changing, you're finished."
3.   Students should be encouraged to pursue personality development, an essential aspect of mature identity attained in adulthood. Appearances may be difficult to change but the kind of person someone aspires to become is a matter of choice that can begin early in life and should be recognized as a context of achievement. Teachers and parents need to know that personality goals is the

realm where they have the greatest opportunity to be seen as models by adolescents.

4. The community should urge involvement in extracurricular activities by supporting expressive as well as instrumental aspects of schooling. This social context builds connections with others who have similar interests. Participation in the expressive culture can result in greater satisfaction at school, lower rates of dropout, and foster healthy adjustment to offset disappointment that occurs in other sectors of life. These benefits are reinforced by evidence that expressive involvement can support coping with pressures, make students less susceptible to stress, and better able to choose appropriate models for relief.

5. Friendship and dating are issues that influence adolescent identity. In many homes parent worry about the potential of early sexual involvement leads them to overlook lessons they should teach on healthy relationships. One result is that the incidence of dating violence is greater than usually supposed. Boys and girls are frustrated by not having opportunities for chances for friendly conversations with members of the other gender. Some discussions on dating can occur in classrooms. All students should know dating rights and responsibilities and recognize where they can turn if abused and be able to refer someone else who is mistreated.

6. Students have more career choices than previous generations and need guided experiences with processes for amending tentative goals. Learning to revise aspirations is usually overlooked as an aspect of decision making that allows a person to figure out when a change in direction is warranted. Teachers should avoid recommending that students persist when what a student may need is more exploration to identify appropriate career goals.

7. Lessons in middle school and high school should be augmented by visual formats that enable concrete thinkers to gain understanding and skills expected of the entire class. There should be an opportunity for students to checkout DVDs from the school library about mathematics and science lessons. DVDs can allow a student repeated exposure to the step-by-step process that does not recur in a classroom where teachers present it only once.

8. Instructional planning should include a balance of direct instruction along with active learning that has greater appeal to most students. This strategy can stimulate motivation, contribute to acquisition of teamwork skills, encourage higher order thinking, and prevent boredom.

CHAPTER 9

TEAM SKILLS FOR
SCHOOL AND WORK

Teachers in middle school and high school can help students acquire
teamwork attitudes and skills by arranging participation in cooperative
learning. This instructional strategy provides opportunities to work with
classmates in small groups while studying the content of a course (Gillies,
2007). Besides learning the curriculum, students get to practice the teamwork skills expected in the work place. There is an understanding that
each team member will contribute something to their team product or
provide insights that could not be attained without extra effort of individuals. The goals of this chapter are to describe origins of interdependence
theory, discuss elements of cooperative learning and its benefits, and
examine challenges of integrating disabled and regular students in the
classroom. The methods that employees use to evaluate one another are
compared with how students are evaluated at school. A rationale is presented for the consideration of a business model and suitable evaluation
tools so students can be well prepared for how things are done at work.

SOCIAL INTERDEPENDENCE THEORY

The theoretical origins of cooperative learning began with Morton
Deutsch (1949a, 1949b) from Columbia University. He informed students
in one of his classes that their course grade would depend on the quality

Learning Throughout Life: An Intergenerational Perspective, pp. 191–218
Copyright © 2012 by Information Age Publishing
All rights of reproduction in any form reserved.

of their discussions. Each student would receive the same grade as teammates reflecting how well they performed as a group. The social interdependence arrangement meant that everyone would have to rely on one another; this was the cooperative situation. Another class, composed of students with similar backgrounds as the first group, was told that grades would be based on performance of individuals in comparison with classmates; this was the competitive situation. Deutsch found that students assigned to the interdependent cooperative situation developed better products and expressed greater satisfaction with their experience than peers in a competitive setting. The cooperative groups generated more and better ideas in discussions, communicated more effectively by considering comments of teammates, liked one another better, and tried to motivate colleagues. In contrast, students from the competitive group tried to dominate or overshadow one another. Results favored the interdependent cooperative situation (Deutsch, 2002).

Building on the findings of Morton Deutsch, Muzafer Sherif (1958) at the University of Oklahoma, discovered that cohesiveness of groups increase if cooperation is required. He randomly placed 22 fifth-grade boys in two groups called the Rattlers and Eagles. They engaged in competitive games of baseball, football, and tug of war at a summer camp. Initially the groups were good sports but soon grew hostile, accusing others of cheating, resorted to put-down statements, and refused interaction. In an attempt to solve the conflict, groups were placed in situations that necessitated cooperation. For example, Sherif deliberately broke the water line that supplied the camp. Then he told all the boys about the problem with the water supply. The Rattlers and Eagles searched for the problem and, after a lengthy collaboration period, found and fixed it. When the boys had to unite, hostility was temporarily set aside. After arranging other cooperative activities, friendships began to emerge between the Eagles and Rattlers. Sherif (1966) replicated the experiment several times with similar results, confirming the importance of interdependence.

Benefits of Cooperative Learning

Cooperative learning can produce numerous benefits when conducted effectively. Some of the observed social-emotional findings include: (a) frequent involvement with peer tutoring, (b) more careful listening to how others see things, (c) encouraging and noting the contributions of teammates, (d) avoiding put-downs or placing blame on others, (e) greater willingness to accept compromise as a way to handle differences of opinion, (f) enhanced sense of belonging, (g) broader perspective, (h) greater willingness to try new and difficult tasks, (i) and increased expression of optimism and hope regarding group success. Cooperative learning research has typically found improvement in academic performance. Students show greater problem solving abilities, more favorable attitudes toward school, added appreciation of cultural and racial diversity, better understanding about principles of democracy, closer relations with classmates, and lower incidence of discipline problems (Forest & Balcetis, 2008).

Social Relations and Achievement

Since Deutsch (1949a, 1949b) carried out his experiments, cooperative learning has been the focus of many studies to find out how social relationships impact student behavior and achievement. The collective findings were summarized in a meta-analysis of 148 studies comparing the relative effectiveness of using cooperative, competitive, and individualistic goal structures (Roseth, Johnson, & Johnson, 2008). These studies included 17,000 students, ages 12-15, from 11 countries. As predicted by social interdependence theory, students from the classrooms with cooperative learning goals where teams worked together were more accurate on test outcomes, and earned higher problem solving scores on reasoning and critical thinking tasks compared to classes in which the focus was on competitive or individualistic learning. In cooperative settings, students felt a greater sense of support from and connection with peers. Some of the implications are that if teachers arrange instruction in a cooperative way, academic gain and social development goals can be promoted simultaneously while the student goals for interaction are also met.

Elements of Cooperative Learning

Five cooperative learning elements are identified by Johnson and Johnson (2003).

Element 1. Positive interdependence among teammates. Teachers can support social interdependence by structuring goals that can only be attained when students function as a team. These shared and mutually understood goals require each member to use whatever resources are necessary to fulfill particular tasks assigned by a team. The interdependence emphasis is on "we" instead of "me." Students that are more talented or assertive are not allowed to dominate the group. Teammates are responsible for their own learning as well as helping peers with tutoring and encouragement. Everyone sinks or swims together since the team product depends on collective performance rather than individual performance. The way to facilitate group success is to design a task that is complex enough to warrant the efforts of a small group, include activities that allow diverse ideas from the perspective of different people or to have limited access to task resources or roles.

Element 2. Face-to-face promotive interaction. Discussion and group consensus can ensure that everyone understands how each task assigned or chosen contributes to the purpose of their team rather than representing independent efforts of individuals that are combined at the end. Peers are encouraged to ask questions and express confusion or doubt. Lessons are reviewed together to improve the comprehension of everyone. Put-downs are unacceptable reactions to frustration with performance of their team.

Element 3. Individual and group accountability. Monitoring progress as well as achievement is essential for productivity. Each member must be responsible for quality work and to help others. The assets of individuals should be used without limiting them to just the particular tasks they perform well. Some students ignore obligation, assuming conscientious peers will do their work for them to avoid failure of the team. An important aspect of accountability is that slackers are not excused nor credited when they do not perform their share of a workload. A single performance standard is relied on with each individual receiving peer feedback.

Element 4. Team and interpersonal skills. These can be accomplished with each student taking a different role or task that supports group goals. In addition, this element helps students be accountable to demonstrate team skills, to help peers learn and to do their fair share of work. Teachers should identify and define teamwork skills everyone is expected to practice and attain. Discussions and reading can be used to ensure there is common understanding of why designated skills are relevant to everyone's occupational future. Besides prescribing the team skills, teachers have to make assignments that encourage and facilitate learning. Group procedure departs from the tradition of a single leader in favor of shared leadership so all teammates get to try this role.

Element 5. Group processing of performance. Teachers agree this element of cooperative learning is the most difficult to manage. The reason is because teacher judgment about quality of team products is only one aspect of appropriate assessment. There is a need to also obtain the observation of students regarding how each member performed teamwork skills. Including the views of students to credit individuals for their team contributions and detect further growth needs requires teacher trust that providing practice in peer and self-assessment can be accurate, fair, and helpful.

EXPANDING EDUCATIONAL OPPORTUNITY

Cooperative learning is a common practice among middle schools, high schools and colleges because favorable results of this approach are well documented. Access to this instructional strategy requires a willingness by faculty to acknowledge students as potential learning sources for peers and arrange for conditions of interaction and evaluation similar to those that can be expected when students enter the workplace.

Collaboration and Unlearning

In *Revolutionary Wealth,* Toffler and Toffer (2006) proposed, "The illiterate of the 21st century will not be those who cannot read or write, but those who cannot learn, unlearn, and relearn." When new ways of doing things become necessary, the greatest challenge can be unlearning. This phenomenon presents concerns for education at every grade level. Unlearning is defined as a willful activity to discard strong habits of mind that require change in order to adjust. In some cases, unlearning can be more difficult than new learning and people often fail as they try to leave behind customary forms of response. Table 9.1 considers some behaviors that people must unlearn to perform well in interdependent teams.

Disabilities and Integration

During adolescence, it is usual to form cliques with classmates that share similar interests. This practice can inadvertently lead to exclusion of classmates, most often those with disabilities. Public reaction to students with disabilities has varied through history. During certain periods, they were seen as enemies, disliked, imprisoned, and even killed. In more modern times, the common response has been to segregate them (Smart, 2011). Fortunately, great improvements have occurred in the past generation based on a realization that persons with disabilities are neither helpless nor hopeless but require some assistance to develop their talents (Burns, 2007).

This perspective is reinforced by government regulations for employment, access to buildings, and education opportunities as well as powerful influence of the positive psychology movement applied to the preparation of professionals. The anticipation that disabled students can be productive contributing members of society is shared by teachers, parents, employers, and the disabled. The transformation of potential to achievement is facilitated when regular teachers and special educators collaborate, family and school are united, appropriate standards of conduct in

Table 9.1.   Student Behaviors to Unlearn for Transition to Collaborative Teamwork

Traditional Behaviors	Collaborative Behaviors
1. Limit reading to content assigned by teachers.	Self-directedness means searching for materials without being told by the teacher.
2. Passive listening without curiosity.	Asking questions should become a norm for everyone in an information-oriented society.
3. Not questioning the views of authorities.	Critical thinking involves examination of logic for school policies, practices, and rules.
4. Define education as in the classroom only.	Growing year round, after graduation, while at work, in retirement, and until life ends.
5. Leader and follower roles for group work.	Differentiated roles are assigned and knowledge merged to increase learning.
6. Teachers are the main source of knowledge.	Students are accountable to share insights and knowledge with teammates.
7. Overreliance on use of textbooks for learning.	Textbook is augmented by electronic sources, teammates, and community input.
8. Defensiveness when criticized by others.	Students learn to constructively process criticism to identify their needs for growth.
9. Dependence upon extrinsic evaluation.	Students evaluate themselves and remain motivated without feedback of others.
10. Gratuitous evaluation of performance for friends.	Students evaluate teammates in an authentic way as expected in the workplace.
11. Ignoring the intended focus of a discussion.	Focus on pertinent issues and good time management reflects student accountability.
12. Individual domination during discussions.	Learn to limit length and frequency of comments so that everyone can be heard.
13. Team suppression of divergent thinking.	Peer encouragement of creative ideas is a necessary condition for group productivity.
14. Inattention and distraction undermine discussions.	Concentrate on agenda, determine implications, and solutions.
15. Uninformed opinions are focus of discussions.	Cite credible references to support personal opinions during discussions.

class are applied, and instruction strategies enable the students with disabilities to integrate with nondisabled peers (Salend, 2005).

The stimulus for reform was a revelation in the 1970s that more than 1 million students were being excluded from public schools and denied any education services (Smart, 2011). Mainstreaming refers to the schooling of special education students attending regular classes, a practice that began when Congress passed the Education of All Handicapped Children

Act in 1975. The traditional duration period for establishing school related laws was waived. Instead, this reform is intended to govern national education policies permanently. Over the past generation the law has been changed several times to reflect needed alterations. A revision known as the Individuals with Disabilities Education Act of 2004 (IDEA) requires the Inclusion of special education students in all aspects of school life including extracurricular activities (Thomas & Loxley, 2007). Thirteen categories of disabilities include autism, specific learning disabilities, speech and language impairments, emotional disturbance, traumatic brain injury, visual impairment, hearing impairment, deafness, mental retardation, deaf-blindness, multiple disabilities, orthopedic impairment, and other health impairments.

Six million students are in special education programs and 70% attend regular classrooms. The conditions for serving this 10-12% of the student population are:

- Free public education provided for all disabled persons between the ages of 3 and 21.

- Access to education in a regular classroom is guaranteed unless a person's handicap is such that services cannot be properly offered there.

- School placement and other education decisions are made only after consultation with a child's parents. Continuation in a program requires a reevaluation once every 3 years based on testing at no cost to the parents.

- Parents can examine and challenge all records bearing on identification of their child as disabled and the kind of educational setting for placement. The expense of this independent educational evaluation is borne by the school.

- Previous federal legislation aimed at elimination of architectural barriers to the physically handicapped is applied to funding school construction and modification (Smart, 2011).

Most people will eventually face disabilities in their family or at the workplace. It can be predicted that a certain proportion of regular students will eventually suffer from impairments or disabilities, whether by accidents, illness, or age. Further, some nondisabled students will grow up to become parents of disabled children or employers of impaired workers. These reasons underscore why learning to accept differences has become an important aspect of school through the curriculum, in cooperative learning and after-school programming.

Inclusion Practice Guidelines

Enabling inclusion practices to succeed requires awareness to prevent repetition of mistakes in the past. The following guidelines can support inclusion practices: (1) recognize a high cost associated with social segregation; (2) develop greater cooperation between the regular teachers and special educators; and (3) arrange cooperative learning to support interaction and avoid social isolation.

(1) Recognize the high cost associated with social segregation. The landmark legislation in the mid 1970s provided economic support to make free and appropriate schooling available for students with disabilities. Part of the directive for schools was to place disabled students in regular classrooms. Before that time many teachers excluded the disabled from their classes by rationalizing that if a student cannot do the work that is required, the rest of the class cannot be abandoned just to assist one person. A special education environment seemed justified because it allowed for a lower pupil-teacher ratio and access to more help. This was seen as a humane and reasonable decision. However, one consequence was the elimination of an equally critical ratio of regular students to disabled students (Lasky & Karge, 2006). When disabled students are separated from their nondisabled peers for the sake of greater teacher attention, the regular population cannot learn how to accept differences. Studies consistently have shown that segregation leads to an unfair assessment by outsiders. This means that, if disabled students are isolated in school, they will remain isolated as adults. This social cost overrides the cognitive benefits of smaller, segregated classes (Burns, 2007; Mannix, 2008).

(2) Develop cooperation between regular teachers and special educators. The initial legislation of Congress presented a strategy seen as more suitable than social segregation. That method of mainstreaming placed special education students within regular classrooms most of the school day to support social integration augmented by extra help given elsewhere from special education teachers. Merging the influences of regular teachers and special educators was seen as sensible. However, getting faculty members to collaborate was underestimated. Disputes arose over a competition for student schedules. Regular teachers complained classes were out of control because special education students would come and go through the day to attend sessions with special educators. These interruptions created a need to repeat lessons for absentees when they returned after instruction had already been given to the rest of the class (Burns, 2007).

Regular teachers were not alone in reluctance to cooperate. Special educators also had misgivings about the benefits of mainstreaming. In their opinion, some regular teachers were not sufficiently committed to the education of students that deviated from the norm. Instead, it was supposed that such children could benefit more by spending their entire day with caring and trained special educators. This rationale led to new categories of disability and programs that grew to include almost 20% of students in some states. Robert Sternberg, in his work at Yale University, referred to the growth rate of special education as an epidemic (Spear-Swerling & Sternberg, 1998). A related concern that continues is the disproportion of minority students in special education. Blacks represent 12% of the school population but 41% of all students in special education and only 3% of the gifted and talented (Sullivan & Artiles, 2011).

Accommodations are distinctive expectations for instruction and assessment of students with disabilities. Accommodations requested of regular teachers by special educators range from extra time to complete tests, less homework, and longer deadlines to finish assignments. Methods, benefits and problems associated with accommodations remain controversial among classroom teachers.

(3) Rely on cooperative learning to facilitate interaction of regular students and students with disabilities. The law focuses on inclusion to ensure special education students participate in nonacademic affairs at school such as lunchtime interaction, assemblies, and extra curricular clubs or organizations. Extending social involvement is intended to further support the development of age-appropriate social skills. It is not enough that regular students learn to accept peers with disabilities. Persons with disabilities should also gain social skills that enable them to become more acceptable to others (Wilmhurst & Brue, 2010).

Research has shown cooperative learning is an effective method for inclusion (Gillies, 2007). More than other approaches, this strategy ensures that students with disabilities have opportunities to interact with nondisabled students. Further, meta-analyses show that cooperative learning favorably impacts classroom management when special education students are present (Roseth, Johnson, & Johnson, 2008). Teachers report special education students in cooperative groups have greater self-esteem, feel less frustrated, and learn to listen better. Peer encouragement enables them to overcome obstacles that they might not surmount if working alone (Newman, Lohman, & Newman, 2007).

EMPLOYMENT AND TEAMWORK

Conditions of employment are undergoing change as more businesses adopt interdependence as their plan to increase productivity. Schools lag behind in preparing students for a group achievement orientation. Understanding the attitudes and skills employers seek in new hires and knowing methods they rely on to evaluate individuals and teams are vital factors to guide the new initiatives that should occur in education.

Expectations for Teamwork

Students are expected to learn skills that they will be expected to demonstrate as adults. Some of the competencies that might be required in the future are unknown but most employers agree that teamwork skills will be essential (Tapscott & Williams, 2010b). In anticipation of the interdependent work environment, teachers can arrange cooperative learning to provide students group experience in problem solving. This strategy reflects a fundamental shift from viewing teachers as the main source of learning to the broader expectation that students should also be sources of knowledge for one another.

A related change in thinking about getting ready for employment is reflected by surveys results on self-impression. In 1950, the Gallup poll asked high school seniors: Are you a very important person? Those who answered yes were 12% of the sample. When the same question was presented a half century later, 80% of students replied, "yes I am a very important person." This shift shows priority given to individualism in the current era and poses a possible reason why most people tend to overestimate their abilities as well as consider themselves to be above average (Brooks, 2011).

Some investigations have concluded that the solution is to help students acquire self-evaluation skills rather than be overreliant on external methods of governing self-esteem (Dunning, Heath, & Suls, 2004). For example, the public expects that schools will convey accurate reports about student progress and achievement. However, over a decade of evidence reveals that students who perform poorly on standardized tests are given high grades (Johnson, Penny, & Gordon, 2009). The misuse of grades to elevate self-esteem of low-achievers is unacceptable because it deceives them about the level of their competence, prevents detection of their learning needs, condones mediocrity, and ignores accountability for students and schools (Solmon, Agam, & Priagula, 2006).

When self-esteem is high and achievement is low, unwarranted confidence can prevent improvement. The Programme for International Student Assessment (PISA) reports that American high school students ranked 24 out of 29 nations for analytic reasoning. Nearly 60% of American 15-year-olds score at or below the basic level of problem solving using single sources of well-defined information to solve challenges such as plotting a destination route on a map. They showed deficiencies in synthesizing, accessing information, expressing complex thoughts and analyzing arguments (National Center for Education Statistics, 2010). In effect, they lack critical thinking skills needed for scientific advancement and engagement with societal decision making.

To make matters worse, students from the United States ranked first in terms of self-confidence (National Center for Education Statistics, 2010). It seems clear that self-esteem can be based on criteria that do not motivate growth. This is one reason peer evaluation of individual performance has gained credibility in the workplace over the past decade. In a similar way, students need feedback from teammates so that their confirmation or challenge to self-impression can be considered in guiding personal development (Twenge & Campbell, 2010).

Besides learning to judge themselves, students should be able to evaluate fairly the contributions of teammates and anonymously report their perceptions. Judgment about individual performance in teams should not be based solely on observation by teachers. Educators acknowledge that evaluation of teamwork is one of their most confusing responsibilities (Johnson, Penny, & Gordon, 2009). The task is difficult because teachers cannot be present to witness interaction of every group nor can they intuit how individual members of a team influence one another. Students also express disappointment with methods used for evaluation of teamwork. Suitable instruments are necessary that define teamwork skills and make known the extent to which individual team members attain them based on collective anonymous observations of teammates.

Job and School Evaluation

Research literature in business describes how coworkers evaluate one another on the job. Education literature shows how students in cooperative learning groups are evaluated in the classroom. Recognizing how these two different approaches can be reconciled offers students the prospect of becoming better prepared for employment.

Understanding the work environment that students will enter includes knowing the methods that are used for evaluating individual employees. Most major corporations like Hewlett-Packard, Intel, Microsoft, and Motorola rely on group ratings as a basis to judge team performance of individuals. The common approach, referred to as 360° feedback, reflects an analogy to the compass. The circular compass is a navigation tool with 360 points of reference to locate direction and also monitor whether the compass reader is on course. The 360° feedback approach consists of reports regarding individual work performance as viewed by multiple sources of observation. There may be differences between self-perception and the way we are seen by others (Dunning, 2010; Dunning, Heath, & Suls, 2004).

During the past decade, nearly all *Fortune 500* companies gave up their reliance on hierarchical personnel evaluation methods, typically judged by a supervisor in favor of implementing the multirater peer performance reviews. Employees prefer multiple sources of observation strategy because coworkers interact with them enough to be able to judge how well they perform required tasks as well as identify shortcomings. Management supports team performance review too because it has been found to improve productivity (Lepsinger & Lucia, 2009).

Because group evaluation is pervasive throughout business and industry as the primary way to determine individual success, secondary teachers should help students gain competencies within this realm that will carry over to their future role as employees. There is benefit in examining this question: How do marketplace models for evaluating individual performance in teams implicate change in evaluation procedures at schools? Three considerations link employment sector conditions and conditions in classrooms.

(1) Emphasis should be on how each individual contributes to the team effort. Faculties commonly contend this is the most appropriate condition for evaluating their own performance. Educators try to help every student in class but, in the final analysis, each student is responsible for personal growth. When the same condition is used to assess how students contribute to the learning of teammates, it means that individuals are responsible for their own conduct but cannot be held accountable for the actions of others. The motivation to support peers increases as students recognize that they will be evaluated based on team skill criteria their peers observe them demonstrate. When students are made aware of the importance that employers attach to teamwork, they usually add cooperative skills to their definition of what it will take for them to succeed (Levi, 2007).

(2) Teachers should share responsibility with students for assessment of learning in team. Educators are subject matter specialists and therefore most qualified to judge work products submitted by student teams. However, teachers do not qualify as the best judges of interaction in groups because they seldom witness dialogue of groups and, even when present, cannot understand how individual initiatives impact teammates. Adolescents are in the best position to identify teammates who influence them and make known the kinds of help given by peers (Gillies, 2007). Evaluation by the team members frees teachers from reliance on their own limited observations as the sole basis for making decisions about the progress of individuals. Instead, teachers can focus attention on being a facilitator while allowing the students to report their more reliable observations based on greater experience within the group.

The importance of teacher trust warrants consideration. Teachers must consider students trustworthy to permit peer and self-assessment. Reciprocal respect between teachers and students can contribute to a favorable transformation of schools. Trusting another person means relinquishing control over some of their behavior. This means that teachers can claim to trust only those allowed to reach their own conclusions and make their own decisions. Without trust, students have fewer opportunities to develop decision-making abilities. Trust is the basis of close and durable relationships. Rather than suppose that teachers who trust students are naive, it could be wise to reflect on whether some adults have left behind the capacity they once had to see the best in others.

(3) Self-evaluation reports should be compared with the observations of peers. Students take national tests, state tests, and teacher-made tests. Feedback about the results of these measures can be helpful. In addition, students can benefit from peer feedback that is related to their performance in group problem solving (Klaus, 2008). Cooperative learning provides an ideal set of conditions for comparing self-evaluation with observations by teammates. Guided practice is needed to become self-critical, an essential attribute for effective performance on a team. Self-evaluation helps students recognize when to think well of themselves and when to modify behavior based upon observations reported by peers. During adolescence, students also acquire the capacity to introspect, apply self-examination to feelings, thoughts, and motives (Goleman, 2006b).

Recognition of Soft Skills

Academic and technical skills that can be taught and measured are referred to as hard skills. In contrast, soft skills are defined as behavioral competencies, sometimes called interpersonal or social skills. These more difficult to measure attributes that are personality related include friendliness, optimism, listening, communication, and etiquette that characterize respectful relationships. Employers value soft skills because they increase customer satisfaction and team productivity. People that have soft skills are more able to motivate others to trust and rely on them. The need for competence in this social context is underscored by recent changes in the admission process of medical schools. Doctors are trained to save lives but some show arrogance in their treatment of nurses, failure to listen to patients, and preference for working alone instead of in collaboration with a professional team. In response, soft skills have begun to be included among the criteria considered for selection of student applicants.

Stanford University and University of California at Los Angeles are among many medical schools that have decided to discontinue the traditional total reliance on grades, test scores, and single 60-minute interview. Instead, candidates that present acceptable academic credentials (hard skills) participate in a process that resembles speed dating. Nine brief interviews are held that force them to show that they possess social skills that are needed to navigate a complicated health care system in which communication is essential. The multiple mini-interview (MMI) process begins as candidates stand with their backs to the door of an interview room. When a bell rings, they turn around and read a sheet of paper taped to the door describing an ethical challenge. In 2 minutes the bell rings again indicating that it is time to enter the room where an interviewer is waiting. After introductions, candidates have eight minutes to discuss the challenge they have read that relates to that particular room. Then, they move to another room where there is a surprise challenge and different interviewer, each of whom score applicants with a number and brief notation.

The tradition of using a single lengthy interview has provided a poor assessment of social skills because it reflects the view of only one interviewer. There can be greater reliability when the views of multiple observers are combined. Secret questions used in the interviews are intended to find out how candidates think on their feet and assess their willingness to work in teams. The most important responses are not to challenges stated on the doors because they have no right or wrong answers but rather to see how individuals respond when someone disagrees with them, something that happens on a regular basis for members of a professional team.

Potential students who rush to conclusions, are easily distracted, do not listen well, and are unwilling to admit uncertainly get poor marks since these behaviors are known to undermine professional teams. In contrast, those who respond to emotions and ideas of an interviewer and ask for more information perform better since these tendencies support reciprocal learning with colleagues and patients. The MMI detects students that look good on paper but lack soft skills needed for success. Development of the process was motivated by studies showing that interviewers rarely changed their scores after the first five minutes, use of multiple interviews removes random bias, and interviews that focus on situations rather than the individual more often reveal character flaws. In fact, MMI scores are highly predictive of medical license scores 3 to 5 years later that test decision-making, patient interaction, and cultural competence. A majority of the medical schools in Canada, Australia, and Israel use multiple mini-interviews.

Several trends account for consideration of soft skills by medical schools. First, as many as 98,000 preventable deaths each year are blamed on poor communication by doctors who may be technically competent but socially inept. When a licensing body reviews the performance of a physician following patient complaints, the most frequent concerns relate to non-cognitive factors such as interpersonal skills, professionalism, and ethical/moral judgment. Second, medicine is moving from an individual practitioner model to a team model. Doctors cannot remain isolated professionals while working for a large health care system. They should be trained for team-based care with colleagues from allied disciplines (Dodson et al., 2009).

STUDENT PARTICIPATION IN EVALUATION

The need for better evaluation of teamwork is widely acknowledged. However, because of a lack of suitable tools educators have been reluctant to approve student involvement with team evaluation. These obstacles must be confronted to promote the concept of teacher and student shared accountability.

Teamwork Skills Inventory

Teacher and student discontent with cooperative learning evaluation motivated development of the Teamwork Skills Inventory (TSI) (P. Strom & Strom, 2011b). In order to help adolescents and adults engage in the low-risk practice that is needed for peer and self-evaluation, this online inventory:

- Gives quick automated feedback to students about their skill set.
- Identifies teamwork skills consistently demonstrated by individuals.
- Provides individual profiles that contain anonymous peer feedback.
- Compares peer observation of performance with self-impression.
- Detects skill deficits of individuals and groups to guide instruction.
- Credits conscientious teammates for initiatives and contributions.
- Discovers slackers that fail to do their fair share of the workload.
- Provides an inflation index that reveals exaggerated evaluations
- Summarizes team skills of individuals for portfolio placement, and
- Enables faculty teaching the same students to intervene together.

The inventory consists of 25 items shown in Table 9.2. These items were based on studies of cooperative learning, group dynamics, creative thinking, critical thinking, and personnel evaluation methods applied in business and industry (Moore & Parker, 2008; Myers & Anderson, 2008; Roseth, Johnson, & Johnson, 2008; Runco, 2006; Tapscott & Williams,

Table 9.2.   Criteria for Evaluation of
Teamwork in Cooperative Groups*

Attends to Teamwork

1	Demonstrates reliability by keeping a record of good attendance
2	Shows dependability by arriving on time for group participation
3	Focuses attention on the team task so there is no waste of time
4	Fulfills rotation roles such as summarizer, discussant and improviser
5	Can be counted on to do a fair share of the team assigned work

Seeks and Shares Information

6	Admits uncertainty when in doubt about what should be done
7	Asks questions that help to understand and complete class lessons
8	Teaches peers by explaining or reviewing concepts and assignments
9	Brings relevant reading materials for teammates to examine in class
10	Refers to reading materials as a basis for enhancing the discussions

Communicates With Teammates

11	Can be counted on to disclose feelings, opinions, and experiences
12	Speaks clearly and uses vocabulary that can be easily understood
13	Limits the length of comments so other people have a chance to talk
14	Listens to everyone in the group and considers their points of view
15	Encourages teammates and recognizes contributions of individuals

Thinks Critically and Creatively

16	Explores viewpoints and suggestions that may not be liked at first
17	Uses logic to challenge the thinking and work methods of the team
18	Practices reflective thinking and avoids making hasty conclusions
19	Combines and builds upon the ideas that are expressed by others
20	Discovers different ways of looking at things and solving problems

Gets Along in the Team

21	Responds well whenever peers disagree or express their criticism
22	Avoids blaming and judging teammates for difficulties or mistakes
23	Accepts compromise when it is the best way to overcome conflicts
24	Keeps trying even when the task or situation becomes demanding
25	Expresses optimism about the team being able to achieve success

*Copyright © P. Strom and R. Strom (2009).

2010a; Torrance, 2000). Items appear in conceptually convenient clusters of five skills each to detect whether a student: (1) attends to teamwork, (2) seeks and shares information, (3) communicates with teammates, (4) thinks critically and creatively, and (5) gets along with teammates. The skills are defined in a document used for student referral during discussions with parents, teachers, and teammates.

Emerging Business Practices

A rationale for each of the TSL clusters is presented here.

Attends to teamwork (Items 1-5). The five items in this cluster focus on acceptable attendance at team meetings, arriving on time for meetings, staying focused on tasks, fulfilling individual roles, and doing a fair share of work expected of everyone.

People with a record of absences and arriving late at work are most likely to lose their jobs. A Pew Foundation national survey of 2,000 adults asked what it takes for young people to succeed (Taylor, 2012). The factor most often identified was having a good work ethic, chosen by 61% of the respondents, followed by knowing how to get along with people at 57%. Just 42% felt getting a college education was as important. Movie director Woody Allen, estimates that 80% of being successful is just showing up. However, being physically present is no guarantee a person can be relied on to perform team assigned tasks.

Life is often set off course by distractions so paying full attention and being able to concentrate are states of mind that seem in decline. Some obstacles are preference for multitasking and insistence on always being connected so as not to miss anything. This orientation causes incessant checking for messages or texting friends, behaviors that can prevent students from doing the work expected of them by teammates.

Neuroscience experiments have consistently found multitasking interferes with information processing, diminishes concentration, and reduces comprehension. These distractions limit student ability to focus on tasks, listen to teammates, and share the workload. Other observers warn that attention itself is in danger because a lifestyle of distraction takes away from being able to maintain concentration, a key factor for productivity and essential for durable intimate relationships. Reliance on technology makes distraction common.

In testimony to the British House of Lords, neurologist Susan Greenfield (2008) of Oxford University reported studies showing that many children are losing the ability necessary to concentrate and remain attentive in class. Experienced teachers of all grades report having observed this trend. Previous generations of students were more able to stay seated, pay attention, and ignore distractions. It is not that students cannot focus but they try to focus on everything. They want to see and hear all that is going on including things that should be blocked out to focus on learning but are not because they are accustomed to monitoring multiple events.

Gloria Mark, professor at the University of California, specializes in an emerging field called "interruption science," the study of effects of disruption on job performance. Her surveys have shown that, in a typical workday, office personnel change tasks, on average, every 3 minutes. E-mail, instant messaging, texting, inquiries on the phone and questions of nearby coworkers present a continual stream of interruptions. Having been interrupted, it usually takes 25 minutes to return to the original task (Mark, Gonzales, & Harris, 2005).

Russell Poldrack, neurologist at the University of Texas, observed that the entire culture is beginning to look like what occurs with attention deficit disorder, where there is difficulty in focusing and distractability. When focus is split, awareness is minimal, ability to gain perspective is compromised, and critical thinking is reduced along with deep learning for creativity (Poldrack, Helchenko, & Hansen, 2009).

Seeks and shares information (Items 6-10). The five items in this cluster focus on admitting when in doubt about what should be done, asking questions to improve group understanding, helping peers by explaining or reviewing lessons, bringing reading materials for the team to examine, and referring to reading materials during team discussions.

Adolescents prefer to learn in teams. Most of them understand the benefits of sharing websites worth visiting, checking with friends about questions on homework, offering encouragement when others are down, and providing tutoring for a review of assignments. When students go online to search or read articles, it is usual to submit their homework to the teacher. This custom prevents peer teaching that can increase knowledge of a group and confirms the value of data sharing. When teams assign the members differentiated tasks, there can be individual accountability followed by oral sharing of homework with teammates before written material is submitted to a teacher. In this way, learning increases for all team members and the importance of interdependence is reinforced.

When teachers maximize conditions for sharing, two prominent deficits can be overcome. These are item 9 (Brings relevant reading materials to examine in class), and item 10 (Refers to reading materials as a basis for enhancing discussions). During data collection, students are surprised they should bring reading material to class without being told by their teacher to do so. Even when they know the topic that will be discussed in class ahead of time and want to engage in self-directed learning, students generally get poor peer ratings for items 9 and 10 on the TSI.

Self-directed learners accept the responsibility to be a source of knowledge for peers. Urging independent learning should be merged with social interdependence that requires practice. The strong desire to dialogue with peers can support productive group work so learning that individuals gain separately can later benefit every team member.

Educators should avoid underestimating what is necessary to transition from a commitment to the concept of independence to also include pursuit of interdependence. This shift is difficult for those who have been nurtured to celebrate the recognition of the individual, and suppose that "its all about me." Immersion in network friendships render many incapable in the beginning to carry out the authentic peer and self-evaluation expected of teams at work.

Adolescent readiness to collaborate grows with an awareness of how businesses are impacted by teamwork. For example, Boeing Aircraft credits interdependence and team skills training for a 50% decrease in engineering problems on their large 777 jets. Federal Express reported a 40% increase in productivity after employees were oriented to how team structures foster greater effectiveness.

Benefit also comes from knowing how collaboration on a global scale is becoming a force for innovation. At Proctor and Gamble, one of the world's largest companies, management determined that even with their 7,500 research employees, they would be unable to sustain a lead over their competitors. Instead of hiring more researchers, unit leaders were directed to source 50% of new products and service ideas from outside the country (Tapscott & Williams, 2010a). As a result, someone can work for Proctor and Gamble without being on the regular payroll. Potential contributors register at InnoCentive network where 90,000 scientists make themselves available to solve difficult research and development (R&D) problems. The reward for acceptable solutions ranges from several thousand dollars to over a million dollars when provided by the posted deadline.

InnoCentive is one of an increasing number of marketplace venues matching scientists with R&D challenges that business seek to innovate. Proctor and Gamble, Dow, DuPont, Novartis, Honeywell, and other major companies rely on these sources for novel ideas, inventions, and qualified minds to help unlock new values in markets. This vast scope of collaboration is expected to replace traditional hierarchies within corporations that have been the main engines of wealth creation (Lesser, Ransom, Shah, & Pulver, 2012).

Communicates with teammates (Items 11-15). The five items in this cluster focus on sharing experiences, feelings, ideas or opinions; speaking clearly and using easily understood vocabulary; limiting length of comments so that others get to talk; listening to everyone and respecting their views; and encouraging and recognizing contributions of others.

The message of Warren Bennis and Patricia Biederman (1998) in *Organizing Genius: The Secrets of Creative Collaboration* is that "None of us is as smart as all of us." They show how networks of talented people have changed the world and methods they used to transform themselves from being independent achievers to collaborative and productive teams. The chronicled groups include those with an enduring impact such as Palo Alto Research Center at Xerox and Apple that were the first to make computers easy to use and widely accessible for nonexperts; aeronautical engineers that built radically new aircraft for Lockheed; scientists that worked on the Manhattan Project at Los Alamos to hasten the conclusion of World War II; and entertainment visionaries responsible for the appeal of Walt Disney Studios. These groups illustrate lessons of value about how teams can become great if individuals are united in purpose and given freedom to do their best.

Most guidelines for how to succeed were devised in a former era when pursuit of excellence was defined in terms of individuality, independence, autonomy, self-reliance, being and making it on your own. These attributes will always be important, but their relevance can no longer be the design for influence or group productivity. The quest for independence should be linked with an appreciation for interdependence shown by communicating perspectives with teammates. Helping employees value and pursue goals that go beyond individual identity is recognized as an enormous challenge for business.

Thinks critically and creatively (Items 16-20). The five items in this cluster relate to considering the views that differ from personal opinion; using logic to challenge group thinking or work methods; thinking carefully about ideas before reaching conclusions; building on the ideas of others; and offering new ways of looking at problems or events.

Encouragement for creative thinking has centered on extraordinary individuals. This support has to expand as companies place greater reliance on the thinking that occurs in teams. Creativity must increasingly be achieved in a social context. The acceptance of divergent thinking should become more common so ideas of creative persons receive fair consideration. Creative individuals must realize that critics will initially express doubts about the worth of their ideas. They may be criticized for novel views, taking a stand, refusing to compromise principles, sharing their faith, raising questions of authority figures or identifying new ways to do things. Creative people need courage to make their contributions and avoid expectation of immediate approval from others.

Employers, politicians, and educators are concerned about a decline in creativity. Kyung Kim from the College of William and Mary, conducted a meta-analysis of 300,000 responses to the Torrance measure of creative thinking. She found that creativity scores had steadily risen in a corresponding way as IQ scores but progression ended in 1990. Over the past 2 decades, scores for creativity have gone down. Students in K-6 have recorded the greatest losses.

These are worrisome signs when contrasted with results of an IBM poll of 1,500 chief executive officers throughout the nation. They identified creativity as the number one leadership competency that will be needed for the future. This view is reinforced by Pasi Sahlberg (2011), author of *Finnish Lessons* and director general of the Center for Mobility and Cooperation in Helsinki. For 10 years, Finland has ranked first in student achievement compared to 31 nations including the United States. Sahlberg is frequently asked what countries can do to prepare students to compete globally. His view is that "Reading, mathematics and scientific literacy remain important but their role as 'core subjects' will increasingly be challenged by a need for creativity and collaboration skills" (p. 142).

Gets along with teammates (Items 21-25). The five items in this cluster focus on willingness to accept criticism; avoid blaming other people for problems; accept compromise as a way to handle conflict; keep trying when a task is hard; and expresses hope about group success.

Research on cooperative learning has assessed how social relationships impact behavior and achievement. A meta-analysis of 148 studies compared effectiveness of cooperative, competitive, and individualistic goal structures. Over 17,000 adolescent, ages 12-15, from 11 nations were examined. As predicted by social interdependence theory, students working in cooperative teams were more accurate on test outcomes and earned higher problem-solving scores for reasoning and critical thinking tasks compared to classes emphasizing competitive or individualistic learning. In cooperative settings, students felt a greater sense of support from and connection with peers. The implications are that when teachers structure class in a cooperative manner, academic achievement and social development goals can be promoted simultaneously while student goals for interaction are also met (Roseth, Johnson, & Johnson, 2008).

The challenge of getting along with teammates should not be underestimated. Jean Twenge (2007), psychology professor at San Diego State, compared results of personality tests by the boomer generation when they were under the age of 30 with students of the millennial generation. Twenge's findings, based on responses from 16,000 students, are reported in *Generation Me* (2007) and *The Narcissism Epidemic: Living in the Age of Entitlement* (Twenge & Campbell, 2010). Two-thirds of college students agreed that their generation is more self-centered and narcissistic. A hyperindividualistic orientation is considered the result of promoting self-esteem independent of behavior or achievement, constantly telling children they are special and protecting them from recognizing their failures, thereby preventing development of the resilience needed to recover and persevere when things go wrong.

Someone who supposes that s/he always performs well is unlikely to seek or consider external criticism. Few students are learning how to process peer observations that could lead to improvement. The result is that defensiveness is a common liability restricting growth because students rely only on themselves to detect their shortcomings and learning needs. Twenge (2007) concluded that child development outcomes of the self-esteem movement have been so poor that this strategy should be abandoned in favor of ways to support empathy, real accomplishment, and diminish egocentrism. By 2015 the Millennials (born since 1980) will represent nearly half the workforce.

Administration and Features

The Teamwork Skills Inventory approach to group assessment appeals to tech savvy students because it is anonymous, avoids laborious hand scoring by teachers, and gives quick feedback to every individual. Students identify specific skills that each member of their team, including self, have demonstrated consistently, without having to estimate how often each of the skills was exhibited. Requiring frequency-type responses regarding observation of 25 teamwork skills as applied to sustained interaction with four or five teammates would be an unreasonable expectation. However, students are able to report their overall impressions about behavior of teammates, whether an individual consistently behaved in certain ways as defined by specific criteria. The proportion of peers who confirm behaviors demonstrated consistently is a more meaningful indicator than frequency no one could accurately recall. This practical response format matches how people make decisions about behavior of others in daily life.

Certain conditions should be met before formative assessment is administered. Teams should work together long enough to support the reliability of their observations. This means that peer judgment should reflect substantial interaction. It is recommended that teams work together a minimum of 4 weeks prior to formative assessment and similar duration between completion of the formative and summative evaluation. Team projects that promise to achieve significant benefits require continuity of membership and sufficient duration of interaction. Sometimes teachers move students from one group to another without regard for real time needed to establish cohesion and interdependence within teams.

Another precondition for assessment are five lessons teachers present to students to acquaint them with the rationale relied on for multirater peer performance reviews of individuals and how this method is applied in the workplace. Students examine the potential benefits of authentic reporting on peer and self-behavior and discuss the obstacles that have to be overcome to prevent flawed assessment. Then they join teams where membership remains constant until there is a formative assessment.

The Teamwork Skills Inventory includes the following practical and novel features.

- Student responsibility for evaluation. Teachers are supposed to evaluate student teamwork skills and deficits. However, they cannot be present to observe all group interactions. TSI results augment teacher insights from the vantage point of the students.

- Anonymous evaluation by teammates. Students want to have their social status protected. Feedback from peers appears on an individual profile that reveals only the proportion of teammates that observed consistent demonstration of each teamwork skill.

- Understanding the assessment criteria. When students want to review a definition for any of the 25 teamwork skills used to assess peers, they click the line for that particular skill and a pop-up message appears providing a definition of the criterion.

- Convenient summary of responses. Students complete the Teamwork Skills Inventory online. Responses are automatically tallied immediately and become available to individuals in profile format as soon as all members of a team finish with their peer and self-evaluations.

- Students assigned Inflation ratings. If a student credits anyone with 20 or more team skills, a popup states— "Are you sure? This is a very high rating." The reminder is to prevent deceptive evaluation that keeps others from learning how to improve.

- Inflation Index of student ratings. A reminder that a very high rating was given urges reflection. The number of high ratings that individuals give appears on the profile as an inflation index to identify those requiring guidance about authentic assessment.

- Enabling teacher collaboration. Teachers of all curriculum subjects are expected to support social development. Access to profiles of individual students across their classes offers a larger picture and enables the faculty to apply united interventions.

- Encouraging student goal setting. After getting formative feedback from their peers, individuals should identify teamwork skills they want to work on. Progress toward these goals can be detected by comparing the formative and summative outcomes.

- Determine needs for intervention. Teachers have access to individual, team, and class profiles. This information recognizes student assets, progress, learning needs, and opportunities to arrange practice for team skills that have yet to be acquired.
- Parent involvement as teachers. Parents need to know how teamwork skills of their child are perceived by teammates. Keeping parents informed of progress in this social context enables them as co-teachers to reinforce skills needed for success.
- Portfolios and social development. Individual student profiles kept in portfolios become a school record of progress in this realm of accomplishment. Portfolios can help students monitor gains, amend goals, and recognize levels of achievement.

Portfolios and Self-Evaluation

Portfolios, a term adopted from the carrying case of paintings or drawings that artists present as proof of their talents, are collections of student work. One of the best opportunities for goal setting is developing a portfolio. During the past decade, portfolios in middle school and high school have gained considerable support and become a familiar component of assessment. Portfolios require a student to state goals, monitor progress, and reflect on performance with feedback from teachers and sometimes peers. This process helps students to become more self-directed and less dependent upon others for always telling them how well they are doing. There is also benefit in students assuming the obligation for improvement of performance instead of placing the blame elsewhere. When failure is experienced, a student is expected to figure out how it happened and identify strategies to get on the right path. The usual outcome of portfolio assessment is a more responsible, self-reliant student who can demonstrate the critical thinking and self-evaluation that is needed for success in school, work, and at home (Kish, Sheehan, Cole, Struyk, & Kinder, 1997; Theobald, 2006).

Some teachers believe that students lack the maturity needed to engage self-evaluation. Others suppose that students are unwilling to adopt the required attitudes of honesty and authenticity. Both arguments against portfolios could be used as reasons for helping students overcome such deficiencies through guided practice (Sunstein, 2000). Most educators favor allowing students to formulate some personal goals, monitor progress, and process feedback from others who critically examine their portfolio. The related dialogue with teachers, peers, and parents acquaints them with aspirations, sponsors reflection, and increases accuracy of self-appraisal (Zubizarreta & Millis, 2009). In addition, empathy often emerges because of the necessity to reconcile multiple perspectives about performance. There is no substitute for direct practice in this process that everyone needs to sustain growth during adolescence and adulthood.

There are limitations of portfolio assessment. Some teachers mistakenly see it as an exercise for showcasing the best and worst work of a student. Instead, the purpose of a portfolio should be to set appropriate goals and evaluate progress by examining the quality of work as it changes over time in specific realms of learning. In this way, teachers have a focus for their conversations that is uniquely relevant to each student. The emphasis on high stakes testing forces teachers to focus exclusively on this kind of assessment. An important step forward is expected as more schools augment subject matter testing with portfolios to track student progress toward personal goals without comparison to classmates (Stefanakis, 2002; Stiggins & Chappius, 2005).

Schools often decide all learning objectives and put them in the course syllabus. As a result, success excludes the attainment of student goals that may differ from the uniform expectations that apply to everyone. Certainly, students are obligated to meet curriculum goals and minimal competency standards for academic skills. Nevertheless, when their learning is restricted to what others expect, students are denied practice in looking within themselves and reflecting on how they should grow as individuals. The schedule at school should include time for students to participate in goal setting, reflect on the future, and examine personal progress (Sadler & Good, 2006).

SUMMARY AND IMPLICATIONS

People who believe that schools should be responsible for curriculum subjects but not social skills underestimate the importance of teamwork in the workplace. In contrast, research has found that when students participate in cooperative learning, academic performance improves, they get along better with classmates, amount of knowledge increases, there is more critical thinking, and incidence of misbehavior declines. Meta-analyses have found that cooperative learning promotes social connections, encourages constructive behavior norms, and motivates an optimistic view that most problems can be solved when collective united action is applied in teams. Employers believe that students would be better prepared for the workplace when schools include practice in learning how to perform well as members of teams.

Teachers support inclusion more effectively when they understand the high cost associated with social segregation, build relationships with special educators, rely on suitable criteria for use in student placement, and arrange cooperative learning that can support interaction and prevents social isolation. Inclusion depends on developing mutual respect among the disabled and regular students and dynamic of their combined effort to plan and solve problems together.

The application of suitable criteria for teamwork evaluation and becoming self-critical are essential elements for social development. Students should get to practice authentic evaluation of teammates and provide feedback that detects learning needs. Productive teamwork also requires self-assessment that can become more accurate when students get anonymous feedback from teammates that verify or challenge self-impressions. Evaluation of progress in this context should no longer be the province of teachers alone because they are unable to continually observe every cooperative group in class. In addition, they cannot interpret how individual students influence one another. Instead, teachers should obligate students to share some responsibility for teamwork skills assessment. Educators who acknowledge teammates are the most relevant source of observation about what occurs in cooperative groups convey trust and respect for student judgment. Reliance on students to share their perceptions improves teacher awareness of demonstrated team skills and deficits of individuals, teams, and classes as a basis for planning instruction.

Most parents have years of employment experience as the basis for providing valuable advice about the workplace application of team skills and consequences of failing to collaborate with others. More than any other sector of education, achieving teamwork skills should include a key role for parents. No matter what their occupation, parents recognize that team skills are a vital ingredient for success at work and in the home. Orienting parents to the specific teamwork criteria expected in a cooperative learning classroom can enable the faculty and family to team teach and reinforce the same skills in both environments. Because parents are obligated to guide children over many years, team skill profiles in individual portfolios allows them to monitor progress.

Parents and teachers sometimes become defensive during their conversations. However, when results of the TSI are the topic, neither party is inclined to blame the other for their inaccurate perceptions about a student. It is not a matter of whether a parent or a teacher has the better perspective. Instead, both are obligated to examine self-reports of one adolescent and how that individual is judged by teammates. In this situation, teachers and parents are motivated to unite in helping individual students reconcile disparities between observations of peers they work with and their self-impressions.

APPLICATIONS FOR TEACHING

1. The distinguishing feature of cooperative learning is reciprocal instruction. Each person on a team is expected to contribute to the knowledge of peers. This approach differs from tutoring where only one party knows a subject or has a skill and tries to pass it on. To establish conditions of interdependence, teachers should structure tasks that students can only attain through teamwork. A sufficient number of tasks should be prepared so each team member has a chance to enlarge the scope of group learning.

2. Cooperation at work differs from the classroom where everyone is roughly the same age. Teamwork skills are supported by assignments that involve collaboration outside class with other generations. Some homework can require teaming with parents and grandparents, such as searching the Internet together, conducting interviews to find out how people of another age group see current situations, performing community service to assist older adults, and taking advantage of unique assets offered by age diversity.

3. A growing number of schools assemble teams of students that devote themselves to academic competitions with peers at other institutions. This group sharing experience acquaints students with the greater possibility that certain problems could be solved when approached collectively than when one individual tries alone to reach a solution.

4. Students should know there is a broader purpose for teamwork activities than meeting requirements for the classroom. These tasks can also develop the foundation of assets that apply to their future as employees. Everyone should pay careful attention and reflect on feedback that peers provide about their team skills. Although a student may believe that s/he has demonstrated a specific skill, if that skill is inconsistently shown, teammates are unlikely to acknowledge it as an asset. Students should also appreciate the added benefit of sharing peer feedback from team skills profile with parents.

5. The emerging workplace requires teamwork skills but teacher efforts to assess student achievement and deficits have been hindered by lack of tools for assessment. The TSI uses peer observation and self-evaluation to establish student accountability, recognize accomplishment, and identify learning needs. Results show students can identify teamwork skills that individuals demonstrate during group work, credit conscientious learners for contributions, detect slackers that fail to complete responsibilities,

compare peer and self-observations of individual performance, and maintain a record of teamwork skills in individual portfolios.

6. Typical group processing, conducted face-to-face, is assumed to be a forum for sharing and receiving peer feedback on teamwork. However, patronizing remarks are often made to retain peer acceptance and avoid disagreement. By using feedback from the TSI, peer assessments can be more authentic because they are not face-to-face and the anonymity in reporting personal observations of teammates remains confidential. This goal is accomplished by providing a summary of the combined view of teammates displayed on each student's individual profile.

7. Some students may suppose that because grades are assigned for subjects but not teamwork skills, these aspects of development are less important than is actually the case. Fortunately, when students understand the importance that employers attach to teamwork, they typically add cooperative skills to their definition of what it is needed to succeed. Comparing peer and self-impressions of performance enables students to understand that each of us is not only the individual who we suppose ourselves to be but also the person seen by others. Learning to unite these separate impressions can result in greater growth and achievement.

CHAPTER 10

PHYSICAL HEALTH AND RISKS

Adolescence is the time in life when people show a greater willingness to take risks. Some of the risks reflect poor judgment and can have damaging consequences. These risks can include pregnancy, sexually transmitted diseases, drug abuse, online predators, lack of sleep, drinking alcohol, truancy, becoming a dropout, joining a gang, involvement with criminal activity, bringing a weapon to school, cheating in education, procrastination in studying, unexcused absence from school, smoking tobacco, lack of exercise, poor nutrition, failing to seek tutorial help when needed, and reckless driving. During adolescence students take greater responsibility for choices that can influence their health. The goals of this chapter are to discuss normative growth, nutritional needs, and benefits of exercise and fitness. In addition, sexual involvement and programs of prevention are discussed with consequence of problems related to substance abuse. The greater willingness of adolescents to take risks should cause adults to help them gauge and monitor judgments that can protect or jeopardize health, adjustment, and opportunity to pursue personal goals.

GROWTH AND DEVELOPMENT

Height and Weight

Many adolescents feel insecure because they are shorter or taller than friends or classmates. Schools should inform all students that the rate of

Learning Throughout Life: An Intergenerational Perspective, pp. 219–242
Copyright © 2012 by Information Age Publishing
All rights of reproduction in any form reserved.

physical growth is not the same for everyone. The physical growth spurt typically begins at age 10 or 11 for girls and peaks by age 12. Most girls stop growing around 15 or 16 years of age. In contrast, the growth spurt for boys begins at age 12 or 13, peaks at 14, and usually ends by 19. As a result, for a brief period in middle school, the girls are taller than boys of their age. However, at the peak of the growth spurt, boys grow faster than girls, sometimes 3 to 4 inches a year. A well recognized indicator of the growth spurt is that an adolescent has outgrown shoes or clothes—again. During growth spurts limbs grow at different rates, leaving teens relatively uncoordinated and clumsy. Sometimes growth is so rapid that connective tissues of tendons and ligaments tighten. For young athletes this implicates stretching before playing sports and growth-related pain is sometimes felt in the knees and lower legs. Many athletes report discomfort in these areas until their bones stop growing (Darst, Pangrazi, Sariscany, & Brusseau, 2011).

Height is not the only physical change during adolescence. While growth spurts occur, both sexes evidence collection of fat on the buttocks and around the abdomen. Boys, however, gain muscle and bone whereas girls add more fat, particularly in their hips and breasts. The result is that, 25% of total body weight for a girl is fat, while fat accounts 15 to 20% of total body weight for boys (Neinstein, Gordon, Katzman, Rosen, & Woods, 2008).

Sexual Maturation

Puberty, the time at which when sexual reproduction becomes possible, is the biological onset of adolescence. Age of puberty in girls has been declining in the past several decades. Frank Biro, director of adolescent medicine at the Cincinnati, Ohio Children's Hospital and his team studied 1,200 girls between 6 and 8 years of age from three regions of the nation (Biro et al., 2010). By 8 years old, 27% of them had begun puberty. Specifically, this represented 18% White, 43% Black, and 40% Hispanic girls. Generally, the development of breasts in girls occurs anytime between ages 8 to 13. The falling age of female puberty is usually attributed to increase in average body weight over the past 30 years. Excess body fat increases blood levels of estrogen that promote breast development. Parents with daughters entering puberty should have conversations, encourage questions, and contribute to reduction of child anxiety.

Puberty for boys typically arrives between ages 9 to 14, later than for girls. The male body prepares for the biological transformation by creating additional androgen hormones. These hormones, made primarily by the testicles, produce the physical changes of puberty. A familiar sign of change is pubic hair at the base of the penis. There is an enlargement and darkening of the scrotum. These alterations occur well before physical growth reaches its peak. Although the penis can become erect from infancy, it is not until 2 years after the onset of puberty and a year after the penis begins to lengthen that it becomes capable of ejaculating semen. The beginning of ejaculation is sometimes spontaneous in reaction to fantasy, nocturnal emission, or outcome of masturbation (Pfiefer & Middleman, 2006).

Another visible change in males is that hair begins to appear under the arms and on the face. As the voice box enlarges, the Adam's apple is more observable. There is a corresponding change as the voice shifts to a deeper tone with periodic cracking as the higher younger voice continues to be heard. During the sexual maturation period, lasting 4 or 5 years, testicles continue to enlarge while the penis grows longer and thicker. By the end of the process, the testicles, penis, and pubic hair are developed and facial hair appears that can form a beard or moustache (Madaras, 2007).

Sexual changes in girls occur because of an increase in hormones produced by ovaries and adrenal glands. The initial visible change is origin of breast development or appearance of light pubic hair. Girls need to know that the two breasts do not typically grow at the same rate. Even when breasts are fully developed, they are unlikely to be exactly the same size. When breast growth is underway for about a year, the overall physical growth reaches its peak. A year after this spurt, girls experience the *men-arche*, their first menstrual period. Menstruation is a monthly process of discharging blood and other matter from the womb that occurs between puberty and menopause in women who are not pregnant. Menstruation signals the need for parents to discuss sexual behavior and contraception (Santelli & Crosby, 2009).

There may be an occasional increase in white or yellow vaginal discharge in the months preceding first menstruation. Girls should be aware that their menstrual periods might be irregular the first year with an average cycle consisting of a 3 to 7 day period that occurs every 24 to 34 days. The first few menstrual periods are not painful but over half of all later adolescent girls suffer mild abdominal cramps during the first day or two of their periods. About 10% experience such pain they cannot follow a normal schedule without reliance on medication (DiClemente, Santelli, & Crosby, 2009).

Vision and Hearing

One out of four students experience sight problems. There is a broad range of visual disabilities, from a need to wear glasses in some situations to total loss of vision. Even blindness is not a unitary concept. There are the legally blind, medically blind, and occupationally blind, as well as partially sighted and visually impaired. People are blind when their better eye tests no better than 20/200 following a correction, and visually disabled when the better eye tests from 20/70 to 20/200 following correction (Sight and Hearing Association, 2012).

Nearsightedness, myopia as it is medically referred to, is a condition where near objects are seen clearly but distant objects do not come into proper focus. Estimates are that 30% of Americans are nearsighted (Kitchen, 2007). *Farsightedness, hyperopia,* is a condition where distant objects are seen clearly but close ones do not come into proper focus. Approximately one-quarter of people are hyperopic, and the incidence increases with age; at least half of the population beyond age 65 have hyperopia. Students with visual problems should have the best seat placement in class so they can easily see the blackboard or overhead visuals. Tasks requiring prolonged focus should be interrupted periodically. The visually impaired also need regular physical exercise.

A hearing handicap is not an either/or phenomenon but matter of degree. Persons may adequately hear low-pitched voices but miss high-pitched voices. Some may hear in a room where there are no competing sounds such as other voices, traffic, fans, and music or where room structure and acoustical tile ceilings minimize echoes. Annual hearing examinations should be available at school because less than 15% of physicians routinely screen for hearing loss in physical examinations (Luxford, Derebery, & Berliner, 2010).

Medical theorists refer to a rising epidemic of ear damage as "a disease of civilization" created by difference between the world bodies are designed for and the environment. Nature designed human ears for detecting predators approaching or prey moving away. However, modern technology has produced a decibel level that exceeds what people can safely handle. Amplifiers have transformed the volume of music for concerts, movies, clubs, home and car stereos and personal listening devices that often jeopardize auditory health. Many teenagers like music as loud as possible on personal listening devices and seem indifferent to the dangers of high decibel levels because the debilitating results for them will not be evident for years (Portnuff, Fligor, & Arehart, 2011). A National Institute of Health study with 2,000 adolescents between the ages of 12 to 19 determined that nearly 20% of them showed hearing loss. The incidence of loss was significantly greater than for adolescents examined a generation ago (Shargorodsky, Curhan, Curhan, & Eavey, 2010).

NUTRITION AND DIET

Nutrition Deficiencies

Sufficient iron is essential in adolescence because of an expanding volume of blood in the body and increase in muscle mass. During growth spurts, extra iron is required because it is vital for muscle development and red blood cells. The need for additional iron is especially acute for girls because of a loss of iron that occurs during menstruation. When there is lack of iron in the diet, the resulting iron deficiency anemia is reflected by a tendency to fatigue, feelings of lightheadedness, loss of appetite, and pale appearance. Teenagers should eat enough iron-containing foods such as meat, fish, poultry, eggs, peas, beans, potatoes and rice (DiClemente, Santelli, & Crosby, 2009).

Another nutrient required by teenagers but often overlooked is calcium (Shanley & Thompson, 2010). Strong bones and teeth depend on calcium. Lack of calcium increases risk for a bone-thinning disease called *osteoporosis*, a common problem for women from middle age onwards. Parents and teachers should encourage calcium as an essential choice for eating lifestyle. Most adolescent girls and boys do not meet the government calcium recommendations of 1,200 milligrams a day for persons aged 9-18 (United States Department of Health and Human Services, 2009).

Dietary Guidelines

Students at 4,500 public high schools were surveyed about their food perceptions (Zullig, Ubbes, & Pyle, 2006). Over 40% reported not eating breakfast in the past week and a similar proportion were trying to lose weight. Excessive diet practices like fasting, diet pills or laxatives and vomiting to lose weight were reported by 25% of the students. Findings suggested that these adolescents are skipping breakfast as part of a patterned lifestyle of unhealthy weight management and that schools must make greater efforts to encourage healthy diets.

An information system to help consumers translate recommendations for nutrition into dietary guidelines was devised by United States Department of Agriculture (2012). The government website describes a healthy diet, by age level, with a focus on fruits, vegetables, whole grains, and low-fat milk and milk products. This diet of lean meats, poultry, fish, beans, eggs, and nuts is low in saturated fats, trans fats, cholesterol, salt (sodium) and added sugars.

Another method to encourage self-monitoring is by helping teenagers become aware of Go, Slow, and Whoa foods identified by The Nemours

Foundation (2012), a leading pediatric health system. Go foods, like skim and low-fat milk, can be eaten anytime whereas Slow foods, like pancakes, should be eaten only sometimes. Whoa foods, like french fries, should be eaten only on occasion as special treats.

Epidemic of Obesity

Adolescents are defined as overweight if their BMI (body mass index) is in the 85th to 94th percentile, and obese when they are in the 95th percentile or higher. From 1980 to 2008 the proportion of overweight among 12- to 19-year-olds more than tripled, increasing from 5% to 18%. The government estimates that 9 million students are fat enough to endanger their health and 5 million more are on the verge of joining the high-risk group. About 25% of Hispanic and Black adolescents are overweight compared with 15% of Whites (Heinberg & Thompson, 2009). Obesity is the result of caloric imbalance (too few calories expended for the amount of calories consumed) and is mediated by genetic, behavioral, and environmental factors.

Obesity is the greatest public health threat, accounting for more fatalities than AIDS, cancers, and accidents combined. The problem begins in childhood with number of fat cells becoming fixed by age 10. Parents should realize that child obesity merits immediate concern. Studies have determined that 7% of children with normal weight parents grow up to be obese while 80% of children with two obese parents will become obese adults. There is an increase in gastric bypass surgery that drastically reduces the stomach capacity, causing people to feel full from meager amounts of food. The medical community is agreed that weight-loss programs generally do not work. A success rate of 1% is the norm. Physical activity must be part of the strategy because exercise and weight management have to go together (Harcombe, 2010).

What concerns health care professionals is the cost in lives. Obese youth are three times more likely than peers of healthy weight to develop high blood pressure and twice as likely to suffer heart disease (Heinberg & Thompson, 2009). There is a saying that "You are as old as your arteries," implying that the condition of your arteries is more important than chronological age in the evolution of heart disease and stroke. Geetha Raghuveer (2010), a cardiologist at the University of Missouri Kansas City, examined 70 obese boys and girls whose average age was 13. Ultrasound imaging was applied to measure the thickness of the inner walls of their carotid arteries in the neck that supply the brain with blood. The intention was to gauge their vascular age, referring to the age at which the level of arterial thickening would be normal. For these teenagers their vascular age generally was 3 decades older than their chronological age; that is, the thickness of their arteries was typical of persons 45 years old.

Other dire predictions indicate that one of every two children will develop Type 2 diabetes because of excess weight, raising the probability that they will die at a younger age than their parents. Diabetes is the sixth leading cause of death and major cause of kidney failure, blindness, and nontraumatic leg amputation. An obese adolescent can expect to live 12 to 14 years less than a peer of desirable weight. The cost of medical treatment for children with obesity is three times more than treating the average child. Reflection is needed because it is easier to prevent obesity than treat it (Codario, 2010).

EXERCISE AND FITNESS

Benefits of Exercise

Choosing to exercise regularly is beneficial because it will contribute to overall health. More specifically, it aids in weight control by using excess calories that would otherwise be stored as fat. Exercise helps to reduce the risk of chronic diseases like diabetes, high blood pressure and cholesterol, heart disease, osteoporosis, and some cancers. Other benefits of exercise include building strong muscles, bones, and joints, improving flexibility and balance, warding off depression, improving mood, sense of well being, and better sleep. Physical activity may include structured activities like walking, running, biking, hiking, basketball, tennis, golf and other sports. It may also include daily tasks like household chores, yard work, or walking the dog. Teens who adopt exercise as a part of their daily regimen are likely to continue the practice in adulthood that may lengthen life expectancy (Darst, Pangrazi, Sariscany, & Brusseau, 2011).

Levels of Exertion

Moderate to intense physical activity is recommended for at least 30 minutes on most, if not all, days of the week. An expert panel reviewed the research on effects of physical activity on young people's health and well-being. More than 850 articles and 1,120 abstracts were examined. The conclusion was that children who participate in moderate to vigorous physical activity one hour or more each day gained significant physiological, health, and psychological benefits. Less than half of all adolescents are physically active on a regular basis. Instead, many maintain a lazy lifestyle that includes sitting at a desk or computer during the school day and watching television or spending time on the Internet while they are home (Darst, Pangrazi, Sariscany, & Brusseau, 2011).

Cultural Differences

Investigations across cultures underscore the relationship of exercise and health. There has been speculation about the extent to which developing type 2 diabetes is due to the genes inherited and our environment (mainly diet and lifestyle). A National Institutes of Health project compared Pima Indians from Arizona with Pima living in the Sierra Madre mountains of Mexico (Schulz et al., 2006). The Pima groups have a similar genetic heritage and, for comparative purposes, resemble identical twins that grow up apart. The Arizona Pima Indians have the highest rate of type 2 diabetes in the world; 34% of the men and 41% of the women are affected. However, prevalence of the disease for the Mexican Pima was previously unknown. When researchers completed a physical examination of 224 Mexican Pima (77% of that population), it was found that only 8% of Pima men in Mexico and 9% of women had diabetes, a rate only slightly above the 7% for 193 other non-Pima Mexicans living in the same area. The pattern was the same for obesity rates.

What aspects of the environment protect Pima south of the border from obesity and diabetes? The diet of Mexican Pima actually contains more fat and less fiber than the Arizona Pima while similar numbers of calories are consumed. The main difference between the groups involves greater physical activity by the Pima in Mexico. Most of them make a living by physical labor and grow their own food. They plow their fields with help of oxen, then plant and harvest by hand. On the other hand, the Pima north of the border in the United States drive trucks or cars and farm with aid of highly mechanized equipment. Most purchase their food at a grocery store. According to researchers, the lower prevalence of type 2 diabetes and obesity in Pima Indians of Mexico than in the United States shows that, even in populations that are genetically prone to these conditions, development is still influenced more by environmental circumstances, thereby suggesting that type 2 diabetes is largely preventable. This investigation offers compelling evidence that changes in lifestyle associated with Westernization has a major role in increasing the global epidemic of type 2 diabetes (Schulz et al., 2006).

SEXUAL ACTIVITY

Sexual Intercourse and Diseases

Early adolescents, ages 10 to 13, usually identify one friend of their same sex as the closest relationship that they have outside the family. During this time teenagers are curious about anything sexual and they want to learn about intercourse. Sexual feelings, especially among boys, are often expressed by telling dirty jokes. When teenagers first become capable of sexual intercourse, they are years away from having the emotional maturity needed for an intimate relationship (Pfiefer & Middleman, 2006). During middle adolescence, age 14 to 16, a shift occurs from being with one friend to spending more time in a group. Most adolescents want to develop a relationship with someone of the opposite sex and their group often influences kind of involvement. Dating and double dating begins and is soon followed by sexual experimentation. Peers can impose pressure to lose virginity, causing some to engage in sexual intercourse. By ages 17 to 20, the perceived social pressure for intercourse is no longer a common main concern (Steinberg, 2011).

Sexually active adolescents are those who have had intercourse at least one time. In the national Youth Risk Behavior Surveillance System, about half (46%) of girls and boys (46%) for Grades 9-12 reported that they had engaged in sexual intercourse, with somewhat higher percentages among Blacks and Hispanics than Whites (Centers for Disease Control and Prevention, 2011b). The average age of first intercourse for girls was 17 and 16 for boys. Most of the girls (73%) and boys (81%) did not use any birth control and 90% never sought testing for sexually transmitted diseases.

Teenagers are at greater risk for sexually transmitted diseases than older age groups partly because they are more likely to have a partner who has been sexually active with others, engage in oral sex, and are least likely to consistently use protection. The rate of sexually transmitted diseases (STDs) among adolescents is growing at an unprecedented rate. According to the Centers for Disease Control (2011a), adolescents represent 25% of the sexually active population but account for 50% of the sexually transmitted diseases.

Each year an estimated 3 million adolescents are diagnosed with gonorrhea, chlamydia, or viral infections like herpes and human papillomavirus (HPV). Most of these diseases are treatable by use of medication but while antibiotics can destroy bacteria, this is not so for the AIDS virus. Medication can slow progression of this disease but there is no cure. Diseases such as herpes and HPV, the leading cause of cervical cancer, may recur even if there has been treatment. The longer STD treatment is delayed, the greater the risk for complications (Sutton 2012).

Gay, lesbian, and bisexual teenagers are often reluctant to identify their sexual preference owing to doubts about the accuracy of their feelings and concerns about potential ridicule and rejection from their peers and relatives (Savage & Miller, 2012). Sexually active adolescent male homosexuals are at far greater risk for chlamydia, hepatitis B, gonorrhea, AIDS, and syphilis. Homosexuals with multiple partners are at even higher risk. A condom can reduce but not eliminate risk of infection (Isay, 2010).

Contraception and Pregnancy

Rates of teen pregnancy have declined in the past 2 decades. Nevertheless, a more targeted approach to prevention seems needed. This is because one in two Latina teenagers (51%) gets pregnant at least once before age 20; this rate is much higher than the national average of 31%. By 2025, estimates are that one-quarter of all American teenagers will be Latino. Whatever happens in this group will undoubtedly affect the nation as a whole (Suellentrop, 2010).

Contraception is prevention of pregnancy by methods like condoms or birth control pills. Sexually active teenagers who do not make use of contraception have a 90% chance of becoming pregnant within a year. Teenagers should understand types of birth control, limitations of each method, and where to access them. Birth control techniques include hormonal contraceptives and the barrier method using a condom or diaphragm. Each kind of birth control has advantages and disadvantages. Condoms provide the most protection from infection but may not be as helpful in prevention of pregnancy (Farber, 2009).

The United States has the highest teenage pregnancy rate among Western nations. Half of these pregnancies occur within 6 months of a girl becoming sexually active. Teenage mothers are more likely than older mothers to have a poor diet, receive welfare, lack prenatal care, and sustain anemia. They have twice the normal risk of delivering a low birth weight baby (less than five-and-a-half pounds) that exposes infants to a higher probability for mental retardation and other developmental problems (Zastrow & Kirst-Ashman, 2010). The main reason why adolescent girls quit school is pregnancy. Less than half of teen mothers graduate and fewer than 2% obtain a college degree. Eight of 10 fathers do not marry the teen mother of their child and rarely pay child support. The daughters of teen mothers are three times more likely to become teen mothers themselves than women who had a child at age 20 or older. Sons of teen mothers are twice as likely to spend time in prison than sons of mothers' age 20 or older. Communities must strive to be more comprehensive in helping teen mothers complete high school, fulfill their parent obligations, and prepare for a job (Suellentrop, 2010).

Abortion is a form of intervention to end a pregnancy by removing an embryo or fetus from the womb. The Supreme Count, in 1973, ruled in the Roe vs Wade case that abortion was legal. During the past decade, abortion rates have declined in every state. Approximately half of 700,000 teenage pregnancies annually end in live births, 35% end by abortion, and 14% end in miscarriage. Teenagers generally do not believe that getting married is the solution for an unplanned pregnancy. About 60% of the adolescents that marry just because of pregnancy divorce within 3 years. Unwed mothers experience less social disapproval today than during the past. Consequently, fewer than 5% surrender their babies for adoption (MacLeod, 2010)

Researchers and policymakers concerned about teen pregnancy focus mostly on romantic relationships between adolescents of the same age. The assumption is that their newfound passion is the main cause of pregnancy. Less well known is that minor-age girls (under 18) are often impregnated by much older men (Cocca, 2004). The evidence was first discovered in the late 1990s when vital statistics for California found that men over age 25 fathered twice as many teenage births than did males under age 18; men over 20 years of age fathered five times more births to middle school girls than middle school males. Data for 46,500 births to mothers aged 10-18 years in California was examined to determine the extent of adult male involvement in school-age childbearing. In 85% of births, father ages were available on birth certificates. In only 34% of all births, the fathers were a school-age peer of mothers; 66% of the fathers were older than high school age adults who were 4.3 years older than the mothers. Post-school-age adult fathers were a majority regardless of ethnicity (67.8% for Hispanic births, 62.9% for Whites, 58.8% for Blacks, and 63.6% for Asians). The younger the mother, the greater the age difference between herself and the father of their baby (Males & Chew, 1996).

To determine whether these figures were unique to the state of California, the Population Reference Bureau carried out a national study. Findings indicated that two-thirds of births to minor age girls throughout the country are fathered by men age 20 or older (De Vita, 1996; Kaestle, Morisky, & Wiley, 2002). The National Longitudinal Study of Adolescent Health data on 2,000 teenage girls were analyzed to find out how the age gap between a minor age female and adult age partner might influence the relationship. Age difference between partners was found to be an important predictor of whether they would engage in sexual intercourse. Adolescent females involved with an adult age partner have higher odds of intercourse with that partner than females do involving partners their own age. Magnitude of this association is most dramatic among the younger females. For example, the odds of intercourse among 13-year old females with a partner 6 years older are 6 times the odds among 13-year old females with a partner of their same age. Females age 17 with partners that are 6 years older have twice the odds of intercourse when compared with those having a same age partner (Halpern, Kaestle, & Hallfors, 2007).

Oral Sex and Risks

There is anecdotal evidence that many adolescents are turning to behaviors that can avoid pregnancy but leave them vulnerable to sexually transmitted diseases, such as herpes, chlamydia, gonorrhea, HPV, and perhaps HIV (Brewster & Tillman, 2008). Although empirical studies are scarce, extant data suggests that half of high school students have given or received oral sex, using their mouth and tongue to stimulate the genitals of a partner. Some researchers believe that combining oral sex and intercourse is becoming a common pattern in relationships (Malacad & Hess, 2010). Researchers at the University of California Division of Adolescent Medicine in San Francisco assessed perceptions of 580 ninth graders on oral versus vaginal sex. More participants reported having oral sex (40%) than vaginal sex (30%). They evaluated oral sex as less risky than vaginal sex and believed that oral sex is more acceptable for their age group in dating and nondating situations (Halpern-Felsher, Cornell, Kropp, & Tschann, 2005). Adolescent girls, especially those in abstinence programs may regard oral sex as a method to preserve their virginity while still providing the intimacy of sensual pleasure. In such cases, they misinterpret public health messages about disease as relating to vaginal sex only.

Comprehensive Sex Education

Comprehensive sex education programs emphasize abstinence as the best way to prevent pregnancy, guidance to avoid sexually transmitted diseases, advice on family planning and contraception, and, when appropriate, prescriptions for contraceptives or referral to a birth control clinic and prenatal care. Medical professionals are in favor of comprehensive sex education because it provides information about abstinence as well as contraception and condoms. Most parents and students feel adolescents have a right to accurate and complete sexual health information as part of their education. This view reflects a belief that knowledge supports better decision making than lack of knowledge and can help teenagers protect themselves from sexually transmitted infections, know how to avoid unin-

tended pregnancy, value abstinence, and make choices that enable fulfillment of personal ambitions while maintaining physical and mental
health.

Comprehensive sex education begins with goal setting, decision making,
and responsibility. There are discussion on topics like masturbation, birth
control, sexually transmitted diseases, premarital sex, abortion, and homo-
sexuality. Research has found this strategy generally promotes favorable
health. Specifically, behavioral outcomes include delaying initiation of sex,
reducing number of partners, curbing incidence of unprotected sex, and
increasing use of condoms and contraception among sexually active participants. The long-term consequences are lower pregnancy rates and less
sexually transmitted disease. From 1998 until 2010, the single approach
supported by federal funds was abstinence-only-until-marriage curriculum.
In these classes, students learned about the failure rate of condoms, were
discouraged from using them to prevent sexually transmitted diseases or
pregnancy, and signed pledges of virginity (Santelli & Crosby, 2009).

The Mathematica Policy Research Institute in Princeton, New Jersey,
carried out a multiyear evaluation of abstinence programs for the Department of Health and Human Services. The purpose was to assess the
impact of four programs on 1,200 students from rural and urban communities in Florida, Wisconsin, Mississippi, and Virginia. Six years after students began the program at age 11 or 12, they were compared with 800
similar peers who had not participated in abstinence classes. Results
showed that the classes had no effect on sexual abstinence. Students
enrolled in the program were just as likely to have intercourse as those not
attending the program (Trenholm et al., 2007).

In 2010, the federal government began to fund sex education programs besides those of abstinence-only that had been the single focus for
over a decade. A grant of $375 million, from 2010-2015, was divided
among 28 programs that have been able to lower pregnancy rates regardless of the curriculum focus. This approach is intended to give adolescents tools they need to make decisions about sex and involves no
matching funds from states. About 30 states maintain abstinence-only
programs that serve one million students. These states still receive $50
million a year in grants but are required to match $3 to every $4 that the
government grants (Rabin, 2010).

The overall conclusion from research on sex education is that encouraging abstinence and contraception are compatible goals. Abstinence-
only-until-marriage curriculum teaches teens about abstinence but not
birth control; this approach makes it more likely that once teenagers
begin sexual activity, they will have unsafe sex and risk greater exposure
to sexually transmitted diseases. Discussions about contraception in comprehensive sex education programs do not increase sexual activity, and

abstinence programs that provide medically accurate information regarding contraceptives for those already sexually active can support better health (Kohler, Manhart, & Lafferty, 2008).

SUBSTANCE ABUSE

The scope of protection that is needed to foster adolescent health goes beyond the sexual domain and includes substance abuse. Public rejection of hard drugs such as cocaine and heroin has been motivated by studies showing how lives are destroyed by dependence upon illegal substances and observation of damage to individuals. A generation ago many adults decided to quit smoking and pay more attention to physical fitness. Attitude shifts were reflected by preferences for beverages with less alcohol. In the past decade, synthetic drugs like methamphetamines have become appealing to adolescents at great cost to health. While the proportion of teen smokers is in decline, this behavior continues to be a hazard with potentially fatal consequence.

Marijuana and Cocaine

Monitoring the Future is an annual survey of 50,000 students from Grades 8, 10, and 12 in 400 schools, conducted by the University of Michigan and National Institute on Drug Abuse. Since these annual studies began in 1975, marijuana has been the most prevalent illicit drug. About 38% of 12th graders, 30% of 10th graders, and 16% of eighth graders report they use marijuana, and it is readily available. The appealing effects are feelings of relaxation, euphoria, elevated self-confidence or altered perceptions of time and space. However, teenagers seldom realize that marijuana is a gateway drug leading to more dangerous substances like cocaine. Similarly, parents who may have used marijuana in the past see it as harmless since they are unaware of how the drug has changed since the time of their youth. Because of technology with hydroponics, plant cloning, and sophisticated lighting systems, the marijuana that adolescents smoke is ten times more potent than a generation ago. Each year more teenagers enter treatment centers with a diagnosis of marijuana dependence than all other drugs combined (Johnston, O'Malley, Bachman, & Schulenberg, 2011).

Two-thirds of marijuana users are younger than age 18. They are less likely to smoke marijuana if their parents strongly disapprove. Only 3% of teenagers whose parents strongly disapprove reported using marijuana compared to 29% of those whose parents do not disapprove. Marijuana can impair judgment, coordination, balance, and ability to pay attention, reaction time in driving accidents and increases the rate of age-related hippocampus neuron loss leading to persistent memory loss. The drug has adverse affects on the respiratory system and associated with bronchitis, emphysema, and lung cancer (Nistler et al., 2006).

Methamphetamine Hazards

Methamphetamine is known by many names such as speed and glass. Use of speed that began as a fad by motorcycle gangs during the 1970s has become a major concern. Law enforcement ranks meth as the number one drug that they have to battle (Weishelt & White, 2009). Congress passed the Combat Methamphetamine Epidemic Act in 2006 (Kennedy, 2006). Teenagers should be aware of how methamphetamine works. Dopamine is the natural pleasure chemical of the brain. Whether it is smoked or injected, methamphetamine has the effect of releasing a powerful stimulant causing the brain to release a surge of dopamine that creates a euphoric high lasting 6 to 24 hours. Meth can also cause a dramatic increase in heart rate, resulting in irreversible narrowing of brain blood vessels, leading to a stroke and severe respiratory problems. The drug also influences the central nervous system, making it difficult to fall asleep. Users often become confused, have tremors, and suffer convulsions, anxiety, paranoia, and aggression. A loss of teeth and sores all over the body are common signs that a person is taking meth. Researchers have found that meth changes wiring of the brain by destroying the dopamine neuroreceptors. Changes in rewiring require a year or more to regrow the receptors. During that time, users often slip into deep depression that may cause relapse (Roll, Rawson, Ling & Shoptaw, 2009).

In Montana, where the epidemic got underway, 85% of women inmates in state prisons have been placed there because of meth-related crimes. Users are entering prison in record numbers while their children often overwhelm the social services system. During the 1990s, foster care in cities increased dramatically because of crack babies but meth originated as a rural phenomenon where batches are more easily cooked in barns without notice of neighbors. As a result, orphans began to appear in places where there are no social service networks to support them when courts took them away from their parents (Owens, 2007).

Montana's effort to confront the meth epidemic has been supported by Thomas Siebel, a Silicon Valley billionaire raised on a ranch in Montana. He began by donating $6 million to fund a prevention campaign that is like no other. In an attempt to learn from adolescents, focus groups were held with them to assess their views on meth. Almost half the students expressed their belief, based on stories they had been told, that meth can be more beneficial than dangerous and worth a try (Weishelt & White, 2009). Civic leaders decided to adopt a novel strategy by presenting striking visual images with stories by teen addicts telling how they became involved and their tragic results. Graphic pictures appear on the Internet, billboards, and television showing addicts and the ways in which their lives have been damaged. Radio spots discourage youth consideration of the drug.

Alcohol and Public Safety

Alcohol use is widespread among teenagers. Forty percent of eighth graders and 73% of 12th graders have consumed alcohol. Over half (56%) of 12th graders and 20% of eighth graders reported being drunk at least once. When asked whether they had consumed alcohol in the past 30 days, 14% of eighth graders, 29% of 10th graders, and 41% of 12th graders indicated yes. Fortunately, overall rate of alcohol use by adolescents is in decline (Johnston, O'Malley, Bachman, & Schulenberg, 2011). The adverse effects that drinking has on schoolwork and behavior are documented (Crosnoe, 2006). Instead of viewing this behavior as a rite of passage, neurological evidence shows that alcohol damages brain development making teenagers more likely to become alcoholics than was once supposed. In a national study of 43,000 adults, 47% who started drinking before age 14 became alcohol dependent compared with 9% of those who waited to drink until they were at least 21 years old (Hingson, Herren, & Winter, 2006).

The recognition that half of all alcohol-related deaths in car accidents involved teenage drivers triggered formation of a group called Mothers Against Drunk Driving (Lerner, 2011). From the outset, this organization planned a campaign to save lives which eventually led all 50 states to raise the age for purchasing and drinking alcohol to 21 years. Nevertheless, automobile accidents continue to be the leading cause of teenage death, accounting for 6,000 lives lost each year—a fatality rate four times higher than for drivers aged 25-69. Many injuries can be prevented by seatbelts. Although driver education courses, school programs, and state laws urge drivers to buckle up, teenagers are less likely than other groups to heed the warning (Wanberg, Timken, & Milkman, 2010).

Smoking and Addiction

The United States Food and Drug Administration (2012) mandated cigarette packages have to present clear and truthful information about smoking by visible graphic health warnings. Nine required warnings are rotated on packages such as "Cigarettes cause fatal lung disease," "Cigarettes cause strokes and heart disease," "Smoking can kill you," and "Quitting now greatly reduces serious risks to your health." Each warning must cover 50% of the front and back of the package and include a national phone number for possible contact by those who seek assistance in becoming able to stop smoking.

The Centers for Disease Control and Prevention (2010) reports that 20% of high school students smoke cigarettes, about the same proportion as adults. Each day an estimated 3,000 persons younger than age 18 start smoking. Tobacco use is the most preventable cause of death, causing 443,000 fatalities a year, more than AIDS, alcohol, accidents, murders, suicides, and drug taking combined. On average, smokers die 13 to 14 years earlier than nonsmokers. Adolescents that smoke underestimate the health risks and overestimate their ability to quit once a habit has been established. The reality is that, among high school seniors who smoke several cigarettes each day, 70% will still be smoking 5 years later. The younger that students are when they begin to smoke, the greater their chances of becoming a heavy smoker as adults (Centers for Disease Control and Prevention, 2012a, 2012b).

For most adolescents, the health commitment needed to refuse tobacco and other drugs comes from supportive families, relatives who do not smoke but listen, make suggestions, encourage goal setting, and provide help. The orientation that makes a family more able to function effectively involves education. According to the Centers for Disease Control (2011b), the likelihood of adolescent exposure to smoking in their family differs substantially by formal education of the parents. Respectively, 8% of parents with a bachelor's degree smoke, compared with 20% that attended some college, 29% of those completing high school and 30% with less than a high school diploma. Parent education on a school web site should try to change these figures.

Peer influence has a powerful effect on the decision to smoke. There is evidence that most adolescents see smoking as an unattractive habit and have developed norms that act as a deterrent to the use of tobacco. The Centers for Disease Control (2005) conducted a national survey of teen opinions about smoking and found reasons why smoking is unpopular. Being exposed to secondhand smoke concerns teenagers who believe they have a right to breathe clean air. The facts supporting this view are that secondhand smoke: produces six times the pollution of a busy highway; causes 30 times as many lung cancer deaths as all regulated pollutants combined; contributes to 300,000 lung infections like pneumonia and bronchitis; produces reddening, itching and watering eyes, wheezing, coughing, earaches, and asthma; fills the air with the same poisons found in toxic waste dumps; and distorts the smell and taste of food while making a person's clothes and hair stink.

All high schools and most middle schools provide some antidrug education. These programs acknowledge that peer influence has greater impact on substance abuse than all other factors (Johnston, O'Malley, Bachman, & Schulenberg, 2011). A longitudinal investigation involving 2,000 adolescents examined five risk behaviors including alcohol, marijuana, smoking, tobacco chewing, and sexual debut. For each risk, friends were identified as the most influential source for adopting unhealthy behavior and enabling cessation. Therapy can produce progress but if adolescents later return to interaction with drug-taking friends, chances are the treatment effect will not last. In such cases, advising someone to adopt refusal skills is seldom effective because the most powerful influence in their lives remains a negative force. This means students need a new group of peers to encourage and monitor a healthier path (Prinstein & Dodge, 2010).

Peer counseling is the most effective form of drug prevention for adolescents (Geldard & Geldard, 2009). Using this strategy, students who sign a contract pledging they will stay tobacco, alcohol or drug-free receive extensive training by the school counseling staff for roles that allow them to act as positive leaders for peers. They learn ways to build self-esteem in classmates that lack friends, provide alternative kinds of support as well as constructive goals for those whose peer group is moving in the wrong direction, and help acquire and practice refusal skills. Peer leaders can be examples in classes, on sports teams, and in extracurricular clubs.

RISKS AND LIFESTYLE

Taking a risk means that something may go wrong, a chance of injury, damage or loss. Risk taking can also bring benefits that would not occur otherwise. Adolescents are generally more willing than adults to take risks. Poor judgment by teenagers is a great concern of parents and teachers. Parents tell daughters and sons to "be careful." This vague advice is meant as a gentle reminder that foolish risks yield disappointment. Everyone has to make decisions about risks throughout life that could jeopardize health, safety, development, and success. Learning to recognize the risks worth taking and ones to avoid is a constant challenge.

Scope of Youth Risks

Adolescents are more willing than adults to take risks. Some of the dangerous risks for youth include: pregnancy, sexually transmitted diseases, drugs, meeting with online predators, lack of sleep, drinking alcohol, truancy, dropping out, joining a gang, participating in criminal activity, and bringing a weapon to school. There are also risks associated with cheating, lying to parents and teachers, procrastination in completing classroom work, smoking cigarettes, chewing tobacco, lack of exercise, poor nutrition, failing to get help if needed, and running away from home. Other risks involve reckless driving, riding with a drunk driver, ghost riding when a driver leaves the car to do stunts while the vehicle is moving, and car surfing where a driver and a stunt passenger lie, kneel or stand atop the car. Adolescents can improve decisions about risks when they know the benefits of risk analysis that can be provided by adults whose perspective and feedback they trust (Amsel & Lightfoot, 2012).

The Centers for Disease Control and Prevention (2011b) Youth Risk Behavior Surveillance System (YRBSS) monitors six types of health-risk behaviors that contribute to the leading causes of death and disability among youth and adults, including (1) behaviors that contribute to unintentional injuries and violence, (2) tobacco use, (3) alcohol and other drug use, (4) sexual risk behaviors, (5) unhealthy dietary behaviors, and (6) physical inactivity.

Origins of Risk Analysis

Some observers believe that teachers should discourage all forms of risk taking including academic failure. An opposite conclusion comes from research on how risks influence behavior. First, being able to accurately gauge risk is a skill everyone needs to learn because it can prevent foolish choices. Consider what can happen when people are unable to accurately assess whether particular risks are appropriate or believe their courage is confirmed by engaging in activities shunned by others as being too risky.

During the Korean conflict in the early 1950s, military leaders introduced a new practice to protect soldiers. Risk analysis involves monitoring ability of individuals to accurately gauge the risks they face. Psychological teams were assigned to conduct risk analysis with air force squadrons (Torrance & Ziller, 1957). The purpose was to identify fighter pilots who should be removed from a battle zone. Prior to this strategy, the only consideration for relief from warfare had been completion of a specific number of combat missions. This policy was amended to include risk analysis for pilots who flew too low or too close to the enemy response system so they jeopardized the lives of crew members, aircraft, and the mission. Because of severe stress associated with their task, some pilots took on the characteristics of high-risk takers. Actually, they were no more courageous than fellow airmen but seemed to lose the common fear that is needed to carry out successful bombing runs. Therefore, whether they had flown the minimum number of flights to justify a furlough, pilots identified by risk analysis as in need of relief were reassigned to Hickham Field in Honolulu for recuperation. The reason for removal from the battle scene was to help pilots recover their usual sense of caution, the normal degree of fear essential to effectively perform their dangerous task (Torrance, 2000).

This risk analysis strategy of psychological teams is credited with saving many lives and reveals that the individual capacity to accurately gauge risk is a fundamental survival skill that can sometimes cease to function, even among highly intelligent people (Vose, 2008). Adults who are concerned about their well-being should continually monitor this aspect of adolescent behavior. Certainly, classrooms do not present dangers comparable to the battlefield. However, school can present significant risks. Students who dropout are more likely to become casualties than survivors (Cosby & Poussaint, 2007).

Monitoring Judgment

Just as the American fighter pilots required external feedback in order to identify when their risk assessment ability was impaired, adolescents need to have teachers and parents help with risk analysis. In particular, it is essential to challenge the personal fable that often causes teenagers to believe they are invulnerable, somehow exempt from the consequences of the risks that others choose to avoid. A broad spectrum of behavior implicated by the personal fable is evident from comments by ninth graders. They confidently announce, "I will not get a sexually transmitted disease because my boyfriend told me that he has never done it with anyone else." "The television warnings are inaccurate; tobacco does not have to be a tumor causing, tooth staining, smelly puking habit because I am an occasional smoker, not a chain smoker."

Another example of taking unreasonable risks can involve driving a car. Teens surpass adults in physical ability to respond quickly. However, they are also responsible for a disproportionate number of car accidents. The leading cause of death among 16- to 20-year-olds is car wrecks. Poor judgment is identified as the primary reason for most fatalities (Medina, 2009). A related consequence is that insurance rates are higher for teenage drivers than for adult drivers. And, the rates for boys, who take greater risks behind the wheel than girls, remain more expensive until age 24 when the risk taking moderates so thereafter similar rates obtain for both genders (Kelly, 2005).

Many teenagers are reluctant to ask adults for their advice before taking risks that could carry a high price. Discussions about gauging risk can be more helpful than trying to instill fear or assuring adolescents that they are trusted unconditionally. There is greater benefit when, in a low-risk setting with adults who care about them, teenagers can calmly reflect on possible outcomes of actions that have not been taken yet than to consider the damage of poor decisions after the fact. A teacher, relative or friend with a reputation for willingness to listen is sometimes permitted by adolescents to review problematic options and the anticipated costs linked with each choice. These dialogues provide adults an opportunity to monitor the risk assessment ability of the adolescent and urge that choices always consider the effects on long-term plans. When students commit themselves to long-term goals, it is easier to avoid foolish risks (Benson, 2010).

When students recognize rewards that can come from growth-oriented risks, they become more willing to take these sorts of risks. For example, setting goals is a risk that can provide a sense of purpose, guide behavior, and minimize boredom. Asking questions in class presents a risk of admitting ignorance but holds the promise of becoming more informed. Providing authentic feedback to teammates in cooperative learning groups is a risk that can enable awareness and preserve honesty. Giving advice is a risk revealing the scope and limits of one's perceptions. Becoming a volunteer is a risk that requires helping others whose needs could be ignored. Self-assertion is a risk that involves acquainting others with how we stand on matters of importance. Sharing differences of opinion poses the risk of conflict but can promote mutual learning. Taking elective courses about unfamiliar topics risks exposing novice frames of reference but offers new perspectives. Trusting friends and relatives is a risk that can be a basis for reciprocal support. Risking spontaneity requires departure from a predictable routine but may offer worthwhile experiences that could not be planned.

SUMMARY AND IMPLICATIONS

A challenging aspect of adolescence is acceptance of a realistic body image. Daily observation of differences between peers and self in height, weight and sexual maturation is a pervasive source of anxiety among adolescents. Appearances matter to them because their identity and status within the group are implicated. Puberty changes for boys include growth of the scrotum and penis, capacity for ejaculation, appearance of body hair, bone and muscle gain, and deepening of the voice. Puberty for girls means breast development and menstruation. There is a need to know in advance that their breasts may not develop at the same rate and menstrual periods could be irregular and accompanied by cramps with possible pain. Parents and teachers should have dialogue with students regarding sexual development and protection from sexually transmitted infections. Schools can also support health by conducting vision screening and hearing tests to identify disabilities that could reduce learning and detract from quality of life.

Teenagers like being the decision makers about what they eat but often choose foods that are not good for them. In 2006, Congress passed a law that brings school menus into compliance with guidelines that support healthy eating habits on campus. Many teenagers who want to conform to the idealized thin body image skip meals and experiment with dieting plans that cut calories but ignore needs for nutrients such as iron and calcium. Exercise is also necessary to support good health. However, most adolescents maintain a sedentary schedule that includes being seated most of the day in school and the habit continues at home with chatting on a computer or watching television. Schools are expected to prepare students for life so curriculum ought to emphasize the importance of a balanced lifestyle that includes time for exercise daily.

Many high school and middle school students report that they have had sexual intercourse. These sexually active youth are less likely than adults to consistently rely on condoms, more likely to have a partner that has also been active with others, and to participate in oral sex. Misinformation about how to prevent pregnancy, underestimates of dangers related to oral sex, and female involvement with partners who are older yield unexpected pregnancies. Half of teen pregnancies result in live births for girls who more often than in the past become single mothers. Comprehensive sex education is widely encouraged as the way to protect the health of teens that might become sexually active and give a more informed message to those pledging to stay abstinent until marriage.

Adolescents want to be independent but lose their ability for self-control if they consume illegal drugs such as cocaine, heroin, and methamphetamine. An effective prevention strategy has been to provide a graphic portrayal of the methamphetamine epidemic including direct reports from addicts who describe the loss of their autonomy. Underage drinking also presents health risks, especially if combined with driving. Car accidents are the leading cause of death among teenagers. Smoking is an addiction for many teenagers who find themselves unable to quit. The forecast that teenage smokers who continue as adults may shorten their life by a dozen years urges schools to create effective methods to help students choose a tobacco free lifestyle.

Adolescents can benefit from adults who assist in monitoring how they assess risks that could place their physical and mental health in jeopardy.

Although peers may be a better source of feedback and guidance for many activities that relate to the youth culture, risk analysis should include input from grownups that have greater maturity than classmates.

APPLICATIONS FOR TEACHING

1. Middle school students should be told that it is normal in their age group to differ from one another in height and weight. Youth who learn about growth patterns are more able to anticipate change and understand their peers also face similar challenges. Body size and sexual maturation are often the focus for teasing. Educators should try to convince students to abandon this unkind behavior.

2. Schools should acquaint adolescents with the increase of hearing loss among people in their cohort, explain potential consequences that can be expected, and describe ways to protect themselves from damage. Faculty, student, and parent initiatives can motivate changes that are necessary.

3. One aspect of lifestyle for adolescents involves fashion, the way they dress and take care of their appearance. When schools invite students to express their views on a poll when adults are getting ready to formulate a dress code for school, teenagers are more likely to believe that their views count, value the rationale for establishing policies, and conform to them.

4. Understanding how to promote and preserve health is an important learning outcome. Districts should provide adolescents with a systematic health curriculum that considers aspects of growth and development, exercise, nutrition, drug awareness, and sexuality. Creating a student norm of healthy lifestyle will support long-term benefits.

5. Oral sex among teenagers is a topic most parents and educators refuse to talk about with students and believe it is a responsibility of someone else. One result of evasion is that teenagers lack a credible source of guidance on this risky behavior. Schools should provide orientation sessions that help faculty and parents confront this issue.

6. Efforts to dissuade adults from tobacco have produced decline in the proportion of smokers. Related initiatives could have a similar effect on teenagers if the schools go beyond just forbidding presence of tobacco on campus to also provide education and mobilize peer influence as powerful means of persuasion.

7. Building relationships with students, providing individualized attention, encouraging peer support, and making sure parents are informed about signs of trouble are aspects of intervention that reduce truancy. Truants typically identify lack of social connections at school as a major reason for staying away. This admission underscores a need to arrange cooperative teams to facilitate social connections and feelings of belonging.

8. Students are more likely to adopt reflective thinking for the management of complex problems if teachers make sure there is enough time to process information, deliberate, and reach thoughtful conclusions. When teachers schedule adequate time for tasks students become more able to understand the importance of time management as a way to prevent unnecessary stress.

9. Students can better avoid poor decisions about lifestyle if adults help them monitor their ability to think about possible consequences of risks. Being a caring listener qualifies adults to provide their more mature perspective than the feedback adolescents receive from people of their own age.

PART IV

EARLY ADULTHOOD (AGES 20-40)

CHAPTER 11

CREATIVE THINKING AND INNOVATION

Public opinion about creative thinking is rooted in mythology. Explanations about the inventive mind and production of novel ideas have usually been derogatory. Ancient man supposed that people demonstrating creative thought must be possessed, driven to originality and unconventional behavior by an unseen divine source that chose them as a medium for revelation. The possibility that innovative views might be a product of learning was overlooked. Instead, because the forces of good and evil were believed to be in constant conflict, nontraditional thinking was always suspected as a possible sign of the dark side. Divergent perspectives were usually interpreted as a form of deception, particularly when creative persons challenged prevailing beliefs and customs of their time (Campbell, 2004; Kaufman & Sternberg, 2010).

The goals of this chapter are to explain how the stigma experienced by people who express imagination is gradually shifting to encouragement. Understanding why creative thinking should be valued to the same extent as intelligence is considered. Progressive steps in the creative thinking process are defined and illustrated along with implications for individuals and institutions to arrange conditions conducive to creativity.

Learning Throughout Life: An Intergenerational Perspective, pp. 245–269
Copyright © 2012 by Information Age Publishing

MODERN VIEWS OF CREATIVITY

Negative evaluation of creative people continued until the late 20th century when a new interpretation emerged about the reasons for unconventional behavior. This view linked imaginative functioning with mental break down. Creative people were no longer seen as the pawns of some invisible deity but instead were personally responsible for their deviation from norms of society. Creative thinking was accepted as an internal function but unrelated to learning. Even though few individuals recognized for their genius also suffered from mental illness, this was viewed as the price of innovative thinking. There was no recognition that willingness of creative people to press their nature to its limits is the supreme test of sanity. Those who failed in such efforts were singled out as proof that creative behavior did not deserve public support (Saunders & Macnaughton, 2005).

Current evidence suggests teachers and parents may unwittingly be taking away from children aspects of the gift that they say they want to nurture. Paul Torrance (1965) tried to find ways to preserve creativity of children. In this context, he presents an "ideal student" concept to educators from five countries. Nearly 1,000 primary and secondary teachers from the United States, Germany, India, Greece, and the Philippines were presented a list of 62 student characteristics, each included because of their previous reliability in discriminating between individuals having high and low creative ability. Teachers were instructed to check characteristics describing the kind of person they would like to see their students become, double check five characteristics that were considered most important, and cross out characteristics that ought to be discouraged. Results showed that the ideal characteristics teachers ranked as being most important reflected a view that it is more important for students to be courteous than courageous, show obedience rather than ask questions, remember well instead of being intuitive, and accept judgment of authorities instead of challenge traditional thought. Recruiting creative people to become teachers may be the single greatest advance that could be made and should replace customary criteria that ignore such abilities in candidates.

A portrayal of strengths and limitations of creative persons is documented by Arnold Ludwig (1995), professor of psychiatry at the University of Kentucky. He carried out a comprehensive study about life histories of 1,000 eminent personalities of the 20th century, using their biographies published by The New York Times Book Review. The purpose of his book, titled *The Price of Greatness*, was to examine the relationship between mental illness and greatness, and detect factors that could predict creative achievement. Using statistical analysis, he scrutinized celebrated figures based on their occupation, relative degree of prominence, and their documented psychological and physiological disorders. His findings reveal what the scientists, writers, musicians, artists, political leaders, and military figures had in common with how they looked at life and aspects of dysfunction shared with others who also made substantial contributions in their field. Incidence of drug taking, depression, mood disorders, attempted suicide, alcoholism, and healthy lifestyles are portrayed in this assessment of famous people.

Valuing Imaginative Abilities

During the past decade officials in China, India, Japan, Singapore, Taiwan, and other countries have decided that making creative thinking a priority in schools is the best way to increase productivity, compete better in a global market, and protect mental health (Lubart, 2010; Sahlberg, 2011). China is decentralizing its curriculum to enable flexibility, and Singapore is trying to promote a creative environment reflected by the guiding principle of "Teach less, learn more." These efforts to innovate depart from the Information Age paradigm that dominated education before 2000 with a near exclusive focus on linear, logical, and analytical thinking. Since then it has become clear that memorization must be joined by learning how to process information which is more accurately stored by technology. The emerging Conceptual Age paradigm reflects a premise that preservation of healthy economies will depend on more support for inventive abilities (Pink, 2009). Computing, calculating, diagnostics, and legal work skills will remain important but lose value. This is because any activity that can be reduced to a set of rules and instructions is likely to become a software program like TurboTax that has replaced many accountants and migrated lower order tasks to populations in less developed countries.

There are conflicting impressions about the best ways to arrange conditions to foster creativity. In *The World is Flat*, Thomas Friedman (2005) contends that location no longer has the impact on creative production that it did in the past. Technology has leveled the global playing field, making the world flat so that anyone can innovate without having to emigrate. An opposite view is expressed by Richard Florida (2008) in *Who's Your City: How the Creative Economy is Making Where You Live the Most Important Decision of Your Life*. Florida provides lists of cities on every continent where creative persons often move because their talents are more commonly accepted, collaborators for novel projects can be found easily, and people like to collaborate on interdependent productions. He suggests that innovation can best be encouraged by the geographic concentration of creative persons, entrepreneurs who know that they can count on one another to allow ideas to flow freely, recommend possibilities to improve products, and implement projects sooner because creators and financial backers are in close contact. A small number of communities and regions like the Silicon Valley in California generate most innovative ideas and products used throughout the world.

Most young adults realize they are less creative than they were during childhood when others assigned high value to their imagination that was applied in fantasy play. Creative thinking begins to decline in the early grades when schools and families urge children to disconnect from reliance on imagination (Torrance, 1995). A more promising practice is to ensure that students in every town and city find acceptance of divergent thinking without having to move to specific places in the country where more favorable reaction to new ways of seeing things are the norm. What is known about the future suggests that efforts are needed to ensure that more children can retain their creative abilities into adulthood. Creative individuals are more able to adapt to new knowledge, cope with complex situations, and think of constructive options to resolve differences. They demonstrate greater ability to generate new ways to improve situations, make independent decisions, and feel comfortable with ambiguity (Runco & Albert, 2010).

Valuing inventive capacity is exhibited by an appreciation for imaginative thought. Human beings are unique in being imaginative, that wonderful attribute that enables us to look beyond the moment and current set of circumstances. Imagination allows us to go back in time and revisit the past as well as look ahead by envisioning ways to create a more desirable future. No one can predict what is going to happen tomorrow but our actions, motivated and shaped by imagination, can influence what life will become. We may be evolving biologically at the rate as other living organisms. However, in cultural terms, people change far more rapidly. As far as we can tell, the cats and dogs that we care about do not change at a corresponding rate. Left to themselves, they seem to do what they have always done and concern themselves with the same things. There is no need to keep checking with them to find out what's new. In contrast, something will always be new in human life because of the way imagination triggers creative thinking and innovation.

Assessing Creative Potential

Much of the school curriculum was designed to help students perform well on state and federal tests. Demonstrating competence on these forms of evaluations is seen as achievement. However, the scope of mental abilities covered by standardized tests has to expand so assessment includes creative thinking. No one knows how much cognitive potential goes unde-tected by the customary reliance on intelligence tests as a measure of abil-ities but studies have long suggested a need for revision of the views (Lehrer, 2012).

Joy Guilford (1950), professor of psychology from the University of Southern California, devoted his presidential address to the American Psychological Association to document the need to broaden the definition of thinking. He described his studies with scientists nominated by col-leagues for making outstanding contributions to their field. Each of the nominees was provided with a list of 28 mental functions and invited to rank order them according to perceived importance for being a factor for success in their discipline. All but one of the traditional intelligence test factors ranked below 20th; that is, 19 of 20 characteristics that inventive leaders reported as most salient for success in their work involved abilities that are not measured by intelligence tests. Guilford believed that the pre-vailing view of mental growth focused too narrowly on convergent think-ing where the emphasis is on knowing the single correct answer for a problem and giving a speedy response. These aspects of achievement should not dominate conceptualization of mental functioning to the exclusion of other dimensions needed for creative thinking. Guilford rec-ommended greater attention to divergent thinking, the ability to branch out and generate alternative answers for problems where there may be more than just one solution, and having the ability to perceive many pos-sibilities in situations (Guilford, 1977).

Michael Wallach, professor of psychology and neuroscience at Duke University, and Nathan Kogan of Educational Testing Service are credited with a landmark study that changed the way scholars think about creativ-ity (Wallach & Kogan, 1965). Their research purpose was to determine whether creative potential is measured by traditional intelligence tests or if creativity is a separate domain of mental functioning that must be gauged by the use of other kinds of measures. *Creativity* was defined as the ability to produce many associations among ideas and many that are unique. The 151 students in the sample were fifth graders attending a suburban public school. These students (70 girls and 81 boys) completed intelligence tests and creativity assessments resembling an earlier battery that was devised by Guilford (1950). In administering measures of creativ-ity, speed and evaluation were de-emphasized in favor of a game-like set-ting without time limits.

Operationally, "intelligence" has focused on abilities needed for read-ing and for mathematics, subjects that are not conspicuously demanding of creative thinking. Even though creativity and intelligence domains have been established as separate, someone might earn high ratings in both sectors. One estimate is that, in a group of either highly creative or highly intelligent students, 30% would qualify in both categories. Torrance maintained that the practice of identifying gifted students as only those persons with IQs of 130 or higher results in the exclusion of 70% of the most creative students (Torrance, 1965, 1995, 2002).

Results of a 50-year follow-up on the Torrance tests of creative thinking demonstrated that these measures have been highly predictive of creative accomplishments in adult life (Millar, 2001). Those able to generate more good ideas as children grew up to become inventors, doctors, scientists, authors, and leaders in other fields. Plucker and Baer (2008), at the University of Indiana, reanalyzed Torrance's data and found the correlation to lifetime achievement more than three times greater for creativity scores than for IQ scores measured in childhood.

Decline in Creative Behavior

Changes in the results of creativity testing during recent years are reasons for concern. Kyung Kim (2010), an educational psychologist from the College of William and Mary, conducted a meta-analysis of 300,000 scores of children and adults on the Torrance measures. She found that creativity scores steadily rose from 1970-1990 when progress ended. During the past 20 years scores declined, with the students in kindergarten through sixth grade recording the greatest losses. These are worrisome signs when contrasted with findings of an IBM poll of chief executive officers. These 1,500 leaders from business and industry identified creativity as the most important leadership competency that will be needed for the future (Bronson & Merryman, 2010).

Sir Ken Robinson (2011) is a spokesman for creative thinking. He chronicles how modern nations have come to agree creativity is as important as literacy, and therefore deserves the same level of support, beginning with recognition of creative potential. He tells the story of a primary school girl who paid little attention in class but became highly motivated when it was time for art. During an art lesson the teacher approached her desk to ask what she was drawing. "I am drawing a picture of God," the girl replied. The teacher reminded the girl that nobody really knows what God looks like. The girl said, "They will in a minute." This story illustrates how young children are comfortable looking at situations in new ways, readily participating in activities that they may have never done before, and showing a willingness to take chances motivated by their curiosity. They are not bothered by the fact that the path they choose may turn out to be wrong.

Unfortunately, many families and schools orient children to believe they should always avoid mistakes, causing them to stop generating original ideas. As students advance through the grades, a fear of being wrong means that making mistakes is unacceptable. In contrast, creative children and adults recognize they have to be wrong repeatedly before the solution to a problem may be discovered. They do not become discouraged by making mistakes but instead are motivated by eliminating options that do not lead to solutions.

Robinson (2011) points out, "If you are not prepared to be wrong, it is unlikely that you will ever come up with anything original." The path to creative thinking usually includes side roads that lead nowhere and require backing up, revise our thinking, and map out a new way to reach a destination. Robinson provides examples like Terrance Tao at UCLA, a recipient of the Fields Medal for Mathematics, the highest possible award in his field. He points out that mathematics is a continuous process of trial and error. Someone comes up with a wrong idea and pursues it for a time until realizing that it does not work. Then, another idea is generated for trial. Eventually, by process of elimination, a solution is achieved. Nobel Prize chemist Harry Kroto from Florida State University expresses a similar description of how problems are pursued. When asked how many of his experiments are failures, he estimated about 95% of them but suggests, "Failure is not the right word. You are just finding out what doesn't work." Albert Einstein observed, "Anyone who claims to have never made a mistake has never tried anything new."

What happens when the students who no longer feel comfortable being wrong are placed on a cooperative learning team with creative teammates who see mistakes as directional signs for improvement? A predictable result is that ideas of creative team members may be dismissed because they do not accord with group consensus. This disappointing response can lead creative students to dislike the team experience, a condition that has to change in order to facilitate greater group productivity. Sometimes college teachers want to stimulate creative thinking by using brainstorming tasks. In the 1950s, brainstorming was popular but later proven not to work when Yale researchers found this method actually reduced team output because of consistent expression of premature judgment by conventional thinkers. That is, the same number of people generate more and better ideas if they work independently than together. Clearly, the willingness of less creative students to listen to divergent thinkers is essential for novel ideas to emerge (Lehrer, 2012).

Creative Thinking Process

Most of what is known about creative thinking comes from anecdotal reports of famous people recognized for extraordinary achievements.

These individuals agree about the process that led to their distinction. Based on these self-reports, respective stages in creative thinking are: (1) preparation, (2) incubation, (3) illumination, and (4) verification (Ghiselin, 1987). Elements of the four stages of the creative process are illustrated in Figure 11.1.

(1) *Preparation Stage.* People are often surprised to find out that preparation is essential for creative thinking. Instead, a common assumption is that 'inspiration' just comes to certain individuals but not others. This impression makes it easier to avoid the struggle that occupies all those who create. Preparation (see Figure 11.1) typically begins after individuals experience vague insights and set out to examine some particular problem or realm of difficulty by literally flooding themselves with the diverse impressions reported by others. Many obstacles that undermine

Source: *From Adolescents in the Internet Age,* by P. Strom & R. Strom, 2009, p. 244. Information Age Publishing Inc., Charlotte, NC.

Figure 11.1.   Stage 1 of the Creative Process—Preparation.* *Search date, begin to question assumptions, brainstorm with a partner, and examine the main problems with a better perspective. This process typically takes the most time.*

production characterize the preparation phase. First, the literature about a particular issue may be so extensive that the task seems overwhelming. This appears the case when many search engines could be applied to locate an enormous database for consideration. At this point the person might decide to withdraw from further exploration in favor of some other less complicated topic.

A second danger is that side issues can capture attention and divert interest from the original purpose. This is a familiar shortcoming among people whose indiscriminate curiosity causes them to depart from their main line of direction. They may be pursuing a particular area of inquiry but along the way websites they explore present links that lead them away from their intention. Remaining focused is fundamental and can be demanding when searching on the Internet or at the library.

Third, the impatience that causes people to grapple with specific issues can destroy their chance for success if they prematurely come to conclusions about data. This is a pervasive hazard in situations where rapid production is an expectation. When teachers set deadlines for student inquiry tasks that are too early, they unintentionally encourage superficial consideration of available data. The emphasis on doing things in a hurry is not conducive to creative thinking. It is necessary to recognize an essential aspect of the preparation phase of the creative thinking process is immersion in the ideas and insights that have already been reported by others. Awareness of these impressions produces the material on which synthesizing ability is applied. Abandoning a problem or a project at this stage is much easier than later because little effort has been invested and the degree of emotional involvement remains minimal.

Many young adults see themselves as lacking creative potential because novel ideas have not come to them without preparation. This view can be revised by reading about lives of eminent individuals who report their failures, successes, and necessity to rely on the resilience produced by courage (John-Steiner, 2000). Courage is necessary to move alone toward uncertainties, express views counter to those held by others, and do battle with personal habits of thinking to accommodate new ways of looking at things. The necessity to confront a task repeatedly calls for acceptance of the failure preceding success. More than most people, creative individuals experience failure because they do not withdraw from complexity. Many people never suffer significant failure because they are so easily discouraged that they quit projects before ever getting into them. At the same time, they can never fully succeed. Curiosity enables creative persons to sustain a question, a problem, or a task and work through to completion. The history of creative persons who have contributed the most is an account filled with endurance and courage.

(2) *Incubation Stage.* The second step in creative thinking is called incubation (see Figure 11.2). During this stage there is an irrational, intuitive encounter with the materials that were gathered in the search process. At this point people experience feelings of unrest and stress as they attempt to produce an ordering structure, a recombination of the data that can result in a unique and practical contribution. The incubating person usually becomes preoccupied with the task. One intended result of trying to avoid any distractions is that the individual sometimes fails to attend to routine tasks expected by others. As they strive to allow intuitive ideas to take conscious form, creative persons are often dissatisfied with themselves and difficult to be around. Sometimes conflicts ensue with relatives or friends who see lack of attention to them as a deliberate insult (Cain, 2012).

During the incubation stage, self-doubt presents a great hazard. Confidence is vital when unconscious activity brings up new possibilities for combination one after another. It is necessary that the conscious mind avoid disapproving of ideas as they emerge, defer judgment until later when a range of unconscious products have become available. Feeling obliged to withhold judgment until the associative flow ends is a very difficult and demanding task that requires a high tolerance for ambiguity and frustration. Mental health is typically delicate in the incubation phase, which can vary from a few minutes to months.

Source: From *Adolescents in the Internet Age,* by P. Strom & R. Strom, 2009, p. 246. Information Age Publishing Inc., Charlotte, NC.

Figure 11.2.   Stage 2 of the Creative Process—Incubation.* *In-depth pondering, sketch or test ideas, get frustrated, recognize paradigm paralysis, look for one's niche.*

Schools cannot foster creative thinking unless students have time for reflection, assigned as homework or tasks in class. Elizabeth Blackburn (2009), a professor of biochemistry at the University of California at Berkeley and 2009 Nobel Prize winner for physiology and medicine, shared advice with young students in her native Australia:

> I think it is important that you engage energetically in your learning but you also need time to daydream, to let your imagination take you where it can. Just do that some of the time because I noticed that among the creative, successful scientists who've advanced things, that was a part of their life. Not that they did not work hard but we sometimes forget about the creative part of science.

Many students express discomfort or boredom when they are expected to focus on anything for very long. Instead of accommodating this dysfunctional inattention by declaring it a norm, educators should strive to find effective ways to implement creative thinking. In addition, the pace of their production often discourages students, that they cannot do everything in a hurry. Teachers add to the frustration when they construe lack of speed as a lack of ability, being slow as a sign of failure. It should be understood that the amount of time needed for production depends on the individual. Mozart and Beethoven represent polarities in the realm of musical production. Mozart conceptualized quartets and symphonies in his head while traveling or exercising. After returning home he would write complete melodies. Beethoven who wrote compositions note by note, fragments at a time recorded in a booklet over years, reflects the opposite circumstance. Often his initial ideas were so clumsy as to make one wonder how, at the end, such beauty could appear (Ghiselin, 1987). Ernest Hemmingway (1964, p. 154) in his retrospective admitted, "I didn't know I would ever write anything as long as a novel. It often took me a full morning of work to write just one paragraph." This giant of literature later wrote classic novels in 6 weeks.

During incubation, anything that is disruptive to concentration is likely rejected. There are some individuals for whom incubation can occur on and off over a long period of time. However, for others the attempt to produce ideas leads to excessive measures to sustain touch with their unconscious in an environment that is noisy and distracting. Not everyone is psychologically capable of spending the same amount of time in the tension-producing phase of incubation. Yet, creative persons commonly prefer to work in long blocks of time so that they can be fully engaged. This is the stage when other people—classmates, relatives, and teachers—should understand the self-absorption that a person experiences. Giving up at this stage is done at great expense since creative persons typically consider not achieving the next stage, called Illumination, as total failure. Albert Einstein observed, "The intuitive mind is a sacred gift and the rational mind is a faithful servant. We have created a society that honors the servant and has forgotten the gift" (Ghiselin, 1987, p. 43).

(3) *Illumination Stage.* If the incubation stage presents what Van Gogh referred to as a "prison" in which people are confined to internal conversation and debate, then the illumination phase is analogous to being released from jail and obtaining a full pardon. Illumination (see Figure 11.3) is viewed as the inspirational moment that the artist Paul Cezanne described as liberation, the mysterious becoming external, and the time when everything falls into place (Ghiselin, 1987). It is the exhilarating triumph creative persons like so much to relive, the time that is beyond words. Charles Darwin, whose search for the theory of evolution came to an end on a dusty lane, recalled the spot on the road while traveling in his carriage that, to his joy and surprise, the solution occurred to him (Darwin & Wilson, 2005). Creative scientists, inventors, artists, and writers all tend to look back in nostalgia at this brief but cherished moment and speak of it as mystical. Illumination lifts the burden of tension and creative persons can regain touch with those around them.

Some creative persons, especially those who have awaited illumination for a long time, make an effort to retain their joy by sharing it. Their accounts of how they reached some new idea is less than exciting to others who view the rapid shift in personality from a total preoccupation with work and seeming depression to happiness and conscious delight as a possible sign of mental illness. They may wonder at extremes in behavior of a creative person and especially the sudden elation expressed about

Source: *From *Adolescents in the Internet Age,* by P. Strom & R. Strom, 2009, p. 248. Information Age Publishing Inc., Charlotte, NC.

Figure 11.3.   Stage 3 of the Creative Process—Illumination.* *"Ah-ha"—finding the answer, loving the idea, taking the leap, and assembling the main pieces that fit well.*

something others do not understand and therefore dismiss as less important than is the case. Further, in returning to a normal state of conscious-
ness, some individuals have trouble figuring out why others have become
distant toward them during the interlude (Ludwig, 1995).

For some persons, the creative process ends with attainment of the illumination stage because they have achieved the tentative answer and shed
stressful tension. At this point, they may choose to move to confront another
problem or interest. Persons of this inclination seldom gain recognition or
contribute as much as possible since they do not go on to make the form of
their invention coherent to others who could support its broader application or modify it to fit a wider range of prevailing situations.

(4) Verification Stage. The stage of verification takes place after an idea
or plan has emerged from unconscious activity and must then be consciously evaluated (see Figure 11.4). Some creative persons find a need for
verification difficult or impossible to accept because emotional certainty
regarding worth of their ideas or products prevent them from accepting
criticism or suggestions for adaptation. Nevertheless, the pleasure of illumination must give way to rational judgment as a determinant of final
production. If a writer is to communicate, the inspired work must become
organized and edited. There must be a coherent flow for readers to
understand the message. Similarly, a successful experiment that produces
elation must be clearly described (Storey & Graeme, 2005).

Unlike the brief illumination phase, verification is often lengthy,
arduous, and at times disappointing to a person whose patience declines
because of eagerness to get on with another project. The hazard awaiting
many writers, scientists, and creators in technology and art is the
temptation to avoid the steps necessary for follow through. This
temptation has prevented good work from becoming public knowledge.
Well-known writers such as Samuel Coleridge and Percy Shelley left

Source: *From Adolescents in the Internet Age,* by P. Strom & R. Strom, 2009, p. 249.
Information Age Publishing Inc., Charlotte, NC.

Figure 11.4. Stage 4 of the Creative Process—Verification.* *Testing final idea to see/
correct faults—"final edition," assessment by outsiders, experience clousure and recognize
success via individual or social judgement criteria.*

fragments of unfinished work because they were unwilling to revise it, feeling their inspiration could not be improved and alteration would depreciate the illumination. Hart Crane was an exacting author. A careful look at his manuscripts reveals revisions involved as much doubt as decision. In contrast, Gertrude Stein disliked the drudgery of revision and responsibility to make her writing intelligible to the public (Ghiselin, 1987). Being willing to consider the criticism of reviewers is necessary at this stage. Sadly, most students have not been taught in school or at home to value criticism of their performance. This means personal growth is limited because introspection is the only source to gauge personal shortcomings. Insight during the writing revision process can improve organization, structure, clarification, and flow of the narrative.

IMPROVING CONDITIONS OF ACHIEVEMENT

Independence has long been considered a key to success. The more recent perspective is that interdependence is also necessary, requiring attitudes and skills of teamwork that facilitate group achievement. Valuing imagination of individuals while encouraging groups to avoid premature judgment of ideas is a challenge young adults face in the workplace. Readiness to accept criticism from teammates and being able to provide constructive recommendations must become more common assets (Lehrer, 2012).

Motivating Creative Production

Two observations based on a decade of studies at Brandeis University provide additional clues about ways to facilitate creativity (McCabe, 1985). First, freedom has been identified as the best method to motivate creative production. Something happens when the interests of individuals are respected, allowing them a chance to decide some of the goals they will pursue and ways to achieve their purposes. Having self-control increases the prospect that a person will explore unlikely paths, take healthy risks, and, in the end, produce something unique and useful. This is the reason Google, Apple, Microsoft and other innovative companies schedule time during working hours for employees to depart from their assigned tasks to pursue their own hunches or dreams related to the mission of the company (Lehrer, 2012).

A second finding about production is that frequent evaluation smothers creativity (McCabe, 1985). This conclusion runs counter to the belief of most young adults that they are able to perform better when provided continuous feedback on their work. This is true when the goal is to master convergent thinking tasks that depend on conformity and therefore do not require departure from conventional thinking. However, if creative thinking is the goal, people do better when production is reviewed less often. Creative people are able to judge their own progress without having to always check with others for confirmation that their evolving ideas will be acceptable. Knowing how to accurately judge personal progress is a characteristic of high achievers and requires confidence that is seldom attained by those who feel compelled to continually seek approval from peers. Persons that are the most inhibited and least capable of expressing imaginative ideas are those engaged in high-pressure occupations where they experience weekly or monthly evaluations (Beghetto, 2005).

Appreciation for Group Identity

Support for creative thinking has centered on extraordinary individuals but this orientation has to expand as greater reliance is placed on teams. This means creativity will increasingly have to be achieved within a social context (Cain, 2012). Educators have been slow to link creative behavior with interdependence. A related concern involves disparity between the work roles needed for global competition and symbolism with which people are able to celebrate their values. Even though there is agreement that teamwork is essential, this asset is often overshadowed by residual priorities from the past. For example, if asked to imagine and describe heroic myths about salesmen, assembly line workers or truck drivers, our vocabulary is strained. Instead, the dominant preference is to honor the cowboy, detective, athlete, or movie icons like James Bond or Superman. These characters embody virtues that we know how to celebrate—individual achievement, individual exploits, and individual strengths.

Guidelines for how to succeed come from a previous era when the pursuit of excellence was defined almost exclusively in terms of individuality, independence, autonomy, self-reliance, being and making it "on your own." These attributes will continue to be important. However, their relevance should no longer be seen as a complete design to enable personal influence or group productivity. The quest for independence should be linked to appreciation for interdependence as shown by teamwork. Helping employees value and pursue goals beyond individual identity is recognized as an enormous challenge for business (Tapscott & Williams, 2010b).

Accepting and Giving Criticism

The willingness to accept criticism contributes to successful adjustment of groups and teams. However, few young adults have been taught to process criticism or benefit from the criticism of others. As a result, defensiveness is common and personal growth is diminished because people rely on themselves alone to detect their needs for growth (Drucker, 2008). Introspection is valuable but cannot provide a comprehensive picture. The tendency to reject criticism reflects a larger societal outlook that keeps people from becoming self-critical, a vital condition to motivate change (Pink, 2009).

Thomas Friedman (2005) in *The World is Flat* explores implications of globalization. He speculates that nations must begin to look at themselves with greater scrutiny. The need is for a strategy analogous to Alcoholics Anonymous where all the members are obliged to see themselves as they really are and make their circumstance known by standing up to announce; for example, "My name is John Jones, and I am an alcoholic." In a corresponding way, nations in the anonymous club might rise and admit to their limitations. The important point is that nations claiming to be part of a global union should go beyond historic self-impressions that center on pride and boasting to include becoming self-critical as well, followed by a decision to make progress, to evolve and become more successful.

Everyone is subjected to occasional criticism. Critics surround creative persons committed to excellence. They are criticized for nontraditional ideas, taking a stand, refusing to compromise principles, sharing their faith, challenging authority figures, or trying new ways of doing things. Creative people require courage to sustain their effort to make contributions and not expect their ideas will have immediate approval of others.

RECOGNITION OF VISUAL LEARNING

Howard Gardner (2011), Harvard University professor of Education has proposed a theory of multiple intelligences involving eight realms of ability. One of these domains is visual intelligence, composed of visual-spatial abilities that enable people to create views of the world and think in pictures. Schools have ignored this asset except for a small minority of students identified as gifted within the visual arts. However, recently it has become obvious that we live in an increasingly image-driven society. The media influence communication, awareness, and decision-making mediated with visual representations offered by computers, digital cameras, cell phones, and television. The observation that "a picture is worth a thousand words" was intuitively recognized during the past. There is reason to believe lessons that include digital images could be retained to a greater degree than those gained only by reading or listening (Williams & Newton, 2006).

Much of what students learn outside of the school attributes to visual images they see on television, the Internet, and video gaming devices. George Lucas, creator of *Star Wars* and other classic films, recommends teaching communication in all its forms instead of the customary narrow focus on written and spoken words. According to Lucas (2005):

> Everyone needs to understand the importance of graphics, music, and cinema which can be just as powerful and, in some ways, more deeply linked with young people's culture. When people talk to me about the digital divide, I think of it not so much about who has access to technology as who knows how to create and express themselves in the new language of the screen. If students are not taught the language of sounds and images, shouldn't they be considered as illiterate as if they had quit college without becoming able to read or write?

Memory for Visual Information

Considerable research has been conducted regarding declarative, procedural, and episodic memory. In addition, there is also an image memory for visual materials. Research has long shown that memory for pictures are much greater than memory for words. Shepard (1967, 1990) presented 600 pictures to students. When students were tested immediately after their observation they correctly identified 98% of pictures. A week later they were able to accurately identify 85% of pictures.

Comparison of text and oral presentations versus pictorial presentations have found visuals are always more effective. When information is presented orally, people recall about 10% when they are tested three days after exposure. The recall rate rises to 65% if a picture or some visual element is added. So great is the advantage of visual memory that it has been designated as the pictorial superiority effect (Brockmole, 2008). The distinction did not matter as much before the Internet began to introduce such a broad range of visual resources. Because of the enormous selection of visuals accessible from Discovery Education (2012), YouTube, and other websites, educators need to incorporate this element to optimize learning.

The dual coding theory of information processing explores superiority of pictures for memory tasks. This theory proposes that human long-term memory contains two distinct and interdependent codes, one verbal and another visual based (Paivio, 1990). One assumption is that the two codes produce additive effects so, if data is coded visually as well as verbally, probability of retrieval doubles. Another assumption is that the manner in which pictures and words activate the two codes differ. Pictures are more likely to be stored visually as well as verbally. For example, someone might recall the title of a book and be able to remember the color or image of the cover. Words alone are less likely to be stored visually. When it comes to memory, two codes seem better than one.

Teachers can increase the probability for information to be dual encoded for long-term memory with a consequent improvement of retention, retrieval and transfer. Dual coding is more likely if lessons are partially presented by imagery, graphics, visual networks of information, and spatial mapping (Orey, McClendon, & Branch, 2006). Graphic organizers such as webbing, concept mapping matrix, flow charts, and Venn diagrams help illustrate, describe, compare, classify, and sequence concepts. Then too, students can transpose more benefit from being referred to observation of streaming videos. The website of a teacher can include advance organizers outlining daily lessons in words or notes and use visual symbols and charts that draw connections between concepts.

An Image Driven Environment

Education reforms to enhance visual learning would sustain benefits that come from customary forms of learning while also becoming capable of accommodating ever-increasing exposure to visual lessons that are provided by media. Many students may be more visually than verbally literate. Boards of education across the nation have expanded the definition of basic skills to include media literacy and make it a high school graduation requirement. The concept of *media literacy* is defined as "ability to communicate competently in all the media forms, print and electronic, as well as to access, understand, analyze and evaluate images, words, and sounds that comprise mass media culture." Media literacy could empower more people to behave as critical thinkers and become creative producers capable of using image, language, and sound (Smith, Moriarty, Barbatsis, & Kenney, 2005).

The Center for Media Literacy in Los Angeles maintains convergence of media and technology for a global environment is changing how people learn about the world and challenging the foundations of education. Being able to read the printed word is no longer a sufficient source of information. Everyone should also acquire abilities needed to critically interpret images in a multimedia culture and express themselves as well in multiple media forms. An inquiry-based theory for learning about media is proposed in conjunction with methods that merge analytical (deconstruction) skills with creative communication (construction/production) skills (Jolls, 2010).

Visual and Verbal Intelligence

How are visual intelligence and verbal intelligence different? People relied on pictures long before written words appeared as forms of communication. Verbal intelligence can be expressive (active) or it can be receptive (passive) but visual intelligence does not have a passive mode for thinking or learning. It appears that visual intelligence has a more prominent function than verbal ability in terms of the process of invention, originality, and discovery. That is, words come later than do images in the creative process and sometimes may be inadequate for communication (Barry, 1997).

Every language has many words people rely on to describe their ideas, feelings, and events. Relatively speaking however, there are fewer corresponding visual prompts that are easily understood. The image of a flashing light bulb is usually presented to illustrate the insight experience in creative thinking, that moment of sudden revelation when the solution for a problem becomes known. It is noteworthy that great thinkers whose insight has influenced history in science, art, mathematics and other fields commonly identify visual thinking or visual images as central to their discoveries. The language of insight is sometimes reported as visual —"I see it now." The English word idea derives from the Greek word Idein, which means "to see." There are many words that link vision with thinking like insight, foresight, hindsight, and oversight (Williams & Newton, 2006).

The famous mathematician Roger Penrose observed visual thinking dominates thinking processes of gifted mathematicians. He explains his own mathematical thought is done visually using nonverbal concepts, although thoughts are often accompanied by inane and near useless verbal commentary such as "that thing goes with this one and this thing relates to that" (Penrose, 2002). His view is corroborated by recollections of other well-known scientists. For example, Albert Einstein maintained written or spoken words did not play an important role in his thinking processes. Instead, physical entities serving as elements of thought were seen as signs in more or less clear visual images Einstein was able to voluntarily reproduce and combine them. He acknowledged that conventional words or other forms of expression had to be reached through struggle only in the second stage of creative thinking, after connection of ideas was sufficiently established and could be reproduced at will.

In a similar way, Frances Galton (1874) explained,

It is a serious drawback to me in writing, and still more in explaining myself, that I do not think as easily in words as otherwise. It often happens that after being hard at work and having arrived at results that seem perfectly clear and satisfactory, when I try to express them in language I feel that I must begin by putting myself on quite another intellectual plane. I have to translate my thoughts into a language that does not run evenly with them (p. 14).

Visual intelligence and media literacy training should become more prominent in the classroom as educators and the public recognizes the limitations of analogies that inappropriately equate the brain with computers. Such common comparisons are based on the capacity of computers for information processing speed and access to data storage. However, what is now known about the brain places it far ahead of computers in higher-order thinking. Specifically, it appears to be in the context of visual functioning, as contrasted to verbal functioning, that the brain is elevated to a higher status (Ward, 2009). This distinction was recognized a generation ago by McKim (1980) who argued that computers are unable to see, dream or create. Computers are language-bound. Thinkers who cannot escape the structure of language rely upon only that small portion of their brain that resembles a computer.

Digital Images and Curriculum

Merging digital images and direct instruction is increasing in schools. Discovery Education (2012), the nation's largest digital video-on-demand service for schools, offers an illustration of how greater exposure to images can support instruction. More than half of American schools enrolling 30 million students use this service. The appeal for teachers is to choose from a library of 50,000 video content clips as brief as 2 minutes, 5,000 full-length titles, 20,000 photographs, and gallery of 1,500 art images.

Discovery Education (2012) videos are categorized by grade and keyed to state department standards for subjects such as mathematics, biology, and American history. The digital materials selected are stored on the local server by subscribing schools. Teachers can upload videos to seamlessly fit a PowerPoint or similar format in the classroom. New videos are continuously added to local servers for consideration. There are closed caption titles for visual impaired learners, hearing impaired, and students acquiring English as a second language.

There is a need for educational research to explore the relationship between use of digital video and the attention span of students. Think about your own experience with movies, video games, and Internet searching. For example, people watching movies seldom stop before the end of a film and even less often claim they had a hard time paying attention. Why is this the case for films that are often 2 or more hours in length? One line of speculation is that films enable the spectators to stay involved because they see pictures and hear soundtrack simultaneously. In contrast, without a stream of images and related sound track, the lectures teachers provide often produce student claims of distraction, loss of attention, and boredom.

Educators lack suitable measures of attention span but often make estimates by observing how long students appear able to concentrate on verbal presentations. The typical conclusion is that students have short attention spans for this aspect of work. Therefore, teachers have been advised to restrict the length of time scheduled for direct instruction. Sometimes attention deficits are attributed to television, supposedly creating a dependency for merging pictures with sound punctuated by predictable interruptions of advertisements.

Multimedia presentations can be implemented by combining video clips and PowerPoint, exemplifying concepts through use of photos, diagrams, props, or artifacts, and Internet sites. In addition to increased visual imagery, it can be helpful to break up lectures with one or more group activities, each lasting for at least 10 minutes. This interaction minimizes monotony and, more importantly, encourages the students to actively process and reflect on material that has just been covered. College students are more attentive in stimulating environments; in a nonstimulating environment, short attention spans are predictable. A promising explanation for teachers is to accept a challenge of providing support for the development of visual intelligence in school and plan instruction so presentations are augmented with digital video and student engagement (Gardner, 2011).

Interpreting Media Experience

When television was introduced in the 1950s, people thought of it as being an extension of human senses, enabling viewers to travel to far away places and observe events vicariously. The assumption was that spectators would be able to make rational decisions about the credibility of content that they saw on the small screen. After all, television was like photography, providing a window on reality while also disseminating information. Technology has since made changes that complicate the processing of visual learning.

The common experience is that images stream past viewers so fast that we are unable to use reflection as a basis for responding to the media-created reality. Even local news stories move quickly to emotionally involve viewers while bypassing their critical thinking. When the video satellite systems present pictures from other countries in real time, accompanied by a brief explanation, spectators must base their reactions primarily on the selected images and verbal excerpts provided them. This prospect of observing events without training related to critical interpretation and reflection caused Marshall McLuhan (1911-1980) to forecast that, in a technological environment, the media becomes the message. McLuhan's contention was everyone experiences more than they will ever understand but it is experience more than understanding that has the greater impact on behavior (McLuhan & Flore, 1967). This is especially the case in relation to media where people can be unaware of the effect that it has on them.

A notable model that established a media-created reality emerged during the 1990s with *ER*, a television program originating in the emergency room of a hospital. Michael Crichton, designer of the show, reported that his formula for success was to speed up the pace with each episode having multiple stories and many speaking parts. This innovative format appealed to millions of viewers who found the rapid action more exciting than customary experience with in-depth treatment. This format is distinguished by a "long-take" in which the vantage points of viewers are moved incessantly, scene changes occur quickly without interruption and visual continuity is retained by using a single camera outlook that drives through the corridors and rooms in a roller-coaster fashion. Some characters lend credibility to the action by using medical terms. There are impressive sound bites that substitute for dialogue. Indeed, the hurried chain of events moves along so rapidly that it is difficult for the characters to convey complex information. Many other programs later adopted the same format.

Nonstop action that imitates truth without being able to cognitively examine what is happening disadvantages spectators because they are denied the active role that is necessary to weigh, balance, and make decisions about what has been seen. Continual exposure to programs in which there is no time or any recognized need to participate in reflective thinking tends to discourage young viewers from acquiring listening habits and responding skills that are fundamental for solving problems and for collaboration. When reflective activities are missing in class, many students announce their conclusion that school is a boring place.

Critical thinking is the habit of mind that resists being deceived by appearances. Everyone should be aware of the emotional power of visual images and the potential they have to exert subconscious influence, how programs as well as advertisements mimic logic while bypassing involvement with critical thought, consequences of abandoning reflection as the basis for making decisions, and implications of individual inattentiveness. Each of these concerns related to visual intelligence warrant consideration owing to a direct influence on media information processing, learning, and behavior.

SUMMARY AND IMPLICATIONS

Creativity and intelligence have been found to be separate domains of mental ability. Divergent thinking promotes the discovery of multiple ways to solve problems when there is no single correct or convergent answer. Inventive thinkers from diverse occupations report similar steps in the creative process they rely upon that includes preparation, incubation, illumination and verification. Creative thinking is in decline for the United States. In response, it seems wise to consider that the prevailing lifestyle of rushing to finish jobs, multitasking, and allowing distractions to interfere with extended concentration prevents the fulfillment of steps in the creative process and undermines the prospect for innovation.

Creativity has traditionally been associated with individuals that pursued ideas on their own, often without encouragement. More favorable conditions have begun to arise. An emerging set of expectations honor the interdependence and productivity expressed by teamwork because this approach can encourage individuals with different strengths to combine their expertise in solving complicated problems. Creativity is most prominent in groups at school and at work where curiosity is the norm, opportunities for reflective thinking are provided, and everyone values imagination. Increased productivity depends upon how creative individuals are treated by less creative teammates. When inventive thought is taken seriously, creative individuals see merit in interdependence and can appreciate teamwork instead of withdrawing to try solving problems on their own. Being talented results in rejection when classmates see creative peers as curve raisers that lower the status of everyone else. In contrast, creative students whose teachers arrange opportunities to help others find that classmates come to see them as a resource and recognize them for their leadership.

Learning to process criticism is an unmet need in most classes. Practice in giving and receiving criticism should be an integral aspect of learning so students become less defensive. Teams are more effective when all members make constructive suggestions and avoid the inclination to judge new ideas without sufficient examination. If growing complaints of students about boredom can be seen as a wake-up call, it can encourage greater emphasis on preservation of imagination and capacity for internal stimulation. When teammates are assigned different tasks as homework, there is greater novelty, less monotony, diminished boredom, increased sharing, and broader scope of group learning.

APPLICATIONS FOR TEACHING

1. Teacher awareness that intelligence and creativity are different domains of mental ability should lead to caution against reaching conclusions about capability of students based entirely on their intelligence test scores. Such measures do not identify highly cre-

ative students. Schools can support creativity by administering appropriate measures that assess ability and plan activities that nurture more divergent thinking.

2.   Students should be familiar with the progressive steps of the creative process and recognize how this information should be used to guide the way assignments and class projects are scheduled, worked on, reviewed, and completed. As students begin to appreciate the importance of classroom planning to support their creative thinking, they should also recognize the corresponding accountability expected of them.

3.   College students have greater opportunity to learn skills of time management when they do not have excessive homework that prevents them from using time after school for other activities. When class projects involve due dates, it is appropriate to have planning discussions with students to decide when certain aspects of their obligation should be completed. This monitoring ensures that procrastination is recognized as unacceptable. There is also merit in discussing the importance of balancing work with play to support optimal mental health.

4.   Creative students must feel comfortable when participating in groups or they tend to withdraw. One way to improve their status is encouraging them to help teammates with difficult tasks or concepts whenever there is lack of comprehension. As classmates begin to view the talented student as an asset to their team, the individual is usually recognized for leadership, valued for willingness to be a source of help, and becomes aware that communal achievement can make individual success more satisfying.

5.   Students who ask lots of questions, enjoy guessing, show preoccupation with tasks, act like visionaries, and show a willingness to take risks are usually creative. Teachers should encourage students to continue these behaviors rather than discourage them. In order to stimulate creative talents, teachers must approve some mental abilities that may be more prominent in the behavior of their students than themselves.

6.   Students should be told that they are expected to enhance the curriculum by searching the Internet or journals for ideas and materials that can enrich content of their course. Their insights, based on self-selected out-of-school learning sources, should be shared in teams or with the whole class as arranged by the teacher. Students accountable for sharing learning with others soon appreciate the concept of interdependence, usually adopt a broader view of the student role, are recognized by peers for leadership in helping

them, and benefit from teammates who reciprocate with their teaching function.

7. Express creativity by combining visual and verbal methods in original ways to convey concepts. Students report they are stimulated by the freedom of being able to seek their own information on the web. The appeal of novelty and its influence on motivation can be experienced by sometimes departing from routine so that students can participate in an unexpected activity or pause to find out how they think a lesson can be applied. Such strategies help sustain interest and link lessons with real life.

8. Every teacher should experiment with ways to help students provide and accept peer criticism. Unless teams are able to process critical feedback in a nondefensive manner, they are likely to forfeit the benefits of insights that can be offered by external observers. Practice in giving constructive suggestions to peer efforts are skills young adults need so they can become more able to contribute to success of their team.

CHAPTER 12

RESILIENCE AND STRESS

Young adults, 20 and 40 years of age, encounter developmental tasks that have implications for the rest of their lives. They are expected to decide about an occupation, complete the education that is needed to qualify for a career, obtain a position, and become financially independent. Other expectations may include finding a suitable partner, maintaining relationships within a social network, getting along with colleagues, and arranging for a healthy balance between time devoted to work and leisure. Fulfilling these plans lead to self-improvement and also increases exposure to stress. The goals for this chapter are to examine: (1) common outcomes of stress, (2) factors that contribute to resilience, (3) influence of anxiety and uncertainty on mental health, (4) workplace effects on morale and productivity, (5) relation of job status to amount of stress, and (6) chemistry of stress. Consideration is also given to: (7) distinctions in the perspective of differing age groups at work, and (8) ways intergenerational understanding can become the basis for a more harmonious and productive environment.

INFLUENCE OF STRESS

Stress and Personality

Emotional health depends on being able to adjust to change, cope with anticipated and unforeseen stress, respond to frustration in a healthy way,

Learning Throughout Life: An Intergenerational Perspective, pp. 271–295
Copyright © 2012 by Information Age Publishing
All rights of reproduction in any form reserved.

avoid excessive anxiety and worry, value diverse points of views, and perform effectively as a team member. Hans Seyle (1956), a professor of medicine from the University of Montreal in Canada, was the first scientific observer to detect connection between stress and health. Seyle identified two kinds of stress. *Eustress* refers to pleasant situations people adapt to such as graduating from college, moving into their own apartment, being hired, and receiving a promotion. The opposite type of stress is distress. This experience occurs when disappointing situations require adaptation. For example, breaking up with a boyfriend or girlfriend, being mistreated by someone with higher status or feeling shunned by another cohort because of disagreements about issues at work that present distress.

People differ in the sources of stress they are exposed to and degree to which external pressures influence them. The weight of specific external stressors is not the only factor that warrants consideration. Another variable is the way people perceive their situation. At one pole of vulnerability are individuals who seem stress resistant in their ability to handle considerable pressure and still carry on effectively. At the other extreme are personalities that appear to collapse whenever they are exposed to even slight pressure. Studies of stress-resistant individuals have determined that they share certain characteristics. Specifically, they (1) are aware of negative forces in their environment but choose not to engage and become preoccupied by them, (2) remain open to possibilities for change, (3) look at new and challenging situations as opportunities for growth, (4) feel a need to become involved when they believe their actions can make a difference, and (5) possess an internal locus of control and feel in charge of most things that happen to them. The contrasting orientation, referred to as external locus of control, describes persons who are convinced that their destiny is controlled by fate, luck, or more powerful people (Shaffer, 2008).

Resilience and Health

Research has discovered that the way someone perceives an event or situation can often be more important than what objectively exists. Those who can readily adapt to new conditions while retaining a sense of personal control possess a psychological hardiness reflected by greater tolerance for stress. This hardiness is a basic element of resilience, working toward a good outcome without being overwhelmed by the risks that could threaten development (Elliott, Menard, Rankin, Elliott, Huizinga, & Wilson, 2006). Resilient people experience doubts and uncertainties like everyone else does but they are more able to recover from setbacks and disappointment that might otherwise cause them to give up. Resilient people are flexible and share faith, hope, and optimism about the future.

The quality of resilience can be observed among low-income students whose surroundings are mostly destructive but who, nevertheless, beat the odds and transcend their circumstance to become adults recognized for achievement.

There is evidence that cognitive styles have an impact on emotions and behavior. The key appears to be an emphasis on accurate thinking more than on positive thinking. For example, resilience is supported in classrooms and households by lessons on the importance of optimism, assertiveness, and flexibility. This strategy improves outlook on life, enhances academic performance, and reduces probability of depression (Reivich & Shatte, 2003). Nearly 20% of young adults indicate that they experience periodic depression, twice the rate reported by their middle-age parents (Twenge, 2007).

To confront this emotional challenge, Martin Seligman (2006), a clinical psychologist and his colleagues from the University of Pennsylvania conducted 19 controlled global studies with 2,000 students, from 5 to 18 years old. In the Penn Resiliency Program, students were taught to think more realistically and flexibly about everyday problems. Teachers emphasized the benefits of slowing down the problem solving process, helping students identify their goals, retrieve information without focus on speed, and generate alternative possibilities to attain their purpose. During the ensuing two years optimism rose while the risk of depression was cut by half. The implication is that conditions at school that nurture emotional well-being can improve health and academic performance.

Seligman, a former President of the American Psychological Association, is cooperating with the United States Army to teach resilience to soldiers before their deployment. The Comprehensive Soldier Fitness Program focuses on resilience training to prepare them for fearful challenges encountered in battle, sometimes leading to depression, suicide, substance abuse, and posttraumatic stress disorder when they return home. The program includes five dimensions (Millerrodgers, 2010):

1. *Physical*—performing and excelling in physical activities that require aerobic fitness, endurance, strength, healthy body composition, and flexibility derived through exercise, nutrition, and training;

2. *Emotion*—approaching life's challenges in a positive, optimistic way by demonstrating self-control, stamina, and good character with choices and actions;

3. *Social*—developing and maintaining trusted, valued relationships and friendships that are personally fulfilling and foster good communication including a comfortable exchange of ideas, views, and experiences;

4. *Family*—being part of a family unit that is safe, supportive, and lov-
    ing, and provides the resources needed for all members to live in a
    healthy and secure environment; and,

5. *Spiritual*—strengthening a set of beliefs, principles or values that
    sustain a person beyond family, institutional, and societal sources
    of strength.

Relatives and friends should recognize the advantages of giving
encouragement to one another, acknowledge setbacks, resolve to overcome obstacles, and identify corrective behaviors to implement. This
"come back" kid type of experience forms the basis for confidence that
difficult challenges in the future can be seen as opportunities for success.
Playing on a sports team that loses regularly calls for an ability to accept
defeat while also aspiring to better performance next time. Failing a
course ought to motivate a request for tutoring, followed by hard work to
achieve the necessary skills. When people try to protect their loved ones
from confronting adversity, these forms of protection frequently have the
effect of rendering a person less capable of surmounting unforeseen challenges experienced by everyone. Development of resilience requires some
exposure to risk.

Ann Masten at the University of Minnesota has conducted a longitudinal study of 205 disadvantaged children to trace their resilience over
time. Thirty years after Project Competence began it continues with 90%
retention of the original sample. Masten's insightful observations have
revealed the ways some participants grew up to become successful despite
significant risk factors like poverty, violence, broken families, and discrim-
ination. An important finding has been that those who overcame the risks
they encountered early in life had access to greater protection and
resources along the way than did less successful peers lacking external
assets. Instead of assuming the course of individual development is forecast by socioeconomic status, there is considerable evidence that dire circumstances can be reversed if healthy goals are supported by community
interventions (Masten & Narayan, 2012).

Cost of Sustained Stress

Individual perspective mediates how stress is perceived. Nevertheless,
sustained stress can erode capacity to cope with adversity and sustain resilience. The relationship of psychological stress to biological aging was initially detected by Elissa Epel and Elizabeth Blackburn (2004) from the
University of California in San Francisco. Their studies have focused on
telomeres, genetic structures at the tip of each of the 46 chromosomes.

Like caps on the end of shoelaces, telomeres function to prevent strands of DNA from unraveling and thereby promote genetic stability. Each time a cell divides and duplicates, a portion of DNA telomeric shrinks by a few basic pairs. Cells reproduce themselves often to strengthen host organs, grow, or fight disease. However, as people age, telomeres shorten and, following many rounds of division, DNA has diminished to such an extent that a cell can no longer further divide or properly carry out its function. Professor Blackburn is credited with the discovery of an enzyme, called telomorease, that helps replenish a portion of the telemorease lost with each division of cells. Blackburn received the 2009 Nobel Prize in Physiology and Medicine for her research showing how chromosomes are protected by telomerase with implications for cancer and longevity studies (Nobel Prize, 2009).

Epel and Blackburn (2004) studied a group of young mothers whose children were disabled. These mothers, who met in a weekly support group, had in common the difficult caretaking task they were obliged to continue for an indefinite period of time. The research hypothesis was that sustained exposure to the extraordinary psychological stress the mothers had to endure would eventually influence length of their telomeres. Blood samples from 39 mothers taking care of a child suffering from chronic type disorders like autism and cerebral palsy were compared with the blood samples of 20 mothers who took care of children that did not have any disabilities.

White blood cells, central to the immune system response to any infection, were examined with particular attention to telomeres. Results revealed that blood cells of mothers who had spent years taking care of their disabled child were genetically more than a decade older than mothers the same chronological age who had less demanding caretaker obligations. The longer the mothers had taken care of a disabled child, the shorter the length of telomeres and the lower their telomerase activity.

Using a self-rating scale, mothers reported the extent to which they were overwhelmed by their daily tasks, and how often they found themselves unable to control matters of importance to them. Mothers who saw themselves as experiencing heavy stress had significantly shortened telomeres compared to those who felt more relaxed, whether they were raising a disabled child or not. This was the first scientific study to quantify the physiological cost of feeling highly stressed and underscores the need to discover ways to manage pressures that relieve a toll on the body. It is sad that these women who gave so much of themselves to help loved ones had to pay such a cost in terms of mental and physical health.

One implication from this line of research is to obtain relief from certain stressors that cannot be eliminated. This means arranging a schedule so there can be attention to personal needs such as getting enough sleep, participation in a social network, physical exercise, and having time to pursue personal interests. This continuing project involving the mothers of children with disabilities is evaluating an array of possible interventions that include meditation, yoga, and cognitive therapy to assess the effects on telomere length and perceived stress to find out what can be done to preserve the capacity for resilience. Mothers in general experience the combined stresses of having multiple responsibilities that include caring for their children, satisfying an employer, managing a household, looking after a husband, and sometimes caring for aging parents. It appears that learning to relax is a lesson more parents should exemplify so their children can observe effective ways to manage stress. Cross-cultural studies have determined that parents typically overestimate their favorable influence in this context as compared to their adolescent daughters and sons who commonly fault them for failing to show how to deal with stress (P. Strom & Strom, 2011c; Strom, Strom, Strom, Shen, & Beckert, 2004).

Anxiety and Uncertainty

Anxiety is the feeling of uncertainty that arises when new or difficult experiences are anticipated. The pace of social change was slower during the past, allowing young adults then to look forward to a more predictable future. By contrast, in a hurry and rush-oriented environment, young adults currently report feeling anxious more often because of increased uncertainty about choice of a career, securing employment that provides satisfaction, maintaining friendships online and in person, establishing intimacy with an awareness that many relationships do not last, and ensuring a lifestyle that is not overscheduled. Feeling uncertain and sensing doubt can be beneficial when the outcome is stimulation of curiosity or greater motivation to participate in creative thinking. However, when the scope of uncertainty becomes excessive, the consequent stress can trigger emotional disturbance. Employers, friends, and relatives should consistently try to help young adults avoid this dangerous outcome of anxiety (Aldwin, 2007).

The preconditions for anxiety are the same as for being human. As far as we can tell, animals do not lie awake at night thinking about problems that make them dread the next day. They do not worry about how to pay the rent or mortgage on the tree where they live in, cover costs of higher education for their many offspring, and whether they might be infected by a sexually transmitted disease. This is because animals lack the capacity to imagine, the wonderful attribute unique to the human mind that leads some people to fret about every conceivable danger. Mankind worries because of awareness that we have a future and what might happen tomorrow is less certain than for people living in earlier times (Blonna, 2006).

The unprecedented degree of uncertainty that young adults encounter can best be dealt with by remaining flexible and calm. Palm trees that flex in high winds usually survive storms without damage while more rigid trees that resist the power of the wind fall down or are uprooted. Flexibility is a capacity to shift from one pattern of thought to another as demonstrated by people whose views are not restricted to their heritage, traditions, and customary social restraints. The reason that flexibility is so valuable is because it promotes cognitive and emotional adaptation. In contrast, rigid thinking is a liability since it relies on ineffective coping with unfamiliar situations.

Remaining calm is also important in dealing with uncertainty because this attitude allows people to control the intensity of their negative emotions like fear, sadness, rage, helplessness, cynicism, and anticipation that the future is bound to be disappointing. Unless these corrosive emotions are controlled, they restrict critical thinking, and inhibit the ability to process information in an organized way. The advantage of staying calm when faced with uncertain events is that a person remains able to generate a broader range of options and choices relevant for making decisions. Staying calm subordinates the emotional brain, the *amygdala*, so the executive logical brain can rationally weigh facts and determine a sensible plan of action (Ward, 2009).

Young adults are more able to manage anxiety and uncertainty when they arrange solitude time to allow for reflection about these self-evaluation questions.

1. What are my educational plans to prepare for an occupation?
2. How can I find reliable friends to be the social group I rely on?
3. How do I feel about the benefits and risks of getting married?
4. Do I want to be a parent and devote effort to raising children?
5. Do I want to stay at home with my parents while in college?
6. How can I get the money that is needed to pay for education?
7. How can I negotiate changes in my relationship with parents?
8. What things could I do to improve my performance on the job?
9. What lifestyle will enable my happiness now and in the future?

Meditation and Relaxation

Stress is part of life so people should learn suitable ways to manage pressures they can expect to encounter in daily life. Stress can be partly controlled by learning to relax. *Meditation*—to empty the mind of thoughts and concentrate—is an effective way to reduce stress (Wallace, 2007). A generation ago, reports on effects of meditation were mostly anecdotal. Since then experiments have assessed the influence using randomized controlled trials. Meditation is included in employee training at American Telephone and Telegraph, Connecticut General, Blue Cross Blue Shield, Armed Forces, and most health maintenance organizations through wellness education programs. In these settings meditation has been found to relieve tension, reduce stress, lower blood pressure, and improve physical and emotional health. Meditators typically describe an enhanced sense of well being, reduced anxiety, improved perception, and less illegal drug and alcohol abuse.

Neuroscientist Andrew Newberg (2000) at the University of Pennsylvania scanned the brains of eight highly skilled meditators from the Tibetan Buddhist School to identify cognitive changes during this activity. Following the injection of a radioactive substance that attaches to red blood cells, the "tagged" blood briefly leaves a trace that can be detected by the imaging machine. Active brain waves reflect more blood than others because neural activity is fueled by blood-born oxygen. *Single photon emission computed tomography* (SPECT) identifies the brain areas working hardest by detecting concentrations of the radioactive marker. Scans reveal different patterns from those typically found in a normal state of mind. Some differences included unusually prolonged and intense concentration, reduced metabolism, less awareness of distractions, and up to 20% greater frontal lobe activity.

Should short periods of solitude, reflection and meditation be a routine part of the daily schedule for students? Such an arrangement would seem particularly important for those from neighborhoods with high rates of crime and violence and families that overschedule them so they lack opportunities to reflect. It is ironic that, as most people have abandoned the traditional practice of setting aside 1 day a week for relaxation, research is affirming restorative power that can come from meditation (Wallace, 2007).

San Francisco's Visitacion Valley Middle School serving 260 students in Grades 6-8 was a place where police routinely were called to make arrests. Lawlessness in the community reflecting drug usage and violence caused students to feel fearful, anxious, and stressed. Then, in 2007, the principal mobilized faculty and parent support to establish Quiet Time, a stress reduction program of transcendental meditation as an optional activity. Twice a day, once at the first bell and again before the final bell, students sit quietly for 15 minutes. They can read, sit with their thoughts or meditate. The time for this activity was not taken from instruction but gained by shaving a few minutes from lunch, a minute from each passing period, and half of homeroom. About 90% of students opt to learn transcendental meditation and get several hours of instruction led by teachers trained in methods to oversee quiet time (Markus, 2012).

The student population at Visitacion is mostly low income as 88% qualify for free lunch. Ethnic origins include 33% Asian, 22% Black, 16% Hispanic, 13% Filipino, 10% Pacific Islander, and 2% White. Over 40% of students are second language learners. Since the introduction of Quiet Time 5 years ago, truancy rates have gone down 60% and suspensions declined by 50%. In 2011, students with unexcused absences were 7%, compared to over 20% before. School grade-point averages have risen. Students like the school, have fewer arguments, and physical fights have become uncommon. These gains have been made despite little change in the violent environment outside the school. In 2011, Ingleside neighborhood had 37 shootings and 10 homicides (Markus, 2012).

The implications for including meditation in secondary and higher education has been largely overlooked. If students could learn to alter their physiological responses through meditation, they might be able to prevent stress that interferes with learning. This is a better option than excessive reliance on caffeine, drugs, alcohol or cigarettes for coping with pressures of daily life. In addition, behavior problems could be dealt with more constructively by urging misbehaving students to withdraw for a time, relax, and find healthy ways of responding to difficulties inherent in modern living (Wallace, 2007).

Researchers at the Medical College of Georgia assessed how exposure to meditation might influence negative behavior at school. The 677 male and female Black students from two inner-city high schools were screened on three separate occasions for blood pressure. Then, 45 students were declared eligible based on systolic rates above the 85th percentile with respect to age, gender, and height. These 15- to 18-year-olds were assigned to a meditation orientation or a health education control group for a year. Students in the meditation group met 15 minutes every day and practiced twice a day at home on weekends. Members of the health education control group attended daily sessions at school focused on lifestyle education (Barnes, Bauza, & Treiber, 2003).

A comparison of pretest and posttest data after 4 months of intervention found that the meditation group showed a significant decrease in school absences as compared to the control group. The meditation group also recorded a significant decline in number of school rule infractions while breaking the rules increased in the control group. Number of suspension days for misconduct also declined in the meditation group by 83% while the control group recorded an increase in suspension time. Anger management was also more effective for the meditators. These outcomes encourage educators to consider stress reduction as a powerful strategy for improving behavior of young adults (Barnes, Bauza, & Treiber, 2003).

As of 2012, nearly 100 schools located in 13 different states are implementing meditation. Preliminary results show that high school students practicing meditation daily have 25% fewer absences, 38% fewer suspension days, and 50% less rule infractions. Similar benefits are reported for students in Grades 1-7 showing significant improvement scores on validated attention skills tests and faculty observed reduction in aggressive behavior (Markus, 2012).

STRESSFUL CONDITIONS AT WORK

Job Status and Stress

There is a common belief that persons in leadership positions experience greater stress than employees who have lower status jobs. A chief executive officer, department manager, or administrative role must present individuals with more stress than is faced by employees whose tasks they monitor and supervise. This assumption is false and well illustrated by studies of Robert Sapolsky, professor of biology and neuroscience at Stanford University and recipient of a Macarthur Foundation Genius Award. Sapolsky's observations contradict the view that high status and greater stress go together. In long-term investigations involving baboons, Sapolsky (2004) discovered greater plaque in the blood vessels, more rapid heart rates, and higher blood pressure among lower ranking baboons while those at the top of the status hierarchy, the ones that exerted control over others and therefore could make their own autonomous decisions had the least hypertension and evidence of stress hormone. In effect, the lower the rank of baboons, the higher their risk for a heart attack, physical disability, and earlier death.

Hierarchy and Mutual Support

Finding ways to prevent conditions that can adversely affect physical and mental health of workers implicate another of Sapolsky's (2004) observations. As he returned to Africa for the annual visit to check on conditions of the baboon troop, he found out that the dominant males had died from diseases they acquired from scavenging in garbage dumps. The departure of these high status troop members fundamentally changed the social dynamic applied for governance of the remainder society. The smaller number of aggressive males and much larger number of socially oriented females created a new set of expectations that assigned the highest priority to congenial interaction. Within a single generation, the way baboons treated one another shifted from exclusive reliance on status hierarchy to a mutual support system characterized by respectful relationships instead of aggressive intimidation.

These results showing that improving a social environment can favorably effect physical health has implications for human beings as well as members of animal troops. Epidemiologist Michael Marmot (2005) from University College London has led a landmark study that continues 40 years since it began in 1967. The initial investigation of 18,000 British male civil servants working in Whitehall found rates of heart disease in proportion to their rank in the bureaucratic pecking order. Results determined that job status was a better predictor of the probability for having a heart attack than obesity, smoking, or high blood pressure. Someone with a low status position like a custodian was four times more likely to suffer a heart attack than a manager or an executive. In fact, even if an executive was overweight, hypertensive or a smoker, s/he was less likely to suffer a heart attack at a given age than was a thin, nonsmoking, low blood pressure custodian. It appears that the lower people are on the pecking order, the less control they can exert over their lives. For workers in the civil service, levels of cholesterol rise not in response to amount of work they do but the extent to which they are ordered about by others who possess greater status.

The Whitehall study of health and job status was replicated in 1988 with 10,000 men and women from a department of the civil service that would soon experience effects of privatization. At the time, civil servants had no concept of what losing their jobs might mean. During a pilot of the survey, workers objected to inclusion of an item asking whether they feared loss of their jobs. It seemed a silly question since the worst situation they could imagine was being transferred from preferred duties to an assignment in another department. However, they soon understood what losing a job could mean as one-third were laid off. A main effect of privatization was to cause people to feel that they were at the mercy of external factors. Stress levels rose and with it came illness with increased signs of poor health than could be explained by changes in diet, smoking, or drinking (Marmot, 2005). The latest wave of data gathering for the Whitehall study was in 2012.

The fact that heart disease is regarded as a symptom of lack of control explains something about its sporadic appearance. More specifically, this could be why many people in senior positions have heart attacks soon after retirement and they begin to "take it easy." From managing a staff or office, they may move to mundane tasks such as washing dishes for the first time, walking their dog or performing other domestic tasks in environments managed by their spouse. Similarly, people seem capable of postponing an illness, even a heart attack, until after a wedding or some major celebration, until the end of busy work periods when they are in control of events. Students also come down with illnesses after periods of examination pressure. The Gulf Oil Crisis in 2010 resulted in large-scale unemployment and welfare dependence, accompanied by high rates of illness, abuse, divorce, and suicide (Walsh, 2011).

Everyone who works in schools should understand the importance of this issue. Administrators are challenged by management tasks involving students, teachers, staff, parents, and community. Teachers must demonstrate discipline, accountability, and often bring their work home at night. And, what about the students who are assigned the lowest status in the school hierarchy? Certain stresses they experience are unprecedented for their age group and therefore underestimated by many adults (Munsey, 2010). Establishing a responsive environment so students feel respected and assured that their views about conditions of learning will be taken seriously can reduce feelings of distress within the school community.

Chemistry of Stress

Cholesterol is a basic element in the intricate biochemistry and genetic systems that integrates the entire body. This small organic compound is soluble in fat but not in water. The body manufactures most of its cholesterol from sugar in the diet and could not survive without it. Five critical hormones are made from cholesterol, each having a different and essential function: progesterone, aldosterone, cortisol, testosterone, and ostradoil. Collectively, these hormones are known as steroids. The relationship between steroids and genes is recognized and unsettling. Here we examine only cortisol, usually referred to as the stress hormone.

Cortisol unites the body and mind by altering configuration of the brain. Chronic stress leads to elevation of cortisol levels, reduction of serotonin and neurotransmitters in the brain, including dopamine. When these chemical systems work normally, they regulate biological processes such as sleep, appetite, energy, and sex drive and allow expression of normal moods and emotions. However, if the stress response fails to shut off and reset following a difficult situation, depression is the typical outcome. Cortisol interferes with the immune system, changes sensitivity of ears, nose, and eyes and alters bodily functions (Ridley, 2006).

Stress is caused by perceptions of the outside world, by anticipation of a difficult test at school, recent death in the family, scary events reported on the nightly news or exhaustion from caring for a disabled relative.

Short-term stressors produce immediate increase in epinephrine and norepinephrine, hormones that cause the heart to beat faster and feet to become cold. These hormones prepare the body for fight or flight response in case of an emergency. Stresses lasting for longer periods of time activate a different path, resulting in a slower but more persistent increase in cortisol levels. A negative effect of cortisol is that it suppresses the immune system. Students who have tests scheduled and show no symptoms of stress are more likely after the examination to develop colds and other infections because the consequence of elevated cortisol is a reduction in number and white blood cells. This result was discussed earlier in relation to young mothers of children with disabilities whose white blood cells were switched on by cortisol and shortening of their telomeres. Cortisol can reduce immunity by switching genes on, only those in cells with cortisol receptors that have in turn been switched on by other triggers (Ridley, 2006).

AGE DIVERSITY AND COLLABORATION

Americans are becoming more age-segregated. This practice has led to a steady decline in the amount of interaction among generations (Rosen, 2010). At the same time, technology has enabled the young to increase interaction with peers by cell phones and the Internet. Some youth report being in contact with friends as much as 70 hours each week while having only meager contact with important grownups in their lives. Adults should carefully consider the cost associated with isolating the young and having them motivated to communicate mainly with others of their age (Rideout, Foehr, & Roberts, 2010).

Effects of Age Segregation

One consequence of age segregation is that a majority of young adults enter the workforce with meager experience in collaborating with people older than themselves. The job is often the first place new hires have consistent and sustained communication with middle age and older adults. This interaction is further complicated because each generation shares distinctive beliefs, values, worldviews, attitudes toward work, views about relationships, impressions regarding seniority, and ways of talking, thinking, and solving problems. These differences can produce disagreements and difficulties that undermine mental health (Lancaster & Stillman, 2010; Lawler & O'Toole, 2008).

Biases of Younger Workers

Studies that chronicle social dynamics in business and industrial settings have found that, when young adults interact with same age peers, they sometimes complain about their relationships with older coworkers. Pejorative comments toward someone of another ethnic group or gender are generally considered unacceptable. However, the same restraint is often ignored when the focus is on individuals of a different age group. The authors surveyed 200 young adults in college and at work. They were asked to describe problems experienced in getting along with middle age and older colleagues. Consider some of their observations.

My 20-year old friend is a host at the dorm front desk and needed to call in sick. There was a protocol to inform the supervisor to avoid the penalty of an unexcused absence as well as facilitate replacement to cover the front desk. The problem was that her boss (my boss too) refused to use text messaging. The boss had no Internet service at home and it was on Sunday so she was 'off the grid.' My friend sent several text messages expressing frustration about what to do because she was unable to reach her supervisor. I often hear this sentiment from friends in similar circumstances. Young adults want all our colleagues to be as accessible as we are but older employees don't want to be bothered outside of work.

Another woman reported this situation.

Young adults like myself typically have supervisors who are middle aged. They are usually seen as distant and aloof. They have a tendency to be less available and less involved than people in my generation would prefer. Being a friend on Facebook does not make sense to them. Maybe this is because they have been employed longer, are closer to retirement or have less energy. They are less motivated to develop relationships that might advance their career path. This poses a problem for us who are younger with goals to cultivate professional work relationships to support promotion.

The following remarks were made by young adults in a discussion group focused on work relationships.

- After the supervisor asked if I would be willing to work overtime, I said, "No way, I have a life and expect to be out of the office by 5 o'clock."
- My unit supervisor gets upset if I call him by his first name.
- Our department head sends me handwritten notes that I am supposed to answer in the same way because he will not use e-mail. When the computer was down and we needed to contact several clients, I texted them and thought my supervisor would view this as a sign of adaptability but he does not want to learn to text. I could teach him and he could do it himself. It's like he does not realize the benefit of reciprocal learning.

Biases of Older Workers

The same morale problems are fueled when middle age and older adults portray their younger co-workers in unfavorable ways. One employee with over 20 years experience describes his impression of newly-hired employees this way:

> They lack professionalism in being overly casual and choosing to ignore business manners. For example, one young woman takes personal calls and gets messages on company time. While she is supposed to be working, she does tasks for herself that have nothing to do with the job. I believe this behavior adversely impacts performance and reflects poorly on our group.

A middle age employee stated her disappointment about younger workers.

- We have one woman who disrupts everything in the office by bringing her infant daughter because a babysitter is not available.
- Another newcomer expects to be promoted and receive a raise after being here for only a few months.
- The discontent goes on as others vent their concerns such as being bothered by a lady who usually arrives late for staff meetings and always blames traffic as the reason for not being on time.
- We have a new employee who claims to be a professional yet he refuses to wear appropriate clothing and comes in wearing a basketball jersey—that would be fine after work but not the office.

During a session of middle age and older workers, the following comments were made about the younger cohorts:

- They seem to be all about money and job benefits that fuel their motivation. This concern about being paid more and working less produces a poor work ethic and lack of loyalty. The desire for money leads them to jump from job to job to make more and that leaves employers with openings to fill, which is a significant change from company loyalty we were taught.
- Too much technology can be a hindrance to productivity since young adults appear more concerned about the latest and greatest gadget, instead of focusing on the tasks of their job. They are often on the phone with their friends that have nothing to do with business.
- We notice too that they prefer to communicate by technology instead of face to face.
- Just as it may seem that older workers are resistant to change, young adults may be too open in a sense because they don't' accept the motto "If it isn't broke, don't fix it," a guide for our group.

- There are many differences that leave older employees questioning the loyalty and dependability of younger recruits, a key criteria for success.
- My observation is that young workers, generally, have an attitude of entitlement. They lack a strong work ethic, sometimes thinking they can come to work when they want to and do not need to learn things about the job that do not interest them.

When these complaints about coworkers of other age groups are expressed, the morale of an organization is jeopardized. Employers agree that training for how to work in groups should begin in adolescence. The qualifications that employers seek in recruiting new personnel always include a record of punctuality and good attendance, willingness to work hard, relevant skill sets, and evidence of ability to get along with others from varied backgrounds. These factors often overshadow school grades that are increasingly regarded as less reliable indicators of employee potential. High schools as well as colleges are expected to require community service so students have some opportunities to interact with middle age and older adults, gaining a broader perspective by sharing skills while engaging in reciprocal learning. The need for intergenerational perspective taking, listening to and respecting colleague views of situations is essential to a setting responsive to everyone and offering common satisfaction (Goleman, 2006b).

Intergenerational communication can also enable stress reduction. Some people are inclined to tell anyone when stress causes them frustration. There are also young adults who talk only with peers of the same age group about their distress (Rosen, 2010). The decision to withhold information about stress can mean that supervisors do not know about situations that undermine well-being and productivity. In such cases, the managers cannot take appropriate action to lessen undue stress that they could control. A more promising outlook is to understand that when young adults are listened to, they may be less inclined to devalue their legacy or abandon customs that could otherwise be revised and retained. Listening is essential to attain the distinctive goals of cultural preservation, cultural evolution, and cultural adjustment.

UNDERSTANDING GENERATIONAL DIFFERENCES

The workforce demographics are changing. Depending upon how differences are perceived, there can be more support for productivity, or greater conflict and poor morale. Efforts are made to maximize the benefits that can come from ethnic and gender diversity. Most employers want these initiatives to continue but also be joined by attention to age diversity issues so generations can work better together.

All employees have certain habits, attitudes, and preferences that identify them as individuals but everyone is also shaped to some extent by peer norms. Members of each generation share an age location in history. They were commonly exposed to the same world events, pop culture trends, and values that were prevalent at the time they were growing up. Understanding elements of motivation, strengths, values, preferences, and concerns—the culture of other age cohorts—can facilitate cooperation, satisfaction, retention, and mental health. Such knowledge is important for educators and counselors whose role includes developing support for appreciation of multicultural concerns. This goal requires awareness of the unique aspects of generations that influence individual sense of self in relation to group identity, priorities, beliefs, expectations, and outlook. Baby Boomers, Generation Xers, and Millenialls are the three generations that account for most of the work force. The common characteristics and perspectives of these groups are examined.

Baby Boomers

This age cohort, born between 1940-1960, is 50 to 70 years old. They have most of the leadership positions in business and industry. It is important to recognize who raised them. Their parents grew up during the great depression at a time when things were scarce, sacrifice was expected, and everyone was told to "save for a rainy day." Government safety nets currently taken for granted like unemployment benefits, social security, welfare, aid to dependent children, and federal deposit insurance on money kept in the bank did not exist. Since national unity was essential to win World War II, students were taught to have faith in the country and show loyalty to basic institutions including family, government, church, and military.

These traditionalist parents of the baby boomers were hardworking, accepted being told what to do, and were usually willing to exceed whatever was expected of them. Generally they accepted a strict moral code as the guide for personal behavior. Over half of all men served in the armed forces where they learned the military chain of command was the best way to get things accomplished. Leaders would give orders and troops followed orders. This top-down style of governance was reflected on the job after the war where a supervisor or manager was in charge and dissent was rare. Given this orientation, it is not surprising that traditionalists applied a similar approach to bringing up their children.

Significant changes in the environment can nurture new ways of seeing things. The baby boomers who grew up during the 1950s were the first child generation to have access to television which provided a new set of references based upon the programs, advertisers, and products they watched which their traditionalist parents were never exposed to while growing up. Optimism is a term that best describes most boomers. Pride in defeating the nation's enemies, broad access to college for returning soldiers, called the GI Bill, referring to government issue, jobs available for almost everyone, and an explosion of consumer goods fostered a perspective that anything was possible.

Unlike their parents whose motivation was rooted in defending the country from Germany and Japan, the idealistic boomers could afford to direct their attention to the domestic issues accompanied by a firm resolve to fix the things they considered to be wrong with the nation. They challenged certain ideals and acted out their opposition by staging protests to support civil rights, women's rights, reproductive rights, and even rights of the earth to fair treatment by promoting ecology (Brokaw, 2004; Erickson, 2008).

Another notable attribute of boomers is competitiveness. As part of the largest cohort in history, 76 million, they felt compelled to compete in almost every sector of life from striving to be selected on sports teams, being among only 20% admitted to college, and surpassing coworkers in order to gain a promotion. Their path for getting ahead was to oppose the chain of command orientation in almost all walks of life that had been the dominant practice of their traditionalist parents. Boomers have a strong work ethic, and their identity is closely tied to jobs, a factor than should be considered in counseling them about retirement. They see higher pay as the preferred compensation for hard work, as compared to younger people who may choose time off as their reward for productivity (Ball & Gotskill, 2010).

As boomers listened to the radio and later television, they celebrated a common set of entertainment icons. In the context of music, this meant a preference for listening to Frank Sinatra, Dean Martin, Bing Crosby, Elvis Presley, Nat King Cole, Johnny Cash, The Beatles, Rolling Stones, Grateful Dead, The Doors, Fleetwood Mac, and Lead Zeppelin.

Generation Xers

Men and women between about 30 to 50 years of age, born between 1960-1980, are referred to as Generation X. Their segment of national population is smaller than the boomer cohort. While Xers were growing up important innovations in communications technology were presented that significantly enlarged individual scope of awareness. Popular exposure to computers, cable and satellite television, video recorders, cell phones, Palm Pilots, and pagers were all introduced to the public during their youth. They were the first generation of children exposed to 24-hour media and tabloid journalism. As a result, they saw some admired personalities in sports, entertainment, business, and government indicted for crimes or identified as unworthy heroes.

Marshall McLuhan (1964) described how powerful the media was becoming in shaping values, ideas, and moods of the nation. His assertion that "The medium is the message" meant that whatever age groups observed in common became a common point of reference for them. Programs targeting youth led Xers to shift from a traditional view of previous generations that maintained considerable trust in the basic institutions of society that include government, military, organized religion, and corporate America. Even security of the family was no longer assured as the divorce rate tripled, proportion of single parents rose, and students returning after school to an empty house became a common experience as a majority of the Baby Boomer mothers became employed (Erickson, 2008).

Xers were the most unsupervised generation in American history and were often obliged to fend for themselves while growing up. Their common set of circumstances motivated the quest to become independent and goal-oriented. A typical response was to adopt caution and skepticism as the guiding principles instead of high confidence in authority figures as had been the previous norm. Downsizing of businesses during the 1990s confirmed what Xers believed, that job security is an illusion and the only real security involves being able to count on yourself. Positive thinking might be regarded as a useful outlook when the world is treating you right but otherwise Murphy's Law seemed to be a more apt interpretation, "anything that can go wrong will go wrong" (Bloch, 2003). The durability of Murphy's Law as an explanation still offered by Xers for many events they anticipate or encounter reflects their pessimistic wisdom. The members of this generation are typically resourceful, self-directed, and dislike the chain of command approach for getting things done. They also dismiss the widespread belief among baby boomers that public institutions can be reformed and made to operate efficiently. Self-reliance, pessimism, and guarded optimism seem to characterize most of the Xers.

Xers claimed their own musical icons, some of whom included Michael Jackson, Billy Joel, Elton John, U2, Bruce Springsteen, Madonna, Cheap Trick, the Bee Gees, Electric Light Orchestra, Kiss, Garth Brooks, Glenn Campbell, and Winona Judd.

The Millennials

The most recent workers to enter the labor force are Millennials, a population of 80 million Americans born between 1980-2000. The eldest are 32 years of age and the youngest are 12. Greater acceleration in the pace of change has led to differences even within the millennial generation, separating those who grew up just a few years apart. To illustrate, we asked graduate students to identify some growing up experiences they had that are no longer common. Some memories were:

- Widespread use of encyclopedias, dictionaries, atlases, and almanacs
- Letters by postal mail to relatives and friends who lived out of town
- Outside play with peers where we made our own decisions
- Mr. Rogers and other education programs designed for children
- Reading books that were considered to be a source of satisfaction
- Reliance on VHS, cassette tapes, and floppy discs for the computer
- Using public pay phones located on street corners and in businesses
- Use of corded telephones as the main method of distance communication

The college students were then asked to describe growing up experiences that are common now but were unavailable to them during the time of their youth:

- Internet as a source of communication and learning
- Cellphones, texting, Ichat, iPad; Skype, data clouds
- Personal video games to serve as the focus for play
- Facebook, MySpace and other social network sites
- Mostly sedentary activities involving electronic devices
- More access to fast foods and greater incidence of obesity
- Less physical exercise in school and at home
- Less time spent doing things together with the family
- Less focus on traditional gender role expectations
- Downloading books to an iPad or Kindle readers
- Being connected with friends almost all of the time

The self-esteem movement that swept the country during the 1980s profoundly influenced how Millennial children were raised. Mr. Rogers told his young television audience that each person was special. Parents adopted this view and they reinforced the significance of being an individual along with the need to feel good about oneself. Whitney Houston captured the sentiment in a number one hit called "The Greatest Love of All," referring to the need to love yourself before you are able to love someone else.

In the 1960s and 1970s about 25% of mothers were employed outside the home. This changed dramatically during the 1980s when rate of maternal employment rose to 85%. As part of the transition, parents allowed their children, for the first time in history, to have a voice in family decision making. Consequently, Millennials are used to being validated and having their opinions seen as important. The societal reorientation also implicated the mission of teachers. Teachers were expected to let their students know that each of them was special. A popular practice used to reinforce individuality was giving students stars or tokens for completing assignments and good performance. Sometimes these rewards could also be traded for gifts to motivate greater incentive (Kohn, 1993). Throughout their education in the home and at school, Millennials have been provided favorable feedback about their behavior so they expect that employers should recognize and celebrate their achievements too (Twenge & Campbell, 2010). By 2015, Millennials will represent nearly half of the entire American workforce (Meister & Willyerd, 2010).

Some favorable attributes demonstrated by Millennials include civic mindedness, optimism about the future, close relationships with their parents, and the preference to solve problems in teams. They take pride in being tolerant of differences, show concern for preservation of the environment, and participate in community service. Millennials grew up with the Internet so online experience helps them feel connected with the larger world. They have built social networks of friends, own cell phones, and have a personal computer to do school assignments. They watched parents make sacrifices for their jobs and are resolved to do whatever they can to avoid the same predicament (Twenge & Campbell, 2010). Instead, they seek a better balance between time for work and time for leisure. Freedom is considered to be a fundamental goal so they are willing to move from one employer to another in order to satisfy expectations for desirable conditions.

Some characteristics Millennials consider to be their assets are often perceived as limitations by people older than themselves. For example, the impression that "it's all about me" explains why so many students crave individual praise, are overly dependent on positive reinforcement, and why standing alone is difficult whenever their personal ideas do not conform to peer opinion. Efforts by parents, teachers and surrogates to promote the self-esteem of Millennials has sometimes prevented them from having to acquire the ability to process criticism necessary on the job to guide self-improvement. This means that certain potential benefits of working in teams cannot happen unless students learn to provide and accept authentic peer feedback as a basis for improving individual performance in groups. Employers often complain about worker retention because new hires have unrealistic expectations including rapid promotion and show impatience by moving from job to job. Millennials want control of their destiny but they commonly fear the risk of making choices that could turn out to be mistakes (Alsop, 2008; Lancaster & Stillman, 2010).

Most (75%) young adults receive financial help from parents who continue to be overly involved in helping them make decisions as was the case in childhood. Schools and employers refer to them as helicopter parents because they always seem to be nearby and hovering. A consensus view among middle age and older adults is that Millennials should learn to think and act more independently. Their greatest worry centers on getting good grades, a stress that motivates many to cheat. They like the shorthand conversations of texting and instant messaging that, when overused can impair writing ability and interpersonal communication skills. Multitasking contributes to their short attention span that in turn jeopardizes learning. College teachers complain that, although Millennials claim they can multitask, they seem unable to hear a lecture and take notes at the same time, a task that requires gaining knowledge by listening and then self organizing it for retention.

Some defining events for Millennials have been the 9/11 tragedy, student shootings at Columbine High School, and Virginia Tech University, the deaths of Michael Jackson and Whitney Houston, U.S. Airways plane crash in the Hudson River, Enron business scandal, Iraq and Afghanistan wars, and hurricane Katrina. Some of the personalities on their evolving list of icons are Justin Bieber, Hanna Montana, Selina Gomez, Enrici Eglacius, Adele, the Black Eyed Peas, and Lady Gaga.

Jean Twenge, a Millennial and psychology professor at San Diego State University, has compared personality test results administered to boomers when they were under age 30 with results from the millennial generation. Twenge's (2007) findings appear in *Generation Me* and *The Narcissism Epidemic: Living in the Age of Entitlement* (Twenge & Campbell, 2010). Her surveys reveal that, as a group, Millennials experience higher rates of anxiety, uncertainty, and depression than older age groups. They have difficulty with ambiguity so they seek specific directions from teachers and supervisors for what to do in school and at work. As a result, *Generation Me* is subtitled *Why Today's Young Are More Confident, Assertive, Entitled and More Miserable Than Ever Before*. Twenge concluded that the poor developmental outcomes of the self-esteem movement means this strategy for raising children should be left behind, replaced by approaches that encourage empathy, real accomplishments, and reduce egocentrism. The most promising assets Millennials bring to employment are technology skills and willingness to work in teams. If they can enjoin these with the acquisition of teamwork skills, it can be a good fit for what is known about the emerging interdependent environment.

SUMMARY AND IMPLICATIONS

The stress and emotional health of young adults seem linked in unprecedented ways. More than previous generations they report anxiety, frustration, uncertainty and depression. Exceptions are resilient individuals who perceive setbacks and failures as opportunities to overcome obstacles and improve their behavior. The optimistic thinking of resilient people motivates them to accept challenges, consistently maintain a positive outlook, and keep on trying when situations become difficult. Resilience is not always related to poverty or contingent upon having to overcome significant odds to succeed. Being disadvantaged can occur when parents try to prevent loved ones from exposure to failure in the belief that setbacks undermine self-esteem rather than contribute to personality.

While positive adaptation is necessary for resilience, sustained stress can erode capacity to cope with adversity. In situations where the stress cannot be eliminated, it is important to arrange a schedule allowing sufficient attention to personal needs including rest, social participation, physical exercise, and pursuit of individual interests. Stresses that continue for long periods lead to elevated cortisol levels that suppress the immune system and thereby increase susceptibility to illness. Mothers are more vulnerable than other groups to high levels of stress because their multiple responsibilities of taking care of children, husbands, employers, and managing the household often prevent them from properly looking after themselves. Parents tend to overestimate their success in helping children learn to cope with daily stress. Being flexible and calm are assets that enable adjustment in situations that present uncertainty and anxiety.

Everyone should be aware of the relationship between stress and job status. Contrary to popular belief, employees in the lowest positions are more likely candidates for high blood pressure, heart attack, physical disability, and early death than are the executives and managers who supervise them. Transforming the workplace so that hierarchical relationships are replaced by conditions of interdependence that honor contributions of everyone can yield greater productivity and better morale. A similar shift is needed in schools where students occupy the lowest status. Building a socially responsive environment in which student views about their conditions of learning are given consideration by adults in authority can reduce amount of distress within the school community.

Segregation based on age means that youth interact with one another more than with adults. One outcome is that beginning employees usually lack enough experience in getting along with and collaborating with older coworkers. Each generation at work has distinctive beliefs, values, worldviews, attitudes, and ways of solving problems. These differences can foster productivity or misunderstanding and increase conflict. A high priority for employers is to ensure that all employees are able to appreciate the assets, motivation, and values of other age cultures to improve cohesion, harmony, and collaboration. Baby Boomers, Xers, and Millennials should become familiar with the outlook and perspective of one another and resolve to combine their separate talents to ensure collective success.

APPLICATIONS FOR TEACHING

1. Recognize the connection between stress and creativity. The qualities needed to manage anxiety and stress can be reinforced by teachers who encourage creativity. Individuals with creative abilities are more able than the general population to accept uncertainty, tolerate ambiguity, look at situations in new ways, exhibit flexibility, and recognize possibilities when faced with a set of unfamiliar or difficult conditions.

2. Depression and reluctance to participate in activities someone previously enjoyed are signs that counseling is needed. When students decide to quit and give up hope, they withdraw by skipping classes, taking illegal drugs, dropping out, or talking about possible suicide. Prompt referral for professional help is a preventive action that can ensure such individuals get the help they need.

3. Resilience is a valuable asset for mental health. Teachers contribute to this attribute by helping students identify and acknowledge failure, detect mistakes and make known ways to correct them, provide feedback on progress, point out when goal amendment should be considered, and encourage a desire to keep trying despite lack of success.

4. Uncertainty produces anxiety on the job or in the classroom that can be minimized by communicating clear expectations for assignments. Young adults should be told that if they are unsure about what is expected of them in particular situations, they should ask a supervisor or teacher to clarify their tasks, specify deadlines, and recommend resources to rely on. Uncertainty is reduced for people when they get confirmation that their electronic message was received. This simple task reflects good manners and should become a habit with the recognition that it contributes to well-being.

5. Avoid assuming that all of the problems experienced by teams can be attributed to generational differences. There are individuals in every cohort whose teamwork skill deficiencies can be detected by peer assessment. Focusing remediation on team skills profiles of

individuals can guide decisions on ways to improve behavior and productivity.

6. During the orientation for age-integrated teams, invite members of each cohort to enhance the presentation by commenting on additional characteristics they feel have been left out, warrant greater emphasis or pose problems for them as they work with colleagues of an older or younger age than themselves.

7. Dispel the myth that high-ranking employees are exposed to more stress than are workers with less status in the hierarchy. This awareness should include a reminder for everyone to consider how their behavior might undermine the morale of others in an organization or contribute to their well being. The common goal should be finding ways to improve the social environment that affects individual and team productivity.

CHAPTER 13

COLLEGE AND FAMILY CHOICES

Young adults share the dream of securing employment that offers middle-class status. They are commonly motivated to complete the educational preparation needed to earn a comfortable income. In the past, this goal was typically met by completing high school, getting a job, and working hard. The plan enabled Baby Boomers (born 1940-1960) and Xers (born 1960-1980) to achieve success. However, times have changed so a high school diploma is not enough to ensure the future for the Millennial generation (born 1980-2000).

This chapter describes (1) reasons to increase the number of students going to college, (2) rates of student success, (3) obstacles that prevent degree completion, and (4) options to improve access to higher learning as well as student achievement. Discussion will also explore lifestyle choices including rationale for cohabitation and motivation of young women to avoid becoming a parent, document the scale of this outlook in terms of global fertility, encourage appreciation for personal choice about parenting, and describe demographic implications for the nation.

Learning Throughout Life: An Intergenerational Perspective, pp. 297–320
Copyright © 2012 by Information Age Publishing
All rights of reproduction in any form reserved.

EXPECTATIONS FOR EDUCATION

Post secondary education is widely recognized as the best path to a middle-class lifestyle. In 1970, only 26% of the middle class had gone to college. Currently, 61% of the middle class has earned a degree or some type of post secondary certificate. That proportion drops to 25% among low-income students. Georgetown University Center on Education and the Workforce published a report about *The Undereducated American* (Carnevale & Rose, 2011). Their conclusion is that the United States needs 20 million more college graduates by 2025 to bolster the economy, retain international leadership, and reduce the hardship suffered by individuals who lack education to join the labor market. Unemployment among those with only a high school diploma is twice as great as for people who have a postsecondary certificate or degree (Bureau of Labor Statistics, 2010).

The Georgetown proposal is that a sharp increase in number of better educated employees would mean wages of all groups would rise and boost the gross domestic product by $500 billion, increase tax revenues by $100 billion, and begin the process of reversing economic inequality. At the current rate, by 2025, it is projected that earnings of workers with bachelor's degrees, on average, will be 96% higher than for those with a high school diploma (Carnevale & Rose, 2011). The present annual gap in income is $20,000 per year (Taylor, 2012).

President Obama set a national goal to have the highest proportion of college graduates in the world by the year 2020 (U.S. Department of Education, 2011a). Twenty years ago the United States was first in the world in percentage of adults ages 25-34 with a postsecondary credential. In 2011, the United States ranked 12th in percentage of young adults with postsecondary education. Countries ranking higher are Korea, Canada, the Russian Federation, Japan, New Zealand, Norway, Ireland, Denmark, Israel, Belgium, and Australia (Lee, Rawls, Edwards, & Menson, 2011).

The Bureau of Labor Statistics (2010) projects that more than half of all new jobs until 2015 will require additional education beyond a high school diploma. Twenty-two of the 30 most rapidly growing career fields necessitate postsecondary education. Bill and Melinda Gates Foundation (2010) is providing $35 million in grants between 2010-2015 to community colleges in several states to double the enrollment of low-income adults who earn a post secondary credential by age 26. The reason that low-income students are targeted is because, for the first time since the government has kept track, the average education level of American workers has declined. This tragedy reflects the fact that, over the next 20 years, the entire net growth in the labor force will come from populations that the education system has been unable to prepare well for work (Passel, Cohn, & Lopez, 2010). This means the nation has a civic and economic imperative to live up to the promise of a good education for all.

Student Success and Failure

Reversing inequality of income by adding 20 million college-educated workers in the next 15 years requires a greater proportion of students to complete their studies and earn a degree. Although families of all ethnic and income groups see higher education as important, student success rates are troubling. Community colleges are serving more and more students, but how well they are serving them is debatable: only 1 in 4 graduates, compared to 3 in 5 at 4-year schools (Schneider & Yin, 2012). This is disappointing for individuals and families involved and represents a serious threat to the nation's ability to compete because it imperils our global position in having the best educated work force (Lee, Rawls, Edwards, & Menson, 2011).

At the same time that many students do not finish a degree, inflation of credentials is also becoming common. The Council on Graduate Schools reports a master's degree has become the new bachelor's degree as entry level expectation for some professions. Emerging degrees are no longer general but specialized. For example, the traditional MBA, master's of business administration, is seen as too broad so the shift is toward programs with a narrow focus such as supply chain management. Even departments of humanities at universities recognize the increasing student need to have credentials that improve their prospect for employment in a competitive job market. This realization has led to professionalizing degrees such as a masters in public history (for positions in a historical society or museum), in art (for managing galleries), and in music (for choir directors or the business side of music). The shift also implicates careers in construction management, fire science, and law enforcement administration where job experience used to matter more than attending classes (Pappano, 2011).

Students aspiring to become teachers, counselors, nurses, and social workers must usually meet community service and internship requirements established by professional organizations that provide accreditation for their curriculum. These requirements include internships that employers use as an additional screening tool to make decisions about recruitment in cases where most job applicants present high grades but differ in potential to perform. There is debate about the worth of professional masters degree programs but it is clear that higher education must assign higher priority to employer needs and help students become more marketable (Datar, Garvin, & Cullen, 2011).

Common College Completion Metrics

Understanding the challenges of career preparation implicates all 50 states. The National Governors Association Center for Best Practices has devised Common College Completion Metrics, a set of guidelines to monitor and compare degree completion rates within and between states and propose initiatives that could improve higher education (Reyna, 2010). Data from the federal government does not give accurate representation of institutional progress because it excludes almost half of all students. For example, the government estimates of success leave out part-time students that represent 37% of all enrollment in higher education. Part-timers are 61% of community college students and 40% of minorities in all the institutions.

Progress of transfer students is also unknown even though 37% of the people earning a bachelor's degree report they have attended more than one institution. Effects of remedial support are also in doubt. About 40% of students at universities and 61% in community colleges enroll in remedial education at an annual cost of more than a billion dollars to the states. The recommendations that states are expected to apply in determining their college completion profiles include two sets of criteria related to outcome metrics and progress metrics.

Outcome Metrics include degrees awarded, rates of graduation, transfer rates, and amount of time taken to earn degrees or certificates. The *Progress Metrics* include student enrollment in remedial education (mathematics and English), rate of success in remedial education classes, success in first year courses (percentage of students that complete entry level mathematics and English within two years) credit accumulation (on schedule completion for full time and part time students), retention rates (enrollment in consecutive semesters) and course completion. Each state is expected to gather data that is comparable from all of its institutions and report progress about outcomes and progress metrics to the federal government. This data will become a basis for improving efficiency and results, identify needed changes in policies, and consider performance in funding decisions, as is already the case in Indiana and Tennessee (Reyna, 2010). The initial steps by the federal government have been to fund a broad range of creative initiatives designed to enable an additional 5 million students to finish higher education degrees or certificates in the next 5 years. Benefactors in the private sector also support higher rates of college graduation.

Myths About Students Who Dropout

Public Agenda conducted a national survey of 600 young adults, 22 to 30 years of age, who had finished at least some college course work. The purpose was to detect contexts where institutional reforms may be needed. Those who started school but left without a degree were asked to explain reasons for dropping out. These views were compared with reports from other students completing a 2-year or 4-year degree. Findings revealed four myths about the experience of college students that provide clues to improve rates of success (Johnson, Rochkind, Ott, & DuPont, 2011).

(1) One myth is that students who quit college before graduation lack motivation to study and are more inclined to experience boredom. This impression overlooks the fact that most students must work to support themselves while going to school. Of students at 4-year institutions, 45% have jobs where they are employed more than 20 hours a week. Only 25% of freshman enroll fulltime and are largely financially dependent on their parents. A small proportion, 14%, live on campus. Similarly, a majority (60%) of community college students work 20 hours or more a week and one-third work over 35 hours (U.S. Department of Education, Center for Education Statistics, 2011). Trying to balance demands of a job and school was a main reason given by 54% of dropouts for their decision to quit. There was not enough time to finish everything that had to be completed. Only 10% identified boredom or difficulty understanding class content as major factors that contributed to leaving school (Johnson, Rochkind, Ott, & DuPont, 2011).

The likelihood that an even greater proportion of students will find it necessary to work and study at the same time is underscored by demographic forecasts. Estimates are that 82% of national population growth between 2010-2050 will involve immigrants who came in that period and their descendants born in the United States (Passel, Cohn, & Lopez, 2011).

For many minority students, the greatest problem is meeting college admission requirements. Only half of the students in the 50 largest cities, where most minorities live, complete high school and earn a diploma. That figure is far below the national high school graduation rate of 75.5% (Balfanz, Bridgeland, Bruce, & Fox, 2012). Great disparity is found when rates of urban districts are compared with suburb school districts. Urban Baltimore graduates 42% of students while suburb districts graduate 81%. The graduation rate for urban Cleveland is 38% compared to 81% in the suburbs. In urban New York City, 54% of students graduate while 83% earn a diploma in the suburbs; Chicago urban schools graduate 56% while suburbs graduate 84% (Swanson, 2009).

The national high school graduation rate by ethnicity for students who finish on time is 92% for Asians, 82% for Whites, 66% for Hispanics, and 64% for Blacks (Balfanz, Bridgeland, Bruce, & Fox, 2012). These figures become more troubling with recognition that Hispanics, the fastest growing minority group, has a high failure rate. The Hispanic subpopulation will double by 2050, resulting in their becoming 29% of the entire population. *Between Two Worlds: How Young Latinos Come of Age in America* is a report from the Pew Research Center indicating that Latinos are more likely than other youth to drop out, live in poverty, become parents as teenagers, and be exposed to gangs (Taylor, 2009).

(2) A second myth about college dropouts is that parents typically pay tuition, or students can obtain loans, scholarships, and other savings plan options. College costs have risen three times faster than household income in the past decade. Sixty percent of students who drop out report that they had to pay for tuition themselves and could not count on financial assistance of families. In comparison, 60% of students who earned a degree received economic support from parents or other relatives. While 70% of dropouts did not receive any financial aid or scholarships, 40% of graduates did (Johnson, Rochkind, Ott, & DuPont, 2011).

(3) A third myth is that high school students have a suitable orientation to making decisions about the particular higher education institutions that match their plans. This impression is conveyed by media reports that often show how affluent families go to great lengths to advantage their child by getting them into the best schools. The fact is more than 60% of students who drop out of college chose an institution solely on the basis of proximity to home, flexible class schedule to allow for employment hours, and having the most affordable tuition. Since more dropouts come from families where the parents never went to college, these students need greater guidance in high school to decide on possible focus for study and institutional choice. Most (62%) dropouts reported that their high school counselor poorly oriented them to the college application process (Johnson, Rochkind, Ott, DuPont, & Hess, 2011).

Family involvement is a factor in the motivation of students at all education levels. Colleges should effectively inform parents about the academic demands, understand what is expected of students, and recognize things they can do to help as well as allow their child to make decisions independently (Alsop, 2008). This is particularly important among minorities where the grownups lack college experience. For example, most Black men in college come from single parent homes and have a lower rate of graduation than any other group of males or females (Bowen, Chingos, & McPherson, 2011). These men usually credit a grandmother with helping them to stay on track in elementary and secondary grades, making sure they stayed out of trouble and did not skip their classes or leave school. Yet, when these students go to college, institutions lack a plan to sustain family involvement and ignore the potential benefit that could be achieved if parents and grandparents are urged to continue monitoring, listening, encouraging, and providing unique support.

In a similar way, Hispanic families prize interdependence and rely on one another in daily affairs to tasks and overcoming difficulties. When Mexican-American mothers go shopping for groceries, family members who can often come along. If someone sees a doctor, the family attends as well. There are emotional benefits of this group orientation and the power of such a support system should not end when a student gets to college. Telling students that they should demonstrate maturity by facing problems alone makes little sense. Indeed, we live in an era when those who have not learned lessons about interdependence at home should be taught them in the school to support teamwork.

Elementary and high school teachers recognize the need to have a partnership with parents because there is evidence that this can support student success. However, the opposite view is taken at college and university level where interaction with families is typically refused except for tours of campus. One line of reasoning is some families would want to monitor evaluation but students have to consent before data is released because this is part of the Family Education Rights and Privacy Act, FERPA (United States Department of Education, 2011b). While this problem does occur sometimes, a more common faculty complaint is that interacting with parents undermines independence of the students and sponsors invasive parenting. Families seeking to remain involved in the education of their children are portrayed as hovering like a helicopter or a snowplow that tries to remove all obstacles to failure. The alleged consequence is that students will remain fragile if they do not get to make decisions or cope with adversity on their own (Alsop, 2008).

(4) A fourth myth is that students who leave without graduating recognize the value of a degree and fully understand the economic consequences of not finishing. Dropouts uniformly agreed that a degree is an asset but many do not recognize the impact that quitting will have on their future. Often they entered college without a specific goal other than hoping it would lead to a better job. They did not consider the degree to be a great accomplishment worth the sacrifice and effort that may be necessary. Dropouts, as a group, were less likely than graduates to strongly agree their parents communicated the importance of college, and they were less likely to agree that people with a degree earn higher incomes. Two-thirds of college dropouts acknowledge that they think about going back to school. Eighty percent of the college dropouts believe that two proposals could improve prospects for graduation: (1) making part-time students eligible for greater financial aid (70% of full-time low income students get Pell grants that do not have to be repaid), and (2) colleges providing more classes in the evenings and weekends so they could keep working while going to school (Johnson, Rochkind, Ott, & DuPont, 2011).

A national random sample of 600 men and women from 26 to 34 years of age was interviewed to compare the perceptions of those who completed 4 year, 2 year, and technical programs with those who went to college for awhile but left before completing a program of study. Compared to graduates, those who did not finish were less confident about their financial future, less likely to believe it is a good idea to borrow money for college, less likely to think getting a degree will pay off, more skeptical about the motives of higher education institutions, and have knowledge gaps that could jeopardize their ability to get a degree in the future (Johnson, Rochkind, Ott, Dupont, & Hess, 2011).

Most studies conducted to determine causes of student failure have not considered time management habits of individuals. However, the way students spend time is bound to impact their academic performance. A sample of 654 students at Louisiana Technical University was surveyed about cell phone use including number of activities performed, time spent per activity, and time of day used. As a group, students spent an average of 5 hours per day interacting with their phone. Of the 5 total hours, 3 were spent making and receiving 12 voice calls with an average duration of 25 minutes a call. Another hour a day was spent sending 100 texts and receiving 120 texts with messages requiring 30 seconds to convey. An additional 30 minutes was devoted to watching videos, with You Tube as the most popular site. The men played video games 30 minutes while women spent only 5 minutes on this activity. Local, national, and world news were largely ignored. About 20% of cell phone use took place between midnight and 2 am, taking away from time needed for sleep (Buboltz, 2012). Some pertinent questions are: How can students spend 5 hours a day on the cell phone and still succeed at school? How time intensive are college program demands for acceptable performance?

Another obstacle to success is poor reading abilities. Based on placement test scores, 43% of students entering community colleges and 34% of freshmen at universities are involuntarily assigned to remedial reading classes without credit (Vandal, 2010). According to American College Testing (2006), ACT, the main cause of remediation is "inability to grasp complex texts." The reluctance to pay attention by reading slowly instead of skim reading is implicated. The greatest predictor that a college student will drop out is a need for remedial reading. Most troubling of all is that the college completion rate for students who enroll in remedial education is extremely low (Shanahan, Fisher, & Frey, 2012). According to the U.S. Department of Education, only 17% of high school graduates who require at least one remedial reading course and 27% who require a remedial math course earn a bachelor's degree (Vandal, 2010).

ENTITLEMENT FOR HIGHER EDUCATION

More lengthy schooling has become a requirement for desirable employment. The education needed for a good job can no longer be met with just an elementary and high school curriculum. However, if students are unable to afford tuition costs for higher education to prepare for entry-level employment, their future is bleak (Trilling & Fadel, 2009). Such conditions could hinder their financial ability to support themselves and their families. The American concept of equal educational opportunity to learn is in jeopardy unless higher education costs are reduced.

Public Support for New Entitlement

Many economists see the growing income gap between poor and affluent as the greatest social problem and agree that equal access to higher education is an aspect of the solution (Bowen, Chingos, & McPherson, 2011). There is a range of imagined outcomes that could occur if access to higher education were to become an entitlement. For students from low-income families, this reform might produce a broader sense of hope, increase motivation to learn, improve attendance and attention in class, increase level of achievement, reduce disruptive behavior in classrooms, diminish the appeal of becoming a gang member, and implement the equal opportunity that our nation has promised itself.

Middle-income families would not have to set aside money over a lengthy period of years to cover expenses of higher education. In turn, this would reduce parent need to borrow funds and allow them to save for retirement. Students could spend less time being employed and devote greater attention to study. This would help them gain the skills needed for an occupation, enter the work force sooner, without a debt, and avoid the anxiety that can be associated with subjecting parents to financial sacrifice. Half of the high school seniors who graduate in the top half of their class do not attend college. They report that their main reason for not going to college is their unwillingness to incur debt (Carnevale & Rose, 2011).

Those who would oppose a higher education entitlement are likely to argue that the nation should maintain its custom of fully funding only schooling that is compulsory. Others may contend that students are better off if they have to pay for tuition because this motivates them to place greater value on an education and devote more effort to studies. Some critics may want to attach conditions before a reform policy is approved. For example, they could insist on discontinuing remedial courses so those who are not fully qualified would have to meet all entry standards before getting to participate in a tuition free program. Some may seek assurances to prevent support of individuals who might seek to be perpetual students by placing limits on number of changes in majors allowed or discouraging studies in subjects with meager future employment forecasts. There could be priority for nondegree programs and fields with favorable job forecasts as in other countries instead of students alone deciding what to study. The Bureau of Labor Statistics reported that 30% of flight attendants, 15% of retail salespersons, and 17% of baggage porters have a bachelors degree or higher (Vedder & Denhart, 2011).

Other restrictions could call for making curriculum more occupation related and practical, improving competence of graduates by increasing number of hours needed for a major, and abandoning the practice of requiring one or more years of general studies before being allowed to study in the chosen field. This is a prominent concern of the National Governors Association, reflected by their efforts to improve graduation rates (Reyna, 2010). Another possible condition may be to direct universities to increase student monitoring by faculty, given the high failure rate that exists without supervision.

The main concern of most parents is no longer whether their children can qualify academically for higher education but how to pay for tuition. Tuition-free learning should include access to vocational training. Previously there has been no compelling reason for middle-age parents to organize as a lobby. The assumption has been that communities would assign high priority to education reforms so youth would have the schooling they need for employment. However, failure of public school bond issues in recent years has led more parents to consider mobilizing to protect the future of their adult children.

A unified initiative by parents might become necessary to override the objections of special interest groups that maintain excessive debt means the nation cannot afford an additional entitlement. However, Social Security and Medicare, on which a large segment of older adults depend, cannot be sustained unless more young people are able to access the education they must have in a globally competitive workplace. No one can be sure when the debate that we propose here will begin on a national scale but we believe it will be soon. In the meanwhile, it is timely to begin reflective thinking about the following questions:

1. Why would I favor or oppose an entitlement for high school students that allowed them to pursue either vocational training or a college degree?
2. What do I expect will be the outcome of public debate about this basic change in access to higher education for all students in the United States?

3. When will disparities in access to higher education be looked upon as sufficiently serious to motivate widespread approval of a national debate?

Faculty and Student Expectations

College teachers and students differ in changes they prefer for higher education. It is common for professors to complain about ignorance of students. Mathematicians, geographers, historians and academics in other specialized fields often suppose their subject is so important that most students must be exposed to it as a basic element of education. On a broader scale, professional organizations periodically allege that the nation's future is in question unless more students become informed about the issues their special interest group considers most important.

Students typically have a different view about how to increase the value of a college education. The main reason most attend is to be prepared for employment. They believe that earning a degree is necessary in this society. As students look to the future, they foresee more global economic competition with personal economic survival dependent on a high level competence based on careful study of a major field they want to enter. They are motivated to take courses related to their career but object to general education requirements that supposedly prepare them to live a more satisfying social, civic, and political life. Students believe these vague goals are attained independent of going to college because of access to the Internet, television, museums, concerts, trade books, videos, travel, and conversations with friends and family. Tuition is expensive and students are of the opinion that their goal of career preparation should trump all other priorities.

Consideration of Compromise Reforms

Institutional change seems necessary to support student motivation and success. However, what reforms would produce the greatest benefit? Is there some way to reconcile opposing views of students and faculty? We believe that compromise is necessary. Suppose the purpose most students give for going to college, preparing for a job, is accepted by faculty as deserving the highest priority. Because most students who quit college do so in the first 2 years when curriculum involves general studies, getting into the major field right away could sustain their motivation and reduce withdrawal. If the requirement of general studies were abandoned, students could finish a degree in less time and the cost would decline. This shift is not without precedent. Many countries including England and Australia allow students to move from high school to professional studies including law and medicine. The doctors and attorneys in these countries are no less competent than our own but they graduate earlier and have a lower debt to repay.

Lamar Alexander was the United States Secretary of Education, President of the University of Tennessee, Governor of Tennessee, and currently serves as senator for the state of Tennessee. He is among many political leaders who believe that American universities can fulfill their mission by becoming more cost conscious. One way to do this is to quicken the pace of schooling so students can graduate in 3 years. George Washington University President Stephen Trachtenberg estimated that a typical college used its facilities for academic purposes little more than half a calendar year. By keeping campuses open year round and requiring students to take at least one summer of study, as Dartmouth does, the bottom line for most schools could improve by millions of dollars and be reflected by lower tuition. By finishing in 3 years students would save money and get a job earlier (Alexander, 2009).

Another reform involves recognition that required general education courses could be more valuable if chosen voluntarily after students graduate and have a job. The interest in lifelong learning is stronger among persons who enjoy the security of a career and earn an adequate income. Steven, an international executive in New York City, exemplifies this conclusion. Looking back on his college days, Steven recalls,

> I disliked courses offered by departments outside the college of business. Now that I have money and time, I read many books for enjoyment. And, because literature courses I attend at night are taken for pleasure instead of credit, my teachers strive to focus on the appreciation value of these subjects.

A related innovation is for college faculties to provide community service in more creative ways. What if, several weeks before each semester, a lecture schedule where professors would welcome visitors was available online and in booklet form to the general community. For September 16, 2013 topics, times, and places for 48 lectures offered that day on campus would be identified. This method to encourage lifelong learning could continue the education of alumni whose contact with the university is mostly monetary requests to subsidize learning for others. In a similar way, retirees who recognize mental stimulation is necessary to retain their cognitive health could attend lectures along with interested parents and grandparents. Faculty could learn from one another in this way as well.

These groups and others could benefit from a broad agenda of topics, from art to aging, family relationships to financial management, health care, literature, history, religion, child and adult development. The faculty willing to participate would list at least two presentations during the next semester that they consider appropriate for the public. Besides improving community learning without any extra effort on the part of the faculty, some constituencies currently disconnected from the university may become supportive. The Parents Association of the university, in cooperation with the university senate and student senate could assume leadership to identify the available lectures, produce and distribute booklets announcing agenda, solicit coverage by the media, and evaluate outcomes of this approach to create and expand a community of learners.

Families and Managing College Costs

The Project on Student Debt (2011) shows, by state, the average amount of debt of college graduates, proportion of students with debt, and in-state tuition costs. Two-thirds of students borrow to pay for tuition. In 2010, the average student graduated from public universities with $25,250 in loans. More money is owed the federal government in student loans than from all credit card holders in the nation. Student loans are provided without regard for ability to pay (Vedder & Denhart, 2011).

Young adults want to go to an accredited institution with low tuition. This decision usually means choosing one of the 1,300 community colleges in the nation. Estimates are that 75% of freshmen and sophomores are in community colleges with even higher proportions among minority students. Students are trained as workers for sectors of the economy that are creating most of the new jobs. For example, 63% of allied health workers in nursing, radiology, sonogram technology, and pharmacy get their initial education from these schools (Clay, 2009).

Many students believe that living at home is a practical way to reduce reliance on loans while making progress toward a degree. Those who choose this option reported that they rarely experience the social stigma once associated with this kind of living arrangement. Hispanic parents, more often than other groups, prefer having their children, especially daughters, stay home while attending college. This position makes financial sense since it minimizes debt.

Parents of young adults who remain at home while in college express a different set of motivations. In the past, the common expectation was that students would leave home after high school when they got a job or went away to college. However, expense of education has risen dramatically at the same time greater numbers of students have concluded a college degree is necessary to achieve their career aspirations. Parents generally agree about the economic practicality of a community college curriculum.

Permitting daughters and sons to live at home is an important contribution to their success. In addition, the student decision to remain with parents during college is sometimes motivated by the allure of keeping their own bedroom, enjoying home cooking, access to laundry, and more opportunity for family dialogue.

Some parents wonder whether having daughters and sons stay home longer will postpone their transition to adulthood. They worry that their children might choose to never move away and establish a place of their own. The opposite reaction is expressed by others that realize they have not developed a sense of identity apart from their parent role and fear isolation of an 'empty nest'. Regardless of the motivations to live together for a longer duration, parents and young adult children should consider renegotiating expectations for their relationship and mutual obligations (P. Strom & Strom, 2004, 2005).

MARRIAGE AND PARENTHOOD

Cohabitation as a Path to Marriage

During the 1980s a nontraditional perspective about marriage emerged that was accompanied by controversy. An estimated 500,000 young adults chose cohabitation even though it was illegal in every state for unmarried couples to live together. Many of them expressed antimarriage sentiments, claiming that the wedding vows were old-fashioned and no longer relevant. Since then the appeal of cohabitation has sharply risen as reflected by involvement of over 60% of young men and women. However, the 5 million people who currently choose this option express a different outlook on marriage than a generation ago. Instead of being opposed to weddings, they acknowledge being fearful of divorce based on statistics showing that chances of marriage failure are roughly the same as for success. Consequently, men and women across races and ethnicities tend to accept the view that it is a good idea to live together in a trial arrangement to determine if they are compatible before reaching an informed decision about marriage (Smock & Manning, 2009).

National Center for Health Statistics report indicates that a majority (51%) of unmarried couples who move in together marry within 3 years, and 65% of them marry within 5 years (Goodwin, Mosher, & Chandra, 2010). The data show that those who live together after becoming engaged and making plans to marry have roughly the same chance of divorce as couples who never cohabited. The government investigation revealed that, between 1990-2005 the proportion of women ages 35-39 who cohabited doubled from 30% to 61%.

Although cohabitation is widespread, little is known about what it means to young adults. A study based on focus groups and in-depth interviews of 140 men and women examined the motivations of each gender (Huang, Smock, Manning, & Bergstrom-Lynch, 2012). Strong gender differences were discovered in perceived advantages of cohabitation. Men saw more frequent opportunities for sex as compared with dating. They tended to regard cohabitation as a "test drive" without particular connection to marriage. In contrast, women tended to view cohabitation as a short interval on the way to marriage with the same partner. Another gendered outcome related to social disapproval of cohabitation, an issue that was mentioned in the women's focus groups far more often than was the case among men.

Women in the study who opposed cohabitation considered it counter productive to their goal of marriage, and therefore a good reason to avoid it. Entry into a marriage-like relationship was thought to carry a risk of delaying marriage by decreasing a male partner's incentive to get married. Men reported the deterrents to cohabitation were loss of personal freedom, restrictions on how their time is spent and with whom, and concerns about partner surveillance. Some men expressed remorse over loss of future sexual opportunities with other women. In contrast, women appeared more inclined to avoid cohabitation because it impedes further commitment and by some men because it requires a further commitment (Huang, Smock, Manning, Bergstrom-Lynch, 2012).

Two-Generational Views of Identity

What do you consider your most important accomplishment? When we have asked 45- to 50-year old men and women this question, most of them say that helping their children grow up is the most significant contribution they have made and the source of greatest satisfaction. In describing aspects of their long-term role, parents tell about continued efforts to motivate child persistence with difficult tasks and to see learning as a lifelong necessity. Parents are expected to demonstrate how to treat others with kindness, respect, honesty, and compassion. They are also supposed to model a productive work ethic. Parents consider themselves responsible to correct the misconduct of children, teach about time management and conflict resolution, preserve family harmony, and provide lessons about friendship, healthy lifestyle, and religious belief. Many orient their children to sexuality, support career exploration, show how to manage stress, and unite their plans with teachers at school to foster student success. Fulfilling these demanding challenges is a basis for pride that parents feel when children show they are becoming mature and independent (P. Strom & Strom, 2009).

Young adult women often express a different perspective from their parents. They acknowledge the love and guidance provided by their mothers and fathers and appreciate the sacrifice and support that they received while growing up. Nevertheless, many of them do not find the role of becoming a parent appealing and have decided to pursue a different path as they set out to define their identity, purposes, and expectations.

Views of Young American Women

Choosing to become a parent is a personal decision that should be based on an awareness of the satisfactions, difficulties, and responsibilities of this important function that is valued by every society. Two hundred young women in the authors' university classes met in small groups to discuss their impressions about why so many of their age group are choosing to avoid having children or postpone a decision about becoming a parent (R. Strom & Strom, 2010). The following reasons were the most common:

- Work toward a career that requires an extensive education
- Seek personal satisfaction first before considering the parent role
- Financial strains that necessitate husband and wife both having a job
- Fear of having an unstable intimate relationship leading to a divorce
- Find the right partner with whom to share the parenting obligation
- Encouragement from friends to choose any domestic role preferred
- Promotion at work seems more possible for women without children
- Motherhood offers less status than jobs, except for poor and minorities
- Defer marriage and parenting decision to a later age than in the past
- Religion is a less powerful influence to force gender role conformity
- Availability of adequate and affordable childcare for working parents

Any strategy to motivate more women to become mothers must emerge from within the cohort of young adults. Twenty years from now, in 2033, when today's young adults reach middle age, we would like to ask the same question presented at the beginning of this discussion: What do you consider to be your most important accomplishment?

WORLD DEMOGRAPHICS

Global Population Shifts

Demography is the scientific study of human populations, including size, growth, density, and distribution, and statistics about birth, marriage, disease, and death. Forecasts show that the world population of 7 billion people in 2012 will increase to 9 billion by 2050. This rise will take place almost entirely in Asia, Africa, and Latin America. Table 13.1 identifies the top ten countries with the highest population in 2011 and projected estimates for 2050. India is expected to move ahead of China as the most populated nation in 2050, while Ethiopia and the Philippines will replace Russia and Japan. Nigeria will rise in rank from 8th to 4th place, while Brazil declines from 5th to 8th (United States Bureau of Census, 2011).

International Fertility Rates

The *fertility rate* for a nation is the expected number of children per woman in her childbearing years, from age 15 to 45 years old. A rate of 2.1 is necessary to replenish a population. The 2012 average world fertility rate is 2.5. Table 13.2 shows fertility rate estimates for 2012 in selected countries. Countries with the top ten highest populations are included along with nations that record low fertility rates (Central Intelligence Agency, 2012). The conditions in some nations with low fertility are briefly described.

Germany. The fertility rate of Germany is 1.41 children per women of childbearing age. By the year 2050, one-third of Germans will be at least 65 years old. Elderly people will outnumber children 2 to 1, and the working age population is expected to decline by one third. This shift is likely to force even greater immigration to prop up the nation's generous welfare system for older people (Federal Statistics Office, 2009). Turkish, Greek, Yugoslav, and Italian guest workers in Germany have much larger families but are denied government allowances for children (Orlow, 2012).

Italy. The scenario in Italy is worse than Germany because the birth rate has been below replacement level for 25 years. The Italian fertility rate is 1.40 (United Nations, Department of Economic and Social Affairs, 2011). This low fertility rate in the most Catholic of countries seems a

**Table 13.1.   Top 10 Countries With the Highest Population 2011 and
2050[a] Expected Population**

Rank by Country	2011 Population	2050 Expected Population[c]
1 China[b]	1,336,718,015	1,303,723,332
2 India	1,189,172,906	1,656,553,632
3 United States	313,232,044	422,554,384
4 Indonesia	245,613,043	313,020,847
5 Brazil	203,429,773	260,692,493
6 Pakistan	187,342,721	290,847,790
7 Bangladesh	158,570,535	250,155,274
8 Nigeria	155,215,573	402,425,535
9 Russia	138,739,892	109,187,353
10 Japan	126,475,664	93,673,826
Top 10 Countries Total	4,054,510,166	5,102,834,466
Rest of the World	2,875,544,988	4,306,202,522
Total World Population	6,930,055,154	9,409,036,988

a. Demographic (population) estimates for years 2011 and 2050 are based on data from the United States Census Bureau website http://www.census.gov/population/international/data/idb/rank.php updated December 31, 2011.

b. The China population data is for the mainland only.

c. 2050 Estimated Population Rankings of Countries as follows: (1) India, (2) China, (3) United States, (4) Nigeria, (5) Indonesia, (6) Pakistan, (7) Ethiopia, (8) Brazil, (9) Bangladesh, and (10) Philippines.

strange contradiction. One explanation comes from surveys indicating that 52% of Italian women between ages 16 and 24 have decided they will not become mothers. The desire for a career is their most common reason (Clark, 2008). Demographers indicate that Italy is heavily dependent on immigrants to bear the load of the nation's deeply indebted pension system. The question troubling Italians is: How can an aging society compete in the global economy with a shrinking number of younger people in the workforce? By 2050, if trends continue, 42% of Italy's population will be at least 60 years of age.

Pope John Paul II expressed alarm in his 2002 presentation to the Italian Parliament. He warned (Population Research Institute, 2002):

The birthrate crisis in Italy is a grave threat that bears on the future of the nation.... There is also ample room for political initiatives which, by upholding recognition of the rights of the family as the natural society founded upon marriage, according to the expression of the Constitution of

Table 13.2. Fertility Rate 2012 Estimates for Selected Countries *

Afghanistan	5.64	Mozambique	5.40
Angola	5.54	Niger	7.52
Bangladesh	2.55	Nigeria	5.38
Brazil	2.16	Pakistan	3.07
Canada	1.59	Philippines	3.15
China	1.55	Portugal	1.51
Congo	5.59	Russia	1.43
Ethiopia	5.97	Somalia	6.26
France	2.08	Spain	1.48
Germany	1.41	Sweden	1.67
India	2.58	Taiwan	1.16
Indonesia	2.23	Thailand	1.66
Italy	1.40	United Kingdom	1.91
Japan	1.39	United States	2.06
Mexico	2.27	Zambia	5.90

* Adapted from Central Intelligence Agency, Estimates for 2012, http://www.cia.gov

the Italian Republic, can make the task of having children and bringing them up less burdensome both socially and economically.

Spain. Once upon a time, Spain was a powerful influence in world exploration and colonization. Two generations ago, under General Franco, large families were given gifts and medals from the state. Today, the Spanish fertility rate is 1.48 and will decline by 25% over the next half century as the number of Spaniards over age 65 increases by 120%. Within one generation, Spain has been transformed from an average family size of eight to a majority of childless couples (United Nations, 2011). Older adults complain that personal comfort seems to be the only thing young people believe in while the customary virtue of sacrificing for others seems to be vanishing (Ross & Richardson, 2008).

Russia. The fertility rate for Russia is 1.43 children per woman of child-bearing age (United Nations, Department of Economic and Social Affairs, 2011). Predictions are that by 2050 the number of children will decline by one-third while the cohort of older adults grows 70%. Two-thirds of pregnancies in Russia are terminated by abortion. On average, Russian women abort three children. This means the national death rate is 70% higher than the birthrate (Connelly, 2010).

Sweden. The fertility rate in Sweden is 1.67. Most of the working population receives 5 weeks annual paid vacation. Mothers, regardless of their marital status, are provided government grants based on their number of children. Retirees have generous pensions. Even the church is provided financial support from the state. There are few prisons in Sweden because the high rate of affluence translates into low rates of crime (Freeman, Swedenborg, & Topel, 2010).

Japan. The fertility rate for Japan is 1.39. Japan has the highest proportion of people age 65 and older (23%). By 2055, the total population is expected to decline to about 90 million, and 36 million (41%) will be age 65 and over (International Longevity Center, 2012). The Japanese worry about lack of younger workers and have tried to compensate through exporting automobile jobs to the United States where workers are more plentiful. There is also greater willingness by Americans to buy Toyota and other foreign cars when they are produced in the United States using its own workforce.

Among Japanese women with children under 14 years of age, only 9% report satisfaction from raising them, compared with 40% to 70% in other developed nations. Government encouragement has failed to persuade women to have children and continue the sacrifice of full-time mothers who are obliged to closely supervise the education of their children. This customary, stressful, and restrictive role is unacceptable to many young women who report that they have given up on the idea of marriage or having a family (R. Strom, Strom, Strom, Makino, & Morishima, 2000; Yu, 2009).

China. During the past generation, the People's Republic of China has undergone profound changes that have influenced standard of living, status of women, and family size (fertility rate 1.55). These shifts have been accompanied by speculation about how departure from tradition is modifying the way that children are raised and what is expected of them in a one-child society with nontraditional parent and gender expectations (Greenhaigh, 2008; R. Strom, Strom, & Xie, 1995). The Chinese public is concerned that the children growing up in small families will become spoiled and egocentric.

The One Child Policy, enacted in 1979, has led to an imbalance in gender population. Boys have always been valued more than girls, particularly in rural areas where they work the land and are obliged by custom to care for their aging parents. Consequently, many Chinese couples have justified aborting females or killing newborn daughters and the government has implemented forced sterilization in some parts of the country. As a result, in certain regions, 80% of the children are boys. Many of them confidently announce that they will get married and become a good farmer. However, when asked where they will find their wife, they suggest she will come from a village far away where there is an abundance of females. Across China millions of boys hope for the same thing although the fact is many will not meet the girl of their dreams (Fewsmith, 2010).

United States. The highest fertility rate in the United States was 3.8 children per family in 1957. Since then, there has been a steady decline to the present rate of 2.06 children (Central Intelligence Agency, 2012). These figures should be viewed in relation to corresponding demographic shifts in longevity. In 1935, when Social Security became an entitlement, the average lifespan was 64 years. Consequently, most people did not live long enough to collect benefits. Today, however, the average lifespan exceeds 80 years. This means that the rapidly increasing older adult population collects social security for a longer period.

There is mounting concern about how it will be possible to sustain economic support for the elderly in view of the decline in fertility rates. Consider that, in 1950, there were 16 people employed for every person receiving social security. By 2000, the ratio fell to 3 workers contributing to the system for every retiree drawing a check. Forecasts for 2050 indicate two working people for every retired person. The government has declared that reducing benefits, increasing FICA taxes, raising the retirement age or some combination of these options must be enacted soon. The reason is that, by 2017, social security benefits will exceed income paid into the system by employees. Estimates are that by 2030 social security will require 60% of the federal budget (Turner, 2011).

Generational support should be reciprocal. Older adults depend on younger people to keep the social security fund solvent. At the same time, younger adults must be able to count on elders to support quality childcare, excellent schools, and college entitlement to get the education they need to be globally competitive. In 1970, about half (47%) of all households included children under 18 years of age. The proportion fell to 30% by 1990. In 2011, school age children live in 26% of American homes; over half of minor-age Americans are minorities but two-thirds of the adult voters are White (Norton et al., 2012). Everybody should become aware of, expected to care about, and respond to the needs of age groups other than their own.

Privileged and Underprivileged Nations

If low fertility rates in the European Union continue, the population under age 15 will decline 40% by 2050 while, in the same period, older adults will increase by 50%. The median age is expected to be 50, highest in history. These figures are not speculation regarding what might happen; instead, they are a mathematical depiction of what is taking place now. There are warnings from demographers that first-world nations must either find ways to reverse the current trends, or be overwhelmed by a third-world population that is already five times larger and predicted to become 10 times greater by 2050. In economically poor countries, half or more of the people are under 25 years old and represent a potentially enormous workforce (Connelly, 2010).

A sobering perspective on global population change emerges from awareness of fertility rates among countries where women are not decision makers about birth control. There seems no end in sight to the birth decline among privileged nations, and all signs suggest that a rising number of women in these favored environments are deciding against becoming mothers. There is a statistical certainty regarding some aspects of demography. For example, Italy cannot have a greater number of young adults of childbearing age in 2020 than it has teenagers and children now unless there were immigrants coming into the country. In contrast, the United States fertility rate is 2.06, which is near the minimum needed to replenish the national population of 313 million. This condition attributes to immigrants and larger family size of 50 million Hispanics (Spanish-language origins of Mexico, Cuba, Puerto Rico, and Central/South America), expected to become 29% of the national population by 2050 (Passel, Cohn, & Lopez, 2011).

SUMMARY AND IMPLICATIONS

Economists warn that, unless the number of students graduating from college in the next few years is increased, disappointing economic and social consequences will occur. Unemployment rates among young people that have only a high school diploma will worsen, income disparity will increase between those who are well educated and others without enough schooling, and the nation is likely to lose its advantage of having the most talented workforce. All 50 of the states have begun using a Common College Completion Metrics approach to assess institutional accountability by revealing the variance in success of students attending different colleges. This data is also being used to decide the relative amount of economic assistance that states provide public institutions. In addition, colleges should begin to consider polling students to determine how to enrich the process of education while also creating free learning opportunities for the community.

Businesses want to recruit college graduates that are knowledgeable, possess attitudes and skills needed for teamwork, and can readily be oriented to fulfill their role within a company. Students going to college so they can get a good job and perform well share these same goals. However, most families have difficulty paying for rising costs of tuition and many potential students express reluctance to assume the debt. Entitlement for free access to higher education deserves urgent consideration. This reform would create career opportunities for more young people and contribute to the economic health of the nation.

Young women in many countries are choosing a future without children. The scope of decline in fertility rates among developed nations is documented along with public policy efforts intended to reverse the course of population change. The initiatives commonly used to persuade women that they should become mothers are monetary incentives and suggestions that attainment of personal maturity requires the sacrifices related to parenting. These solutions, devised by middle age and older adults, rarely include intergenerational dialogue that recognizes goals and apprehensions of young women in the present environment or explores what society should do to make parenthood a role that is more appealing and more frequently chosen.

APPLICATIONS FOR TEACHING

1. Students in middle school and high school benefit from continuing orientation to the labor market outlook, projections for specific occupations, and career exploration. This awareness can ensure greater knowledge of the shifting patterns and demands in the evolving workplace, emphasize planning, and identify myths about employment.

2. The way most students begin career exploration is searching the Internet to find out about requirements for preferred jobs. School counselors for districts should work as teams to formulate a list of web sites that can be helpful, accompanied by explanations about the unique contributions provided by each of the sites.

3. Parents should be partners with children in career exploration programs. This is because most mothers and fathers have substantial influence on student decisions about work, usually provide economic support throughout the education process, and need sufficient information to participate in family discussions about readiness for jobs.

4. Society has insisted that students be educated to understand their obligations to others. Young adults should insist that this circumstance apply in reverse as well. That is, the adult members of society should become informed about the needs of families for access to quality child care, excellent schools, and education entitlement

with free access to higher education to supply a modern workforce while preserving the social security system. These conditions seem essential before more women can seriously consider whether becoming a parent is appealing and realistic for them.

5.   The status associated with a role influences the extent to which it will be chosen. In American subcultures with the highest fertility rates, being a mother has more status and involves a greater investment of time. For society in general the role of mother is often seen as providing less status than a job. As a result, women are conflicted as they decide between employment alone or combining work with being a mother. Every segment of society should understand the childrearing choices made by women from different cultural backgrounds and respect the options they choose.

PART V

MIDDLE ADULTHOOD (AGES 40-60)

CHAPTER 14

SELF-EVALUATION AND MATURITY

Many middle-age adults report that their fast paced schedule prevents them from being able to spend time reflecting about challenges, amending goals, and determining how to achieve their purposes. Instead, they feel pressured for completing a relentless to-do list. The pursuit of an agenda that is too ambitious leads people to rationalize why they cannot give attention to the self-examination that is necessary to identify sectors of life that should become the focus for self improvement. The goals of this chapter are to describe the importance of self-evaluation in how development is advanced or arrested during middle age, and how assessment of learning needs can become more accurate when based on the observations of two generations. There is also an exploration of how parent conflict with adolescent children can promote mutual growth when guidelines are established that foster constructive disagreement. The relevance of conflict goals as a context for gauging development is discussed. Challenges of family configuration are examined with implications for community support.

Learning Throughout Life: An Intergenerational Perspective, pp. 323–349
Copyright © 2012 by Information Age Publishing

GOAL SETTING IN MIDDLE AGE

Psychologists agree that reassessment of personal direction seems necessary at midlife, between 35 and 45 years of age (Cavanaugh & Blanchard-Fields, 2010). However, there is a lack of agreement about the particular goals middle-age people should attempt to achieve. This lack of consensus is actually beneficial because it encourages each individual to focus self-evaluation on the specific issues deserving attention in their unique circumstance.

Discontent as Motivation

Midlife is a time to figure out how to cope with new perspectives about aging. It is important for people to take stock of their lives, particularly long-standing illusions that have motivated achievement of occupational goals, intimate relationships, and what an individual really wants out of life. By age 35 to 40, people are typically aware of where they stand in achieving plans that were made in early adulthood and how much farther they can reasonably expect to go. If there has been failure in reaching aspirations, there is some regret as well as adjustment that come with accepting that knowledge. Even individuals who are seen by others as highly successful, those whose occupational goals have been met and surpassed, report having to cope with feelings of futility and meaninglessness. In fact, discontent is such a pervasive experience during middle age that it should be seen as a normal aspect of personality development (P. Strom & Strom, 2011c).

What seems to happen is that certain previously obvious truths, basic beliefs and supporting values, suddenly come into question. A sense of disparity between "what I have attained and what I really wanted" instigates a search for "what I want now." Many people find it difficult to amend their dreams. They hold on to fantasies that should be replaced; uncertainty keeps others from making changes. Yet, the necessity to construct a more appropriate dream should be recognized as the main developmental task of middle age. Everyone needs to restructure earlier goals in such a way that the worthwhile and mature dimensions of their original form are retained while new priorities consistent with being middle aged are added.

Sources of Discontent

Anecdotal reports show that feelings of discontent trigger the motivation to modify aspirations but do not provide the direction for change.

Because people differ in source(s) of their discontent, they vary in the kinds of questions suitable for self-evaluation. When marriage is regarded as the main reason for unhappiness, people think about what is missing in the relationship with a spouse (Cherlin, 2009). Persons in this circumstance usually ask: Do I want to stay with my husband or my wife now that our children are no longer home, and they are old enough to adjust if we divorce? Should I make an effort to recover the passion we enjoyed earlier in our life together? Should I have an extramarital affair to compensate for a loss of affection and sexual pleasure?

Some men and women consider a spouse their greatest source of satisfaction so they would not ask these kinds of questions. Instead, what bother them the most are adverse conditions at work. Dual career couples represent 70% of the households with parents and children (Freedman, 2010). These adults often review their commitment to a job and struggle to decide whether the effort they have put into this aspect of their life has been as worthwhile as they once supposed. Whether they are bored or pressure-ridden, their questions are similar: Do I want to keep doing the same job for the rest of my career? Is it too late to change my line of work? Is it reasonable for me to begin a different occupation at this stage of life? These questions usually occur at about the same time adolescent sons and daughters begin thinking about their own career opportunities. It is unfortunate that, as adolescents reflect about their options for work, their parents who are heavily engaged in self-evaluation seldom share the processes they use to support decision-making and healthy adjustment.

The physical decline that comes with middle age can often be a major cause of discontent. In these cases declining efficiency of the body causes some individuals to become anxious and worry about heart disease, leads others to consider a more moderate lifestyle, and still another group to become preoccupied with changes in their appearance and the possible effects on relationships (Sharkey & Gaskill, 2006). Some prominent questions may include: What habits must I give up or renew to improve my prospects for good health? What can I do to keep my body youthful and attractive? An army of middle-age persons who join health clubs and exercise programs, diet clinics, and cosmetic services reflect these concerns. Just as puberty signals the onset of adolescence, physical changes inform parents they are entering middle age. Usually this occurs at the same time daughters and sons are starting to develop attractive bodies and appealing physiques.

Discontent can also center on the inconsistencies between religious values or philosophical beliefs and less mature behavior shown by individuals. Carl Jung, a renowned psychoanalyst, was sought out for treatment by people throughout the world. In his book, *Modern Man in Search of a Soul*, Jung (1955) summarized his experience:

Among all my patients in the second half of life, there has not been an individual whose problems in the last resort was not one of finding a religious outlook on life. It is safe to say that every one of them fell ill because s/he had lost that which the living religions of every age have given their followers, and none of them had been really healed that did not regain a religious outlook.

Self-examination in each of these contexts center on consistency of lifestyle. For example, if my children matter so much to me, then why do I spend so little time with them? How can my definition of success enlarge to go beyond just things I do at work to also include my other roles as a husband, father, wife, mother, and adult child? Why do I resolve to pursue a healthy lifestyle yet continue to avoid getting regular exercise and having a good diet? What changes are needed to reconcile how I act with the beliefs that I have chosen to guide my life? (Wolpe, 2009).

Intensity of Discontent

Individuals differ not only in the source of their discontent but intensity as well. Severity of discontent seems to account for why self-evaluation during middle age produces only slight changes in some people but significantly alters the future for others. Clinical psychologists whose mission is to help people with mental health have been responsible for most of the literature about middle age. As a result, public perspective has been imbalanced toward expectations for middle-age crises. Some scenarios suggest that introspection and self-evaluation without the guidance of professionals could be a gateway to depression, alcoholism, sexual disorder, divorce, obesity, and other dysfunctions. Certainly, some people are overwhelmed by their situations and should be encouraged to seek professional counseling (Anderson, Goodman, & Schlossberg, 2011).

For most people, however, middle age is not a crisis but a time of transition for further development that can initiate greater maturity and happiness. This transition is shown by a higher level of intimacy in marriage, increased satisfaction at work, better attention to health issues, and greater commitment to moral principles. The way parents look at adolescent children often changes as well. They assign greater importance to emotional growth and take pride in the kind of person their daughter or son is rather than limiting their approval to the child's academic or athletic achievements. Parents encourage youth to set some goals and take credit for personal accomplishments. Mothers and fathers become more willing to listen and give undivided attention to what children say. It is difficult to overstate the relationship gains that can accompany healthy self-evaluation during middle age.

FLAWED SELF-ASSESSMENT

Self-evaluation is essential to determine whether personal goals have been met, remain appropriate, or should be amended. However, research has repeatedly found that self-assessment of skill and character is often flawed. Generally, self-impressions correlate with actual behavior to a moderate or meager extent. The majority of people report seeing themselves as "above average" in skill, overestimate their demonstration of commendable behavior, tend to give overly optimistic speculation about when they will complete future projects, and reach judgments based on more confidence than is warranted (Dunning, Heath, & Suls, 2004). Despite our best efforts, it seems that none of us are able to fully detect all our learning needs by relying on self-evaluation alone. There can be benefit in having at least a second opinion, someone who sees us on a regular basis, understands the goals we are pursuing, and wants to support us so we reach our potential. Accordingly, observations of a spouse, friends, or teammates can improve the accuracy of self-evaluation (Goleman, 1996).

A Balanced Perspective

There may be differences in the criteria required to become successful at work and to perform well in a family. Many people assume that being in the fast lane is the best way to travel through life. This is the view embraced by 40-year old Jeff Hansen, husband of Ann and father of three sons. As the manager of a prospering insurance company, Jeff earns a high salary allowing Ann the choice to stay at home and more carefully supervise their children. During a typical week, Jeff spends 70 hours at work. The reason for his demanding schedule is that making personal contacts requires time and he likes the job. Jeff's devotion to the company means that he may unintentionally neglect his wife and children. He is proud that the needs of his clients are taken care of immediately. In contrast, family needs often must wait until a slowdown in activity occurs at the office.

It is not surprising that Jeff identifies lack of time as his greatest limitation. When company demands have been met, there does not seem to be enough hours or energy left to do things with Ann, take the children places, listen to concerns of loved ones, or think about monitoring his goals as a parent. Although he is not sufficiently involved with the family, Jeff arranges time to have workouts at the gym, play tennis or golf, and participate in other activities that he says reduce his stress and allow him to stay fit. He admits that his children are the source of more worry and stress than all other sources including his job.

The attributes Jeff depends on to fulfill his responsibilities as a father differs from those he relies on for success in his business. At the office, Jeff finds intensity and determination are key factors for increasing sales. He is also accustomed to having a high level of control at work, a condition that cannot be duplicated in his relationships with relatives. Teenagers especially need to assert themselves and exhibit behaviors that Jeff would not approve of by subordinates at work. Perfectionism and efficiency may be factors that contribute to progress on the job but the qualities that are more helpful in raising healthy children are patience and willingness to spend time together.

Jeff often comes home late. One night Ann was already sleeping but 16-year old Larry was watching a television program in his bedroom. The room was in disarray with clothes, books, papers, money, tapes and discs scattered around the floor. Jeff took one look and made this comment: "When are you ever going to become responsible?" Larry did not reply. The next morning when Jeff told his wife about the incident, she listened and said, "You haven't talked to Larry much over the last few weeks. It should please you to know that he has been volunteering for the Sierra Club in planting trees. He is concerned about the environment beyond his bedroom, the entire planet, and future of people whom he has never met. I believe that Larry is developing a broader sense of responsibility than we had at his age and there are better ways to gauge his progress than how he maintains the bedroom." Perhaps it is time for Jeff to reevaluate his lifestyle (Harrington & Van Deusen, 2010).

Valuing Adolescent Views

Surveys of middle age parents show that they feel their role is most difficult and least satisfying when children become adolescents (P. Strom & Strom, 2009). At this stage, mothers and fathers discover the parent-child relationship must be renegotiated. The adolescent quest for autonomy has traditionally led to friction and sometimes bitter disputes in families. The influence of Internet, other media, and peers on the norms of youth accelerates the social distance that separates children and parents.

Many adults suppose there are greater differences among ethnic groups than age groups. This long-standing impression assumes that members of the same ethnicity must share beliefs, values, and ideas that are independent of their age. Middle age politicians who agree with this view usually claim they speak for their whole subpopulation even though they do not consult with people younger than themselves about the way they look at things. The reality is that the traditional definition of culture is no longer sufficient because it does not include influence of technology and social evolution. There was a time, in yesterday's world, when ethnicity, language, heritage, nationality, and traditions were preeminent influences that shaped child and adolescent development. However, that changed with a revolution in communications that has resulted in people of the same age having more experiences in common no matter where they live or background of their family. The impact of global media has allowed cohort influence to become more prominent than ever while eroding the overall influence adults have on younger people. In turn, youth look to one another for guidance and intergenerational communication is decreasing.

In modern societies, youth can rely on many sources of learning. Consequently, the cyber environment has a powerful effect on the way adolescents interpret situations, build friendships, share views on social networks, and think about the future. This basic change creates differences in generational views so people of the same ethnicity but from different age groups increasingly possess dissimilar perspectives. Nevertheless, the elements that continue to dominate attention of adults are ethnicity, language, and religion. Those who write and speak about multicultural issues generally overlook age as an aspect of culture in favor of outdated definitions. Such incomplete pictures ignore the way people process information, organize data, and create meaning. Because adolescents of many nations are exposed by social networks to similar messages, age norms are communicated on a broader scale than in the past. One outcome is that youth have like-minded views on issues that separate them from adults including those of their family and ethnicity. This explains in part why teenagers in Tokyo, Atlanta, and Moscow agree with each other more than they do with their parents (R. Strom & Strom, 2011).

When generation is considered an important factor in defining culture, the impressions of adolescents get greater attention. In addition, adults become less inclined to act as advocates for youth and instead want the teenagers to speak for themselves. In hierarchical societies, adolescents have been discouraged from stating personal opinions that may contradict views of older relatives, educators or others in authority. Youth in these environments who express ideas contrary to those of adults are often characterized as lacking respect. Given these impediments to authentic dialogue, some teenagers remain silent. In turn, this can cause adults to mistakenly suppose absence of opposition means the generations are in agreement.

Parent Learning Needs

A more promising outlook is to recognize that when adolescents are heard, they are less inclined to devalue their legacy or abandon customs they might otherwise have revised. One context in which adolescent observations can contribute to development of middle age people is in detection of strengths and learning needs of parents. These insights become known by administering the Parent Success Indicator, PSI (R. Strom & Strom, 2009). This instrument identifies favorable qualities of parents and aspects of behavior that warrant improvement.

The PSI contains 60 items equally divided in six scales of ten items. The scales are:

1. Communication—skills of advising children and learning from them;
2. Use of time—making decisions about the ways time is used;
3. Teaching—scope of guidance and instruction expected of parents;
4. Frustration—adolescent behaviors that are bothersome to parents;
5. Satisfaction—aspects of being a parent that bring satisfaction; and
6. Information needs—things parents need to know about their child.

There are two versions of the inventory, one for parents and the other for 10- to 14-year-olds. Mothers and fathers provide self-assessments while children describe observations about their parents. The reason for inviting two generations to assess parent behavior is because adults can make better decisions about self-improvement when they know perceptions of those they seek to influence. Parents care more about how their children feel that they succeed and fail than they do about judgment of experts who give advice in the media. Parents know some of their assets and shortcomings but certain abilities and deficiencies are overlooked if adults are the only source of judgment on their behavior. By relying upon a two generational perspective of family interaction, a more balanced picture of parental competence and learning needs comes into view along with a more realistic portrayal of how adults influence their children.

Success for most middle-age people is defined by how well they carry out their guidance role. Like educators in a classroom, parents can benefit from feedback about their instruction. To provide this insight, a sample of 1,544 Black, Hispanic, and White parents and their adolescents completed the Parent Success Indicator (R. Strom, Strom, Strom, Shen, & Beckert, 2004). The following four main lessons emerged for parents.

(1) The results showed that parents should learn time management before they can teach this important behavior to their children. In *Fellowship of the Rings*, Gandalf says that everyone has the same challenge: "All we have to decide is what to do with the time that is given us" (Tolkien, 2003, p. 50). Time management is recognized as a goal that must be

attained to ensure a desirable quality of life. Individuals who arrange time so their priorities get sufficient attention feel more in control of their lives, report greater satisfaction, and have a more productive work record. Parents who schedule too much activity prevent themselves from spending time with children. Many adolescents are as busy as their parents, juggling after-school events, time on the phone, and interacting with friends on social networks. Adolescents need the lifestyle balance time management can provide so they avoid taking on too many activities, breaking promises, and ignoring people who matter most to them.

Independent variables were examined to determine individual significance to each item response for mothers (R. Strom, Strom, Strom, Shen, & Beckert, 2004). Amount of time that mothers spent interacting with adolescents had the greatest influence on perceptions of maternal success as reported by both generations. In contrast, household income had a relatively small effect on the perceptions of maternal success. Variables that can be manipulated, like "mother and adolescent time together," should become more prominent criteria for how parents see themselves. Mothers and fathers cannot readily change their amount of income or education level but can choose to take advantage of the powerful influence that comes from spending time with their adolescent. Similar findings have been obtained in studies involving 517 American fathers and their adolescent children (Beckert, Strom, & Strom, 2006).

(2) Parents should learn how to cope with stress. This need was detected solely by their adolescent children. Adolescents in all three ethnic groups gave their mothers unfavorable ratings for teaching them how to deal with stress. Learning to relax is fundamental to support mental health, a path more parents should demonstrate for children as a way to deal with stress. Parents commonly overestimate their favorable influence in this context. In order to provide advice about stress, a parent must be perceived by daughters or sons as demonstrating this capacity in their own lives. A good reason to occasionally retreat from tasks is to recover a sense of perspective. It is troubling that mothers in each ethnic group gave themselves low scores for being able to manage their time. Their inability to schedule leisure for themselves was ranked the lowest among things mothers do well, 60th out of 60 items and 57th out of 60 as observed by adolescents (R. Strom, Strom, Strom, Shen, & Beckert, 2004).

This familiar situation should not be interpreted as another example of maternal sacrifice. The fact is adolescents need their mothers to show them how to deal with stress by setting aside time for themselves and ways to manage time to have a sense of personal control. Some items on the Information Needs scale such as how to help children with fears and worries, set goals, deal with conflict, explore careers, address concerns about sex and bullies can only be met by listening to the children. Careful listening takes time and involves conversations that avoid distraction. Mothers who invested over 10 hours a week talking with and doing things with their adolescents were seen as more successful by adolescent children and in their own estimate. Adolescent access to parents is a factor that can be manipulated and should be a lesson parents learn.

The American Psychological Association carries out annual surveys using a nationally representative sample of 1,500 adults and 1,200 children ages 8 to 17 about stress in America (Munsey, 2010). Findings show that many parents do not know what bothers their children so stress symptoms commonly go unnoticed. This applies to headaches, reported by 33% of the children and sleeping difficulties cited by 44% of them. Inattentive parents supposed that only 13% of children have these problems. Twenty percent of children said they worried a lot but only 3% of the parents were aware of this sign of stress. Children worry about doing well in school, getting into college, and whether their family will have enough money. Again, parents seemed unaware of stresses that can undermine the psychological and physical health of youth.

Many parents find it difficult to set aside time for conversations with daughters and sons about matters of consequence. If mothers and fathers are unavailable or seem preoccupied during conversations, children conclude that they are a burden and should not bother busy parents with their problems. Among the parents, mothers reported much greater stress than fathers. Using a 10-point scale with 10 being the highest level of stress, 15% of mothers rated their level as 10 compared to 3% of fathers. To ease the maternal burden, fathers must assume a greater share of domestic tasks (Munsey, 2010).

There are things parents can do to reduce stress of their children. These recommendations require reflection and effort on the part of mothers and fathers (P. Strom & Strom, 2009):

1. Arrange dialogues every day that focus on child ideas and concerns.
2. Encourage reflective thinking rather than rely on impulsive thinking.
3. Demonstrate patience in waiting for the child to answer questions.
4. Set aside time for you and know that this is an important example.
5. Make sure a child has discretionary time so its value is recognized.
6. Avoid planning too many activities in favor of chances to set goals.
7. Learn to assess child stress and help with the amendment of goals.
8. Take small breaks regularly so work is not viewed as undesirable.
9. Participate in exercise so health becomes a common family goal.

10. Help children monitor stress and ask for adult help when needed.
11. Realize that a hectic type lifestyle makes you a dysfunctional model.
12. Recognize that online learning allows students to control their pace.
13. Understand that parents have to acquire coping skills to teach them.
14. Break tasks into small pieces so they are considered manageable.

(3) Parents should teach about friendship and dating. Parent unwillingness to discuss adolescent concerns about dating was seen by both generations as a serious shortcoming. The fact that adolescents saw this as the most prominent learning need for their parents might seem surprising. After all, schools make a concerted effort to teach about sexual relationships and safe sex practices. However, student responses suggest that parent instruction leaves out how to get along with the opposite gender. Adolescents need conversations with adults regarding expectations for dating and building friendships to demonstrate mutual respect and self-restraint in an evolving relationship with dating partners.

Both generations from all three ethnic groups (Black, Hispanic, White) felt that parents should become more engaged in discussing adolescent concerns about dating. Adolescents often begin to date well before they possess adequate knowledge about this kind of relationship. Curiosity and lack of information leads to greater anxiety and premature sexual activity. Dating involves a complicated process of friendship formation and can be distressing because it implicates peer status as emotionally or socially competent. While adolescents can turn to peers for information, this can lead to unfortunate results. Parents should accept the obligation to guide adolescents about dating at the same time they listen to teenagers about their concerns and experience.

(4) Parents need to learn from their children. Adolescents from all three ethnic groups assigned their parents unfavorable ratings for being willing to learn from them. Furthermore, the time that mothers spend with adolescents made considerable differences in this context. The more time mothers and adolescents in all ethnic groups spent together, the more favorable maternal ratings were reported by both generations. It appears that when mothers and children spend a lot of time together, both parties conclude mothers learn from their child.

Fathers also received higher scores for listening to children than for their willingness to learn from them (Beckert, Strom, & Strom, 2006). Because of vast changes in technology, youth possess a considerable amount of valuable information. Because parenting is transactional, views of adults and children should be more closely related. Fathers must be provided ways to access ideas, feelings, and opinions of their children as well as techniques for examining the logic of adolescents. Listening is necessary to understand how another person sees things, but fathers must go beyond listening to recognize the need for reciprocal learning in family relationships. This combination of attributes characterizes effective teachers at home and in the classroom.

LEARNING FROM CONFLICT

During middle age, the scope of self-evaluation for those who are parents must grow because of increased conflicts that surface as children transition to adolescence. There are 95 million American adults raising middle school, junior high, and high school students. These adolescents, who at younger ages seemed so agreeable, now appear to have issues that provoke daily debates. Arguments usually center on procrastination for not completing assigned chores, cleaning a bedroom, monopolizing the bathroom, scheduling transportation, spending more than was budgeted, and agreeing on time for curfew. Adolescents consider these topics appropriate agenda to leverage their independence. The resulting hassles motivate parents to renegotiate how they communicate with their children in more equitable ways (Barkley & Robin, 2008).

Parent-Child Disagreements

Family disputes typically center on resources, needs, and values. Issues about resources such as the car, television, cell phones, and computers are easiest to resolve by negotiation, additional purchases or having someone be a mediator who establishes a schedule for sharing use of limited resources. Arguments focused on personal needs for status, esteem, and power are more difficult because the reasons precipitating these differences are often unclear. A problem solving approach that allows adolescents to state their hopes and express discontent is usually effective as a way to settle such disagreements.

Guidelines for Disputes

The best method for adults to address disagreements with children is always take the high road and show maturity. Getting back at the other party should not be seen as an option. A Chinese proverb informs us that

"Those who pursue revenge dig two graves." Conflicts over values present the greatest difficulty. When the benefits and the goals that generations prize are challenged, they might feel their sense of self is at risk. Conflicts that involve values necessitate careful listening along with the realization that the people we love may adopt certain beliefs with which we disagree. Because youth values deviate from parent values more so than in the past, the following guidelines can help with family conflicts.

(1) *Respectful relationships are based on self-disclosure.* Every person should express their point of view so fair consideration can take place. Parents need to be aware of the adolescent perspective to offer guidance that is relevant. In turn, adolescents should feel obligated to enable fulfillment of this goal by providing continuous insight about how they see and feel about events and ideas. The resulting dialogue ensures that a certain amount of disagreement is inevitable because it meets the necessary conditions for getting to know each other.

(2) *Establish ground rules together that will be used to guide arguments.* Put downs, shouting, and sarcasm should be out of bounds because they contradict the goal of both parties to demonstrate self control, an agreed upon indicator of maturity. The speaker/listener role can be applied so while one person talks, others listen and do not interrupt. Listeners should restate what a speaker says to confirm that what was expressed has been understood. Adolescents should avoid statements like "Everybody else's parents let them do it…" and parents should avoid comments like "When I was your age….".

(3) *Agree on a definition of the issues so conversation has a common focus.* It can be frustrating to find out at the end of a lengthy talk that both parties are still unaware of the main concerns felt by the other. For a daughter, an argument over curfew may be a challenge to her maturity whereas the parents see it as a matter of safety. There is a great difference between telling an adolescent "I don't trust you" and saying "I am afraid for you because most car accidents happen after midnight." Parent fears, worries, and concerns always warrant expression and deserve to be heard.

(4) *Set aside uninterrupted time to discuss bothersome matters.* Most arguments arise in response to particular events but certain disputes are continuous. These issues require attention when neither party is distracted and is able to spend time in a serious conversation. If anger surfaces, either person should call time-out and bring the topic up again later. At every age, anger makes us temporarily unable to access divergent thinking or show consideration for the needs and feelings of others.

(5) *Examine options that you may not like at first consideration.* Building an addition to the house so an adolescent has more space could be a parent response to the frustration of continually viewing a crowded bedroom. However, this situation could also motivate practical options such as wall

shelves to add storage or donation of old clothes to a charity. Almost every solution to an argument is more difficult for one party than for the other. If either person feels their position has not been fairly assessed, the search for more solutions should continue until there is agreement. The best resolutions often involve more than a single strategy. Finding storage space in some other room and showing restraint in comments about how teenagers maintain their bedroom could combine to minimize a dispute. Agree on a schedule for evaluating whether trial options are succeeding or new ones are necessary.

(6) *Acknowledge the existence of disagreements.* Parents who do not spend enough time with adolescents tend to ignore conflicts by making concessions. This denial of disagreements overlooks the benefits parents can offer adolescents by giving them opportunities to practice emerging debate skills in a safe and constructive environment. The family should be the ideal setting for learning to disagree with others since parents love their children and generally are able to show greater maturity. This should enable adults to respond with restraint instead of anger. Greater maturity also allows the grownups to enact important social skills such as listening, empathy, negotiation, compromise, and independent thinking. Parent and adolescent disputes also confirm that people can disagree and still love each other.

(7) *Encourage constructive behaviors you have yet to master.* Acting as a model does not imply having knowledge about how to succeed in all situations. Instead, people qualify as models by being further along the path toward achievement. Adolescents who recognize that parents can be effective teachers while they also improve themselves understand this condition. A powerful way to help adolescents go beyond the example of older family members is encouraging them to set conflict learning goals and monitor their attainment.

(8) *Everyone's views should be heard without interruption.* Some Native American tribes solve some problems by use of a talking circle. At Good Samaritan Hospital in Phoenix, a Navajo family let us observe this procedure. In the hospital room, the leader of the circle began by holding an arrowhead above his head. Then he said,

> Sometimes older people in our tribe must come to the city for medical care. This is a time of worry and feeling bad because they lack spiritual support of their traditional medicine man. What can be done to help the Indian who is disoriented when placed in the hospital, recuperation center or nursing home? How can others help during this time of difficulty?

Then the leader passed the arrowhead to the person standing on his right. That person then had the opportunity to speak and make suggestions. In turn, each person in the circle was given a chance to comment.

The order of speakers was determined by their seating and they always held the arrowhead, passing it on only when s/he was finished talking.

This practice differs from television programs where experts invited to state their views routinely interrupt one another and try to dominate the conversation. Some of the talking circle speakers expressed agreement with the views of others who had spoken before them. Often the speaker supported a position or elaborated some idea that had already been stated. Sometimes a novel solution was presented. At the end, the initial speaker summarized what those in the circle had proposed. When an elder is at the hospital, it would be possible for the medicine man to visit, conduct ceremonies on the reservation in absentia, bring religious artifacts that were blessed by the medicine man, play video or audio messages recorded by the medicine man, and use the hospital computer center for patients to have iChats with loved ones from the reservation.

(9) *Rely on search skills to resolve factual disputes about people, places, and things.* Knowing the correct answers for issues that relate to dates, locations, events, and outcomes can trigger disagreement. Before access to the Internet it was common practice to challenge the view of an opponent by asking, "What do you want to bet?" as if determination of the correct answer should cost one party something instead of resulting in mutual benefit. A better strategy is to begin the family practice of going to the Internet to look up matters of fact or confirm events that represent the disagreement. This encourages curiosity and searching for answers as the key to reciprocal learning and settling differences.

(10) *Recognize that conflict can provide opportunities for everyone to learn.* Parents can be more motivated to pursue opportunities for modeling if they realize that family disagreements can yield benefits for both parties. Adolescents are acquiring the ability to examine logic so they carefully monitor the reasoning of others. They tend to practice this newfound ability mostly by debating with parents and teachers. Continual challenges to their ideas are reported by parents as an exhausting experience. Mothers and fathers who do not recognize these daily arguments as chances to share feelings and engage in reciprocal learning usually attribute their turmoil to the undesirable influence of their child's peer group (Cherlin, 2009). A more accurate appraisal is that youth are motivated to initiate conflicts so parents can show them how differences can be dealt with in a civil way.

(11) *Take initiative for reconciliation that can restore harmony.* This guideline is based on research of Franz de Waal (2009), professor of biology and director of the Yerkes Primate Research Center at Emory University. Before his studies, primatologists were reluctant to assert that animals are capable of thinking. There were exceptions such as Wolfgang Kohler (1925) who documented that chimpanzees recognize cause and effect by showing insights

needed for problem solving. Gordon Gallup (1982) found that chimpanzees could recognize themselves in a mirror. Jane Goodall (1986) observed animals that used self-made tools to hunt for food below ground. Nevertheless, the prevailing custom of primatologists had been to follow the behaviorist conclusion that, because what animals feel or think cannot be known by mankind, there is no point talking about it. Most investigations of chimpanzees tracked them in the wild with the limitation that the animals could not be continuously seen. Thousands of social contacts took place in dense undergrowth or in trees where the animals could not be observed. Consequently, the few interactions that were witnessed served as a basis for describing behavior that was much more complex.

In contrast, Franz de Waal (2009) went to the only place in the world where a colony of chimpanzees had been confined and could be observed at all times. Over a 6-year period, he took daily notes and photos to detail the social life of 23 chimps living on two acres of forest surrounded by a moat at Burgers Zoo in the Netherlands. His observations revealed how closely the social organization of chimpanzees with their continual struggle for power resembles the organization patterns of humans. The data that de Waal collected about conflict determined that after all of their frequent and loud disputes the chimps quickly resumed contact to reconcile. As a rule, this took only a few moments before they would come together, kiss, embrace, and begin to groom one another. This pattern was universal even when the process was delayed for several hours. Until the combatants reconciled, both parties demonstrated observable tension. These findings, corroborated by subsequent primate studies, illustrate how reconciliation fulfills a necessary purpose of repairing valuable relationships between individuals with close ties and a cooperative partnership.

Consider this question: Can people learn lessons about relationships from the chimpanzees? Some adults seem uninformed about how they can repair damage in their important associations. On the other hand, adolescents are often reminded that, when they become angry, say hurtful things or mistreat others, they should try to make amends. Grownups who refuse their obligation to model reconciliation forfeit valuable opportunities to teach children to accept expression of differences and retain harmony. Everyone can make progress toward maturity by considering the chimpanzee example demonstrating reconciliation, starting over, and building bridges.

Goals for Living With Conflict

Children need to learn more than they are taught about living with conflict. When this goal is stated in general terms, it seems vague and overwhelming. However, when we divide the goal into a larger number of manageable tasks, a more complete picture of conflict learning begins to emerge. In addition, it becomes clear that certain lessons should be dealt with at school and other lessons should be learned at home. In both environments, the way parents and teachers can begin is by choosing objectives they are willing to pursue. Consider the list of conflict goals and identify the ones you are currently trying to reach. Share this information with other family members so they are aware of your goals and can provide observational feedback using examples of your behavior as a gauge for progress. Invite them to make known their conflict goals from this list in order to help one another move toward greater maturity.

1. Recognize that people who love each other may experience conflict.
2. Helping others may involve conflict.
3. Decide to talk things over instead of trying to settle issues by fighting.
4. Be able to accept changes in people that we would wish to prevent.
5. Know that self-conflict is essential for moral behavior (conscience).
6. Develop the ability to respect others by willingness to compromise.
7. Be able to accept defeat when this is the outcome of a competition.
8. Have will power to stand alone when it appears necessary to do so.
9. Accept that living with a certain amount of uncertainty is necessary.
10. Find ways to disagree on things without a loss in status or affection.
11. Be willing to apologize after making hurtful comments about anyone.
12. Realize that there might be some differences which are irreconcilable.
13. Learn to share possessions as well as take turns with other people.
14. Realize that respect for personal property is a way to reduce conflict.
15. Listen to others when they express contrary feelings or opinions.
16. Analyze conditions that are needed to result in mutual reconciliation.
17. Share dominance and demonstrate an ability to be cooperative.
18. Cope with complex situations that present unfamiliarity and anxiety.
19. Learn to assert personal opinion without having feelings of guilt.
20. View differences as possible opportunities for reciprocal learning.

FAMILY CONFIGURATION

Common Need for Support

Children are increasingly exposed to risks and dangers unrelated to family configuration, income or ethnicity. This awareness is replacing the customary view that only certain readily identifiable types of families are subject to risk that requires external support. This has been the premise of compensatory education since the 1960s. Even though enormous changes have occurred in society, narrow criteria continue to be used in defining families that deserve help. The fact is that most parents are neither poor nor single but encounter obstacles that exceed their ability to respond in effective ways. Yet, they are led to feel it is inappropriate to seek or receive assistance from the community.

A more informed observation is that low-income families are sometimes resilient and possession of economic surplus does not prevent dysfunction or keep children from getting into trouble. An assumption that families with similar configurations are uniform in experience does not take into account the variation within single, blended, nuclear, and extended families. Family structure and income level are less influential factors on child development than parent behavior and community support. Efforts to protect youth should support all families in their struggle for success.

Single Parent Households

There are 15 million American single parents raising 22 million children, about 26% of the youth population. Mothers (84%) are usually the custodial parent although fathers (16%) also assume this obligation. This situation is complicated by the fact that 40% of the 4 million annual births involve unwed mothers (Bloom, Cohen, & Freeman, 2011). Table 14.1 shows the rise in percentage of births to unwed mothers over a period of one generation in selected countries (Ventura, 2009). Out-of-wedlock proportion of births for Black women is 72%, 51% for Latinos, and 28% of Whites. When the California Cryobank, the nation's largest sperm bank, was established in the 1970s, 99% of the business centered on couples struggling with male infertility. That market is now 14%. Each year over 50,000 mothers who give birth are single by choice (Morrissette, 2008). Manning, Cohen, and Smock (2011) estimate that 40% of single parents are not divorced or separated but two-parent cohabitants. In this arrangement, the nonparent partner does not have explicit legal, financial or custodial rights or responsibilities toward a child or his partner.

During the 1980s, the divorce rate tripled leading some observers to speculate there was little difference between growing up in a single-parent home and living in a two-parent family. However, with the accumulation of evidence, it has become clear that this family configuration has greater risk for particular problems. Everyone can be more helpful when they become aware of unique challenges experienced by mothers, fathers, and children in one-parent families (Wallerstein & Lewis, 2004).

Students need gender role models. Most juvenile offenders, 74%, do not have access to a father at home (Lamb, 2010). Father absence also correlates positively with violent behavior, teen pregnancy, dropout, drug abuse, gang affiliation, and welfare dependence. Hopefully, adolescents can stay in contact with their fathers even though they cannot live together. However, a national survey of 1,000 teenagers whose parents divorced a decade earlier found that 42% had not seen their father in the previous year; less than 15% saw him weekly (Popenoe, 2009).

There is agreement that children benefit from being with a male adult surrogate. Big Brothers of America is a program to assist single parents.

Table 14.1. Unmarried With Children Percentage of Births to Unwed Women in 1980 and 2007*

Country	1980	2007
Japan	1	2
Italy	4	21
Spain	4	28
Canada	13	30
Germany	12	30
Ireland	5	33
Netherlands	4	40
United States	18	40
United Kingdom	12	44
Denmark	33	46
France	11	50
Norway	15	54
Sweden	40	55
Iceland	40	66

**Source:* S. J. Ventura (2009). *Changing patterns of nonmarital childbearing in the United States.* National Center for Health Statistics data brief, no 18, Hyattsville, MD.

This national organization provides companionship for boys from father-absent homes while giving mothers relief time for themselves. In cases where dad has custody, Big Sisters of America is often a suitable resource. Participating adult mentors spend time with a teenager and develop a close relationship that lasts several years. The expenses associated with activities are borne by the organization that gives the pair complementary tickets to sports events, concerts, and other forms of entertainment.

School results for students with Big Brothers were compared with a control group lacking such help. Findings based on teacher reports indicated that: 64% of mentored students developed more favorable attitudes toward school; 58% attained higher grades in required subjects; 60% established better relations with adults; 56% were more able to express their feelings; 64% developed self esteem and 62% were more likely to trust teachers (Tierney, & Grossman, 2000). Single parent families also benefit when children get involved with sports like Pop Warner football, Little League baseball, Boys Scouts, Girls Scouts, and church or synagogue teams. These groups offer opportunities for youth to interact with adult models of their gender.

Arrange tutorial help for students who fall behind. The National Association of Elementary School Principals examined achievement of students from nuclear and single parent homes. This study of 18,000 children from 18 states was carried out to discover ways for educators to better serve a growing number of single-parent households. Findings showed that 30% of two parent elementary school students ranked as high achievers as compared with 17% from single parent homes. At the opposite pole, 23% of children in two parent homes scored as low achievers versus 38% of those in single parent households. Students of single parents were absent more often and twice as likely to quit school (Frymier & Joekel, 2004).

Help students overcome feelings of isolation. When students exhibit worry, anger, resignation, or an inability to get along with others, consideration should be given to support group participation. Four goals are pursued in support groups at school led by a trained counselor. One goal is to let a student know s/he is not alone. A 25-year follow-up study about effects of divorce on 60 families in Marin County California, showed a high rate of intense loneliness in children (Wallerstein & Lewis, 2004). They did not like coming home to an empty house and having no family activities to participate in on weekends.

Provision of pleasure is the second goal of support groups since children often feel miserable and deprived. An environment that is friendly makes being in a group enjoyable for those who otherwise feel trapped by depression. Divorce is regarded by some clinical psychologists as the single greatest cause of child/adolescent depression (Seligman, 2011). Children may be less resilient than adults suppose in recovering from the tragedy of divorce. It is estimated that 70% of clients seen by child guidance clinics are from nonintact homes; 80% of adolescents in psychiatric hospitals are from broken homes; 75% of suicides involve children from single parent homes. In a review of family backgrounds for several hundred children who were treated consecutively for evaluation by the Psychiatry Department at the University of Michigan, it was found that children of divorce showed up at twice the rate of their occurrence in the general population (Bray & Stanton, 2009).

The health disadvantages of children from single-parent homes are identified by studies in other nations. However, investigations that compare children in two-parent and one-parent families rarely include sufficient sociodemographic data to adjust for key confounding and mediating variables. Such conditions were met in a Swedish study that followed up the mortality, severe morbidity, and hospital inpatient use of nearly a million children over 9 years, the largest study of its kind. The main findings were that, after controlling for confounders, Swedish children of single parents had over double the risk of psychiatric illnesses such as severe depression or schizophrenia, suicide, and attempted suicide, and to develop alcohol related diseases. Girls were three times more likely to become drug addicts if they lived with a single parent and boys were four times more likely than peers from nuclear households. Bear in mind that financial hardship, poverty, is rare for Swedish single parents so low income is not a feasible explanation (Weitoft, Hjem, Hagland, & Rosen, 2003).

The third goal of support groups in schools is to be with a sympathetic adult who listens to children and lets them know s/he cares. This condition can seldom be met at home because, while the mother is willing to listen to the child about most topics, she may not be willing to hear about her former spouse and would not claim to be objective on the subject. Instead of denying the student a chance to talk about a topic that is so much on her or his mind, it is best that someone other than the mother be expected to listen to these conversations.

The fourth goal of support groups is to center group discussion on daily issues children face. For example, what can I do when angry or worried that will make me feel better? How can visitation with my parent be improved? What things can I influence and which are beyond my control? Overall, child participants in support groups feel better when they realize what is going on, feel more understood, and when difficulties are interrupted by occasional relief and pleasure.

Prepare teachers to value and assist single-parents. Teachers often feel sorry for children of divorce but wonder how to help (Harvey & Fine, 2010). One consideration implicates expectations in a classroom. Students of all grade levels are adversely affected by family breakup. When this occurs in

344 P. S. STROM and R. D. STROM

college, students can be advised to reduce credit hours or stop taking classes for a semester because preoccupation with difficulties could cause poor performance and jeopardize grades. However, when parents of a high school freshman decide to go separate ways, the teenager cannot be counseled to take a year off from school.

Temporary emotional disturbance for such students is predictable so teachers should not expect them to behave as though conditions were normal. Instead, allowances may need to be made such as shorter assignments or less frequent homework with longer limits. Schools offer such accommodations to special education students but ignore emotional challenges of students in separating households. Teachers are more responsive when they observe single parent support groups discuss problems experienced with schools. Teachers should also learn to detect signs of stress in students, know how to monitor problematic behavior, and convince more students they care and want to help (Beckert, Strom, Strom, Darre, & Weed, 2008).

Family structure is not destiny. Even though students from single parent homes are, on average, more likely to engage in at-risk behaviors, it does not mean that such problems are inevitable. Many children in single parent homes thrive while classmates from nuclear families fail to attain success (Seligman, 2011). What matters most is the nature of interaction in families and the support system available. Single parents and educators perform their roles better when they know some dangers are more prevalent in this family structure and take precautions to prevent and minimize difficulties.

Help parents process their feelings. Parents Without Partners (2011) gives parents who have no spouse valued opportunities for interaction. Some schools provide support groups too. When the needs of these women and men have for communication are not met, loneliness can trigger depression and cause them to be less effective in raising children. It is a mistake for single parents to suppose they can rely on their children as confidants. Sharing certain feelings with daughters and sons who do not understand a situation reflects poor judgment. The Parent Buddy System is a more promising approach that involves a skilled nonprofessional friend who phones each week. This contact allows single parents to express emotion when there are no other adults to hear their feelings. Besides the described concerns, single parents also must arrange supervision and substitute care on a limited budget. The biggest contributor to poverty is instability of families. When partners split up, poverty generally follows. In two-parent families, the proportion in poverty is 5% whereas the poverty rate is 30% for single parents (Sowell, 2011). Other concerns are to obtain periodic relief, get job preparation to be more self-sufficient, and set aside time for the children. Most parents are unable to manage these tasks alone and need support from relatives, friends, and the community.

Blended Family Challenges

Divorce ends an intimate relationship but may not end involvement with marriage. Most divorced men (83%) and women (76%) remarry. Nearly half (46%) of all marriages are blended where one or both spouses have a child or children from a previous marriage (Cherlin, 2009). Consider some challenges they share.

Get married and become a parent at the same time. Husbands and wives in blended families are denied the opportunity most other newlyweds have for getting used to each other and solidify their bond before becoming parents. This obstacle is further complicated by the fact that most remarriages occur before there is recovery from the loss of a previous relationship. This is particularly the case for children who may still be struggling to adjust to having an absent parent. They often resent the new arrangement that is being thrust upon them.

Establish new expectations for success and failure. Every member of a blended family brings expectations. They experienced certain right, responsibilities, and roles in their prior situation that may have to be renegotiated in a new setting. Some former rituals, traditions, and aspects of lifestyle might conflict with what others in the new group feel should be the rule. There is a lot of uncertainty about how decisions will be made, questions about what issues should be subject to compromise, and doubts about the pace at which change should occur. These situations can yield considerable anxiety.

Expand the source of family authority and discipline. The basis for effective discipline is mutual trust and caring. These elements of a close relationship take time to develop so blended families can initially expect to have problems in this context. Because most children in a blended family live with their biological mother and a stepfather, the stepfather usually experiences the greatest frustration. Perhaps his wife expects him to take responsibility for discipline but her children want continuity. Therefore, they resist change from their usual source of advice and punishment. Going slow and working things out together are essential.

Determine the rules of equity and avoid favoritism. Children will inform parents when they suppose stepsiblings are being treated better than themselves. Acting fair and even handed in the disposition of time, money, and other resources are difficult for intact families too. However, the situation of blended parents predisposes them to certain hazards. For example, a stepfather may be trying to win the friendship and trust of a stepson by spending a lot of time with him. Although this motive is commendable, his biological son may feel cheated and dislike the stepsibling for getting too much attention. There is a need for continued parent awareness about how everybody feels about things.

Maintain realistic expectations about the new relationship. It is unreasonable to expect immediate affection between stepparents and children. Yet, many adults are surprised when their attempts to establish a sense of closeness with a stepdaughter or a stepson are rejected. Other stepparents complain that many things are not appreciated by stepchildren who ought to show gratitude more often. Some adults do not recognize they are coming on too strong until a child reacts saying "You are not my real dad and you never will be."

Stepparents have to demonstrate great patience and believe that, in time, their steady commitment may lead to the friendship and trusting relationship they see. One reason this hopeful orientation is less common than it should be is because life in a fast-paced society conditions people to expect quick feedback for most things they do. However, happiness among blended families is rarely immediate. Instead, on average, the process of adjustment to one another on which happiness can be built usually takes from 3-5 years (Bray & Kelly, 1999). That is a long time and favorable results are not guaranteed but it is worth the effort.

Expect siblings with different parents to get along. Stepsiblings compete for affection and rival for attention. They may challenge the territory of one another and, in the opinion of their parents, seem to engage in perpetual conflict. This behavior upsets parents who sometimes get involved by taking the side of their biological child. Then a conflict becomes a matter of "You better straighten out your child." "No, you better straighten up your kid." A more helpful strategy is let children know they must resolve their differences just as they do with peers outside the home.

Understand developmental stages of stepchildren. Michael has brought a 6 year old son, Richard, to the blended family while his new wife, Amy, has a 15-year old daughter Sharon. The knowledge Michael has gained about guiding young boys is inadequate for his role as stepfather of an adolescent girl. By finding an appropriate parent class, Michael can be informed about adolescence and find out how the parent-child relationship during this period can best proceed.

There are other cautions suggested by Michael's new situation. It seems wise for Sharon, his 15-year old stepdaughter, to avoid parading around the house in underwear. Until Michael and Sharon emotionally bond as parent and child, he might see her mostly as an attractive young woman. One reason stepparents should accept legal adoption is because it establishes incest as a taboo in the reconstituted family. Whether this works depends on individuals but reports of sexual abuse occur eight times more often in blended families than other family configurations (Wenck & Hansen, 2009).

Many stepfather-stepdaughter relationships could improve if the man understood how his daughter defined affection and differentiated intimacy from sexuality. For men, affection tends to be physical and demonstrated by hugs, kisses and other forms of touching. In contrast, children consider affection as verbal and to be expressed through compliments and friendly conversation. Different interpretations of affection can create problems. In new stepfamilies, girls may respond negatively to a stepfather because of the kind of affection he offers.

Take time to build a close relationship with the spouse. James Bray, former president of the American Psychological Association and professor of Family Medicine at Baylor University conducted a 9-year study of 100 stepfamilies for the National Institute of Health (Bray & Kelly, 1999). He found the array of daily complications of managing a blended family requires a close relationship between husband and wife. This is why counseling therapy centers on ways for couples to grow together, remain in touch, and provide mutual support. Unless husband and wife take time to be with each other, their union can easily be threatened. The risk of giving up is reflected by a 60% rate of divorce among blended families. Furthermore, whereas first marriages typically end because of infidelity or disputes over money, the most common reason men and women give for ending a blended marriage is their partner's children. Michelle explained her decision, "It was not my husband but his sons I had to divorce."

SUMMARY AND IMPLICATIONS

The most important questions in middle age are those we ask ourselves. Self-evaluation motivates individuals to pay attention to conditions that cause discontent and encourages goal amendment. This process motivates detection of learning needs and fosters progress toward maturity. However, others who ask themselves similar questions fail to spend time for reflection that is needed to respond by altering their outlook or lifestyle. Personality development is the usual outcome and benefit for those who choose self-improvement as a goal whereas those who decide against amending goals may remain fixed in a permanent stage of arrested development.

Having access to a second opinion increases awareness of changes that may be needed in personal conduct as well as facilitates closer and more durable relationships. A spouse or friend can sometimes offer this benefit. Similarly, adolescent children can be sources of feedback on parenting and learning needs. Parents should recognize important lessons they fail to provide children. Teaching adolescents to manage stress, create a healthy balance in how time is spent, discussing friendship building before focusing on education about sexual relationships, and being willing to listen and learn are contexts in which many parents perform poorly in the estimate of their daughters, sons, and themselves. Yet, these lessons are vital to enable adjustment.

A fundamental value of democracies is allowing everyone to make their opinion known without fear of rejection. Teaching this value becomes important in adolescence when conflicts with adults accelerate and students struggle to become independent. The emerging ability to monitor logic motivates adolescents to frequently engage the adults in disputes. These confrontations can have value since they offer chances to practice debating skills needed for constructive conflict. Parents should realize that arguments give opportunities to demonstrate problem solving and to show tolerance for opposing views. There is also merit in modeling self-conflict, allowing daughters and sons to witness how adults examine and judge themselves. The capacity to introspect emerges in adolescence so youth benefit from adoption of healthy criteria for self-evaluation. They also benefit from recognizing this form of assessment is often a key to conflict resolution because reflection can produce changes in personal behavior.

Most parents recognize that arguments are a normal occurrence in adolescence and can facilitate the transition to adulthood. However, this awareness does little to ease the anxiety of mothers and fathers who sometimes suppose their teenager has a mission to engage them in perpetual arguments. Reliance on practical and respectful guidelines to conduct civil conflict can allow everyone in the family to feel comfortable expressing differences while they also gain a broader perspective.

Nuclear families are no longer the dominant household configuration. There is a greater proportion of single parents, blended households, and cohabiting couples with children. This means the longstanding premise that only low income or minority ethnic homes deserve assistance should be replaced with recognition that people in diverse family settings are more likely to succeed if schools, professionals, and communities become aware of their unique needs and respond in ways that enable well being for all children, adolescents, and adults.

APPLICATIONS FOR TEACHING

1. Middle age adults sometimes rely on a friend to listen to their discontent. If listeners suppose the friendship role is to always reassure that changes in personal behavior are unnecessary, this inauthentic evaluation can have the adverse outcome of setting self-criticism off course and foreclose further personal development. Evidence that someone is a friend is shown by always providing honest observations.

2. Some important life lessons can only be taught by example. For middle age mothers, this means arranging a schedule that allows time to pursue personal interests, maintain a healthy perspective, and demonstrate how to manage daily stress. Mothers are more able to take this initiative when fathers assume a greater share of the domestic tasks.

3. Parents who invite their adolescent children to share observations can help mothers and fathers detect their learning needs and offer insight to guide decision making about personal improvement. When teenagers feel respected as observers whose perceptions are used to support parent development, this transactional relationship renders them more willing to accept the reciprocal observations of parents.

4. The tendency to interpret every disagreement as a competition in which the only goal is to defend one's point of view is a narrow outlook that prevents the reflective processing of another person's perspective. Adults should encourage adolescents to recognize that taking time to weigh opinions that differ from their own is an aspect of appreciating diversity, causing us to change our minds, and adopt new paradigms to guide behavior.

5. Helping teenagers live with disagreement should include consideration and adoption of specific conflict goals, the desire to strive toward their attainment, and a willingness to consider feedback on personal progress from trusted others who see us on a regular basis. Giving attention to this domain of development is more often seen as important when adults reveal the conflict goals they are trying to reach on a more consistent basis.

6. Parents should be willing to apologize to their daughters, sons, colleagues or anyone they offend. When adults do not acknowledge their mistakes, youth may refer to such behavior as a justification for their own similar actions. Reaching out to make amends, asking for forgiveness, and seeking reconciliation to restore harmonious relationships is a sign of humility, one of the important aspects of maturity.

7. Communities should recognize and respond to the needs of everyone. Even though families having the same household configuration vary in experiences, they also face similar challenges. Appreciation of cultural diversity is shown by making an effort to understand these unique conditions and respond in ways that support mental health.

CHAPTER 15

RECIPROCAL LEARNING AND TEACHING

Some adults suppose that since children and adolescents have to attend school, their age groups should assume the main burden for adapting to social and technological change. A more practical strategy is to obligate everyone to participate in some aspects of social transformation together. This broader perspective could produce awareness that cultural harmony and cohesion call for the continual adjustment of more than a single generation. People of all generations need to know how age groups other than their own interpret events, recognize the values that guide their behavior, become aware of their vision for the future, and be willing to trade places in providing instruction when this shift is needed. These conditions define reciprocal learning, mutual growth based on consideration of the feelings, ideas, methods or perspective of another person or group.

Moving away from hierarchical relationships toward more equitable forms of interaction will require significant attitude change. The goals of this chapter are to describe: how reciprocal learning can increase productivity while improving relationships at school, at home, and at work; reasons why traditional criteria for granting identity status should be replaced with criteria that are more relevant in a digital society; guidelines for adolescents who teach adults; and lessons adolescents expect grownups to provide them. An explanation is given for why a positive view toward mistake making is essential to increase healthy risk taking and achievement.

Learning Throughout Life: An Intergenerational Perspective, pp. 351–371
Copyright © 2012 by Information Age Publishing

BENEFITS OF TRADING PLACES

Freaky Friday is a movie about 13-year old Anna and her mother Tess
(Rodgers, 1972). They disagree about almost everything including fashion, men, and Anna's passion to join a rock band. One night the biggest
freak out ever occurs when both mother and daughter undergo a mysterious transformation and find themselves trapped in each other's body.
Tess is supposed to get married in a few days so they have to hurry and
find a way of switching back to their own identity. Forced to walk in each
other's shoes, the pair has to learn a lot about each other in a short time.

Mentoring at Work

Mentoring was first described in Greek mythology. When Odysseus left
home to fight in the Trojan War, he asked his friend, Mentor, to assume the
responsibility for educating his son Telemachus. Currently a *mentor* is
defined as someone who serves as a trusted advisor, tutor, coach, counselor,
and faithful friend. A common practice in business and industry is to
provide new employees with a mentor, typically someone of middle age who
understands company expectations, procedures, and worker anxieties. This
practice reflects a belief that experienced personnel have valuable insights,
seniority includes responsibility to share knowledge with newcomers,
advice from veterans can minimize costly mistakes, and the need for
interdependence is communicated as necessary for success of individuals,
teams, and the company (Allen, Finkelstein, & Poteet, 2009).

Most employers recognize the worth of arranging conversations
between new employees and mentors but have given less attention to
merits of reverse mentoring. The concept of *reverse mentoring* involves
turning around the usual relationship by which an older person mentors
someone who is younger. In effect, shifting roles or trading places is
required. Reverse mentoring first received national attention when the
General Electric Corporation conducted an experiment. Jack Welch, the
chief executive officer, realized that his senior executives were unfamiliar
with the tools of technology needed for effective communication in the
emerging cyber environment. Rather than send the management officials
back to school or arrange expensive training for them, Welch paired 500 of
his top leaders with younger workers who had recently joined the company.
The task that younger workers were assigned was to teach senior colleagues
how to navigate the Internet and speed up interaction by using electronic
mail (Welch & Welch, 2005). This shift in roles acknowledged the greater
technology skills of young adults, confirmed for them that the company
valued these assets, and called on upper level managers to perceive their

younger mentors as important sources of learning. The experiment was successful, introduced the continuous practice of sharing expertise, and improved productivity for the company. Since then many businesses have adopted the General Electric reverse mentoring model and confirmed that it increases profitability (Tapscott & Williams, 2008, 2010b).

Career exploration is a source of motivation for most adolescents. Researching occupations, identifying skills that are required for positions, and thinking about relative advantages and difficulties of particular work paths should begin during middle school. The impact that middle age mentors can have on adolescent students is strong even if the parties never meet face-to-face but interact on the Internet. A prominent example of how influence of online mentors can foster career awareness including recognition of characteristics needed for job success is a program known as the Computer Clubhouse. Boston's Museum of Science and the Media Laboratory at Massachusetts Institute of Technology operate the joint venture. This center, and 75 others like it throughout the world, provide youth in underserved communities with an after-school environment where they can explore career choices, acquire job related skills, and gain confidence about what it takes to perform well on the job. Students select a mentor after reviewing biographical sketches including visuals that have been prepared by adult volunteers willing to dialogue with them. All of the mentors have successful careers, and most of them are middle aged. They try to convey the importance of integrity, civility, and time management. Mentors also emphasize resilience for coping with disappointment, ways to support harmony, and the value of reflective thinking (Kafai, Peppler, & Chapman, 2009).

Mentoring at School

The Olympic school district located in suburban Seattle, Washington, decided to integrate technology with their curriculum at all grade levels. Organizers agreed that schools have been slow to embrace innovation, mainly because learning methods that students prefer are ignored. The tools of technology can encourage students to question, challenge, and disagree, thereby increasing the potential to become critical thinkers. The Internet urges students to read, conduct searches for information, respond to messages, interact with friends or relatives, and pursue teamwork. Because students enjoy the Internet, this tool could motivate those whose dislike of school prevents them from paying attention, completing assignments, and performing well. The Internet has potential to make school and homework satisfying for more students (Cole, 2009).

For the first time in history, students possess greater skills in using tools needed for learning in the future than do the adults who are expected to educate them (Collins & Halverson, 2009). This unprecedented lag in proficiency of adults presents students with frustrating situations. Many report that life online after school hours is disconnected from instructional methods that teachers depend on during class. Middle age teachers, the largest cohort, grew up before the communications revolution. Many of them concede that their lesser technology skills along with a prevailing emphasis on high stakes testing combine to prevent greater use of the Internet for instruction and assignments (Cole, 2009).

The Olympia strategy for applying reverse mentoring was to pair students with a partner-teacher at school. These student-teacher teams plan a curriculum project to be enhanced by some technology application. Teachers provide the knowledge regarding a topic, awareness of learning needs, and steps to guide lessons. The student is expected to contribute a visual element to make the instructional presentation appealing and more easily understood. This collaborative creation becomes part of the curriculum offered by the partner-teacher. This process allows students to practice and refine computer skills for practical projects while gaining interdependence experience needed for employment. The advantage for teachers is having access to technology support that compliments direct instruction and being able to learn new skills shared by their younger mentor.

The teaming of students and teachers benefits both parties. Studies consistently have found that lessons containing visual components are retained to a greater extent and longer period than instruction provided orally or in text form. So great is the advantage of visual memory that it is designated as the *pictorial superiority effect*. Experiments have shown that people remember pictures with more than 90% accuracy several days following exposure even if the pictures were seen for only a few seconds. A year later the accuracy rate for visual memory still exceeded 60% (Brockmole, 2008). Comparisons of text and oral presentations versus pictorial presentations have found that visuals are always more effective. When information is given orally, people recall about 10% when they are tested three days following exposure. The recall rate rises to 65% if a picture or visual element is added (Medina, 2009).

The pictorial superiority effect had less relevance before the Internet introduced a broad array of visual resources. Given the expansive range of choices that are provided by United Streaming, YouTube, and other websites, educators with help from student mentors should emphasize incorporation of visuals to optimize motivation and learning. The shift can also include a place for three dimensional conversation tools and chat rooms available on some social sites.

Exciting technologies are emerging at such a rapid rate that teachers are unable to keep up. Reverse mentoring allows teachers to benefit from how fast students learn the latest technical skills and how willing the adolescents are to assume a mentor role. Professional development has relied on instructional specialists to train teachers during in service sessions in the hope that this method will translate into improved learning for students. The favorable experience of the Olympia school district suggests that more can be gained by reverse mentoring. Allowing students to practice technology skills and help enhance the quality of teacher instruction improves learning while reducing boredom.

The optimal reverse mentor relationship should be explored because it could provide clues about how teacher-student interaction should evolve in the future. Each party participates in setting goals to guide collaboration. A curriculum lesson requires both to share complimentary strengths reflecting interdependence. The teacher does not control the student but instead conveys freedom and trust that is vital for teamwork. Student and teacher alternate in taking responsibility for leadership. This sharing of dominance is a departure from the custom in which the teacher is always the leader.

Over 1,200 schools have adopted the instructional model of Olympia Washington for integration of technology with curriculum. This kind of on-the-job technology training in which teachers participate in reverse mentoring with tech savvy students has proven to be an effective way for promoting educational reform. Classroom experience should become more interactive, collaborative, and related to life applications. These outcomes are more likely when teachers realize the possibilities of using a team problem solving approach, are willing to alternate leadership and relinquish control in favor of supporting self-directed learning. Enthusiastic advocates for reverse mentoring are students whose projects can be examined at Generation YES (2011).

Mentoring at Home

An inversion of authority has modified some of the dialogue that occurs between adolescents and their parents. Both groups recognize that youth are more competent in using technology tools. Researchers at Carnegie Mellon University in Pittsburgh carried out an experiment to find out how this factor changes communication and relationships (Kraut, Brynin, & Kiesler, 2006). There were 170 subjects from 73 middle class homes in Pittsburgh. All of the families included an adolescent and received a free computer with Internet access. None of the families had previously been connected. During the orientation researchers explained that computers would be remotely monitored to find out how often they were used, length of time that was spent online, and sites visited but not the content. At several month intervals parents and teenagers completed surveys that described self-defined computer skills, amount of time spent together online, and how often they helped one another to solve computer problems.

Monitoring detected that, on average, the time teenagers spent online was six times greater than their parents. Adolescents received ten times as much electronic mail as parents and explored the Internet to a greater extent. Another source of data were videotapes made during home visits to observe how each family used their computer. Researchers did not help when participants they were watching experienced technical difficulties. Problems were rampant in 89% of families where the usual reaction of adults reflected helplessness. Grownups offered a broad range of excuses for their inability to solve computer problems. On the other hand, teenagers seldom complained in facing difficulties and experimented until completing tasks (Kraut, Brynin, & Kiesler, 2006).

Everyone was invited to phone the Home Net line anytime to obtain assistance. However, the adults were more inclined to turn to daughters and sons for guidance. If adolescents were not home, adults usually chose to abandon a task rather than make their needs known and seek support from the Home Net. Those who phoned the help desk most often were teens, the same people who demonstrated the best performance. It appears that individuals possessing the most skill realize what they do not yet know and exhibit more confidence in challenging themselves to try ever-more-difficult tasks. Knowledge trickled upward in a majority of the families as teenagers claimed the most authority, acting as consultants to their parents.

PRINCIPLES FOR RECIPROCAL LEARNING

One way to reduce the risks associated with the authority inversion is to help adolescents acquire attributes that characterize good teachers. Possession of a skill does not ensure that someone can convey that particular asset to others. Patience and encouragement are implicated in teacher effectiveness. In contrast, impatience and lack of feedback can erode the motivation of students and cause them to doubt their capacity to teach. The Home Net study revealed that adults are frequently more inclined than are adolescents to give up when confronted by an unfamiliar learning situation that involves technology tools. For this reason, the adolescents who are expected to teach grownups should understand that emotional support is essential so adult learners remain willing to keep trying after they experience setbacks and failure (Kraut, Brynin, & Kiesler, 2006).

Challenges for Adult Considerations

Discovering opportunities for adults and adolescents to trade places as teachers will be a challenge for society from now on. Success requires experimentation with new methods of instruction that involve more equitable relationships. Eight important challenges are identified.

(1) Reciprocal learning can enable society to grant identity status to youth. There is general agreement that a well-defined role is needed for a favorable sense of identity. This is especially important in adolescence when the common goal is working toward being accepted as an adult and gaining an individual sense of meaning, purpose, and direction (Temple, 2006). Nevertheless, permitting youth to have a significant place in society appears more difficult within a technological setting than in previous times. The customary procedure has been for society to bestow status when young people are hired for a full time job, get married, become a parent, or no longer need financial help from the family. However, these conditions occur later than in the past. The extensive schooling that is needed to get ready for employment along with a high cost of living often necessitates continued economic support from parents, even after young adults have obtained a full time position.

Adolescents rely on technology for conversations with friends. These same tools can expand the social context for youth identity through interaction with adult mentors, relatives, community leaders, elders, and persons from other cultures. Efforts to enlarge the contextual base of identity acknowledge that the emerging social self could be too narrow if it is defined exclusively by interaction with peers online or by face-to-face dialogue with one's own generation. Generally, it is appropriate to credit adolescents for having technology skills needed for learning and job performance in the future and accept this strength as a criterion for granting identity status.

Robert Epstein shares the impression that teenagers and some young adults are unfairly being denied identify status. In *The Case Against Adolescents*, Epstein (2007) explores fallacies in how adults see youth as incapable of responsibility, to be shielded from tasks of adulthood, and unable to make reasoned decisions. Epstein describes the "artificial extension of childhood" by which teenagers are isolated from the people they are about to become and traps them in a meaningless world controlled by peers and media figures that cater to them. He argues that society has forgotten how capable young people can be but adolescents are aware of their potential and feel frustrated.

The new equation for the identity status youth seek should be based upon their competence with technology tools. This response is more reasonable than to continue no longer attainable conditions that could lead to alienation and excessive reliance of adolescents on peers for communication and respect. The high involvement level with social network sites such as MySpace and Facebook illustrates common dependence on age mates for interaction. Talking to peers is easier because it is based on equality, a condition that is less common in conversations with adults. Because computer skills are valued, those who possess them deserve status, should be given responsibilities, and expected to communicate with older and younger people to support harmony (Wallace, 2008).

(2) Sharing dominance is an essential aspect of reciprocal learning, allowing the other person to sometimes assume the leadership role. Successful relationships are characterized by shared dominance instead of unilateral control based on age, gender, or rank. People who prize and rely on strengths of one another develop a partnership. Before emergence of the Internet adults were rarely in a position to consider youth as possible sources for their learning. Grownups should strive to demonstrate maturity and humility recognizing that, in certain situations, hierarchy is unreasonable.

(3) Listening is fundamental to reciprocal learning. Students are told and reminded they should listen to teachers because this behavior will influence how much they learn. Ironically, divided attention and distraction of teachers is a concern. A nationwide study of achievement used results from National Assessment of Educational Progress (NAEP) measures. Results showed that students from the lowest 10% of the school population made good improvement in test scores between 2000-2007. In contrast, students in the highest achieving 10% did not improve much (Duffert, Farkas, & Loveless, 2008).

To probe for possible reasons why gains were made by one group but not the other, 900 teachers from Grades 3-12 were surveyed. These teachers reported that, because of No Child Left Behind testing mandates, many school administrators have made struggling students the top priority at their school. Most teachers, 81%, agreed this meant low achievers are more likely to get one on one attention in their classroom. The teachers (92%) felt that the right thing is to give equal attention to all students, regardless of their achievement level. These contradictory views indicate that teachers are conflicted about the differences between what they believe and the way they are expected to behave (Duffert, Farkas, & Loveless, 2008). When the parents of average or higher achieving students are informed by their children that attention from the teacher is unequal, they are disappointed and sometimes transfer their student to a private institution where teachers are expected to show greater equality of attention to everyone.

(4) Teaching includes evaluation of learning. Trusting students to participate in peer and self-evaluation of group dynamics is necessary. Teachers cannot know the interaction in multiple teams and how students teach their peers. Cooperative learning provides an ideal environment for comparison of self-impressions with the observations provided by teammates. The ability to self-evaluate helps people know when to think well of themselves and when to change behavior so their actions more closely resemble the person they wish to become. Students complete the Teamwork Skills Inventory that calls for peer and self-evaluation on 25 team skills easily detected after interaction for a reasonable period of interaction and observation. Each student receives an individual profile with anonymous feedback from teammates on personal strengths and learning needs (P. Strom & Strom, 2011b).

(5) There are many adults who overestimate their willingness to learn from adolescents. Chapter 14 described the Parent Success Indicator that assesses perceptions of two generations—parents and children ages 10-14. This instrument identifies views about the role performance of mothers and fathers. One item on the adult version states, "I am good at learning from my child." Optional responses include always, often, seldom, and never. The corresponding version showing adolescent observations states, "My parent is good at learning from me." Significant differences were identified in generational responses of several thousand adults and adolescents from Japan, Republic of China, and Black, Hispanic, and White families in the United States. For all these cultures, adolescents gave unfavorable ratings to their parents for learning from children while most parents portrayed themselves favorably as willing to learn (Beckert, Strom, Strom, Yang, & Singh, 2007; Strom, Strom, Strom, Makino, & Morishima, 2000; Strom, Strom, Strom, Shen, & Beckert, 2004).

(6) Reciprocal learning is facilitated by mutual awareness of the possible benefits. Providing feedback to adolescents on their instruction helps them realize the favorable influence they can have on others, motivates improvement of how well they teach, and encourages them to provide similar feedback to their own teachers at home and in the classroom. Teenagers are accustomed to frequent feedback on the computer so they crave this same kind of response from adults. However, few recognize how feedback can motivate classroom teachers to continue their difficult tasks and sustain enjoyment in their job. Students and parents honored teachers more often in the past, a bygone custom that should be restored. By trading places as a teacher, adolescents can better appreciate the prob-

lems educators face as they try to arrange learning for individual students who collectively present a broad range of performance levels.

(7) Some lessons schools should learn from adolescents will not be acquired by usual methods of inquiry. Discussions of ways to motivate and engage students should consider inviting their views about conditions of learning. Trading places should include some procedure for adolescents to comfortably express how they feel about school (P. Strom & Strom, 2009). Focus groups can require a high risk for identified students who make known their negative impressions. The range of views in the student population can never be fully represented by focus groups. School improvement requires electronic anonymous student polling to determine their preferred ways for learning and perceived obstacles to achievement. Accordingly, efforts should be made to assess feelings about the quality of their schooling. Equality is defined as having the opportunity to be a student but not to have input regarding educational reform.

(8) Reciprocal learning should be fostered for every student when assigned online homework to support interdependence. Individuals can be assigned as a single member of their team to examine particular web sites. Specific tasks could include summarizing content, identifying material to augment course curriculum, and describing implications drawn from reading. These tasks appeal to students because they prefer to work online, like to share knowledge that classmates and their teacher have not acquired, recognize others depends on them to provide an accurate report, and observe greater learning that occurs when each student is accountable as an educator (Prensky, 2010).

Guidelines for Adolescents as Teachers

By middle school, most students gradually surpass other relatives in technology skills. This deficit in the competence of adults should not be regarded as a put down. Instead, young people should be helped to carry out their emerging responsibility for trading places in the provision of instruction. Students should discuss the following guidelines to prepare for their opportunities to become effective teachers of adults.

(1) Adults prefer teachers who show patience by not rushing the lessons. When learners feel hurried, the usual outcome is a reduction in comprehension. If enough time is arranged to practice newly acquired skills, satisfaction and success become common.

(2) While explaining the steps of a sequence task, illustrate using slow transitions between steps. Always describe your behavior in the manner that sports commentators do when they tell fans about the way a particu-

lar play was executed. This strategy allows adult learners to observe and understand a series of actions for doing a task.

(3) Repeat examples several times to allow more opportunities for observation. People of all ages rely on observation as a valued method for learning. Sometimes teachers who know particular processes well think of them as being simple so they provide an abbreviated explanation causing learners to become confused or feel disappointment.

(4) Monitor adult learner behavior and provide favorable feedback when a task is done correctly by saying, "You did it; that's the correct way." When behavior is incorrect, ask the person to try again while you watch and figure out possible sources of error and then explain how to make the correction.

(5) Arrange situations where the adult is given enough time and opportunity to go through a process several times. Continue to supervise actions until the person is able to complete the task repeatedly without making any errors.

(6) Ask the adult to explain the steps in doing a task that you have taught. Tell them to provide reasons for each of the actions they suggest. All students should go beyond memorizing to show understanding that is verified by an accurate explanation.

(7) Encourage the continued effort that is needed to become computer literate and motivated to stay up-to-date. Bear in mind that some adults may be inclined to give up after failure with technology tasks so offering emotional support to them is important.

(8) Recognize that a common problem of adolescent teachers is showing an adult how to do a task without then insisting that the person perform the same process while you observe. Modeling how to do something without engaging the learner is meant to save time but the usual outcome is continued and unnecessary dependence.

(9) Invite questions to find out what the person finds confusing or wants to know more about a specific task. Good teachers of every age group encourage questions in order to detect learning needs that observers may be unable to see.

(10) Speak clearly and take your time because adults often process information more slowly than adolescents. Explain terms since beginners may not know as much about the language associated with use of computers.

(11) All adolescents should be involved with reverse mentoring, including those in hierarchical cultures where adults prefer traditional criteria to grant status of identity and are less willing to trade places. In these circumstances, the youth strategy should be to express a willingness to teach as well as affirm their belief that adults can learn.

(12) Discover the satisfactions of teaching and find enjoyment in this leadership role. Students of every age can tell when a teacher likes to work with them.

(13) There can also be benefit in getting feedback from adults who are taught by adolescents. Table 15.1 provides a list for adults to give feedback to adolescents about their teaching performance.

Table 15.1.   Adolescent Teacher Performance: Feedback From Adult Learners

Directions: Check each statement that describes behaviors consistently demonstrated by this teacher.

——Encourages learner to try again after mistakes are made.

——Carefully shows the steps needed to complete a process.

——Detects errors by watching learner show and explain steps.

——Recommends practice while continuing to act as observer.

——Keeps learner actively engaged instead of in a passive role.

——Gives honest feedback about how well the learner is doing.

——Accepts the pace that is most comfortable for the learner.

——Allows time for reflection after a question has been asked.

——Invites learner to judge the progress that s/he is making.

——Willing to acknowledge things s/he does not understand.

——Does not get discouraged when the rate of progress is slow.

——Conveys belief in learner ability to understand the lesson.

——Welcomes questions about aspects of learning process.

——Gives full attention to the learner and avoids distractions.

——Enjoys teaching and providing guidance to adult learners.

——Offers logical reasons to explain the ways things are done.

——Shares personal experiences about overcoming hardships.

——Speaks clearly and uses words that are easily understood.

——Lets learners know their ideas and opinions are important.

——Cares about learner and seen as a reliable source of help.

——Allows learner to set some goals that will guide teaching.

——Is organized and well prepared to provide the instruction.

——Uses visuals to urge interest and support comprehension.

——Exhibits enthusiasm about the importance of each lesson.

——Helps the learner to keep a record of what has been taught.

Describe other behaviors you saw that are not on this list.

Lessons Adolescents Expect of Adults

The rising proportion of adults willing to learn from adolescents is evidence of progress. At the same time, adolescents recognize their need to learn important life lessons from adults. Parents and teachers try to establish suitable expectations for detection of student learning needs, assessment of development, and recognition of achievement. A reciprocal learning perspective requires adults to look at needs from the viewpoint of adolescents. Teenagers believe that adults are not teaching some lessons that are essential for success. Adults should focus on improving the instruction they provide for the lessons identified in Table 15.2.

Table 15.2. Adolescents Want Adults to Teach These Lessons

1. Present continuous lessons on how to manage daily stresses.
2. Be listeners that pay careful attention by avoiding distractions.
3. Illustrate self-control by showing up for appointments on time.
4. Model healthy nutrition and have exercise on a regular basis.
5. Discuss concerns about dealing with friendships and dating.
6. Model goal-setting behavior that demonstrates self-direction.
7. Assist with the process of review and amendment of goals.
8. Encourage time alone for reflection and for creative thinking.
9. Show how to disagree with others in a civil, respectful way.
10. Establish a safe, supportive, and satisfying environment.
11. Confirm importance of trust as the basis for relationships.
12. Apply teamwork skills that are needed at home and work.
13. Rely on reciprocal learning to enrich personal relationships.
14. Dialogue on possible occupations and alternative lifestyles.
15. Hold youth accountable for their misbehavior and correction.
16. Monitor and provide feedback on reaching personality goals.
17. Confront issues with careful planning, hope, and optimism.
18. Detect causes of failure and follow up with renewed effort.
19. Give the highest priority for arranging time to be together.
20. Be fair and honest to illustrate the value of trustworthiness.
21. Disclose personal goals and ask teens to evaluate progress.
22. Model the resiliency that is necessary to confront adversity.
23. Continue personal development to remain a lifelong learner.
24. Devote volunteer efforts intended to improve the community.

(Table continues on next page)

Table 15.2.   Continued

25. Respect privacy but monitor teen actions and whereabouts.

26. Receive encouragement, love, and genuine sense of caring.

27. Consistency of responses in dealing with issues of correction.

28. Set rules that must be kept in the home and in the classroom.

INFLUENCE OF ANTICIPATION

Self-Fulfilling Prophecy

Robert Merton, professor of sociology from Columbia University, introduced the concept of a *self-fulfilling prophecy,* defined as setting an expectation for others that may affect behavior toward them in a way that causes the anticipation to be fulfilled. Merton (1948) maintained that, once an expectation has been set, even if inaccurate, people will tend to behave in a way that is consistent with the anticipation conveyed to them. The result is that, as though by magic, the expectation often turns into reality.

The Roman poet, Ovid (43 B.C.–A.D. 18), was the first to illustrate how the self-fulfilling prophecy works in his myth titled *Pygmalion and Galatea.* The story is about a lonely sculptor who had given up hope of getting married (Lind, 1957). While Pygmalion carved an ivory figure of his ideal woman, he became attracted to the clay figure named Galatea and talked to her as though she was alive. When he went to the Venus festival, Pygmalion prayed, "If the gods can give what they wish, grant me a wife like her." After returning home, Pygmalion's prayer was answered. Galatea was transformed into a human being who became his lifelong partner.

George Bernard Shaw (1856-1950), Nobel Prize winner for literature, published his own version of *Pygmalion* in 1912. Shaw's work was subsequently adapted in 1956 by Alan Jay Lerner and Frederick Lowe to become the famous Broadway musical play and film *My Fair Lady.* One hundred years have passed since Shaw's popular book first appeared, and it is still available at the bookstore and online. In the play *Pygmalion*, Professor Henry Higgins made a bet that he could transform a young woman with little formal schooling into a lady who would be accepted into the status group of the social elite of London. Henry won his wager and then fell in love with the person the young woman had become. Again, the sequence was the same—high expectations were established and conveyed to the individual who was treated accordingly. In turn, the person reciprocated, thus transforming the original expectation into a reality.

High Expectations

How can the self-fulfilling prophecy be applied to teaching? Kenneth Clark (1963), Black psychologist and civil rights leader, argued that the low expectations that are common among inner-city teachers threatens minority student achievement. Many observers agreed with Clark but were unable to substantiate his claim. Then, Lenore Jacobson, principal of a public school serving low-income families in San Francisco, read an article by Robert Rosenthal (1963). Rosenthal described his studies about experimenter effects on animal behavior. Specifically, he misled college students to suppose that randomly chosen rats they would be training were genetically superior or inferior. Depending upon what students were told, they treated their rats differently. Those who believed the rats they cared for were highly capable handled them gently, talked to them often, observed them with careful attention, expressed encouragement, and portrayed the rodents as pleasant and likable. They set high expectations for the rats to solve maze puzzles.

Another group of students were led to believe that the rats they were responsible for did not have much chance for success. They tended to handle the rats roughly, seldom spoke to them, gave meager encouragement, referred to the rodents as unpleasant, and held low expectations for their maze performance. When the experiment ended, it was determined that the rats provided a supportive environment and exposed to high expectations performed better than those with similar capabilities to learn but seen by their caretakers as dull and treated in less nurturing ways. In his conclusion, Rosenthal (1963) wondered whether teachers who expected students to be slow contributed to a self-fulfilling prophecy.

Jacobson was intrigued so she wrote to Rosenthal proposing that "If you ever graduate to working with children, let me know if I can help." Soon the principal and the researcher agreed to collaborate. Jacobson pointed out that it would be naive to think her teachers could be told that certain students had previously unrecognized potential. Instead, some test that the teachers were unfamiliar with had to be taken by students. So, the faculty was informed that Rosenthal had invented a new measure, the Harvard Test of Inflected Acquisition. His test, administered to all students, would identify those *about to blossom* and show surprising growth over the next eight months. However, Rosenthal did not have such a test but instead gave students a nonverbal intelligence test that was not recognized by the teachers. Then, 20% of students from each class were chosen at random and identified for teachers as the *about to blossom* group (Rosenthal & Jacobson, 1968).

At the end of the school year, students were reexamined using the same test. Considering the school as a whole, students from whom the teachers were led to expect greater gains improved achievement scores to a higher degree than a control group of similar age, sex, and ability, but not labeled as about to blossom. In Rosenthal's experiment, there was no intervention, no special projects, no unique challenges for identified students. The only distinction was a favorable shift in teacher outlook—a change in their expectations that Rosenthal called the *Pygmalion Effect.* When the expectations of teachers rose, students made better use of their mental capacities (Rosenthal & Jacobson, 1968).

Establishing high expectations for their children is one way for parents to show that they recognize potential. However, wishful thinking about a child's future is never enough to bring about the desired outcome. Instead, parents must also set high expectations for themselves as their child's only long-term teachers. The Pygmalion Effect and the Blossom Experiment should motivate parents to increase the amount of time they spend talking with children, listening to their feelings, ideas, and opinions, learning from them, and helping them acquire the attitudes and skills needed for success.

Mistakes and Perseverance

Many airline pilots acquire their navigation skills by flight simulator practice. This experience allows the beginning aviators to learn from their mistakes without being exposed to the costly consequences that might occur during an actual flight. In effect, pilots get to assess the risk of certain maneuvers and then correct their errors without expense. In this way, they can make mistakes without also making headlines. Simulator training was used to prepare astronauts and is implicated in video games where players pretend they are race car drivers or downhill skiers who take risks and then correct their poor judgment without being exposed to physical injury (Lee, 2005). Because the cost of making mistakes is certain to be low and the feedback about performance is constant, flight instruction by simulators requires less time, is not as expensive, and produces better performance ratings.

The principle of lowering the cost of making mistakes in class would seem appropriate. However, it conflicts with the strongly held and contrary belief many teachers have about self-esteem. According to this view, mistakes could place student self-confidence at risk and jeopardize motivation to learn (Twenge & Campbell, 2010). Students in our classes affirmed the impression that mistakes are undesirable in school. Curious as to how prospective teachers saw student mistakes, we included the following item on a true-false quiz in class. "Student mistake making in class should always be discouraged." Most of the soon-to-be-teachers agreed that the statement was true. On the contrary, there is abundant evidence that making mistakes is basic for development. From the time infants take their first tumble when they begin to walk, mistakes are an essential aspect of living and the experience of anyone willing to approach tasks that are new or difficult. Making mistakes is the way people discover what they can do and have yet to learn.

Continued effort following mistakes has long been confirmed as a factor in improved performance. The pleasure of success occurs when previous defeats are overcome. In addition, exposure to mistakes can generate courage, stamina, and resilience (Warrell, 2008). Progress throughout history has been dependent on sustained efforts of individuals who made mistakes repeatedly but did not see their setbacks as a sign of inability. Instead, they recognized the value of staying engaged with a task to pursue solutions rather than giving up. The success that follows mistakes triggers continued motivation and hope to keep trying during the next difficult venture.

Teachers do not have the power to prevent students from making mistakes but they can usually control the cost related to mistakes. The reason the cost must be low is that some amount of mistakes are needed for learning to happen. When students fear making mistakes, they avoid practicing or exploring methods that could bring about changes in their thinking. The impression that success is possible without making mistakes contradicts common experience. Students are more willing to make mistakes when they are allowed to explore tasks without getting a grade, choose unfamiliar topics for projects, and try new ways of reporting by using formats such as photographs or pod casting. In these situations students are willing to take a chance, mindful that the mistakes they are bound to make can be corrected, will probably lead them to success, and will not undermine the status of their grades.

When teachers make the cost of mistakes low enough so that students are comfortable looking at things in new ways, there tends to be a corresponding rise in achievement. Teachers show a willingness to correct mistakes when they: (a) revise the scale of a task, (b) extend the deadline for an assignment, (c) take the same tests they expect students to complete and post their own responses to test items, (d) discuss obstacles that delay a project, and (e) amend team goals that appear unattainable. In classrooms where all students anticipate making mistakes and accept lower success levels in the beginning, they become less defensive about errors and more inclined to learn from mistakes (Dweck, 2006; Pink, 2009).

Parents have an important role in supporting this realistic orientation on mistake making in the classroom and outside of school. If they accept the notion that denial of failure is a way to protect their child and preserve self-esteem, they unintentionally prevent experiences needed to grow up and cope with events where first tries are not enough and quitting is a poor choice. The capacity to succeed in tasks and relationships requires detection of mistakes, resolve to correct them, renewed effort using more appropriate steps, and remaining confident about the eventual outcome. These kinds of responses to failure help youth to look at new and unfamiliar tasks as opportunities for learning instead of evidence that they are incompetent. Resilience needed to overcome problems in life cannot be gained without the practice of patience. This means that encouraging mistakes, controlling costs of errors, and getting corrective feedback are worthwhile.

The hopeful attitude needed to process failure is reinforced by sharing our own experiences. Many adults suppose that the memories they describe should feature personal achievements with only rare mention of mistakes. However, the willingness to acknowledge failure causes adolescents to see these adults as capable of understanding their struggles. Because most people fail often, there are a range of situations to choose from in talking with teenagers about these questions.

1. In what activities will you risk failure to learn something new?
2. What situations are the ones where you are most likely to fail?
3. Of all your failures, what was the most difficult one to accept?
4. Who usually helps identify your failures and ways to recover?
5. Which friendship failures would you now handle differently?
6. What are some of your plans that turned out to be unsuccessful?
7. What failures bother you less than they bother other relatives?
8. How do you respond to relatives when they encounter a failure?
9. What failures have you later looked back on with some pleasure?
10. How do family members react when they learn you have failed?

President Barak Obama (2009) offered this advice to the Wakefield High School students in Arlington, Virginia:

> You won't succeed at everything the first time you try. That's ok. Some of the most successful people are those who have had the most failures. The first *Harry Potter* book by J.K. Rowlings' was rejected 12 times before it was published. Michael Jordan was cut from his high school basketball team, and he lost hundreds of games and missed thousands of shots during his career. Jordan said, "I have failed over and over again. And that is why I succeed." These people all succeeded because they understood that you cannot let your failures define you. Instead, let failures teach you what to do differently the next time.

SUMMARY AND IMPLICATIONS

Trading places offers possibilities to go beyond the limitations of traditional instruction, improve communication and respect across generations, support better adjustment to new ways of thinking and doing things, and create a society where interdependence and harmony are more common. Nevertheless, trading places is difficult because reciprocal learning contradicts the attitudes and behaviors parents were taught at the time they were growing up and may be unwilling to give up. Arranging opportunities for trading places at work, in the classroom, and in the home can help define a broader vision of human development and learning.

Parents are critical about the quality of schools their children attend but seem less critical of their own learning needs. Instead of complaining that adolescents spend too much time communicating with peers, adults should grant the identify status that adolescents deserve based on competencies with technology tools that is essential for learning in the future. In addition, adults should expect far more interaction with youth using the current modes of communication. In many homes, family members are so preoccupied by their daily tasks that they fail to arrange time for important conversations and doing things together. Access to sensible guidelines for teaching and learning from each other can enable adults and adolescents to leave behind customary hierarchical relationships in favor of more equitable dialogue that respects the strengths and limitations of both generations. Getting to know daughters and sons is necessary to provide advice they consider relevant.

Reciprocal learning often depends on the preferences valued most by teachers. Because adolescents are highly motivated by technology, they favor mentoring in this context (Collins & Halverson, 2009; Rosen, 2010). The focus may include skills where their competencies exceed adults such as surfing the Internet, skimming text, visual-spatial skills, and multitasking. In contrast, adults have different assets that can support development. Providing a consistent example of the capacity for extended attention span, concentrating without distraction, finding value in reading entire books, withdrawing from electronic stimuli to reflect and to gain perspective, and processing failure to develop resilience can support acquisition of greater knowledge, inductive analysis, critical thinking, imagination, creativity, and adjustment. The greatest value of reciprocal learning, based on differing generational orientations, can be a mutual willingness to acquire important survival attitudes and skills possessed by the other.

Some teachers complain that their job prevents them from having any power. A different way to look at teaching is to recognize that educators have power to exercise enormous influence on student attitudes by lowering the cost of mistakes that happen during learning in the classroom. Many students are misled to suppose that making errors is unacceptable and therefore should be avoided or denied. A better strategy to process failure experience is by understanding that learning usually begins with mistakes that have to be detected, corrected, and then result in confidence about being able to perform a specific task. When students fear that a low grade will be the outcome of making mistakes, they may refuse to get involved with the inevitable setbacks and struggles that are bound to precede success. In classrooms where all the students anticipate mistakes and accept lower levels of success in the beginning, they become less defensive about doing things wrong, more inclined to benefit from their mistakes, and gain the competence required for completion of their course. Teachers should continually remind students about the importance of resilience and being able to deal with new and unfamiliar challenges.

APPLICATIONS FOR TEACHING

1. There are things that students know more about than teachers and parents because the Internet has made it more convenient than ever before to carry out research. This shift means that direct instruction is no longer the gateway for most learning. Instead, the role of teachers is transitioning to become facilitators as they provide clues, monitor direction, give feedback, and offer advice. These functions permit students to become active learners who are more self-directed which makes teaching a more exciting task.

2. When teachers acknowledge that the technology skills students possess exceed their own, a more equitable relationship emerges based on shared leadership and reciprocal learning. This choice enables students to grow through further practice with technology, and learn to work cooperatively with adults. Teachers benefit by learning from student mentors who share their technology skills.

3. Inventors are building low cost hardware that could diminish the extensive digital divide. Schools have an important role too. One task is to make sure that parents understand the importance of having a computer at home by preparing assignments that include family involvement on the web, provide free classes for the parents, and maintain a multiple language school website to address academic and social needs.

4. Students prefer the Internet as their main source for learning. Teachers should take advantage of this common motivation by developing creative homework and projects allowing application of

research skills, collaboration with teammates, critical thinking to judge the worth of suggestions reported on web sites, and encourage exploration of personal goals related to higher education and possible careers.

5. Most students want to learn by doing, find out some things on their own rather than gaining all of their knowledge by being told. This quest for self-direction should include accountability to report the cyber path taken on the Internet and sharing new knowledge that has been acquired. Encouraging a strategy of greater self-direction also implicates teachers in monitoring individual differences in interest and ability. When the discovery approach to learning has been established, it can continue to motivate and guide personal growth after formal schooling ends.

6. Students should be oriented to recognize mistake making is an aspect of learning. Everyone should expect to fail but know that repeated efforts after mistakes can help to reach an acceptable standard. In turn, achievement increases confidence to confront another set of problems for which the answers may be unknown. Adults who encourage children to avoid or deny failure undermine the development of resilience and motivation that are needed to overcome obstacles.

CHAPTER 16

CAREGIVERS AND AGING PARENTS

One sign of the longevity revolution is that the population of Americans reaching retirement age is forecast to double by 2030 (Friedman & Martin, 2011). As the country considers ways to provide health care for the 72 million people of this baby boomer generation, the impact it will have on caregivers has begun to emerge. No one looks forward to taking care of aging relatives. However, as more people live longer, they will eventually need additional care. This responsibility is presently being met by 45 million members of the "sandwich generation," so-named because of their place between two age groups that depend on them for financial assistance and care (Bertini, 2011).

Understanding the importance of their role causes many middle-aged women and men (40 to 60 years of age) to wonder how they will manage all that is expected of them. The goals of this chapter are to: (1) describe needs of aging parents and their middle age caregivers, (2) identify workplace practices that can ease the task of caregivers, and (3) glimpse telemedicine prospects to monitor and enhance the lives of older adults who are at home alone. The motivations of (4) retirees who choose age-segregated peer communities is discussed along with (5) a need to create opportunities for intergenerational learning within the context of religion, and (6) the abuse of older people is examined along with prevention methods.

Learning Throughout Life: An Intergenerational Perspective, pp. 373–396
Copyright © 2012 by Information Age Publishing

UNDERSTANDING MUTUAL CHALLENGES

Eighty percent of American retirees have adult age children. Most of these elders live in their own home, usually within 1 to 2-hour drive from their younger relatives. The majority, 68%, live in households with a spouse or other relatives including 34 million who reside in extended families. During the past decade, 4 million older adults have moved in with their adult children, an increase of 67%. The remainder group of elders live alone, are housed in nonfamily settings like assisted living, or share rooms with friends (Metlife Mature Market Institute, 2011). Whatever their circumstance, both generations try to offer mutual support. However, increased longevity means that parents will require more assistance. On average, middle age adults spend about 10% of their household income on caring for their parents. The estimated annual economic value of their unpaid contribution is $450 billion (Feinberg, Reinhard, Houser & Choula, 2011). While this situation seems predictable, most daughters and sons admit that they are unsure about how to negotiate the role reversal that comes with being a caregiver of someone who looked after them while they were growing up (Gross, 2012).

Communication of personal needs is essential for a good relationship between aging parents and adult children. Both parties should be aware of what elders require and reasonable contribution to expect of the adult child. Each person should agree to make known their opinions about needs of the parents. At the outset elders may require weekly help with housekeeping or yard care. If it is affordable, they should be urged to hire someone outside the family to perform these chores instead of relatives. Some elders have enough money but are reluctant to give up longstanding frugal habits that are inappropriate in this situation. Persuasion may be needed for them to realize that outside assistance is a wise expenditure.

Later, when elders must give up driving, their needs expand to include transportation to the grocery store, visiting a doctor, getting their hair fixed or going to church. They may also want to talk with grandchildren. Unless these needs are expressed, they may not be met. Adult children cannot anticipate all elder needs without being told by them. Many families rely on intuition when it is more sensible to depend on communication (Gillman, 2005).

Aging parents may have needs they do not realize but are detected by adult children. For example, most conversation should focus on current events so everyone feels obliged to keep up and share interpretations of what is occurring in the family, community, nation, and world. Emphasizing the present discourages excessive reminiscence, talking mostly about the past. In this connection, some midlife adults discover that their parents are becoming isolated because they refuse socialization outside the family. When this realization occurs, it should be brought to the attention of the parent. Adult children must be willing to make known their impressions about other parent needs too such as continued involvement with learning, volunteer service, and adapting to change. Aging parents who pursue these goals are less egocentric and more concerned about the needs of others.

Recognition of Parent Needs

There is benefit in knowing ahead of time some conflicts that are likely to occur in conversations. More families must become willing to talk about the things that matter most. A common explanation is that neither party wants to worry or upset the other. Therefore, no one introduces legal concerns like estate planning, completing a will or trust, power of attorney, burial preferences, and medical choice about life support. Because tragedy can take place suddenly, it is never too soon to discuss possible situations. Consider these observations from middle age discussion groups who were asked to tell about their conflicts related to the needs of aging parents.

(1) *The need for interdependence.* Laura reports,

> My dad is 81. He wants to do everything around the house but can no longer safely manage some tasks. I worry if he gets on a ladder or does heavy lifting because it can be dangerous. When I make known my willingness to get someone else to come over and take care of a job, he gets mad and tells me "No thanks."

Families should talk about how expectations of society are changing. In the past demonstrating independence was the way to judge success and attain respect. Depending too much on others was seen as a sign of failure and identified someone as a burden. The young still need independence to gain employment skills but are also expected to become interdependent to work in teams and solve problems by sharing assets and assisting others. Families must make the same transition to foster obligation and harmony. Middle age workers can orient elders to interdependence in the emerging workplace and its application to family life. People of all age groups must adapt to change by pursuing both independence and interdependence.

(2) *The need to expand scope of social interaction.* Gladys observed,

> My dad died 2 years ago. Mavis, my mom, lives alone several miles away from my husband and I and our two children. Each day I phone or visit to check in, talk about what is happening, and find out whether

she needs anything. Mom likes to see me and enjoys coming to our house for meals and visits but does not socialize outside the family. When I suggest that she get involved with the senior center, she refuses and explains that being around other old people does not interest her and offers no benefit.

Gladys should visit the senior center to find out the kinds of activities that could benefit her mother. She should also tell Mavis that students must learn group process skills not taught in the past but that are needed now for productive intergenerational conversation. These skills can be acquired and practiced in discussions with peers at the senior center. Another advantage of peer discussions is that seniors can monitor the thinking process of one another, detect sloppy thinking habits, and remind of repetitive storytelling. Discussions led by facilitators help respect divergent opinion, limit speaker time, avoid interruptions, wait for responses, challenge statements, urge clarification, and maintain optimism. These assets support more mutually satisfying discussions with loved ones.

(3) *The need to retain a sense of purpose and meaning*. Jenny is a single parent whose responsibilities and schedule are difficult to reconcile. She is disappointed that calls and visits with Max, her recently retired father, center on his complaints about lack of satisfaction with retirement. In early and middle adulthood having a job is recognized as a major influence on self-esteem. The chance to spend time however one pleases in retirement supposedly replaces a job as a key factor promoting favorable self-esteem. Nevertheless, many elders report that retirement is accompanied by loss of purpose that must be restored to provide a sense of meaning. Some older adults discover community service is a worthwhile use of their time and recognize that obligations toward others are the basis of maturity. This is why everyone is better off when retirees volunteer and share talent with society.

(4) *The need to consider moving into a long-term care center*. Roger is middle aged, single, and wondering how to convince Martha, his mother, that she should think about exploring what life could be like in a long-term care center. Martha does not take care of herself. On several occasions Roger found she left the stove on, blood pressure and other medications were forgotten, the front door was left unlocked, and water was running on the outside hose. When Roger brings up the topic of changing residences, Martha responds with comments intended to create guilt, "You don't care about me, or you would never suggest making me leave the home I love." Visiting a long-term care center demystifies the stereotype held by many older adults. Arranging an orientation answers many questions, identifies advantages and limitations of this lifestyle, and offers data for discussion about what both parties saw instead of perpetuating fear of the unknown.

(5) *The need to become involved with communications technology.* Arthur and his family live in another state than his parents. They visit at Christmas and come for summer vacation. The three grandchildren have cell phones and computers but do not interact with grandparents except brief comments during family phone calls. Arthur told his parents that he would like to buy a computer for them. They refused and explained that their lack of experience meant it would be impossible to operate a computer. Arthur should realize his parents have to experience the benefits of having a computer before they can be motivated to own one. Arthur could take them to a senior center where they might go online for an iChat with their grandchildren. At the center they can also find out when free classes are held that introduce the wonders of Internet learning, how to use e-mail, and skills for using search engines. After such an experience, Arthur's parents would be more likely to accept his offer and stay in touch using the tools of technology.

Needs of Middle-Age Caregivers

Care for aging relatives must take into account the needs of those who provide care. Adult children have to decide what they can reasonably expect of themselves and still be a source of assistance for their parents. There is concern about being able to merge the caregiver role with responsibilities that typically involve a spouse, children, employer, and home management (Cohen, 2012). It is also important to recognize that 70% of elders give financial support to adult children and grandchildren. Some reasons are that many need money to go to college, pay back student loans, cover the rent, cope with layoffs, unemployment or require funds to deal with overmortgaged homes. The toll on emotional health for caregivers are reflected by stress, sadness, worry, and loss of sleep for many middle-age women (Sheehy, 2010).

A Gallup-Healthways Well-Being Index (2010), based on one million surveys, completed over three years to track the nation's health, ranked middle-age women as lowest in personal well-being and having the highest incidence of depression, regardless of whether they were employed or homemakers. The American Psychological Association's annual online Stress in America Survey of 1,200 adults determined that 56% of elder caregivers felt overwhelmed by their daunting task (Anderson, 2011).

Codependence is the term used to define an inclination to act in overly passive or excessively caretaking ways that can undermine relationships and quality of life. For some middle-age caregivers this means assigning low priority to personal needs while becoming preoccupied with needs of an elderly parent. The resulting behaviors, thoughts, and feelings go beyond what is considered to be normal self-sacrifice. Codependent caregivers often assume the role of a martyr. By constantly placing the wishes, demands and needs of aging parents above their own, they fail to take care of themselves and sometimes ignore their obligations to others including a spouse or children. In conflict situations, those who are codependent caregivers often set themselves up as the "victim." When they do stand up for themselves, they also feel guilty. Codependency does not refer to all caring behavior but only response patterns that are excessive to an unhealthy degree (Ranji & Salganicoff, 2011).

Estimates are that 90% of elder caregivers are middle-age daughters who may spend more years looking after their aging parents than bringing up their own children (Gross, 2012). Given the workload carried by these middle-age women, it should not be surprising some feel emotionally exhausted, have high cholesterol, high blood pressure, obesity, and depression. Others dislike being tied down by a daily care schedule and resent giving up their preferred social and recreational lifestyle. Still another segment of caregivers report being discouraged because the parents are never satisfied no matter what is done to make their life more comfortable. Elders should remind one another that adult children deserve gratitude for their efforts. Ungrateful people make the task of helping them more difficult. Research has found that caregivers are three times more likely than those they assist to experience depression, and four times more likely to report feelings of anger. When these stress signs continue over a long period, the consequence can threaten a marriage, undermine relationships with children, and lead to other forms of dysfunction (Feinberg, Reinhard, Houser, & Choula, 2011).

The numerous roles assumed by middle-age caregivers commonly include:

- Giving companionship and emotional support
- Helping with household tasks that are necessary
- Handling bills and dealing with insurance claims
- Providing personal care like bathing and dressing
- Managing multiple medications including injections
- Identifying and arranging for coordinated services
- Hiring and supervising care workers in the home
- Transporting elders to their medical appointments
- Communicating with the health care professionals
- Advocating and interpreting at medical appointments
- Coordinating for transition from hospital to home

A need for periodic relief from providing care implicates siblings, employers, and community agencies. Brothers and sisters who do not regularly provide care should substitute for siblings so they get occasional time off. Those who live elsewhere should come to visit parents while a sister or brother has an uninterrupted vacation. Alternately, noncaregivers may pay to fly elder parents to visit them. Besides sharing caretaking with siblings, there is benefit in becoming familiar with services that can lighten the load. For every adult in long-term care, two others stay home where they get assistance like Meals-On Wheels. This federal program ensures that homebound get a hot meal each day. There is also a social purpose met by the person delivering a meal. S/he stays a few minutes to engage the older adult in conversation. Other services available in most places are housekeeping assistance, reassurance phone calls, friendly visitors, adult day care, dial-a-ride transportation, and socialization activities at the senior center. The Area Agency on Aging provides advice about local resources.

A popular and incorrect assumption is that adults in the past showed greater devotion to care of aging parents. A more accurate picture is that families provide 75% of the care received by older adults whose population is far larger now because, on average, people live longer. Two-thirds of all caregivers have part-time or full-time jobs (Ranji & Salganicoff, 2011). Some employers offer seminars for caregivers and support groups. IBM was the first corporation to arrange elder care for employees. Related efforts have increased so 40% of all medium and large companies provide programs. Some elements are referral services, counseling, long-term care insurance, and flexible hours, the most often chosen benefit. Two-thirds of Fortune 500 companies offer flextime (Employee Research Institute, 2009).

The burden of caring for elders can be great, frequently detracting from worker concentration. The Employee Research Institute reports 91% of employees caring for elderly relatives identify mostly negative changes in their work habits. For example, 56% acknowledged they worried at work about elderly relatives, and 48% used the phone more than usual to check on them. Elder care causes 37% of employees to arrive late or leave early, and 35% are distracted enough to admit that their productivity is diminished (Employee Research Institute, 2009).

Employers view elder care as one of their most troubling personnel issues. As baby boomers move beyond middle age, community services for them will become an even greater concern of businesses than other family issues. This priority is justified because of greater longevity, larger numbers of older people, more mobility separating families, growing employment of women, high divorce rates, and increase of single parents whose ability to provide care for older relatives is diminished (Gross, 2012).

Education programs are necessary for adult children and for aging parents to help both groups adjust to their situation. For example, care involves more than just getting groceries, helping maintain a home, and providing transportation. When these difficult tasks become a sole focus, not enough attention is given to sustaining mutually satisfying relationships. When elders move to a long-term care facility, some middle age adults suppose their support obligations are finished and staff at the facility should fulfill future caring. In effect, some family caregivers conclude 'I have done my share; now it's someone else's turn. A dire consequence from anecdotal reports given by a majority of long-term care residents is that they lack regular visitors Certainly staff can provide care but cannot substitute for family relationships. Lack of visitation is a sign of neglect implicating self-esteem, loneliness, peer reliance, and communication (Victor, Scrambler, & Bond, 2008).

There are two sides to this equation. Some grandparents between ages 50 to 75 devote almost all of their energy and time to the pursuit of personal interests. During this long period they provide little help to younger relatives, often excusing themselves with a claim that they do not want to interfere. Later, when they become frail, those who have been selfish with their time when they had greater energy may expect daughters and sons to care for them. This familiar circumstance indicates that the issue of elder care should be linked with grandparent education. Studies on relationships between aging parents and adult children seldom describe obligations of older adults. When grandparents are encouraged to assume some share of nurturing while they are young, healthy and independent, adjusting later to a less viable status is easier and less often a source of resentment by relatives. There is a reason to merge concerns about what families should expect of grandparents and what aging parents should expect of children.

Motivation for Generativity

People choose to become parents with responsibilities for childcare. However, none of us can choose whether to have parents. Motivation to care for mothers and fathers during their final years is supported by a common desire generated as an aspect of personality development. The most important developmental task of middle age is choosing between generativity and stagnation. *Generativity* is defined as a reduction of selfish concerns in favor of caring more about the well being of other people. Increased awareness about the brevity of human existence urges a resolve to leave a legacy of value, to make a positive contribution to mankind.

Some middle-age people decide to continue living for the moment as demonstrated by always assigning the highest priority to personal desires. As a result, these individuals effectively halt their development, a condition known as *stagnation* (Erikson & Erikson, 1998). The insensitive and money-possessed character Scrooge portrayed in Charles Dickens' (1843) novel, *A Christmas Carol*, exemplifies stagnation. Scrooge eventually decides that generativity is the path to attaining a sense of purpose and meaningful life.

There is reason for concern about the future. Changes in family structure such as delayed marriage and childbirth, high rates of divorce, and smaller family size mean that the burden of care will fall on fewer people in a family. There are also increasing numbers of women who have no children. Nearly 20% of older women do not have children today compared to just 10% a generation ago (Feinberg, Reinhard, Houser, & Choula, 2011).

Elders Home Alone

Many people of middle age recall a movie called *Home Alone* (Hughes, 1990). This story centers on the adventures of Kevin McAlister, an 8-year old boy played by Macauley Culkin. Kevin is the youngest of five children and often picked on. The first film opens to chaos as Kevin and extended family (two parents, two brothers, six cousins, an uncle and aunt) are preparing for Christmas vacation in Paris, France. One plane ticket is mistakenly thrown out during a sibling altercation and Kevin is banished to the attic by his angry mother. On the way upstairs, he tells her that he wishes the whole family would disappear. Kevin's mom leaves him to sulk. There is a storm that night and a tree falls down, cutting electricity and producing a power outage. Two shuttle drivers knocking at the front door wake the family up. Pandemonium ensues with the realization everyone overslept and may not be on time for their flight. A faulty headcount is taken as people enter two minibuses. They leave the house without Kevin who is still asleep in the attic.

Kevin wakes up and cannot understand why the house is so quiet. He finds that cars are still in the garage, prompting him to think the family has not left for France. Soon he concludes his Christmas wish has come true and somehow he made the family disappear. Meanwhile, his mother thinks they have forgotten something and, in midflight, discovers that it is Kevin. She worries that he will be unable to look after himself. However, Kevin is doing fine and starting to stand on his own two feet. He takes care of the laundry, showers, and shops for groceries. The only potential danger are two local burglars who spotted the family leaving the McAllister house and see it as an easy target. The rest of the film follows Harry and Marv as they try to burgle the (almost) vacant house versus Kevin as he does a great job at defending it with homemade booby traps. Deterrents include flying paint cans, a bb gun, and a doorknob heated with an electric charcoal lighter. Kevin's mother tries to return and arrives Christmas morning. The rest of the family also walk in, sick of France, and glad to be home.

Fast forward to 2020. By then there is expected to be 70 million Americans over age 65. Nearly all people of that age now report they would like to grow old in their own home rather than go to an assisted living facility. Economically, institutional long-term care is not a sustainable model in a longevity society. The prevailing view among older adults is fear about spending the end of their days in a facility. One business that supports the elder goal to stay home alone is GrandCare Systems (2012). They install motion sensors in every room and on all exterior doors. Sensors monitor motion, tracking whether a resident seems to be wandering or fails to get up from a chair or bed, falls down, how often doors open and close, and checks room temperature. The system connects wirelessly and monitors vitals as well as blood pressure, blood sugar levels and other health indicators such as whether medicines are taken on time, and relays data in real time to doctors or relatives.

The communication base that elders use is connected to a television or monitor and Internet source, wired or wireless. This system provides a continuous display menu of options on a touch pad that only requires pressing from a list of choices to obtain e-mail, brain exercises, favorite web sites, games, wellness information, music, family photos, the weather, spiritual guidance, and health information. A person can check how well s/he is doing on the touch monitor at the desk.

The University of California Los Angeles School of Nursing and Wireless Health Institute reports similar advances in telemedicine. The 700,000 Americans with congestive heart failure need methodologies for prevention, monitoring and treatment of heart disease on a daily basis. Researchers found that people relying on a remote health monitoring system had a 6% reduction in abnormal weight and blood pressure. This instrumentation takes relevant measurements and sends readings to health providers without scheduling visits with a doctor (Suh et al., 2011).

Another researcher group is testing robots that can help care for elders, keeping them company with conversation, and giving sponge baths. Jeffrey Kaye, director of the Oregon Center for Aging and Technology, indicates this kind of monitored all-the-time life will be common among older adults by 2015 and become a norm soon thereafter (Kaye, Pavel, Jimison, & Hayes, 2009). Robert Jennings, a middle-age man, lives in another state than his mother. He pays $300-$400 a month for a system to monitor his home-alone parent. This is much less expensive than

$4,000 a month that it would cost for nursing care. The option is cheaper and allows Bob peace of mind. His mother is grateful because she gets to stay home. Bob and his mother agreed to let her remain at home alone as long as possible. That may be quite awhile thanks to telemedicine.

SOCIAL INTERACTION AND MENTAL HEALTH

Many adults share a wish that, after their years of employment are over, they can spend retirement in a more climate-favored location. What are the social implications of this choice and what effect does it have on mental health? There are other older adults whose wish is to be well treated by the people who take care of them so they can avoid suffering fear and abuse.

Life in Retirement Communities

The dread of becoming a burden to their middle-age children is common among older adults and can lower self-esteem. Therefore, it can be predicted that, the stronger the desire for family respect, the greater the motivation to remain independent as long as possible. Most surveys indicate that about 75% of retirees would prefer to live in age-segregated communities apart from relatives (Butler, 2008). Retirement centers located in climate-favored states like Arizona, Florida, Nevada and Texas continue rapid growth (Brandon, 2012).

Importance of Age Norms

The motivations of older adults who move to a retirement community are often misunderstood. Young adults usually suppose that living in an age-segregated place would be uniform, dull, and depressing. In contrast, surveys of people age 50 and over consistently reveal that most would prefer living in a community consisting of people their age (Hunt, 2006). To account for differing perceptions in how older and younger adults perceive age-segregated living, it is relevant to consider the loss in roles, norms, and reference groups that accompany aging.

During childhood boys and girls are reminded to "act your age." This advice implies that, at least in the initial stages of life, there are predictable sets of expectations from which a departure will be disapproved. However, after adolescence, most people substitute their occupation, place of work, and relationships required in this setting as the basis for expectations about how to act. Still later, when age dictates retirement, many find themselves for the first time without a reference group to rely on to guide their behavior. To be without norms is to be alone in the worst sense because a person is unaware of the criteria that should be applied for self-evaluation. This is especially important in later life when what little people know beforehand about aging supports fear. So, to be old and lack norms is to wonder: Do other people of my age have the same physical problems as I do? Am I different or about the same as other people who are my age? The need to rely on a physician as a substitute for norms is shown by a high frequency of office visits where there is no evidence of organic disease (Butler, 2008).

Suicide and Lack of Norms

For certain people the result of role and norm loss can be fatal. This danger was first identified in 1897 by Emile Durkheim, a French sociologist who sought to determine the reasons why people commit suicide. He concluded the most common explanations for self-destruction were intense loneliness, coupled with a lack of clear expectations resulting from a marginal social position (Durkheim, Simpson, & Spaulding, 1997). Current research confirms that the 30,000 American suicides annually can often be attributed to a loss of roles, norms, and reference groups. It is more than coincidence that suicide rates rise after age 60, particularly among White men who take their own lives more than any other segment of the population (Heisel & Dubertstein, 2005).

Marvin Miller (1979) studied the suicides of older White men who took their lives over a 6-year period in Phoenix, Arizona. His findings revealed that role and identity losses at retirement were significant influences. The results also showed that physicians, relatives, and friends should become more responsive to depression signs. For example, Miller found that three out of four suicide victims had visited a doctor within a month before taking their life; 60% presented verbal or behavioral clues to their family. However, these signs went unrecognized or were not taken seriously.

The typical reaction was to reprimand a victim for sharing such views and insisting they should not feel that way. Most of us have given similar poor advice to others that have shared their anxieties or fears. We may have urged them "don't worry about it," or "try to forget it." A more helpful response is, "I did not realize you felt that way and will make sure you get professional help to restore your feelings of hope and confidence." Referral is an important helper role.

If normlessness contributes to self-destructive behavior, what can be done to compensate for the inevitable loss in roles people will experience at retirement? Gerontologists contend that age-segregated housing can be an effective solution. They contend older adults in regular communities are disadvantaged by a lack of roles, social networks, and norm expectations. Since they have few recognized functions or norms to guide their conduct, the way to increase norms is deliberately create an age reference group through residential concentration. In bringing many older adults together, a retirement community can become valuable for socialization into old age and for the development of age-appropriate expectations.

Socialization and Fitness

Retirement communities offer many benefits that are unrecognized by outsiders. A common expectation is that everyone who is able will strive for fitness. Most places have golf, swimming, workout centers, walking tracks, bowling, bike paths, and other forms of exercise. Residents encourage and remind one another to avoid a sedentary schedule. This constructive peer pressure contributes to better physical health. When illness does occur, geriatric hospitals like Del Webb and Boswell in Sun City, Arizona, are staffed by specialists with greater training and experience in treating older patients than physicians in facilities that serve patients from a broader age range. When retired residents require help, they know volunteers from their community can be counted on. The most comprehensive and satisfying arrangements are known as Continuing Care Retirement Communities. This means that, when residents become frail, alternative care facilities are locally available so there is no need to move to another community (Delehanty, Ginzler, & Pipher, 2008).

The high priority assigned to health is joined by an emphasis on socialization and developing a social network made up of companions and friends. There are abundant opportunities to participate in activities that offer mental stimulation, recognized as an important form of protection against dementia. Fashion continues to be a concern for older women and men but they are frequently disappointed with the choice of clothing available to them at malls catering mainly to younger customers. The clothing stores in retirement communities stock garments designed specifically for older adults. The price of housing is also less expensive because the single developer of a community is able to build homes at a lower cost than in an age-integrated community (Hunt, 2006).

Most residents in retirement communities come from other parts of the nation. Still, they prefer to preserve a sense of original place by having their community phone book list the city and state where they previously lived and perhaps identification of their former occupation. This resource provides yet another way to meet people of similar backgrounds. Typically, younger relatives are allowed to visit for a maximum of 10 days and are welcome to participate in all facilities. A greater proportion of retirement community residents are tech savvy, communicate by e-mail or iChat, enjoy traveling and take grandchildren on trips. They are generally more affluent and many help finance the cost of college tuition for their grandchildren.

Intergenerational Religious Education

Older adults should have opportunities for intergenerational learning. One promising but commonly overlooked possibility involves religious institutions. The practice of going to church, parish or synagogue increases with age. In addition to spiritual guidance, older adults consider their place of worship as a source of social support. Generally they view faith to be an essential aspect of their lives. They usually reject the assumption that moral development can proceed without reliance on religious beliefs to guide ethical conduct and govern decision making. Retirees no longer attend school or go to work. They seldom get to interact with younger people about issues that could support personal goals and maturity.

The current segregation of age groups should motivate religious educators to consider innovative alternatives for intergenerational dialogue while supporting spiritual development. The paradigm proposed here is intended to be a basis for education to foster reciprocal transmission of values and reciprocal learning that is consistent with the stated purposes of religious education.

Purpose. Religious education aims to build moral character over a lifetime. In most churches, all age groups come to the sanctuary for worship, inspiration, and instruction led by the minister, priest, rabbi or lay leader. At the end of this activity, everyone leaves to convene again in a few minutes with others of their same age. Age-segregation is the typical arrangement for religious education. For example, preschoolers are brought to a room where adult volunteer teachers provide lessons. Adolescents get their instruction in another location. Grownups are also categorized by age to meet in separate places based on whether they are young adults, middle aged or retired. Marital status is sometimes a criterion for determining the appropriate group younger adults are expected to join.

One goal of intergenerational education can be to broaden the perspective of individuals by learning from people of the same age as other family members Sharing responses to common sets of questions enables different age groups to acquaint one another with concerns, views, and challenges that resemble those of loved ones in the same generation. In turn, this orientation can help respond to relatives in a more informed and sensitive way.

Participants. Discussion groups include five people, each representing a different age group balanced for gender. One person is an adolescent from 15-20 years of age, another is 20-30. Additional members are 30-40, 40-60, and another over age 60. There is considerable evidence that people learn more from interaction with people across a broad age spectrum. Unless older adults engage in such forums, many are involuntarily denied conversations that can inform them about the outlook of younger people. In turn, capacity of elders to respond to the needs of others is diminished,

Focus. One curriculum focus should emphasize emotional development. This aspect of growth gets little attention even though it is a basic motivation for maturity and essential for spiritual health. Some possible topics could include:

1. Honesty and Ethics (Cheating in school, at the workplace and the family)

2. Family Communication (going beyond communication with one's age cohort)

3. Defining success (setting goals and amending goals at different stages of life)

4. Coping with stressful situations (in school, at work, home and leisure settings)

5. Failure and resilience (managing anxieties and feelings of disappointment)

6. Fears and worries (portrayed by different ages in what they find bothersome)

7. Challenges to faithful living in the current setting (distractions from the faith)

Format. One week ahead of time all team member receive a copy of some questions that will guide discussion at the next session. This advance agenda that can be seen as homework encourages reflection, urges note taking, and satisfies people who prefer structure in preparing for group conversations. For those who prefer to access the questions online, they can be placed on the church website.

A discussion leader can follow any progression such as calling on the youngest or oldest member to respond first and then ask others for comments. In most cases, however, allowing whoever wants to speak first and then ensuring everyone has input encourages spontaneity. Color-coded name cards (by age) can be worn to place comments in age perspective. Members can also be asked to state their age group when making remarks. The discussion always begins with the reminder that no one speaks for their entire age group but greater familiarity with norms of their cohort helps outsiders understand better than would otherwise be the case.

For some topics church members of a single age group might be invited to discuss a topic that is heard by the multiage class. For example, discussing the stresses experienced in going to college could best be expressed by those who are having these experiences. Emphasis on a single cohort is useful for topics where the goal is to inform everyone more than intergenerational comparisons.

Agenda. Discussion agenda invite members to share experiences about the present, past, and future. The present is the way things are: These accounts clarify how people differ in feelings and thoughts. By ourselves, none of us fully comprehend the present, even though we experience a part of it. The past, the way things were is another focus for concentration. Memory reveals the range of experiences in a group and makes known a personal reference of members. Long-term memory favors older adults but reminiscence should not be given undue emphasis. The future, the way things could be: People of all ages should motivate others to explore beyond what can be directly observed and imagine what is possible, thinking mostly about possibilities, optimism instead of cynicism.

Depending on the topic and relative ease of discussion, four or five agenda questions are recommended for each unit of instruction. One question should invite anyone to share a religious reference—from the old or new testament in the *Bible, Torah, Book of Mormon* or other sacred source that appears relevant, a story or incident, or recommended reflection. This option for sharing allows those familiar with religious literature to contribute particular insights for reflection.

Presentation. A 10-15 minute lesson about the topic can be presented with a handout outlining the main points. For certain topics structured discussions and minilectures can be offered on a weekday in additional sessions attended mostly by older adults who have time to come to church and socialize over coffee. This attempt to augment the regular curriculum with related sessions can make elders more aware of divergence of younger people's experience (sometimes viewing video discussions of younger age groups offering their response to specified questions) as well as increase the amount of mental stimulation.

Schedule. The education component we envision is not a substitute for existing worship. Participants would attend regular services in the sanctuary of a parish, church, synagogue or temple. The schedule to unite generations for interaction is the period now devoted to age-segregated Sunday school.

Lifespan Learning. Each stage in life presents new adjustments that can support further development. In addition, there are challenges related to social transformation and role changes that depend on reciprocal learning by all age groups. Table 16.1 presents a list of 30 learning needs that older adults, people of middle age, young adults, adolescents, and children have in common and should strive to address together. These topics can be used in discussions where people of different ages can get together to explore reciprocal learning.

In summary, the choice of methods to acquire values should be seen in broad perspective. One older person recalls:

> When I was in second grade, a man who lived down the street, Mr. Thompson, would detain any of us who ventured too near his property or walked on his lawn. He always gave a warning that ended with, "And don't you forget, I'm a taxpayer." Since I was only 7 years old, I supposed that Mr. Thompson must be the only taxpayer in our small town. Later, my grandfather informed me that paying taxes was not a distinction. In fact, Grandpa said, the law requires that everyone pay taxes. Since then I have discovered that whether men and women go beyond this minimal contribution to society and make an effort to improve life for others depends mostly on their values and level of social maturity.

Table 16.1. Reciprocal Learning Themes for Intergenerational Group Discussion

Cope with stressful experiences	Build intergenerational friendships
Manage time schedule wisely	Protect the environment
Share fears and anxieties	Avoid multitasking habits
Communicate with other generations	Choose an unhurried lifestyle
Recognize conflict as opportunity	Show patience toward others
Reciprocal learning and teaching	Accept differences in lifestyle
Develop methods of self-control	Build creative abilities
Establish and amend goals	Accept and give criticism
Detect and process failure	Use Internet resources
Fair evaluation of peers and self	Ask for help and help others
Delay immediate gratification	Minimize distractions
Become a self-directed learner	Follow healthy lifestyles
Independence and interdependence	Build resilience
Share vision and future goals	Adapt to family role change
Continue learning throughout life	Express honesty and concern

These aspects of development require greater attention in a society that aspires to global leadership. Religious institutions have an essential responsibility for communicating ethics. Therefore, efforts involving intergenerational teams of learners deserve encouragement and creative experimentation.

PREVENTION OF ELDER ABUSE

Caring for aging parents is a stressful responsibility but can bring mutual satisfaction. In contrast, in some families older adults are denied compassionate treatment. Child abuse became a prominent issue in the 1960s, followed by the 1970s recognition of spousal abuse. Congressional hearings convened again in the 1980s about elder abuse and prevention. Since the 1990s, a global network has been devising interventions and researching elder abuse (Malley-Morrison, Nolido, & Chawla, 2006).

Most of the 5.5 million abuse victims are at least 75 years old and female. In fact, 94% of the cases involve females while only 6% implicate males. The most frequent perpetrators are overstressed daughters and sons (Nerenberg, 2007). The population of elders reliant on middle-age children for assistance is forecast to double by 2030, with families offering 80% of care. These figures implicate caregiver education as well as public support systems (Brandl, Dyer, Heisler, Otto, Siegel, & Thomas, 2007).

Forms of Mistreatment

Abuse takes many forms. Physical abuse can be slapping, beating, kicking, or sexual assault. Sometimes forcible restraints are applied to confine someone by being tied to a bed or a chair. Overmedications with tranquilizers or sleeping pills are used to make people more manageable. Financial abuse involves exploitation by stealing social security checks, credit cards, forcing a victim to sign a will or turn over stocks and savings. Calling a person names, making threats to institutionalize them, withholding companionship, and imposing social isolation are forms of psychological abuse. Withholding food, medicine, personal care, and taking vital supports like eyeglasses, hearing aids, and dentures reflects active neglect. Passive neglect, which means being ignored, left alone, and forgotten is the most prevalent form of elder abuse. Only 5% of elders reside in assisted living facilities so the abuse occurs far more often in private homes where they live alone, with relatives or companions (Butler, 2008). Statistics about elder abuse by state are available online at *Elder Assistance Daily* (2012).

Barriers to Detection

Authorities maintain that only 10% of elder abuse cases are reported (Nerenberg, 2007). Societal beliefs about family life represent an obstacle to detection. The way that relatives interact has long been regarded as a private matter beyond interference of outsiders. This view is reinforced by an assumption that, as the basic unit of society, the family is a harmonious support system capable of providing members with the affection, guidance, and protection they need. These sometimes false impressions can combine to insulate a family from external social monitoring for humane care.

Finding out whether individuals are mistreated is further complicated by the fact that elders are comparatively isolated. Because they no longer have a job, there is no interaction with coworkers. They do not go to school so there have no classmates to see them. Consequently, there may not be a window of observation for people outside of the family to detect whether a person is mistreated in private. Unlike children who are often in contact with the public through teachers that are expected to recognize their needs and assist them, elders lack such resources. When abused elders are in poor health and housebound, this prevents detection by restricting their contacts with outsiders (Brandl, Dyer, Heisler, Otto, Stiegel, & Thomas, 2007).

Detection of abuse also depends on willingness of victims to make mistreatment known. When cases are verified, only 25% of discoveries occur because victims reported them. About 35% of victims deny visible evidence of their abuse (Nerenberg, 2007). Some reasons for victim reluctance to reveal the truth about their mistreatment are as follows:

1. They may depend on abusers for survival and fear retaliation.
2. They accept the blame for being the cause of their abuse.
3. They worry about being forced to move somewhere else.
4. Their bonds of affection for the abuser are stronger than a desire to leave the situation.
5. They feel guilt about having a relative that mistreats them.
6. They are concerned about loss of family status if abusive behavior became known.
7. They believe that what happens in a family should be private.

Comparison of Elder Abuse and Child Abuse

There are four areas of correspondence between child abuse and elder abuse:

(1) Adults who were abused as children are far more likely to behave the same way toward their aging parents. This reverse cycle suggests that revenge can be a motive for mistreatment. Studies indicate that people who were not treated violently when they grew up mistreat their parents in adulthood by a ratio of 1 in 400. In comparison, adults that were abused in childhood and adolescence have a record of mistreating their parents by a ratio of 1 to 2 (Summers & Hoffman, 2006).

(2) Another similarity has to do with reasons perpetrators give for their behavior. Often mistreatment occurs because previous attempts to control unacceptable conduct did not achieve the intended effect. Noncompliant elders who are unaccustomed to accepting authority of their adult children or willing to comply with demands expose themselves to greater risk for abuse. When young children oppose parent expectations by refusing to eat, having toilet accidents or crying, these reactions may be interpreted as acts of defiance. Yet, when frail elderly exhibit these forms of resistance, they present unanticipated problems to be overcome. In exasperation, an adult caregiver who acts against an aging parent sounds much like an abusive parent of a child who says "she made me hit her. She was asking for it all day."

(3) The most common expression of child abuse by adult males is physical violence directed toward female children. This is similar in elder abuse where most victims are female. In contrast, neglect is the dominant form of abuse adult females use toward children and aging parents.

(4) Child abuse and elder abuse occur in a society which is reluctant to acknowledge the widespread existence of family violence.

Some people believe physical punishment of children is necessary to correct behavior but this strategy to deal with noncompliance of elders is considered a violation of their rights. As a result, those who mistreat elders are less likely to admit it, knowing their actions are unacceptable to others. Dissimilar expectations of the young and old are also implicated. Generally, children are seen as more vulnerable and in need of greater protection than the elderly who are stereotypically viewed as being a burden to their family. The elderly have more legal, economic, and emotional independence than children, including the right to refuse an offer of assistance and intervention by professionals. Consequently, government agencies to protect families usually assign higher priority and more resources to prevention of child abuse (Brandl et al., 2007).

Victims of elder abuse are often mentally and physically frail whereas abused children, although dependent, typically do not have any disabilities. Then too, it is more difficult to detect abuse of older adults. They do not live public lives so there is limited contact with external agencies or perhaps anyone other than their abusers. They do not attend school or have regular medical checks. In addition, the norms of development are well established for children so deviation from them may trigger investigation. However, the situation is more complex with elders. The differing extent of acute and chronic illness in old age means less accurate indicators of normality. Therefore, it can be medically difficult to determine the difference between a deliberate injury and accidental fall.

Another difference implicates the future. In the case of most children, it is possible for the parents to look forward to a time when their dependency and the related stress will end as children acquire greater independence to provide self-care. In contrast, as people age they are likely to become more dependent and place even greater demands on those who care for them. It is not always possible for caregivers to foresee a satisfactory outcome or know the time frame that will be required before they can expect relief. Death of a dependent elder may be only a partial solution if caregivers are left with unresolved guilt or remorse about their behavior (Summers & Hoffman, 2006).

(4) In a longevity society, many adult children who take care of aging parents may themselves be elderly and suffer from poor health or disabilities. It is increasingly common for people in their 50s and 60s to be caring for parents in their 70s and 80s, some of whom are in better health than the children and may outlive them. Finally, in child abuse, the relationship is of recent origin whereas elder abuse is based upon a relationship of years. Abuse may arise from longstanding disagreements.

Societal Support Systems

Employers are encouraged by workers unions and advocacy groups to offer flexible schedules for employees who have responsibilities for elder care. There are increasing requests to provide supervision of older relatives at the workplace in the same way care of young children is a benefit given by leading companies. Efforts are being made to sponsor support groups to relieve caregivers whose obligations produces high levels of stress. Elders themselves should be made aware that adult day care could be a better alternative for them than staying home alone. From the perspective of a daughter or son, low cost day care offers assurance that the aging parent will get attention, a hot meal, medication on time, socialization with peers, help when needed, and supervision to ensure safety. Adult day care also offers relief for many wives responsible for care of their often older and less viable husbands. Enabling these men to attend day care and return at night supports mental health (Bowden & Lewthwaite, 2009).

Families should recognize the majority of elder abuse cases involve self-neglect by persons living alone who are unable to properly care for themselves. Usually these widows are malnourished, prefer not to cook because no one else eats with them, seldom change clothes or bathe, and fail to keep their residence clean. In these circumstances adult children can arrange for home health care and personal maintenance programs. When this help is not enough, long-term care should be considered as a solution to preserve the health and safety of aging mothers and fathers.

SUMMARY AND IMPLICATIONS

Maintaining a satisfying relationship with aging parents is a goal for most middle age people. Fulfilling this intention depends on mutual awareness regarding the needs of each other. Conversations that focus on important issues as defined by each party foster greater respect and adjustment. Providing elder care requires generativity, the mature base of perspective that motivates concerns for welfare of others and contributes to personality development.

The forecast for population growth of elders is accompanied by innovations in telemedicine that enable new ways to provide care that requires less time from middle age relatives and at a fraction of the cost. The advantages of monitoring vital signs that are communicated in real time can detect health problems and intervention needs. Social isolation is reduced because the older adult has access to response options that stimulate mental functioning, connect to relatives by e-mail, check favorite websites, and pursue personal interests. The high cost of long-term care may not be feasible in the future so trial of creative alternatives should be encouraged.

Understanding the appeal of a retirement community can help younger relatives avoid misimpressions about strength of family ties for relatives choosing to move away when they retire. Peer norms are important at every age because they represent the criteria that most individuals rely upon as a basis for self-evaluation. Age-segregated retirement communities encourage physical fitness and participation in social networks. These assets are less prominent in age-integrated communities where sedentary habits more often characterize elder lifestyle and diminish the prospects for good health.

The potential of religious institutions for leadership in providing intergenerational learning to support spiritual development and ethical conduct requires experimentation. Bringing successive age groups together can increase awareness that is necessary to facilitate social transformation and harmony. Departure from age-segregated learning is an option that requires ministers, priests, rabbis and governing boards to recognize how experimenting with new forms of instruction could benefit the entire congregation.

Elder abuse is more pervasive than is reflected by number of reported cases. Older adults live private lives that can keep neighbors or other outsiders from knowing when abuse occurs. This situation is further complicated by an unwillingness of most victims to report or to confirm their mistreatment. In later life, as in childhood, females are more often the targets of abuse. Overstressed middle age adults are the source of most mistreatment but many elders also suffer from self-neglect. Employers have an important obligation to allow flexible work hours, make elder day care available on site, sponsor caregiver support groups and counseling services. Siblings should share their obligation for parent care instead of expecting the main caregiver to assume all of the responsibility. All daughters and sons should assume a fair share of financial costs and, by providing occasional relief, enable the main caregiver to sustain resilience.

APPLICATIONS FOR TEACHING

1. Aging parents do not recognize some of their own needs that may be observed by adult children. These insights should be shared so both parties understand the full scope of conditions they need to work on together. Some observations by middle age children can reduce elder egocentrism by clarifying expectations that allow them to retain a sense of purpose by continued learning, volunteering, and adapting to change.

2. Middle age women carry a disproportionate share of the load for providing elder care. The combined responsibilities for younger and older relatives as well as obligation to employers means main caregivers should be helped by siblings who do not regularly care for parents. Failure to assist caregivers exposes middle age women to depression, loss of hope, and vitality that makes them the resource others rely on for support.

3. Families should be willing to talk about matters of importance instead of avoiding sensitive issues so that no one becomes upset. Discussions about health and death concerns should be welcomed by everyone so later the wishes and expectations of elders are not in doubt. Denying loved ones the information that they need shows lack of trust and unwillingness to confront reality.

4. Older adults benefit from norms of socialization and fitness established by peers. The powerful teaching influence that others of the same age can have includes expectations to exercise on a regular basis, participate in classes, maintain social interaction, rely on friends to hear reports of joy and concern, and help one another to monitor the quality of their thinking.

5. Elder caregivers need classes provided by municipal governments to acquaint them with available community resources. Churches,

civic groups, and fraternal organizations can identify caregivers and attempt to ensure that their needs are not overlooked.

6. Classes at senior centers should include personal safety and well being in old age. This discussion forum can consider knowledge of mistreatment by caregivers and actions that prevent abuse and rehabilitate abusers without fear of further retaliation.

7. Religious education should include reciprocal intergenerational learning so older adults are not isolated from the ideas and concerns of younger age groups. Middle age daughters and sons who may be leaders of church boards should express their willingness to assume responsibility for implementing this new concept in religious education.

CHAPTER 17

GRANDPARENTS
AND GENERATIVITY

Generativity is the term used to describe concern for establishing and guiding the next generation (Erikson, 1950). One sign of maturity is the ability to look beyond oneself, to want to give back to society, and to provide care that others may need. These characteristics have been a longstanding expectation of older adults. They are supposed to pass on lessons about effective ways of doing things, along with attitudes and beliefs that enable healthy perspective. When grandparents behave in these ways, they are regarded as important resources by family, friends, and community. This aspiration is becoming possible for more women and men because of greater longevity and better physical health.

GOALS FOR GRANDPARENTS

The average life span of 85 years has lengthened the duration of being a grandparent (Goossens, 2010). Most people become grandparents between age 50 to 55, allowing them an opportunity to provide continuity of affection, care, and guidance to their grandchildren from infancy until early adulthood. Over 90% of retired persons are grandparents; half of them will live to see their great grandchildren. These men and women can be a great asset when certain conditions are met. This chapter describes current expectations of grandparents, redefinition of their role,

Learning Throughout Life: An Intergenerational Perspective, pp. 397–418
Copyright © 2012 by Information Age Publishing

397

purposes to guide behavior, and ways to improve intergenerational relationships with daughters, sons, and grandchildren. The goals and new traditions that are described in Table 17.1.are intended for grandparent consideration. Readers can also use this report card to mark their observations regarding the performance of a particular grandparent.

Reinforce Parent Goals for Children

Amy invited Margaret to join her at a weekly class for grandparents. Margaret replied, "Why should I take a course on how to be a grandparent when the role comes naturally to me? I raised three children. They all turned out well so I must have known something." Certainly, raising three responsible children is an accomplishment. However, being a good parent does not ensure being a successful grandparent. One reason is that the grandparent role must be defined in part by other family members. The goals parents have chosen for bringing up their children are the most important factor to guide grandparent behavior. It is essential to become aware of these expectations as a basis to reinforce lessons parents are trying to teach their daughters and sons. This information is not revealed by intuition; it does not come naturally.

What does come naturally is enthusiasm for a grandparent-grandchild relationship that focuses mainly on entertainment, with little attention to

Table 17.1.   Grandparent Report Card

Directions: Some goals for grandparents remain the same over time while others emerge to fit the uniqueness of current events. The purpose of this report card is to think about the behavior of a particular grandparent. For each statement, circle the rating that reflects your observation of how frequently the grandparent fulfills each goal and new tradition.

Goals and New Traditions	Behavior of this Grandparent			
1. Reinforce parent goals for their children.	Always	Often	Seldom	Never
2. Define role in cooperation with the family.	Always	Often	Seldom	Never
3. Express feelings, ideas, and perceptions.	Always	Often	Seldom	Never
4. Spend time together to build relationships.	Always	Often	Seldom	Never
5. View grandchildren as sources of learning.	Always	Often	Seldom	Never
6. Expect to be included in grandchild schedule.	Always	Often	Seldom	Never
7. Show optimism about people and events.	Always	Often	Seldom	Never
8. Encourage gender equity within the family.	Always	Often	Seldom	Never
9. Pursue self-improvement through education.	Always	Often	Seldom	Never
10. Compare parent practices of past and present.	Always	Often	Seldom	Never

acting as a partner for parents. Doing what comes naturally typically means ignoring responsibility. Grandparents who suppose their main function is to fulfill the wishes of grandchildren unintentionally support selfishness and egocentrism. Helping children consider the needs of others is a more important contribution that fosters personality development. Grandparents can support family plans when they understand the intentions of parents. Some grandparents claim, "I don't want to interfere in my children's lives; they should be allowed to guide their family the way I did." Yet, grandparents do interfere if they are unaware or choose to ignore the childrearing goals of parents. The grandparent role is first and foremost a supportive partnership with parents (R. Strom & Strom, 1997).

Grandparents may disagree with some aspects of current parenting practices, particularly ones that contradict those they followed when raising their own children. There must also be awareness that, as the growing up process changes in response to new environments, some corresponding shifts are needed in how parents fulfill their role. When grandparents understand how the middle generation perceives their obligations, they can be better informed, less critical, and more ready to help.

Grandparents often underestimate the contribution they should make to socialization of grandchildren. When asked if being a grandparent is easier or more difficult than expected, the usual response is that being a grandparent is easier and less demanding because parents have all the responsibility. In contrast, mothers and fathers rarely report that being a parent is easy. One conclusion is that the obligation for bringing up children is disproportionate in many families, with grandparents assuming less than their share of responsibility. Certainly, there are families in which surrogates have a heavy load because they are the primary child caregivers. Nevertheless, there is a vast difference between being mostly responsible for the well being of grandchildren and the more common practice of insufficient involvement. The desirable pattern is to share some obligation with parents who accept a far greater portion of the load.

Define the Grandparent Role

Grandparents want to think well of themselves. However, it is difficult to gain the respect they seek when it depends on fulfilling an ambiguous role (Goossens, 2010). Defining any role requires setting goals, pursuing a course of direction, and engaging in periodic evaluation to gauge progress. It follows that, unless grandparents try to carry out particular responsibilities, they cannot claim to succeed in achieving them. This then is the grandparent dilemma—they aspire to success but often lack a set of reasonable rights and responsibilities to use as criteria for self-evaluation.

Grandparents need to have norms of constructive behavior so their role can be influential and satisfying (R. Strom & Strom, 1997). Table 17.2 encourages three generations—grandparents, parents, and grandchildren—to collectively define rights of grandparents. Table 17.3 defines responsibilities of grandparents according to three generations. In combination, these tables can provide a description of the grandparent role as defined by a specific family.

Express Feelings, Ideas, and Opinions

When grandparents are asked to describe their relationship with grandchildren, most of them portray the bond as being much closer than is described by boys and girls. One explanation for the difference in perception is that children make themselves known by sharing their ideas, opinions, and feelings. In contrast, older people are often less willing to communicate emotions so understanding how they feel becomes more difficult. Moreover, when grandparents refuse to disclose their ideas and feelings, they cannot gain from give-and-take family conversations that could sometimes persuade them to change their minds about people, events, and themselves.

Steven, a teenager, said, "One of the things that I like about my grandma Marie is her readiness to discuss politics, business, or anything else; she is always willing to let me know what she thinks and wants to hear about current ideas." It is true that people can learn more about topics they are willing to discuss. Most children are brought up to express their thoughts and listen to others, even when they disagree. There may be topics that each person prefers to avoid but the list should not be so long it prevents family members from getting to know grandparents. Paul realized his limitations, "I need to understand ways to express my feelings with grandchildren. I have strong opinions but keep them to myself so that no one gets upset—including me."

Relationships can also suffer when grandparents establish a reputation for being intolerant of how other people feel. Eleanor learned this lesson the hard way. After 2 weeks as a guest at her son's home, she got up one morning and found her 4-year old granddaughter Joyce playing alone in the backyard sandbox. While they talked Joyce mentioned, "Grandma, I have to be good only two more days." Eleanor asked, "Why is that?" Joyce replied, "Because that's when you go home." Some families do not behave normally when grandparents come to visit. There is an attempt to put on a performance because it is assumed that grandparents cannot accept typical family behaviors. Some parents explain that their temporary suspension of routine and normal activity is easier than for grandparents to

Table 17.2. Defining Rights for Grandparents*

The grandparent role is better understood when defined by the whole family. First, look over the lists of grandparent rights and responsibilities. Then, circle the G (for grandparent) column beside each of the rights and responsibilities that you consider appropriate for yourself. Add more items to the lists if you wish.

Next, give the lists to your daughter or son and their child(ren). Ask them to make their views known by circling the P (for parent) and GC (for grandchild(ren) column beside items on the lists of rights and responsibilities they think should be expected of you. Encourage adding more items if they wish.

After all three generations complete their task, review the lists together to find areas of agreement and disagreement. Where disagreement about a particular item exists, negotiation may be possible. Many people go through life without knowing what relatives expect of them. This process of defining your role in the context of your family can help set more appropriate expectations and identify responsibilities mutually agreed on and understood by everyone. Use these same directions for Table 17.3. Defining Responsibilities for Grandparents.

			As a grandparent, I would like the right to:
G	P	GC	1. Hear from my grandchildren on a regular basis.
G	P	GC	2. Spend time with my grandchildren.
G	P	GC	3. Share my interests and hobbies.
G	P	GC	4. Say "No" sometimes to requests for babysitting.
G	P	GC	5. Participate in special events of grandchildren.
G	P	GC	6. Give advice to my children and their spouses.
G	P	GC	7. Give advice to my grandchildren.
G	P	GC	8. Be told about grandchild problems and success.
G	P	GC	9. Know about school progress of grandchildren.
G	P	GC	10. Maintain the rules of my home during visits.
G	P	GC	11. Get to visit grandchildren if there is a divorce.
G	P	GC	12. Express my view about religious beliefs.
G	P	GC	13. Discuss financial needs of family members.
G	P	GC	14. Talk about things that are right and wrong.
G	P	GC	15. Be able to vacation travel with grandchildren.
G	P	GC	16. Choose a lifestyle that reflects my preference.
G	P	GC	17. Expect grandchildren to have obligations to me.
G	P	GC	18. Know parent goals of sons/daughters/in-laws.
G	P	GC	19. Receive feedback about my role performance.
G	P	GC	20. Rely on the family for encouragement to learn.

* Adapted from *Adult Learning and Relationships*, by P. Strom & R. Strom, 2011, p. 172. Information Age Publishing Inc., Charlotte, NC.

Table 17.3.   Defining Responsibilities for Grandparents*

				As a grandparent, I would like the responsibility to:
G	P	GC	1.	Tell grandchildren about their parents' childhood.
G	P	GC	2.	Communicate some of the traditions of our family.
G	P	GC	3.	Give advice to my children and their spouses.
G	P	GC	4.	Give advice to granddaughters and grandsons.
G	P	GC	5.	Be an example of mature concern for others.
G	P	GC	6.	Cooperate with the other set of grandparents.
G	P	GC	7.	Keep learning so improvement is continuous.
G	P	GC	8.	Find out views and feelings of grandchildren.
G	P	GC	9.	Take care of grandchildren if parents cannot.
G	P	GC	10.	Devote some leisure time to volunteer tasks.
G	P	GC	11.	Maintain the rules of my home during visits.
G	P	GC	12.	Understand current goals of raising children.
G	P	GC	13.	Share financial resources with grandchildren.
G	P	GC	14.	Communicate regularly with grandchildren.
G	P	GC	15.	Act as a family example of personal stability.
G	P	GC	16.	Support school improvement for all children.
G	P	GC	17.	Be honest in expressing feelings and needs.
G	P	GC	18.	Reinforce parenting goals of daughters/sons.
G	P	GC	19.	Encourage grandchildren to value creativity.
G	P	GC	20.	Understand goals of individual grandchildren.

*Adapted from *Adult Learning and Relationships*, by P. Strom & R. Strom, 2011, p. 173. Information Age Publishing Inc., Charlotte, NC.

accommodate a lifestyle that differs from their own. The result of this charade is that grandparents are misled, they are not expected to adjust, and reciprocal learning seldom occurs.

Spend Time Building Relationships

"She is one of a kind." This comment suggests that someone is recognized as unique, possesses qualities that differentiate her or him from others. Every grandchild should be seen in this way. Grandparents deny individuality when they say, "I want to be fair and not play favorites so I treat all my grandchildren the same way." On the contrary, if the goal is to demonstrate equality, then it is necessary to identify, accept, and encourage differences in talents and interests. When grandchildren are known as individuals, they can have a greater impact on grandparents and motivate efforts to remain in touch.

One of the joys grandparents can experience is establishing a unique relationship with each grandchild. This goal is more difficult when grandchildren increase in number. There is no merit in merely counting grandchildren as though they were status symbols—"I have 4, 6, 10 or 12 grandchildren." What matters most is that each individual is sufficiently well known so it becomes possible to support self-esteem, distinctiveness, individual sense of direction, and provide feedback on progress toward growing up (McGovern, Ladd, & Strom, 2006).

To attain these goals, grandparents must communicate often. Most elders admit that they find it difficult to keep a conversation going with grandchildren. The exchanges never last long enough to yield insight, enable mutual understanding, or establish a close relationship. Table 17.4 provides a set of questions that a grandchild can ask grandparents to get to know them better.

Table 17.4. Getting to Know Me

Directions: Grandchildren should get to know their grandparents. Show this list of questions to grandparents and ask them to answer the items they are willing to share.

1. Who are some famous people you have admired most?
2. What did you like and dislike most about going to school?
3. What things are more important at this age than earlier in life?
4. What did you find most satisfying and difficult about your job?
5. What do you regard as your most important achievements?
6. What was better or worse about growing up during your time?
7. What do you see as your major strengths and shortcomings?
8. Which experiences as a parent stand out as fond memories?
9. What goals and dreams are you trying to achieve at this time?
10. What regrets do you have as you look back upon your life?
11. What traditions do you hope will be preserved by the family?
12. What are the activities that help you feel good about yourself?
13. What changes do you anticipate for the future of our country?
14. What things do you remember about the place you grew up?
15. What advice can you give about the ways to find happiness?
16. What would you like to understand better about the grandchildren?
17. What things do your daughters and sons do that you admire?
18. How does raising children now differ from your own parenting?
19. What are some words you think accurately describe yourself?
20. What should be expected of older adults in a longevity society?

ESTABLISH NEW TRADITIONS

Recognize Grandchildren as Teachers

Social change requires new traditions so intergenerational relationships can be mutually supportive and satisfying. Grandparents admit that knowing grandchildren is one of their greatest learning needs. Lack of this awareness is costly because youth tend to seek advice from those they believe understand their struggles, doubts, and concerns. There is little benefit in identifying older relatives as the most mature and then nullify their potential by refusing to keep them informed. This response increases ambiguity of the grandparent role and relegates their position in the family to an honorific status without a sense of purpose or meaning. There is a related obstacle. Mary describes the familiar problem.

> I don't like it when my daughter and son in law act as reporters about the behavior of my grandchildren. They tell me all of the good things that are happening, achievements in the classroom, victories on sports teams, and other ways my grandchildren perform well. Disappointing events or failures are never mentioned even though my grandchildren certainly must have such experiences. The difficult side of life is never told to me because the parents suppose I need to be proud and avoid worries. However, for me it is more important to be accurately informed. I would like to encourage grandchildren when they have hard times; that is when I am needed the most but cannot be responsive if I am given only favorable news. I cannot be a listener or source of guidance if everything is always "Just fine, grandma." My grandchildren must wonder sometimes if I even care to console them.

Partial or biased reporting prevent grandparents from knowing what is happening and denies them a chance to give the emotional support children need to develop resilience. Parent reports that leave out the difficulties of grandchildren cause some grandparents to suppose that growing up at the present time must be relatively easy and free of worries or stress. This situation reflects how the grandparent role is defined in some families. Grandparents may want to question whether the family does not take them into their confidence. Even friends share more with each other than just reports of the good times. Grandparents should tell relatives that they want to hear directly from grandchildren. This means that they expect grandchildren to speak for themselves by phone, e-mail, or visiting, without parent involvement as messengers or interpreters.

Parents can tell children that grandparents want to be helpful but cannot offer useful advice without relevant information. Grandchildren who describe their experiences acquaint older relatives with the complexities of growing up in the current environment and stimulate involvement in family problem solving. Grandchildren will decide the extent to which they share feelings and information, but this behavior is almost always increased when grandparents demonstrate a similar readiness for sharing the highs they enjoy and lows they struggle to overcome.

Expect Inclusion in Grandchild Schedule

American, Chinese, and Japanese grandparents who spend the greatest amount of time interacting with their grandchildren are identified by three generations as more successful than grandparents who spend less time with interaction (R. Strom, Heeder, Strom, 2005; R. Strom, Lee, Strom, Nakagawa, & Beckert, 2008; R. Strom et al., 1995; R. Strom et al., 1997). Arranging time together often depends more on the availability of busy grandchildren than the schedule of grandparents. Parents should teach their children that they have an obligation to be in frequent touch with grandparents and keep them informed about the full scope of their experiences. When this does not happen, the grandparents should question daughters and sons about the flexibility of a child's schedule. Taking this action can often avoid being assigned just a cheerleader role invited to attend grandchildren participation in competitive activities and performances with their peers.

Members of a grandparent class shared reactions to this question: What obligations do you expect of your grandchildren? Alice, who previously assigned herself a lengthy list of responsibilities as a grandparent, said, "I don't feel that my grandchildren should have any obligations toward me." Then Alice was asked, "How can your grandchildren ever grow up to become responsible when you deny them a sense of obligation to members of their own family?" If grandchildren are expected to show concern for loved ones, they are more likely to become adults with caring attitudes. Linda expressed her perspective: "When I think about obligations of my grandchildren, I want them to have compassion toward me when I am sick or do not feel well." The woman next to Linda inquired, "How do grandchildren who live far away know when you are not feeling well?" Linda admitted they probably could not know because she never tells them, supposing they may worry or think she is a hypochondriac. The point is that just as grandparents want to know when grandchildren feel down and need encouragement, younger relatives should be aware of times when grandparents are depressed and need cheering up. Mutual self-disclosure and being able to count on each other is a foundation for close relationships.

Show Optimism as Basis of Adjustment

The behavior of children often reminds adults about the optimism that grownups should model. Betty stopped by the apartment of her recently divorced son awarded custody of Justin, his 7-year old boy. Betty came by early to pick up Justin knowing that it would require some effort to get him ready for church the next morning.

> According to Betty, my plan was to get Justin new shoes and a haircut. I felt confident that whatever else he might need would be in the large sack of dirty laundry I had taken out of his room and brought home to wash. Then I discovered there was no underwear in the whole mess of wash, not one pair. "There were no undershorts in the laundry, Justin," I said while heading toward the bathroom. "I'll wash the ones you have on while you take a shower before bed." "I don't have undershorts on, Grandma," he replied. "There were none in my drawer all week so I just didn't wear any." "You mean you've gone to school the whole week without underwear?" I asked amazed while my mind scrambled to think of stores that might be open at 9:30 Saturday night. "Don't worry grandma," Justin said, "My pants are real thick, and tomorrow no one will know I don't have underwear on except you and me." So, we went to church with no one knowing except us.

The willingness of Betty to share her grandson's sense of possibility, to make the best of an undesirable situation, was an effective way to handle the stress. She later took steps to make sure more pairs of underwear would be available and without sacrificing the boy's respect for Justin's father.

Attitudes qualify or disqualify adults chosen by children as sources of emotional support. Whether grandparents are optimistic or pessimistic, these basic attitudes become a significant aspect of their legacy. If the grandparent role, particularly in middle class White families, continues to decline in importance, many children will lose a potentially valuable resource while grandparents become more vulnerable to feeling that their life lacks purpose and meaning. The aging process itself leads to physical and psychological limitations that can encourage negative self-impressions. An important insight for grandparents is to realize that when grandchildren are exposed to continuous pessimism, they can lose the creative capacity to perceive possibilities, including their own happiness. Observing optimistic grandparents motivates a favorable outlook that children need to shape their future.

Encourage Gender Equity in the Family

The convenience provided by microwave ovens, dishwashers, and other appliances has made housework easier. Nevertheless, in many homes, couples do not share domestic tasks. Shifts in responsibility do not come easily for some men who seem to think domestic chores are just for women. Some older women did not have jobs. They stayed home to take care of children and the household. A residual effect is continued avoidance of older husbands to share domestic obligations, claiming, "I am too old to change." In many of these families, women continue to take care of the home with little help. The good news is a much greater proportion of young men are partners with wives who are dual wage earners (McClain & Grossman, 2009).

Grandfathers are advised to share responsibility at home because it helps their wives and allows younger relatives to see them as a constructive influence in the family. In contrast, when grandfathers hold on to traditional division of labor expectations, grandchildren are likely to dismiss them as sources of guidance about gender relationships. Children are oriented to a more equitable model of how families should cooperate. The media, schools, classmates, and parents teach that girls and boys are equal. One result is that children dislike watching grandma do all the cooking, shopping, washing, ironing, and housecleaning without help from grandfather. They interpret this as gender inequity and are reluctant to view grandfather in the way he wishes to be seen.

More is involved than just stubbornness of husbands to change. Attitudes of wives are implicated too. When husbands begin to participate in household tasks, their initial performance will not match the standard of their wives. Instead of saying "You're hopeless in the kitchen," or, "It's easier to do the job myself," wives should consider more motivating responses. By showing several times the way to perform a task, giving constructive feedback, encouraging another try after mistakes, and making favorable comments about progress, grandmothers help grandfathers learn how to share domestic tasks and become a better example for the family.

Pursue Education for Self-Improvement

Society must educate all generations simultaneously to ensure everyone stays in touch with the present and future of other age groups. Expectations for learning should go beyond preparation for work to include retirees. Grandparents should become as critical of their own development and maturity as they are about the education of grandchildren. By themselves grandparents may be unable to motivate peers to pursue the learning they need. One reason is that many older adults think of retirement as a time when they should be allowed to withdraw from responsibility and spend time doing whatever pleases them. Other retirees often support the concept that being carefree is a lifestyle they deserve for their many years of employment. A more mature outlook is that people stop working when they retire but should never stop learning.

The best way to "respect our elders" in a technological community is make certain they have access to education that helps them adjust to change. Some grandparents do not believe they remain capable of learning. This harmful self-impression is perpetuated if young people have low expectations for them. To illustrate, grandparents of Mexican-American background usually depend on relatives for self-esteem, and obtain most of their recognition from loved ones (Strom, Buki, & Strom, 1997). These conditions suggest that some grandparents who do not express interest in classes might be willing to participate if encouraged by their family. Just as children are motivated to learn at school to please parents, grandparents can be motivated to gain new knowledge to satisfy expectations of the family.

During the first session in the grandparent courses, participants are asked to tell something about their reasons for taking the class.

> Esther said, "When my daughter and 9-year-old grandson heard I was planning to attend a course for grandparents, they told me, 'Grandma you don't need a course. We love you just the way you are.' Their remarks were intended as a compliment so I replied, "I'm glad you think I do well, but learning is needed at every age in life. I try to understand how things change and what it means for me. Learning is the best way for me to know what's new and how to adjust. So, please encourage me to grow. I appreciate it more than your supposing I don't need to keep learning." Esther took the initiative to establish suitable expectations for her growth. She resembles others who have been told by friends less motivated to learn that "Your behavior is ok so don't bother to take a grandparent course."

When young relatives encourage further education, elders should interpret this as a sign of confidence. Grandparents can understand that loved ones want them to become an example in the family by demonstrating continued learning is essential at every age for adjustment. Some important learning can only be attained in the family. Middle age mothers and fathers discover gaps in grandparent understanding about modern parenting and usually provide explanations that improve interpretation. An additional way to detect contexts where the grandparents need advice is by discussion of the questions in Table 17.5 that focus on what parenting is like today. Parents and children should let grandparents know they expect them to keep growing, invest time in the family, offer guidance to younger relatives, and show concern for their community. When the norms for grandparent behavior include learning and responsibility, older men and women can have a sense of purpose and continue making important contributions to their family and society.

Table 17.5. What is Parenting Like Today?

For discussion by grandparents and parents.

1. How do you suppose being a parent is easier and more difficult now?
2. What parent behavior of your daughter or son do you really admire?
3. What methods of raising children do relatives use that disappoint you?
4. What is most satisfying about the relationship with your adult children?
5. What should the children be taught to expect from their grandparents?
6. Why do you suppose grandparents find it difficult to become advisors?
7. What is your experience giving advice to children and grandchildren?
8. In what ways could your performance in providing advice be improved?
9. What kind of advice would you benefit from given by younger relatives?
10. How are parents today more successful than parents were in the past?

GIVE AND SEEK ADVICE

Become an Informed Advisor

Parents can access more sources of advice than ever before about how to raise children. Authors seek to explain strategies for teaching children, counselors answer questions on radio or television shows, and educators offer classes on family relations. So many professionals claim expertise about the growing up process that mothers and fathers are often perplexed and wonder whose advice is best. Despite the uncertainty that comes with having many choices, parents are grateful to have these alternatives. Children also benefit when families have access to a broad range of potential advisors. However, there may be other consequences for grandparents. When they are no longer seen as relevant sources of guidance, grandparents are deprived of feeling that their experience matters, their ideas are worthwhile, and younger relatives value their point of view.

Some people wonder whether it is sensible to always tell the truth. The answer is Yes. No one should not say only what others want to hear on the assumption this is necessary to preserve relationships. Inauthentic comments cannot preserve relationships; they merely maintain a social arrangement. Relationships are always based on self-disclosure because this is the only way to really know someone.

Mary came to this realization during a visit. She had bought 8-year-old grandson Todd a yellow sweater for his birthday and knew that it would look great on him. After Todd opened the package and looked at the sweater he said, "Grandma, I don't like it." Mary's feelings were hurt, so she told her daughter the details. Todd's mother listened and then pointed out, "Mom,

I'm sorry Todd isn't as excited about the sweater as you are, but we're raising him to tell the truth, to be honest. This means that sometimes he will say things we would rather not hear, but Todd's feelings will be made known and we think that is the most important thing."

When grandparents are asked to respond to Todd's story, their reactions illustrate how a single event can be seen in a number of ways. Wanda expressed concern about how Todd responded to his grandmother's choice. She said, "I like it that Todd is honest but wish he would not have hurt his grandmother's feelings." Mavis focused on adjusting to the grandmother's choice, "My grandbaby got a pink shirt from a relative but he did not want to wear it because he considered it to be a girl's color. Then a neighbor girl got the same kind of shirt but it was purple- so they traded. Apparently purple is ok for boys in his group." Leona's emphasis was on enlarging the grandparent choice. She said, "I think the grand-mother should have said to Todd before giving him a sweater-Todd, what are your favorite colors in clothes? Grandparents should find out what grandchildren like rather than assume that they will be pleased with whatever they are given."

Optimistic people do not fear the cost of honesty about stating their feelings because they recognize worthwhile qualities in others; they view the world and their own situation in terms of possibilities rather than limitations. In this respect, they resemble young children whose preference for seeing life in an intuitive way provides them with optimism and sense of trust—both essential attitudes for ensuring mental health. In many families grandparents need to recover this sense of optimism and trust so children and grandchildren can consider them as advisors.

Benefits of Giving Advice

Grandparents need to know how family conversation has changed. Grandparents often express disappointment that parent-child relationships are no longer characterized by obedience. However, it is a mistake to suppose that child and parent disagreement reflects disrespect by children. The same dialogue grandparents interpret as a breakdown of parent authority may be considered a healthy exchange of opinion by younger relatives. Comparative studies over the past 50 years show that the order in which parent goals are ranked have been reversed. The shift is away from strict obedience toward encouraging autonomy and account-ability (Berns, 2009).

Grandparents report that it is sometimes frustrating to accept how grandchildren treat adults, particularly their own parents. After witness-ing her family express their differences, one grandmother told her daughter, "When you were a child, you never talked back to me like that." Grandma's memory is correct because in those days respect was reserved for fewer people. There was less concern about equality of minorities, women, disabled, and children. Currently students are taught from an early age that every person is different and important. They are encouraged to view self-assertion as a healthy way to act as a positive influence and attain identity. Unlike coercion, imposing our will on others, self-assertion is stating how we see things and what we stand for.

Self-disclosure is necessary to be a family advisor. Many grandparents are reluctant to offer suggestions or comments for fear that it may produce conflict. Others prefer to keep their opinion to themselves unless someone asks for it. However, if grandparents say only what others want to hear, being a source of guidance is diminished. Consider Judy's story:

> My 3-year-old grandson, Randy, had just told me "No" about my suggestion that he move his toys away from the door. My son-in-law scolded him, "I don't ever want you to tell your Nana 'no.' In fact, and I don't want you to say 'no' to any adult." After Randy went out to play, I approached his father, "You know, it may be dangerous to teach a child they must never say 'no' to an adult. There are some pretty awful people in this world. What about an adult that might say, 'Come here little boy, and I'll give you candy,' or 'Let's play a game, but you must never tell mommy or daddy.' Immediately my son-in-law called Randy into the room. "Son," he said, "I'm sorry, but daddy told you something a while ago that was wrong. There are some times when mommy and daddy would want you to say 'no' to adults."

Suggestions should be made without having to be asked, especially when grandparents see possible danger or trouble their children or grandchildren do not recognize. When some people need advice the most, they are the least inclined to seek it. Bear in mind that, whenever a person is emotionally upset, s/he cannot engage in creative thinking, the ability to generate alternative practical solutions for problems. In these times, caring advisors are needed to propose options for consideration. Suggesting courses of action is part of the advisor role; being a listener is not enough.

Parents should be able to think of grandparents as sources of advice. Some grandparents excuse themselves from this obligation by stating, "My children have a lot more schooling than I do so my advice would not be worth much." Exaggeration of how schooling equips people for dealing with life's problems is costly if it excludes insightful observations of elders. Indeed, if grandparent impressions are considered, a broader perspective can emerge. Conversely, if family members dismiss recommendations of grandparents, this should not be interpreted as an insult. No one should expect or wish that their advice would always be implemented.

Moreover, older adults should not be defensive as if their wisdom is in question. Most families should engage in independent decision making.

There is evidence that people are educable at every age and can change their minds. However, grandparents deny that possibility if they withhold advice and prevent family members from determining for themselves whether the suggestions are suitable and deserve to shape their behavior. Certainly, there is a risk in giving advice because it exposes personal perspective. Moreover, risk-taking declines with age. Taking some risks is essential to grow and remain influential. If grandparents choose not to advise children and grandchildren, they lose a chance to present insights that could improve family decisions; they forfeit a chance to be seen as helpful, and share the benefit of their experience. No one gains from our experience unless it is made known, until it is expressed. Experience has to be shared to continue its value for subsequent generations (Levine, 2004).

Grandparents should realize that disagreements are looked upon differently today, and older adults should assert themselves in the same manner expected of other age groups. Younger relatives should encourage grandparents to offer them advice that will then be subject to their individual examination and decision making. Even teenagers give parents advice. In the best relationships advice giving is reciprocal, not unilateral. Each person can accept or reject the advice of others. However, when people do not share their views, their impressions about the best course of action remain unknown.

The chance to observe grandparents in disagreement can show grandchildren that older relatives are willing to expose their thinking to the same scrutiny as others do. Grandparents who decide against offering advice that family members can critically examine deprive themselves of a benefit the rest of us enjoy—external monitoring of our thinking processes that is important for continued mental viability. Being retired usually means getting less critical feedback about thinking than occurred during employment. For example, Scott, Julia's 14-year old grandson, was walking with her in the mall when Julia spotted a "punker." She said, "Look at that guy, the one with green hair, crazy clothes, and blank stare. He's really strange." Scott, a high school freshman, replied, "Grandma, don't be so quick to judge. Maybe he just wants attention. He might be just as nice inside as anyone else."

Ask for and Accept Advice

Another important new tradition is to seek help as well as provide it (P. Strom & Strom, 2011c). Unfortunately, asking younger relatives for advice is uncommon among grandparents. This is because many are embarrassed to acknowledge ignorance when making decisions, even though they urge daughters, sons, and grandchildren to ask them for advice. For example, this question is presented in grandparent classes: How do you suppose grandchildren and children could help you deal with your worries? Emma replied, "My grandchildren tell me about troubles of their brothers and sisters so I recognize when they need me." Eleanor thought the family could help her most by behaving properly. In this way, she would not have to worry as much about them. Sam admitted, "It is hard for me to see how my grandchildren could help with my worries since they don't have my experience." Not one of these older adults recognized the potential of relatives to help by listening to worries.

Telling someone about worries means acquainting them with our doubts and concerns, making known uncertainty, confusion, and indecision. This is particularly difficult for older adults who suppose that seeking advice reflects an admission of weakness, a sign that they lack independence. This old fashioned view should be abandoned. No one should mistake isolation for independence. People who are independent do take care of themselves but also call on others for advice so they handle their affairs wisely. This is similar to getting a second opinion in matters of health (Raeff, 2005).

Grandparents who fail to ask for advice convey an impression that they can do without the resources younger people welcome and rely on. For the grandchildren this behavior confirms that a grandparent is out of date. Telling confidential problems to a listener can help organize thinking. Then too, the observations that advisors share can often increase options and enhance reasoning used for making decisions. Recognize too that, when the worries of a grandparent are unknown to the family, grandchildren do not know when to offer consolation. Boys and girls should learn to show compassion for family members so they can respond the same way to needs of outsiders later on. Grandparents deny grandchildren this opportunity for growth when they fail to let them know about their emotional need for comfort and assurance.

Prayer and Guidance

Everyone can benefit from prayer and, because older adults typically are more religious, they pray more often than younger people. Some grandparents respond to worrisome situations by choosing to pray about them. These prayers should include requests for better communication skills, greater trust in people who love us and want to help, ability to see more possibilities and determine those that are worthwhile, and willingness to consider changes within ourselves that may be needed. Guidance can be gained from conversations with relatives and friends, followed by reflective thinking and prayer to weigh the merits of their advice. God is reported to work in mysterious ways but, as the author of logic, He works in practical ways too. Solutions often require change in the actions of more than one person, including the individual who prays for others to improve their behavior.

Some grandparents are critical of younger relatives because they less often rely upon prayer to resolve difficulties. This difference can attribute in part to the greater maturity of grandparents, and their willingness to be governed by faith. In contrast, young people may be more inclined to use the talents that God has given them, to think of themselves as being capable of influencing the outcomes for most of their problems. They may pray but also consult with an expert and ask friends in their social network to provide suggestions. God wants people to seek direction through prayer, but He is also the source of talents acquired by others who can offer suggestions or acquaint us with the availability of resources that can contribute to solutions.

Present Advice Carefully

The way advice is given matters as much as the message. Participants in a grandparent class were discussing in-law relationships. In-laws include sons-in-law, daughters-in-law, and their parents. It was generally agreed in-law relationships should not be confined to visiting at weddings, funerals, and graduations. Both sides of the family share a desire to support a healthy and happy relationship for their children rather than present the couple with frustration and disappointment over who gives the most gifts, who demands priority for holiday visits, and who is identified as interfering the most. In-laws should make an effort to communicate with each other on a regular basis. Consider the insights of two women.

> Just before the coffee break, Sally, who recently returned from a two-year civilian work assignment on an air force base in Japan, described problems that younger women there associate with their dominating mothers-in-law. She pointed out that the mother-son bond superseded the husband and wife relationship, and this often causes bitterness, conflict, and jealousy between the older and younger women.
> After coffee, Maria, a Mexican-American grandmother said, "I want to share a personal experience in trying to deal with potential jealousy of two women who could compete for the attention, affection, and time of someone they both love. I am a widow and have one son named Eddie. Shortly after he got married, Eddie and his wife Salina came to visit for dinner. He

had just washed his hair so it was shiny and nice. I ran my fingers through his hair as I had so often done while he was growing up. Then, when I went into the kitchen, I overheard Salina comment, "When are you ever going to cut loose from mother's apron strings?" I did not say anything. Instead, I waited until they had enjoyed their meal. At that time, I spoke, "Salina, I heard what you told Eddie. Let me ask—Do you love your mother?" "Of course," Salina said. "Well, there are two great loves in the life of most men——the love they have for their wife and their love for a mother. They are very different kinds of love. I hope Eddie's love for both of us doesn't cause jealousy between you and I." Salina started to cry and said, "I'm sorry, Mom—I love you." Salina and I get along very well, and we are willing to offer each other advice, knowing that both of us want to be successful in our complimentary roles.

Maria's story drew applause from the class. Another grandmother, Marilyn, wanted to say something about one of her in-laws. There may be times when people have to go beyond giving advice and actually implement it for the sake of a loved one who cannot evaluate the benefit it can give them. One of the greatest problems I experienced was wondering how to help my mother-in-law who seemed to be slowly killing herself with alcohol. She would not admit to a problem and her son, my husband, denied it by saying that Mom is not that bad and she doesn't hurt anyone. Yet, one time when she was babysitting for our 2-year old son Luke, she passed out at the mall and we had to pick up Luke at the police station. I decided to take control of the situation. My father, a psychologist, scheduled an appointment for my mother in law with a physician that specializes in alcohol abuse. On the day of the appointment, we were unsure how to handle expected resistance. As it turned out we had to abduct her to the clinic where she received a complete examination and counseling. This appointment convinced my mother-in-law that she needed help. She has been sober for several years, goes to Alcoholics Anonymous meetings, and supports our family including valuable advice for me.

Some grandparents exemplify patience, a wonderful asset to promote self-restraint and harmony. Grandparents can also share advice on setting goals that go beyond doing well in school and at work. A broader perspective of life can enable mental health, family cohesion, and maturity. Children need a healthy definition of success that will evolve and help sustain further development. Having this orientation that illustrates what it takes to be successful in a longevity society can cause parents and grandchildren to view grandparents as a valued source of guidance.

SUMMARY AND IMPLICATIONS

The grandparent role presents some people with an unexpected loss of purpose, sense of direction, and need for guidance to understand their place in the family. The possibility of being viewed as informed family advisors increases by being aware of current challenges, concerns, and joys associated with bringing up children. Attending family development classes, reading self-help books directed to parents, joining discussion groups, and volunteering in schools can improve understanding about growing up today. These sources provide general knowledge.

In addition, each grandparent should have conversations with their adult children to determine particular goals they want to achieve in raising daughters and sons. The challenge to stay in touch with grandchildren is essential because these interactions are the context for discovery of child goals, satisfactions, and worries. The grandparent-grandchild bond is closer when reciprocal learning is a goal because it will motivate adults to listen carefully and show a willingness to self-disclose so younger relatives get to know them better.

Giving and seeking family advice is more effective when certain conditions are met. A basic requirement for grandparents is willingness to replace traditional attitudes and habits that no longer govern family interaction. It is not surprising to find that well-informed people are the ones that parents consider as their best sources of advice. An implication for grandparents is to gain awareness about the challenges of younger relatives and try to use this knowledge as a basis for providing relevant advice. Another shift is to realize that, although children in the past were marginal participants in family conversation, their current involvement, including assertive comments, is necessary to discover feelings, ideas and concerns they have that might otherwise remain unknown.

Loved ones sometimes choose some other path than the one grandparents recommend. This motivates yet another change, accepting decisions of relatives as a product of deliberation instead of viewing their contrary choice as an insult. No one should desire or expect that others will always follow advice they offer. Grandparents should strive to be seen as consistently telling the truth instead of saying just what others want to hear. This behavior qualifies a person as someone who can be relied on to describe situations as they are perceived. Grandparents should solicit advice from the family and consider grandchildren to be essential sources of learning. Finally, arranging time with grandchildren and learning to use the communication tools they prefer shows adjustment and can support more frequent conversations.

APPLICATIONS FOR TEACHING

1. Grandparent success depends on having appropriate goals and getting feedback on how well these purposes are met. The way to

begin is having periodic conversations with the parent(s) of a grandchild to find out their expectations. This dialogue can be uneasy because most parents are not accustomed to identify, define, and explain their priorities. A good strategy is to tell them your intent is to reinforce their goals while interacting with grand-children. This allows grandparents to be a partner and minimize contradiction of the parents. Some mothers and fathers appreciate an invitation to clarify their plans, another group is defensive and declare such goals are obvious without being expressed, and still others may consider questions intrusive. Think about the relation-ship with adult children as a basis to guide how to approach them and make sure to invite feedback about your behavior.

2. Defining the grandparent role in cooperation with the family clari-fies expectations but parents cannot be responsible for building a grandparent-grandchild relationship. This bond requires spending time together and exchanging feelings and ideas by using the com-munication methods preferred by grandchildren. In addition to phone calls locally, long distance, or Skype, grandparents should stay in contact by e-mail, texting, instant messaging, iChat, social network, and other venues grandchildren use daily to interact with friends.

3. Family advice should be offered that has not been requested. When a grandparent becomes aware of a situation that could present danger or pose problems unforeseen by others, s/he should report it to parents. The possible benefits from this course of action should outweigh misgivings about whether someone initially views the advice as intrusive. Bear in mind that when people need help the most, they may be the least inclined to seek support.

4. Talking to grandchildren can be difficult because the process is dif-ferent from the way things were when, as children, today's grand-parents were taught to show deference to elders and not disagree with them. These memories associated with reminders about respect should be set aside and replaced with acceptance of grand-children as equal contributors to conversations. Allowing the young to express their views is the only way adults have to compre-hend what growing up is like now. As boys and girls share their feelings and thoughts, grandparents must do the same so that grandchildren can get to know them well.

5. Everyone should ask for help when they are unable to manage situ-ations. The education grandparents received in school and at home led them to believe that people who seek assistance may be seen as failures because this behavior reflects a lack of indepen-

dence, the key ingredient for self-esteem in the past. Today students are taught to value interdependence, being able to count on others in teams at work and family at home. Benefits that come from pursuing independence and interdependence should be included in education of older adults so they see why a dual emphasis can improve performance of individuals and productivity of groups.

CHAPTER 18

COGNITIVE HEALTH AND EDUCATION

Young adults may wonder about the quality of life they can expect in old age. Some of their assumptions could resemble those of Lemuel, the ship captain and surgeon whose adventures were described as *Gulliver's Travels* by Jonathan Swift (1726, 2008). When Gulliver was told about the immortal people, referred to as Struldbrugs, he wanted to meet them. His impression was that immortals would never experience the depression and anxiety felt by the rest of us regarding the prospect of our death. It must be wonderful to be around someone who has acquired enormous knowledge because of so many years of experience. Gulliver fantasized that, if it had been his good fortune to be born a Struldbrug, he would devote himself to the study of arts and sciences. In addition, he would take great pleasure from interaction with other immortals generating new ideas, creating wisdom, and making discoveries to make life better for everyone.

As Gulliver shared these ambitions with his friends, one of them who had been with the immortals interrupted to set the matter straight. The facts are when Stuldbrugs reach 80 years of age, they cease to exhibit any curiosity. Instead, they become narrow-minded and incapable of close relationships. Their prevailing passions are envy and desires they are no longer able to fulfill. They do not remember much except some irrelevant information that was learned hundreds of years ago in their youth. They forget the names of people, even their nearest relatives and friends. For

Learning Throughout Life: An Intergenerational Perspective, pp. 419–441
Copyright © 2012 by Information Age Publishing

the same reason, they are unable to amuse themselves by reading because their memory cannot carry them from the beginning of a sentence to the end. No wonder they are seen by others as an economic burden, people who do not benefit the rest of society.

Gulliver was hopeful that the negative description of Struldbrugs was untrue. However, a visit with some of them confirmed that the disappointing observations reported by his friend were accurate. This sobering experience led Gulliver to revise his thinking and conclude that his earlier wish to become immortal had vanished. Instead, he now understood that there are worse things than death, especially being alive without a sense of purpose, meaning, or opportunities to be viewed by others in a favorable way.

There are no Struldbrugs yet. However, if the life expectancy for developed nations continues to increase, more than half the children born since 2000 in the United States, Canada, Denmark, France, Germany, Italy, Japan, and the United Kingdom could celebrate their 100th birthday (Christensen, Doblhammer, Rau, & Vaupel, 2009). A longitudinal study of 2,972 identical twins concluded that longevity is only moderately heritable. The estimates are that about 25% of how long people live depends upon genetics while 75% relates to lifestyle (Herskind et al., 1996).

To improve common understanding about how to make wise choices in lifestyle, a collaborative investigation was carried out by the National Institute of Aging and National Geographic (Buettner, 2008). The team began its work by identifying locations throughout the world where people live the longest and have the healthiest habits. In these places men and women reach age 100 at rates that are significantly greater than elsewhere. Four confirmed zones include (1) Okinawa, Japan, (2) Sardinia, Italy, (3) Nicoya Penninsula, Costa Rica, and (4) Loma Linda, California. The food centenarians eat, company they keep, their daily activities, and outlook on life were documented. The examples these exceptional people provide can enable anyone willing to adopt some of their habits a chance for extending life by as much as a decade.

Modern nations are in the process of revising customs and economic systems created to meet the needs of past generations that had a shorter life span. The plan is to establish policies that will sustain greater longevity while also improving quality of life. The goals of this chapter are to examine cognitive potential in old age based on interdisciplinary studies, discuss the effects of mental dysfunction, examine methods of detection for Alzheimer's disease, and document the protective element offered by education and social networks for building cognitive reserve.

COGNITIVE POTENTIAL

Capacity for Learning

Before retirement became a norm during the 1980s, the mental ability of older adults was not regarded as an important topic for research. Prior to that time, most older adults were taken care of by relatives as part of an extended family. Individuals who did not have a family or who could not be cared for by them were placed as the last resort in "old people's homes." Consequently, the initial studies of cognitive aging centered mostly on convenience samples consisting of institutionalized elders. Because the reports documenting mental deficits of these residents became the primary sources of public information about aging, society was led to underestimate potential for learning in old age (Salthouse, 2010).

A more accurate impression has since emerged from longitudinal studies tracing changes within age groups over time. Warner Schaie (2005) monitored the mental abilities of 5,000 adults, tracking some over 50 years. The subjects recruited for his dissertation at the University of Washington, in 1956, were healthy volunteers between 20 to 80 years of age. Follow-up assessments at 7-year intervals detected how mental functioning changes, when detectable age decrements occur in cognitive abilities, and the extent of loss. Schaie found that, at every retest, a majority of subjects retained mental competence as they grew older. These findings eventually replaced a common incorrect assumption that intelligence peaks about age 17 and thereafter begins an inevitable decline for the rest of life (Nisbett, 2009).

Even when mental competence begins to diminish, training can sometimes slow or reverse decline. Because certain abilities erode earlier and appear less amenable to restoration, most interventions have centered on spatial orientation and inductive reasoning, abilities for which men and women respectively show the greatest loss after the age of 65. Mental performance of 200 men and women, aged 65 to 95, was tracked over 14 years. Half the participants recorded some loss while the others remained stable. The conclusion was that mental skills can atrophy through disuse but stimulation can remove deficits. After just five hours of training, 40% of the subjects were able to equal or exceed their earlier scores on problem solving and visualization skills. Bingo does not improve cognitive ability because it does not require mental stimulation; however, vocabulary-oriented games like crossword puzzles can have a beneficial effect (Schaie, 2005).

Paul Baltes (2006), a developmental psychologist in Germany, reported mental benefits following brief training provided for specific tasks. He determined that gains equal to amount of decline observed from ages 60-80 in longitudinal tracking. Consistent evidence caused Baltes to assert that age-related losses of particular aspects of intelligence can be offset by compensation efforts to improve the performance of other abilities that have become subject to measurement during recent years such as social interaction, mature thought, and wisdom.

Readiness to Change

An important requirement for adjustment is a readiness to change. There are four conflicting hypotheses about this capacity in older adults (Visser & Krosnick, 1998). One assumption suggests that openness to new ideas is greatest during early adulthood and thereafter declines steadily for the remainder of life. This view suggests that elderly hold unyielding opinions, so they are stereotyped as stubborn and set in their ways. The explanation is that, with the passage of time, people acquire habits that provide a sense of stability but at the price of becoming more resistant to new ways of looking at things. Age-segregation can also enter an effect by restricting the social network so that elder communication is mostly with others whose similar experiences reinforce rather than challenge attitudes and beliefs.

A second set of assumptions maintain that readiness to change is highest in the late teenage years and early adulthood when, for the first time, people can participate in the political process, join the work force full time, or enlist in the military. The speculation is that attitudes about life adopted in this period tend to become fixed, causing a sharp decline in openness to change that remains in place from middle age onwards.

A third assumption accepts that susceptibility to attitude change is the highest in early adulthood and bottoms out during middle age but then rises again in later life. This U-shaped experience curve comes about because older adults are confronted with the need to redefine themselves, owing to retirement or the death of a spouse. These and related experiences diminish social support for long-standing attitudes and force older people to alter their perceptions about the world. A fourth assumption is that, because certain mental skills are known to decline, older adults become less able than they once were to present counter arguments to those who would persuade them to change their minds.

To determine relationship between age and susceptibility to change, researchers from Princeton and Ohio State University exposed 8,000 adults of differing age groups to the same set of change-inducing situations (Visser & Krosnick, 1998). During multiple experiments opinions of men and women were reviewed on topics such as gun control, death penalty, defense spending, abortion, environmental protection, and racial policies. For example, persons interviewed by phone were asked to express their views on using tax dollars to assist minority students and use of racial preferences in admission policies at universities. Immediately after expressing their answer, each respondent was given a counter attitudinal challenge to assess whether they were willing to change their mind. Those who favored preferential admissions to college for Black students were asked if they would still feel the same even if it meant a reduction in opportunities for qualified Whites. Those who expressed opposition to racial preference were asked if they would still feel the same if it meant hardly any Blacks would be able to attend the best schools.

The investigators found that readiness to change attitudes declined after early adulthood but rose again during later life. It seems that the role transitions experienced by many older adults present them with new demands and expectations leading to a resocialization. In addition, more than younger groups, elders find it difficult to generate counter arguments when presented with persuasive appeals, thereby increasing their susceptibility to attitude change. Society should welcome this more optimistic estimate of the potential of older adults to modify their thinking. Their perspective about changing times could also be enhanced by arranging opportunities to interact with young people, particularly adolescents whose homework could include more service situations that involve intergenerational interaction and reciprocal learning (R. Strom & Strom, 2011).

Brain Cell Stimulation

Physiological studies support optimism about learning potential in later life. Brain cells are stimulated by use and can grow at any age in response to mental enrichment. The evidence has been confirmed for every species that has been studied including primates. Discovery began in the 1960s at the University of California, Berkeley, where rats corresponding to the human age of 75 were given an enriched environment until they reached the equivalent human age of 90. For rodent lifestyle, an impoverished environment consists of a one square foot bare wire cage with a single occupant. An enriched environment is a one square yard cage where a dozen rats share toys like ladders, wheels, and mazes.

Results showed that elderly rats exposed to stimulating environment differed from impoverished rats in that their brains showed a thickening of the cortex, reflecting an increase in brain cell size and activity. In turn, the enriched rats proved better at learning how to successfully make their way through a maze (Diamond, 1985). One generation later, researchers using parallel and innovative techniques from the Salk Institute for Biological Studies found that adult mice provided enriched living conditions grew 60% more neurons and performed better on learning tasks than genetically identical control animals (Kempermann, Kuhn, & Gage, 1997).

Human anatomy studies also provide insight about cognitive health. The outer layer of the brain, cerebral cortex, has long been recognized as subjected to relentless deterioration. It has been shown there is loss of cells with age as well as degenerative change in the dendrites, the nerve branches that spread to send or receive messages from other cells. In the 1970s Paul Coleman at University of Rochester challenged prior research by finding that, in the absence of disease, dendrites in the cortex continue to grow into old age. Coleman's autopsy team compared brains of normal elderly ranging from 68 to 92 years of age, normal middle-age adults between 44 and 55, and people 70 to 81 that had died of Alzheimer's. While dendrites of some cells appeared to have shrunk, brains of normal elderly had longer and more extensive branches than brains from either of the other two groups. Dendrites in the Alzheimer victims had stopped growing or degenerated; the longer the history of the disease, the less extensive the branches. This is significant because dendrites that Coleman examined were in the cortex region that provides information to the *hippocampus*, the area of the brain crucial for memory and learning (Coleman & Buel, 1979).

Coleman's study was the first to find that there is a greater degree of growth than there is deterioration in the normal older adult brain. Coleman's findings represent only one aspect of a lifelong process but he speculated that the brain might be compensating for a loss of some cells over time. Perhaps, at some point, the cells that are dying begin to outnumber those surviving and growing, but Coleman was unable to find the age at which that may happen—and the oldest brain he examined was 92 years of age (Coleman & Buel, 1979).

Gage and Kempermann (2007) demonstrated the capacity of the brain to repair itself through neuronal regeneration in the hippocampus region where memories are formed. Generation of new cells suggests that a stimulating environment in later life could be a key mechanism to enable greater viability. The greater the brain activity, the higher the performance level stays and higher the ratio of synapses to neurons. Brains stay dense the more they are used. Therefore, the advice to "use it or lose it" has empirical support (Kempermann, 2011).

Memory Performance

Older adults often express concern about deterioration of memory. Declarative memory refers to content that can be consciously remembered such as facts, rules, principles, or paradigms. People communicate with one another using these common frames of reference. There are two categories of declarative memory, episodic and semantic. First, episodic memory relates to storage of autobiographical experiences including events, places, times, emotions, and contextual knowledge that can be explicitly stated. People can recall where they were on 9/11 and when they got their first bicycle. Episodic memory of events is implicated whenever someone forgets where they left their glasses, parked a car, or name of someone they just met.

Episodic memory functions well until about age 65 when there is a slight drop followed by a more pronounced loss after age 70. This decline appears to be triggered more by the lifestyle of retirement than by aging. For most people, retirement does not include as much mental stimulation, as often a need to monitor their thought processes so others will think well of them or as much critical feedback provided by coworkers about the accuracy of their comprehension and quality of judgment (Bosma, van Boxtel, Ponds, Houx, & Jolles, 2003).

In order to manage episodic memory loss, older people typically compensate by writing notes to themselves, identifying things they want to remember, and asking others to remind them of details they might fail to recall. Most memory research has dealt with episodic testing of how well people can retain letter patterns, objects, or word groupings to which they have just been exposed. As a result, it was long assumed that memory is destined to worsen in later life. Consider some investigations about episodic memory. A National Institute of Aging study focused on 79 men and women from 23 to 93 years of age (Kandel, 2006). They were asked to recall details of events that occurred over a 2-day visit at a research center. Everyone was retested the following week by telephone, and one-third were tested again 18 months later. Findings indicated that older adults had the poorest recollection of details. However, there were no significant differences among age groups in ability to recall data needed to take further action. There is much to be said for selective memory.

A long overlooked aspect of episodic memory that has been given more attention since the advent of the Internet is the importance of image memory containing visual information drawn from pictures, observations, photographs and media exposure. There is evidence that older adults are able to use nonverbal memory codes to support long-term retention as effectively as younger people. In one study of 160 adults, ages 51-97, the *pictorial superiority effect* of visual memory as an episodic phenomenon persisted into the ninth decade of life for healthy elders. It seems appropriate for researchers to incorporate visuals in assessment tools to better gauge cognitive function and methods that can counteract a decline in verbal recall (Cherry et al., 2008).

The second category of declarative recall involves semantic memory. These memories consist of the stored meanings, understandings, and the concept-based knowledge that is independent of personal relevance. Some good news is that semantic memory, the ability to recall aspects of the overall store of information and experience accumulated over a lifetime, often remains robust into old age. Memories of things that happened many years ago are for stories and emotional moments people have thought about and reviewed many times, keeping them vivid and accessible.

Researchers at Southern Methodist University (SMU) compared semantic memory of 48 men and women from 57 to 83 years of age with a similar size group of younger people 18 to 34 years old (Mitchell, 2009; Mitchell, Brown, & Murphy, 1990). The older group consisted of SMU alumni or spouses while those in the younger group were students taking psychology courses at the university. A vocabulary test of word meanings revealed significantly higher scores for the older group, leading researchers to conclude that semantic memory grows with age. James Birren from the UCLA Center on Aging shared this conclusion. His estimate was that the average college graduate has half the vocabulary (22,000 words) s/he will possess by age 65 (45,000 words) (Birren & Schaie, 2005).

Memory Manipulation

There are times when everyone feels that it would be beneficial to forget some things because remembering them brings disappointment, worry and undermines a sense of well-being. What if it were possible to erase certain memories so that a person could be spared from revisiting a traumatic loss, avoid recurrent regrets, and inhibit fears and addictions? What if it was possible to help Alzheimer's patients access their memories of events, people, and places so they could remain viable, maintain close relationships, and delay the onset of suffering from mental dysfunction?

All of us edit and revise the memories of stories that we tell others and ourselves after they are recovered from their storage in long-term memory. Imaging technology makes it possible to watch the brain fire as it searches for a memory and shows how a single event divides into components that are stored in separate regions of the brain and then reassembled with different elements added after the original experience.

Todd Sacktor is a professor of neurology at the State University of New York. He discovered a chemical that blocks functioning of a molecule that is essential for being able to retain memories (Shema, Sacktor, & Dudai, 2007). In the initial experiments rats learned to walk around a plate that, if stepped on, would provide them with a mild shock. However, when the rats were injected with the chemical, they walked back on the plate. Inhibiting some memories and perpetuating others are anticipated as being possible treatments in the future.

Sacktor's breakthrough discovery was related to earlier experience with his mentor Erik Kandel (2006). When Erik was 9 years old, his family fled from Vienna, Austria, to the United States because Adolph Hitler had seized power in Germany and established persecution of the Jews. While at Harvard University, Kandel sought to examined the history of intellectuals who supported the Nazis. He later studied psychiatry as a way of understanding processes of the mind.

At the time neuroscience did not exist, and biological connections had not been explored. Erik wanted to find out all he could about the biology of the mind. He started by focusing on a giant sea snail that had some cells, which could be seen by the naked eye in addition to 20,000 neurons, as compared to 100 billion neurons in the human brain. Scale matters. He determined that when a single neuron was stimulated, the snail would move its gill. Kandel's search for an understanding of human cruelty had brought him to respiration, the most basic function of all living creatures. His team observed that the snail learned responses to different types of stimuli and these could be tracked by changes in the spaces between nerve cells that would thereafter become known as synapses. For his pioneer efforts, Erik Kandel of Columbia University received the Nobel Prize for Medicine in 2000. The steps of Kandel's journey are presented in his books, *In Search of Memory* (2006), and *The Age of Insight* (2012).

One of the graduate assistants in Kandel's laboratory was Todd Sacktor who later found a way to make old memories stronger without interfering with them as they form or are recalled. When a memory is made, the brain builds new synapses, the communication channels between nerves. To retain a memory, that synapse must endure. Scientists have not known exactly how to strengthen synapses to keep memories stable over time. In 2007, Sacktor and colleagues erased long-term memories that rats had formed weeks earlier using a drug that inhibited an enzyme protein PKMζ (Shema, Sacktor, & Dudai, 2007). The hypothesis is that memories are maintained by constant presence of the PKMζ enzyme.

Sacktor and his international team alleviated the concerns of other neuroscientists about specificity of the blocking drug by using genetic tools in rats to disrupt PKMζ and also boost the enzyme in the neocortex of the brain, the presumed repository for long-term memory storage. One week after rats became ill from drinking sweet lithium-laced water, they were given injections that contained genetic elements that would either block or increase activity of PKMζ. Rats with abundant PKMζ in their neocortexes remembered that sweet water caused illness. They did not try the sweet water when it was served again a week following their injection. Meanwhile, the rats with reduced PKMζ actively drank. The same thing happened with salty, lithium-laced water given a week before treatment and again a week after. Sacktor's colleague Yadin Dudai, neuroscientist at the Weizmann Institute of Science in Israel, reports that PKMζ is persistently active for months after animals learn. Without it, memories of those lessons won't persist. The main challenge is to turn the enzyme on and off selectively so only targeted individual memories will be affected (Shema et al., 2011).

Some observers express concern about erasing memories, warning that nature may have arranged for a decline in memory capacity in order to prevent the hard disk of human beings from being overloaded. Perhaps the difficulties older adults experience in remembering is due to complexity of access to a growing store of information that accumulates with longevity. Restoring memories to victims of mental dysfunction could be detrimental unless it was also possible to impact a corresponding decline in judgment and related functions. Other critics warn that trying to manipulate memory improvement to produce people with superior intelligence might become a goal for families and society, thereby shifting from a proper emphasis on healthy social and emotional development. Still another group is enthused because they believe this line of research could reveal ways to diminish the memory deficits of Alzheimer victims that result in a loss of independence and relationships. Therefore, studies on manipulation of memory warrant encouragement and support (Shema et al., 2011).

COGNITIVE DYSFUNCTION

Alzheimer's Disease

The term *dementia* is used to describe a broad range of symptoms exhibited because of loss in cognitive skills like remembering, thinking and reasoning that are so severe an individual has difficulty performing daily activities. Sometimes dementia can be the result of neurodegenerative conditions like Parkinson's disease. A stroke in the memory or language part of the brain can produce cognitive impairment because of vascular disease. There are side effects from medication that can mimic dementia but these are treatable. However, the most prevalent cause of dementia is Alzheimer's disease (AD), an irreversible and progressive disorder resulting in death of brain cells. This incurable condition that tangles nerve endings of the brain and destroys normal thought processes is named for Alois Alzheimer, the Austrian-born neurologist who discovered it in 1907 (Hoffman, Froemke, & Galant, 2009).

The population of Americans suffering from Alzheimer's disease is 5.4 million. Estimates are that the number of victims will increase to 16 million by 2050. According to the Alzheimer's Association (2012), older adults in minority groups are at greater risk. Blacks are two times more likely and Hispanics 1.5 times as likely to develop AD than Whites even though minorities have a shorter lifespan. Elders from both minority groups are also less likely to be aware that they have AD. People of low income generally have less access to quality health care. There is a taboo in Hispanic households against placement of a loved one in an assisted living facility. This reflects a belief that the family is everything so keeping an elder home is viewed as essential no matter how difficult it might be to provide the necessary care.

AD is age-related. A longer life expectancy of women means females are two-thirds of AD victims. AD kills approximately 100,000 people annually, making it one of the leading causes of death for older adults (Alzheimer's Association, 2012). Those with AD live an average of 8 years after symptoms become noticeable to others but survival following diagnosis ranges from 4 to 20 years. In the course of this feared disease, human development processes are reversed illustrating how a disease mercilessly unravels a lifetime of neurological connections. The process begins as the connections that govern higher cognitive function steadily move backward along a development path until only the most basic and primal of emotions remain (Hoffman, Froemke, & Golant, 2009).

The primary symptoms include difficulty recalling recent events, not recognizing familiar people or places, trouble finding the words to express thoughts or name objects, problems planning and carrying out tasks such as doing calculations, balancing a checkbook, following a recipe, writing a letter, trouble exercising judgment such as knowing what to do in the event of an emergency, inability to control mood and behavior, demonstrating depression and agitation or aggression, and not maintaining personal care like grooming or bathing. Relatives readily detect a victim's memory loss, diminished comprehension, hesitancy in using speech, loss of words for expressing feelings, and inability to remember common objects. A related loss is the ability to organize information, often resulting in disorientation. AD patients are unable to screen out distractions. As a result, situations that are new or different tend to startle them (Alzheimers Association, 2012).

In the AD ward of long-term care facilities, patient shouting includes incessant calls for help. Sufferers report they are trying to find something but whatever they discover frightens them. Over time delusions emerge and there is a failure to recognize loved ones. If a person does not die of another illness like pneumonia, complete helplessness occurs. Brain scan studies have shown damage of AD is not confined to structures involving memory but impact emotion and self-control too. Over half of Alzheimer's victims exhibit agitated behaviors like aggression, shouting, verbal abuse, hyperactivity, and irritability. Disruptive behavior such as physical violence or wandering involves 70% of patients (Daviglus, Bell, & Berretti, 2010).

Although antipsychotic drugs seem the most effective medication for agitation, there is concern these drugs are overused in long-term care. Daniel Levinson (2011), United States Inspector General of the Department of Health and Human Services, reported that over 300,000 elderly nursing home residents that had no diagnosis of psychosis were still prescribed antipsychotic drugs that can cause deaths and cost Medicare billions of dollars a year. These patients include 40% of residents exhibiting cognitive impairment or behavior problems. The problem also represents a daunting challenge to families that provide care. They must suffer the grief of losing someone twice, first when the patient dies mentally and again at the time of physical death.

The Wandering Dilemma

Victims of AD have a hard time remaining still, a condition that makes caring for them more difficult. Healthy adults are able to devote attention to a television program, read a book, or interact socially with another person. This is not the case for someone who has lost the ability to understand the meanings of words and images. They view stillness as a type of prison. Consequently, they share a common inclination to wander. This concerns families because a victim's desire to walk outside could mean getting hit in the road by a car or getting lost while out in the neighborhood. Recently global position system devices have been devised that track AD individuals who are permitted to walk alone, making their whereabouts known and ensuring they do not go beyond the boundaries established by caregivers (Hoffman, Froemke, & Golant, 2009).

Additional restrictions are necessary in assisted living facilities where AD victims tend to wander up and down the hallways in an obsessive quest to escape from deprivation. This problem implicates mentally alert residents when a person with AD enters their room without permission and begins to rummage through their dresser drawers, closets, or cabinets, looking for something that they cannot identify or locate. The anxiety and fear these intruders trigger in mentally stable but frail patients are a growing concern.

Half of the 3 million residents in nursing homes suffer from AD or other forms of dementia related to vascular disease. Most facilities were designed to assist physically impaired but mentally healthy patients instead of patients who are mentally impaired but physically healthy. For a long time managing this situation depended on restraining AD victims by tying them down, strapping them to a bed or wheelchair or using chemical restraints to prevent wandering, falling down, bothering or frightening others or leaving the facility that would require staff supervision. These methods were considered inhumane and increased the cost of care since residents who lack exercise have greater health problems than those permitted to walk. Nursing care costs are expected to double in the next two decades, largely because of the rising population of elders with AD (Alzheimer's Association, 2012).

Risk Factor Prediction

Unlike heart disease for which risk factors are well know, it has been difficult to predict Alzheimer's. Initially, most of the research was focused on genetic precursors to detect biological factors such as family history. People that have one or more parents who were afflicted are three times as likely to develop Alzheimer's than those without a family history. About 5% of all AD cases are of the inherited type and characterized by an early onset of the disease, before age 60. However, biological markers do not completely explain the incidence of dementia. Indeed, psychosocial risks are implicated in 95% of late onset cases, after age 60. This form impacting the fastest growing age segment emerges from defects in the individual during a life history, starting anytime after conception and is not passed on to offspring (Salthouse, 2010).

Alzheimer's and other dementias are the main reason for placement of older adults in long-term care centers. More individuals suffer from AD than in the past because they are living long enough to be stricken. The incidence of AD is less than 1% for 40-year-olds, 6% among 65-year-olds, 40% at age 80, and 50% by 85. For people still alive in their late 80s, however, the incidence of dementia actually declines. This unexpected finding implicates what is referred to as critical age. The most dangerous decade for threats to health is 70 to 79 years of age. After this age threshold, health relatively stabilizes. Rates of dementia decline for people in their late 80s, and by age 95 the prevalence is 30%, less than half the rate among 80-year-olds. Investigations of centenarians, people 100 years of age or older, are being conducted throughout the world to determine how they were able to avoid AD compared to younger groups. It is important to realize that dementias are diseases; they are not aspects of normal aging. Therefore, fears about getting AD are usually unwarranted (Alzheimer's Association, 2012).

Detection of Dementia

Marilyn Albert at Johns Hopkins University found that AD patients demonstrate impairment when they encounter new learning situations.

The speed in which new information is lost to episodic memory is evident after showing them several objects to remember and then involving them in a brief conversation before asking what objects were presented earlier (e.g., a ball, an orange and a pencil). Persons with AD show an increased rate of forgetting, losing very early what was learned. This limit differentiates them significantly from normal peers whose primary problem is usually a slower rate of learning with more time needed to gain new information. However, once information is grasped, normal elderly demonstrate understanding as well as younger people (Albert, Blacker, Moss, Tanzi, & McArdle, 2007).

Most experts believe Alzheimer's may originate 10 years or more before symptoms are detectable, and, by then, effective intervention may be less possible. Therefore, being able to identify beginning stages of the disease could make it feasible to monitor individuals, determine how long before symptoms emerge, study the effects of drugs intended to slow or halt progression, and assess efficacy of mental stimulation programs to delay the onset of dementia. Doctors have relied on brain imaging and psychiatric tests. Blood tests are increasingly used for diagnosis. These procedures have a high degree of accuracy, exceeding 96%, in identifying AD before symptoms like memory loss appear (De Meyer et al., 2010).

COGNITIVE PROTECTION

Effects of Education

Formal education provides protection from Alzheimer's disease. This conclusion has been a consistent finding in independent studies conducted for more than a generation in Australia, China, Finland, France, Israel, Italy, Sweden, and the United States. Robert Katzman (1993) at the University of California in San Diego directed an international team that examined 5,500 residents from Shanghai, China. The subjects were 55 to 75 years of age. Prevalence of Alzheimer's disease was 5% in the overall sample. However, other factors being equal, persons lacking any formal education had twice the risk of being demented as those who had completed elementary or middle school. After comparing effects of education and age, researchers speculated that dementia might be delayed by as much as 7 to 10 years because of protective effects given by formal education (Barnes & Yaffee, 2011).

Tia Ngandu at the University of Kuopio in Finland led a longitudinal study of 1,400 participants over 21 years, from their middle age into later life. Participants were divided in three levels: those having five or less years of education, (low), 6 to 8 years (medium) and 9 or more years of schooling (high), equivalent to elementary, middle school and high school. Findings indicated that, compared to people having a low educational level, those with a medium level had 40% lower risk of developing dementia and those with a high education level had 80% lower risk (Ngandu et al., 2007).

British researchers investigated 870 brain donors, 56% of whom were found to be demented at autopsy. The subjects varied in length of formal education, from 4 years to 11 years. Greater number of school years was associated with decreased risk of dementia and greater brain weight, but unrelated to neurodegenerative or vascular pathologies. The correlations between neuropathological variables and clinical dementia differed as a function of the dose of education, with more formal schooling associated with diminished dementia risk independent of severity of pathology. More education seemed to mitigate impact of pathology on the expression of dementia before death (Brayne et al., 2010).

The National Institute of Health published an independent state-of-the-science report that included a comprehensive systematic review of the evidence related to risk factors for AD and cognitive decline. Several modifiable factors were identified as being associated with increased risk of cognitive decline or AD or both (Daviglus, Bell, & Berrettini, 2010). Another review centered on the literature related to each of these risk factors. One factor, cognitive inactivity or low educational attainment, implicated twice the risk for being demented. Data from 146 countries suggest 15% of people worldwide have not received any formal schooling. An additional 25% have only attained primary school, giving a total of 40% with low educational attainment. The estimates are that 19% (6.5 million) of the AD cases worldwide are potentially attributable to low education (Barnes & Yaffee, 2011).

Language and Work

The National Institute of Aging has supported a long-term project at the University of Kentucky called the Nuns study. Those participating have included 4,000 Sisters of Notre Dame. Each subject agreed to participate in annual assessments of her cognitive and physical function, physical examinations, have blood drawn, and allow full access to medical records. Each participant also consented to donate her brain at the time of death for neuropathological study (Snowdon, 2002).

One nun investigation sought to determine whether linguistic ability in adolescence is a predictor of mental impairment during later life. Cognitive functioning was assessed in 93 nuns, from 75 to 95 years of age. Each person underwent seven neuropsychological tests for dementia. Results were then compared with their autobiographies that were written 58 years earlier when the nuns took vows at around age 22. This was one way to gauge vocabulary, complex thinking, and intelligence. It was determined that low idea density and low grammatical complexity were associated with low cognitive scores in later life.

Among 14 nuns who died, pathology confirmed that Alzheimer's was present in all of them with low idea density in early life and none with high density. Nuns in the lowest third of intelligence group had a rate of AD 10 to 15 times greater than college educated sisters who were teachers most of their lives. The researchers suspect this outcome has more to do with cognitive ability in early life than lifestyle because nuns had the same reproductive and marital histories, did not drink or smoke, had similar social activities, occupations, and income, ate the same food, lived in the same housing, and had the same medical care from early adulthood (Snowdon et al., 1996).

Most nuns do not retire although the scale of activities moderates as they grow older. Collectively, they have about the same rate of Alzheimer's disease as the general population. Nevertheless, for them the good news is that onset of the disease occurs later, and symptoms are less severe. Their active lifestyle does not prevent them from getting Alzheimer's but may help postpone it. David Snowdon (2002), who directs the Nuns project speculates that if onset of Alzheimer's could be delayed by 5 years, the number of people who have it could be reduced by half almost immediately since it develops at such a late age that half of those afflicted would have died before the disease caused mental impairment for them.

The Religious Order Study at Rush Medical Center in Chicago has also detected an association between high level of cognitive activity and reduced risk of AD. Older nuns, priests, and religious brothers were asked to describe amount of time they devoted to seven information processing activities including conversations, reading a book, listening to the radio, watching television, reading newspapers, playing puzzles, and going to museums. After 4 years of follow-up the risk of developing AD was, on average, 47% lower for those who performed the activities most often than for those that did them least often. People in the bottom 10% for current activity level were three times as likely to develop Alzheimer's as those in the top 10% of involvement with activities (Bennett, Schneider, Tang, Arnold, & Wilson, 2006).

Few studies have explored the reasons why lack of formal education is closely related to accelerated cognitive decline in middle and old age. Mental stimulation and the education process are usually hypothesized as mechanisms. Conditions of employment such as mental workload might be another mechanism. The Maastricht University Brain and Behavior Institute in the Netherlands conducted a 3-year study with 700 workers. It was found that persons with the least education recorded greater decline in information processing speed, memory, and general cognitive functioning as compared to persons with higher levels of education (Bosma, van Boxtel, Ponds, Houx, & Jolles, 2003).

The low prevalence of mental stimuli and challenges at work among poorly educated subjects explained about 42% of this association. This indicates that it may be helpful to look beyond the mechanisms operating in childhood for prediction of cognitive change occurring in later life. Factors in adulthood, after the highest level of education has been attained, warrant attention as well because these are more modifiable. The contribution was similar across measures of cognitive functions. Some questions presented were: Is your job mentally demanding? Do you have to concentrate to do your tasks? Does your work require great precision? Do you regularly have to work under stress? A substantial part of the association between low education level and accelerated cognitive decline appears to be mediated by few mental demands at work among poorly educated participants. This suggests that the gap in risk of age-related cognitive decline between poorly and highly educated might be substantially narrowed by increasing work-related mental stimuli and challenges (Bosma et al., 2003).

Social Engagement

Besides education, other environmental factors also correlate with a lower incidence of Alzheimer's disease. The most prominent factor is social engagement and relationships. Researchers at the Stockholm Gerontology Research Center in Sweden interviewed 1,200 nondemented elders, age 75 or older, in a community-based study. The participants were grouped according to whether they lived alone, if they had friends with whom they interacted, and whether they had an unsatisfying relationship with their children. Subjects were monitored over three years. By the end of that time 176 subjects had developed dementia and 300 others had died. Those disadvantaged in all three dimensions (they lived alone, lacked friends, and had unsatisfying relationships with family) were categorized as having a poor social network; those with two factors were considered to have a limited social network (Fratiglioni, Wang, Ericcson, Maytan, & Winblad, 2000).

In combination, the limited and poor social network groups had a 60% higher chance of developing dementia than those having just one negative aspect or an extensive social network. When the factors were examined independently, persons living alone were 50% more likely to develop dementia than those who were friendless. Separating effects of living alone from marital status is problematic but the data suggests that being single carries the highest risk. For example, no differences in risk exist between widowed and divorced persons living alone and widowed or divorced persons living with others. Further, patterns show that satisfaction from relationships with children, friends, and relatives is more important than the frequency of contact with them. A poor relationship with children doubled the chances of older adults becoming demented.

In a critique of the Stockholm study, Berkman (2000) from Harvard University expressed concern about the finding that risk for dementia is higher among elders having unsatisfactory contact with children than for those without children. Social relations may challenge people to maintain effective communication with persons they value and in this way promote cognitive organization. Thus, the power of interaction and the consequent fulfillment could be the way in which social networks serve to offset mental decline and onset of dementias. It appears that being alone is what is risky, not living alone. The risk of mental confusion rises with increase in social isolation. Diversity of relationships seems important because having only one strong bond, marriage or close contact with an adult child, may not be enough. Risks are lowest among those with strong relationships in several domains.

Availability of jobs often means young people must accept positions elsewhere than where they grew up or would prefer to live (Gray, 2009). The resulting dispersion of family populations makes elders more reliant on nontraditional support sources. Researchers at the University of Essex in England used longitudinal survey data from 1,900 subjects, drawn when they were nearly 50 years old and again after 60. The purpose was to determine how they perceived their social and emotional support system had changed over a period of 12 years. Relatively poor social support was found among elders who were childless or who were continuously without a partner. In contrast, those who had frequent contact with others and perceived their neighborhood as a positive social environment reported relatively rich support. Belonging to organizations had less effect on social support than informal social contacts. Among varied organizational activities, the only ones that had a positive association with perceived social support were contact with others by religious activities and sports clubs (Gray, 2009).

The National Institute of Aging Memory and Aging project, directed by David Bennett, discovered an association between higher levels of social engagement and better cognitive functions over time (Bennett et al., 2006). Bennett has approached brain activity by considering how people must develop their semantic memory, generalized knowledge that does not involve a specific event, each time they interact with someone they know. The brain is obliged to work hard to maintain an expansive social network.

If a woman meets someone she has not seen for years, she may be able to recall in an instant how she knows her, whether she was in the same class, appeared to be smart or considered attractive. This challenge stimulates the brain. Then, the old information is integrated with latest data for storage in the memory bank so she is able to recover it next time they meet.

People who have complex social networks, whether maintained on MySpace, Facebook, the workplace, at school or church are continually engaging with others in this way, necessitating an update of brain files. Perhaps, like education, social networking may stimulate the brain and add to cognitive reserve. This possibility accords with studies revealing that individuals with many friends and those who often participate in social activities have less cognitive decline and a decreased risk of dementia. Even though friends sometimes get on our nerves, it seems they also provide greater benefit than some of us realize.

The Center for Aging Studies at Flinders University in South Australia followed 1,500 older people for 10 years. Subjects with a large network of friends outlived those with fewest friends by 22%. Researchers speculated that good friends discourage unhealthy behaviors like smoking and heavy drinking. Their companionship may ward off depression, elevate self-esteem, provide emotional support, and help confront adverse events. As people age they become more selective in choosing friends and spend more time with them. In contrast, close relationship with adult children and other relatives had almost no effect on longevity. Family ties were seen as important but had little effect on survival (Giles, Glonek, Luszcz, & Andrews, 2005).

Cognitive Reserve

The mechanism by which the brain is able to learn, remember, and think is the synapse, a connection allowing one cell to communicate with others. Synapses are constantly changing as some strengthen because of learning while others weaken by disuse. Unused connections disappear while others emerge with the formation of new memories. The number of synapses can grow or decline by 25% or more, depending on amount of exposure a brain has to learning. The more experiences a person has the more connections that are formed between brain cells. A brain with more connections can afford to lose more to Alzheimer's disease before memory loss or other symptoms develop (Barnes & Yaffee, 2011).

Autopsy studies have determined this is precisely what happens. More highly educated people whose neocortex was riddled with enough plaque from damaged cells to qualify for a diagnosis of Alzheimer's nevertheless did not suffer memory loss. They had a larger number of neurons and greater brain weight than nondemented subjects in a control group of the same age without Alzheimer's. Conversely, people with less education but similar amount of brain plaque showed symptoms of Alzheimer's disease (Katzman, 1993; Scarmeas & Stern, 2004).

The term, cognitive reserve, is defined as the ability of an individual to tolerate progressive neuropathology damage without demonstrating clinical cognitive symptoms. In general, the more schooling someone has the less likely that person is to present symptoms. Speculation is that mental activity develops a surplus of brain tissue that compensate for tissues damaged by the disease. It is hypothesized that, for those with more formal education, greater brain reserve in the form of increased synaptic density in the neocortex might delay the onset of Alzheimer's disease by several years and thereby substantially reduce the prevalence of dementia.

David Bennett at Rush Medical Center in Chicago wondered why some 90-year-olds presented no evidence of memory loss yet they had considerable amyloid beta plaque at time of autopsy. He is interested in whether efficiency of the brain plays a role in allowing certain people to withstand significant damage. His team has examined family, income, and cognitive performance background of 2,300 individuals and retirement home residents including Catholic nuns, priests, and brothers from 40 different communities throughout the nation. All the participants have agreed to donate their brain to science when they die. Over 700 brains have been contributed. One-third found at autopsy to have AD plaque pathology showed no signs of cognitive decline. Cognitive reserve may prevent people from presenting clinical indicators of AD. A brain with reserve may have more paths and connections that can rewire themselves when challenged by disease (Bennett et al., 2006).

Studies suggest the more complex and resonant a brain can become through interaction, the better protected a person is against the ravages of Alzheimer's disease. Mental stimulation appears to provide a safety net so people have further to fall before the disease process begins to show itself. Persons advantaged by education while growing up are more protected in later life than those who grew up with less schooling. Disadvantaged populations in the first 2 decades of life are the same who will suffer more again in old age (Fratiglioni & Chengxuan, 2011).

Society must recognize the high stakes associated with motivating young people to stay in school and graduate. The purpose of education is to prepare for a job but, in a longevity society, this goal should expand to include building cognitive reserve needed later to help delay the onset of dementia. Consider a look at the future of students A and B. Student A quits school in Grade 9 while B graduates from high school and goes on to get a college degree. Sixty years later, students A and B have Alzheimer's pathology with plaques and tangles in the brain. However, student A is the only one to exhibit symptoms of AD. The explanation is that having a more stimulating life because of education, occupation, and leisure skills has reduced the risk of student B for exhibiting dementia. Generally, those with cognitive reserve are 40% less likely to manifest the disease. Pathology still occurs but a victim can better cope with the neurological damage. A person may not be diagnosed as AD because s/he does not present symptoms (Carper, 2012).

A review of brain reserve literature concluded that persons who remain mentally active throughout life reduce their risk of Alzheimer's disease. Data from 29,000 subjects across 22 studies from countries around the world examined the influence of education, occupational complexity, and mentally stimulating lifestyle. Neuroscientists Valenzuela and Sachdev (2006) at the University of New South Wales in Australia reported that the "Use it or lose it" recommendation was confirmed. Results showed that persons with high brain reserve had a 46% decreased risk of dementia compared to those with low brain reserve. Instead of assuming that brain reserve is a static property, determined by early life experiences such as education and income status, mental stimulation in later life is also associated with protective effects.

Valenzuela's (2009) research projects found that, after five weeks of memory-based mental exercises, brain chemistry markers increased in an opposite direction as observed in AD. The change was concentrated in the hippocampus, the brain region that is first affected by dementia. A related 5-year investigation of 488 subjects, age 75 to 85, determined that for the 101 people who developed dementia, the greater the number of stimulating activities they engaged in, the longer their rapid memory loss was delayed. The stimulating activities consisted of reading, writing, crossword puzzles, board or card games, group discussions, and playing music (Hall et al., 2009).

A similar type of investigation was conducted with 1,321 randomly selected elders from age 70 to 89. Some of the subjects, 197, had been diagnosed with mild cognitive impairment. Findings indicated that reading books, playing games, computer activity, and crafts such as pottery or quilting was associated with a 30 to 50% decrease in development of memory loss compared to people who did not participate in these activities (Geda, 2009, 2010).

People benefit from mental stimulation at every stage of life. The brain is less active at 80 years of age than at 30. However, findings from animal and human studies clearly show that it is possible to counteract adversity by building better brain structures until death. There is enough evidence to motivate field-testing of innovative education programs to offer learning as a mechanism for additional protection against dementia (P. Strom & Strom, 2011c).

SUMMARY AND IMPLICATIONS

Science has corrected false assumptions about mental potential in later life. The view that older adults cannot learn has been abandoned because of evidence that training can restore atrophied skills or reduce rate of decline. Episodic memory fades but reliance on nonverbal memory codes can boost retention to match the level exhibited by younger adults. Semantic memory remains robust as illustrated by a larger size vocabulary of elders who have continued to learn, compared to vocabulary of younger adults. Experiments have found that providing elderly rats a stimulating environment increases brain size and greater activity. Similar interventions involving humans have determined that the greater the amount of brain activity, the higher the level of cognitive performance. Retired people do not have to keep working but should continue to learn.

Brain dysfunction caused by Alzheimer's disease increases with age, a fact that is more troubling in view of forecasts for greater longevity. Formal education provides protection from dementia by building cognitive reserve that enables people to remain capable even when significant indicators of pathology are present. Mental stimulation in old age can also contribute to brain reserve, offering further resistance to devastating effects of dementia. Having a rich social network and a regimen of physical exercise are other protective mechanisms that can contribute to brain health and lifestyle.

APPLICATIONS FOR TEACHING

1. Education programs should reflect the cognitive reserve theory that brains with more connections can afford to lose more to Alzheimer's disease before evidence of memory loss and related symptoms emerge. The compensation principle can be communicated to elders and motivate their participation in programs for mental stimulation.

2. Albert Einstein observed, "Wisdom is not a product of schooling but a life long attempt to acquire it." The desire of retirees to continue being learners must become common, used to motivate the design of innovative programs for them, implicate indigenous leadership, and reflect a practical curriculum that supports personal development.

3. Modern nations seek to establish policies that can sustain longevity while improving quality of life. This goal should include creative initiatives to build education programs that appeal to elders, help

improve their ability to adapt, and retain a sense of purpose, meaning, and satisfaction.

4. Maintenance of cognitive health should be motivated by younger relatives, organized groups of elders, and local community. This expectation should replace the current view that retirement is a stage of life without obligation. The older adult cohort should become more active in influencing its members to view retirement as a time to protect mental viability and maximize social interaction.

.

CHAPTER 19

LONGEVITY AND IDENTITY CHANGE

Archeological records suggest that ancient mankind had an average lifespan of about 20 years, with very few people surviving to age 50. In contrast, the residents of wealthy nations now, on average, can expect to live 80 years and perhaps become as old as 100 if they were born since the millennium (Christensen, Doblhammer, Rau, & Vaupel, 2009). The rate of population increase among older Americans is greater than other cohorts. This longevity revolution presents a new set of challenges for policy makers, health care providers, employers, schools, religious institutions, families, and individuals.

The goals for this chapter are to (1) explore how role reciprocity can create a renewed sense of purpose and meaning that is often diminished in retirement, and (2) consider ways older adults can help students manage mental, emotional, and social challenges. Additional discussion involves (3) stages of grief experienced by persons who suffer the loss of a loved one, (4) changes in identity that follow death of a spouse, (5) the path that can lead to recovery and adjustment, and (6) ways to provide emotional support for people who struggle with sorrow.

Learning Throughout Life: An Intergenerational Perspective, pp. 443–464
Copyright © 2012 by Information Age Publishing
All rights of reproduction in any form reserved.

ROLE RECIPROCITY IN RETIREMENT

The sense of identity changes as people leave employment and retire. Whether older adults live with their spouse, alone or in an extended family, what matters most is how they evaluate themselves and the consequent importance they attach to their lives. Two factors usually combine to reduce self-esteem and the feeling of having a purpose. One is anticipation of becoming a burden to the family; the other is retreat from a sense of obligation. In the first instance, becoming a burden means involuntary assignment to a social status that lacks *role reciprocity*, having something to offer others in return for care provided by them. When because of age someone is defined as having nothing of value to trade, then any claim that person makes on others is evidence of dependency and likely to motivate feelings of guilt.

Some cultures expect older adults to contribute to their community. Whether the elders are perceived as having something of value for exchange is largely a matter of cultural definition. In primitive cultures, elder status depends upon serving the younger members in exchange for subsistence and protection. Unless older adults are disabled, they are supposed to take responsibility for particular tasks and, as a result, by cultural definition, have something of value to trade. It is essential that all generations agree this is an important and mutually beneficial arrangement for the society (Robine, Crimmins, Horiuchi, & Zeng, 2007).

The concept of role reciprocity has been successful in nonindustrialized settings. However, can technological societies establish expectations that incorporate talents of older adults? The answer depends on how deeply committed the public is to a youth-oriented way of life. If people are frightened by the prospect of old age, banishing the old may seem to be a good idea. Conversely, if old people are not heard or taken seriously, more of them will choose to live together in peer-segregated communities. If aging is seen as just another social problem, the public may welcome migration to retirement villages. Further, if society believes the young can avoid spending time with the old but still understand the past, appreciate the benefits maturity brings, and prepare for their own aging, then older adults can be said to have nothing of value to offer. In a youth-oriented society, the old may be seen as superfluous and expected to stay out of sight.

On the other hand, if Americans are willing to consider human development in the same way as some other cultures, life will be seen as concluding with a final sense of integrity, wisdom, and mature philosophy that should be shared. When life is viewed in this way, as a whole, rather than worthwhile only through the years of employment, it becomes possible to shift away from a youth-oriented society to a humanistic one where people are valued for themselves instead of having a premium placed on their age. At the same time, younger generations correct their evaluation of elders, many older adults should alter their self-impression. In particular, they should recognize that retirement does not signal the end of their responsibility to society.

Maintain Self-Esteem

During early adulthood (ages 20-40) and in middle age (40-60 years old), having a job is a major influence on self-esteem. It is generally assumed that the freedom to spend time as one pleases during retirement will replace a job as the key to favorable self-impression. Many people look forward to the day when they will be able to quit working. Yet, surveys of older adults consistently show that the average 15 years of retirement is generally accompanied by loss in purpose that must be restored so life can continue to have meaning. Everyone benefits when retirees decide to share their talents. It all begins with volunteering—at hospitals, libraries, churches, long-term care centers, and schools.

Providing assistance to children can motivate a positive perspective and restore a zest for living. Teachers sometimes complain about having too many students and not enough help. The preferred solution is smaller classes. This goal is rarely met because of budget constraints. Another way to improve education is by recruiting volunteers to help in public school classes. The cooperative orientation that is necessary is evident when teachers are willing to increase the sources of insight students can rely on. This need is partially met by retirees who represent one of the few natural resources that is increasing. Older adults are currently 90% of the 3 million volunteers who work in classrooms (Bortz & Stickrod, 2010).

The motivation to help and willingness to devote time to students would seem to predict success. In addition, teachers and administrators have observed that particular attributes make some volunteers more effective. Those who demonstrate the behaviors valued at work, like dependability, punctuality, dedication, persistence, and adaptability, are recognized as most reliable. Some possess qualities such as flexibility, spontaneity, patience, curiosity, and humor. Being a volunteer offers opportunities to develop these assets further. The importance of modeling desired personality attributes is illustrated by the following examples of flexibility and spontaneity.

Flexibility as an Asset

Although many older adults worry about memory loss, they tend to overlook the significant loss of cognitive flexibility. Inflexible individuals are easily detected at every stage in life but this pattern increases with age.

The inflexible are often described as people who are set in their ways. This means that they like things to remain the same, prefer predictable situations, and do not appreciate exposure to surprises. The main disadvantage of being inflexible is that it prevents growth that results from seeing people, events, and conditions in new ways. Amy and Gwen demonstrate inflexibility.

> Every week they come to the senior center for the session where people like to listen to music from the big band era. The two women have occupied the same front row seats since the program began 3 years ago. Recently, the center installed a new sound system. Amy and Gwen felt that the sound system was too loud but said nothing. Finally, they went to the director who listened to their concerns and replied, "Most people tell me the sound level is about right. An exception is the hard of hearing folks who always want the volume higher. I suggest that you move back a few rows and, if the music is still too loud, go to the adjoining room and enjoy the band from there." Amy and Gwen chose to ignore the advice and did not change their habit to solve the sound problem. They refused to move from the front row seats that they had come to regard as their own. Each week they sat there, imprisoned by their need for sameness, locked in a routine, stuck in a rut of their own making due to lack of flexibility.

Flexibility is an essential ingredient for adjustment. Being flexible means knowing how to integrate new and different experiences into the fabric of life without producing major disruption. Volunteers who can demonstrate flexibility are more likely to have a favorable influence on students. For example, Lois is willing to accept the ever-changing feelings, mood shifts and opinions of the sixth to eighth graders with whom she works. Students value Lois for making an effort to understand the way they see things and for considering their ideas as important. She also tries to help them look at situations from other views, including ones that they may not like at first, and encourages their careful consideration of optional ways to solve problems. Lois is just as willing to learn from the students as she is committed to supporting their development. Students at every grade level appreciate volunteers who consider new ideas and show flexibility in their thinking.

Value of Spontaneity

It is important for classroom volunteers to possess spontaneity. This is shown by the readiness to do some things without a lot of planning, being willing to depart from an agenda when it is appropriate and take advantage of unforeseen opportunities as they arise. Most people become less spontaneous as they get older. This appears to be the case with Grace. She lives in a retirement complex a few miles from her son Marshall and his family. Marshall works construction, which makes it difficult for him to know in advance when he will have free time. When Marshall does get a break from the job, he usually invites Grace for a family activity later on that same day or the next day. These impromptu invitations bother Grace, who is accustomed to living according to a strict schedule. She prefers a lifestyle that allows her to know what is going to happen next and permits plenty of time to make a shift from one activity to another without feeling stress. Consequently, Grace frequently tells Marshall that she cannot get ready with such short notice or is unable to join him because of previous plans to do something else like her laundry. If Grace postponed her laundry, she would still have enough clean clothes. Her unwillingness to ever act on the spur of the moment, to amend plans or accommodate someone else's schedule may carry a high cost. One outcome is that Grace forfeits opportunities to enjoy the only times the family can arrange to be with her. In a broader sense, giving up spontaneity may mean missing enjoyable interaction and the excitement that can be associated with doing some things that are unplanned.

Sometimes teachers deny students spontaneity by overscheduling them. The defense may be that there is a limited amount of time to cover so much material and therefore the class cannot wander from the topic or it will fall behind schedule. Another view is that that spontaneity creates more opportunities for learning. Student motivation increases as they learn to cope with uncertainty and balance living in the present with living for the future. When children cannot depart from what adults have planned for them, creative learning may seem off limits and result in complaints about boredom.

To illustrate, Evelyn is a retiree who volunteers in a fourth grade class. She has come to appreciate why lesson plans the teacher makes are tentative. Evelyn has observed that plans often must be revised in the process of a lesson depending upon how well children respond to the instructional tasks. This means both the teacher and Evelyn have to improvise, react spontaneously to student difficulties, and forego anticipated activities in favor of others that have to be given a higher priority. On the one hand, it seems obvious to Evelyn that fourth graders are more present-oriented than adults are so they need practice in setting goals, amending aspirations, and realizing their need to delay gratification. Evelyn also found that interaction with the students has increased her spontaneity. She believes they contribute to her self-improvement by their insistence on preparing for the future without sacrificing spontaneity.

Older adults bring many valued characteristics to the classroom which include: (a) patience as shown by a willingness to wait for correct responses of students and gauge progress in their growth, (b) good humor as a way to deal with setbacks, (c) curiosity about how others see things, (d) a sense of wonder about reasons for why certain events happen, (e) enthusiasm and optimism, (f) kindness and compassion, (g) attentive listening, (h) empathy toward student needs, (i) keen appreciation of individuality and cultural heritage, and (j) modeling effective communication skills.

The activities older people engage in affirms that what they believe is worth doing. If their schedule includes concern for others, they will be viewed in a favorable way. For example, a request was made for 700 retired persons to identity personal aspirations. Two profiles emerged. Those whose aspirations centered on self-preservation were closely associated with poor self-rated physical health, being burdened by difficulties, lack of purpose and meaning, dissatisfaction with life, and pessimistic expectations for the future. In contrast, participants who held aspirations of personal improvement and concern for the welfare of others were associated with feelings of well being in later life. These outcomes suggest that having mature goals support healthy longevity (Lapierre, Bouffard, & Bastin, 1997).

BECOME A SCHOOL VOLUNTEER

Identify Specific Tasks

Successful partnerships are based on mutual consideration. When the needs of both partners are considered, relationships are more productive and longer lasting. This general principle can be applied to intergenerational programs that link schools with the community. Educators should know how to maximize effectiveness of volunteers. The degree of influence volunteers have on students and degree of satisfaction that they experience depends on level of support given by the faculty. Recognizing the potential of volunteers and using their talents wisely supports the teacher-volunteer relationship.

Although most teachers like the idea of having volunteers in their classroom, they may be uncertain about what tasks can be expected of a volunteer. When expectations are poorly defined, volunteers sense anxiety and are more inclined to drop out. A better strategy is for the school principal to provide a volunteer assignment request form to each participating faculty member. The teacher completes the form to identify the tasks where volunteer help is needed. The list of possible tasks can include: (a) listening to students read, (b) giving corrective feedback about arithmetic problems, (c) review spelling words, (d) going over lessons that a child missed because of absence, or (e) practicing use of vocabulary. Tasks that require group support could include: (a) playground supervision, (b) before and after-school care, (c) flash card drill and practice, (d) leading topical discussions, and (e) giving encouragement to troubled children.

In a survey of inner-city teachers to identify priorities for volunteer support, it was determined that 60% sought assistance for encouraging troubled children. When asked why they made this request, many teachers stated their belief that there are many more troubled children than is generally known. The teachers saw patience in interacting with such students as a vital quality for volunteers. The typical view expressed by young and middle aged teachers was that retired persons in their classes possess patience to a greater degree than themselves. One teacher described her situation in this way:

> Some children in my room need more time than they get from adults. In most cases, parents are employed and teachers are busy. The result is that older adult volunteers are the only people to listen without rushing children or cutting them off with promises to resume a conversation later. I am grateful for volunteers who fulfill this need that parents and faculty seem unable to meet.

Clerical help by retirees allows teachers to carry out other important tasks. Volunteer assignments may include grading papers, preparing bulletin boards, copying materials, locating library resources, and recording attendance that is confirmed by the teacher. Older volunteers might also assume leadership for special activities, such as: (a) supervising arts and crafts projects, (b) monitoring computer tasks, (c) discussing hobbies, (d) reading or telling stories, and (e) giving language drills. Over the long run, these efforts can enhance student achievement.

Most students comprehend lessons and make good progress. Volunteers in this environment soon recognize age norms, observe the benefits of their assistance, and develop confidence in the helper role. In contrast, persons assigned to assist students with problems in learning usually feel unsure of themselves, fail to see progress, and may decide to give up. Unless volunteers receive special training, they should work with normal achievers and have faculty apply their skill with exceptional children.

Choose Interests and Assignments

An information form should be provided for volunteers to provide personal data needed at any work place. For example, it is necessary to know a person's place of residence, phone number, health status, and who to contact in event of an emergency. In addition, volunteers should be asked to indicate their preferences for the days and times they want to volunteer and where they would like to be assigned in grade level, or subject matter. They can place check marks beside tasks given on a list. Knowledge about hobbies, talents, and occupational experience can be used to make individualized matches between students and volunteers.

Every volunteer should have a range of optional assignments. This arrangement should allow for an easy exit without detailed explanation or embarrassment when some particular task is unacceptable to the volunteer. For example, someone might suppose that helping first-graders would be satisfying but conclude after spending time with them that this age is too demanding or they make too much noise. Another volunteer might believe initially that work with the upper grades would offer a mental challenge for them but then find out that students in this age are moody and outspoken. From the beginning, volunteers should have choices of the age groups they prefer to work with on a regular basis. It is unreasonable to expect binding decisions before they have direct experience with students. Getting involved with various tasks also helps volunteers feel comfortable knowing they do not have to continue with a teacher to whom they were first assigned.

Screening, Training and Schedule

Security screening of volunteers is essential. School districts vary in the kinds of personal information sought from volunteers. Data forms should include a place for disclosure of an arrest record by the police. There are federal and state laws to protect students from encountering convicted felons seeking access to schools as staff, faculty, or volunteers. This legislation requires that districts participate in a national data bank designed to track abusers. Volunteers should be informed of this practice and be told that similar investigations are routinely required for anyone getting teacher certification. Efforts to safeguard children do not always work well. Nevertheless, there should be a high standard of screening for everyone who interacts with students.

Teachers and staff should show volunteers how assigned tasks should be performed. Later, educators can observe the volunteer performance and provide constructive feedback. Periodic training should emphasize child development and difficulties that can arise in a classroom. This education shows volunteers how to be more helpful and contribute to understanding standard procedures at school. Specific topics for training may vary but any topic that is covered should include discussion of views and concerns of faculty, students, and volunteers.

The schedule of each volunteer should be flexible to allow variability of individual responsibilities. Men and women differ in their obligations outside of school. Some have relatives or friends who count on them for personal care or other types of support. They may also differ in health and energy level. Thus, some persons need a slower pace and prefer relatively short work periods. Compared with these individuals, others are more energetic and may be available to help for longer periods. Most retired people devote less than 1 hour a week to volunteer efforts but some of them will make further time commitments when they feel comfortable with the tasks. Being able to choose the time they arrive at school is important and faculty should respect this choice. The teachers, staff, board of education, students, and parents should assure every volunteer that the schedule they prefer is acceptable and appreciated.

Sometimes faculty members think that one way to show respect for volunteers is increase the level of their responsibility. For example, Nancy had done an excellent job shelving and checking out books. Because of this success, the school librarian decided to put Nancy in charge of four other volunteers. However, when Nancy was informed of her new role as a supervisor, she quit volunteering. This loss of a volunteer could have been prevented had the librarian talked to Nancy about her plans before implementing them. The assignment shift the librarian saw as a promotion was viewed by Nancy as a more stressful obligation. Many volunteers have said they would never complain about an assignment but would welcome some revision in what is expected if a teacher raised the possibility. Faculty members and the school coordinator should periodically check with each volunteer about their comfort level with the workload and type of assignment.

Performance Feedback and Recognition

Volunteer performance should be evaluated periodically. Men and women often assert that participation in this kind of activity enriches their lives. Because most are eager to perform well, they are disappointed when no feedback is forthcoming about their performance or how they could become more effective. The potential benefits of offering feedback to volunteers may include increasing their awareness of personal influence in the classroom and using data to identify specific attitudes and behaviors where there is a need for change.

The School Volunteer Report Card presented in Table 19.1 was developed to provide feedback to volunteers regarding their performance (R. Strom & Strom, 1995). Sixteen criteria are used to record observations of volunteer behaviors as perceived by students, teachers, and the older adults themselves. The students are assured that their names will not be provided in the feedback given to a volunteer. In order to fulfill this promise, volunteers get a summary profile combining the reports of multiple student observers. The simple form presents task specific items, eases recording observations, and covers a broad range of activities. Many educators who use this instrument express the belief that feedback to volunteers bolsters self-esteem, supports motivation, and contributes insights on personal improvement needs.

Most teachers receive compliments from parents for the instruction and guidance they provide students. These comments motivate the continued hard work and personal development of teachers. Volunteers can benefit in a similar way when their contributions are recognized. To illustrate, one of the authors was chairman of the board of directors for the

Table 19.1.   School Volunteer Report Card*

Name of Volunteer_____

Directions: Place a check beside statements that describe this volunteer.

1. ___ Encourages students to try again after they make mistakes

2. ___ Helps students to become self-confident in solving problems

3. ___ Speaks clearly and uses words that can be easily understood

4. ___ Shows willingness to learn about new things from the students

5. ___ Gives students honest feedback on how well they are doing

6. ___ Allows students enough time to think before giving answers

7. ___ Wants students to ask questions about what they're studying

8. ___ Likes to spend time with students that are at this grade level

9. ___ Tries to get along with students who are difficult to be around

10. ___ Protects students when they are mistreated by other people

11. ___ Allows the students to judge some of their own schoolwork

12. ___ Lets students know their ideas and opinions are important

13. ___ Cares about students and is viewed as being a good friend

14. ___ Admits ignorance about the things that s/he does not know

15. ___ Cooperates with teacher and other school staff members

16. ___ Keeps on trying to solve problems when they are difficult

You may have observed other things this volunteer does well or behaviors you do not like and wish could be improved. Write your ideas here.

*Adapted from *Adult Learning and Relationships,* by P. Strom & R. Strom, 2011, p. 202. Information Age Publishing Inc., Charlotte, NC.

Phoenix Retired Senior Volunteers Program. The customary method for recognition of volunteers was to meet with them every three months in churches or synagogues and provide pins and certificates for specified numbers of hours to 1,200 volunteers who were providing service in non-profit settings like hospitals, libraries, and schools. These recognition ceremonies were usually attended by the volunteers with occasional appearance of city officials. A decision was made to have the recognition shifted to public schools. The volunteer awards are given during ceremonies that also honor students and faculty accomplishments. By thanking older adult volunteers in a public forum, schools offer students a lesson about the merits of involvement with community service throughout life (Friedman & Martin, 2011).

DEATH AND STAGES OF GRIEVING

A predictable change in identity that often occurs in later life involves grief. Most people try to avoid thinking about their own death or loss of someone they love because emotions of sadness and helplessness are bound to arise. Death of a spouse typically takes place in old age. Annually 1 million women lose husbands and remain widows for another 14 years. There are 11 million widows and 3 million widowers in the United States. These people often report being misunderstood by family, friends, and coworkers (Seiden, Bilett, & Thornton, 2008).

Grief is the price each of us pays for caring deeply about someone. Everyone suffers feelings of loss at some time or another during life. People who cherish a pet eventually have to deal with losing their companion. Separation from a spouse or a parent because of divorce brings grief to greater numbers of people than ever before. When a son or daughter leaves home to go to school or begin a career, parents must cope with their absence. Some men and women grieve over loss of their career at the time of retirement. Most situations involving separation from someone we love force a change in our perspective so that we can regain mental health. However, death of a spouse presents the greatest adjustment and is considered the most devastating loss (Rock & Rock, 2006).

Elizabeth Kübler-Ross (1926-2004) was a psychiatrist and the medical director for Family Service and Mental Health Center of Chicago. She was also a cofounder of the Hospice movement. After she conducted interviews with hundreds of terminally ill patients, Kübler-Ross (1997) concluded that people who are dying and those left behind to grieve for them pass through five similar emotional stages. These stages of grief include denial, anger, bargaining, resignation, and acceptance. Individuals differ in the length of time that they remain in each stage, intensity of the feelings they experience, sequence in which stages are encountered, and how often some of the stages might be repeated. Nevertheless, there is agreement that stages to be described are an accurate portrayal of the grieving process and can provide insight for those wanting to provide support (Kübler-Ross & Kessler, 2007).

Denial

The first response of people who are grief-stricken is always shock. Their typical reaction is, "No, it just can't be true. I don't believe it." The benefit provided by shock is that it temporarily protects us from being overwhelmed with sorrow and having to face the truth all at once. It takes time for terrible news to be fully accepted. This means that denial is a healthy form of escape from reality provided that it lasts for only a few days. Friends are often misled by the behavior of a widow during proceedings of the funeral. What they see as an example of courage and presence of mind is actually the result of numbness, a buffer effect induced by denial. This natural defense helps people to get through obligations to the public before they can withdraw to deal with their grieving.

Initially, it is common for a widowed person to want to make frequent visits to the cemetery, to be near the body of the loved one. The survivor might stand beside the grave and make an effort to communicate, even though this is a one-way conversation. This evidence of denial is normal and shows that the grieving person is still unwilling to completely concede the separation. Relatives and friends should not discourage these gravesite visits, unless the practice becomes a compulsion and the widow feels it has to be incorporated in the daily routine.

Anger

Sorrow is sometimes accompanied by feelings of anger. The target for anger can be anyone, including the deceased. If the widowed person has been accustomed to suppressing anger, s/he can be stuck for a longer period of time in the denial stage. For example, Jane's husband recently died of lung cancer but she cannot bear to show anger toward him and rationalizes that his two-pack a day cigarette habit was not enough to cause the disease. In contrast, MaryAnn's husband also died from a lung disorder and she is furious with him for ignoring her pleas to give up smoking when he was aware of the possible consequences. Whether widows and/or widowers are religious or not, they often inform God that He is to blame for the injustice of taking their spouse when the world has so many bad people who should have been chosen instead.

Sometimes widowed persons express anger about their own behavior, supposing that, if they had done certain things, the deceased would still be alive. Anger can also implicate friends who have not bothered to come for a visit since the funeral, or relatives who tend to treat the bereaved person like a child. At times anger centers on what is perceived as an unreasonable effort by doctors to keep a terminally ill and suffering person alive. Grieving persons need someone who will help monitor their anger response and tell when it becomes excessive.

Bargaining

Death is the end of life, a condition that cannot be changed. Still, some widowed persons convince themselves that the loss they are suffering might have been prevented and punish themselves with comments like: "If only we had gone to the Mayo Clinic for the best diagnostic testing, she would still be alive," "If only he had taken early retirement when I wanted him to," "If only he would have stayed on the low cholesterol diet that his doctor recommended to him." Whether these precautions would have altered the course of events may never be known and no longer matter after someone dies.

Since God has not responded to angry pleas, it is supposed that He may consider a more kindly type of appeal. Therefore, widowed persons, or those whose spouse is terminally ill, may resort to promises of good behavior, public service, and compensation to the world if only the dying person is permitted to live a while longer. Such attempts to bargain for more time reveal that a grieving person is locked into thinking about the present and cannot deal with their future. The best thing that can be done by relatives and friends who hear the bereaved person pray for the impossible is to provide comfort, express affection, and pray themselves with an emphasis on thanksgiving for the life of the deceased as well as appeals for strength so the survivor can endure their loss.

Resignation

When people abandon their hope of being reunited with a loved one, they frequently experience depression. Feelings of depression are demonstrated by a lack of interest in the future. During such times, people report feeling that they are useless. Their outlook indicates that life no longer has a purpose and it will never again provide them with a sense of meaning. Fortunately, it is possible for most men and women to occasionally be distracted from thinking about their situation and experience short intervals of joy. Then a memory, familiar place, or event activates the depression once again. Studies have determined that from

15% to 30% experience clinically significant depression in the year after the death of a spouse. Some of the signs that depression is continuing for too long are neglect regarding personal appearance, poor eating habits, and withdrawal from all social involvement. These symptoms indicate a need to obtain professional counseling (Carr, Neese, & Wortman, 2005).

The goal at this stage of grieving is to assume greater control of life, to achieve a balance of moods, in order that satisfaction is more prevalent in the overall scheme of things. This is difficult because a lot of energy is devoted to feeling sorry for oneself. A helpful way to offset the poor self-impression that typically comes with depression is to spend time with others who are able to stimulate a positive picture of self-worth. This can happen by participation in support groups such as the AARP Widow to Widow program and by volunteering at an elementary school. Young children are often the most persuasive source to confirm for a survivor that s/he has value as a single person. Spending time trying to help children does not end personal sorrow, but it can renew joyful feelings, boost self-esteem, and demonstrate the orientation bereaved persons need to regain an optimistic view about their future.

Acceptance

There comes a time when the widowed person recognizes, "I have survived and can go on living without someone who was very important to me. I am ready to resume my interest in the future, to establish new goals for myself, and invest energy in relationships again." This constructive attitude is possible because emotional balance has gradually replaced the one-sided pessimistic view of life. The person is no longer preoccupied with events of the past nor overcome by uncertainty about their future. They enjoy some aspects of the present, express their feelings to other people, and show more confidence in making decisions instead of always guessing what their spouse would want them to do.

Of course, the habit of planning with two people in mind is difficult to break, because it calls for looking at tomorrow with a new perspective. No one becomes the old self again since his or her identity has been changed. This means that for a while it is best to look ahead only a short distance and set goals that can be attained within a matter of hours, days, or weeks. Dealing with more than one task at a time remains difficult, so it helps to write lists of things that have to be done and then decide their order of priority. This simple procedure can ensure that everyday chores are accomplished without feeling overwhelmed.

ELEMENTS OF SUCCESSFUL ADJUSTMENT

Most people accept the concept of uniqueness as it applies to the physical world. For example, it is understood that fingerprints are just one of a kind. Nevertheless, we often deny the possibility of uniqueness in the realm of emotional experience. However, the fact is that widowed men and women vary considerably in how they manage to cope with grief, in the duration, intensity, and sequence of the grieving stages, the outlook they bring to the tragedy and their rate of recovery. Therefore, it is wise to accept first-hand accounts of how someone feels rather than judge him or her as overreacting, or not behaving as they should be based strictly on our experience in observing how others dealt with grief. There are many factors that have an impact on coping including the previous losses a person has faced, support they are receiving, closeness of relationship to the deceased, the role the spouse had in their life, circumstances surrounding the death, religious beliefs about the afterlife, age of both parties, and other experiential elements. All these factors urge consideration of the individual. Consider some practical guidelines that can ease the process of adjustment to widowhood.

Take Time to Finish Grieving

Some men and women whose lives parallel the rapid pace of today reject the old saying that "Time heals all wounds." They are accustomed to expect quick solutions for most problems and tend to be impatient in situations that require prolonged effort before there is evidence of progress. There is no doubt that inventions that speed up various processes like microwave cooking have led to greater convenience. Nevertheless, an emphasis on speed can impair mental health when it is applied to emotional recovery. What happens is that people are willing to accept the grief of someone, providing the person works through it in a hurry. Sometimes this rush to terminate grieving comes from relatives. If they expect a member of the family to resume a normal life before it is possible, recommend reading this presentation to help them become aware of the slow recovery that is needed to adjust to crisis of attachment. Most widowed persons require at least a year and sometimes two years to adjust to their new situation. Even then, events like birthdays, anniversaries, and holidays can retrigger feelings of grief.

Most people are poorly informed about grief so they persist with maintaining the view that widowed persons should recover in a short time. Co-workers and employers are the most likely to avoid or reject someone in grief because they may feel uncertain about what to say and how to relate to them. The insensitive statements they make can be an unintended source of stress and cause feelings of alienation and hurt.

Continue to Communicate Feelings

Husbands and wives usually count on their spouse as the person who will listen to their concerns, care for them if they are ill, help them make decisions, monitor the quality of their thinking, provide corrective feedback on their behavior, share meals and conversations, set goals and plan with them, participate in leisure activities together, look out for their safety, and promote self-esteem. These basic needs continue after a spouse dies and must be met by someone else.

Telling relatives and friends about feelings makes them more aware and can diminish the griever's sorrow. The new listeners must be prepared to hear some negative feelings that are brought on by occasional depression. There will be times too when some enjoyable experience takes place and bereaved persons find themselves with no one to share. Instead of talking to the deceased partner, it is more sensible to speak with the new confidants who can give feedback. Recognize that joyful experiences can still be shared, even though the grieving process continues. Taking a trip with grandchildren can build memories with them. They can have a larger and more influential role if more time is spent together.

Keep Making Personal Decisions

When healthy widowed persons review their recovery, they often conclude that maintaining a degree of independence was important in helping them overcome grief. At the time, it would have been easier to permit other family members to make decisions for them. However, it is better to accept some assistance initially when relatives check out aspects of funeral arrangements but leave the choice of coffin, nature of burial service, and other details up to the widow/widower. A close friend or relative who can look out for the best interests of the family should accompany someone who is grieving. Taking this approach will lead to learning important procedures, such as determining how many death certificates are needed, how to change or stop social security payments, and prepare insurance forms. Time spent on such tasks provides distraction from self-examination, and confirms that the person is capable of managing personal affairs.

It is a wise practice to avoid major decisions, particularly ones that may involve lifestyle change like moving to another place, selling the house, or getting married again. These kinds of judgments are premature during the first year after the death of a spouse and frequently lead to regret. People who make such choices too soon usually do so with the hope of reducing their loneliness. However, being lonely is a continuous burden for widowed persons no matter where they go, and it will persist until they recover.

Newly widowed persons are able to handle everyday choices but they should not overestimate their emerging capacity to deal with issues that may involve greater significance. This is a time when people commonly experience insomnia, absentmindedness, problems trying to concentrate, failure of memory, the intrusion of unpleasant thoughts, and a tendency to repeat the same things over and over again. In combination, these limitations can make it too difficult to sort out and evaluate long-term choices. It is better to wait until a sense of perspective returns.

Enlarge the Circle of Friends

Widowed persons identify loneliness as their most difficult problem. Eight months after the death of her husband, Pearl wrote this note to her nephew:

> It is so lonesome without Gordon that some days I wonder whether I can make it. My life seems to have no future at all. Then I scold myself and remember what good children I have, wonderful friends who are standing by me, and my church. After that I thank God for all of my blessings. During widowhood, the most important relationship in life is gone, and can never be replaced.

By developing new friendships, experiences can still be shared. Whether or not the family lives close by, an effort should be made to meet new people. Studies have shown that widowers seem to adjust better socially than widows. One reason may be that the identity of women, until recently, has centered on their husband, as symbolized by taking his last name to become their own. When a husband dies, the lifestyle of his wife radically changes because, until recently, fewer women had an employment career. The problems of making decisions, handling finances, concerns about personal safety, and worry about dependent children seem to outweigh the difficulty widowers have learning to get by in the kitchen and managing the house.

Widows frequently complain that friends whom they have known for years, particularly couples, exclude them from their activities. The explanation widows usually give is that women friends consider them as a potential threat to their marriage. It is less often recognized that being around a widow reminds a couple of the husband's mortality and the condition his own wife may someday face. It is not surprising that widows want to spend some time with men. However, instead of blaming old friends, try to make new ones. Some of the new friends may be younger, and they can do much to enlarge perspective. It takes initiative to enlarge the social circle.

So much of grieving is talking about confused feelings that it is worthwhile to seek out those who are willing to give their undivided attention. Some of the best listeners are women or men who have been widowed. They have already endured the suffering, confused feelings, and loneliness. Many people say, "I just didn't feel that I could make it until I heard stories of other widowed persons." Sharing stories is the essence of a support group. They provide evidence that others have traveled a similar difficult path and emerged as independent persons (Silverman, 2004).

Support groups also provide assurance that to worry about one's mental state is normal. There is often fear about the unknown workings of the mind. When a person knows what to expect ahead of time, s/he is less likely to be overwhelmed. During grief, even supernatural events seem common. From 20% to 50% of widowed persons report seeing, hearing, or sensing the presence of the deceased (Victor, Scambler, & Bond, 2008). They seldom share these experiences because grievers suppose that other people will consider them mentally ill. Some men and women prolong their grief by staying home to avoid the prospect that others will discover their mental confusion. They want to reduce the risk of making a fool of themselves in public. Nevertheless, the risk of making mistakes, learning new things, and sharing feelings with others are worth taking. Withdrawal is not the key to recovery; the gradual achievement of acquiring a new perspective is what matters most.

Besides family, friends, and other widowed persons, talking to a family counselor who is trained to work with bereaved persons can help. Wives that have forewarning of their husband's death usually adjust better than those who unexpectedly are widowed. The critical advance time appears to be two weeks which gives people a chance to say goodbye, express affection, ask for forgiveness, renounce regrets, make promises, say things that should be told, and try to settle issues that were previously unresolved.

More men than women remarry after the death of a spouse. Some explain this difference by suggesting that men have greater opportunities to remarry. A less often mentioned view is that older women prefer not to remarry because they know how to take care of themselves and have close ties with their children and grandchildren. Some women also prefer to be free of previous constraints, do not want to take care of another sick man, and they may fear possible objections from their children. Daughters and sons frequently disapprove of remarriage for their mother because they idealize the deceased father, question motives of a boyfriend, and have concerns about their own inheritance (Worden, 2008).

Call a widow a few days after the funeral to ask whether it is possible to come by for a visit. If she prefers to wait awhile, call her back later. There is nothing anyone can say that matters as much as "I care about you." Listen to the person's feelings, provide comfort and make known that you will be available whenever she wants to have a talk. Sometimes there may be little conversation but it helps to sit together, watch a television program or take a walk. If the widow expresses concern about personal safety and does not have family living nearby, offer to establish a phone check-in system so someone is there if needed. Find out his/her favorite food, and bring it in a disposable container so s/he will not worry about returning it. Help the person get out of the house by taking a walk in the mall, going out for coffee or lunch, visiting church, or running errands. Plan to watch a movie or attend some sporting event together.

Always express optimism; it can often have a therapeutic effect. Talk about the deceased and the good times that are remembered, funny things that happened, and special qualities that were admired about the person. It is wrong to say nothing about the deceased and pretend as though s/he never existed. The departure of someone should not end the sharing of memories about him or her. Seneca, the ancient Roman philosopher, expressed this insight, "As a tale, so is life: not how long it is, but how good it is that matters." Knowing how to spend time with a widowed person may be difficult but realize that being there shows a concern for welfare and confirms s/he is important. Being the friend that is needed can be of great benefit.

Think Ahead About Widowhood

Husbands and wives can help each other by annually reviewing their business affairs. Both partners along with sons and daughters should know where all-important papers are kept. Spouses should understand that they are required to notify the Social Security Administration soon after the death. The survivor of any age is given additional benefits if s/he takes care of the deceased's child to age 19, and children get benefits at any age if they are disabled before age 22 and remain disabled. In cases of divorce, a former spouse may still qualify for benefits. Making a will and assigning power of attorney is also appropriate.

Both spouses should be informed of family commitments. This knowledge will help when s/he has to assume responsibilities. Sharing takes time but it lessens the burden for a spouse later. Depend on each other, but maintain the ability to fend for self. This means that women should keep driving the car instead of always relying on husbands to do so. Support the personality development of your spouse and take pride in his or her growth and achievements. Have good times together and let each other know how grateful you are for the partnership. Build good memories because they will be the most important gifts that are left to your spouse, children, and grandchildren.

SUMMARY AND IMPLICATIONS

Most people are reluctant to think about the prospect of their death. Exceptions are those who suffer from severe pain related to illness, injury or psychological trauma. Healthy emotional development through life improves adjustment to bereavement and reduces fear and anger. An increased level of acceptance is fortunate because death rates rise dramatically among people that have reached the age of retirement.

The mental health of widowed persons can improve when family and friends are informed about evolution of the grieving process. Those who mourn the death of a loved one typically experience predictable stages of grief including denial, anger, bargaining, resignation, and acceptance. It is also helpful for grieving persons to follow practical guidelines that can ease their adjustment. Some important considerations are: take enough time to complete the grieving process even though others may try to hurry the length of this ordeal; continue to communicate feelings and rely on new confidants to provide feedback; continue making decisions in order to maintain a sense of control and gradually regain independence; take initiative to enlarge the circle of friends; seek comfort from other widowed persons who are the most able to confirm the normality of your experience; respond to acquaintances as they struggle with the loss of someone dear to them; think about widowhood ahead of time by reviewing family responsibilities and financial planning; and, finally, acknowledge the relationships for which you are grateful.

Many older adults have reduced their ambition to compete in favor of pursing the secondary values of society. Some of these values are concern for others rather than domination, cooperation rather than self-seeking acclaim, and self-acceptance instead of struggling to attain status. These are the role reciprocity behaviors elders have to offer and represent the assets that are needed by all societies. Therefore, inviting older adults to become a source of help in the classroom could be one of the tasks expected of them. By recruiting elders to volunteer in schools, the community acknowledges that mature influence has an important place in the education of children and older people have a responsibility to share themselves. Use of this strategy mean shifting the focus from "Are older people still able to learn?" to "How can we ensure that elders share with us what they already know?" Edna St. Vincent Millay (1921), in a poem entitled *Lament*, observed that, "Life must go on. I forget just why." This sad conclusion can become less common among older adults by bringing them back into our lives and, in the process, gain something ourselves that cannot be found elsewhere.

APPLICATIONS FOR TEACHING

1. Everyone should be informed about stages of grieving and the mourning process. This awareness is necessary to support those who are coping with personal loss and create empathy about the emotional conditions experienced when a loved one passes away. Understanding the need for enough time to complete the grieving process can ensure that someone in mourning is not expected to resume a normal life in a short period. No words can eliminate sadness or loneliness of survivors but they recognize friendship as the best way to provide them with emotional support.

2. The loss of a spouse forces a change in identity and, for a time, narrows perspective because processing ideas and feelings have to take place without the partner. Initially, life may seem to have lost meaning so looking ahead and planning does not get attention. However, joining a widow support group can be a source of valued guidance and finding a confidant who listens and monitors thinking can be a factor in recovery.

3. Husbands and wives should review together their business affairs several times a year. This practice acquaints both partners with each other's wishes about the end of life. It can also make decision making less difficult for a survivor while s/he is grieving.

4. Well-intentioned relatives and friends may express a willingness to act in widow's behalf to ease burdens. However, retaining independence is a key factor for recovery because it confirms that someone is still able to manage her or his own affairs. Major decisions such as selling a house or moving should be deferred until perspective has been restored.

5. The identity of older adults changes when they leave employment for retirement. As a group, older adults are the primary providers

of volunteer service in the public schools. They can perform tasks more effectively when principals arrange continuing education for them, respect their choice of preferred assignments and schedule for participation, provide feedback about performance as observed by students and teachers, and recognize their contribution to school improvement.

6. Volunteering at school can help elders grow by developing a readiness to be more flexible, spontaneous, patient, and possess good humor. Flexible people are able to look at situations in new ways, an essential asset when volunteering to help students whose generation has a different perspective. Spontaneity means willingness to deviate from a plan when appropriate in favor of improvising to attain unforeseen opportunities. Patience avoids impulsive thinking and good humor motivates an outlook that setbacks are not defeats but opportunities to improve.

7. Role reciprocity for older adults seems more difficult to arrange in modern societies where social security and savings means that elders usually do not have to depend on trading their services for survival. On the other hand, self-esteem needs, aspiration to become more mature, and desire for favorable status in the community can motivate public service. When some elders do not take the initiative to determine how they can help their community, local institutions should make known the places where assistance is needed and recruit older adults to participate in community service.

REFERENCES

Adams, D., & Hamm, M. (2006). *Redefining education in the twenty-first century: Shaping collaborative learning in the age of information*. Springfield, IL: Charles C. Thomas.

Agliata, A., Tantleff-Dunn, S., & Renk, K. (2007, January). Interpretation of teasing during early adolescence. *Journal of Clinical Psychology, 63*(1), 23-30.

Albert, M., Blacker, D., Moss, M., Tanzi, R., & McArdle, J. (2007). Longitudinal cognitive change among individuals with mild cognitive impairment. *Neuropsychology, 21*, 158-169.

Aldwin, C. (2007). *Stress, coping and development*. New York, NY: Guilford

Alexander, L. (2009, October 26). The three-year solution. *Newsweek, 26-29*.

Alexander, P. (2005). *Psychology in learning and instruction*. Upper Saddle River, NJ: Prentice-Hall.

Allen, T., Finkelstein, L., & Poteet, M. (2009). *Designing workplace mentoring programs: An evidence based approach*. New York, NY: Wiley-Blackwell.

Alsop, R. (2008). *The trophy kids grow up*. San Francisco, CA: Jossey-Bass.

Alzheimer's Association (2012). *Alzheimer's disease facts and figures*. Retrieved from http://www.alz.org. Chicago, IL: Alzheimer's Association.

American College Testing (2006). *Reading between the lines: What the ACT reveals about college readiness in reading*. Iowa City, IA: ACT.

Amsel, E., & Lightfoot, C. (2012). *Making sense of adolescent risk taking: Issues, implications, and integration*. London, England: Psychology Press.

Anderman, E., & Murdock, T. (2006). *Psychology of academic cheating*. San Diego, CA: Academic Press.

Anderson, M., Goodman, J., & Schlossberg, N. (2011). *Counseling adults in transition: Linking Schlossberg's theory with practice in a diverse world* (4th ed.). New York, NY: Springer.

Anderson, N. (2011 January). Stressed in America. *Monitor on Psychology, 42*(1), 60.

Anti-Bullying Bill of Rights Act, State of New Jersey. (2011, January 5). Retrieved from http://www.njleg.state.nj.us/2010/Bills/AL10/122_.PDF

Bakan, J. (2011). *Childhood under siege: How big business targets children*. New York, NY: Free Press.

Balfanz, R., Bridgeland, J., Bruce, M., & Fox, J. (2012, March). *Building a grad nation: Progress and challenges in ending the high school dropout epidemic*. Washington, DC: Americas Promise Alliance.

Ball, K., & Gotskill, G. (2010). *Surviving the Baby Boomer exodus: Capturing knowledge for Gen X and Y employees*. Belmont, CA: Course Technology PTR.

Baltes, P. (2006). *Lifespan development and the brain: The perspective of biocultural constructivism*. New York, NY: Cambridge University Press.

Barkley, R., & Robin, R. (2008). *Your defiant teen*. New York, NY: Guilford Press.

Barnes, D., & Yaffe, K. (2011). The projected effect of risk factor reduction on Alzheimer's disease prevalence. *The Lancet Neurology, 10*(9), 819-828.

Barnes, V., Bauza, L., & Treiber, F. (2003). Impact of stress reduction on negative school behaviors in adolescents. *Health and Quality of Life Outcomes, 1*(1), 10.

Barry, A. (1997). *Visual intelligence.* Albany, NY: State University of New York Press.

Bauerlein, M. (2010). *The dumbest generation: How the digital age stupefies young Americans and jeopardizes our future.* New York, NY: Penguin.

Bauman, S. (2010). *Cyberbullying: What counselors need to know.* Alexandria, VA: American Counseling Association.

Baumeister, R. (2005). *The cultural animal: Human nature, meaning, and social life.* New York, NY: Oxford University Press.

Baumeister, R., Campbell, J., Krueger, J., & Vohs, K. (2003, May). Does high self-esteem cause better performance, interpersonal success, happiness or healthier lifestyle? *Psychological Science in the Public Interest, 4,* 1-2.

Baumeister, R., & Tierney, J. (2011). *Willpower: Rediscovering the greatest human strength.* New York, NY: Penguin.

Beaty, J. (2009). *Observing development of young children.* Upper Saddle River, NJ: Prentice-Hall.

Beckert, T., Strom, P., Strom, R., Darre, K., & Weed, A. (2008). Single mothers of early adolescents: Perceptions of competence. *Adolescence, 43*(170), 275-290.

Beckert, T., Strom, R., & Strom, P. (2006). Black and White fathers of early adolescents: A cross-cultural approach to curriculum development for parent education. *North American Journal of Psychology, 8*(3), 455-469.

Beckert, T., Strom, R., Strom, P., Yang, C., & Singh, A. (2007). Parent Success Indicator: Cross-cultural development and factorial validation. *Educational and Psychological Measurement, 67*(2) 311-327.

Beghetto, R. (2005, Spring). Does assessment kill creativity? *The Educational Forum, 69*(3), 254-263.

Belsky, J. (2008). Quality, quantity and type of child care: Effects on child development in the USA. In G. Bentley & R. Mace (Eds.), *Substitute parenting.* London, England: Berghahn Books.

Bennett, D., Schneider, J., Tang, Y., Arnold, S., & Wilson, R. (2006, May). The effect of social networks on the relation between Alzheimer's disease pathology and level of cognitive function in old people: A longitudinal cohort study. *The Lancet Neurology, 5*(5), 406-412.

Bennis, W., & Biederman, P. (1998). *Organizing genius: The secrets of creative collaboration.* Reading, MA: Addison-Wesley.

Benson, P. (2010). *Parent, teacher, mentor, friend: How every adult can change kids' lives.* Minneapolis, MN: Search Institute.

Beran, T., & Shapiro, B. (2005). Evaluation of an anti-bullying program: Student reports of knowledge and confidence on manage bullying. *Canadian Journal of Education, 28*(4), 700-717.

Berkman, L. (2000, April 15). Which influences cognitive function? Living alone or being alone. *The Lancet, 355*(9212), 1291-1292

Berns, R. (2009). *Child, family, school, community socialization, and support.* Belmont, CA: Wadsworth.

Bertini, K. (2011). *Strength for the sandwich generation: Help to thrive while simultaneously caring for our kids and our parents.* Westport, CT: Prager.

Binet, A. (1905). New methods for the diagnosis of the intellectual level of subnormals. *L'Année Psychologique*, 12, 191-244. Retrieved from Classics in the History of Psychology http://psychclassics.yorku.ca/Binet/binet1.htm

Biro, F., Maida, P., Galvez, L., Greenspan, C., Succop, P., Vangeepuram, N., Pinney, S., Teitelbaum, S., Windham, G., Kushi, L., & Wolff, M. (2010). Pubertal assessment method and baseline characteristics in a mixed longitudinal study of girls. *Pediatrics, 126*(3), e583-e590.

Birren, J., & Schaie, K. W. (Eds.) (2005). *Handbook of the psychology of aging* (6th edition). San Diego, CA: Elsevier Academic Press.

Blackburn, E. (2009, February 18). *Daydreaming*. A presentation to Moriah College, Sydney, Australia.

Blackhurst, R. (2008, June 22). A class apart. *Financial Times*, 1-2.

Bloch, A. (2003). *Murphy's Law: The 26th anniversary edition*. New York, NY: Penguin.

Blonna, R. (2006). *Coping with stress in a changing world*. New York, NY: McGraw-Hill.

Bloom, B., Cohen, R., & Freeman, G. (2011). *Summary health statistics for U.S. children*. Washington, DC: United States Department of Health and Human Services.

Bodrova, E., & Leong, D. (2006). *Tools of the mind: The Vygotsky to early childhood education*. Upper Saddle River, NJ: Prentice-Hall.

Bortz, W., & Stickrod, R. (2010). *The roadmap to 100: The breakthrough science of living a long and healthy life*. New York, NY: Palgrave Macmillan.

Bosma, H., van Boxtel, M., Ponds, R., Houx, P., & Jolles, J. (2003). Education and age-related cognitive decline: The contribution of mental workload. *Educational Gerontology, 29*, 165-173.

Bourke, J. (2005). *Fear, a cultural history*. London, England: Virago Press.

Bowden, A., & Lewthwaite, N. (2009). *The activity yearbook: A week by week guide for use in elderly day and residential care*. Philadelphia, PA: Jessica Kingsley.

Bowen, W., Chingos, M., & McPherson, M. (2011). *Crossing the finish line: Completing college at America's public universities*. Princeton, NJ: Princeton University Press.

Bowlby, J. (1988). *A secure base: Parent-child attachment and healthy human development*. London, England: Routledge.

Bowlby, J. (1999). *Attachment*. New York, NY: Basic Books.

Brandl, B., Dyer, C., Heisler, C., Otto, J., Stiegel, L., & Thomas, R. (2007). *Elder abuse detection and intervention*. New York, NY: Springer.

Brandon, E. (2012, January 9). 65-and-older population soars. *U.S. News & World Report*.

Bray, J., & Kelly, H. (1999). *Stepfamilies*. New York, NY: Random House.

Bray, J., & Stanton, M. (Eds.). (2009). *Handbook of family psychology*. Boston, MA: Blackwell/Wiley.

Brayne, C., Ince, P., Keage, H., McKeith, I., Matthews, F., Polvikoski, T., & Sulkava, R. (2010). Education, the brain and dementia: Neuroprotection or compensation? *Brain, 133*(8), 2210-2216.

Brewster, K., & Tillman, K. (2008). Who's doing it? Patterns and predictors of youth's oral sexual experiences. *Journal of Adolescent Health, 42*(1), 73-80.

Brockmole, J. (Ed.) (2008). *The visual world of memory*. New York, NY: Psychology Press.

Brokaw, T. (2004). *The greatest generation*. New York, NY: Random House.

Bronson, P., & Merryman, A. (2010, July 10). The creativity crisis. *Newsweek*.

Brooks, D. (2011). *The social animal*. New York, NY: Random House.

Brown, S., & Vaughan, C. (2010). *Play: How it shapes the brain, opens the imagination, and invigorates the soul*. New York, NY: Penguin.

Buboltz, W. (2012, February 16). *College student cell phone usage: How much is too much?* Presentation to the American Association of Behavioral and Social Sciences Annual Conference, Las Vegas, Nevada.

Buettner, D. (2008). *Blue zones: Lessons for living longer from the people who've lived the longest*. Washington, DC: National Geographic.

Bureau of Labor Statistics (2010). *Back to college*. Washington DC: The Bureau

Burns, E. (2007). *The essential special education guide for the regular education teacher*. Springfield, IL: Charles Thomas.

Butler, R. (2008). *The longevity revolution: The benefits and challenges of living a long life*. New York, NY: Perseus Books.

Cain, S. (2012). *Quiet: The power of introverts in a world that can't stop talking*. New York, NY: Crown.

California Fair Accurate Inclusive Respectful Education Act (Senate Bill 48) (2011, July 14). Retrieved from Legislative Information website at http://www.leginfo.ca.gov/pub/11-12/bill/sen/sb_0001-0050/sb_48_bill_20110714_chaptered.html

Campbell, J. (2004). *Pathways to bliss: Mythology and personal transformation*. Novata, CA: New World Library.

Carey, K. (2011, July 19). *The good news in the Atlanta and D.C.'s schools cheating scandal*. Retrieved from Education Sector, http://www.educationsector.org

Carlson, M. (2000). *Developing self and emotion in extreme social deprivation*. Retrieved from the Project on the Decade of the Brain, Library of Congress, available at http://www.loc.gov/loc/brain/emotion/Carlson.html

Carnevale, A., & Rose, S. (2011). *The undereducated American*. Washington, DC: Georgetown University Center on Education and the Workforce.

Carper, J. (2012). *100 Simple things you can do to prevent Alzheimer's and age-related memory loss*. New York, NY: Little, Brown & Co.

Carr, D., Nesse, R., & Wortman, C. (Eds.) (2005). *Spousal bereavement in late life*. New York, NY: Springer.

Carr, N. (2010). *The Shallows: What the Internet is doing to our brains*. New York, NY: W. W. Norton.

Carrabine, E. (2008). *Crime, culture and the media*. Boston, MA: Polity.

Carroll, L. (1865/2004). *Alice in wonderland*. London, England: Macmillan.

Cassidy, D., Lower, J., Kintner-Duffy, V., Hegde, A., & Shim, J. (2011, January-March). The day-to-day reality of teacher turnover in preschool classrooms. *Journal of Research in Childhood Education*, 25(1), 1-23.

Cattaert, C. (1963). *Where do goldfish go?* New York, NY: Crown.

Cavanaugh, J., & Blanchard-Fields, F. (2010). *Adult development and aging*. Belmont, CA: Wadsworth.

Caveon Test Security (2012). *Cheating detection and prevention*. Retrieved from http:/
/www.caveon.com

Center for the Digital Future. (2010, December 17). *Parents souring on the Internet*.
Los Angeles, CA: University of Southern California. Retrieved from http://
www.digitalcenter.org/

Centers for Disease Control and Prevention. (2005). *Teen opinions on smoking survey*. Atlanta, GA: Centers for Disease Control and Prevention. Retrieved from
http://www.cdc.gov

Centers for Disease Control and Prevention. (2010). *Youth and tobacco use*. Atlanta,
GA: Centers for Disease Control and Prevention. Retrieved from http://
www.cdc.gov

Centers for Disease Control and Prevention. (2011a). *Adolescent and school health:
Sexual risk behavior: HIV, STD, & teen pregnancy prevention*. Retrieved from
http://www.cdc.gov/healthyyouth/sexualbehaviors/index.htm

Centers for Disease Control and Prevention. (2011b). *Adolescent and school health:
Youth Risk Behavior Surveillance System (YRBSS)*. Retrieved http://www.cdc.gov/
healthyyouth/yrbs/index.htm

Centers for Disease Control and Prevention. (2011c, April 22). Bullying among
middle school and high school students. *Morbidity and Mortality Weekly Report,
60*(15), 1-3.

Centers for Disease Control and Prevention. (2012a). *Health effects of cigarette smoking*. Retrieved from http://www.cdc.gov

Centers for Disease Control and Prevention. (2012b). *Smoking & tobacco use: Fast
facts*. Retrieved from http://www.cdc.gov/tobacco/data_statistics/fact_sheets/
fast_facts/

Central Intelligence Agency. (2012). *The world factbook: Country comparisons total fertility rate*. Retrieved from http://www.cia.gov.

Chemelynski, C. (2006, July 18). When mean girls turn to female violence. *School
Board News*, 8.

Cherlin, A. (2009). *The marriage-go-round*. New York, NY: Random House.

Cherry K., Hawley, K., Jackson, E., Volaufova, J., Su, L., & Jazwinski, S. (2008,
October). Pictorial superiority effects in oldest-old people. *Memory, 16*(7),
728-741.

Children's Internet Protection Act. (2000). Public Law No. 106-554 USC.

Children's Online Privacy Protection Act of 1998. (2012). Retrieved from http://
www.ftc.gov/ogc/coppa1.htm

Christensen, K., Doblhammer, G., Rau, R., & Vaupel, J. (2009, October 3). Aging
populations: The challenges ahead. *The Lancet, 374*(9696), 1196-1208.

Christie, C., Jolivette, K., & Nelson, M. (2005). Breaking the school to prison
pipeline: Identifying school risk and protective factors for youth delinquency.
Exceptionality, 13(2), 69-88.

Chugani, H. (1998, November). Biological basis of emotion: Brain systems and
brain development. *Pediatrics, 102*(5) Supplement, 1225-1229.

Clark, K. (1963). Educational stimulation of racially disadvantaged children. In A.
Harry Passow (Ed.), *Education in depressed areas* (pp. 142-162). New York, NY:
Teachers College Columbia University.

Clark, M. (2008). *Modern Italy, 1871 to the Present* (3rd ed). Upper Saddle River, NJ: Pearson.

Clay, R. (2009, December). Community colleges' increased role. *Monitor on Psychology, 40*(11), 67-68.

Cocca, C. (2004). *Jailbait: The politics of statutory rape.* Albany, NY: State University of New York Press.

Codario, R. (2010). *Type 2 diabetes, pre-diabetes, and the metabolic syndrome.* New York, NY: Humana Press.

Cohen, P. (2012). *In our prime: The invention of middle age.* New York, NY: Schribner.

Cole, J. (2009). *Seventh annual Internet study of Internet use by children.* Los Angeles, CA: University of Southern California Center for the Digital Future.

Coleman, P., & Buel, S. (1979). Dendritic growth in the aging brain and failure of growth in senile dementia. *Science, 206,* 854-856.

Collins, A., & Halverson, R. (2009). *Rethinking education in the age of technology: The digital revolution and schooling in America.* New York, NY: Teachers College, Columbia University.

Coloroso, B. (2009). *The bully, the bullied, and the bystander.* New York, NY: William Morrow.

Compton, M. (2009). *Clinical manual of prevention in mental health.* Arlington, VA: American Psychiatric Publishing.

Conley, D. (2004). *The pecking order.* New York, NY: Random House.

Connelly, M. (2010). *Fatal misconception: The struggle to control world population.* Cambridge, MA: The Belknap Press of Harvard University Press.

Consumer Reports Magazine (June 2011). *That Facebook friend might be 10 years old, and other troubling news.* Retrieved from http://www.ConsumerReports.org

Cosby, B., & Poussaint, A. (2007). *Come on, people: On the path from victims to victors.* Dallas, TX: Thomas Nelson.

Cromie, W. (1998, June 11). Of hugs and hormones: Lack of touch puts kids out of touch. *Harvard University Gazette.*

Crosnoe, R. (2006, January). The connection between academic failure and adolescent drinking in secondary school. *Sociology of Education, 79*(1), 44-60.

Cukras, G. (2006, Winter). The investigation of study strategies that maximize learning for underprepared students. *College Teaching, 54*(1), 194-197.

Damasio, A. (2005). *Descartes error: Emotion, reason and the human brain.* New York, NY: Penguin.

Darst, P., Pangrazi, R., Sariscany, M., & Brusseau, T. (2011). *Dynamic physical education for secondary school students.* San Francisco, CA: Benjamin Cummings.

Darwin, C., & Wilson, E. (Ed.) (2005). *From so simple a beginning: Darwin's four great books.* New York, NY: W. W. Norton.

Datar, S., Garvin, D., & Cullen, P. (2011). *Rethinking the MBA: Business education at a crossroads.* Boston, MA: Harvard Business Press.

Davidson, A. (2005, March). Spiritual state. *National Geographic, 207*(3), 31.

Daviglus, M., Bell, C., & Berrettini, W. (2010). National Institutes of Health State-of-the Science Conference statement: Preventing Alzheimer's disease and cognitive decline. *Annals of Internal Medicine, 153,* 176-181.

Davila, T., Epstein, M., & Shelton, R. (2006). *Making innovation work: How to manage it, measure it, and profit from it.* Upper Saddle River, NJ: Pearson.

Davis, S., Drinan, P., & Gallant, T. (2009). *Cheating in school.* New York, NY: Wiley.

De Meyer, G., Shapiro, F., Vanderstichele, H., Vanmechelen, E., Engelborghs, S., De Deyn, P., et al. (2010). Diagnosis-independent Alzheimer's disease bio-marker signature in cognitively normal elderly people. *Archives of Neurology, 67*(8), 949-956.

De Vita, C. (1996, March). The United States at mid-decade. *Population Bulletin, 50*(4).

de Waal, F. (2009). *Primates and philosophers: How morality evolved.* Princeton, NJ: Princeton University Press.

Debevec, K., Shih, M., & Kashyap, V. (2006, Spring). Learning strategies and performance in a technology integrated classroom. *Journal of Research on Technology in Education, 38*(3), 293-308.

Delehanty, H., Ginzler, E., & Pipher, M. (2008). *Caring for your aging parent.* New York, NY: Sterling.

Deletant, D. (1995). *Ceausescu and securitate: Coercion and dissent in Romania 1965-1989.* Armonk, NY: M.E. Sharpe.

Deutsch, M. (1949a). A theory of cooperation and competition. *Human Relations, 2*(2), 129-152.

Deutsch, M. (1949b). An experimental study of the effects of cooperation on group process. *Human Relations, 2*(3), 199-231.

Deutsch, M. (2002). Social psychology's contributions to the study of conflict resolution. *Negotiation Journal, 18*(4), 307-320.

Diamond, M. (1985). *Enriching heredity: The impact of the environment on the anatomy of the brain.* New York, NY: Free Press.

Dickens, C. (1843). *A Christmas carol.* London, England: Chapman & Hall.

DiClemente, R., Santelli, J., & Crosby, R. (Eds.) (2009). *Adolescent health: Understanding and preventing risk behaviors.* San Francisco, CA: Jossey-Bass.

Discovery Education. (2012). *About Discovery Education.* Retrieved from http://www.discoveryeducation.com

Dodson, M., Crotty, B., Prideaux, D., Carne, R., Ward, A., & De Leeuw, E. (2009, January). The multiple mini-interview: How long is long enough? *Medical Education, 43*(2), 168-174.

Dolgin, K. (2010). *The adolescent: development, relationships and culture.* Upper Saddle River, NJ: Prentice-Hall.

Drucker, P. (2008). *Managing oneself.* Cambridge, MA: Harvard Business Press.

Duffert, A., Farkas, S., & Lovelass, T. (2008). *High-achieving students in the era of No Child Left Behind.* Washington, DC: Thomas Fordham Foundation.

Dunning, D. (2010). *Social motivation.* New York, NY: Psychology Press.

Dunning, D., Heath, C., & Suls, J. (2004, December). Flawed self-assessment: Implications for health, education and the workplace. *Psychological Science in the Public Interest, 5*(3), 69-106.

Durkheim, E., Simpson, G., & Spaulding, J. (1997). *Suicide.* New York, NY: Free Press.

Dutton, D. (2007). *The abusive personality: Violence and control in intimate relationships* (2nd ed.). New York, NY: Guilford.

Dweck, C. (2006). *Mindset: The new psychology of success.* New York, NY: Ballantine Books.

Education of All Handicapped Children Act (1975). Pub. L. 94-142, 20 USC 1400.

Elder Assistance Daily (2012). *Elder abuse data and statistics.* Retrieved from http://www.eadaily.com

Eliot, G. (1861). *Silas Marner.* New York, NY: Simon & Schuster. (Original work published 1861)

Elkind, D. (2006). *The hurried child: Growing up too fast too soon.* Cambridge, MA: Perseus Press.

Elliott, D., Menard, S., Rankin, B., Elliott, A., Huizinga, D., & Wilson, K. (2006). *Good kids from bad neighborhoods.* New York, NY: Cambridge University Press.

Employee Research Institute (2009). *Fundamentals of employee benefit programs.* Washington, DC: The Institute.

Epel, E., & Blackburn, E. (2004). Accelerated telomere shortening in relation to chronic stress. *Proceedings of the National Academy of Sciences, 101,* 17312-17315.

Epstein, R. (2007). *The case against adolescents: Rediscovering the adult in every teen.* Sanger, CA: Quill Driver.

Erickson, T. (2008). *Retire retirement: Career strategies for the Boomer generation.* Boston, MA: Harvard Business School Press.

Erikson, E. (1950). *Childhood and society.* New York, NY: W. W. Norton.

Erikson, E. (1968). *Identity: Youth and crisis.* New York, NY: W. W. Norton.

Erikson, E., & Erikson, J. (1998). *The life cycle completed.* New York, NY: W.W. Norton.

Espelage, D., & Swearer, S. (2010). *Bullying in North American schools.* New York, NY: Routledge.

Eysenck, M., & Keane, M. (2005). *Cognitive psychology.* Philadelphia, PA: Psychology Press.

Family Watchdog. (2011). *Awareness is your best defense.* Retrieved from http://www.familywatchdog.us/

Farber, N. (2009). *Adolescent pregnancy: Policy and prevention services.* New York, NY: Springer

Farkas, S., Johnson, J., Duffett, A., Wilson, L, & Vine, J. (2002). *A lot easier said than done: Parents talk about raising children in today's America.* New York, NY: Public Agenda.

Farrell, M. (2012). *New perspectives in special education.* New York, NY: Routledge.

Federal Statistics Office. (2009, November 18). Germany's ageing population heading for massive decline. *The Local Europe GmbH.*

Fein, R., Vossekuil, B., Pollack, W., Borum, R., Modzeleski, & Reddy, M. (2002). *Threat assessment in schools: A guide to managing threatening situations and to creating safe school climates.* Washington, DC: United States Secret Service and United States Department of Education. Retrieved from http://www.ustreas.gov/usss/ntac_ssi.shtml

Feinberg, L., Reinhard, S., Houser, A., & Choula, R. (2011). *Valuing the invaluable, 2011 update: The growing contributions and costs of family caregiving.* Washington, DC: American Association of Retired Persons Public Policy Institute.

Fewsmith, J. (Ed.) (2010). *China today, China tomorrow: Domestic politics, economy, and society.* Lanham, MD: Rowman & Littlefield.

Fitzpatrick, C., & Costantini, K. (2011). *Counseling 21st century students for optimal college and career readiness: A 9th-12th grade curriculum*. New York, NY: Routledge.

Florida, R. (2008). *Who's your city? How the creative economy is making where you live the most important decision of your life*. New York, NY: Basic Books.

Fohee, V., & Langwick, S. (2010). *Safe dates*. Center City, MN: Hazelden Information and Educational Services.

Forest, K., & Balcetis, E. (2008, February). Teaching students to work well in groups. *Observer, 21*(2), 27-29.

Fosnot, C. (2005). *Constructivism: Theory, perspectives, & practice*. New York, NY: Teachers College Press.

Frank, S. (2010, November 9). *Hyper-texting and hyper-Networking linked to teen sex, drug use*. Presentation to the American Public Health Association Annual meeting in Denver, Colorado.

Franke, T. M. (2000). Adolescent violent behavior: An analysis across and within racial/ethnic groups. In D. de Anda & R. Becerra (Eds.), *Violence: Diverse populations and communities* (pp. 47-70). New York, NY: Haworth Press.

Fratiglioni, L., & Chengyuan, Q. (2011, September). Prevention of cognitive decline in ageing: Dementia as the target, delayed onset as the goal. *The Lancet* Neurology, *10*(9), 778-779.

Fratiglioni, L., Wang, H., Ericcson, K., Maytan, M., & Winblad, B. (2000, April 15). Influence of social network on occurrence of dementia: A community based study. *The Lancet, 355*(9212), 1315-1319.

Freedman, M. (2010). *Shift: Midlife opportunity and the transition to a new stage of life*. New York, NY: Perseus Books.

Freeman, R., Swedenborg, B., & Topel, R. (2010). *Reforming the welfare state: Recovery and beyond in Sweden*. Chicago, IL: University of Chicago Press.

Frey, K., Kirschstein, M., & Snell, J. (2005, May). Reducing playground bullying and supporting beliefs: An experimental trial of the "Steps to Respect" Program. *Developmental Psychology, 41*(3), 479-490.

Friedman, H., & Martin, L. (2011). *The longevity project*. New York, NY: Penguin.

Friedman, T. (2005). *The world is flat: A brief history of the twenty-first century*. New York, NY: Farrar, Strauss & Giroux.

Frymier, J., & Joekel, R. (2004). *Changing the school environment*. Bloomington, IN: Phi Delta Kappa.

Gage, F., & Kempermann, G. (2007). *Adult Neurogenesis*. New York, NY: Cold Springs Harbor Laboratories.

Galbraith, L. (1998). *Romanian orphans, adopted daughters: A parent's story about international adoption, growth and attachment*. Fayetteville, AR: Stoneridge.

Galinsky, E. (2000). *Ask the children: The breakthrough study that reveals how to succeed at work and parenting*. New York, NY: Harper.

Gallant, T. (2010). *Creating the ethical academy: A systems approach to understanding misconduct and empowering change*. New York, NY: Routledge.

Gallup, G. (1982). Self-awareness and the emergence of mind in primates. *American Journal of Primatology, 2*, 237-248.

Gallup-Healthways Well-Being Index. (2010). *One million surveys reveal portrait of Americans' well-being.* Retrieved from http://www.well-beingindex.com/findings.asp

Galton, F. (1874). *English men and science: Their nature and nurture.* London, England: Macmillan.

Gardner, D. (2009). *The science of fear: How the culture of fear manipulates your brain.* New York, NY: Plume.

Gardner, H. (2011). *The unschooled mind: How children think and how schools should teach.* New York, NY: Basic Books.

Gardner, S., & Birley, S. (2008). *Blogging for dummies.* Hoboken, NJ: Wiley.

Gates Foundation (2010). *Foundation launches $35 million program to help boost community college graduation rates.* Seattle, WA: Bill and Melinda Gates Foundation.

Geda, Y. E. (2010). A purpose-oriented life: Is it potentially neuroprotective? *Archives of Neurology, 67*(8), 1010-1011.

Geda, Y. E. et al. (2009). *Cognitive activities are associated with decreased risk of mild cognitive impairment: The Mayo Clinic population-based study of aging.* Presented April 28 at the American Academy of Neurology, 61st Annual Meeting, Seattle, Washington.

Geldard, K., & Geldard, D. (2009). *Counseling adolescents: The proactive approach for young people.* Thousand Oaks, CA: Sage Publications.

Generation YES (Youth and Educators Succeeding) (2011). *Free resources from Generation YES.* Olympia, WA: Generation YES. retrieved from http://www.genyes.com/freeresources/

Ghiselin, B. (1987). *The creative process.* New York, NY: New American Library.

Giles, L., Glonek, G., Luszcz, M., & Andrews, G. (2005, July). Effect of social network on 10-year survival in very old Australians: The Australian longitudinal study of aging. *Journal of Epidemiology and Community Health, 59*(7), 574-579.

Gilliam, W. (2005). *Prekindergarteners left behind: Expulsion rates in state prekindergarten systems.* New Haven, CT: Yale University Child Study Center.

Gillies, R. (2007). *Cooperative learning: Integrating theory and practice.* Thousand Oaks, CA: SAGE.

Gillman, C. (2005). *You and your aging parents: How to balance your needs and theirs.* London, England: Hodder & Staughton.

Ginsburg, K. (2011). *Building resilience in children and teens.* Elk Grove Village, IL: American Academy of Pediatrics.

Glassner, B. (2010). *The culture of fear: Why Americans are afraid of the wrong things.* New York, NY: Basic Books.

Golding, W. (1954). *Lord of the flies.* New York, NY: Riverhead Books.

Goldstein, S., & Brooks, R. (2012). *Handbook of resilience in children.* New York, NY: Springer.

Goleman, D. (1996). *Vital lies, simple truths: The psychology of self deception.* New York, NY: Simon & Schuster.

Goleman, D. (2006a). *Emotional intelligence.* New York, NY: Bantam Books.

Goleman, D. (2006b). *Social intelligence: The new science of human relationships.* New York, NY: Bantam.

Goodall, J. (1986). *The chimpanzees of Gombe: Patterns of behavior.* Cambridge, MA: Harvard University Press.

Goodwin, P.,, Mosher, W., & Chandra, A. (2010). Marriage and cohabitation in the United States: A statistical portrait based on Cycle 6 (2002) of the National Survey of Family Growth. National Center for Health Statistics. *Vital Health Statistics, 23*(28).

Goossens, C. (2010). *Family life: Roles, bonds, and impact.* Hauppauge, NY: Nova Science.

Graham, K. (2012, March 6). Amid cheating allegations, district appoints "Integrity advisor". *The Philadelphia Inquirer.* Retrieved from http://www.philly.com

GrandCare Systems. (2012). *The GrandCare Systems Homepage.* West Bend, WI. Retrieved from http://www.grandcare.com

Gray, A. (2009). The social capital of older people. *Ageing and Society, 29,* 5-31.

Greenfield, S. (2008). *The quest for identity in the 21st century.* London, England: Sceptre.

Greenhaigh, S. (2008). *Just one child: Science and policy in Deng's China.* Berkeley, CA: University of California Press.

Gross, J. (2012). *A bittersweet season: Caring for our aging parents—and ourselves.* New York, NY: Vintage Books.

Guilford, J. (1950, September). Creativity. *American Psychologist, 5*(9), 444-454.

Guilford, J. (1977). *Way beyond the IQ.* Buffalo, NY: Creative Education Foundation.

Hall, C. B., Lipton, R., Silwinski, M., Katz, M., Derby, C., & Verghese, J. (2009). Cognitive activities delay onset of memory decline in persons who develop dementia. *Neurology, 73*(5), 356-361.

Halpern, C., Kaestle, C., & Hallfors, D. (2007). Perceived physical maturity, age of romantic partner, and adolescent risk behaviors. *Prevention Science, 8,* 1-10.

Halpern-Felsher, B., Cornell, J., Kropp, R., & Tschann, J. (2005, April). Oral versus vaginal sex among adolescents: Perceptions, attitudes, and behavior. *Pediatrics, 115*(4), 845-851.

Harcombe, Z. (2010). *The obesity epidemic: What caused it? How can we stop it?* York, England: Columbus.

Hardy, K., & Laszloffy, T. (2006). *Teens who hurt: Clinical interventions to break the cycle of adolescent violence.* New York, NY: Guilford.

Harlow, C. (Ed.). (1986). *From learning to love: The selected papers of H. F. Harlow.* Westport, CT: Praeger.

Harlow, H. (1958). The nature of love. *American Psychologist, 13*(12), 573-685.

Harlow, H., Harlow, C., & Suomi, S. (1971, September/October). From thought to therapy: Lessons from a primate lab. *American Scientist, 59*(5), 538-549.

Harrington, B., & Van Deusen, F. (2010). *The new dad: Exploring fatherhood within a career context.* Boston, MA: Boston College Center for Work and Family.

Hart, B., & Risley, T. (2002). *The social world of children learning to talk.* Baltimore, MD: Paul Brookes.

Harvey, J., & Fine, M. (2010). *Children of divorce.* Grand Rapids, MI: Baker Academic.

Harwood, V. (2005). *Diagnosing disorderly children.* New York, NY: Routledge.

Havighurst, R. (1972). *Developmental tasks in education*. New York, NY: David McKay.

Hawaii Department of Health. (2011). *Healthy Start*. Retrieved from http://hawaii.gov/health/family-child-health/mchb/programs/hs.html

Headden, S., & Silva, E. (2011, December 1). *Lessons from D.C.'s evaluation system*. Retrieved from http://www.educationsector.org

Heinberg, L., & Thompson, K. (2009). *Obesity in youth: Causes, consequences, and cures*. Washington, DC: American Psychological Association.

Heisel, M., & Dubertstein, P. (2005). Suicide prevention in older adults. *Clinical Psychology Science and Practice, 12*(3), 243.

Hemmingway, E. (1964). *A moveable feast*. New York, NY: Charles Scribners.

Henkin, R. (2005). *Confronting bullying*. Portsmouth, NH: Heinemann.

Herskind, A., McGue, M., Holm, N., Sorensen, T., Harvald, B., & James W. Vaupel (1996). The heritability of human longevity: A population-bases study of 2872 Danish twin pairs born 1870-1900. *Human Genetics, 97*, 319-323.

Hess, R., & Shipman, V. (1973). Early blocks to children's learning. In R. Strom & P. Torrance (Eds.), *Education for affective achievement* (pp. 28-38). Chicago, IL: Rand McNally.

Heward, W., & Haring, N. (2011). *Exceptional children*. Upper Saddle River, NJ: Prentice-Hall.

Hingson, R., Herren, T., & Winter, M. (2006). Age at drinking onset and alcohol dependence. *Archives of Pediatrics & Adolescent Medicine, 160*, 739-746.

Hirsch, B., & Hudnell, R. (2009). *The computer clubhouse*. New York, NY: Teachers College Press.

Hirsch, M., & Narayan, M. (1971). *Leela and the watermelon*. New York, NY: Crown Publishers.

Hirschland, D. (2008). *Collaborative intervention in early childhood: Consultation with parents and teachers of 3- to 7- year olds*. New York, NY: Oxford University Press.

Hoffman, J. M. (Director). (2002). *The Emperor's Club* [Movie]. Hollywood, CA: Universal Studios. Retrieved from http://www.theemperorsclub.com

Hoffman, J., Froemke, S., & Golant, S. (2009). *The Alzheimer's project: Momentum in science*. New York, NY: Perseus Books.

Horak, R. (2007). *Telecommunications and data communications handbook*. New York, NY: Wiley Interscience.

Huang, P., Smock, P., Manning W., & Bergstrom-Lynch, C. (2012, February). He says, she says: Gender and cohabitation. *Journal of Family Issues, 32*(7), 876-905.

Huesmann, L. (2007). The impact of electronic media violence: Scientific theory and research. *Journal of Adolescent Health, 41*, S6-S13.

Hughes, J. (Producer), & Columbus, C. (Director). (1990). *Home alone* [Motion picture]. United States: Fox.

Hunt, B. (2006). *Where should I live when I retire?* New Hyde Park, NY: Square One Publications.

Individuals with Disabilities Education Act (2004). Pub. L. 108-446, 20 USC 1400.

International Longevity Center. (2012). *A profile of older Japanese 2012*. Tokyo, Japan: International Longevity Center.

Isay, R. (2010). *Being homosexual: Gay men and their development.* New York, NY: Vintage.

Jackson, M. (2009). *Distracted: The erosion of attention and the coming dark age.* Amherst, New York, NY: Prometheus Books.

James, W. (1890/2007). *Principles of psychology* (Vol. I). New York, NY: Cosimo Classics.

Jasper, M. (2006). *Missing and exploited children.* New York, NY: Oxford University Press.

Jennings, L., & Likis, L. (2005, March). Meeting a math achievement crisis. *Educational Leadership, 62*(6), 65-68.

Jinks, C., Knopf, H., & Kemple, K. (2006 Summer). Tackling teacher turnover in child care. *Childhood Education, 82*(4), 219-226.

John-Steiner, V. (2000). *Creative collaboration.* New York, NY: Oxford University Press.

Johnson, D., & Brooke, J. (1999, April 22). Portrait of outcasts seeking to stand out. *The New York Times,* pp. 1, 26.

Johnson, D., & Johnson, R. (2003). *Joining together: Group theory and group skills.* Boston, MA: Allyn & Bacon.

Johnson, J., Duffett, A., & Ott, A. (2005). *Life after high school: Young people talk about their hopes and prospects.* Retrieved from http://www.publicagenda.org

Johnson, J., Rochkind, J., Ott, A., & DuPont, S. (2011). *With their whole lives ahead of them.* New York, NY: Public Agenda.

Johnson, J., Rochkind, J., Ott, A., DuPont, S., & Hess, J. (2011). *One degree of separation: How young Americans who don't finish college see their chances for success.* New York, NY: Public Agenda.

Johnson, R., Penny, J., & Gordon, B. (2009). *Assessing performance.* New York, NY: Guilford.

Johnston, L. D., O'Malley, P., Bachman, J., & Schulenberg, J. (2011). *Monitoring the future national results on adolescent drug use: Overview of key findings, 2010.* Ann Arbor, MI: Institute for Social Research, University of Michigan.

Jolls, T. (2010). *Literacy for the 21st century: Theory/overview of media literacy (2nd ed.).* Los Angeles, CA: Center for Media Literacy.

Josephson Institute of Ethics. (2010). *The ethics of American youth.* Los Angeles, CA: Josephson Institute. Retrieved from http://josephsoninstitute.org/

Jung, C. (1955). *Modern man in search of a soul.* New York, NY: Harcourt.

Kaestle, C., Morisky, D., & Wiley, D. (2002, November/December). Sexual intercourse and the age difference between adolescent females and their romantic partners. *Perspectives on Sexual and Reproductive Health, 34*(6), 304-309.

Kafai, Y., Peppler, K., & Chapman, R. (2009). *The computer clubhouse.* New York, NY: Columbia University Teachers College Press.

Kagan, J. (2007). *An argument for mind.* New Haven, CT: Yale University Press.

Kamphaus, R., & Frick, P. (2006). *Clinical assessment of child and adolescent personality and behavior.* New York, NY: Springer.

Kandel, E. (2006). *In search of memory: The emergence of a new science of mind.* New York, NY: W. W. Norton.

Kandel, E. (2012). *The age of insight: The quest to understand the unconscious in art, mind, and brain, from Vienna 1900 to the present.* New York, NY: Random House.

Katzman, R. (1993). Education and the prevalence of dementia and Alzheimer's disease. *Neurology, 43,* 13-20.

Kaufman, J., & Sternberg, R. (2010). *The Cambridge handbook of creativity.* New York, NY: Cambridge University Press.

Kaye, J., Pavel, M., Jimison, J., & Hayes, J. (2009). Technologies for an aging population. *The Bridge, Linking Engineering and Society, 39*(1), 5-12.

Kelly, K. (2005, May 10). Driving to early deaths. *U.S. News & World Report, Mysteries of the Teen Years Special Edition,* 51-54.

Kelsey, C., & Kelsey, C. (2007). *Generation MySpace: Helping your teen survive online adolescence.* New York, NY: DeCapo Press.

Kempermann, G. (2011). *Adult neurogenesis 2.* New York, NY: Oxford University Press.

Kempermann, G., Kuhn, H., & Gage, F. (1997, April 3). More hippocampus neurons in adult mice living in an enriched environment. *Nature, 386,* 493-495.

Kennedy, A. (2006, April). Nation caught in meth's grip. *Counseling Today, 48*(10), 1, 32-34.

Khadaroo, S. (2011, September 28). SAT cheating scandal. *Christian Science Monitor,* 1-2.

Kim, K. (2010). Measurements, causes, and effects of creativity. *Psychology of Aesthetics, Creativity and the Arts, 4*(3), 131-135.

Kindlon, D. (2006). *Alpha Girls: Understanding the new American girl and how she is changing the world.* Emmaus, PA: Rodale.

Kirkpatrick, K. (Director). (2009). *Imagine that* [Motion picture]. United States: Paramount Pictures.

Kish, C., Sheehan, J., Cole K., Struyk, L., & Kinder, D. (1997). Portfolios in the classroom: A vehicle for developing reflective thinking. *The High School Journal, 80*(4), 254-260.

Kitchen, C. (2007). *Fact and fiction of healthy vision: Eye care for adults and children.* Westport, CT: Praeger.

Klaus, P. (2008). *The hard truth about soft skills: Workplace lessons smart people wish they had learned sooner.* New York, NY: Harper Collins.

Klich, K., & Muller, H. (2002). *Children of Ceausescu.* Brooklyn, NY: Umbrage Editions.

Kohler, P., Manhart, L., & Lafferty, W. (2008, April). Abstinence-only and comprehensive sex education and the initiation of sexual activity and teen pregnancy. *Journal of Adolescent Health, 42*(4), 344-351.

Kohler, W. (1925). *The mentality of apes.* New York, NY: Vintage.

Kohn, A. (1993). *Punished by rewards: The trouble with gold stars, incentive plans, A's, praise and other bribes.* New York, NY: Houghton Mifflin.

Kosciw, J., Dias, E., & Greytalk, E. (2008). *The 2007 national school climate survey: The experience of lesbian, gay, bisexual and transgender youth in our nation's schools.* New York, NY: Gay, lesbian, and Straight Education Network.

Kovarik, B. (2011). *Revolutions in communication: Media history from Gutenberg to the digital age.* New York, NY: Continuum International Publishing.

Kowalski, R., Limber, S., & Agatston, P. (2008). *Cyberbullying: Bullying in the digital age.* Malden, MA: Blackwell.

Kraut, R., Brynin, M., & Kiesler, S. (2006). *Computers, phones, and the Internet: Domesticating information technology.* New York, NY: Oxford University Press.

Kübler-Ross, E. (1997). *On death and dying.* New York, NY: Scribners.

Kübler-Ross, E. & Kessler, D. (2007). *Grief and grieving.* New York, NY: Scribners.

Lamb, M. (2010). *Role of the father in child development.* New York, NY: Wiley.

Lancaster, L., & Stillman, D. (2005). *When generations collide.* New York, NY: Harper Collins.

Lancaster, L., & Stillman, D. (2010). *The M-factor: How the Millennial generation is rocking the workplace.* New York, NY: Harper Business.

Langman, P. (2009). *Why kids kill: Inside the minds of school shooters.* New York, NY: Palgrave Macmillan.

Lapierre, S., Bouffard, L., & Bastin, E. (1997). Personal goals and subjective well-being in later life. *International Journal of Aging and Human Development, 45*(4), 287-303.

Larson, J. (2008, January). Angry and aggressive students. *Principal Leadership, 8,* 12-15.

Larson, J., & Lochman, J. (2005). *Helping school children cope with anger.* New York, NY: Guilford.

Lasky, B., & Karge, B. (2006, March). Meeting the needs of students with disabilities: Experience and confidence of principals. *National Association of Secondary School Principals Bulletin, 90*(1), 19-36.

Lathrop, A., & Foss, K. (2005). *Guiding students from cheating and plagiarism to honest and integrity: Strategies for change.* Englewood, CO: Libraries Unlimited.

Lawler, E., & O'Toole, J. (2008). *America at work: Choices and challenges.* New York, NY: Palgrave Macmillan.

Lee, A. (2005). *Flight simulation: Virtual environments in aviation.* London, England: Ashgate.

Lee, J. M., Rawls, A., Edwards, K., & Menson, R. (2011). *The college completion agenda 2011 progress report.* Washington, DC: The College Board.

Lehrer, J. (2012). *Imagine: How creativity works.* New York, NY: Houghton Mifflin Harcourt.

Lepsinger, R., & Lucia, A. (2009). *The art and science of 360-degree feedback.* New York, NY: John Wiley.

Lerner, B. (2011). *One for the road: Drunk driving since 1900.* Baltimore, MD: The Johns Hopkins University Press.

Lesser, E., Ransom, D., Shah, R., & Pulver, B. (2012). *Collective intelligence: Capitalizing on the crowd.* Somers, NY: IBM Global Services.

Levi, D. (2007). *Group dynamics for teams.* Thousand Oaks, CA: SAGE.

Levine, M. (2006). *The price of privilege: How parent pressure and material advantage are creating disconnected and unhappy kids.* New York, NY: HarperCollins.

Levine, R. (2004). *Aging with attitude.* Westport, CT: Praeger.

Levinson, D. (2011, May). *Medicare atypical antipsychotic drug claims for elderly nursing home residents.* Office of Inspector General, Department of Health and Human Services, OEI-07-08-00150. Retrieved from http://oig.hhs.gov/oei/reports/oei-07-08-00150.pdf

Liau, A., Khoo, A., & Peng, H. (2005). Factors influencing adolescent engagement in risky Internet behavior. *CyberPsychology & Behavior, 8*(6), 513-520.

Lind, L. (1957). *Latin poetry in verse translation*. Boston, MA: Houghton Mifflin.

Liu, Z. (2008). *Paper to digital: Documents in the information age*. Westport, CT: Libraries Unlimited.

Lodge, J., & Frydenberg, E. (2005, Fall). The role of peer bystanders in school bullying: Positive steps toward promoting peaceful schools. *Theory Into Practice, 44*(4), 329-336.

Lubart, T. (2010). Cross-cultural perspectives on creativity. In J. Kaufman, & R. Sternberg (Eds.), *The Cambridge handbook of creativity* (pp. 265-278). New York, NY: Cambridge University Press.

Lucado, M. (2009). *Fearless: Imagine your life without fear*. Nashville, TN: Thomas Nelson.

Lucas, G. (2005). *Teaching communication*. Retrieved March 1, 2012, from Edutopia, San Rafael, CA. Retrieved from available at http://www.edutopia.org

Ludwig, A. (1995). *The price of greatness: Resolving the creativity and madness controversy*. New York, NY: Guilford Press.

Luthar, S., & Latendresse, S. (2005). Children of the affluent: Challenges to well-being. *Current Directions in Psychological Science, 14*(1), 49-53.

Luxford, W., Derebery, M., & Berliner, K. (2010). *The complete Idiot's guide to hearing loss*. New York, NY: Penguin.

MacKinnon, D. (1962 July). The nature and nurture of creative talent. *American Psychologist, 17*(7), 484-495.

MacKinnon, D. (1978). *In search of human effectiveness*. Buffalo, NY: Creative Education Foundation.

MacLeod, C. (2010). *Adolescence, pregnancy, and abortion*. New York, NY: Routledge Academic.

Madaras, L. (2007a). *What's happening to my body: Book for boys*. New York, NY: Newmarket Press.

Mahoney, J., Larson, R., & Eccles, J. (2005). *Organized activities as contexts of development*. Mahwah, NJ: Erlbaum.

Malacad, B., & Hess, G. (2010). Oral sex: Behaviors and feelings of Canadian young women and implications for sex education. *The European Journal of Contraception and Reproductive Health Care, 15*(3), 177.

Males, M., & Chew, K. (1996). The ages of fathers in California adolescent births. *American Journal of Public Health, 86*(4), 565-568.

Mallay-Morrison, K., Nolido, N., & Chawla, S. (2006). International perspectives on elder abuse: Five case studies. *Educational Gerontology, 32*, 1-11.

Manning, W., Cohen, J., & Smock, P. (2011). The role of romantic partners, family, and peer networks in dating couples' views about cohabitation. *Journal of Adolescent Research, 26*(1), 115-149.

Mannix, D. (2008). *Social skills for secondary students with special needs*. San Francisco, CA: Jossey-Bass.

Mark, G., Gonzales, V., & Harris, J. (2005). No task left behind? Examining the nature of fragmented work. In *Proceedings of the ACM CHI Conference on Human Factors in Computing Systems* (pp. 321-330). New York, NY: ACM Press.

Marks, I. (2005). *Living with fear: Understanding and coping with anxiety*. New York, NY: McGraw-Hill.

Markus, D. (2012, February 22). *Risking peace at a troubled school.* Retrieved from http://www.edutopia.org

Marmot, M. (2005). *The status syndrome: How social standing affects our health and longevity.* New York, NY: Henry Holt.

Mason, G. (2007). *Spectacle of violence.* New York, NY: Taylor & Francis.

Masten, A., & Narayan, A. (2012). Child development in the context of disaster, war, and terrorism: Pathways of risk and resilience. *Annual Review of Psychology, 63,* 227-257.

Mate, G. (2011). *When the body says no: Exploring the stress-disease connection.* New York, NY: Wiley.

McBride, N. (2011). *Child safety is more than a slogan.* National Center for Missing & Exploited Children. Retrieved from the http://www.ncmec.org

McCabe, E. (1985, August 1). Creativity. *Vital Speeches of the Day, 51*(2), 628-632.

McClain, L., & Grossman, J. (Eds.). (2009). *Gender equality: Dimensions of women's equal citizenship.* New York, NY: Cambridge University Press.

McGovern, M., Ladd, L., & Strom, R. (2006). Online assessment of grandmother experience in raising grandchildren. *Educational Gerontology, 32*(8), 669-684.

McKim, R. (1980). *Thinking visually: A strategy for problems solving.* Los Angeles, CA: Dale Seymour.

McLuhan, M. (1964). *Understanding media: The extension of man.* New York, NY: McGraw-Hill.

McLuhan, M., & Fiore, Q. (1967). *The medium is the massage: An inventory of effects.* Corte Madera, CA: Gingko Press.

McQuade, S., Colt, J., & Meyer, N. (2009). *Cyber bullying: Protecting kids and adults from online bullies.* Westport, CT: Praeger.

Medina, J. (2009). *Brain rules.* Seattle, WA: Pear Press.

Meister, J., & Willyerd, K. (2010). *The 2020 Workplace: How innovative companies attract, develop, and keep tomorrow's employees today.* New York, NY: HarperCollins.

Meltzer, L. (Ed.) (2007). *Executive function in education.* New York, NY: Guilford.

Merton, R. (1948, Summer). The self-fulfilling prophecy. *Antioch Review,* 193-210.

Metlife Mature Market Institute. (2011). *The Metlife study of caregiving costs to working caregivers.* Westport, CT: Metlife Mature Market Institute.

Millar, G. (2001). *The Torrance kids at mid-life.* Westport, CT: Greenwood.

Millay, E. St. Vincent (1921). *Second April.* New York, NY: Mitchell Kennerley, 64-65.

Miller, M. (1979). *Suicide after 60.* New York, NY: Springer.

Millerrodgers, M. (2010, September 27). *Comprehensive soldier fitness marks change in Army culture.* Retrieved from http://www.army.mil

Minnesota Early Childhood Family Education Program. (2011). Retrieved from http://ecfe.mpls.k12.mn.us/

Mischel, W., & Ayduk, O. (2004). Willpower in a cognitive-affective processing system: The dynamics of delay of gratification. In R. Baumeister & K. Vohs (Eds.), *Handbook of self-regulation: Research, theory, and applications* (pp. 99-129). New York NY: Guilford.

Mischel, W., & Peake, P. (1990). Predicting adolescent cognitive and self-regulatory competencies from preschool delay of gratification. *Developmental Psychology, 26*(6), 978-986.

Mishna, F., Scarcello, I., & Pepler, D. (2005). Teachers' understanding of bullying. *Canadian Journal of Education, 28*(4), 718-738.

Mitchell, D. (2009). Nonconscious priming after 17 years: Invulnerable implicit memory. *Psychological Science, 17*(11), 925-929.

Mitchell, D., Brown, A., & Murphy, D. (1990). Dissociations between procedural and episodic memory. *Psychology and Aging, 5*(2), 264-276.

Mitra, S. (2003). Minimally invasive education: A progress report on the "Hole-in-the wall" experiments. *British Journal of Educational Technology, 34*(3), 367-371.

Mitra, S. (2006). *The hole in the wall: Self-organizing systems in education.* New Delhi, India: Tata-McGraw-Hill.

Mitra, S. (2012a). *Beyond the hole in the wall: Discover the power of self-organized learning.* New York: NY: TED Books.

Mitra, S. (2012b, March 26). *Sugata Mitra - Keynote Speaker @ 21st Century Learning Conference,* presented in Hong Kong. Retrieved from http://www.youtube.com

Mitra, S., & Dangwal, R. (2010). Limits to self-organizing systems of learning: The Kalikuppan experiment. *British Journal of Educational Technology, 41*(5), 672-688.

Moore, B., & Parker, R. (2008). *Critical thinking.* New York, NY: McGraw-Hill.

Moore, M. (2002). *Bowling for Columbine* [Movie]. Los Angeles, CA: United Artists, Alliance Artists and Dog eat Dog Films.

Moore, R., & Robillard, A. (2008). *Pluralizing plagiarism: Identities, contexts, and pedagogies.* Portsmouth, NH: Boynton/Cook.

Morrisey, K., & Werner-Wilson, R. (2005, Spring). Relationship between out-of-school activities and positive youth development. *Adolescence, 40*(157), 67-86.

Morrissette, M. (2008). Choosing single motherhood. New York, NY: Harcourt Mariner Books.

Munsey, C. (2010, January). The kids aren't all right. *Monitor on Psychology, 41*(1), 23-25.

Murray, C., & Herrnstein, R. (1996). *Bell curve: Intelligence and class structure in America.* New York, NY: Free Press.

Myers S., & Anderson, C. (2008). *Fundamentals of small group communication.* Thousand Oaks, CA: SAGE.

Naglier, T., & Goldstein, S. (2009). *Practioners guide to assessing intelligence and achievement.* New York, NY: Wiley.

National Association of Child Care Resources and Referral Agencies. (2011). *High cost of child care.* Arlington, VA: The Association.

National Center for Education Statistics (2010). *Program for International Student Assessment (PISA) results for 2009.* Washington, DC: United States Department of Education.

National Center for Missing and Exploited Children. (2012, January 23). *Number of registered sex offenders in the US nears three-quarters of a million.* Retrieved from http://mcmec.org

National Institute of Child Health and Human Development Early Childhood Care Research Network. (2006, February/March). Child care effect sizes for the NICHD study of early childhood care and youth development. *American Psychologist, 6*(2), 99-116.

Neinstein, L., Gordon, C., Katzman, D., Rosen, D., & Woods, E. (Eds.). (2008). *Handbook of adolescent health care.* Philadelphia, PA: Lippincott, Williams & Wilkins.

Nemours Foundation. (2012). *Go, Slow, and Whoa! A kids guide to eating right.* Retrieved from http://kidshealth.org/kid/nutrition/food/go_slow_whoa.html

Nerenberg, L. (2007). *Elder abuse: Emerging trends and promising strategies.* New York, NY: Springer.

Newberg, A. (2000). *Why God won't go away.* New York, NY: Ballantine Books.

Newman, B., Lohman, B., & Newman, P. (2007, Summer). Peer group membership and a sense of belonging: Their relationship to adolescent behavior problems. *Adolescence, 42*(166), 1-23.

Ngandu, T., von Strauss, E., Helkala, E., Winblat, B., Nissinen, A., Tuomilehto, et al. (2007). Education and dementia: What lies behind the association? *Neurology, 69,* 1442-1450.

Nisbett, R. (2009). *Intelligence and how to get it: Why schools and cultures count.* New York, NY: W. W. Norton.

Nistler, C., Hodgson, H., Nobrega, F., Hodgson, J., Wheatley, R., & Solberg, G. (2006, September). Marijuana and adolescents. *Minnesota Medicine, 89,* 1-7.

Nixon, J. L. (1974). *The alligator under the bed.* New York, NY: G.P. Putnam & Sons.

Nobel Prize. (2009). *The Nobel Prize in Physiology or Medicine 2009.* Retrieved from http://nobelprize.org/nobel_prizes/medicine/laureates/2009/

Norton, M., Sheriff, C., Blight, D., Chudacoff, H., Logevall, F., & Bailey, B. (2012). *A people and a nation: A history of the United States, Volume II: Since 1856* (9th ed.). Boston, MA: Wadsworth Cengage Learning.

Obama, B. (2009, September 8). *Goals, work, and success.* Presentation to the students of Wakefield High School in Arlington, Virginia.

Olfman, S. (2005). *Childhood lost: How American culture is failing our kids.* Westport, CT: Praeger.

Ophir, E., Nass, C., & Wagner, A. (2009, August 24). Cognitive control in media multitaskers. *Proceedings of the National Academy of Sciences, 106*(34), 15583-15587.

Orey, M., McClendon, V., & Branch, R. (Eds.) (2006). *Educational media and technology yearbook* (Vol. 31). Englewood, CO: Libraries Unlimited.

Orlow, D. (2012). *A history of modern Germany: 1871 to Present* (7th ed.). Upper Saddle River, NJ: Pearson.

Orpinas, P., & Horne, A. (2006). *Bullying prevention: Creating a positive school climate and developing social competence.* Washington, DC: American Psychological Association.

Owens, F. (2007). *No speed limit: The highs and lows of meth.* New York, NY: St. Martin's Press.

Paivio, A. (1990). *Mental representations: A dual coding approach* (2nd ed.). New York, NY: Oxford University Press.

Pappano, L. (2011, July 22). The master's as the new bachelor's. *The New York Times.*

Parents Without Partners. (2011). *Who we are*. Retrievedf rom http://www .parentswithoutpartners.org

Passel, J., Cohn, D. & Lopez, H. (2011, March 24). *Hispanics account for more than half of the nation's growth in past decade*. Washington, DC: Pew Research Center.

Penrose, R. (2002). *The Emperor's new mind. Concerning computers, minds and the laws of physics*. New York, NY: Oxford University Press.

Peterson, N. (2005, Spring). Early 20th century photography of Australian Aboriginal families: Illustrations or evidence. *Visual Anthropology Review, 21*(1 & 2), 11-26.

Pfiefer, K., & Middleman, A. (2006). *American Medical Association boy's guide to becoming a teen*. San Francisco, CA: Jossey-Bass.

Piaget, J. (1954). *The construction of reality in the child*. New York, NY: Basic Books.

Piaget, J. (1963). *Origins of intelligence in children*. New York, NY: Norton.

Piaget, J. (1969). *Psychology of intelligence*. New York, NY: Littlefield, Adams.

Piaget, J. (1970). Piaget's theory. In P. Mussen (Ed.), *Carmichael's manual of child psychology* (Vol. 1, pp. 702-732). New York, NY: John Wiley.

Pierce, J. (2011). *What adolescents ought to know*. Amherst, MA: University of Massachusetts Press.

Pink, D. (2009). *Drive: The surprising truth about what motivates us*. New York, NY: Penguin Group.

Plato, A. (2008). *Republic*. New York, NY: Oxford University Press. [First publication of *Republic* by Plato appeared in 380 B.C.)

Plucker, J., & Baer, J. (2008). *Essentials of creativity assessment*. New York, NY: Wiley.

Poldrack, R., Helchenko, Y., & Hansen, S. (2009). Decoding the large-scale structure of brain functioning by classifying mental states across individuals. *Psychological Science, 20*, 1364-1372.

Popenoe, D. (2009). *Families without fathers*. Piscataway, NJ: Transaction

Population Research Institute. (2002, November 14). Pope addresses Italian Parliament: Italian birthrate in crisis, says John Paul II. *PRI Review, 12*(6), Retrieved from http://www.pop.org

Portnuff, C., Fligor, B., & Arehart, K. (2011, November/December). Teenage use of portable listening devices: A hazard to hearing? *Journal of the American Academy of Audiology, 22*(10), 663-677.

Prensky, M. (2010). *Teaching digital natives*. Thousand Oaks, CA: Corwin Press.

Prinstein, M., & Dodge, K. (2010). *Understanding peer influence in children and adolescents*. New York, NY: Guilford.

Privateer, P. (2006). *Inventing intelligence*. London, England: Blackwell.

Proctor, C. (2008). *Behavioral indicators as attachment difficulties: The case of Romanian adopted children*. Saarbrucken, Germany: VDM Verlag.

from http://projectonstudentdebt.org.

Rabin, R. (2010, May 10). New spending for a wider range of sex education. *The New York Times*, Retrieved from http://www.nytimes.com

Raeff, C. (2005). *Always separate, always connected: Independence and interdependence in cultural contexts of development*. Philadelphia, PA: Erlbaum.

Raghuveer, G. (2010, May). Lifetime cardiovascular risk of childhood obesity. *American Journal of Clinical Nutrition, 91*(5), 1514S-1519S.

Ranji, U., & Salganicoff, A. (2011). *Women: Health Care Chartboard key findings from the Kaiser women's health survey.* Menlo Park, CA: Kaiser Family Foundation.

Rathvon, N. (2008). *Effective school interventions: Evidence based strategies for improving student outcomes.* New York, NY: Guilford Press.

Reivich, K., & Shatte, A. (2003). *The resilience factor.* New York, NY: Broadway Books.

Rescoria, L., & Rosenthal, A. (2004, March). Growth in standardized ability and achievement test scores from 3rd to 10th grade. *Journal of Educational Psychology, 96*(1), 85-96.

Reyna, R. (2010). *Common college completion metrics.* Washington DC: National Governors Association Center for Best Practices.

Reynolds, A., Temple, J., Suh-Ruu, O., Artega, I., & White, B. (2011). School-based early childhood education and age-28-well-being: Effects of timing, dosage, and subgroups. *Science, 333*(6040), 360-364.

Rideout, V., Foehr, U., & Roberts, D. (2010, January). *Generation M²: Media in the lives of 8-to-18-year-olds.* Menlo Park, CA: Kaiser Family Foundation.

Rideout, V., & Hamel, E. (2006). *The media family: Electronic media in the lives of infants, toddlers, preschoolers and their parents.* Menlo Park, CA: Henry J. Kaiser Family Foundation.

Ridley, S. (2006). *Genome.* New York, NY: Harper.

Ripkin, C., & Wolff, R. (2006). *Parenting young athletes.* New York, NY: Penguin Books.

Robine, J., Crimmins, E., Horiuchi, S., & Zeng, Y. (2007). *Human longevity, individual life duration, and the growth of the oldest-old population.* New York, NY: Springer.

Robinson, K. (2011). *Out of our minds: Learning to be creative.* West Sussex, England: Capstone.

Rock, J., & Rock, M. (2006). *Widowhood: The death of a spouse.* Bloomington, IN: Trafford.

Rodgers, M. (1972). *Freaky Friday.* New York, NY: HarperCollins.

Rogers, C. (1961). *On becoming a person.* Boston, MA: Houghton Mifflin.

Roid, G. (2004). *Essentials of Stanford-Binet Intelligence Scales assessment.* New York, NY: Wiley.

Roll, J., Rawson, R., Ling, W., & Shoptaw, S. (2009). *Methamphetamine addiction: From basic science to treatment.* New York, NY: Guilford.

Rosen, L. (2010). *Rewired: Understanding the iGeneration and the way they learn.* New York, NY: Palgrave Macmillan.

Rosen, M. (1996). *This is our house.* Cambridge, MA: Candlewick Press.

Rosenthal, R. (1963). On the social psychology of the social psychological experiment. *American Scientist, 21,* 268-283.

Rosenthal, R., & Jacobson, L. (1968). *Pygmalion in the classroom: Teacher expectations and pupils' intellectual development.* New York, NY: Holt, Rinehart & Winston.

Roseth, C., Johnson, D., & Johnson, R. (2008, March). Promoting early adolescents' achievement and peer relationships: The effects of cooperative, competitive, and individualistic goal structures. *Psychological Bulletin, 134*(2), 223-246.

Ross, C., & Richardson, B. (2008). *Contemporary Spain* (3rd ed.). London, England: Hodder Education.

Rowling, J. (1999). *Harry Potter and the chamber of secrets.* New York, NY: Arthur A. Levine Books.

Ruffman, T., Slade, L., Devitt, K., & Crowe, E. (2006). What mothers say and what they do: The relation between parenting, theory of mind, and conflict/cooperation. *British Journal of Development Psychology, 24,* 105-124.

Runco, M. (2006). *Creativity: Theories and themes: Research, development and practice.* San Diego, CA: Academic Press.

Runco, M., & Albert, R. (2010). Creativity research: A historical view. In J. Kaufman & R. Sternberg (Eds.), *The Cambridge handbook of creativity* (pp. 3-19). New York, NY: Cambridge University Press.

Rycik, M. (2006, Spring). 9/11 to the Iraq war: Using books to help children understand troubled times. *Childhood Education, 82*(3), 145-152.

Sadler, P., & Good, E. (2006). The impact of self and peer-grading on student learning. *Educational Assessment, 11*(1), 1-31.

Sahlberg, P. (2011). *Finnish Lessons: What can the world learn from educational change in Finland?* New York, NY: Teachers College Press.

Salend, S. (2005). *Creating inclusive classrooms: Effective and reflective practices for all students.* Columbus, OH: Merrill.

Salmivalli, C., Kaukiainen, A., & Voeten, M. (2005, September). Anti-bullying intervention: Implementation and outcome. *The British Journal of Educational Psychology, 75*(3), 465-487.

Salthouse, T. (2010). *Major issues in cognitive aging.* New York, NY: Oxford University Press.

Santelli, J., & Crosby, R. (2009). *Adolescent health: Understanding and preventing risk behaviors.* San Francisco, CA: Jossey-Bass.

Sapolsky, R. (2004). *Why zebras don't get ulcers.* New York, NY: Henry Holt.

Saunders, C., & Macnaughton, J. (2005). *Madness and creativity in literature and culture.* New York, NY: Palgrave Macmillan.

Savage, D., & Miller, T. (2012). *It Gets Better: Coming out, overcoming bullying, and creating a life worth living.* New York, NY: Plume Penguin.

Savage, J. (2007). *Teenage: The creation of youth culture.* New York, NY: Penguin.

Savage, T., & Savage, M. (2009). *Successful classroom management and discipline: Teaching self-control* (3rd ed.). Thousand Oaks, CA: SAGE.

Sax, L. (2005). *Why gender matters: What parents and teachers need to know about the emerging science of sex differences.* New York, NY: Doubleday.

Scarmeas, N., & Stern, Y. (2004, October). Cognitive reserve: Implications for diagnosis and prevention of Alzheimer's disease. *Current Neurology and Neuroscience Reports, 4*(5), 374-380.

Schaie, K. W. (2005). *Developmental influences on adult intelligence: The Seattle longitudinal study.* New York, NY: Oxford University Press.

Schneider, M., & Yin, L. M. (2012, April 3). *Completion matters: The high cost of low community college graduation rates.* American Enterprise Institute for Public Policy Research, No. 2, Washington, DC.

Schneier, B. (2003). *Beyond fear: Thinking sensibly about security in an uncertain world.* New York, NY: Springer.

Schulz, L., Bennett, P., Ravussin, E., Kidd, J., Kidd, K., Esparza, J., & Valencia, M. (2006). Effects of traditional and western environments on prevalence of type 2 diabetes in Pima Indians in Mexico and the U.S. *Diabetes Care, 29,* 1866-1871.

Seiden, D., Bilett, J., & Thornton, E. (2008). *When your spouse dies.* Parker, CO: Thornton.

Seligman, M. (2006). *Learned optimism.* New York, NY: Vintage.

Seligman, M. (2011). *Flourish: A visionary new understanding of happiness and wellbeing.* New York, NY: Basic Books.

Seyle, H. (1956). *The stress of life.* New York, NY: McGraw-Hill.

Shaffer, D. (2008). *Social and personality development.* Belmont, CA: Wadsworth.

Shanahan, T., Fisher, D., & Frey, N. (2012, March). The challenge of challenging text. *Educational Leadership, 69*(6), 58-62.

Shanley, E., & Thompson, C. (2010). *Fueling the teen machine* (2nd ed.). Boulder, CO: Bull.

Sharez-Orozco, M. (2005, November). Rethinking education in the global era. *Phi Delta Kappan, 87*(3), 209-212.

Shargorodsky, J., Curhan, S., Curhan, G., & Eavey, R. (2010). Change in prevalence of hearing loss in US adolescents. *The Journal of the American Medical Association, 304*(7), 772-778.

Shariff, S. (2008). *Cyber-bullying: Issues and solutions for the school, the classroom, and the home.* New York, NY: Routledge.

Sharkey, B., & Gaskill, S. (2006). *Fitness and health.* Champaign, IL: Human Kinetics.

Shaw, G. B. (2011). *Pygmalion.* Seattle, WA: CreateSpace. (Original work published 1912)

Sheehy, G. (2010). *Passages in caregiving.* New York, NY: Morrow.

Shema, R., Haramati, S., Ron, S., Huzvi, S. Chen, A., Sacktor, T., & Dudai, Y. (2011). Enhancement of consolidated long-term memory by overexpression of protein kinase M? in the neocortex. *Science, 331,* 1207-1210.

Shema, R., Sacktor, T., & Dudai, Y. (2007). Rapid erasure of long-term memory associations in the cortex by an inhibitor of PKM?. *Science, 317,* 951-953.

Shepard, R. (1967). Recognition memory for words, sentences, and pictures. *Journal of Verbal Learning and Verbal Behavior, 6,* 156-163.

Shepard, R. (1990). *Mind sights.* New York, NY: Freeman.

Sherif, M. (1958). Superordinate goals in the reduction of intergroup conflict. *American Journal of Sociology, 63*(4), 349-356.

Sherif, M. (1966). *In common predicament: Social psychology of intergroup conflict and cooperation.* Boston, MA: Houghton Mifflin.

Siegel, L., & Welsh, B. (2007). *Juvenile delinquency.* Belmont, CA: Wadsworth.

Sight and Hearing Association. (2012). *Sight Center.* Retrieved from http://www.sightandhearing.org/sightcenter

Silverman, P. (2004). *Widow to widow.* New York, NY: Brunner-Routledge.

Singer, D., & Singer, J. (2011). *Handbook of children and the media.* Thousand Oaks, CA: SAGE.

Smagorinsky, P. (2011). *Vygotsky and literacy.* Rotterdam, Netherlands: Sense.

Smart, J. (2011). *Disability across the developmental lifespan.* New York, NY: Springer.

Smith, K., Moriarty, S., Barbatsis, G., & Kenney, K. (Eds.) (2005). *Handbook of visual communication: Theory, methods, and media.* Mahwah, NJ: Erlbaum.

Smock, P., & Manning, W. (2009). New couples, new families: The cohabitation revolution in the United States. In B. Risman (Ed.), *Families as they really are.* New York: NY: W.W. Norton.

Snowdon, D. (2002). *Aging with grace.* New York, NY: Bantam Books.

Snowdon, D., Kemper, S., Mortimer, J., Greiner, L., Wekstein, D., & Markesbery, W. (1996). Linguistic ability in early life and cognitive function and Alzheimer's disease in late life: Findings from the Nun study. *Journal of the American Medical Association, 275*(7), 528-532.

Solmon, L., Agam, F., & Priagula A. (2006). *The challenges of school reform.* Charlotte, NC: Information Age.

Sowell, T. (2011). *Economic facts and fallacies.* New York, NY: Basic Books.

Spear-Swerling, L., & Sternberg, R. (1998, January). Curing our epidemic of learning disabilities. *Phi Delta Kappan, 79,* 397-401.

Stefanakis, E. (2002). *Multiple intelligences and portfolios.* Portsmouth, NH: Heinemann.

Steinberg, L. (2011). *You and your adolescent.* New York, NY: Simon & Schuster.

Sternberg, R., & Subotnik, R. (Eds.). (2006). *Optimizing student success in school with the other 3 Rs: Reasoning, resilience and responsibility.* Charlotte, NC: Information Age.

Stevenson, R. (1915). *A child's garden of verses.* New York, NY: Holt.

Stevenson, R. L. (1886). *The strange case of Dr. Jekyll and Mr. Hyde.* New York, NY: Scribners.

Stiggins, R., & Chappius, S. (2005, October). Putting testing in perspective: It's for learning. *Principal Leadership, 6*(2), 16-20.

Storey, J., & Graeme, S. (2005). *Managers of innovation: Insights into making innovation happen.* Malden, MA: Blackwell.

Strauss, S. (2011). *Sexual harassment and bullying: A guide to keeping kids safe and holding schools accountable.* Lanham, MD: Rowan & Littlefield.

Strom, P., & Strom, R. (2004). Entitlement: The coming debate in higher education. *The Educational Forum, 68*(4), 325-335.

Strom, P., & Strom, R. (2005). Parent-child relationships in early adulthood: College students living at home. *Community College Journal of Research and Practice, 29*(7), 517-529.

Strom, P., & Strom, R. (2009). *Adolescents in the Internet age.* Charlotte, NC: Information Age.

Strom, P., & Strom, R. (2011a). Cheating in middle school and high school. In K. Ryan & J. Cooper (Eds.), *Kaleidoscope: Contemporary and classic readings in education* (pp. 49-56). Belmont, CA: Wadsworth.

Strom, P., & Strom, R. (2011b). Teamwork skills assessment for cooperative learning. *Educational Research and Evaluation, 17*(4), 233-251.

Strom, P., & Strom, R. (2011c). *Adult learning and relationships.* Charlotte, NC: Information Age.

Strom, P., Strom, R., Walker, J., Sindel-Arrington, T., & Beckert, T. (2011). Adolescent bullies on Cyber Island. *NASSP Bulletin, 95*(3), 195-211.

Strom, P., Strom, R., & Wing, C. (2008, December). Polling students about conditions of learning. *National Association of Secondary Schools Bulletin, 92*(4), 292-304.

Strom, P., Strom, R., Wingate, J., Kraska, M., & Beckert, T. (2012). Cyberbullying: assessment of student experience for continuous improvement planning. *NASSP Bulletin, 96(2)*, 137-153. doi: 10.1177/0192636512443281

Strom, R., Amukamara, H., Strom, P., Beckert, T., Strom, S., & Griswold, D. (2000). Parenting success of African American fathers. *Journal of Research and Development in Education, 33*(4), 257-267.

Strom, R., Beckert, T., Strom, P., Strom, S., & Griswold, D. (2002). Evaluating the success of Caucasian fathers in guiding adolescents. *Adolescence, 37*(145), 131-149.

Strom, R., Buki, L., & Strom, S. (1997). Intergenerational perceptions of English-speaking and Spanish-speaking Mexican-American grandparents. *International Journal of Aging and Human Development, 45*(1), 1-21.

Strom, R., Heeder, S., & Strom, P. (2005 March). Performance of Black grandmothers: Perceptions of three generations of females. *Educational Gerontology: An International Journal, 31*(3), 187-205.

Strom, R., Lee, T., Strom, P., Nakagawa, K., & Beckert, T. (2008). Taiwanese grandmothers: Strengths and learning needs as perceived by grandmothers, mothers and granddaughters. *Educational Gerontology, 34*(9), 812-830.

Strom, R., & Strom, P. (2009). *Parent Success Indicator Manual*. Bensenville, IL: Scholastic Testing Service.

Strom, R., & Strom, P. (2010). *Parenting young children: Exploring the Internet, television, play, and reading*. Charlotte, NC: Information Age.

Strom, R., & Strom, P. (2010). Personal goals and global awareness of American community college women regarding parenthood. *Community College Journal of Research and Practice, 34*(3), 277-286.

Strom, R., & Strom, P. (2011). A paradigm for intergenerational learning. In Manuel London (Ed.), *The Oxford handbook of lifelong learning* (pp. 133-146). New York, NY: Oxford University Press.

Strom, R., & Strom, S. (1995). Intergenerational learning: Grandparents in the schools. *Educational Gerontology, 21*(4), 321-335.

Strom, R., & Strom, S. (1997). Building a theory of grandparent development. *International Journal of Aging and Human Development, 45*(4), 255-286.

Strom, R., Strom, P., Strom, S., Shen, Y., & Beckert, T. (2004). Black, Hispanic, and White American mothers of adolescents: Construction of a national standard. *Adolescence, 39*(156), 669-686.

Strom, R., Strom, S., Collinsworth, P., Sato, S., Makino, K., Sasaki, Y., Sasaki, H., & Nishio, N. (1995). Grandparents in Japan: A three-generational study. *International Journal of Aging and Human Development, 40*(3), 209-226.

Strom, R., Strom, S., Fournet, L., Wang, C., Behrens, J., & Griswold, D. (1997). Learning needs of African-American, Caucasian, and Hispanic grandparents. *Journal of Instructional Psychology, 24*(2), 119-134.

Strom, R., Strom, S., Strom, P., Makino, K., & Morishima, Y. (2000). Perceived parenting success of mothers in Japan. *Journal of Family Studies, 6*(1), 25-45.

Strom, R., Strom, S., & Xie, Q. (1995). The small family in China. *International Journal of Early Childhood, 27*(2), 37-46.

Subrahmanyam, K., Greenfield, P., & Tynes, B. (2004, November). Constructing sexuality and identity in an online teen chat room. *Journal of Applied Developmental Psychology, 25*(6), 651-666.

Suellentrop, K. (2010). *Effective and promising teen pregnancy prevention programs for Latino youth.* Washington, DC: National Campaign to Prevent Unplanned Pregnancy.

Suh, M., Chen, C., Woodbridge, J., Tu, M., Kim, J., Nahapetian, A., Evangelists, L., & Sarrafzadeh, M. (2011, May 25). A remote patient monitoring system for congestive heart failure. *Journal of Medical Systems, 35*(5), 1165-1179.

Sullivan, A., & Artiles, A. (2011). Theorizing racial inequality in special education. *Urban Education, 46*(6), 1526-1552.

Summers, R., & Hoffman, A. (2006). *Elder abuse: A public health perspective.* Washington, DC: American Public Health Association.

Sunstein, B. (2000). *The portfolio standard: How students can show us what they know and are able to do.* Portsmouth, NH: Heinemann.

Sutton, A. L. (2012, in press Nov 2012 release). *Sexually transmitted diseases sourcebook.* Aston, PA: Omnigraphics.

Swanson, C. (2009). *Cities in crisis 2009: Closing the graduation gap.* Bethesda, MD: Editorial Projects in Education.

Swift, J. (1726). *Travels into several remote nations of the world.* Reprinted as *Gulliver's travels* (2008). New York, NY: Oxford University Press.

Tally, B., & Goldenberg, L. (2005, Fall). Fostering historical thinking with digitized primary sources. *Journal of Research on Technology in Education, 38*(1), 1-21.

Tapscott, D. (2009). Grown up digital: How the net generational is changing your world. New York, NY: McGraw-Hill.

Tapscott, D., & Williams, A. (2010a). Macrowikinomics: Rebooting business and the world. New York, NY: Portfolio Penguin.

Tapscott, D., & Williams, A. (2010b). *Wikinomics: How mass collaboration changes everything.* New York, NY: Portfolio Trade.

Taylor, M. (1999). *Imaginary companions and the children who create them.* New York, NY: Oxford University Press.

Taylor, P. (2009). *Between two worlds: How young Latinos come of age in America.* Washington, DC: Pew Research Center

Taylor, P. (2012). *Is college worth it?* Washington, DC: Pew Research Center.

Temple, P. (2006). *Identity theory.* San Francisco, CA: MacAdam/Cage.

Terman, L. M. (1916). *The measurement of intelligence.* Boston, MA: Houghton Mifflin.

Theobald, M. (2006). *Increasing student motivation: Strategies for middle and high school teachers.* Thousand Oaks, CA: Corwin.

Thomas, G., & Loxley, A. (2007). *Deconstructing special education and constructing inclusion.* New York, NY: Open University Press, McGraw-Hill Education.

Thompson, C. (2008). *The best of technology writing 2008.* Ann Arbor, MI: University of Michigan Press.

Thorndike, R., & Hagen, E. (2011). *Measurement and evaluation in psychology and education.* Upper Saddle River, NJ: Prentice-Hall.

Tierney, J., & Grossman, J. (2000). *Making a difference: An impact study of Big Brothers/Big Sisters*. New York, NY: Public/Private Ventures.

Tizard, B., & Hughes, M. (2003). *Young children learning*. New York, NY: Wiley-Blackwell.

Toffler, A., & Toffler, H. (2006). *Revolutionary wealth*. New York, NY: Alfred Knopf.

Tolkien, J. (2003). *The fellowship of the ring (The lord of the rings, Part I)*. Boston, MA: Houghton Mifflin.

Torrance, E. P. (1965). *Rewarding creative behavior*. Englewood Cliffs, NJ: Prentice-Hall.

Torrance, E. P. (1995). *Why fly? A philosophy of creativity*. Norwood, NJ: Ablex.

Torrance, E. P. (2000). *On the edge and keeping on the edge*. Westport, CT: Greenwood.

Torrance, E. P. (2002). *Torrance Tests of Creative Thinking*. Bensenville, IL: Scholastic Testing Service.

Torrance, E. P., & Ziller, R. (1957). *Risk and life experience: Development of a scale for measuring risk-taking tendencies*. Lackland Air Force Base, San Antonio, TX: Research report AFPTRC-TN 57-23-ASTIA Document No. 09826.

Trenholm, C., Devaney, B., Fortson, K., Quay, L., Wheeler, J., & Clark, M. (2007, April). *Impact of four Title V, section 510 Abstinence education programs*. Princeton, NJ: Mathematica Policy Research Institute, Inc.

Trilling, B., & Fadel, C. (2009). *21st Century skills*. San Francisco, CA: Jossey-Bass.

Turkle, S. (2011). *Alone together: Why we expect more from technology and less from each other*. New York, NY: Basic Books.

Turner, J. (2011). *Longevity policy: Facing up to longevity issues affecting social security, pensions, and older workers*. Kalamazoo, MI: W. E. Upjohn Institute.

Twenge, J. (2007). *Generation me: Why today's young Americans are more confident, assertive, entitled—and more miserable than ever before*. New York, NY: Free Press.

Twenge, J., & Campbell, W. (2010). *The narcissism epidemic: Living in the age of entitlement*. New York, NY: Free Press.

Underwood, M., & Rosen, L. (2011). *Social development*. New York, NY: Guilford Press.

United Nations, Department of Economic and Social Affairs, Population Division (2011). *World population prospects, the 2010 revision*. New York, NY: United Nations.

United States Bureau of the Census. (2011). *United States interim projections by age, sex, race, and Hispanic origin: 2000–2050*. Retrieved from http://www.census.gov/ipc/www/usinterimproj/

United States Department of Agriculture. (2012). *Choose my plate*. Retrieved March 1, 2012, from http://www.choosemyplate.gov

United States Department of Education. (2011a, March 11). *Meeting the nation's 2020 goal: State targets for increasing the number and percentage of college graduates with degrees*. Washington, DC: Author.

United States Department of Education. (2011b, April 7). *U.S. Education Department launches initiatives to safeguard student privacy*. Retrieved from http://www.ed.gov, Washington, DC.

United States Department of Education, Center on Education Statistics. (2011). *Conditions of Education, 2011*. Washington, DC: Author.

United States Department of Health and Human Services. (2010). *Child maltreatment*. Washington, DC: Author.

United States Department of Health and Human Services, National Institutes of Health. (2009 August). *Take charge of your health: A guide for teenagers*. Washington, DC: NIH Publication No. 09-4328?.

United States Department of Homeland Security (2012). *Are you ready? Guide*. Retrieved February 25, 2012, http://www.ready.gov/are-you-ready-guide.

United States Department of Justice. (2012). *A Parent's Guide to Internet Safety*. Retrieved from http://www.fbi.gov/publications/pguide/pguidee.htm

United States Food and Drug Administration. (2012). *Cigarette health warnings*. Retrieved from http://www.fda.gov/TobaccoProducts/Labeling/ CigaretteWarningLabels/ucm259214.htm

Valenzuela, M. (2009). *It's never too late too change your mind*. Sydney, Australia: ABC Books.

Valenzuela, M., & Sachdev, P. (2006). Brain reserve and dementia: A systematic review. *Psychological Medicine, 36*(4), 441-454.

Vandal, B. (2010). *Getting past go: Rebuilding the remedial education bridge to college success*. Retrieved from http://www.gettingpastgo.org

Vedder, R., & Denhart, M. (December 2, 2011). *Why does college cost so much?* Retrieved from http://www.cnn.com

Ventura, S. J. (2009). *Changing patterns of nonmarital childbearing in the United States*. NCHS data brief, no. 18. Hyattsville, MD: National Center for Health Statistics.

Victor, C., Scambler, S., & Bond, J. (2008). *The social world of older people: Understanding loneliness and social isolation in later life*. New York, NY: McGraw-Hill.

Visser, P., & Krosnick, J. (1998). Development of attitude strength over the life cycle: Surge-decline. *Journal of personality and social psychology, 75*(6), 1389-1410.

Vose, D. (2008). *Risk analysis: A quantitative guide*. New York, NY: John Wiley

Vossekuil, B., Fein, R., Reddy, M., Borum, R., & Modzeleski, W. (2002). *The final report and findings of the safe school initiative*. Washington, DC: United States Secret Service and United States Department of Education. Retrieved from http://www.ustreas.gov/usss/ntac_ssi.shtml

Vygotsky, L. (1978). *Mind in society*. Cambridge, MA: Harvard University Press.

Vygotsky, L. (1994). The development of thinking and concept formation in adolescence. In R. Van der Veer & J. Valsiner (Eds.), *The Vygotsky reader* (pp. 185-265). Cambridge, MA: Blackwell.

Vygotsky, L. (1998). The collected works of L. W. Vygotsky. In R. Rieber (Ed.), *Child psychology*. New York: Plenum.

Wahlberg, M., & Mahr, J. (2011, August 28). State paid sex offenders as baby sitters. *Chicago Tribune*. Retrieved from http://articles.chicagotribune.com/ 2011-08-28

Wallace, B. (2007). *Contemplative science: Where Buddism and neuroscience converge*. New York, NY: Columbia University Press.

Wallace, M. (2008). *50 Years from today*. Dallas, TX: Thomas Nelson.

Wallach, M., & Kogan, N. (1965). *Modes of thinking in young children of the creativity-intelligence distinction*. New York, NY: Wadsworth.

Wallerstein, J., & Lewis, J. (2004). The unexpected legacy of divorce: Report of a 25-year study. *Psychoanalytic Psychology, 21*(3), 353-357.

Walsh, B. (2011, April 20). The biggest casualty of the oil spill: Mental health. *Time*. Retrieved from http://www.time.com

Wanberg, W., Timken, D., & Milkman, H. (2010). *Driving with care: Education and treatment of the underage impaired driving offender.* Thousand Oaks, CA: SAGE.

Ward, J. (2009). *The student's guide to cognitive neurosience.* New York, NY: Psychology Press.

Wargo, E. (2009). Resisting temptation. *Observer, 22*(1), 10-17.

Warrell, M. (2008). *Find your courage.* New York, NY: McGraw-Hill.

Washington State Office of the Attorney General. (2012). *Dating Rights and Responsibilities.* Retrieved from http://www.atg.wa.gov/ProtectingYouth/TeenDatingViolence/DatingRights.aspx

Watters, A. (2011, November 3). *Plagiarism differences in high school and college students.* Retrieved from http://www.mindshift.kqed.org

Weigel, D., Martin, S., & Bennett, K. (2005). Ecological influences of the home and the child-care center on preschool-age children's literacy development. *Reading Research Quarterly, 40*(2), 204-233.

Weishelt, R., & White, W. (2009). *Methamphetamine: Its history, pharmacology, and treatment.* Center City, MN: Hazelden.

Weitoft, G., Hjem, A., Hagland, B., & Rosen, M. 2003). Mortality, severe morbidity, and injury in children living with single parents in Sweden. *The Lancet, 361*(9354), 289-295.

Welch, J., & Welch, S. (2005). *Winning.* New York, NY: HarperCollins.

Wenck, S., & Hansen, C. (2009). *Love him, love his kids: The stepmother's guide to surviving and thriving in a blended family.* Avon, MA: Adams Media.

Whitley, B. E., Jr., & Keith-Spiegel, P. (2002). *Academic dishonesty: An educator's guide.* Mahwah, NJ: Erlbaum.

Whitten, L. (2011). *High school student opinion polling on career exploration.* Auburn, AL: College of Education, Auburn University.

Willard, N. (2007). *Cyber-safe kids, Cyber-savvy teens: Helping young people learn to use the Internet safely and responsibly.* San Francisco, CA: Jossey-Bass.

Williams, R., & Newton, J. (2006). *Visual communication.* Mahwah, NJ: Erlbaum.

Wilmhurst, L., & Brue, A. (2010). *Complete guide to special education.* San Francisco, CA: Jossey-Bass.

Wolak, J., Mitchell, K., & Finkelhor, D. (2007). Does online harassment constitute bullying? An exploration of online harassment by known peers and online-only contacts. *Journal of Adolescent Health, 41*, S31-38

Wolpe, D. (2009). *Why faith matters.* New York, NY: Harper.

Wong, G. (2005). *Skills for going to school.* Los Angeles, CA: Horizon Research Corporation.

Worden, J. (2008). *Grief counseling and grief therapy.* New York, NY: Springer.

Wormeli, R. (2006, April). Differentiating for tweens. *Educational Leadership, 63*(7), 14-19.

Ybarra, M., Diener-West, M., & Leaf, P. (2007). Examining the overlap in Internet harassment and school bullying: Implications for school intervention. *Journal of Adolescent Health, 41*, S42-50.

Yu, W. (2009). *Gendered trajectories: Women, work, and social change in Japan and Taiwan*. Stanford, CA: Stanford University Press.

Yuill, N., & Ruffman, T. (2009). *The relation between parenting, children's social understanding and language* (Grant # RES-000-23-0278). Brighton, England: Department of Psychology, University of Sussex.

Zastrow, C., & Kirst-Ashman, K. (2010). *Understanding human behavior and the social environment*. Belmont, CA: Cengage.

Zeigarnik, A. (2007). Bluma Zeigarnik—A memoir. *Gestalt theory, 29*(3), 256-268.

Zubizarreta, J., & Millis, B. (2009). *The learning portfolio: Reflective practice for improving student learning*. San Francisco, CA: Jossey-Bass.

Zuckerberg, M. (2011, May 18). *Innovation and entrepreneurship: What it takes*. Presentation to NewSchools Summit 2011, New Schools Venture Fund and the Aspen Institute, Burlingame, CA.

Zullig, K., Ubbes, V., & Pyle, J. (2006, March). Self-reported weight perceptions, dieting behavior, and breakfast eating among high school adolescents. *The Journal of School Health, 76*(3), 87-92.

CPSIA information can be obtained
at www.ICGtesting.com
Printed in the USA
FFOW04n0508170617
36808FF

9 781623 960469